HIGHER EDUCATION LAW

HIGHER EDUCATION LAW

EDITED BY

David Palfreyman MA, MBA, LLB
Bursar and Fellow, New College, Oxford

AND

David Warner MA
Principal, Swansea Institute of Higher Education

JORDANS
2002

Published by
Jordan Publishing Limited
21 St Thomas Street
Bristol BS1 6JS

British Library Cataloguing-in-Publication Data
A catalogue record for this book is available from the British Library.

ISBN 0 85308 730 X

Typeset by Mendip Communications Ltd, Frome, Somerset
Printed by MPG Books Ltd, Bodmin, Cornwall

PREFACE

This second edition (originally *Higher Education and the Law: A Guide for Managers*, Open University Press, 1998) explores the implications for HEIs of *Clark v University of Lincolnshire and Humberside* (2000) (CA) in relation to breach of the HEI–student contract to educate; *Phelps v Hillingdon London Borough Council* (2000) (HL) in relation to the tort of 'educational malpractice'; *University of Nottingham v Fishel* (2000) (QBD) in relation to the employment contracts of academic staff; and *R v HM Treasury ex parte University of Cambridge* (2000) (ECJ) in relation to whether an HEI is a 'public authority' for the purposes of the EU public procurement regulations; as well as numerous cases impacting on the HEI as the manager of IT facilities, as the provider of residential accommodation, as a 'caring' employer, and as the exploiter of intellectual property.

There is also consideration of recent legislation similarly affecting the management of HEIs: the Trustee Act 2000, the Human Rights Act 1998, the Data Protection Act 1998, the Race Relations (Amendment) Act 2000, the Freedom of Information Act 2000, the Regulation of Investigatory Powers Act 2000, the Special Educational Needs and Disability Act 2001, and numerous sets of Regulations, along with various EU Directives; as well as there being new material on academic freedom, on academic tenure and on the legal aspects of alumni relations.

In preparing this edition, the General Editors are most grateful to the various contributors, whether revising their chapters from the 1998 first edition or adding completely new material. We are also thankful for the efficiency of Jordans as our publishers.

The book is updated to the end of February 2002: further updating will be available on-line at the OxCHEPS website at www.new.ox.ac.uk/oxcheps.

David Palfreyman and David Warner
Oxford
March 2002

DEDICATION

This book is dedicated to Julia, Tessa and Laurence
(David Palfreyman)

EDITORS AND CONTRIBUTORS

The Editors

David Palfreyman, MA, MBA, LLB, is the Bursar and a Fellow of New College, Oxford. With David Warner he has edited *Higher Education Management* and *The State of UK HE*; they are also the General Editors of the 20-volume *Managing Universities and Colleges* series. With Ted Tapper he co-authored *Oxford and the Decline of the Collegiate Tradition*. David is a member of the editorial boards of the journals *Education and the Law* and *Perspectives: Policy and Practice in Higher Education* (the journal of the Association of University Administrators, AUA), and a Consultant Editor for *ADR, Mediation and Negotiation*. David is the founding Director of OxCHEPS (the Oxford Centre for Higher Education Policy Studies).

David Warner, MA, is the Principal, Swansea Institute of Higher Education, having been a Pro-Vice-Chancellor at the University of Central England in Birmingham and having also worked at the University of Warwick and at the University of East Anglia. His previous books include *Managing Educational Property*, *The Income Generation Handbook* and *Human Resource Management in Higher and Further Education*. David is the Deputy Director of OxCHEPS.

The Contributors

The law firms contributing are Eversheds, Linnells, Manches, Martineau Johnson, Mills & Reeve, Pinsent Curtis Biddle, Shakespeares and Travers Smith Braithwaite. Other contributors include Emma Chamberlain (Barrister), Oliver Hyams (Barrister) and David Isaac (Solicitor).

TABLE OF CONTENTS

Preface		v
Dedication		vii
Editors and contributors		ix
Table of Cases		xix
Table of Statutes		xxxvii
Table of Statutory Instruments, Codes of Practice, etc		xliii
Table of EC and International Materials		xlvii
Table of Abbreviations		li
PART 1	CONTEXTS	1
Chapter 1	Setting the Scene	3
	Rationale for this book	3
	The growth of consumerism	4
	Other recent works	8
	The objectives of this book	10
	A note on terminology	13
	Legal problems in HE	13
	Final thoughts	19
	Acknowledgements	19
	A Note on the University of Oxford's statement to students	19
	A case-book on HE and the law and on-line updating	23
	Appendix to Chapter 1	24
Chapter 2	What is a Higher Education Institution as a Legal Entity?	27
	Editors' introduction	27
	The corporation	28
	Powers	29
	Charitable status	30
	Public body	30
	Community	31
PART 2	GOVERNANCE	33
Chapter 3	Governance, Accountability and Personal Liability	35
	Editors' introduction	35
	Governance under scrutiny	40

Back to constitutional basics   45
Personal liability   54
Avoidance of personal liability   62
Conclusion   63

Chapter 4   **Charity Trusteeship and Personal Liability**   65
Editors' introduction   65
Charity trusteeship   67
Charity trustees   72
Trustee Act 2000   77

Chapter 5   **The Law of Meetings**   81
Editors' Introduction   81
The essential elements   81
Defamation   88
Delegation, agency and vicarious liability   90

PART 3   **THE HIGHER EDUCATION INSTITUTION AND ITS
             STAFF AND STUDENTS**   99

Chapter 6   **The Higher Education Institution–Student Contract**   101
Editors' introduction   101
Scope of this chapter   112
Is there a contract?   113
When things go wrong   119
Practical preventive or remedial action   123
Conclusions   125
A Note on references   125
Appendix 1 to Chapter 6   127
Appendix 2 to Chapter 6   132

Chapter 7   **The Regulation of the Community: Student Discipline,
             Academic Appeals and Complaints**   137
Editors' introduction   137
Scope of this chapter   139
General principles   139
Human Rights Act 1998   141
Discipline   146
Academic appeals   154
Complaints   157
Discrimination   159
Conclusion   161

Chapter 8   **Disputes I: The Role of the Visitor in Chartered
             Institutions**   163
Editors' introduction   163
Introduction   165

	Background	166
	What are the benefits of the visitorial system?	166
	Drawbacks to the visitorial process	168
	Human Rights Act 1998	170
	Alternatives	172
	Conclusion	175
Chapter 9	**Disputes II: The Scope for Judicial Review in Statutory Institutions**	**177**
	Editors' introduction	177
	Introduction	180
	Development of judicial review	180
	Nature of judicial review	182
	Grounds and remedies	185
	Contractual arrangements	186
	Students	188
	Reducing the risk of judicial review	190
	Procedure and costs	198
Chapter 10	**Disputes III: Selected Employment Law Issues ('Academic Freedom', 'Tenure' and 'Good Cause')**	**201**
	Editors' introduction	201
	Introduction	204
	HEIs where there is a Visitor	206
	Academic freedom	209
	Powers and duties of the Commissioners: tenure, redundancy, good cause	210
Chapter 11	**Termination of Employment and the Model Statute: and Notably the Position of Fixed-Term Staff**	**215**
	Editors' introduction	215
	Introduction	215
	The contractual importance of the model statute	216
	Unfair dismissal and the model statute	234
	Particular issues in respect of fixed-term contracts	242
PART 4	**THE HIGHER EDUCATION INSTITUTION AND ITS ACADEMIC ACTIVITY**	**247**
Chapter 12	**Intellectual Property, Copyright and Trade Marks**	**249**
	Editors' introduction	249
	Introduction	251
	What is intellectual property and why is it important?	252
	Three general concepts	252
	National character	254
	Types of intellectual property	254
	Creation and acquisition	259

Ownership 260
Management of intellectual property 267
Summary 268
Appendix 1 to Chapter 12: Tables 270
Appendix 2 to Chapter 12: HEI photocopying of
'copyrighted' material 272

Chapter 13 **Data Protection and Freedom of Information** 275
Editors' introduction 275
Introduction 277
Some key definitions 278
'Categories' of personal data 279
Manual records 280
Transitional relief 280
Access by data subjects: a data subject right 280
Exemptions 281
Powers of the Information Commissioner 281
Application of the DPA 1998 281
Freedom of Information Act 2000 282
Appendix to Chapter 13: the Part II exempt
information 288

Chapter 14 **The Internet: A Modern Pandora's Box?** 289
Introduction 289
Data protection 291
'Hacking' and computer misuse 292
'Theft' of data 292
Pornography 293
Intellectual property: patents, copyright, databases,
trade marks 294
Defamation 294
Threatening e-mails 296
Conclusion 297

PART 5 **THE HIGHER EDUCATION INSTITUTION AS A
BUSINESS** 299

Chapter 15 **Trading Companies** 301
Editors' introduction 301
Introduction 304
Taxation 307
VAT 309
Powers of the HEI 310
Relationship between HEI and trading company 310

Liability 311
Starting the company 312
Members 314
Directors 315
Company secretary 316
Minority shareholdings 316

Chapter 16 **Mergers and Acquisitions** 319
Editors' introduction 319
Introduction 320
Legal framework 321
Big issues to watch out and prepare for 333

Chapter 17 **Franchising** 337
Editors' introduction 337
What is franchising? 338
The contractual structure 341
Terms of the contract 345
The impact of recent developments 357
Conclusion 357

Chapter 18 **The Private Finance Initiative** 359
Editors' introduction 359
Introduction 360
What is a PFI transaction? 360
Position of HEIs 360
Risk 361
How is a PFI transaction achieved? 363
Assets or services? 363
PFI in higher education 364
Anatomy of a PFI transaction 367
Conclusions on PFI and practical considerations 374
Other private sources of finance 375
Conclusions 376

Chapter 19 **The Legal Status of the Students' Union** 377
Editors' introduction 377
Definition 379
The requirements of the EA 1994 380
Freedom of speech 382
Status 384
The SU and charity law 385
Risk and liability 387
Potential HEI liability 389

Reducing the risks by incorporation   390
Conclusions   393

PART 6   THE HIGHER EDUCATION INSTITUTION AND ITS
              PROPERTY   395

Chapter 20   Security: Surveillance, Trespass, 'Reasonable Force'
              and 'Clamping'   397
              Editors' introduction   397
              Introduction   400
              Occupiers' liability   400
              Health and safety   402
              Security guards: powers of arrest and use of reasonable
                  force   405
              Security of property   407
              Freedom of speech   408
              Close circuit television   409

Chapter 21   Houses in Multiple Occupation and What is a 'House'?   411
              Editors' introduction   411
              Introduction   411
              What is an HMO?   412
              Effect of a student residence being an HMO 415
              Availability of grants   419
              Future developments   420
              Conclusions   420

Chapter 22   The Implications for Higher Education Institutions of
              the Disability Discrimination Act 1995   423
              Editors' introduction   423
              Introduction   425
              Multi-faceted HEIs   425
              The definition of disability   426
              Employment   427
              Provision of services   430
              Education: Impact of the SEND 2001   432
              Human Rights Act 1998   435

Chapter 23   Student Accommodation: Lease or Licence, Eviction
              or Quiet Enjoyment?   437
              Editors' introduction   437
              Introduction   438
              Lease or licence   438
              Discipline in student accommodation   451

Conclusion   452

Chapter 24   **Risk Management and Insurance**   453
              Editors' introduction   453
              Introduction   455
              The risk management process   456
              Legal risk management   459
              Conclusion   468

Chapter 25   **Alumni: Friend-raising to Fund-raising** 471
              Editors' introduction   471
              Alumni   471
              Alumni associations   471
              Charitable giving   474
              Data protection   480
              Confidentiality   488
              Conclusion   489

Chapter 26   **A Note on Personal Property within the Law of
              Property: Lost Property, Treasure Trove, Bailment**   491

PART 7   CONSEQUENCES   495

Chapter 27   **A Guide to Litigation**   497
              Editors' introduction   497
              Introduction   498
              Types of dispute   499
              The resolution of disputes   500
              The structure and jurisdiction of the courts   503
              Litigation procedures: overview   505
              Litigation procedures: step by step   505
              Arbitration   509
              Alternative dispute resolution   511
              Remedies   512
              Enforcement of orders   513
              Safeguards for the HEI   514
              The future of dispute resolution   517

Chapter 28   **The Impact of European Law**   519
              Editors' introduction   519
              Introduction   520
              The main laws   521
              Public procurement   523
              Fees and awards   531
              Free movement of academic staff and students   533
              The HEI as employer   535
              Mutual recognition of degrees and qualifications   536

| | Anti-competitive practices | 540 |
| | Future developments | 546 |

Chapter 29	**A Note on Consumer Law**	549
	Introduction	549
	The legislative framework	553
	Conclusion	559

Chapter 30	**A Bibliographical Essay on the Visitor**	563
	Introduction	563
	The history and evolution of the Visitor	565
	The strengths and weaknesses of the Visitor model	568
	The jurisdiction of the Visitor	570
	The Visitor's powers of enforcement and ability to award damages	574
	The procedures for visitation	574
	Judicial review of the Visitor	576
	A comparison of the Visitor in Australia, Canada, England, New Zealand and Nigeria	578
	The Visitor post-Nolan Report (1996)	581
	Notes on key cases referred to in Chapter 30	584

Further Reading	587
Bibliography	603
Contact Details for Contributors	615
Index	617

TABLE OF CASES

References are to editors' introductions (§), paragraph numbers and chapter appendices

AAUP v Bloomfield College 322 A 2d 846, NJ Super Ct Ch Div 1974; *affirmed* 346 A 2d 615, App Div 1975 §10.5

A-G v De Winton [1906] 2 Ch 106, 75 Ch 612, 70 JP 368 3.37

A-G v Ross [1986] 1 WLR 252, [1985] 3 All ER 334, (1985) 130 SJ 184 19.15

A-G v Talbot [1747] 3 Atk 662, 1 Ves Sen 78 30.25, 30.27, 30.28, 30.29, App 30

A-G's Reference (No 2 of 1999) [2000] QB 796, [2000] 3 WLR 195, [2000] 3 All ER 182, [2000] 2 BCLC 257, CA 20.8

Abbeyfield (Harpenden) Society Ltd v Woods [1968] 1 WLR 374, [1968] 1 All ER 352n, 19 P&CR 36, CA 23.9

Abdelsayed v Narumanchi 668 A 2d 378, Ct App 1995 5.17

Adams v Cape Industries plc [1990] 2 WLR 786, HL; [1990] Ch 433, [1991] 1 All ER 929, CA §15.2

Adams and Another v Rhymay Valley DC [2000] Lloyd's Rep PN 777, [2000] 39 EG 144, [2000] NPC 83, CA §6.25

Addis v Gramophone Co Ltd [1909] AC 488, 78 LJKB 112, [1908–10] All ER Rep 1, HL 29.38

Agorà Srl v Ente Autonoma Fiera Internazionale di Milano (C-223/99) [2001] TLR 412, (2001) *The Times*, June 26, ECJ §28.2

Akbarali v Brent London Borough Council; Abdullah v Shropshire County Council; Shabpar v Barnet London Borough Council; Shah (Jitendra) v Barnet London Borough Council; Barnet London Borough Council v Shah [1983] 2 AC 309, [1983] 2 WLR 16, [1983] 1 All ER 226, HL 28.33

Albert v Lavin [1982] AC 546, [1981] 3 WLR 955, [1981] 3 All ER 878, HL 20.12

Allue (Pilar) and Coonan (Mary Carmel) v Università degli Studi di Venezia (Case C-33/88) [1989] ECR 1591, [1991] 1 CMLR 283, (1989) *The Times*, June 16, ECJ 28.43

Altschuler v University of Pennsylvania Law School 1997 US Dist LEXIS 3248, SDNY 21 March 1997; *affirmed* 201 F 3d 430, 3d Cir 1999 §6.13

Andre v Pace University 618 NYS 2d 975, City Ct Yonkers 1994; *reversed* 655 NYS 2d 777, NY App Div 1996 §6.12

Ansari v New York University 1997 US Dist LEXIS 6863, SDNY 1997 §6.12

Anya v University of Oxford [2001] EWCA Civ 405, [2001] ICR 847, [2001] IRLR 377, [2001] ELR 711, (2001) *The Times*, May 4, (2001) ELJ 2(4) 227, CA 7.63, §10.1

Anyanwu and Another v South Bank Student Union and Another and Commission for Racial Equality [2001] UKHL 14, [2001] 1 WLR 638, [2001] 2 All ER 353, [2001] ELR 511, HL §19.2, 19.24

Apfel v Huddleston 50 F Supp 2d 1129, D Utah 1999 §6.5

Appleford's Case. *See* R v Appleford

Aranitis v Land Berlin (Case C-164/94) [1996] ECR I-135, ECJ 28.53

Arroyo v Rosen 648 A 2d 1074, Md App 1994 5.17

Arthur v Anker [1995] NPC 187, (1995) *The Times*, December 1, CA 20.9

Arthur JS Hall & Co v Simmons [2000] 3 WLR 543, [2000] 3 All ER 673, HL §6.24

Ashburn Anstalt v Arnold (WJ & Co) and Another [1988] 2 All ER 147,
   (1988) 55 P&CR 137, (1987) 284 EG 1375, CA 23.4

Ashdown v Telegraph Group Ltd [2001] Ch 685, [2001] 2 WLR 967, [2001]
   2 All ER 370, (2001) *The Times*, February 6 §12.4

Ashley v Sutton London Borough Council [1995] Crim LR 657, (1994) 156 JP
   631, (1995) Tr LR 350, QBD 29.27

Associated Provincial Picture Houses Ltd v Wednesbury Corporation [1948] 1
   KB 223, [1948] LJR 190, [1947] 2 All ER 680, CA   9.37, 9.40, 30.63, App 30

Atkins v DPP [2001] 1 WLR 1247 14.10

B v Manchester Metropolitan University ex parte Nolan (1993) unreported, 15
   July 30.55

Baillie v Oriental Telephone and Electric Co Ltd [1915] 1 Ch 503, 84 LJ Ch
   409, 112 LT 569, CA 5.3

Baldry v Feintuck [1972] 1 WLR 552, [1972] 2 All ER 81, (1971) 115 SJ 965   19.14

Barber v Manchester Regional Hospital Board [1958] 1 WLR 181, [1958] 1 All
   ER 322, 122 JP 124, QBD 11.56

Barings plc (No 5), Re [1999] 1 BCLC 433, ChD §15.3

Barnes v Sheffield City Council (1995) 27 HLR 719, [1995] NPC 87, CA   21.7, 21.8

Barrett v Ministry of Defence [1995] 1 WLR 1217, [1995] 3 All ER 87, (1995)
   The Times, January 13, CA §6.22

Bartholomew v London Borough of Hackney [1999] IRLR 246, CA 6.38

Baxter v Camden LBC. *See* Southwark LBC v Mills; *sub nom* Southwark LBC v
   Tanner; Baxter v Camden LBC

Bayley-Jones v University of Newcastle [1990] 22 NSWLR 425 30.50

Beckett v Cohen [1972] 1 WLR 1593, [1973] 1 All ER 120, (1972) 71 LGR
   46, DC 29.27

Bell v University of Auckland [1969] NZLR 1029 30.52

Bishopsgate Investment Management Ltd (in Liquidation) v Maxwell (No 2)
   [1994] 1 All ER 261, [1993] BCLC 1282, (1993) *The Times*, February 16,
   CA 3.39

Blank v Board of Higher Education of the City of New York 273 NYS 2d 796,
   NY Sup Ct 1966 5.21

Bloch v Temple University 934 F Supp 387, ED Pa 1996 §10.3

Blum v Schlegel 18 F 3d 1005, 2d Cir 1994 §10.3

Boff's Case (1523) unreported App 1

Bolam v Friern Barnet Hospital Management Committee [1957] 1 WLR 582,
   [1957] 2 All ER 118, 101 SJ 357 §6.25, 29.13

Bolitho (Deceased) v City & Hackney Health Authority [1997] 3 WLR 1151,
   [1997] 4 All ER 771, (1997) 141 SJLB 238, HL §6.25

Booth v Arnold [1895] 1 QB 571, 59 JP 215, 64 LJQB 443, CA 5.2

Botzen v Rotterdamsche Droogdok Maatschappij BV (No 186/83) [1985] ECR
   519, [1986] 2 CMLR 50, ECJ 17.32

Boulting v Association of Cinematograph, Television and Allied Technicians
   [1963] 1 QB 606, [1963] 2 WLR 529, [1963] 1 All ER 716, CA §15.3

Boyo v Lambeth London Borough Council [1994] ICR 727, [1995] IRLR 50,
   CA 10.11

Bradley v Greater Manchester Fire and Civil Defence Authority EAT/253/00 §22.7
Brighton Corporation v Parry (1971) 70 LGR 576, (1972) 116 SJ 483 §9.8
British Airways Board v Taylor [1975] 1 WLR 1197, [1975] 3 All ER 307,
    [1975] 2 Lloyd's Rep 434, DC 29.27
British Broadcasting Corporation v Farnworth [1998] ICR 1116, (1998) *The
    Times*, October 7, EAT 11.27
British Gas v McCaull [2001] IRLR 60, EAT §22.7
British Telecommunications plc v One in a Million Ltd, Marks & Spencer plc
    v One in a Million Ltd; Virgin Enterprises Ltd v One in a Million Ltd,
    J Sainsbury plc v One in a Million Ltd; Ladbroke Group plc v One in a
    Million Ltd [1999] 1 WLR 903, [1998] 4 All ER 476, [1999] FSR 1, CA 14.11
Brown v Knowsley Borough Council [1986] IRLR 102, EAT 11.16
Brown v South Bank University (1999) Case No 2305234/97, 86 EOR 15, 22,
    23, EAT §22.6
Bruton v London and Quadrant Housing Trust [1999] 3 WLR 150, [1999] 3
    All ER 481, (1999) 31 HLR 902, HL 23.5, 23.6, 23.30, 23.31, 23.32, 23.34
Bryan v UK (1996) 21 EHRR 342, [1996] 1 PLR 47, [1996] 2 EGLR 123,
    ECHR 7.19
Buller ex parte (1855) 3 WR 447 App 30
Bulmer (HP) v Bollinger (J) SA [1974] Ch 401, [1974] 3 WLR 202, [1974] 2
    All ER 1226, CA 28.1
Burrows v University of York [1999] EdCR 586, Visitor (University) §7.7, 10.6,
    30.24, 30.63
Butler v Louisiana State Board of Education 331 So 2d 192, La 1976 5.21

Cadells v Balfour (1890) 17 R 1138 App 6(1)
Cambridgeshire County Council v Hogan (2001) unreported, EAT 11.19
Camden LBC v McBride [1999] CLY 3737, Clerkenwell Cty Ct 23.27
Campbell and Fell v United Kingdom (1984) 7 EHRR 165, ECHR §8.4, 30.62
Carleton v Glasgow Caledonian University (1993) unreported App 6(1)
Carroll v Manek (1999) *The Times*, August 18, ChD 23.11
Casson v University of Aston in Birmingham [1983] 1 All ER 88 30.37, 30.38,
    App 30
Centre Belge D'Etudes de Marché Télé-marketing v Compagnie
    Luxembourgeoise de Télédiffusion et Information Publicité Bénélux
    (Case 311/84) [1986] 2 CMLR 558, ECJ 28.59
Ceylon University v Fernando [1960] 1 WLR 223, [1960] 1 All ER 631, 104
    SJ 230, PC §9.8
Charnock v Liverpool Corporation [1968] 1 WLR 1498, [1968] 3 All ER 473,
    112 SJ 781, CA 29.14
Chiavarelli v Williams 681 NY S 2d 276, NY Sup Ct App Div 1998 5.17
Claridge's Patent Asphalte Co Ltd, Re [1921] 1 Ch 543, 90 LJ Ch 273, 125 LT
    255 3.39
Clark v University of Lincolnshire and Humberside [2000] 1 WLR 1988,
    [2000] 3 All ER 752, [2000] ELR 345, CA §6.13, App 6(1), §7.6, §9.3, 9.7–9.9,
    §27.4, 30.55, 30.62, App 30
Cohen v San Bernardino Valley College 92 F 3d 969, 9th Cir 1996; *reversing*
    883 F Supp 1407, CD Cal 1995 §10.3
Coleman Taymar Ltd and Others v Oakes and Another [2001] 2 BCLC 749,
    [2001] TLR 540, (2001) *The Times*, September 3, ChD 3.39

Commissioners of Customs and Excise v University of Leicester Students'
    Union [2001] STC 550   §19.2
Conservative and Unionist Central Office v Burrell [1982] 1 WLR 522, [1982]
    2 All ER 1, [1982] STC 317, CA   19.10
Copeland v Smith and Another [2000] 1 WLR 1371, [2000] 1 All ER 457,
    [2000] CP Rep 14, CA   §6.24
Corporation of Mercer University v Smith 371 SE 2d 858 (Ga 1988)   4.26
Cotran v Buckingham University (1998) unreported, 24 February, CA   App 6(1)
Cotton v Derbyshire Dales District Council (1994) *The Times*, June 20, [1994]
    CLY 4286, CA   20.6
Courtaulds Northern Spinning Ltd v Sibson [1988] ICR 451, [1988] IRLR
    305, CA   29.5
Cowl and Others v Plymouth City Council (2002) *The Times*, January 8, CA
    App 6(1), §9.3, §27.4
Cowan v Scargill [1985] Ch 270, [1984] 2 All ER 750   4.18
Cox v Sun Alliance Life Ltd [2001] EWCA Civ 649, [2001] IRLR 448, CA   6.38
Crédit Suisse v Allerdale Borough Council [1997] QB 306, [1996] 3 WLR 894,
    [1996] 4 All ER 129, CA   2.3
Crédit Suisse v Waltham Forest London Borough Council [1997] QB 362,
    [1996] 3 WLR 943, [1996] 4 All ER 176, CA   2.3
Cusumano and Yoffie, Re [US Government v Microsoft] 162 F 3d 708, 1st Cir
    1998   §10.5
Customs and Excise Commissioners v Hedon Alpha Ltd [1981] QB 818,
    [1981] 2 WLR 791, [1981] 2 All ER 697, CA   3.39

D v Queen's University of Belfast [1997] ELR 431, (1996) *The Times*,
    December 16, NICA   10.7
Dean v Wissman 996 SW 2d 631, Mo Ct App 1999   5.17
Derby v National Trust [2001] PLSCS 24, CA   20.6
Dickson v Pharmaceutical Society of Great Britain [1970] AC 403, [1968] 3
    WLR 286, [1968] 2 All ER 686, HL   10.13, 10.21
D'Jan of London Ltd, Re; Copp v D'Jan [1993] BCC 646, [1994] BCLC 561   3.39,
    §15.3
D'Mello v Loughborough College of Technology (1970) 114 SJ 665, (1970)
    The Times, June 16, [1970] CLY 2888   6.18
Doane v Mount Saint Vincent University 74 DLR (3d) 301, Canada   29.6
Dudzinski v Kellow [1999] FCA 390 (8 April 1999), FCA 1264 (27 August
    1999) Australia   App 6(1), 29.3
Duomatic Ltd, Re [1969] 2 Ch 365, [1969] 2 WLR 114, [1969] 1 All ER 161   3.39

EC Commission v Spain (Madrid University) (Case 24/91) [1992] ECR
    I-1989, [1994] 2 CMLR 621, ECJ   28.15
East London College v University of East London (2001) unreported, 15
    February, QBD   §17.1
Edmunds v Brown and Tillard (1688) 1 Lev 237   3.44
Edwards v California University of Pennsylvania 156 F 3d 488, 3d Cir 1998   §10.3
Eelheimer v Middlebury College 869 F Supp 238, D Vt 1994   §6.13
Enderby Town Football Club Ltd v Football Association Ltd [1971] Ch 591,
    [1970] 3 WLR 1021, [1971] 1 All ER 215, CA   7.35

Esso Petroleum Co Ltd v Fumegrange Ltd (1994) 68 P&CR D15, [1994] 46
    EG 199, [1994] NPC 106, CA   23.10
Euro Express, Re [2000] 2 WLR 907, CA   §15.2
Excelsior Snc de Pedrotti Bruna and C v Ente Autonoma Fiera Internazionale
    di Milano (C-260/99) [2001] TLR 412, (2001) *The Times,* June 26, ECJ §28.2

FC Sheppard & Co Ltd v Jerrom [1987] QB 301, [1986] 3 WLR 801, [1986] 3
    All ER 589, [1986] IRLR 358, CA   11.19
FDIC v Providence College 115 F 3d 136, 2d Cir 1997   5.21
Fahy's Will Trusts; Mcknight v Fahy [1962] 1 WLR 17, [1962] 1 All ER 73,
    106 SJ 15   25.3
Farley v Skinner [2001] UKHL 49, [2001] 3 WLR 899, [2001] 4 All ER 801,
    [2001] 49 EG 120, HL   29.38
Feldman v Ho 171 F 3d 494, 7th Cir 1999   §10.3
Fennell v Australia National University [1999] FCA 989 (22 July 1999),
    Australia   App 6(1), 29.3
Flanagan v University College Dublin [1988] IR 724, [1990] CL 1808   App 6(1),
                                                                         7.37
Forster, ex parte, Re Sydney University [1963] SR (NSW) 723   §9.8
Foster v Board of Trustees of Butler County Community College 771 F Supp
    1122, D Kan 1991   5.21
Frabotta v Meridia Huron Hospital School 657 NE 2d 816, Ohio Ct App 1995 §6.13
Framlington Group plc and Another v Anderson and Others [1995] BCC 611,
    [1995] 1 BCLC 475, ChD   3.39
Francovitch and Bonifaci v Republic of Italy (Joined Cases C-6 and C-9/90)
    [1991] ECR I-5357, [1993] 2 CMLR 66, [1995] ICR 722, ECJ   28.10

Gebhard v Consiglio dell'Ordine degli Avvocati e Procuratori di Milano (Case
    C-55/94) [1995] ECR I-4165, (1995) *The Times,* December 13, ECJ   28.54
Gebroeders Beentjes BV v The Netherlands (Case 31/87) [1990] 1 CMLR 287,
    [1988] ECR 4635, ECJ   28.17
Gencor ACP Ltd v Dalby [2000] 2 BCLC 734, ChD   §15.2
Ghosh v General Medical Council [2001] UKPC 29, [2001] 1 WLR 1915,
    [2001] All ER (D) 189 (Jun), (2001) *The Times,* June 25, PC   §7.1
Gill v Franklin Pierce Law Center 899 F Supp 850, DNH 1995   §22.5
Glazewsksa v Sweden (1985) 45 DR 300   22.32
Glynn v Keele University [1971] 1 WLR 487, [1971] 2 All ER 89; *sub nom*
    Glynn v University of Keele (1970) 115 SJ 173   §7.6, §9.8, 9.25
Glynn v University of Keele. *See* Glynn v Keele University
Godfrey v Demon Internet Ltd [1999] 4 All ER 342, [1999] EMLR 542,
    [1999] ITCLR 282, QBD   14.12, 14.13
Goodwin v Patent Office [1999] ICR 302, [1999] IRLR 4, [1999] Disc LR 104,
    EAT   22.4
Grand Duchy of Luxembourg v European Parliament and Council of the
    European Union (Case C-168/98) (2000) unreported, 7 November, ECJ   28.51
Greater Glasgow Health Board's Application [1996] RPC 207, (1996) 19(1)
    IPD 6, Pat Ct   12.38
Green v Peterhouse (1896) *The Times,* February 10   App 6(1), §7.2
Green v Rutherforth (1750) 1 Ves Sen 463   30.25, 30.36

Greenaway v Tesco (1998) unreported   20.6
Groener v Minister of Education and City of Dublin Vocational Education
    Committee (Case C-379/87) [1989] ECR 3967, [1990] 1 CMLR 401,
    (1989) *The Times*, December 1, ECJ   28.44

Hadden v University of Dundee Students' Association [1985] IRLR 449, EAT   19.20
Hanlan v University of Huddersfield [1999] Disc LR 82, EAT   §22.6
Harries v Church Commissioners for England; *sub nom* Lord Bishop cᶠ Oxford
    v Church Commissioners of England [1992] 1 WLR 1241, [1993] 2 All
    ER 300, (1991) 135 SJLB 180   3.35, 4.18, 4.20
Harrison v Hearn [1972] 1 NSWLR 428   19.16
Hatton v United Kingdom (2001) ECHR, 2 October   §7.1
Hedley Byrne & Co v Heller & Partners [1964] AC 465, [1963] 3 WLR 101,
    [1963] 2 All ER 575, HL   §6.25
Hegel v Langsam [1971] 29 Ohio Misc 147, 237 NE 2d 351, 55 Ohio 2d 476   §6.5
Heinz (HJ) Co Ltd v Kenrick [2000] ICR 491, [2000] IRLR 144, (2000) IDS
    Brief 657/3, EAT   §22.7
Henderson v Merrett Syndicates Ltd; Hallam-Earnes v Same; Hughes v Same;
    Arbuthnott v Feltrim Underwriting Agencies; Deeny v Gooda Walker (in
    Liquidation) [1995] 2 AC 145, [1994] 3 WLR 761, [1994] 3 All ER 506,
    HL   §6.26
Henry v The Delaware Law School of Widener University Inc 1998 Del Ch
    LEXIS 7, Ct Chan Del 1998; *affirmed* 718 A 2d 527, Del 1998   5.17
Herring v Templeman and Others [1973] 3 All ER 569, (1973) 117 SJ 793,
    (1973) 72 LGR 162, CA; [1973] 2 All ER 581   §9.8, 9.25, 30.31, App 30
Hines v Birkbeck College [1986] Ch 524, [1986] 2 WLR 97, [1985] 3 All ER
    156   30.29, 30.49, 30.61, App 30
Hogg v Historic Building and Monuments Commission for England [1989]
    CLY 2573, Truro Cty Ct   20.6
Home Treat Ltd, Re [1991] BCC 165, [1991] BCLC 705   3.39
Hugo Fernando Hocsman v Ministrie de l'Emploi et de la Solidarite (Case
    C-238/98) [2000] 3 CMLR 1025, ECJ   28.53
Hydrodam (Corby) Ltd (in Liquidation), Re [1994] BCC 161, [1994] 2 BCLC
    180, (1994) *The Times*, February 19, ChD   15.18

IBM/Computer Programs (T935/97); *sub nom* IBM Corp's European Patent
    Application (No 96305851.6) (T935/97) [1999] RPC 861, [1999] EPOR
    301, [1999] Info TLR 135, Technical Bd App   14.11
Income Tax Special Purposes Commissioners v Pemsel [1891] AC 531,
    [1891–4] All ER Rep 28, 55 JP 805, HL   4.3
Iqbal Sandhu v University of Central England. *See* R v University of Central
    England ex parte Sandhu (Iqbal)
Islington LBC v Rogers; *sub nom* Rogers v Islington LBC [2000] EHLR 3,
    (2000) 32 HLR 138, [1999] 3 EGLR 17, [1999] NPC 106, CA   21.8

JD Williams & Co Ltd v Michael Hyde & Associates Ltd; *sub nom* Michael
    Hyde & Associates Ltd v JD Williams & Co Ltd [2000] Lloyd's Rep PN
    823, [2000] NPC 78, (2000) *The Times*, August 4, CA   §6.25
Jackson v Horizon Holidays [1975] 1 WLR 468, [1975] 3 All ER 92, 119 SJ
    759, CA   17.9, 29.38

Jacob v Tesco (1998) unreported, 5 November, CA 20.6

Jarvis v Swan Tours Ltd [1973] 1 QB 233, [1972] 3 WLR 954, [1973] 1 All ER
71, CA 29.38

Jeanette Winterson v Mark Hogarth (WIPO Case No D2000-0235, 22 May
2000) 14.11

Jebson v Ministry of Defence [2000] 1 WLR 2055, [2000] ICR 1220, [2000]
PIQR P201, CA §6.22

Jeff Erpelding v Ministrie de la Santè (Case C-16/99) (2000) unreported, 14
September, ECJ 28.53

Jenkin v Pharmaceutical Society of Great Britain [1921] 1 Ch 392 10.13

Jex-Blake v Senatus Academics of the University of Edinburgh [1873] 11 M
784 App 6(1), 29.7

Jimenez v Almodovar 650 F 2d 363, 1st Cir 1981 §10.5

Johns Hopkins University v Ritter 689 A 2d 91, Ct App Md 1996 5.21

Johnson v Nottinghamshire Combined Police Authority; Dutton v Same
[1974] 1 WLR 358, [1974] ICR 170; *sub nom* Johnson v Nottinghamshire
Combined Police Authority, Dutton v Nottinghamshire Combined Police
Authority [1974] 1 All ER 1082, CA 11.27

Johnson v Unisys [1999] 1 All ER 854, [1999] ICR 809, [1999] IRLR 90, CA 29.38

Jolley v London Borough of Sutton [2000] 1 WLR 1082, [2000] 3 All ER 409,
[2000] BLGR 399, HL 20.3

Jones v The Post Office. *See* Post Office v Jones

Jones v Tower Boot Co Ltd [1997] 2 All ER 406, [1997] ICR 254, [1997]
IRLR 168, CA 5.25

Jones v University College Aberystwyth (1995) unreported 30.59

Jones v Welsh Rugby Football Union; Jones v Pugh (1997) *The Times*, March
6, QBD 7.29

Kaye v Croydon Tramsways Co [1898] 1 Ch 358, 67 LJ Ch 222, 14 TLR 244,
CA 5.3

Kent v University College London (1992) 156 LGR 1003, (1992) *The Times*,
February 18, CA 28.33

Kirby's Coaches Ltd, Re [1991] BCC 130, [1991] BCLC 414 3.39

Kirker v British Sugar plc [1998] IRLR 513 §24.4

Knoll v Board of Regents of the University of Nebraska 601 NW 2d 757, 1999 §6.4

Krakunas v Iona College 119 F 3d 80, 2d Cir 1997 §10.3

Kraus v Land Baden-Württemberg (Case C-19/92) [1993] ECR I-1663, (1993)
The Times, April 6, ECJ 28.51

Krotkoff v Goucher College 585 F 2d 675, 4th Cir 1978 §10.5

Kuwait Asia Bank EC v National Mutual Life Nominees Ltd [1991] 1 AC 187,
[1990] 3 WLR 297, [1990] 3 All ER 404, PC §15.3

Lalu Hanuman v UK [2000] ELR 685, ECHR 7.18, §8.4, 9.43, 30.62

Langlois v Rector and Members of Laval University [1974] 47 DLR (3d) 674 30.32

Lavarack v Woods of Colchester Ltd [1967] 1 QB 278, [1966] 3 WLR 706,
[1966] 3 All ER 683, CA 11.49

Le Compte, Van Leuven and de Mayere v Belgium (1980) 4 EHRR 1, ECHR 9.43

Lee v Lee's Air Farming Ltd [1961] AC 12, [1960] 3 WLR 758, [1960] 3 All
ER 420, PC §15.2

Leeds and Hanley Theatres of Varieties, Re [1902] 2 Ch 809, 72 LJ Ch 1, 87
LT 488, CA 3.37

Leicester University Students' Union v Mahomed [1995] ICR 270, [1995]
    IRLR 292, (1994) *The Times*, December 6, EAT   19.20
Levin v Harleston 770 F Supp 895; *affirmed* 966 F 2d 85, 2d Cir 1992   §10.2
Lewis v University of Bristol and Ultra Violet Light Properties (Third Party)
    (2001) unreported, 15 June, CA   20.8
Linkage Corporation v Trustees of Boston University 679 NE 2d 191, Mass
    1997   5.21
Lister and Others v Hesley Hall Ltd [2001] UKHL 22, [2001] 2 WLR 1311,
    [2001] 2 All ER 769, [2001] 2 FLR 307, HL   5.25
Liverpool and District Hospital for Diseases of the Heart v Attorney-General
    [1981] Ch 193, [1981] 2 WLR 379, [1981] 1 All ER 994   3.35
Livingstone v Rawyards Coal Co (1880) 5 App Cas 25, 44 JP 392, 28 WR 357,
    HL   29.38
Lloyd v Alpha Phi Alpha and Cornell University 1999 US Dist LEXIS 906,
    NDNY (1999) 26 January   §6.4
Lloyd v Director of Public Prosecutions [1992] 1 All ER 982, [1992] RTR 215,
    [1991] Crim LR 904, DC   20.10
Lo-Line Electric Motors Ltd, Re, Companies Act 1985, Re [1988] Ch 477,
    [1988] 3 WLR 26, [1988] 2 All ER 692   §15.2
London Borough of Hammersmith and Fulham v Farnsworth [2000] IRLR
    691, EAT   §22.7
London College of Science and Technology v Islington London Borough
    Council [1997] ELR 162, [1997] COD 33, (1996) *The Times*, July 23,
    QBD   §2.1
London Hospital Medical College v Inland Revenue Commissioners and
    Others [1976] 1 WLR 613, [1976] 2 All ER 113, [1976] TR 29   19.16
Lord Bishop of Oxford v Church Commissioners of England. *See* Harries v
    Church Commissioners for England
Lyall v Service (1863) 2 M 115   App 6(1)

MFI Warehouses Ltd v Nattrass [1973] 1 WLR 307, [1973] 1 All ER 762,
    [1973] Crim LR 196, DC   29.27
M v London Guildhall University [1998] ELR 149, CA   App 6(1), 7.51, §9.8, 9.12
M v Secretary of State for Education [2001] 2 FCR 11; *sub nom* R v Secretary
    of State for Education and Employment and Another ex parte McNally
    [2001] TLR 231, (2001) *The Times*, March 23, CA   7.37
Macquarie University, Re, ex parte Ong [1989] 17 NSWLR 119   30.50
Majid v London Guildhall University (1993) *The Times Higher Educational*
    Supplement, 12 November, CA   9.19
Malcolm v Chancellor, Masters and Scholars of the University of Oxford (t/a
    Oxford University Press) [1994] EMLR 17, (1990) *The Times*, December
    19, CA   5.22
McFadyen ex parte [1945] 45 SR (NSW) 200   30.47, 30.48
McGill v the Regents of the University of California 52 Cal Reptr 2d 466, Ct
    App Cal, 4th Dist 1996   §10.6
McGuinness v University of New Mexico School of Medicine 170 F 3d 974,
    10th Cir 1998   §22.5
McLeod v Hunter (John) [1987] CLY 1162, Westminster Cty Ct   29.38
McNeil v Wagner College 667 NYS 2d 397, Sup Ct App Div 1998   §6.21

Marchant v Charters [1977] 1 WLR 1181, [1977] 3 All ER 918, (1976) 34
    P&CR 291, CA   23.9

Marshall v Harland and Wolff Ltd [1972] 1 WLR 899, [1972] 2 All ER 715,
    [1972] IRLR 90, NIRC   11.19

Mayberry v Dees 633 F 2d 502, 4th Cir 1981   §10.6

Mehta v Royal Bank of Scotland plc [1999] L&TR 340, (1999) 78 P&CR D11,
    [1999] 3 EGLR 153, QBD   23.5

Merrett v Babb [2001] EWCA Civ 214, [2001] 3 WLR 1, [2001] EGCS 24,
    (2001) *The Times*, March 2, CA   §6.25

Michael Hyde & Associates Ltd v JD Williams & Co Ltd. *See* JD Williams &
    Co Ltd v Michael Hyde & Associates Ltd

Milmo v Carreras [1946] KB 306, [1946] 1 All ER 288, 115 LJKB 278, CA   23.30

Mittra v University of Medicine and Dentistry of New Jersey 719 A 2d 693, NJ
    Ct App 1998   §6.13

Moran v University College, Salford (No 2) [1994] ELR 187, (1993) *The*
    Times, November 23, CA   6.3, 6.7, 6.15, App 6(1), 9.16

Morrison v Kappa Alpha Psi Fraternity 738 So 2d 1105, La Ct App 1999   §6.4

Morse v Wiltshire County Council [1998] ICR 1023, [1998] IRLR 352,
    (1998) 44 BMLR 58, EAT   22.9

Molton Builders Ltd v City of Westminster LBC (1976) 30 P&CR 182, (1975)
    119 SJ 627, CA   23.16

Mozart v State [of New York] 441 NYS 2d 600, NY Ct Cl 1981   5.21

Murdoch University v Bloom (1980) unreported, 16 April, Australia   30.49

Murphy v Epsom College [1985] ICR 80, [1984] IRLR 271, (1985) 82 LS Gaz
    199, CA   11.27

Murray v Foyle Meats Ltd [1999] 3 WLR 356, [1999] 3 All ER 769, [1999]
    ICR 827, HL   11.23, 11.24

Napolitino v The Trustees of Princeton University 453 A 2d 263, NJ Sup Ct
    App Div 1982   App 6(1)

Nash v Chelsea College of Art and Design [2001] EWHC Admin 538, [2001]
    All ER (D) 133 (Jul), [2001] TLR 471, (2001) *The Times*, July 25,
    QBD   App 6(1), 7.40, §9.9

National Car Parks v The Trinity Development Company (Banbury) Ltd
    [2000] EGCS 128, ChD; (2001) unreported, CA   23.3, 23.10, 23.11

National Trustees Co of Australia v General Finance Co of Australia [1905]
    AC 373, 74 LJPC 73, 92 LT 736, PC   3.39

Naylor v Cornish (1684) 1 Vern 311n(1)   3.44

Neberry v East Texas State University 161 F 3d 276, 5th Cir 1998   §22.4

Nedder v Rivier College 908 F Supp 66, DNH 1995; 944 F Sup 111, DNH
    1996   §22.4

Nessa v Chief Adjudication Officer [1999] 4 All ER 677, HL   28.32

Noah v Shuba [1991] FSR 14, [1991] CLY 570   17.16

Norman v Theodore Goddard (Quirk, Third Party) [1992] BCC 14, [1992]
    BCLC 1028   §15.3

Norrie v Senate of the University of Auckland [1984] 1 NZLR 129   30.33, 30.52,
    30.55, App 30

Norwich City Council v Harvey (Paul Clarke) [1989] 1 WLR 828, [1989] 1
    All ER 1180, (1989) 133 SJ 694, CA   17.9

Norwich Union case (1997) *The Times*, July 18   14.1, 14.12

Oakes v Sidney Sussex College, Cambridge [1988] 1 WLR 431, [1988] 1 All
    ER 1004, (1988) 132 SJ 416   30.32, 30.61, App 30
O'Brien v Associated Fire Alarms Ltd [1968] 1 WLR 1916, [1969] 1 All ER 93,
    4 KIR 223, CA   29.5
Ohio Civil Rights Commission v Cane Western Reserve University 666 NE 2d
    1376, Ohio 1996   §22.5
Ord v Belhaven Pubs Ltd [1998] BCC 607, [1998] 2 BCLC 447, (1998) *The
    Times*, April 7, CA   §15.2
Ostasz v Medical College of Ohio 691 NE 2d 371, Ct Cl Oh 1997   5.17
Oxford v Moss (1978) 68 Cr App R 183, [1979] Crim LR 119, DC   14.9, §20.8
Oxford University Press v Commissioner of Income Tax 2001 SOL Case No
    053 (2001) January 1, Supreme Ct of India   4.17

Paal Wilson & Co A/S v Partenreederei Hannah Blumenthal [1983] 1 AC 854,
    [1982] 3 WLR 1149, [1983] 1 All ER 34, HL   11.18
Pace v Hymas 726 P 2d 693, Idaho 1986   §10.5
Palmer (Sigismund) v R; Irving (Derrick) v R [1971] AC 814, [1971] 2 WLR
    831; *sub nom* Palmer v R [1971] 1 All ER 1077, 55 Cr App R 223, PC   §20.6
Parker v British Airways Board [1982] QB 1004, [1982] 2 WLR 503, [1982] 1
    All ER 834, CA   26.2
Patel v University of Bradford Senate [1979] 1 WLR 1066, [1979] 2 All ER
    582, (1979) 123 SJ 436, CA; *affirming* [1978] 1 WLR 1488, [1978] 3 All
    ER 841, (1978) 122 SJ 791   8.4, 30.23, 30.29, 30.31, 30.33, 30.48, 30.61,
                                                                     App 30
Pearce v University of Aston in Birmingham [1991] 2 All ER 461, CA   30.33, 30.61,
                                                                     App 30
Petrie v Universita degli Studi di Verona (Case C-90/96) [1998] CEC 117,
    [1998] CLY 2153, ECJ   28.44
Phelps v Hillingdon London Borough Council [2000] 3 WLR 776, [2000] 4
    All ER 504, [2000] LGR 651, HL   §6.24, §6.26, §6.28, 6.27
Philips v Bury [1692] 1 Ld Raym 5, 2 TR 347, Skin 447, 4 Mod 106   30.28, 30.29,
                                                                30.44, 30.61, App 30
Pinion, Re, Westminster Bank v Pinion [1965] Ch 85, [1964] 2 WLR 919,
    [1964] 1 All ER 890, CA   4.6
Pitre v Louisiana Tech University 655 So 2d 659, La Ct App 1995; *reversed*
    673 So 2d 585, La 1996   §6.5
Polkey v AE Dayton Services Ltd [1988] AC 344, [1987] 3 WLR 1153, [1987]
    3 All ER 974, [1987] IRLR 503, HL   11.46, 11.47
Post Office v Jones [2001] EWCA Civ 558, [2001] ICR 805; *sub nom* Jones v
    The Post Office [2001] IRLR 384, (2001) *The Times*, June 5, CA   §22.7
Prestwick Circuits Ltd v McAndrews [1990] IRLR 191, 1990 SLT 654   29.5
Produce Marketing Consortium Ltd (in Liquidation), Re [1989] 1 WLR 745,
    [1989] 3 All ER 1, [1989] BCLC 513   3.39
Prudential Assurance Co Ltd v London Residuary Body and Others [1992] 2
    AC 386, [1992] 3 WLR 279, [1992] 3 All ER 504, HL   23.4

Queen on the application of Ahmed v University of Oxford (2000)
    unreported, 7 November   App 6(1), §9.9

Queen on the application of B v Head Teacher of Alperton Community School
[2001] EWHC Admin 229, [2001] ELR 359; *sub nom* R v Secretary of
State for Education and Employment ex parte B (2001) *The Times*, June 8
9.43
Queen on the application of Isolyn Burgess v South Bank University [2001]
ELR 300–310 App 6(1)
Queen on the application of Jemchi v the Visitor of Brunel University (2001)
unreported, 23 April, QBD §8.4
Queen on the application of Greenwich Property Ltd v Commissioners of
Customs and Excise §18.4
Queen on the application of Liverpool Hope University College v Secretary of
State for Education and Employment [2001] EWHC Civ 362, (2001)
unreported, 15 March §2.1
Queen on the application of M v University of the West of England [2001]
ELR 458 App 6(1), §9.9
Queen on the application of McNally v Secretary of State for Education and
Metropolitan Borough of Bury [2001] ELR 772 9.42, 9.43
Queen on the application of Mitchell v Coventry University and the Secretary
of State for Education and Employment [2001] ELR 594–606 28.32
Queen on the application of Oxford Study Centre Ltd v British Council
[2001] EWHC Admin 207, [2001] ELR 803 App 6(1), §9.1, 9.20
Queen on the application of Persaud v Cambridge University [2001] EWCA
Civ 534, [2001] ELR 480, CA App 6(1), 9.9, 9.42
Queen on the application of Udemba v South Bank University (2000)
unreported, 2 November App 6(1), §9.9
Quinn v Schwartzkopf Ltd [2001] IRLR 67, (2001) IDS Brief 679/9 EAT §22.7

R v A Local Authority and Police Authority in the Midlands ex parte LM
[2000] 1 FLR 612, [2000] UKHRR 143, [2000] COD 41, QBD 9.38
R v Absolam (1989) 88 Cr App R 332, [1988] Crim LR 748, CA 14.9
R v Adams (1985) 7 Cr App R (S) 97, CA 20.17
R v Appleford (1672) 2 Keb 861; *sub nom* Appleford's Case (1672) 1 Mod Rep
82; *sub nom* R v New College, Oxford 84 ER 545 30.29
R v Avro plc (1993) 157 JP 759, (1993) 157 JPN 490, (1993) 12 Tr LR 83, CA
29.27
R v Bishop of Chester (1747) 1 WM Bl 22, 1 Wils 206 30.27, 30.29, App 30
R v Bishop of Ely. *See* St John's College, Cambridge v Todington
R v Board of Governors of the London Oratory School ex parte Regis (1988)
The Times, February 17 9.20
R v Board of Governors of the Sheffield Hallam University ex parte Rowlett
[1994] COD 470, (1995) EdLM 2(4)11, QBD App 6(1), 9.29, 9.43, 9.48
R v Bow Street Magistrates Court and Allison A.P. ex parte Government of the
United States of America [1999] 4 All ER 319 14.8
R v Bow Street Metropolitan Stipendiary Magistrate ex parte Pinochet Ugarte
(No 2) [2000] 1 AC 119, [1999] 2 WLR 272, [1999] 1 All ER 577, HL 9.48
R v Bowden [2000] 2 WLR 1083, CA 14.10
R v Breeze [1973] 1 WLR 994, [1973] 2 All ER 1141, [1973] Crim LR 458,
CA 29.27
R v Cambridge University ex parte Beg [1999] ELR 404, (1999) 11 Admin LR
505, (1999) 163 JPN 755, QBD App 6(1), 9.40
R v Chelsea College of Art and Design ex parte Nash [2000] ELR 686, [2000]
Ed CR 571, QBD App 6(1), §9.9

R v City of Bath College Corporation ex parte Bashforth [1999] ELR 459,
    QBD §3.12, 9.22
R v Committee of the Lords of the Judicial Committee of the Privy Council
    acting for the Visitor of the University of London ex parte Vijayatunga
    [1990] 2 QB 444, [1989] 3 WLR 13, [1989] 2 All ER 843, CA; [1988] 1
    QB 322, [1988] 2 WLR 106, [1987] 3 All ER 204, DC 30.35, 30.61, App 30
R v Cranfield University Senate ex parte Bashir [1999] ELR 317, [1999] Ed
    CR 772, CA App 6(1), 7.53
R v de Montfort University ex parte Cottrell (1996) unreported App 6(1)
R v Derbyshire County Council ex parte Noble [1990] ICR 808, [1990] IRLR
    332, CA 9.21
R v Disciplinary Committee of the Jockey Club ex parte Aga Khan [1993] 1
    WLR 909, [1993] 2 All ER 853, [1993] COD 234, CA 9.19
R v Dunsheath ex parte Meredith [1951] 1 KB 127, [1950] 2 All ER 741, 94 SJ
    598, DC 30.29
R v East Berkshire Health Authority ex parte Walsh [1985] QB 152, [1984] 3
    WLR 818, [1984] 3 All ER 425, [1984] ICR 743, CA 9.21, 10.12
R v Fellows (Alban); R v Arnold (Stephen) [1997] 2 All ER 548, [1997] 1 Cr
    App R 244, [1997] Crim LR 524, CA 14.10
R v Fernhill Manor School ex parte A [1994] ELR 67, [1993] 1 FLR 620, QBD
    9.20
R v Flintshire CC ex parte Armstrong-Braun [2001] LGR 344, [2001] TLR
    186, (2001) *The Times*, March 8, CA 5.6
R v Gold; R v Schifreen [1988] 1 AC 1063, [1988] 2 WLR 984, [1988] 2 All
    ER 186, HL 14.8
R v Gough (Robert) [1993] AC 646, [1993] 2 WLR 883, [1993] 2 All ER 724,
    HL 9.48
R v Governors of Haberdashers' Aske's Hatcham College Trust ex parte T
    (1994) *The Times*, October 19, (1994) *The Independent*, October 12,
    [1994] CLY 24 9.20
R v HM Treasury ex parte University of Cambridge (Case C-380/98) [2000] 1
    WLR 2514, [2000] All ER (EC) 920, [2001] CEC 30, [2000] CMLR
    1359, ECJ §28.2, 28.16, 28.17
R v Hereford and Worcester County Council ex parte Wimbourne (1983) 82
    LGR 251, [1984] CLY 1174 28.32
R v Higher Education Funding Council ex parte Institute of Dental Surgery
    [1994] 1 WLR 242, [1994] 1 All ER 651, [1994] COD 147, QBD §9.1, §9.9,
    9.10
R v Hull University Visitor ex parte Page; *sub nom* R v Lord President of the
    Privy Council ex parte Page [1993] AC 682, [1992] 3 WLR 112, [1991] 4
    All ER 747, HL 2.2, 9.18, 10.2, 11.8, 30.44, 30.45, 30.61, App 30
R v Leeds Metropolitan University ex parte Manders [1998] ELR 502,
    QBD App 6(1), 9.10
R v Liverpool Corporation (1759) 2 Burr 723, 97 ER 533 5.3
R v Liverpool John Moores University ex parte Hayes [1998] ELR 261,
    QBD App 6(1), §9.8, 9.31
R v Lloyd (Sidney); R v Bhuee; R v Ali (Choukal) [1985] QB 829, [1985] 3
    WLR 30, [1985] 2 All ER 661, CA 14.9
R v London Borough of Newham ex parte X [1995] ELR 305 9.13
R v Lord President of the Privy Council ex parte Page. *See* R v Hull University
    Visitor ex parte Page

R v Manchester Metropolitan University ex parte Nolan [1994] ELR 380,
(1993) *The Independent*, 15 July, DC   App 6(1), 7.53, 9.13, 9.26, 9.29, 9.40
R v Ministry of Agriculture, Fisheries and Food ex parte First City Trading
[1997] 1 CMLR 250, [1997] Eu LR 195, (1996) *The Times*, December 20,
QBD   9.40
R v Ministry of Defence ex parte Murray [1998] COD 134, (1997) *The Times*,
December 17, (1997) *The Independent*, December 18, QBD   9.46
R v New College, Oxford. *See* R v Appleford
R v North and East Devon Health Authority ex parte Coughlan [2000] 2 WLR
622, [2000] 3 All ER 850, [1999] COD 340, CA   9.41
R v Nottinghamshire County Council ex parte Jain [1989] COD 442, (1989)
The Independent, January 23, [1990] CLY 1759, DC   28.33
R v Oxford University ex parte Bolchover (1970) *The Times*, October 7   §9.8, 30.17
R v Panel on Takeovers and Mergers ex parte Datafin [1987] QB 815, [1987]
2 WLR 699, [1987] 1 All ER 564, CA   9.19, 10.11
R v Rochdale MBC ex parte Schemet [1994] ELR 89   9.41
R v Scriba [1998] Crim LR 68   14.12
R v Secretary of State for Education ex parte Prior [1994] ELR 231   9.31
R v Secretary of State for Education ex parte S [1995] ELR 71, [1995] 2 FCR
225, [1995] COD 48, CA   9.42
R v Secretary of State for Education and Employment ex parte B. *See* Queen
on the application of B v Head Teacher of Alperton Community School
R v Secretary of State for Education and Employment and Another ex parte
McNally. *See* M v Secretary of State for Education
R v Secretary of State for the Environment ex parte Holding and Barnes plc; R
v Secretary of State for the Environment ex parte Alconbury
Developments Ltd and Others; Secretary of State for the Environment v
Legal and General Assurance Society Ltd [2001] UKHL 23, [2001] 2
WLR 1399, [2001] 2 All ER 929, (2001) *The Times*, May 9, HL   §7.1, 7.19
R v Secretary of State for the Home Department ex parte Daly [2001] 2 WLR
1622, HL   9.40
R v Secretary of State for Transport ex parte Factortame [1990] 2 AC 85,
[1989] 2 WLR 997, [1989] 2 All ER 692, HL   App 1
R v Self [1992] 1 WLR 657, [1992] 3 All ER 476, (1992) 95 Cr App Rep 42,
CA   20.11
R v Sheffield Howlett University Board of Governors ex parte R [1994] COD
470, QBD   App 6(1)
R v Smith (Morgan James) [2000] 3 WLR 654, [2000] 4 All ER 289, [2000]
Crim LR 1004, HL   §20.7
R v Somerset County Council and ARC Southern Ltd ex parte Dixon [1997]
COD 323, [1997] JPL 1030, [1997] NPC 61, QBD   9.14, 9.51
R v South Bank University ex parte Burgess (2000) unreported, 4
October   App 6(1), §9.9
R v South Bank University ex parte Coggeran [2000] ICR 1342, (2000) 97
(40) LSG 41, [2001] ELR 42, CA   App 6(1), §9.9
R v Sunair Holidays [1973] 1 WLR 1105   29.27
R v the Teacher Training Agency ex parte University of Exeter [2001] EWHC
Admin 264, unreported   §9.1
R v Thames Valley University Student Union ex parte Ogilvy [1997] CLY
2149, (1997) 4(8) ELM 6, QBD   9.19, §19.2

R v University College London ex parte Idriss [1999] EdCR 462, [1999] CLY
1928, QBD App 6(1), 9.45

R v University College London ex parte Riniker [1995] ELT 213, (1995) EdLR
2(6)1 9.22

R v University of Aston Senate ex parte Roffey [1969] 2 QB 538, [1969] 2
WLR 1418, [1969] 2 All ER 964, DC App 6(1), 7.50, §9.8, 9.25, 30.40

R v University of Cambridge (Dr Bentley's Case) (1723) 1 Str 557, Fortes Rep
202, 2 Ld Raym 1334 §9.8, 30.17

R v University of Cambridge ex parte Evans [1998] ELR 515, [1998] EdCR
151 §9.6, 9.32, 30.18

R v University of Cambridge ex parte Evans (No 2) [1999] EdCR 556, [1999]
CLY 1930, QBD §9.6, 9.22

R v University of Cambridge ex parte Persaud [2000] EdCR 635, QBD App 6(1)

R v University of Central England ex parte Sandhu (Iqbal) [1999] ELR 419,
[1999] EdCR 766, CA; *affirming* [1999] ELR 121, [1999] EdCR 594,
QBD App 6(1), 7.53, 9.36

R v University of Essex ex parte McPherson (2001) unreported, 23 March,
QBD §8.4

R v University of Humberside ex parte Cousens [1995] CLY 1947, (1995)
EdLM 2(6)11, CA App 6(1), 9.29, 9.45

R v University of Liverpool ex parte Caesar-Gordon [1991] 1 QB 124, [1990]
3 WLR 667, [1990] 3 All ER 821, DC 9.22, 19.7, 20.19

R v University of Nottingham ex parte K [1998] ELR 184, CA App 6(1), 7.51, 9.18

R v University of Portsmouth ex parte Lakareber [1999] ELR 135, [1999] CLY
1933, CA App 6(1), 9.10

R v University of the West of England ex parte M [2001] ELR 77 App 6(1), §9.9,
9.38

R v Visitor to University of East Anglia ex parte Hanuman [1999] EdCR 781,
CA §8.4, 30.62

R v Visitor to Brunel University ex parte Jemchi [2001] EWCA Civ 1208,
unreported, CA 30.42

R v Visitors to Inns of Court ex parte Calder; Same v Same ex parte Persaud;
Calder v General Council of the Bar; *sub nom* R v Visitors to Lincoln's Inn
ex parte Persaud; R v Same ex parte Calder; Calder v General Council of
the Bar [1993] QB 1, [1993] 3 WLR 287, [1993] 2 All ER 876, CA 30.46

R v Visitors to Lincoln's Inn ex parte Persaud; R v Same ex parte Calder;
Calder v General Council of the Bar. *See* R v Visitors to the Inns of Court
ex parte Calder; Same v Same ex parte Persaud; Calder v General Council
of the Bar

R v Warwickshire County Council ex parte Collymore [1995] ELR 217,
[1995] COD 52, QBD 9.34

R v Whiteley (1991) 93 Cr App Rep 25, (1991) 135 SJ 249, [1993] FSR 168,
CA 14.8

R v Williams (Gladstone) [1987] 3 All ER 411, (1984) 78 Cr App Rep 276,
[1984] Crim LR 163, CA §20.3

R (on the Application of Greenwich Property Ltd) v Commissioners of
Customs & Excise [2001] STC 618, QBD §18.4

Raspin v United News Shops [1999] IRLR 9, EAT 11.53, 11.54

Ratcliffe v McConnell [1999] 1 WLR 670, [1999] EdCR 523, [1999] IIQR
P170, CA 20.5

Reagan v State 654 NYS 2d 488, NY App Div 1997 §6.21

Reed v Hastings Corporation (1964) 62 LGR 588, 190 EG 961, 108 SJ 480,
    CA   21.3
Reed v Wastie [1972] Crim LR 221, (1972) *The Times*, February 10   §20.4
Reference under s 48A of the Civil Appeal (Northern Ireland) Act 1968 (No 1
    of 1975) [1976] 2 All ER 937, 120 SJ 524, HL   §20.6
Reilly v Daly 666 NE 2d 439, Ind 1996   §9.5
Revill v Newbury [1996] QB 567, [1996] 2 WLR 239, [1996] 1 All ER 291,
    CA   20.13
Rialto, The (No 2). *See* Yukong Lines Ltd of Korea v Rendsburg Investment
    Corporation of Liberia (The Rialto) (No 2)
Ribee v Norie [2000] NPC 116, (2000) *The Times*, November 22, CA   §24.3
Rigg v University of Waikato [1984] 1 NZLR 149   30.52
Rogers v Islington LBC. *See* Islington LBC v Rogers
Romulus Trading Co Ltd v Comet Properties Ltd [1996] 2 EGLR 70, [1996]
    48 EG 157, [1996] NPC 52, QBD   23.18
Rondel v Worsley [1969] 1 AC 191, [1967] 3 WLR 1666, [1967] 3 All ER
    933, HL   §6.24
Ross v Creighton University 957 2d 410, 7th Cir 1992   §6.12
Ross v St Augustine College 103 F 3d 338, 4th Cir 1996   5.17
Rothbard v Colgate University 652 NYS 2d 146, NY App Dist 1997   §6.4
Royal British Bank v Turquand (1856) 6 E&B 327, 119 ER 886, [1843–60] All
    ER Rep 435, Exch Ch   5.24
Ruxley Electronics and Construction Ltd v Forsyth [1996] AC 344, [1995] 3
    WLR 118, [1995] 3 All ER 268, HL   29.38
Ryan v Shipboard Maintenance Ltd [1980] ICR 88, [1980] IRLR 16, EAT   11.16

St David's College, Lampeter v Ministry of Education [1951] 1 All ER 559, 95
    SJ 137, [1951] WN 131   §2.1
St John's College, Cambridge v Todington (1757) 1 Burr 158, 1 Keny 441; *sub*
    nom R v Bishop of Ely 1 Wm Bl 71   30.29, App 30
Saloman (Aron) (Pauper) v Saloman (A) & Co Ltd; Saloman (A) & Co Ltd v
    Aron Salomon [1897] AC 22, 66 LJ Ch 35, [1895–9] All ER Rep 33, HL   §15.2
Sammy v Birkbeck College (1964) *The Times*, November 3   6.18
Scholz (Ingetraut) v Opera Universitaria di Cagliari (C-419/92) [1994] ECR
    I-505, (1994) *The Times*, March 29, ECJ   28.43
Secretary of State for Trade and Industry v Deverell [2000] 2 WLR 907,
    [2000] 2 All ER 365, [2000] 2 BCLC 133, CA   §15.3
Seleh v University of Dundee (1992) *The Times*, December 23   App 6(1)
Shah (Jitendra) v Barnet London Borough Council. *See* Akbarali v Brent
    London Borough Council
Shaw's Will Trusts, Re; National Provincial Bank v National City Bank [1952]
    Ch 163, [1952] 1 All ER 49, 95 SJ 803   4.6
Shell-Mex & BP Ltd v Manchester Garages Ltd [1971] 1 WLR 612, [1971] 1
    All ER 841, 115 SJ 111, CA   23.10, 23.21
Sibley Hospital case. *See* Stern v Lucy Webb Hayes National Training School
    for Deaconesses and Missionaries
Silva v University of New Hampshire 888 F Supp 293, DNH 1994   §10.3
Silvey v Pendragon plc [2001] IRLR 685, CA   11.54
Simmon Box (Diamonds) Ltd, Re [2000] BCC 275, ChD   §15.3
Sirohi v Lee 634 NYS 2d 119, Sup A Ct App Div 1995   §6.12
Smith v Atkins 622 So 2d 795, La App 1993   5.17

Smith and Others v Nottinghamshire County Council [1981] CLY 1520,
(1981) *The Times*, November 13, HL   §23.1, 23.16, 23.18, 23.34
Smoldon v Whitworth [1997] ELR 249, [1997] PIQR P133, (1996) *The Times*,
December 18, CA   §6.21, §6.22, 6.27
South Staffordshire Water Co v Sharman [1896] 2 QB 44, [1895–9] All ER
Rep 259, 65 LJQB 460   26.2
Southwark LBC v Mills; *sub nom* Southwark LBC v Tanner; Baxter v Camden
LBC [1999] 3 WLR 939, [1999] 4 All ER 449, [1999] NPC 123, HL   23.19
Southwark LBC v Tanner. *See* Southwark LBC v Mills
Speight, Re; Speight v Gaunt (1883) 22 Ch D 727, CA   4.27
Spijkers v Gebroeders Benedik Abattoir CV (C-24/85) [1986] 2 CMLR 296,
[1986] 3 ECR 1119, ECJ   17.31
Spring v Guardian Assurance plc [1995] 2 AC 296, [1994] 3 WLR 354,
[1994] 3 All ER 138, [1994] IRLR 460, HL; *reversing* [1993] 2 All ER
273, [1993] ICR 412, CA   5.15, 6.38, §24.3
Spruce v University of Hong Kong [1993] 2 HKLR 65   §9.8
Staples v West Dorset DC (1995) 93 LGR 536, [1995] PIQR P439, (1995) 139
SJLB 117, CA   20.6
Stark v Post Office [2000] ICR 1013, [2000] PIQR P105, (2000) 144 SJLB
150, CA   20.8
Stein v Kent State University Board of Trustees 994 F Supp 898, ND Ohio
1998; *affirmed* 181 F 3d 103, SD NY 1994   §10.6
Stern v Lucy Webb Hayes National Training School for Deaconesses and
Missionaries 381 F Supp 1003 (DDC 1974)   4.26
Stratton Dakmont Inc v Prodigy Services Co 1995 WL 323710 (NY Supp, 24
May 1995)   14.14
Street v Mountford [1985] AC 809, [1985] 2 WLR 877, [1985] 2 All ER 289,
HL   23.2, 23.3, 23.5, 23.6, 23.7, 23.8, 23.10, 23.12, 23.21
Swain v Natui Ram Puri [1996] PIQR P442, [1996] CLY 5697, CA   20.6
Swartley v Hoffner 734 A 2d 915, Pa Super 1999   §6.13
Sylvester v Texas Southern University 957 F Supp 944, SD Tex 1997   §6.13

Target Holdings Ltd v Redferns (a firm) and Another [1942] 2 All ER 337 3.39
Tawil-Albertini v Ministre des Affaires Sociales (Case C-154/93) [1994] ECR
I-451, (1994) *Financial Times*, February 15, ECJ   28.53
Thirunayagam v London Guildhall University (1997) unreported, 14 March,
CA   §6.17, App 6(1)
Thomas v Sorrell (1673) Vaugh 330, [1558–1774] All ER Rep 107, 1 Lev 217,
Ex Ch   23.1
Thomas v University of Bradford [1987] AC 795, [1987] 2 WLR 677, [1987] 1
All ER 834, HL   §8.2, 30.24, 30.30, 30.33, 30.34, 30.38, 30.49, 30.55, 30.61,
App 30
Thomas v University of Bradford (No 2) [1992] 1 All ER 964   30.41
Thomson v University of London (1864) 33 LJ Ch 625, 10 LT 403, 10 Jur NS
669   30.29, 30.32, App 30
Thorne v University of London [1966] 2 QB 237, [1966] 2 WLR 1080, [1966]
2 All ER 338, CA   App 6(1), 7.54, §9.8, 30.29, 30.32, 30.61, App 30
Tolman v CenCor Career Colleges, Inc 851 P 2d 203, Cols App Ct 1992;
affirmed 868 P 2d 396, Cols 1994   §6.12
Trustees of Dartmouth College v Woodward (1819) 17 US 518   30.20

Trustor AB v Smallbone and Another [2001] 1 WLR 1177, [2001] 3 All ER
    987, [2001] 2 BCLC 436, [2001] TLR 247, ChD   §15.2
Tuttle v Edinburgh University 1984 SLT 172   §6.20
Tweddle v Atkinson (1861) 1 B&S 393   17.8

United Bank Ltd v Akhtar [1989] IRLR 507, EAT   29.5
United States v Morris (1991) 928 F 2d 504   14.8
University College London v Newman (1986) *The Times* January 8, CA   28.32
University of Baltimore v Peri Iz 716 A 2d 1107, Md Ct Special App 1998   §10.6
University of Essex v Djemal and Others [1980] 1 WLR 1301, [1980] 2 All ER
    742, (1980) 41 P&CR 340, CA   §19.3, 20.17
University of Melbourne, Re, ex parte De Dimone [1981] VR 378   30.50
University of Nottingham v Fishel [2000] ICR 1462, [2000] IRLR 471, [2000]
    ELR 385, QBD   §10.4, 10.24, §12.3
University of Oxford v Humphreys (1999) unreported, 19 December   16.19
University of Warwick v De Graaf and Others [1975] 1 WLR 1126, [1975] 3
    All ER 284, 119 SJ 528, CA   §19.3, 20.17
University Patents Inc v Kligman 762 F Supp 1212, ED Pa 1991   §12.2
Uratemp Ventures Ltd v Collins [2001] UKHL 43, [2001] 3 WLR 806, [2002]
    1 All ER 46, [2001] 43 EG 186, HL; [2000] L&TR 369, [1999] NPC 153,
    (1999) *The Times*, December 10, CA   23.11, 23.12
Urofsky v Gilmore 167 F 3d 191, 4th Cir 1999; 2000 WL 806882, 4th Cir
    23/06/2000   §10.3

Vanek v Governor of the University of Alberta [1975] 3 WWR 167, [1975] 5
    WWR 429   30.32, 30.51
Vine v Waltham Forest London Borough Council [2000] 1 WLR 2383, [2000]
    4 All ER 169, [2000] RTR 270, CA   20.9

Walker v Northumberland County Council [1995] 1 All ER 737, [1995] ICR
    702, [1995] ELR 231, QBD   §6.22, 6.27, §24.3, §24.4
Ward v Bradford Corporation (1972) 70 LGR 27   §9.8
Watson v British Boxing Board of Control Ltd and Another [2001] QB 1134,
    [2001] 2 WLR 1256, [2001] PIQR P213, CA   §6.21, §6.22
Watts v Morrow [1991] 1 WLR 1421, [1991] 4 All ER 937, (1991) 23 HLR
    608, CA   29.38
Waverley Borough Council v Fletcher [1996] QB 334, [1995] 3 WLR 772,
    [1995] 4 All ER 756, CA   26.2
Webb v Board of Trustees of Ball State University 167 F 3d 1146, 7th Cir 1999
    §10.3
Welfab Engineers Ltd, Re [1990] BCC 600, [1990] BCLC 833   3.39
Westminster City Council v Clarke [1992] 2 AC 288, [1992] 2 WLR 229,
    [1992] 1 All ER 695, HL   23.9, 23.10
Wheat v Lacon (E) & Co [1966] AC 552, [1966] 2 WLR 581, [1966] 1 All ER
    582, HL   20.2
Wiltshire County Council v National Association of Teachers in Further and
    Higher Education and Guy [1978] ICR 968, [1978] IRLR 301, (1978) 77
    LGR 272, EAT   11.16
Wislang's Application, Re [1984] 5 NIJB, [1984] CLY 2462   30.34, 30.38, App 30

Wisniewski v Central Manchester Health Authority [1998] PIQR P324, [1998]
    Lloyd's Rep Med 223, CA   §6.25

X v United Kingdom (1980) 23 DR 228   22.32

Young v Naval, Military and Civil Service Co-operative Society of South Africa
    [1905] 1 KB 687, 74 LJKB 302, 92 LT 458   3.50
Yukong Lines Ltd of Korea v Rendsburg Investment Corporation of Liberia
    (The Rialto) (No 2) [1998] 1 WLR 294, [1998] 4 All ER 82, [1998] 2
    BCLC 485, QBD   §15.2

Zemco Ltd v Jerrom-Pugh [1993] BCC 275, CA   3.39
Zeran v Amenio Online Inc 129 F 3d 327 (4th Cir 1997), cert denied 118 S Ct
    2341 (1998)   14.13

TABLE OF STATUTES

References are to editors' introductions (§), paragraph numbers and
chapter appendices

Access to Justice Act 1989
  s 11   9.52
Administrative Law (University
  Visitor) Act 1985 (Victoria)   30.50
Americans with Disabilities Act
  1990 (USA)   §22.2, §22.3, §22.4,
                    §22.5
Arbitration Act 1996 8.21, 27.41, 27.70,
                    30.60
  ss 89–92   29.24

Business Names Act 1985   §2.1

Charitable Uses Act 1601   4.2, 4.3
  preamble (Statute of Elizabeth
    I)   4.2
Charities Act 1992   4.2, 25.19
  s 58   25.19
  s 60(7)   25.19
  s 63(1)   25.19
Charities Act 1993   3.35, 15.3
  s 8   4.13
  s 13   4.14
  s 16   4.14
    (5)   4.14
  s 18   4.13
  s 26   4.14
  s 27   4.19
    (4)   4.19
  s 29   4.24, 4.26
  s 36   4.13
  s 38   4.13
  ss 41–46   4.17
  s 47(2)   4.17
  s 72   4.18
  s 96   4.10, 4.11
    (1)   4.10

  s 97   4.18
    (1)   3.35
  Sch 2   3.35, 4.8, 4.11, 19.11, 25.6
    category (w)   4.11, 19.30
Companies Acts   3.12, 3.34, 3.38
Companies Act 1985   §2.3, §15.1, 19.28
  Pt X   §15.3
  s 1(4)   15.24
  s 15(1)   15.24
  s 288   15.29, 19.31
  s 292   15.27
  s 303   15.27
  s 317   15.28
  s 320   15.28
  s 370   15.23
  s 378   15.23
  s 379A   15.23
  s 459   15.30
  s 727   3.29, 3.38, 3.39, 3.40, 3.45,
               §4.4, 4.21
  s 741(3)   §15.3
Companies Act 1989   5.24
Companies Consolidation
  (Consequential Provisions)
  Act 1985
  s 10   15.24
Competition Act 1998   17.43, 28.57,
              28.68, 28.69
  Ch I   28.68, 28.69
  Ch II   28.68, 28.70
Computer Misuse Act 1990   14.8
  s 1   14.8
Consumer Credit Act 1974 25.28, 27.23
Consumer Protection Act 1987   25.29,
              29.12, 29.37
  Pt III (ss 20–26)   29.29
  s 20   25.28
  s 21   25.28
    (c)   29.29

Consumer Protection Act 1987 – *cont*
s 39   29.30
Contracts (Rights of Third Parties) Act 1999   17.9, 17.10
Copyright Designs and Patents Act 1988   12.24, App 12(2), 17.15, 17.16
Criminal Damage Act 1971   14.8
Criminal Justice Act 1988   14.10
Criminal Justice and Public Order Act 1994   1.15, 14.10, 20.18
s 69   20.18
Criminal Law Act 1967   20.13
Criminal Law Act 1977   23.24

Data Protection Act 1984   13.1, 13.8, 14.7
Data Protection Act 1998   1.37, 2.8, 6.38, 9.42, 10.16, §13.1, §13.2, 13.1, 13.2, 13.3, 13.6, 13.7, 13.8, 13.9, 13.10, 13.11, 13.12, 13.13, 13.14, 13.16, 13.22, 13.24, 13.25, 14.5, 14.7, 14.10, 19.29, 20.20, 20.21, 20.22, §23.2, §24.3, 25.4, 25.11, 25.20, 25.25, 25.38
Pt II   App 13(1), 25.25
Pt III   25.25
Pt IV   13.23
s 10   13.23, 25.35
s 11   25.34
   (2), (3)   25.34
s 28   §13.2
s 29   §13.2
Sch 1, paras 11, 12   25.36
Sch 2   25.20, 25.25
   para 1   25.35
   para 2   25.21, 25.35
   paras 3, 4   25.35
   para 6   25.21
Sch 3   25.21
   para 1   25.21
Defamation Act 1996   14.14
ss 2–4   5.14
Digital Millennium Act 2000 (USA)   14.17

Disability Discrimination Act 1995   7.12, 7.64, 10.19, 11.78, §22.1, §22.2, §22.6, 22.1, 22.2, 22.3, 22.4, 22.5, 22.6, 22.7, 22.8, 22.9, 22.13, 22.15, 22.16, 22.19, 22.20, 22.21, 22.22, 22.25, 22.28, 22.29, 22.32, §24.4, 24.23
Pt II   22.2
Pt III   22.2
s 1   22.4
s 3   22.4
s 28R   22.22
Sch 1   22.4

Education Act 1994   1.37, §19.2, 19.1, 19.2, 19.3, 19.4, 19.17, 19.29
s 20   19.2
   (1)   19.1
   (4)   19.3
s 22   §19.2, 19.4, 19.17
   (2)(a)   19.4, 19.10
   (4)   19.6
Education (No 2) Act 1986
s 43   9.22, 19.6, 19.7, 20.19
   (1)   19.7
   (8)   20.19
Education Reform Act 1988   §2.1, 2.1, 4.16, §7.1, 8.13, 9.1, 10.5, 10.10, 11.8, 15.15, 16.10, 23.16, 25.3, 30.33, 30.34
Ch II   9.27
s 105   9.20
s 124   16.13, 25.3
   (2)   2.3
    (e)   16.13
    (f)   2.3, 16.13
s 124A   16.2
s 125A   19.11
s 128   3.43, 16.10, 16.11
ss 202–207   10.9, 10.14
s 202   10.14
   (2)   10.14
    (a)   §10.1
    (3)   10.18
ss 203–207   §10.1, 10.14
s 203   10.17, 10.19, 10.23

Education Reform Act 1988 –
   cont
   s 203(1)   10.18, 10.22
         (a), (b)   10.20, 10.23
         (d), (e)   10.5, 10.6, 10.8
         (2)   10.20
         (3)   10.22
         (4)   10.7, 10.19
         (5), (6)   10.19
         (7), (8)   10.19
   s 204   10.17, 10.20
   s 204(1)–(9)   10.23
   ss 204–206   10.19
   s 206   2.2, 8.3, 10.8, App 30
         (1)   10.5, 10.6, 10.7, 10.8, 10.9
         (2)   App 30
         (3)   10.5
         (4)(a)   10.8
           (b)   10.7
   Sch 7   16.2
   Sch 12, para 64   3.35
Employment Protection Act 1975   §7.1
Employment Protection
   (Consolidation) Act 1978   11.9,
                       11.10, 30.33
   s 55   11.9
Employment Relations Act 1999
   s 18   11.80
Employment Rights Act 1996   10.19,
         11.9, 11.10, 11.14, 11.17,
         11.21, 11.22, 11.24, 11.25,
         11.43, 11.65, 11.66, 11.77
   Pt X   10.19, 10.20
   ss 1–7   29.5
   s 95   11.9, 11.60
   s 98   11.61
         (4)   11.47
           (a), (b)   10.20
   s 139   11.21
Estate Agents Act 1979   29.35

Finance Act 1990
   s 25   25.9
Finance Act 2000   15.12
Freedom of Information Act
   2000   §13.5, 13.14, 13.15, 13.16,
         13.17, 13.19, 13.20, 13.21,
                   13.22, 13.25
   Pt VII (ss 67–72)   13.24
   s 67   13.24

   s 68   13.24
   Sch 1   13.18
Further and Higher Education
   Act 1992   13.18, 16.4, 30.6
   Pt II   13.18
   s 18   17.25
   s 22   16.2
   s 65   13.18
   s 72(3)   13.18
   Sch 8, para 69   3.35

Health and Safety at Work etc
   Act 1974   §6.21, 20.7
Hotel Proprietors Act 1956   26.6
Housing Act 1985   21.23
   s 32(3)   23.6, 23.30
   s 345(1), (2)   21.3
   s 350   21.17
   s 352   21.23
Housing Act 1988   23.11
   s 1(1)   23.11
         (b)   23.12
   s 45(1)   23.11
   Sch 1   23.11
       para 8   23.13, 23.25
Housing Act 1996   21.16, 21.19, 21.21,
          21.33, 21.34, 21.35, 23.13,
                         23.25
   s 65(1)   21.20
   s 73   21.25
Housing Grants, Construction
   and Regeneration Act 1996   21.30
Human Rights Act 1998   1.10, 1.11,
        App 1, 2.2, 2.6, 6.22, 6.31,
       §7.1, 7.1, 7.3, 7.6, 7.7, 7.8,
       7.20, 7.34, 7.35, 7.39, 7.64,
      §8.4, 8.1, 8.3, 8.4, 8.8, 8.12,
       8.18, 8.19, 8.20, 8.21, 8.23,
        8.24, 8.25, 8.26, 9.1, 9.3,
       9.15, 9.17, 9.23, 9.28, 9.36,
       9.40, 9.50, 9.51, §10.1,
       10.10, 10.16, §12.4, 13.18,
       19.5, 20.22, 22.1, 22.31,
       22.32, 23.29, 24.23, 25.26,
       28.4, 29.12, 29.24, 29.26,
                         30.62
   s 6   App 1, 9.33

Income and Corporation Taxes
   Act 1988
   s 205   25.18

Income and Corporation Taxes
  Act 1988 – *cont*
  s 339   15.12
  s 389   25.9
  s 505   15.4, 15.10
    (1)(e)   15.4, 15.5
  s 506   15.10
  Sch 20, Pts 1, 2   15.10
Inheritance Tax Act 1984
  s 23   25.7
Insolvency Act 1986
  Pt V   3.43
  s 213   15.18
  s 215   15.18
Interpretation Act 1978
  s 7   5.3

Landlord and Tenant Act 1985
  s 11   23.30
Learning and Skills Act 2000   16.4
  s 145   3.29, 3.49, 4.21
  Sch 9, para 15   2.3
Licensing Act 1964
  Sch 7   19.32

Misrepresentation Act 1967   29.27

National Audit Act 1983   3.25

Occupiers' Liability Act 1957   20.2,
                     20.3, 20.6, 24.13
Occupiers' Liability Act 1984   §6.21,
           20.2, 20.3, 20.4, 20.6, 24.13
  s 1(6)   20.5
  s 2   20.3
Official Secrets Acts   25.4
Oxford and Cambridge Act 1571
                                           2.1

Partnership Act 1890   16.13
Patents Act 1977   12.12, 12.38
Police and Criminal Evidence
  Act 1984
  s 24   20.11
Powers of Criminal Courts Act
  1973   23.24

Private Security Industry Act
  2001   §20.8
Protection from Eviction Act
  1977   23.25
  s 5(1A)   23.25, 23.26
Protection from Harassment Act
  1997   §7.4, 14.16
Protection of Children Act 1978   14.10
Public Interest Disclosure Act
  1998   1.37, §3.6, 3.26, §10.8
Public Order Act 1986   25.4
  s 11   1.37
Public Records Act 1958   13.16

Race Relations Act 1976   7.60, 19.24,
                              §24.4, 24.23
  s 33(1)   19.24
Race Relations (Amendment)
  Act 2000   7.16, 7.62, §10.1
  Sch 1   7.62
Regulation of Investigatory
  Powers Act 2000   13.13, 14.10,
                                         20.20
Rehabilitation Act 1973 (USA)   §22.3
Rent Acts   23.8

Sale of Goods Act 1979
  s 14   29.13, 29.36
Sex Discrimination Act 1975   7.60,
                              §24.4, 24.23
School Standards and
  Framework Act 1998   13.18
Scotland Act 1998   7.7
Special Educational Needs and
  Disability Act 2001   7.64, §22.3,
           §22.6, 22.1, 22.2, 22.3, 22.7,
           22.22, 22.23, 22.25, 22.26,
           22.27, 22.28, 22.29, 22.30,
                                         22.32
  Ch 2   22.22
Supply of Goods and Services
  Act 1982   29.12, 29.13
  s 13   29.13, 29.16, 29.36
  s 14   29.14
  s 15   29.15
Supreme Court Act 1981
  s 31(3)   9.51

Supreme Court of Judicature Act
  1873
  s 34   30.10
Supreme Court of Judicature
  (Consolidation) Act 1925
  s 56(2)(a)   30.10

Taxation of Charitable Gains Act
  1992
  s 2   25.8
  s 8   25.8
Teaching and Higher Education
  Act 1998   28.34
  s 26   29.29
  s 28   29.29
  s 39   §2.1
Telecommunications Act 1984   14.16
  s 43   14.10
Theft Act 1968   §20.8
  s 21   20.9
Tort (Interference with Goods)
  Act 1977   20.9
Trade Descriptions Act 1968   29.12,
     29.37

s 14   29.9, 29.27, 29.28, 29.35, 29.39
ss 24, 25   29.28, 29.30
Trade Practices Act 1974   App 6(1),
     29.3
Trade Union and Labour
  Relations (Consolidation)
  Act 1992   11.90, 13.7
Treasure Act 1996   26.3
Trustee Act 1925
  s 61   3.29, 3.36, 3.40, §4.4, 4.21
Trustee Act 2000   4.27, 4.29
  s 19(4)   4.27
Trustee Investment Act 1961   4.27

Unfair Contract Terms Act 1977   6.28,
     6.29, 19.21, 20.5, 20.16,
     23.26, 29.12, 29.20
  s 2   29.16
  s 3   29.17
  s 8   29.18
  s 11(1)   29.19
  s 25(1)   29.5
Universities and Colleges Estates
  Act 1964   4.15

TABLE OF STATUTORY INSTRUMENTS, CODES OF PRACTICE, ETC

References are to editors' introductions (§), paragraph numbers and chapter appendices

ACAS Code of Practice 1: Disciplinary and Grievance Procedures (September 2000)   11.72
Accounting Standard FRS 5   18.5, 18.30
Assured and Protected Tenancies (Lettings to Students) Regulations 1998, SI 1998/1967
   reg 3   23.25

Cadbury Code of Best Practice   15.28
Charitable Institutions (Fundraising) Regulations 1994, SI 1994/3025   25.19
Civil Procedure Rules 1998, SI 1998/3132   27.10, 27.11, 27.22, 27.26, 27.70, 27.71
   Pt 8B   23.24
   Pt 36   27.28, 27.36
   Pt 54   9.50
   Pt 55   23.24, 23.25
Code of Practice for the elimination of discrimination in the field of employment against disabled persons or persons who have had a disability   22.9
Code of Practice for Users of Close Circuit Television   20.20
Code of Practice: rights of access to goods, facilities, services and premises   22.17
Combined Code on Corporate Governance (Turnbull Report)   24.4
Companies (Single Member Private Limited Companies) Regulations 1992, SI 1992/1699   15.27
Copyright and Rights in Databases Regulations 1997, SI 1997/3032   14.11
Consumer Protection (Code of Practice for Traders on Price Indications) Approved Order 1988, SI 1988/2078   29.29
   Pt II, art 2.2   29.29
Consumer Protection (Distance Selling) Regulations 2000, SI 2000/2334   6.14, 14.4, 24.23, 29.12, 29.32, 29.33
County Court Rules 1981, SI 1981/1687
   Ord 24, r 1(1)   23.24

DoE Circular 12/86   21.5
DoE Circular 12/93   21.5
DoE Circular 3/97   21.19
DETR *Houses in Multiple Occupation Guidance on Standards* (28 April 1999)   21.15

Disability Discrimination (Meaning of Disability) Regulations 1996, SI 1996/
    1455   22.4

Education (Fees and Awards) Regulations 1997, SI 1997/1972   28.32
Education (Fees and Awards) (Amendment) Regulations 1998, SI 1998/1965
                                                                       28.32
Education (Student Support) Regulations 2000, SI 2000/1121   28.32, 28.34
Education (University Commissioners) Order 1995, SI 1995/604   10.17
European Communities (Recognition of Professional Qualifications)
    (Amendment) Regulations 2000, SI 2000/1960   28.49

Further Education Funding Council Circular 95/25   18.37
Further Education Funding Council Circular 96/06   17.25
Further Education Funding Council Circular 98/36   16.4
Further Education Funding Council Circular 99/09   17.25
Further Education Funding Council Circular 99/37   17.25

*Guidance on matters to be taken into account in determining questions relating
    to the definition of disability*   22.4

HEFCE Circular 17/95   18.10
HEFCE Circular 5/96   18.34
HEFCE Circular 24/00 *Accounts Direction to Higher Education Institutions for
    2000/01*   24.4, 24.5
HEFCE Circular 00/47 *Guidance on PFI and Student Accommodation*   §18.3

Health and Safety Regulations 1992   20.7
Houses in Multiple Occupation (Fees for Registration Schemes) Order 1997,
    SI 1997/229   21.20
Houses in Multiple Occupation (Fees for Registration Schemes)
    (Amendment) Order 1998, SI 1998/1813   21.20

Immigration (European Economic Area) Order 1994, SI 1994/1895   28.37, 28.38,
                                                         28.39, 28.40, 28.41
Immigration (European Economic Area) (Amendment) Order 1997, SI 1997/
    2981   28.37
Indictment Rules 1971, SI 1971/1253
    r 5(1)   7.31
Inland Revenue Extra Statutory Concession C4   15.5
Inland Revenue *Guidance Notes for Charities* (November 2000)
    para 3.16.3   15.13

LSC Circular 01/10   16.4

Package Travel, Package Holidays and Package Tours Regulations 1992,
    SI 1992/3288   29.35, 29.36

Provision and Use of Work Equipment Regulations 1992, SI 1992/2932
    reg 6(1)   20.8
Public Contracts (Works, Services and Supply) (Amendment) Regulations
    2000, SI 2000/2009   18.17, 28.27, 28.29
Public Services Contracts Regulations 1993, SI 1993/3228   18.17, 28.13, 28.29
    reg 10(2)(b)   18.19
    regs 14–20   18.21
    Sch 2, Pt D   18.21
Public Supply Contracts Regulations 1995, SI 1995/201   28.13, 28.20, 28.27, 28.29
Public Works Contracts Regulations 1991, SI 1991/2680   18.17, 28.13, 28.27

Rules of the Supreme Court 1965, SI 1965/1776
    Ord 113   20.17

Statutory Maternity Pay (General) and Statutory Sick Pay (General)
    (Amendment) Regulations 2001, SI 2001/206   28.29

Telecommunications Law (Businesses Practice) Regulations 2000, SI 2000/
    2699   14.10
Telecommunications (Data Protection and Privacy) Regulations 1999,
    SI 1999/2093   25.31
Town and Country Planning (Use Classes) Order 1987, SI 1987/764
    Class C3   21.14
Transfer of Undertakings (Protection of Employment) Regulations 1981,
    SI 1981/1794   10.3, 16.1, 16.15, 16.18, 16.19, 16.20, 16.21, 16.26, 16.36,
        16.37, 16.38, 17.30, 17.31, 17.32, 17.33, 17.34, §23.2
    reg 5   17.30
    reg 8(1), (2)   17.30
    reg 10   17.30
Turnbull Report. *See Combined Code on Corporate Governance*

Unfair Terms in Consumer Contracts Regulations 1994, SI 1994/3159   10.10, 20.16
    reg 4   23.27
    Sch 2   29.22
    Sch 3   29.23
Unfair Terms in Consumer Contracts Regulations 1999, SI 1999/2083   6.19, 6.29,
        6.35, 10.10, 20.16, §23.2, 23.26, 23.33, 29.12, 29.20, 29.22, 29.24,
        29.26, 29.39, 30.60
    reg 3(2)   29.26
    reg 4(1)   29.20
    reg 5(1)   23.26
    reg 6   6.35, 29.25
      (3)   6.29
    reg 8   23.27
    reg 10   6.30, 23.27
    Sch 2   6.29, 29.23
Utilities Supply and Works Contracts Regulations 1992, SI 1992/3279   28.27

Working Time Regulations 1998, SI 1998/1833   §24.4, §28.2

TABLE OF EC AND INTERNATIONAL MATERIALS

References are to editors' introductions (§), paragraph numbers and chapter appendices

Agreement on trade-related aspects of Intellectual Property Rights (GATT Uruguay Round) concluded 15th December 1993   28.30

Berne Convention for the Protection of Literary and Artistic Works, Berne 9th September 1886   12.21
Bologna Declaration (1999)   §28.3

Directive 68/360 on the Abolition of Restrictions on Movement and Residence within the community for workers of Member States and their families, OJ 1968 L257/13   28.38
Directive 77/187, on the approximation of the laws of the Member States relating to the safeguarding of employees' rights in the event of transfers of undertakings, businesses or parts of businesses (Acquired Rights Directive), OJ 1977 L61/26   17.30
Directive 77/453 concerning the co-ordination of provisions laid down by law, regulation or administrative action in respect of the activities of nurses responsible for general care, OJ 1977 L176/8   28.46
Directive 78/686 concerning the mutual recognition of diplomas, certificates and other evidence of the formal qualifications of practitioners of dentistry, including measures to facilitate the effective exercise of the right to establishment and freedom to provide services, OJ 1978 L233/1   28.53
Directive 86/361 on the intial stage of the mutual recognition of type approval for telecommunications terminal equipment, OJ 1986 L217/21   28.21
Directive 87/95/EEC on standardisation in the field of information technology and telecommunications   28.21
Directive 89/48 on a general system for the recognition of higher-education diplomas awarded on completion of professional education and training of at least three years' duration, OJ 1989 L19/16   28.47, 28.48, 28.49, 28.50, 28.51, 28.53, 28.54
    Art 1(a)   28.48
    Art 7   28.52
Directive 90/314 on package travel, package holidays and package tours, OJ 1990 L158/59   29.36
Directive 92/50/EEC relating to the co-ordination of procedures for the award of Public Service Contracts, OJ 1992 L209/1   18.17, 28.13, 28.29

Directive 92/51 on a second general system for the recognition of
    professional education and training to supplement 89/48, OJ 1992
    L209/25   28.47, 28.50
Directive 93/13/EEC on unfair terms in consumer contracts, OJ 1993 L95/29
    Art 7.2   6.30
Directive 93/36 co-ordinating procedures for the award of public supply
    contracts, OJ 1993 L199/1   28.29
Directive 93/37/EEC concerning the co-ordination of procedures for the
    award of public works contracts, OJ 1993 L199/54   18.17, 28.13, 28.14, 28.17,
                                                                             28.27
    indent 3   28.17
    Annex 1   28.15
Directive 93/96/EEC Public Supply Contracts Directive   28.13, 28.28, 28.38, 28.41
    Annex B   28.28
Directive 98/5/EC   28.51

EC Directive 99/70/EC, European Framework Directive on Fixed Term
    Work   11.17, 11.80
EC Treaty (Treaty of Rome 1957)   2.6, 28.2, 28.7, 28.12, 28.51, 28.59
    Art 8(a)   App 1
    Art 12   28.8, 28.32, 28.35
    Arts 23–31   28.8
    Art 39   28.36, 28.43, 28.45
    Arts 39–42   28.8
    Arts 43–48   28.8
    Art 43   28.36, 28.45
    Art 47   28.45
    Art 49   28.8
    Art 52   28.54
    Art 81   28.8, 28.55, 28.56, 28.60, 28.61, 28.62, 28.63, 28.64, 28.65, 28.66, 28.68,
                                                                             28.69
    Art 82   28.8, 28.57, 28.58, 28.60, 28.62, 28.66, 28.68, 28.69, 28.70
    [new] Art 149   28.2, 28.8
    [new] Art 150   28.2, 28.8
European Convention for the Protection of Human Rights and Fundamental
    Freedoms, Rome 4th November 1950   2.6, 7.7, 7.8, 7.9, 7.10, 7.12, 7.28, 9.3,
                                     9.17, 9.23, 9.51, 10.16, 22.31, 22.32, §23.2, 28.4
    Art 6   6.21, 7.17, 7.18, 7.19, 7.20, 7.22, 7.23, 7.24, 7.34, 8.18, 8.19, 9.36, 9.42,
                                                 9.43, 9.44, 9.46, 9.50, 10.10
        (1)   App 1, §7.1, §8.4, 8.18, 10.10, 29.24, 30.62, 30.64
    Art 8   App 1, 9.38, 9.38, 10.16, 20.22, 25.26
    Art 10   10.16, §12.4
    Art 11   App 1
    Art 14   7.12, 7.64, 9.47, 22.32, 25.26
    Protocol 1, Art 2   22.31, 22.32
EU Copyright Directive   14.17
European Patent Convention, Munich 5th October 1973   12.12, 12.19
European Trade Mark Convention   12.32

General Agreement on Tariffs and Trade, Geneva 30th October 1947   28.30

Government Procurement Agreement signed at Marrakesh 1994   28.30

Maastricht Treaty (Treaty of European Union) 7 February 1992   28.2, 28.3, 28.7,
28.12, 28.73
Art 3(q)   28.2
Madrid Agreement concerning the International Registration of Marks,
Madrid 14th April 1891   12.32
Madrid Protocol concerning the International Registration of Marks, Madrid
27 June 1989   12.32

New York Convention on the Recognition and Enforcement of Foreign
Arbitral Awards 1958   17.39

Paris Convention for the Protection of Industrial Property, Paris 20th March
1883   12.17, 12.32
Patents Cooperation Treaty, Washington 19th June – 31st December 1970   12.18
Prague Declaration (2001)   §28.3

Regulation 1612/68 on freedom of movement for workers within the
Community, OJ 1968 L257/2   28.38
Regulation 418/85 on the application of the EEC Treaty, art 85(3) to
categories of research and development agreements, OJ 1985 L53/5   28.65
Regulation 295/91 establishing common rules for a denied-boarding
compensation system in scheduled transport, OJ 1991 L36/5   29.38
Regulation 240/96 on technology transfer licensing agreements   28.64
Regulation 2790/99 on vertical agreements and concerted practices   28.66
Regulation 2659/2000 on research and development agreements   28.65

Single European Act 1986   28.2, 28.7

Treaty of Amsterdam 1997   28.7, 28.12
Treaty Establishing the European Community 1997   28.7

United Nations Convention on the Rights of the Child, 20th November 1989
(UN General Assembly Resolution 44/25)   22.32
Universal Copyright Convention, Geneva 6th September 1952   12.21

TABLE OF ABBREVIATIONS

1998 Act	Competition Act 1998
1999 Act	Contracts (Rights of Third Parties) Act 1999
ADR	alternative dispute resolution
AfC	Association for Colleges
AGM	Annual General Meeting
AUA	Association of University Administrators
AUP	Acceptable Use Policy
AUT	Association of University Teachers
BAFO	best and final offer
CCTV	close circuit television
CDPA 1988	Copyright, Designs and Patents Act 1988
CIF	Common Investment Fund
CIPFA	Chartered Institute of Public Finance and Accountancy
CJPOA 1994	Criminal Justice and Public Order Act 1994
CLA	Copyright Licensing Agency
CPA 1987	Consumer Protection Act 1987
CPR 1998	Civil Procedure Rules 1998
CPD	continuing professional development
CPDA 1988	Copyright Designs and Patents Act 1988
CPE	Common Professional Examination
CPS	Crown Prosecution Service
CRE	Commission for Racial Equality
CUA/AUA	Conference/Association of University Administrators
CUC	Committee of University Chairmen
CVCP	Committee of Vice-Chancellors and Principals
DDA 1995	Disability Discrimination Act 1995
DES/DfES	(see DfEE)
DETR	Department of the Environment, Transport & the Regions
DfEE	Department for Education and Employment
DGFT	Director General of Fair Trading
DPA 1984	Data Protection Act 1984
DPA 1998	Data Protection Act 1998
DRC	Disability Rights Commission
DSR 2000	Consumer Protection (Distance Selling) Regulations 2000

EA 1994	Education Act 1994
ECHR	European Court of Human Rights
ECJ	European Court of Justice
EEA	European Economic Area
EGM	Extraordinary General Meeting
EPCA 1978	Employment Protection (Consolidation) Act 1978
ERA 1988	Education Reform Act 1988
ERA 1996	Employment Rights Act 1996
EU	European Union
FE	further education
FEC	further education corporation
FEFC	Further Education Funding Council
FEI	further education institution
GATT	General Agreement on Tariffs and Trade
GDP	gross domestic product
GPA	Government Procurement Agreement 1994
HSWA 1974	Health and Safety at Work etc Act 1974
HE	higher education
HEC	higher education corporation
HEFC	Higher Education Funding Council
HEFCE	Higher Education Funding Council for England
HEFCW	Higher Education Funding Council for Wales
HEI	higher education institution
HERO	Higher Education Regulatory Officer
HEQC	Higher Education Quality Council
HMO	house in multiple occupation
HND	Higher National Diploma
HRA 1998	Human Rights Act 1998
HSE	Health & Safety Executive
ICTA 1988	Income and Corporation Taxes Act 1988
IP	intellectual property
ISP	internet service provider
IVF	in vitro fertilisation
LEA	local education authority
NACUA	National Association of College and University Attorneys
NAO	National Audit Office
NATFHE	National Association of Teachers in Further and Higher Education

NUS	National Union of Students
ODPC	Office of the Data Protection Commissioner
OFSTED	Office for Standards in Education
OFT	Office of Fair Trading
OIC	Office of the Information Commissioner
OJ/OJEC	Official Journal/of the European Communities
OLA 1957	Occupiers' Liability Act 1957
OLA 1984	Occupiers' Liability Act 1984
OUP	Oxford University Press
PAC	Public Accounts Committee
PFI	Private Finance Initiative
PSBR	Public Sector Borrowing Requirement
QAA	Quality Assurance Agency for higher education
RAE	Research Assessment Exercise
RRA 1976	Race Relations Act 1976
SEND 2001	Special Educational Needs and Disability Act 2001
SGSA 1982	Supply of Goods and Services Act 1982
SHEFC	Scottish Higher Education Funding Council
SRI	socially responsible investment
SU	students' union
TDA 1968	Trade Descriptions Act 1968
TPS	Telephone Preference Service
TUPE	Transfer of Undertakings (Protection of Employment) Regulations 1981
UCAS	Universities Central Admissions Service
UCELNET	Universities and Colleges Education Law Network
UCTA 1977	Unfair Contract Terms Act 1977
UFC	Universities Funding Council
UGC	University Grants Committee
UTCCR 1999	Unfair Terms in Consumer Contracts Regulations 1999
UUK	Universities UK
WTO	World Trade Organisation

Part 1
CONTEXTS

Chapter 1

SETTING THE SCENE

David Palfreyman and David Warner

RATIONALE FOR THIS BOOK

1.1 Higher education (HE) in the UK is big business in every sense of the term, and it is growing. At the time of writing, the three national funding councils for England, Scotland and Wales directly fund 134, 13 and 19 HE institutions (HEIs) respectively, plus, in the case of the first named, a large number of further education (FE) institutions for their HE work. It should be noted that these figures change almost annually. In addition, the Department for Education in Northern Ireland funds several HEIs and there are a number of private institutions, such as the University of Buckingham, the Royal Agricultural College and the Royal Academy of Dramatic Arts. The sector employs approximately 250,000 staff and teaches more than 1½ million students on award-bearing courses alone. It is not surprising, therefore, that financial turnover is also massive. On 18 June 1996, Professor G Roberts, then Chairman of the Committee of Vice-Chancellors and Principals (CVCP), commented:

> 'The annual turnover of the higher education sector has now passed the £10 billion mark. The massive increase in participation that has led to this figure, and the need to prepare for further increases, now demands that we make revolutionary advances, in the way we structure, manage and fund higher education.'

1.2 The Editors entirely agree with these sentiments and, for similar reasons to those enunciated by Professor Roberts, jointly edited *Higher Education Management: The Key Elements.*[1] That volume ended with a section entitled 'Notes on the Legal Framework within which HEIs Operate'. The first edition of this book took those Notes as a starting-point and expanded them into a full-length book.[2] This second edition is inevitably even longer, but it is still not a law textbook: we give many references to legal texts in both the Further Reading and Bibliography. This book is a *guide* for busy HEI managers who need to familiarise themselves with the legal context in which HE operates and who, from time to time, need to purchase legal services on behalf of the HEI. That said, it should also be of interest to legal practitioners by helping them to understand where an HEI client might be coming from, and perhaps especially

---

1   Warner and Palfreyman (1996, second edition due 2003).
2   *Higher Education and the Law: A Guide for Managers* (Open University Press, 1998).

if the solicitor does not regularly advise students over their 'contract to educate' with the HEI.

THE GROWTH OF CONSUMERISM

1.3   There is no doubt that we live in an era of increasing consumerism and, indeed, 'charterism', if that is the correct description of Government policy in the early 1990s. Each year, full-time students pay either directly or through their families a larger percentage of the costs of their time in HE and it seems quite possible that in the future they will contribute even more towards their tuition. The majority of part-time students, who are increasing rapidly in numbers, already pay for tuition fees at the full cost or economic rate, although a few will have their fees paid for by employers. As paying customers, students will readily resort to the law if they feel that their HEI has not provided value for money. *The Times Higher Educational Supplement* on 12 July 1996 carried an Editorial: 'The natives are restless', referring to the student community 'getting stroppy', to 'a growth in litigiousness', to 'slow, anachronistic, secretive or apparently excessively cosy' complaints procedures and to the risk of UK HE 'getting mired in expensive and unsatisfactory litigation which can only undermine public confidence'. That kind of media attention to UK HE helped prompt the first edition of this book, as did Laurie Taylor in his column for *The Times Higher Educational Supplement* a few weeks later when he addressed the issue of student consumerism in his inimitable style:

> '"More and more students are suing their universities over marks and grades" (Leading article in *The Independent*, 22 August).
>
> Lapping speaking.
>
> Ah, good morning, Professor Lapping. It's Gerald Stiggins, of Stiggins, Upton and Harcourt.
>
> Good morning, Gerald. How's tricks?
>
> Not bad at all. We've a sexual harassment in philosophy, an unfair dismissal in earth sciences, and the usual crop of student business. In fact, we are currently representing a Miss Rebecca Tomkins who has recently completed her first year in your department.
>
> Tall with fair hair and a tattoo?
>
> My client is small and dark haired with no tattoos.
>
> That Rebecca Tomkins. Small, dark, un-tattooed Rebecca Tomkins. How is she?
>
> Not at all well, Professor Lapping. She feels strongly that her C brackets plus mark on her Coronation Street essay may jeopardise her chances of obtaining a good degree and pursuing her chosen career in facilities management. She alleges that the marking system in your department is arbitrary and unreasonable and that in any case her low essay mark was a direct result of inadequate supervision by her senior tutor, a certain Professor Lapping. She intends to pursue these matters through the High Court.
>
> And, purely as a matter of curiosity, what mark does Rebecca feel she might have obtained if her essay had been appropriately marked and supervised?
>
> An A plus.
>
> A plus!

Imagine the scene in the High Court, Professor Lapping. Your marking system held up to judicial scrutiny.

How about a B double minus?

Imagine the usher's voice: "Call Professor Lapping. Call Professor Lapping".

B-minus. And I'll throw in a year's subscription to *Media Studies* and a three-drawer filing cabinet.

And two dozen A4 lined pads.

Agreed.

A Daniel come to judgement. And now if I might have Doctor Piercemuller's extension number.

With great pleasure.'[1]

1.4 Already the 'grapevine' suggests that some international students from outside the European Union (EU), and especially those from the USA, have threatened legal action, reflecting the more litigious culture back home and also the heightened sense of grievance at having paid increasingly large sums of money for their allegedly inadequate British university courses. From the mid-1990s, newspapers have carried headlines such as:

SUE THREAT TO COLLEGES

STUDENT CAN SUE FOR LOW GRADE

STUDENTS SUE FOR 'INADEQUATE TEACHING'

STUDENT TO SUE OVER CHEATING ACCUSATION

BUILDERS BOTHER UNFRESH FRESHERS

DUBAI TEACHER PURSUES COMPENSATION FOR 'WASTED' PhD EFFORT

All types of HEI are involved: for example, Northumbria, Open, Manchester, Bath, Oxford, London Guildhall, Edinburgh, Leicester, East London, Aston, Lincolnshire and Humberside, Manchester Metropolitan, De Montfort, Sheffield Hallam, Nottingham, UCL, Glasgow, Dundee, Glasgow Caledonian, Liverpool John Moores.

1.5 Even the Senior Proctor of the University of Oxford, on demitting office at the end of his year, was prompted to make the following comments in a speech to Congregation:

'Traditionally the Senior Proctor has been concerned with graduate examinations, predominantly the DPhil. Complaints have, very approximately, tripled over the last decade (or doubled, proportionately to student numbers).

Echoing the words of my predecessor of last year, I have to report that nearly 70 per cent of all graduate examination complaints have come from overseas students. I have no single explanation for this, since not everything can be explained by cultural differences.'[2]

---

1   This column first appeared in *The Times Higher Education Supplement* on 30 August 1996, and is reproduced with permission.

2   *Oxford University Gazette*, 21 March 1996, vol 126, no 4396.

Since the Senior Proctor uttered his words of warning, the University has joined the 20 or 30 others against which disgruntled students have commenced legal action and, in Oxford's case, perhaps uniquely an unhappy student also launched an action in the USA, for a mere $1 million!

1.6　In a somewhat different publication from the *Oxford University Gazette*, Brendan O'Neill wrote:

'More students are turning to the courts to challenge their university's failure to provide the education they require, claiming that they failed their degrees because of inadequate teaching and a lack of resources. Educational lawyers predict that growing numbers of dissatisfied students will demand compensation through the courts.'

A solicitor, Jaswinder Gill, specialising in student complaints, is quoted:

'there are those who are aggrieved at the mark awarded for their degree, so they go through the normal appeals mechanism at their university. But they feel that the appeals mechanism has also let them down so legal action becomes necessary. These cases can usually be resolved by way of a judicial review. The second, more serious grievance is where students feel they have not received the service for which they paid ... I am arguing that a student is a consumer, no different to a consumer purchasing any other kind of product or service. Like other consumers I think that students should have recourse if a university fails in its obligation to provide a satisfactory course or full programme of study.'[1]

1.7　Another solicitor, Ivan Walker (Lawfords & Co), is cited in the same article, establishing the HEI perspective: '... sometimes the reason they have failed is simply that it is part of a university's function in life to pass some students and to fail others, that is what higher education is all about'. Dennis Farrington is also reported as commenting:

'the relationship between university and student is not as straightforward as that between provider and consumer. I see the contract as a bi-lateral one. There are obligations on the institution to provide certain things, but there are also obligations on the student to participate fully: to attend lectures, to participate in seminars, to hand essays in on time. It is a partnership approach, rather than a commercial consumer approach.'

1.8　In fact, the author of the *Living Marxism* article concludes:

'The fact is that students are much more than consumers and university is not the same as school ... Higher education should demand that students work hard and contribute fully to their own learning ... Establishing a legal precedent that students are consumers can only degrade higher education and the role of the student within it even further. And who will benefit from that?'

Yet for those fearful of the student empowered as a consumer there is another devastating prospect – the spectre of 'parent power', and especially of pushy middle-class parents who have already invested huge sums via private school fees in the education of their offspring and now are keen to ensure that the HEI also provides value for money with access to a good job at the end of it (see 'On the march to fight tuition fees' and 'When parental power becomes over-bearing'[2]).

1　　'Should failed students sue?' *Living Marxism*, April 1997.
2　　*The Times Higher Educational Supplement*, 8 December 2000, pp 6 and 7.

1.9 On 9 February 1997, the *Sunday Times* carried a front-page article 'Students Sue Over Course Failures', in which it was reported that three ex-students, with public funding, were suing their former HEI 'in legal test cases that could pave the way for a flood of costly compensation claims'. They were seeking damages for loss of future earnings arising from allegedly unsatisfactory courses which were claimed to have reduced their job prospects. Their solicitor was quoted as saying that: 'Universities have a duty to provide a proper programme of study . . . People are increasingly having to pay for their own tuition and they have every right to expect what they are promised'. The same article also reported on a separate case where a student who failed the first year of a Higher National Diploma (HND) course at another HEI, allegedly because of inadequate teaching, was claiming 'more than £120,000'. Further afield, an article in *The Times Higher Educational Supplement* on 21 February 1997 reported that four graduates were suing a New Zealand university over an allegedly sub-standard masters course. Their legal costs were being met by the New Zealand equivalent of the National Union of Students (NUS). One of the claimants was quoted as declaring: 'this is the 90s, and quality is what it is all about. It was a huge cost for us to do this course, and we haven't got time to muck around'.

1.10 If, however, the concept of the student as a customer causes difficulty for any UK reader at the present time, it should be noted that the earliest reference to the student-customer that the Editors have come across is, unsurprisingly, from the USA, although even for the norms of US HE, the year (1888) is perhaps surprisingly early, especially given the then tendency for US colleges to adopt the Oxbridge Christian/Liberal Arts 'young gentlemen' model (Duke (1996)): 'College administration is a business in which trustees are partners, professors the salesmen and students the customers', as quoted from the inaugural address of the new President of Princeton University. Closer to home, chronologically and geographically, student leaders from more than 100 European HEIs have met several times to draw up an international charter of student rights: 'the essential defence of the right to a higher education, the harmonisation and integration of credits systems throughout Europe and free access to all Europe's universities for all European students'.[1] Finally, an amusing article entitled 'Do undergraduates have rights?'[2] set out as an Appendix to this chapter, light-heartedly but tellingly explores the potential impact of the Human Rights Act 1998 (HRA 1998) on the HEI:student legal relationship.

1.11 Meanwhile, following problems of management at a number of HEIs and FE institutions in recent years, Lord Nolan explored 'governance' and engendered a general debate about the legal liabilities of governors/members of council. The result seems to have been a fairly clean bill of health, that 'mismanagement, maladministration, and misconduct seem to be isolated occurrences'. There was, however, a recommendation for 'publicly available

---

1   *The Times Higher Educational Supplement*, 28 July 2000.
2   *Oxford Magazine* Eighth Week, Michaelmas Term, 2000.

registers of interests' in relation to members of council/governing body. In addition, the Nolan Committee (1996) recommended that a system be established to allow senior managers complaining about (or even 'whistle-blowing' over) issues of governance and students challenging procedures and decisions to take their disputes to an independent review panel/appeals body. However, it is not entirely clear whether such independent, external mechanisms will supplement or replace the traditional role of the Visitor in the chartered HEIs and whether the mechanism for the statutory HEIs will be based on the Visitor (or an enhanced version of same) in the chartered HEIs, or whether the whole UK HE system will end up with an Ombudsperson, or some similar regulatory authority: note that the National Audit Office Report (January 1997) on 'a breakdown in both governance and management' at Swansea Institute of Higher Education floated the concept of an Ombudsman for HE, as have conferences and seminars surrounding the implementation of the HRA 1998. (See Chapter 29 'A Note on Consumer Law', and Palfreyman (2000).)

OTHER RECENT WORKS

1.12 All of the points raised so far make the legal status of the (changing) student–university relationship (contract) topical and emphasise the need for the fiduciary duties of governors/members of council to be clarified and stressed. In 1990, *Universities and the Law*, edited by Farrington and Mattison, was published by the Conference of University Administrators (CUA, now the Association of University Administrators (AUA)). This was followed by Farrington *The Law of Higher Education*.[1] Also, in 1994, the immensely readable report of Sir Michael Davies as the Visitor examining a dispute at University College, Swansea, was published in book form – the first time a Visitor report has been made so widely available (Davies (1994)). Attention is also drawn to the journals *Education and the Law* and *Education Law Journal*, and to the series of law reports: *Education Law Monitor, Education Law Reports* (available online at www.lawreportsonline.co.uk) and *Education Case Reports*. In addition, a major book by Oliver Hyams on education law emerged in 1998.[2] In 1996 Farrington established UCELNET (Universities and Colleges Education Law Network). Prior to Farrington in 1994 and the first edition of this book in 1998, along with the chapters on HE in Hyams, there had been virtually nothing on the law of HE until one reaches back as far as 1910, when Butterworths published *The Law of the Universities* by Williams, who noted that there were 'very few works dealing directly with the law of a university or universities' and that coverage for the topic 'has hardly been done before in England', or indeed (until the 1990s) since. The latest publication is Evans and Gill *Universities and Students: A Guide to Rights, Responsibilities and Practical Remedies* (2001), aimed squarely at the student-consumer.

---

1   1994, second edition 1998.
2   See also Kaye (2002, forthcoming) and the 2001 reissue of vol 15 on Education in *Halsbury's Laws of England* (4th edn).

1.13 In the USA, by contrast, extensive modern coverage of the interaction between the law and the academic world was to be found as early as 1979 in the first edition of Kaplin *The Law of Higher Education*, which noted: 'The law has arrived on the campus . . . The challenge is to make law more a beacon and less a fog'. The second edition (1985) ran to over 600 pages, and the third (Kaplin and Lee (1995a)) came to 1023 pages. Its *Supplement* (2000), barely 5 years later, ran to a further 725 pages. The third edition notes:

> 'In the decade since publication of the second edition, many new and newly complex legal concerns have arisen on the campuses. It is difficult to think of any other entities . . . that are subject to as great an array of legal requirements as colleges and universities are . . . Litigation has extended into every corner of campus activity . . . It is said that the law reaches too far and speaks too loudly . . . Traditionally, the law's relationship to postsecondary (or higher) education was much different from what it is now . . . The higher education world, moreover, tended to think of itself as removed from and perhaps above the world of law and lawyers.'[1]

Some 1500 cases are cited. The third edition certainly stresses 'student (or educational) consumerism', citing Riesman (1998): 'An increasing emphasis on students as consumers of education with attendant rights, to whom institutions owe corresponding responsibilities, has further undermined the traditional concept of education as a privilege'.[2] There is also an entirely new chapter on relationships between HEIs and 'the business/industrial community' in the third edition. We will refer to US law and to Kaplin and Lee where appropriate in our 'Editors' Introduction' at the start of each chapter and give the US perspective (including key cases) as part of the Further Reading at the end of this book. Kaplin and Lee (1997) is a version for student affairs officers at US HEIs of their 1995 wider-ranging text, with a little new material concerning a few significant cases since 1995 and a section on campus computer networks (see Chapter 14). In addition, there is a *Supplement* to Kaplin and Lee (1995a) and (1997) in the form of Kaplin and Lee (2000), which will also be referred to where appropriate throughout this book. The Americans, moreover, have the following journals: *College Law and University Law*, *Synthesis: Law and Policy in Higher Education*, and *College Law Digest*. This US material is cited not only to illustrate the very wide range of matters within the HEI which can potentially give rise to legal conflict and ultimately to litigation, but also on the assumption that generally what happens in the USA today surfaces in the UK sooner or later.

1.14 There appears to be no equivalent of Farrington or Kaplin and Lee for Australia, Canada or New Zealand, whose case-law, as Commonwealth countries broadly sharing the English common law system, would be of relevance to cases in English courts. A 1975 publication from the Legal Research Institute at the University of Manitoba, *Universities and the Law* (ed Thomas), noted, even then, that in the context of Canadian universities: 'Life

---

1   Kaplin and Lee (1995a), preface and pp 1 and 4.
2   Ibid, p 8.

becomes more legalistic by the day ... Administrators, in response, are also turning to legal advisors with increased frequency'. Certainly, over the last three decades, Canadian courts do seem to have considered a number of cases generated over the university–student contractual relationship: Farrington, for instance, cites an article by Lewis, 'The legal nature of a university and the student–university relationship'[1] which discusses the relevant Canadian cases (see also Lewis, 1985).

THE OBJECTIVES OF THIS BOOK

1.15 We set ourselves three objectives in preparing the first edition of this book; and they remain the same, 3 years later, in working on the second edition. First, this is not an encyclopaedia which covers every aspect of the law applicable to HE. There are numerous texts covering those legal issues which apply to all organisations and employers, whether they relate to individual employees, premises or whatever. We mention, however, as potentially interesting areas of development within employment law, the issues of employee claims for work-related/work-induced stress[2] and of employee actions and/or claims in relation to the Criminal Justice and Public Order Act 1994 (CJPOA 1994), which created a new criminal offence of intentional harassment (largely aimed at the 'stalker' problem, a problem not unknown in HE circles;[3] and possibly also applicable to bullying in the workplace). Otherwise, we have concentrated on those topics which are peculiar to HE (and in many cases other sectors of education), such as the discipline and dismissal of academic staff; legislation on houses in multiple occupation and its relationship to halls of residence; academics and intellectual property; and the status of student unions in relation to contract and tort. In particular, we have also attempted to cover some of the topics not fully covered in the excellent work by Farrington, which tries in only a little extra space to be more ambitiously comprehensive than this book. It is interesting to note that the recently launched Continuing Professional Development (CPD) programme for HEI managers, which will probably lead eventually to something like a 'Postgraduate Certificate in Professional Practice (Higher Education Administration)', contains a module on 'The Legal Framework'. Arguably, a basic skill for any competent HEI manager, alongside the principles of marketing and the essentials of management accountancy for costing and pricing, is a level of 'legal literacy' that incorporates at least contract law, agency, employment law, and due process, with charity law, company law, and intellectual property law being also significant for certain specialists.

1.16 Secondly, whenever possible, we have asked the contributors to attempt to solve problems rather than just to identify them. This is not, of course,

---

1   1983, *Ottawa Law Review*, XV.
2   See Edworthy (2000).
3   Fine (1997).

always practicable because many of the points at issue have not yet been tested in the courts. However, the aim is for each chapter to be a clear, comprehensive and concise explanation of the relevant law, with concrete examples of how it affects day-to-day management within institutions, including identification of the legal pitfalls and the provision of possible avoidance mechanisms. The book is intended above all to be 'hands on' and accessible to the non-lawyer. Moreover, it is intended not only to help the HEI manager get good value from expensive legal advice, but also to give the HEI manager as the client the confidence to remain firmly in control of the client : lawyer relationship – as Bagley (1999) notes:

> 'Finally, managers should realize that legal disputes are inevitable ... Instead of delegating such disputes to attorneys, successful managers realize that every legal dispute is a business problem requiring a business solution. Too often managers treat the law as a black box and leave it up to the lawyers, rather than taking responsibility for disputes.'[1]

Bagley's text is especially useful for the non-lawyer manager struggling to understand the litigation process (pp 96–119) and ADR (Alternative Dispute Resolution: Negotiation, Mediation, Arbitration, pp 124–155), even if it is written for the US commercial and legal context. (On the management of risk, see Chapter 24.)

1.17 Finally, we have eschewed the single-author approach and have brought together a team of solicitors who, as individuals, are all experts in the particular topics with which they are dealing and whose firms have a significant number of HE clients. However, the 'insider' experience of the HE manager has not been lost because we have added an 'Editors' Introduction' at the head of each chapter. Inconsistencies have been removed, but we have not attempted to homogenise individual styles, nor to eliminate repetition which is necessary to understand a chapter read in isolation. Further Reading is cited, both generally and chapter by chapter, at the end of the book. Readers should also use the index and the tables of cases and statutory materials to help locate relevant material, as well as consulting the follow-up reading material listed in the Further Reading and Bibliography. There is also a valuable facility at www.bristol.ac.uk/armed as the site of the Higher Education Funding Council for England (HEFCE)-funded project 'Active Risk Management in Education' which has information on many aspects of the law relating to HEIs (for example, student discipline, student debt, public interest disclosure, work permits, research misconduct).

1.18 There is one objective, however, which we have not set ourselves, namely to make the book relevant to the whole of the UK. The law used throughout is the law of England and Wales, and hence we regret that the book is of less value to those managing institutions in Scotland and in Northern Ireland. Nevertheless, we trust that it will still be of some value to them. Farrington (1998) does, however, cover both English and Scottish law. In this

---

1   *Financial Times* 'Guide to Mastering Management' part 9, p 4, 27 November 2000.

book the various chapters (as indicated in brackets in the list below) map
across to the broad divisions of English law as follows:

Private law

1. Law of obligations, comprising
   (a) Contract law (6 and 7), including
       –   Agency (5)
       –   Employment law (10 and 11)
       –   Franchising (17)
       –   Insurance law (23)
       –   Consumer law (29)
   (b) Tort law (6 and 7), including
       –   Defamation (5)
       –   Professional negligence (6)
       –   Occupier liability (20)
   (c) Law of restitution (indirectly relevant)
2. Law of corporations (2 and 3), including
       –   Law of meetings (5)
       –   Company law (15)
       –   Unincorporated associations (19)
3. Law of property, including
       –   Intellectual property (12)
       –   Landlord and tenant (23)
       –   Personal property (26)
4. Trusts law/charity law (4, 8 and 30)
5. Litigation (27)

Public law

6. Administrative law, including
       –   Due process/natural justice (5, 7 and 9)
       –   Judicial review
7. EC Law (28)
8. Criminal law (20)
9. Discrimination law (22)

(Some topics within the 30 chapters, however, do not readily and neatly fit the
above scheme: 13, on data protection and freedom of information; 14, on the
internet; 16, on mergers and acquisitions; 18, on the private finance initiative;
21, on houses in multiple occupation (HMOs); 25, on alumni.)

1.19   This second edition has also benefited from comments in reviews of the
first edition, pointing out gaps in its coverage and textual errors: for example,
Harvey (1999) and Neave (1998).

A NOTE ON TERMINOLOGY

1.20   In the first chapter of the first edition of this book, we argued that the debate over the use of the terms 'administrator' or 'manager', 'administration' or 'management' is a sterile one and adds little to understanding. Nevertheless, the 'm' word has emotively good connotations (similar to 'marketing' which is always used in educational circles rather than 'selling') and, therefore, that is the term which will be used throughout this book (except in quotations and in historical context). It will also be used to describe both academic and other managers.

1.21   The language of HE is in need of significant overhaul because, as yet, there is no generally accepted terminology to distinguish between those institutions which gained the title of 'university' as a result of the Further and Higher Education Act 1992 and those which already had it. Many commentators use 'old' and 'new', but how could we accept these terms as one of us is a Fellow of New College, Oxford (founded 1379) and the other has worked at the University of East Anglia and Warwick University, both of which were previously called 'new universities'? 'Modern' is slightly better, but perhaps a little jaded. The word 'managed' is sometimes used to describe the former polytechnics, perhaps implying that the rest are unmanaged, ill-managed or under-managed. Suffice it to say that we have decided on 'chartered' and 'statutory', even though we know that some pre-1992 institutions were founded by Act of Parliament (see Chapter 2) and that a small number do not have charters. In any case, this debate completely omits the colleges of higher education which are legally, and, in most cases, managerially in the same category as statutory universities. Wherever possible, therefore, we have used 'higher education institution' (HEI).

LEGAL PROBLEMS IN HE

1.22   While organising the conference which provided part of the stimulus for writing the first edition of this book, we realised that there was little or no information available about the nature and frequency of legal problems which HEIs face or about the way in which they are handled. Consequently, we prepared a questionnaire survey which was sent to the registrars/heads of administration of all HEIs in the UK. Putting on one side the definitional problem of deciding exactly how many HEIs there are in the UK, 162 questionnaires were sent out: 62 to chartered universities, 41 to statutory universities and 59 to colleges/HEIs. The response to a single questionnaire, which was not followed up by a prompt, was very good as Table 1.1 indicates. Within these categories there are, of course, wide variations in size. By almost every criterion, the University of Birmingham is at least 15 times larger than St David's University College, Lampeter, and Southampton Institute has 30 times more students than Rose Bruford College. However, the categories reflect historical differences which still have management implications and, therefore,

Table 1.1   Response rates

	Number sent out	Number returned	Percentage return
Chartered university	62	38	61
Statutory university	41	24	59
College of HE	59	29	49
Overall	162	91	56

they have been used for the analysis of the survey results. The questions asked were as follows.

What types of legal problems arise in institutions and approximately how often in an average year?

1.23 In order to keep the questionnaire brief and, thereby, increase the likelihood of it being answered, explanations of terminology were kept to a minimum. As a result, the majority of respondents interpreted 'legal' in the narrow sense of requiring the expertise of a lawyer, whereas others used a broader definition along the lines of 'contravening the institution's rules, regulations, etc, and requiring significant action or judgment'.

1.24 The 13 areas in Table 1.2 were prompted with the average and median results as set out for an individual HEI.

Table 1.2   Type and annual frequency of legal problems

	Chartered		Statutory		HE Colleges		All	
	Average	Median	Average	Median	Average	Median	Average	Median
Employment issues	16	5	16.1	10	5.4	5	12.2	5
Staff discipline	4.8	2	7.5	3	3.5	2	5.4	2
Student admissions issues	2	2.5	2.7	2	2.7	2	2.7	2
Student matriculation issues (including examinations)	2.1	2	12.2	5	2.6	2	6.1	2
Student discipline	3.7	2.5	7	5	3	2	4.6	2
Students' union issues	3.4	2	3	3	1.5	1	2.7	2
Health and safety	2.3	2	12	5	3	2	5.3	2
Residential accommodation	3	3	6.2	5	2.8	3	4.1	2
Property-related issues	9	10	8.9	10	5.3	4	7.8	6
Charitable status issues	4.5	1	3.9	3	2.1	2	3.7	2
Trading company issues	3.9	3	9.7	9	3.2	2	5.4	3
Intellectual property and similar	38.1	3	7.3	3	1.8	1	16.7	2
Security issues	1.5	1	5.3	5	2.7	2	3.3	2

There are several interesting conclusions which can be drawn from these responses. First, the statutory universities have, on average, more legal problems than the chartered universities. This is entirely to be expected because, on average, the statutory universities:

—   are larger than the chartered universities;

- have just undergone significant constitutional and human resource management changes;[1]
- have many more part-time and mature students.

1.25   Secondly, a number of chartered universities are experiencing considerable difficulties with intellectual property and related issues. Again, this is not especially surprising given the stimulus the Research Assessment Exercise (RAE) has given to this area. We would predict a similar growth in those statutory universities and colleges of HE which are putting an increasing emphasis on research. Thirdly, there arises, on average, one substantial legal issue in every HEI in the UK every working week of the year.

1.26   Respondents were also asked to indicate which other types of legal problem had occurred in their institution. Some 29 separate topics were mentioned, but about half of these could be subsumed in the categories just given. Of the new issues, the most common were of a constitutional nature (for example, concerning the charter or the function of the Visitor) or involved finance (at the corporate level, VAT, raising of loans and, especially, debt collection). Other interesting references were to defamation, medical negligence and licensing.

Are legal problems increasing or decreasing in institutions?

1.27   The results, expressed as a percentage, unequivocally point to an increase in legal activity (see Table 1.3). Indeed, the overall increase would probably have been slightly higher had there not been a decrease by the late 1990s in activity in the statutory universities and colleges of HE resulting from the completion of the incorporation process begun in 1992 and the consequent difficult asset transfer issues.

Table 1.3   Frequency of legal problems: increasing or decreasing?

	Increasing	Decreasing	Constant
Chartered university	86.8	0	13.2
Statutory university	87.0	0	13.0
College of HE	76.7	3.3	20.0
All institutions	83.8	1.2	15.0

Do principals and/or heads of administration have any legal qualifications?

1.28   The results set out in Table 1.4 are self-explanatory. It would perhaps have been of even more interest to have found out the actual subject discipline of each of the principals. Would engineering or physics have been more common than sociology or management? However, that is another story. It is of significance to note that several universities (for example, the Universities of

---

1   See chapters 2, 3 and 12 in Warner and Crosthwaite (1995).

Birmingham, Leeds, Oxford and Salford) have appointed an internal legal officer/adviser. This is a trend which is almost certain to continue, at least among the larger institutions. (Note the existence of the National Association of College and University Attorneys (NACUA) in the USA and its many excellent publications, for example NACUA (1989) and (1994).)

Table 1.4   Whether senior management legally qualified?

	Chartered universities %	Statutory universities %	HE colleges %	Overall %
Principal	10.5	4.1	7.2	7.5
Head of administration or similar	15.8	33.3	10.7	18

Are legal problems dealt with internally or externally?

1.29   This question foundered a little on the difficulty in defining a 'legal problem' as mentioned earlier. Suffice it to say that virtually all HEIs employ a mixed economy. When asked to specify what internal processes are used, the following responses were all given:

1. *refer to individuals*:
   - chair of the board of governors
   - clerk to the board of governors
   - deputy director/vice principal
   - head of human resources
   - legal officer/part-time solicitor
   - head of finance
   - office of academic affairs
   - head of personnel
2. *use procedures*:
   - informal approach
   - disciplinary committee
   - internal tribunal
   - NATFHE/UNISON
   - reference to agreed procedures
   - use *Croner's Law Line* for reference and advice.

Clearly, HEIs would benefit from the identification and publication of some good practice case-studies. Perhaps the establishment of UCELNET by Farrington has helped.

If legal problems externally dealt with, how many firms of solicitors are used?

1.30   Table 1.5 gives these results.

Table 1.5   Number of legal firms used

Chartered universities	Statutory universities	HE colleges	Overall
2.4	1.9	1.7	2.1

Is a tender procedure used to select the main firm of solicitors?

1.31   These results (in Table 1.6) are particularly interesting because they indicate that many HEIs may be breaking their own financial rules. We did not ask how much each institution spends each year on legal advice, but anecdotal information leads us to believe that the figure is in excess of £100,000 for many large institutions (indeed, one university budgets for around £100,000 pa but in the last couple of years has spent approximately £250,000 and £500,000 respectively). Not only would this financial level normally entail a tendering procedure, but, of course, the arrangement is effectively perpetual. To be fair, however, several HEIs did indicate that they were about to introduce or were considering a change in their practice towards tendering.

Table 1.6   Whether legal firm(s) selected and appointed on the basis of tendering

Chartered universities %	Statutory universities %	HE colleges %	Overall %
31.4	52.4	28.5	34.5

What criteria are used for selecting solicitors?

1.32   All of the following are used and, in most cases, in combination (for example, cost was only mentioned on its own by one institution):

- competence
- expertise
- quality of individual solicitor involved
- specialisms (for example, corporate law)
- suitability
- familiarity with institution and knowledge of procedures
- efficiency
- good working relationship with client
- track record
- response time
- speed
- by recommendation
- by references
- insurer's solicitor
- price
- competitive tender

–   value for money
–   proximity to institution.

1.33   In order to secure a good response from busy people, many of whom are suffering from 'survey overload', we deliberately produced a brief question-naire. The results, as given earlier, are tantalising – at best, they provide some important new insights, and at worst they raise far more questions than they answer. Indeed, this whole area seems to us to be ripe for further in-depth research. Who will take up the challenge? Certainly, the survey results show that HE and the law is an expanding territory in the UK, just as Kaplin and Lee (1995a) trace the already greatly increased impact of the law on US HEIs. They introduce the concept of 'legal audits' to check whether an 'office or function is in compliance with the full range of legal constraints to which it is subject'.[1] The contrast between firefighting, defending and reacting in legal terms, and a 'preventive law' approach is drawn: the latter 'focuses on initiatives that an institution can take before actual legal disputes arise … this approach becoming increasingly valuable as the presence of law on the campus increased [since the 1980s]'. Reference is made to *The Formbook* produced by the US NACUA (1994) as including 'nearly one hundred legal forms and checklists covering a wide range of institutional functions and transactions … A practical resource'. How long before we need something similar for UK HEIs? It would be much cheaper than each HEI independently employing law firms to reinvent the wheel.

1.34   For this second edition, we have not troubled busy colleagues with another survey only a few years after the last one, but we have telephoned a number of those who kindly responded to our original survey and in this way we have updated the 1997 assessment. Not much has changed.[2] Finally, in a Note at the end of this chapter we have examined the 2000/01 edition of the University of Oxford student handbook and we cross-reference from it to the different chapters in this book concerning the many areas of law which Oxford clearly feels it necessary to clarify for its relationship with its students. Many of those legal aspects simply would not have been on the agenda ten years ago (just as a book like this was much less necessary), let alone in need of highlighting to students. In a sense the University's booklet is a good example of a 'legal audit' having been undertaken and the carefully worded booklet emerging as a 'preventive law' approach to student discipline and complaints problems, as doubtless other HEIs have also been through a similar review process.

---

1   Pages 44/45, and 64.
2   See Elleven *et al* (1997a and 1997b), for a similar survey of legal issues for US HEIs.

FINAL THOUGHTS

1.35 It hardly needs pointing out to anyone who works in HE how rapidly the system changes, particularly those aspects of the system which are determined by external agencies. Legislation which impinges on HE (and almost all legislation seems to do so) changes equally rapidly. New laws are introduced, existing laws are amended and, above all, new interpretations and rulings are made. This last point is especially important to HE because many issues of relevance have simply not yet been tested in the English courts, let alone at the European Court of Justice (ECJ) as appropriate. It is stressed, therefore, that, although we and the contributors have made all reasonable efforts to ensure that this book is comprehensive and useful, none of us can accept any responsibility or liability if a reader and his or her institution rely on the material within this book. It is advised that up-to-date legal advice should always be taken in relation to each particular set of circumstances.

ACKNOWLEDGEMENTS

1.36 We would like to thank the following for commenting, for the first edition in 1997, on the scope of the book in relation to the perceived needs of HEI managers: John Lauwerys, Registrar, University of Southampton; David Neave, then Secretary-General, Brunel University; and Harold Thomas, HE Consultant. Thanks are also due to Kate Hunter at New College for her patience and skill in coping (for two editions) with the handwriting of one of the Editors, to Maureen Harvey at Swansea Institute of Higher Education and to Laurence Palfreyman for his computing assistance. This book arises from a seminar held in March 1996, at New College, Oxford, on 'Key issues in the Law of HE', at which the following provided valuable commentaries on papers given by solicitors: Peter Cane (1996), Harvey McGregor, QC (1997), Hubert Picarda, QC (1999), and Michael Shattock OBE (1994); and at which Sir Michael Davies, QC (1994), spoke on the role of the Visitor. We gratefully acknowledge the kind permission of Laurie Taylor for the reproduction of two of his columns in *The Times Higher Educational Supplement* (in this chapter and in Chapter 12), and the Editor of the *Oxford Magazine* for generous permission to reproduce the article set out in the Appendix to this chapter. For this second edition we also thank all those who commented so helpfully on the first edition: remaining errors and omissions, however, are solely the responsibility of the Editors.

A NOTE ON THE UNIVERSITY OF OXFORD'S STATEMENT TO STUDENTS

1.37 The University of Oxford used to issue its student rules in a quaintly entitled and distinctly not user-friendly *Proctors' Memorandum*. Now it sets them out in a very accessible, comprehensive, concise and clear booklet (*Essential Information for Students*), covering all the potential points of conflict between student and University. Few students, of course, will ever read the neat new booklet, but, in court, at least they will not be able to claim that they were never told about X, Y, Z as follows:

- *Foreword* – 'Welcome to this booklet. *PLEASE KEEP IT*: it is a work of reference to help you get the most out of your Oxford career. It contains some information that is essential, other information that you may find useful from time to time, and statutory requirements of the University for which this serves as formal notification.'

- *Equal Opportunities and Harassment* – 'The University has a committee with terms of reference to consider equal opportunities matters within the University. The role of the committee is to co-ordinate and monitor steps taken by the University to prevent discrimination in the fields of employment and student admissions; and to advise on and/or investigate general issues relating to equality of opportunity ... Most colleges have Codes of Practice and have appointed special advisers or advisory panels to respond to complaints of harassment. If your college has no special arrangements, people you might approach within college could include the dean, tutor for women, or chaplain.

  The University regards harassment as unacceptable behaviour and has introduced a Code of Practice designed to protect its students, staff and other people for whom it has a special responsibility. For the purposes of this Code, harassment is regarded as unwarranted behaviour directed towards another person which disrupts the work or reduces the quality of life of that person. Forms of harassment covered by the Code include one or more acts of bullying, verbal or physical abuse, harassment relating to another's sex, sexual orientation, religion, race or disability, where the effect is to create or maintain a hostile studying, working or social environment.

  The University has a Harassment Advisory Service comprising:

  - departmental or faculty confidential advisers;
  - the Advisory Panel on Harassment;
  - college confidential advisors, where notified.

  These advisers may be approached by any student or member of staff of the University suffering from harassment. The panel has also prepared a pamphlet, *Harassment: what it is and how you can deal with it*.'

- *Personal Safety* – 'Personal security is a matter of being aware of your surroundings and avoiding situations which you believe may become confrontational. Oxford is generally a safe place to study and socialise, and with a few simple precautions you can significantly reduce your chances of falling victim to an attack. Violence is rare, but it is always worth being alert to the risks ... If you are concerned about personal safety, there is a very useful set of web pages which can be found on the Internet at http://info.ox.ac.uk/oxford/crime-prevention.'

- *Theft* – 'If you have important data on a personal computer or floppy discs (lecture notes, draft dissertations, etc), make back-up copies and keep these separately. Proctors do not look sympathetically on requests for late submission of theses, etc, on the grounds that back-up copies of data were not made or were stolen along with a computer.'

- *Insurance* – 'Students are strongly recommended to take out insurance for their personal possessions, whether in college or living in lodgings.'

- *Students Union* – 'All universities have to draw up and publish a code of practice explaining how the requirements of the Education Act 1994 relating to student unions are being carried ... The University's Code of Practice is published in full in Appendix B of this booklet, together with current guidelines to student unions from the Department of Education and Employment ... ' (See Chapter 19.)

- *Clubs and Societies* – ' ... the University does not accept liability for the club's activities and financial affairs. No club should claim to be acting on behalf of the University without express authority to do so; and each club is responsible for any debts incurred.' (See Chapter 19.)

- *Data Protection Act 1998* – 'Anyone holding or intending to keep personal data of any kind ... must comply with the provisions of the Data Protection Act 1998. This is an individual responsibility ... ' (See Chapter 13.)

- *Defamation in Student Newspapers* – 'Students are reminded that, whether or not a publication is formally registered with the Proctors, the individuals involved in the production and distribution are legally responsible for all material ... ' (See Chapters 5 and 19).

- *Plays* – 'Organisers of plays, college balls and other entertainments need to know that there may be complicated issues about licensing and legal requirements ... even if an entertainment or performance does not require a licence, [organisers] may be held responsible if inadequate precautions are taken to ensure the safety of the performers and the audience; the law's requirements regarding such matters as obscenity, incitement to racial hatred, etc, apply equally to private performance of plays ... '

- *Computing and IT* – 'All authorisation [to use the University's computing and IT facilities] is conditional on the user's obeying the rules of the body operating any particular facility or service. Computer misuse is in many cases an offence in law ...'. A later section gives a lengthy list (a-l) of what users are not allowed to do, covering cyber-porn, cyber-libel, cyber-harassment, cyber-fraud, 'spam'-mail, infringement of copyright, e-trading for private gain, deliberately or recklessly introducing a virus into the University network ... Similarly, the user is required to respect confidentiality, comply with data protection legislation, follow University guidelines concerning web-pages, accept monitoring by 'System Administrators.' (See Chapter 14.)

- *Intellectual Property* – 'The University in its Statutes claims ownership of certain forms of intellectual property (IP) which students may create in the course of, or incidental to, their studies. By accepting a place at Oxford as a student, you agree to be legally bound by the University's IP provisions ... The full text of the Statute relating to Intellectual Property is given in Appendix D ...' (See Chapter 12.)

- *Complaints about the conduct of examinations* – on how to complain to the Proctors, who, however, 'have no remit to question the academic judgement of Examiners.' (See Chapters 6–9.)

- *Cheating* – 'No candidate shall make use of unfair means in any University examinations ... examples of "unfair means" include (but are not limited to) the following: collusion ... cheating ... fabricating experimental results ... plagiarism [which is then further defined as "including words or ideas from another author in your essay, thesis, etc, without proper attribution, so as to lead the examiners to believe that the words or ideas are your own"] ...' (See Chapters 6–9.)

- *Degradation* – 'The University has the statutory power (rarely [but recently] used) to deprive somebody of a degree or other qualification after this has been awarded, if it is proven that the degree etc. was obtained falsely (*eg* a thesis is found to contain plagiarised material or falsified data).' (See Chapter 6).

- *General student conduct* – the Statute on University Discipline is extensively quoted, stressing that a student should not 'intentionally or recklessly' disrupt University activities, prevent the lawful exercise of freedom of speech, obstruct University employees, damage University property, occupy University premises, forge University documentation or falsely claim University degree results, harass other University members, use or supply illegal drugs, etc. The University's Code of Practice Relating to Harassment is given as Appendix A to the booklet, and its Code of Practice on Freedom of Speech is given in Appendix C to the booklet. (See Chapter 7.)

- *Marches and processions* – 'The Public Order Act 1986, Section 11, requires the organiser of a procession to give at least six days' notice in advance of the date of the event to the [Police] ... ' (See Chapter 20.)

- *Payment of academic fees* – a student not paying by the due date 'is liable to be suspended from access to University premises and facilities ...' (See Chapter 6.)

- *University Police* – '... all members of the University are obliged to obey the University Constables ...'. As with US HEIs and their private (armed) police forces, Oxford's 'bulldogs' in their bowler hats (but unarmed!) are 'officially a police force constituted under Act of Parliament.' (See Chapters 7 and 20.)

- *Disciplinary Procedures* – 'preliminary investigations', 'disciplinary hearings', 'the disciplinary court', 'the appeal court', etc, are all described, with comments that: 'The standard of proof is the balance of probabilities'; the student may decide 'whether to have the case heard in public or private; the student can be accompanied/represented by 'a barrister or solicitor' or indeed (at 'appeal court' level) by 'anyone whom they choose (including professional lawyers)'. There is even a user-friendly flow-chart showing the various stages of the University Disciplinary Procedures. (See Chapters 7–9.)

- *Medical incapacity* – 'In cases where a student's conduct creates a need for urgent action, the Proctors [usually the Vice-Chancellor at most HEIs] have the power to suspend him or her immediately for a period of up to 21 days, pending investigation. Students have the right of appeal to the Vice-Chancellor against such an order ...' (See Chapter 7.)

- *Complaints about teaching, graduate supervision, and other University services* – may be made to 'the Proctors and Assessor as "Ombudsmen"' ... [who have authority] within the University system to investigate complaints and, where possible, provide redress ...' (See Chapters 6–9.)

- *Public Interest Disclosure Act 1998 (Whistle-blowing)* – 'The University has a code of practice and procedure under this Act, available both to staff and students ... Individuals who make malicious or vexatious allegations may be liable to disciplinary action.' (See Chapter 10.)

- *Academic integrity in research* – 'The University expects all staff and student members ... to observe the highest standards in the conduct of their research. It has been established a Code of Practice and Procedure for Academic Integrity in Research ...' (See Chapters 6, 8, 10 and 12.)

1.38 Impressively clear and comprehensive as the University's booklet undoubtedly is, there is (perhaps unsurprisingly) no mention in the context of complaints of the Visitor jurisdiction applying within the colleges, and similarly no reference to the student–University legal relationship technically being mainly based on a contract and hence ultimately open to adjudication within the courts. The booklet refers to 'Student Membership' and to students as 'Junior Members', thereby emphasising the traditional and indeed medieval concept of the student as a part of the academic endeavour within the 'universitas',[1] rather than the modern trend towards defining the student as being merely a 'consumer' of a mass higher education 'service industry' which supposedly needs external bureaucratic policing to maintain its 'teaching quality' and hence provide 'value-for-money' for its 'customers' (see Chapter 29). The University's booklet in taking this approach would be firmly in line with the colleges' perspective on 'the student learning experience',[2] and hence possibly increasingly at odds with the harsh reality of 'big' business UK HE plc in 2002.

A CASE-BOOK ON HE AND THE LAW AND ON-LINE UPDATING

1.39   It is hoped to produce, as a companion to this volume, a case-book on the student–HEI legal relationship giving case reports and commentaries for the leading cases cited here, and providing other material useful for those wrestling with the impact of the law on HEIs. The case-book will probably be electronic, hosted on the OxCHEPS website referred to below. It is also intended that, in due course, both this volume and the case-book can be updated between editions by referring to the website of OxCHEPS (Oxford Centre for Higher Education Policy Studies), accessible at www.new.ox.ac.uk/oxcheps. (See in addition Ruff (2002, forthcoming) and the *Lawfords UK Higher Education Casebook* at www.lawfordslaw.co.uk.) Relevant HE cases can also be increasingly accessed electronically. In recent years the English courts have made cases available on the web, giving them a 'neutral citation': UKHL (United Kingdom House of Lords), EWCA (England and Wales Court of Appeal), EWHC (High Court), and with sub-divisions (for example, 'EWCA Civ' for the Civil Division of the Court of Appeal, or 'EWHC Admin' for the Administrative Court, or 'EWHC Ch' for the Chancery Division). Thus a recent case may be reported not only in the standard published law reports ('All England', etc) but is also available in its, as it were, official 'neutral' form (for example, *Smith v Jones* [2002] EWHC 873 (Ch), or *BCCI v Ali* [2001] UKHL 8).

---

1   Cobban (1988, 1999).
2   Tapper and Palfreyman (2000), chapter 5; Palfreyman (2001).

APPENDIX TO CHAPTER 1

(Reproduced, with permission, from the *Oxford Magazine*, 8th week, Michaelmas Term, 2000.)

Piffle v. St Luke's College
(Do undergraduates have rights?)

ANON (with apologies to A.P. Herbert)

The House of Lords today delivered judgment in the notorious 'vexatious student' case.

LORD LAUD: My Lords, in my many years in the law, in which I have eaten almost as many dinners in Oxford as I did when I was myself an undergraduate, I do not think that I have ever come across a case which seemed so clear on its face, but which, on deeper examination, threatened as much legal and social revolution as the case that we have had outlined before us.

The facts of the case are not simple, and it may be my first duty to lay out these facts in the language of the simpleton, which is to say in terms that even an undergraduate averaging less than a beta mark in his tutorial essays may comprehend. The main incident, and the one from which all other proceedings in this case have stemmed, happened on the Tuesday of Noughth Week of this Michaelmas Term, when the hapless undergraduate, without seeking permission from his College Dean, walked into the centre of Oxford.

The initial facts of the case
Sergeant Crump of the University of Oxford Police attested that Mr Piffle was, indeed, sighted walking not only within three miles of Carfax, but within a few hundred yards of that central location, thus contravening the regulations of his College. Piffle later acted in a number of despicable ways, so as to compound the felony. Before the end of that very same day, the undergraduate had been accused of going against the regulations of his College by:
(*a*) Entering within three miles of Carfax outside of Full term without prior permission of his College;
(*b*) Attending an unauthorised party on College premises; and
(*c*) Blocking the path of the Junior Dean of the College when she tried to enter the party to reprimand the party-goers.

Mr Piffle's College Governing Body thereupon accused the undergraduate of the above offences, and, at a private meeting at the beginning of Michaelmas Term, convicted him. Mr Piffle accepted that he had done all of which he was accused, but denied that he had committed any offence under law. The Governing Body felt that,

given the acceptance of the Acts of Mr Piffle by his own testimony, they had no option but to convict him.

Such is the normal process of law. If a young man is accused of doing something, and pleads in evidence that he did, in fact, do it, then, according to historical precedent and the rule of law, he is convicted and sentenced. The College Regulations have been so applied to countless generations of young men throughout five hundred years.

The College in Court
But Mr Piffle has no regard for such tradition and precedent, and he subsequently brought a case in the Courts against the College. He sought to overturn these five centuries of practice through the use of the Human Rights Act 1998. Arguing that the College was a 'Public Authority' under section 6 of the Act, he stated that the College had breached the following rights accorded to him under the European Convention on Human Rights: (i) Article 6(1) (the right to a fair hearing), by failing to ensure the independence of the complainant, prosecutor, and jury when charging him with the stated offences; (ii) Article 8 (the right to privacy of person and abode), by failing to respect his privacy and that of the host of his party by seeking entry without due warrant under law; and (iii) Article 11 (the right to freedom of association), by seeking to prevent him and others exercising their right to free and peaceable assembly.

Furthermore, it was alleged that the College had infringed the undergraduate's right to freedom of movement, which had been conferred on all citizens of the European Union by Article 8(*a*) of the European Communities' Treaty (as amended).

The College's defence
In its defence, the College cited a great deal of historical precedent as justification for its action, thus proving, at last, that having the Regius Professor of Middle-Ages Jurisprudence among the Fellowship can have its advantages. In doing so, they presented a coherent, imaginative, and witty argument, showing that since the time of Boff's Case (1523) it has been established law that

undergraduates have no rights against the whim of the College Dean, acting on behalf of the Governing Body. Moreover, they showed how, in the last Century, following the clarification by the University Commissoners of the laws relating to Colleges' powers, Gilbert M. R. pronounced that 'An Oxford College's Governing Body has no kind of fault or flaw, for a Governing Body, My Lords, emobides the Law'. Although it was not possible for undergraduates to have rights defined in law, this was said not to disadvantage them: as Avril Dicey, the Eminent Victorian Constitutional Lawyer, wrote in 1885: 'The benevolence of a Governing Body is worth a hundred Bills of Rights'. The defendant's case so impressed the Court with its style and eloquence that the defendant was acquitted by the court.

The case before your Lordships' House

However, the Court in coming to its findings in the initial hearings of this case, did not take account of the latest developments in the New Jurisprudence. Since the Human Rights Act 1998 came into effect on 2 October, 2000, it is no longer the case that the style of argument in defence, or the age of the precedents cited, should, by themselves, determine the resolution of the Court. In the stead of these factors have been placed some new-fangled ideas: namely that the Court must take notice of what the Law says today, especially with regard to the rights of the citizen, in preference to what it said in the time of Coke and Blackstone.

What the Law does say today is that Oxford Colleges must, as any Public Authority must, obey the Law. Moreover, the same Law states, with unusual clarity, that Public Authorities must act according to certain provisions of the European Convention on Human Rights, including the right to receive a fair hearing, the right to associate freely, and the right to enjoy privacy.

In the case before Your Lordships, the restrictions placed upon the undergraduate do not seem to be 'necessary in a democratic society' in the interests of national security, for the prevention of crime, or for the protection of public health; and the restrictions are not, therefore, permitted by the Convention. Moreover, the restrictions are not embodied in Law: to the best of my (if I may say so, extensive) knowledge, the Queen-in-Parliament has never passed a Being Within Three Miles of Carfax (Vacation) Act, or a Junior Dean (Party Pooper) Act. Contrary to the claims of the Counsel for St Luke's College, the pronouncements of Governing Body do not have the status of Primary Acts of Parliament.

Moreover, even if Parliament had passed a Being Within Three Miles of Carfax (Vacation) Act, the original charge by the College against the undergraduate would not be compatible with the fundamental law of the European Union, which grants to the citizens of the European Communities the right to move freely within Member Nations. It is clear, following the decision of Your Lordships' House in the case of *R. v. Secretary of State for Transport (ex parte Factortame)*, that Acts of the Sovereign Parliament cannot transgress the provisions of such freedoms.

The conclusion of these considerations can be no other than that, since October 2000, and possibly earlier, an undergraduate has rights against his College. In the original hearing of this case, Mr Justice Grapple, summing up, borrowed from the language of the prominent jurist Light, L. C. J. Grapple deemed the claim, made by the Counsel for the Undergraduate, that students have rights, to be 'like the thirteenth stroke of a crazy clock, which not only is itself discredited but casts a shade of doubt over all previous assertions.' However, Mr Justice Grapple did not take into account the momentous recent juridical developments. There can be no doubt that the conclusion in this case, which is brought about directly by the passage of the Human Rights Act, will cause a revolution in legal and educational circumstances. Contrary to all the previously accumulated wisdom of reasoned man through the ages, undergraduates do have rights.

I am therefore left with no option but to find for Mr Piffle in all instances.

LORD LUNK assented enthusiastically, adding that this sort of case gave Jurisprudence undergraduates an excellent opportunity to gain first-hand practical experience of litigation.

LORD MILQUETOAST agreed, but lamented the passing of gown-wearing as a daily undergraduate activity.

LORD TOSH dissented, noting that being sent down from Oxford had never harmed his career.

Chapter 2

WHAT IS A HIGHER EDUCATION INSTITUTION AS A LEGAL ENTITY?

Nicola Hart (Martineau Johnson)

EDITORS' INTRODUCTION

§2.1   The observations in this chapter are intended to provide an introductory platform for diving into any other chapter in this book, by generally and briefly setting out some fundamental concepts one needs to be aware of in applying the law to an HEI and cross-referencing to the relevant chapter(s) where the issue is explored in greater detail. A 'university' is not an easy thing to define in law: like an elephant it is hard to describe, but you know one when you see it, as the judge commented in *St David's College, Lampeter v Ministry of Education*[1] (in which he concluded that a university must have its own charter). In essence, a UK university will either have a Royal Charter from the Crown, or be created by statute. The issue is complex and there is not space to explore it here (see Farrington (1998), pp 6–58). (See also *London College of Science and Technology v Islington London Borough Council*[2] where the College as a limited company was trading as the 'American University in London': the issue was whether using the word 'university' was an offence under the Business Names Act 1985.) Suffice to say that, in practice, the Privy Council controls the award of the title 'University', and hence it recently upset Bolton Institute of Technology (BIT) by rejecting its bid to be upgraded to university status, while, similarly, Liverpool Hope University College has not been allowed to retain the word 'University' in its title following a 1999 clamp-down on the (ab)use of the u-word. LHUC challenged that decision, based on s 39 of the Teaching and Higher Education Act 1998, but was unsuccessful (*The Queen on the application of Liverpool Hope University College v Secretary of State for Education and Employment*).[3]

§2.2   A key concept is that the HEI has perpetual and separate legal personality as a corporation, as in law an artificial person rather than a natural person or human being, the corporation being in the case of an Oxbridge college, for example, the Warden and Fellows – here it is worth recalling Bracton, a thirteenth-century lawyer: '. . . for in colleges and chapters the same body [the corporation] endures for ever, although all [the corporators] may die one after the other, and others may be placed in their stead; just as with flocks of sheep, the flock remains the same though the sheep die. . . .'.[4]

---

1   [1951] 1 All ER 559.
2   (1996) *The Times*, July 23, [1997] ELR 162.
3   [2001] EWHC Civ 362, (2001) unreported, 15 March. See also *Halsbury's Laws of England* 15(1) 'Education' paras 567 and 568 concerning 'bogus' or 'unrecognised' degrees 'awarded' by 'degree mills': an area policed by Trading Standards under s 214 of the ERA 1988.
4   Folio 374b of his 'Notes', quoted in Pollock and Maitland (1923), vol 1, p 508, n 1.

§2.3   In civil law countries there is the legal entity of the 'foundation' not found in
common law systems, where it would be a cross between the exempt charity
statutory or chartered corporation (ie universities and colleges; see this
chapter and Chapter 3) and the registered charitable trust (for example,
'Oxfam'; see Chapter 4), with elements of the unincorporated association (as
often is the Students' Union; see Chapter 19) and the registered company as
another kind of corporation duly registered under the Companies Act 1985
(as HEIs have trading companies; see Chapter 15). There is, however, talk of
legislation to create the 'Charitable Incorporated Institution' as a new legal
form in English law more closely fitted to the running of charities.

§2.4   Thus we have:

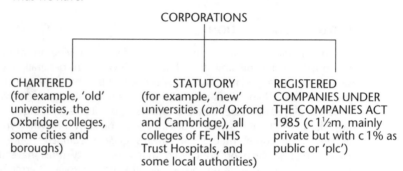

CORPORATIONS

CHARTERED	STATUTORY	REGISTERED
(for example, 'old' universities, the Oxbridge colleges, some cities and boroughs)	(for example, 'new' universities (*and* Oxford and Cambridge), all colleges of FE, NHS Trust Hospitals, and some local authorities)	COMPANIES UNDER THE COMPANIES ACT 1985 (c 1½m, mainly private but with c 1% as public or 'plc')

THE CORPORATION

2.1   An HEI is a peculiar kind of legal entity, probably best generally
described as a corporation. A corporation is a body of persons recognised by
the law as having a personality distinct from the separate personalities of its
members. It is a distinct legal entity, which continues in existence as its
members change from time to time. HEIs fall into various sub-categories of
corporation. The basic distinction is between those created by statute (for
example, the Oxford and Cambridge Act 1571 and the Education Reform Act
1988 (ERA 1988)), and those founded by grant of a charter. Only the Crown
can grant a charter. The distinction is important because statutory and
non-statutory corporations have different powers. A chartered university has
power, generally speaking, to do anything in law which could be done by an
individual. Express powers do not need to be spelled out in its charter or
statutes. Although a chartered university, as a corporation with all the powers
of an individual, will not generally be susceptible to claims that it has acted
beyond its powers, in practice there are restrictions on its freedom. If the
university acted in direct contravention of its charter, in theory the charter
might be revoked by the Crown. More realistically, an individual member
could sue the university or petition its Visitor to enforce the charter's
provisions.

POWERS

2.2   The notion of an Alsatia in England (where, as a result of the Visitor's jurisdiction, 'the King's writ does not run') is, however, becoming increasingly attenuated for chartered universities. There have been a number of warning signs in recent years. The role of the Visitor has been curtailed by Parliament's enactment of the Education Reform Act 1988, s 206, removing the Visitor's jurisdiction in employment disputes and introducing the role of the University Commissioners (see Chapters 10 and 11). In the case of *R v Hull University Visitor ex parte Page*,[1] the House of Lords decided that there were (limited) circumstances in which a University Visitor could be subject to judicial review by the High Court. Of even greater significance is the fact that the Visitor is now subject to the provisions of the Human Rights Act 1998 (HRA 1998). Kaye (1999) points out that unless visitorial procedures are substantially reorganised, decisions of Visitors will almost certainly no longer amount to the final word; those aggrieved will be able to seek redress either in an application for judicial review or in the county court. (See Chapters 8 and 30 on the Visitor.)

2.3   While the previous paragraph suggests that the distinction between the powers of old and new universities is starting to be eroded, a statutory as opposed to a chartered university is a creature of its originating statute and its only rights and powers to act are those expressly or impliedly conferred by that statute. The ERA 1988, s 124(2) provides for a subjective test: that which *appears to it to be necessary or expedient* in the exercise of its principal powers, the corporation has power to do. The exercise of this judgment is still distinct from the exercise of the powers of a chartered university: while the subjective test provides some comfort to members of the corporation, the power in question, as an express statutory one, is clearly subject to the usual public law requirements that it should be exercised reasonably and for its proper purpose. The courts will generally take a narrow view of the powers of statutory corporations, following the Court of Appeal's decisions in the *Allerdale* and *Waltham Forest* cases[2] (about local authorities' powers to participate in companies and to give guarantees). Hence, s 124(2)(f) of the ERA 1988 has perhaps been amended by para 15 of Sch 9 to the Learning and Skills Act 2000 specifically to clarify and explicitly to confirm that a statutory HEI can indeed set up a company for trading purposes.[3]

2.4   Generally, under the terms of the enacting statute, a statutory HEI will have power to delegate its duties and functions, subject to any restriction as to those which may only be carried out by the governing body itself (see Chapter 5). Acting beyond its express powers may lead to transactions being set aside as

1   [1993] AC 682, [1992] 3 WLR 112 (*sub nom R v Lord President of the Privy Council ex parte Page*.

2   *Crédit Suisse v Allerdale Borough Council* [1997] QB 306; *Crédit Suisse v Waltham Forest London Borough Council* [1997] QB 362.

3   See Chapter 15, and Farrington (2000b).

of no effect in law. The impact of this may be felt in areas where a statutory HEI tests the boundaries of its freedom to operate commercially (for example, borrowing, lending or giving guarantees in relation to the operations of subsidiary or joint venture companies). The statutory HEI may be required to demonstrate to a commercial lender that it has power to enter into a particular commercial arrangement. While in theory the risk might rest with the lender, in practice the HEI, first, needs the funds, and, secondly, does not want the scheme called in as a nullity, with the implication that new and unfavourable terms could be substituted. Students may also challenge a statutory HEI's actions, if they are beyond its powers (*ultra vires*), by way of judicial review (see Chapter 9).

CHARITABLE STATUS

2.5   An HEI will also usually be a charity (see Chapter 4). Although (in most cases) exempt from the jurisdiction of the Charity Commissioners, it will be subject to the control of the High Court. The principal advantages of the HEI's charitable status are: first, that a charity has a special status in society, which will assist it in areas such as fund-raising; secondly, that particularly favourable tax treatment is available to charitable bodies; and, thirdly, that the parameters of the charity's operations and essential nature are clarified by a body of statute and case-law. These advantages are partly offset by the impact charitable status has on the HEI's ability to engage in commercial operations (see Chapter 15). The questions which generally need to be asked are: whether trading is permissible; whether the HEI may properly establish subsidiary non-charitable trading companies; and the extent to, and way in which, the HEI may fund, guarantee or otherwise facilitate the operations of such companies. Charity law may also have an impact on the HEI since duties equivalent to those of charity trustees may be imputed to those in charge of its governance (see Chapters 3 and 4).

PUBLIC BODY

2.6   The HEI will be treated as a public body for certain purposes in law. This classification introduces further complications and brings the HEI within the jurisdiction of various external regimes. There seems little doubt, for example, that an HEI is a 'public authority' for the purposes of the HRA 1998. HEIs are, therefore, under an obligation to ensure that they do not act in a way that breaches any of the rights included in the European Convention for the Protection of Human Rights and Fundamental Freedoms 1950 (European Convention on Human Rights) (and some of the related Protocols). Such rights include the right to freedom of conscience and expression and the right to respect for private and family life. It also seems inevitable that an HEI will be classified as a 'emanation of the State' for the purposes of European Community law. The consequences of such classification would include the possibility of claims by individuals under the Treaty of Rome (for example, on equal pay issues) being made directly against the institution. Other obligations also arise in connection with European law, such as, for most (but not all) HEIs, the requirement to advertise in the *Official Journal* for tenders for public works contracts over a certain value (see Chapter 28).

2.7 External control and regulation may be exerted on the HEI from a number of different quarters. The State has power, through Parliament, to make constitutional changes. Ministers make regulations with statutory force (see, for example, Chapters 21, 22 and 23). Governmental bodies and agencies – the funding councils and Quality Assurance Agency for higher education (QAA) for example – impose their requirements and criteria unilaterally. Statutory inspectorates – for example in Health and Safety, Pollution, Radiation, Food Hygiene – inspect and prosecute in the criminal courts. The setting up of some sort of ombudsman's office to deal with complaints about all HEIs, whether chartered or statutory, is a possibility currently under review, whereas the High Court continues to provide third parties with the opportunity of judicial review of a statutory HEI's decisions (see Chapter 9). The Visitor in chartered universities also has wide powers to intervene and right wrongs (see Chapters 8 and 30).

COMMUNITY

2.8 The HEI is a community, originally of academics but ultimately encompassing a wide range of individuals and groups with correspondingly diverse interests: academic and non-academic staff, undergraduates, post-graduates, honorary post-holders, administrators and managers. These are examples of interest-groups or stakeholders within the university – they could be grouped under the name of the 'home community'. In relation to any of these, the HEI may be one or more of, for example: employer (see Chapters 10 and 11); supplier of educational services and qualifications (see Chapters 6, 7 and 28); landlord (see Chapter 23); co-shareholder of a limited company (see Chapter 15). In addition to these various internal groupings, the HEI will also have 'foreign relations' at a variety of diplomatic or other levels with, for example: other HEIs; the media; legislators; Parliament and civil servants; the courts; funders; commercial partners; external validating agencies; and people, institutions and governments outside the UK jurisdictions. The way in which the members of its home community interact with these outsiders is also a subject likely to be of interest from the legal point of view (see, for example, Chapters 16, 17 and 18). The HEI's relationship with the Students' Union (SU) is, in legal terms, somewhere between the 'home community' and a matter of 'foreign relations' (see Chapter 19). Similarly, the relationship between the HEI and its alumni is both a family affair and one covered by the Data Protection Act (see Chapters 12, 13, 14 and 25).

2.9 The HEI arguably has an obligation to regulate its home community and activities, to ensure that good order is maintained for the benefit of all participants. This obligation (in the context of both the home and foreign communities) has to be seen as the basis for the HEI's ability to require its students to sign up to a system of disciplinary regulations. The regulations form part of the HEI–student contract (see Chapter 6), and the HEI, as well as its students, is, therefore, obliged to act within the terms of the regulations, or risk a disciplinary decision being overturned by its Visitor or a court. Students will only be bound by the regulations they signed up to: unilateral changes will not be effective. It is, therefore, of particular importance to ensure that disciplinary regulations are kept up to date and cover all the circumstances in which they might need to be used (see Chapter 7).

2.10 All of these internal and external legal relationships need managing, whether in terms of minimising liability risk (the theme of this book throughout, as detailed in Chapter 1), covering that liability with appropriate insurance (see Chapter 24), or handling any litigation (see Chapter 27).

Part 2
GOVERNANCE

Chapter 3

GOVERNANCE, ACCOUNTABILITY AND PERSONAL LIABILITY

John Hall (Eversheds) and Oliver Hyams (Barrister)

EDITORS' INTRODUCTION

§3.1 'Governance' is a rather pompous term for the total management of an HEI. It is, however, useful in a wider sense than simply 'the management of an HEI' in circumstances where 'the management' within an HEI has become distorted or confused about its power and duties. Sometimes 'the management' in any organisation can assume too readily that *its* best interests as a constituency and as an interest group are automatically the same as those of the organisation *as a whole*. The role of governors also extends beyond control of the executive to encompass defending the HEI against external pressures or acting as a conduit for society's increasing demands for the academic community to be accountable. It might well all be subsumed under the phrase: 'the taking of sound collective decisions for the overall benefit of the corporate enterprise' (and 'sound' includes careful risk management – see Chapter 24).

§3.2 Hence, we have seen difficulties at University College, Cardiff, in the late 1980s, and during the 1990s at Portsmouth, Glasgow Caledonian and Huddersfield, with governance problems also occurring in the colleges of higher education at Southampton and Swansea (plus, in the FE sector, at Derby Wilmorton College and at St Philips Roman Catholic Sixth Form College, as well as at Bilston College). Such problems prompted the extension of the original Nolan Inquiry (1995) into an investigation of HE and FE governance in the UK. The result seems to be a fairly clean bill of health from Nolan (1996):

> 'On the evidence we received, the rare cases of mismanagement, malad-ministration and misconduct, seem to be isolated occurrences. We have been impressed by the remedial action which has been taken by regulators, funding bodies, and representative associations ... Many of the institutions have evolved systems of governance over many years and it would require evidence of substantial misconduct to justify sweeping changes. We received no such evidence.'

§3.3 The inquiry does, however, call for 'publicly available registers of interests'. However, a later Nolan Report (1997), while noting that there has been a willingness to take up the Nolan (1996) anti-sleaze and whistleblowing recommendations in principle, also commented that implementation in practice has been slow and that there is complacency. That said, goverance failure in HE pales into insignificance when compared with corporate failure in the private sector (for example, Barings, Enron, Independent Insurance, Equitable Life, Railtrack, Marconi and Robert Maxwell's business empire in the UK).

§3.4   At Portsmouth University, the governing body has recently established a
Chancellor's Court to consider complaints presented by a minimum of four
governors. This kind of move, with variations on the theme at other statutory
HEIs, reflects a search for the equivalent of the Visitor to be found in the
chartered universities (see Chapters 8 and 30). At the Swansea Institute, a
governor resigned over the conduct of a governors' meeting, the alleged use
of 'a gagging order', and the alleged lack of independence of the governing
body.[1] Certainly, the Government White Paper response to Nolan[2] called for
HEI governing bodies to receive guidance on best practice – see Committee of
University Chairmen (CUC) (2001) as the latest issue of what was originally
CUC (1994); see also Association for Colleges (AfC) (1995) and later issues:
the original 1995 edition in its Foreword referred to the responsibilities of
governors as being 'onerous', and to their liabilities as 'awesome' and as yet
'not even fully tested'.

§3.5   The concept of governance is about checks and balances within the HEI to
ensure that it is well managed, about the allocation of responsibility and
appropriate power to fulfil that responsibility, and about other duties. It links
with the concept of trusteeship explored in Chapter 4, and to the conduct of
meetings and the concepts of delegation and agency examined in Chapter 5.
It also rapidly blends into other areas beyond the law – the concept of the
culture of an organisation, of its management style and of managerial lines of
reporting. These aspects of the collegiality/shared-values: managerialism/
corporatism debate are all explored in Warner and Palfreyman (1996, second
edition due 2002/2003), chapters 1, 2 and 6; see also Tapper and Palfreyman
(1998 and 2000), pp 17–24, with Bargh *et al* (1996), Bolton (2000), pp 10–13
and Watson (2000), pp 6–8, and especially Shattock (forthcoming). This
chapter, however, examines, governance from the legal perspective, which is
essentially:

–   what functions exist and their tasks;
–   how the functions are distributed within an HEI's management structure
        (officers, governing body, committees); and
–   the duties, responsibilities and potential liability of members of govern-
        ing bodies, individually and collectively as committees.

§3.6   The relevant sections and recommendations in Dearing (1997) on HEI
governance[3] are significant. Dearing proposed a code of practice for
institutional governance, and a review of the effectiveness of the governing
body and of the HEI to be undertaken at least once every 5 years. It is also
proposed that governors should have effective arrangements to address
complaints by students (see Chapters 6–9, and 30; on confidentiality or
'gagging clauses', see Davies (1994), pp 78–80. In essence, Dearing follows
Nolan (1995, 1996) and endorses the steps already taken by way of the 'good
practice' guides referred to above (in addition to which the CUC has speedily
produced 'Advice on Whistleblowing', CUC (1997)). Nolan (1997) seems to
feel, however, that HEIs have been a bit slow in establishing appropriate
practice in 'whistleblowing' even if the principle on how to handle it is
accepted. Note, for example, the furore in 1997 at Glasgow Caledonian
University surrounding the 'whistleblowing' of a former member of academic
staff over the alleged undermining of academic standards by putting financial

---

1   *The Times Higher Educational Supplement*, 5 July 1996.
2   *The Governance of Public Bodies: A Progress Report*, January 1997.
3   Paragraphs 15.32–15.68 of the main report, pp 236–247; Recommendations 54–60.

interests first, and note the now long-running 'Whistleblowers' column in *The Times Higher Educational Supplement* which has featured in disputes at Anglia Polytechnic University, Middlesex University and Oxford University. The 'whistleblowing' charity providing advice and legal support to concerned employees in relation to the Public Interest Disclosure Act 1998 is *Public Concern at Work* (020 7404 6609; www.pcaw.co.uk). See Lewis *et al* (2001) and Lewis (2001).

§3.7   It is worth quoting extensively from Steve Cannon's chapter in Warner and Palfreyman (2001), pp 112–113 where he describes governance from the perspective of the Scottish HEIs and the Scottish Higher Education Funding Council (SHEFC):

> 'It is this view of universities as "first and foremost corporate enterprises" that encouraged SHEFC to look to corporate governance arrangements in the private sector to provide a lead. In England the universities had taken the initiative themselves through the Committee of University Chairmen who in 1998 produced a *Guide for Members of Governing Bodies of Universities and Colleges in England, Wales and Northern Ireland* (CUC (1998)). The Funding Council in Scotland took a different line. *The Guide for Members of Governing Bodies of Scottish Higher Education Institutions and Good Practice Benchmarks* (SHEFC (1999)) goes much further than its English counterpart and promotes and develops a set of good practice guidelines against which individual institutions could benchmark and develop their own specific arrangements. The guide makes a series of recommendations in respect of the roles, responsibilities, size and composition of governing bodies. In addition it discusses the procedures these bodies should follow and makes recommendations in respect of the role of the Secretary or Clerk, the remit of committees of the governing body and the regulation of the relationship between the institution and its related companies. Finally it invites the governing body to adopt a range of performance measures related to the institution's strategic objectives. As with similar codes that govern practice in the private sector, the objective is not to be prescriptive but rather to define what the Council considers to be good practice and compare their existing practices with these benchmarks, and indicate in their Annual Reports where and why they consider it to be either inappropriate or impractical to follow them (SHEFC (1999)).
>
> There are a number of flaws in this analysis. Unlike company boards, the governing bodies of HE institutions have on the whole not been designed for strategic management but rather as representative bodies of a wide constituency of interests. Governing bodies, particularly in the older universities, derive from an age when their roles and responsibilities were more symbolic than real, when the "dignified" as opposed to the "efficient" elements of governance were emphasised (Bargh *et al* (1996)). A university is primarily defined by its business of teaching and research, and, while it must remain solvent, looks principally not to profits but to the value of its outputs (CUC (2000)). In addition, and uniquely, in many of the older universities the core business – academic matters – lies outside the governing body.
>
> Evidence from recent National Audit Office (NAO) studies at a number of institutions in the higher education sector (NAO (1997a, 1997b and 1998)) supports recent research findings that effective governance is likely to depend more on interpersonal and largely informal relationships

than on constitutional or structural arrangements (Bargh *et al,* 1996).

Research undertaken by Bargh *et al* suggests that, although the majority of governors acknowledge their strategic role in taking responsibility for determining the institution's strategic mission, "in the complex world of university governance only 'knowledgeable actors' can operate effectively"; not all governors are invited to play an "acting role" and those that are often find themselves in minor roles or bit parts.

They further suggest that within governing bodies a relatively small "core group" of governors control the governance process to the extent that "some groups of governors are effectively marginalized from important areas of influence". Moreover the process appears to be self-perpetuating despite the guidance in both the Cadbury Report (1992) and the *Guide for Members of Governing Bodies* (Committee of University Chairmen, 1998). While most, if not all, universities have established a Nominations Committee, the researchers found that in practice the process of seeking new members draws heavily on existing members, informal networks via personal recommendations (Bargh *et al*, 1996).

The ability of independent governors to initiate strategic proposals depends, to a large extent, on their background knowledge of higher education issues and their degree of self-confidence to express and volunteer ideas in the company of seasoned executive professionals. This disadvantage is compounded by the fact that lay governors are frequently almost entirely dependent on the executive for information. The executive decides what information it thinks the governing body needs rather than the governing body specifying what it requires to fulfil its responsibilities. Under such circumstances governors are likely to become passive and reactive, shunning the proactive behaviour necessary for the effective performance of their strategic function. In both old and new universities the evidence suggests that it is the executive, the senior management team, which takes the 'efficient' or most proactive role in the governance process (Bargh *et al*, 1996).'

(See also Hurrell (2001); Shattock (1999 and forthcoming); plus the CUC *Report on University Governance, 1997–2000* as, to some extent, updating Bargh *et al* (1996).)

§3.8   HEIs really do have to get governance right: they are *not* bright and breezy dot.coms; they are quasi-public bodies which must have an innate sense of propriety, procedures and protocol. If they do not get it right, they deserve headlines like: 'Cambridge admits errors in filling positions'[1] and a story which begins with 'Cambridge University has been breaking its statutes ...' (professors having been appointed *ultra vires* as a result of procedural 'sloppiness'). Indeed, as Brown (2001) comments on the many Public Accounts Committee (PAC), NAO and QAA investigations into management and governance abuse at HEIs over the past decade:

'If there is one common feature running through these reports it is the difficulty which these institutions had in controlling the behaviour of a strong chief executive who was often closely associated with a small group of key Governors who may have bypassed a largely supine Governing Body,

---

1   *The Times Higher Educational Supplement,* 30 March 2001, p 4.

many of whom were not sufficiently knowledgeable either about higher education matters or about their own rights and responsibilities as members of the supreme decision-making body of a higher education institution.'

§3.9 Nor are HEI administrators and managers personally immune; they, like their governors and council members, need to have a code of best practice or ethics. For example, in CUC (2001) there is material on the role of the Secretary of State in relation to the Governing Body. Given below is the *Code of Professional Standards* for members of the UK Association of University Administrators (AUA) (see also Skinner (2001)). The code of values and principles establishes the framework within which AUA expects its members to set the highest standards of professionalism. In order to demonstrate this professionalism and their commitment and contribution to higher education, AUA members are expected to:

- provide high quality professional services;
- develop an appreciation of the academic culture, of the traditions and values of the organisations and institutions through which it is sustained, and of the roles of colleagues at all levels and all branches of higher education;
- be sensitive to the multiplicity of clients served by the higher education administrator and to the need to balance conflicting demands;
- act with integrity, honesty, fairness, professional impartiality and diligence without discrimination;
- observe due care, objectivity and respect for confidentiality;
- be explicit and straightforward in their dealings with colleagues and clients;
- ensure that personal interest does not override the needs of clients;
- accept responsibility for their actions;
- challenge existing practices and ideas when necessary;
- be committed to their own personal and professional development by seeking new knowledge and skills to enhance professional performance;
- foster the development of others by sharing expertise and good practice and by encouraging employers to support professional development.

§3.10 The function of the HEI governing body is wide in scope, covering not only its role as a check on the abuse of executive power but also, for example, the protection of the rights of individuals within the HEI (see Chapter 10 on academic tenure and freedom and Chapter 19 on the freedom of speech in relation to the HEI's supervision of the Students' Union. See also the OxCHEPS Occasional Paper 'Proper Governance in the English Chartered University' (Palfreyman (2002, forthcoming)): access to the OxCHEPS website is detailed in para **1.39** above. This paper, inter alia, comments on the governance and management implications of the University of Cambridge 'CAPSA' financial/management accounting £9m IT fiasco (see also Chapter 5).

§3.11 The way in which HEI governing bodies go about their business is under constant review and development (see the latest CUC governance guidance as CUC (2001), and the CUC *Report on Governance* (2000).[1] Yet, despite this general progress, HEIs are (like further education institutions (FEIs) and schools, or indeed charities generally) finding it increasingly difficult to fill

---

1   The editors wish to thank Mike Shattock OBE for his valuable comments on the complex issue of governance as discussed in this chapter. We very much look forward to Shattock's

the ranks of governors/members of council, at least in terms of finding folk of appropriate experience and expertise with also the time to serve (and especially once put on committees and working parties). As discussed in this chapter, the (admittedly very remote) threat of personal liability hanging over HEI governors as, after all, unpaid volunteers is not helpful in recruiting a vibrant team.

§3.12　　Finally, concerning the removal of governors, see *R v City of Bath College Corporation ex parte Bashforth*.[1]

GOVERNANCE UNDER SCRUTINY

3.1　　For the past 15 years, the spotlight of public scrutiny has turned with increasing intensity on the governance and management of HEIs. The Jarratt Report contained seminal recommendations to the CVCP (now rebranded 'Universities UK', 2000) and the University Grants Committee (UGC) which embraced the important acknowledgement that universities are, first and foremost, corporate enterprises headed by a 'Chief Executive' Vice-Chancellor to which the academic community is accountable. The granting of corporate independence to the former polytechnics and higher education colleges from local authority control in 1989 gave impetus to the move to a more corporate model of governance in higher education, the enhancement of the principal's role as chief executive, the growth in the power of the governing body (Council or Board) in relation to the supreme academic authority (the Senate or Academic Board), and a recent demand for more effective but less burdensome public accountability (see *Better Accountability for Higher Education* (HEFCE (2000))). These developments coincided with the harsh economic climate of the late 1980s, which placed the work of the Cadbury Committee (1992) in the eye of the storm following BCCI, Maxwell, and public disquiet about executive pay and pay-offs. The quest for effective governance thus became an imperative in the private sector. The country's economy depends on the drive and efficiency of its companies. Thus the effectiveness with which their boards discharge their responsibilities determines Britain's competitive position. They must be free to drive their companies forward, but exercise that freedom within a framework of effective accountability. This is the essence of any system of good corporate governance.

3.2　　Close on the footsteps of Cadbury followed a flurry of reports which emphasised the importance of independent remuneration committees to curb the worst excesses of executive pay, culminating in the Greenbury Report and Code (1995). This was, in large measure, prompted by fierce media criticism of the chief executives of privatised utility companies and the accusation that too many 'fat cats' were being rewarded for failure. There emerged from the gloom, in gleaming armour, 'the new philosophy of full transparency' (proclaimed with a transatlantic accent), which required company shareholders to have

---

forthcoming book *Managing Governance* in the Open University Press 20-volume series *Managing Universities and Colleges*. In the meantime, we note his particular comments.

1　　[1999] ELR 459.

access to all information which they might reasonably require to enable them to assess a board's policy on issues such as executive pay and packages.[1] Wider and wider was cast a net for governance structures which would command public confidence. Studies were undertaken into comparative models in other countries, but these only emphasised the diverse range of corporate governance systems worldwide. Perhaps inevitably the quest for good governance moved to that most indefinable and controversial area of human conduct – ethics. A fall in public confidence in the financial probity of Members of Parliament and other holders of public office (exemplified by the public furore concerning 'cash for questions') and the development of a 'culture of sleaze' led to the then Prime Minister setting up the Committee on Standards in Public Life under the chairmanship of Lord Nolan (October, 1994). The terms of reference of Lord Nolan's Committee were drawn in the widest possible terms:

> 'To examine current concerns about standards of conduct of all holders of public office, including arrangements relating to financial and commercial activities, and make recommendations as to any changes in present arrangements which might be required to ensure the highest standards of propriety in public life.'

3.3 The challenge was taken up with alacrity. The Committee's First Report (Nolan (1995)) concentrated on Members of Parliament, ministers and civil servants, executive quangos, and National Health Service bodies. Certain weaknesses in the procedures for maintaining and enforcing appropriate standards of behaviour in public life were identified, and the Committee recommended 'urgent remedial action'. In particular, the Committee identified seven principles of public life to serve as a yardstick against which the personal qualities and conduct of those charged with public responsibilities could be measured and to which they should aspire:

- *selflessness*: holders of public office should take decisions solely in terms of the public interest. They should not do so in order to gain financial or other material benefits for themselves or their families or friends;
- *integrity*: holders of public office should not place themselves under any financial or other obligation to outside individuals or organisations that might influence them in the performance of their official duties;
- *objectivity*: in carrying out public business, including making public appointments, awarding contracts or recommending individuals for rewards and benefits, holders of public office should make choices on merit;
- *accountability*: holders of public office are accountable for their decisions and actions to the public and must submit themselves to whatever scrutiny is appropriate to their office;
- *openness*: holders of public office should be as open as possible about all the decisions and actions that they take. They should give reasons for their decisions and restrict information only when the wider public interest clearly demands;

---

1   See also the Reports of the Hempel Committee on corporate governance, 1998, and the Turnbull Committee on risk, 1999.

–   *honesty*: holders of public office have a duty to declare any private interests relating to their public duties and take steps to resolve any conflicts in a way that protects the public interest; and

–   *leadership*: holders of public office should promote and support these principles by leadership and example.

3.4   The Nolan Committee then announced (June, 1995) a second inquiry which would review local public spending bodies, that is to say, 'not-for-profit' bodies which are neither fully elected nor appointed by ministers, but which provide public services, often delivered at local level, and which are wholly or largely publicly funded. Thus, in response to this remit the Nolan Committee turned its sights on HEIs, together with their FE counterparts and grant maintained schools. As a catalyst for the submission of evidence it produced an 'Issues and Questions' paper, which identified three 'common threads' as mechanisms for maintaining standards of conduct and attaining the seven principles of public life, namely: the use of codes of conduct; the encouragement of independent scrutiny; and the availability of guidance and training for governing bodies and managers. The Committee also made plain in the issues and questions paper that it intended to focus its attention on three broad themes as follows: the appointment and accountability of board members; the role of boards in relation to the officers and staff; and safeguards in respect of conflicts of interest. The Nolan Committee published its Second Report in May 1996 (Nolan (1996)). While acknowledging the existence of high standards of conduct in the governance of HEIs, the Committee made several recommendations directed at FE and HE which are considered later in this chapter. In the main, such recommendations were aimed at the achievement by HEIs of greater consistency in standards of openness and responsiveness, rather than any radical overhaul. The recommendations made in the report were not binding on the Prime Minister or Government of the day, but carried considerable moral authority.

3.5   The Second Nolan Report was received with particular interest since HEIs have been no strangers to allegations of 'mismanagement and maladministration' in recent years. It is beyond the scope of this chapter to chronicle the well-publicised governance problems in 1994 at two statutory universities (Huddersfield and Portsmouth), and in 1994 and 1995 at two further education colleges (Derby Tertiary College, Wilmorton and St Philip's Roman Catholic Sixth Form College). These have been fully analysed elsewhere (NAO (1995); Lever (1995); Further Education Funding Council (FEFC) (1994a and b)).[1] In the wake of the resultant media coverage, universities, colleges and their representative associations issued guidance for members of governing bodies,[2] codes of conduct and ethics, and other governance advice, while at the same time the Funding Councils tightened their disclosure requirements for the purposes of financial accounting. However, it must be recognised that despite all this action, significant damage was inflicted on the reputation of

---

1   See also Shattock (1994), re the financial fiasco at University College, Cardiff, in 1986/87.
2   CUC (1995 and revised 1999 and 2001); CEF (1995); AfC (1995).

universities and colleges by the media treatment of these and other *causes célèbres*: see the official reports published by the NAO, Funding Councils, Department for Education and Employment (DfEE), PAC and QAA into Swansea Institute (1997), Thames Valley University (1998), Glasgow Caledonian University (1998), Southampton Institute (1999), and many FE Colleges (notably the highly critical reports of the FEFC, NAO and PAC into Halton College, 1999). Whether or not one considers that such treatment was over-blown, the public was not accustomed to thinking in terms of its universities as tainted by 'sleaze'. In seeking to explain those cases, it has been suggested that the constitutional structure of the statutory universities, with its stress on corporate managerialism, a mainly 'lay' board, and optional staff and student board members, may make those institutions particularly susceptible to misgovernance.[1] There has been a pejorative reaction on the part of some critics of the statutory university management style (Warren (1994); Ryder (1996)). This response was probably unwarranted, and detracted from a cogent argument that the governance systems of all universities, chartered and statutory, needed urgent review particularly with regard to their effectiveness and performance.

3.6 For example, at the University of Oxford the Commission of Inquiry established under the chairmanship of the Vice-Chancellor, Dr Peter North, and following on from a similar review and updating exercise for the University of Cambridge by way of its 1989 Wass Report, issued a consultative paper on the University's objectives, structure, size and shape (Oxford (1995)), following which consultants, Coopers & Lybrand, prepared a detailed report into the University's decision-taking systems (Oxford (1996)). (See also Franks (1966).) This has led to substantial changes to the pluralistic governance structures of the University and its scheme of delegation (from October 2000). Other more far-reaching action was taken by governing bodies of HEIs following the Report of Sir Ron Dearing's Committee (Dearing (1997)), and the CUC Guide (now in a 2001 edn) – including reducing the size of the Councils of chartered universities, clarifying where responsibility for decision-taking lies (for example, with the Council rather than the court), exchanging good practice and carrying out periodic effectiveness reviews.[2] It is too easy to dismiss the ancient universities of Oxford and Cambridge as unrepresentative of their pre-1992 counterparts. Despite the improvements in governance introduced since 1997, there is concern that many chartered universities are continuing to operate inefficiently because of a participative committee structure which is unwieldy and wasteful of academic time, and that governance and management in HE is often conducted by a small *cadre* of senior university officers in a manner which is not explicitly provided for by charter, statutes or regulations. Expressed another way, there is a surrealistic detachment between, on the one hand, what the constitutions of many chartered universities provide *de jure* and, on the other, how, in practice, the

---

1   See National Association of Teachers in Further and Higher Education (NATFHE) *Survey of Governance in the post-1992 Universities and Colleges of Higher Education*, 1999.
2   See also Progress Report of CUC Working Party (CUC (2000)).

governance and management of those universities are conducted *de facto*. It is outside the scope of this chapter to describe the different types of governance models in higher education, or explain how they evolved.[1] Suffice to say that many of the chartered universities have developed historically in such a way as to render aspects of their constitutional structures, at best, outmoded and, at worst, misleading. Thus, if some statutory universities resemble giant tower blocks with design faults caused by the speed of their construction, many of their chartered counterparts give the appearance of labyrinthine mansions, built to a specification of another age and now requiring comprehensive redesign.

3.7 The premise on which this chapter is based is, therefore, very simple. Notwithstanding the importance of higher education for economic growth and social development, the funding of UK HEIs is in crisis (Taylor Report (2001)), as it is in other industrial and developing countries throughout the world (World Bank (1994)). In response to this crisis and the challenge of how to preserve or improve the quality of HE as budgets are squeezed, government has decentralised key management functions to HEIs in order to promote funding diversification and a more efficient use of resources. This increased autonomy makes it more important than ever for HEIs to have decision-taking structures which work efficiently and effectively, contain safeguards against impropriety, and command public confidence. Although there are other important ways in which the decision-taking process at HEIs can be improved (for example, by promoting more effective leadership at all staffing levels – Dearlove (1995a and b), HEIs should continue to examine their constitutional structures, and ask themselves several questions:

–   What are the structures intended to achieve?
–   Do they promote or impede effective decision-taking at a time when higher education is faced with an investment crisis?
–   Are the constitutional structures sufficiently explicit to be understood by members of the governing body, staff, students and other members of the university, in addition to the general public which has a legitimate interest in the well-being of HEIs as part of the fabric of our national life (whatever the level of public funding)?

3.8 The essence of this chapter is that, notwithstanding the need for continuing diversity, there remains an alarming lack of coherence across the sector with regard to governance structures. In the spotlight of public scrutiny, many HEIs still compare unfavourably with other corporate models which have more coherent and clearly defined constitutions. Higher and further education institutions thus find themselves part of a broader canvas in which corporate governance itself, in the UK and worldwide, is under scrutiny. This chapter will now consider how, by returning to some simple constitutional basics – and drawing on the political theory of earlier generations – guidance

---

1   See Bargh *et al* (1996); Warner and Palfreyman (1996); Gray (1997); Warren (1997), Farrington (1998), and the clear and concise general account in the CUC *Guide for Members of Governing Bodies* (CUC (2001)); plus Shattock (forthcoming).

can be obtained which may help to answer the questions which have been posed above.

BACK TO CONSTITUTIONAL BASICS

Governance and effective governance

3.9   Governance in the higher education sector is essentially the process whereby independent corporate enterprises which conduct teaching and research take collective decisions. Typically, such decisions should cover three main areas:

–   the planning and determination of strategy. This function focuses on the goals and ends of a corporate enterprise;
–   the implementation of planning, and putting into effect of strategy. This function focuses on the objectives and means of achieving an enterprise's goals and ends. It consists of executive day-to-day decisions taken when managing an enterprise; and
–   the monitoring and supervision of the executive management of the enterprise, and the evaluation of management decisions against goals and ends. Supervision may lead to decisions being taken by the corporate enterprise to modify its strategy or the means of implementation.

3.10   Of these three elements, the first and last are often described as board functions, exercised by simple majority decisions at quorate meetings of the governing body of an enterprise or by delegation to a board committee or officer; whereas the second is usually allocated to the enterprise's management, often in the person of the most senior manager or chief executive. The means whereby the governing body controls executive management is by exercising the sole authority to appoint, appraise and, if necessary, dismiss the most senior manager or chief executive. In the context of higher education, it is important not to confuse the determination of strategy, which is a board function, with the method whereby the strategy takes shape and is proposed to the board. In practice, of course, strategy will often be based on or shaped by the vision of the academic staff, whose views will be put to the governing body via the Chief Executive or senior staff. Having identified what governance is, or should be, the next step is to identify what makes one decision-taking process more efficient and effective than another. In answering this question, much will turn on the particular circumstances of an HEI, its culture and history, rate of growth, main sources of funding, and tradition of democratic accountability to its own members. However, at the risk of over-generalisation, it is possible to discern certain dynamic qualities which, when properly harnessed, seem to promote a decision-taking process which is more effective in coping with the planning, management and supervision of change and the associated problems.

3.11   In particular those qualities include:

– the encouragement of leadership and the sharing of an institution's vision and strategic planning throughout its staff, in contrast to 'command and control' management from the top down;[1]

– striking the right balance of experience, skills and expertise on the governing body, and ensuring that there are sufficient numbers of 'lay' persons on the governing body who have relevant experience of business (and hence the planning and use of business resources) and the necessary enthusiasm, commitment, and understanding of their responsibilities and of public sector values or 'independence';

– reducing the size of governing bodies to enable members to participate more actively in the decision-taking process, coupled with controlled delegation to fewer committees and a greater use of full-time managers;[2]

– a regular and self-critical approach by governing bodies to the review of their effectiveness and of the performance of their institutions.[3]

3.12 It is axiomatic that, for the decision-taking process of a corporate enterprise to be effective, it must also command the confidence of all those who have a stake in the enterprise's business. In the case of companies registered under the Companies Acts, it is the trust and confidence of the shareholders that matter. With regard to HEIs, the constituency of persons who have a legitimate interest or stake in the well-being of a particular university or college is much greater, embracing not only the members who normally comprise the corporate body of the institution (that is to say, lay members of the court and council, academic staff, graduates and students), but also the tax payer and the wider community – the general public. Accordingly, there must be mechanisms which:

– provide safeguards against impropriety, especially in relation to the misapplication of public money; and

– establish clear lines of accountability in the sense not only of giving a financial account upwards to the ultimate paymaster (and increasingly to the QAA in respect of academic standards)[4] but also encouraging a genuine responsiveness to all those persons who have a stake in the enterprise.

Dark forces

3.13 In order to understand what constitutional safeguards (checks and balances) should be put in place to safeguard against impropriety, one needs to

---

1   See *Strategic Planning in Higher Education* (HEFCE (2000)).
2   See the Report of the Dearing Committee (Dearing (1997)) which recommended the appointment of a majority of 'lay' members to promote governing bodies subject to a ceiling of 25.
3   See Progress Report of CUC Working Party (CUC (2000)), following the Government's endorsement, in 1998, of the specific recommendations of the Dearing Committee.
4   See QAA Report on degree awarding powers, 1999, and the Government's response to that report which contained the ominous warning that, 'Ministers agree that, where there is persistent failure to maintain acceptable degree standards, the power to award degrees should no longer be exercised', October 1999.

ask the question: what are the main obstacles to propriety? This requires an understanding of the flesh and blood of human nature, and in particular three 'dark forces', which have manifested themselves throughout human history and at least as early as the third chapter of the Book of Genesis. The first dark force is *power* or, more specifically, the abuse or misuse of power either as a result of its exploitation by one person or a group of persons working in concert, or as a result of the abandonment of power. Throughout history, whether in relation to the governance of States or social and business organisations, the abuse or misuse of power has proved to be a corrupt and corrupting crown – the outward manifestation or, in legal terminology, the *actus reus* of misgovernance ('Power tends to corrupt and absolute power corrupts absolutely'). The second dark force is *greed* or, to put it another way, self-interest, which may be either individual or collective self-interest, seeking to misuse positions of authority and power for self-advancement. This provides the motivation for misgovernance or, in legal parlance, the *mens rea* of the offence. The third dark force is *secrecy* which provides the opportunity for the abuse or misuse of power and the advancement of self-interest. Secrecy offers an environment in which misgovernance is likely to thrive. The sum total of these three dark forces produces the following simple equation: abuse or misuse of power + self-interest + secrecy = corruption, dishonesty and tyranny. In safeguarding against impropriety, it should, therefore, be the aim of every enterprise (and, therefore, of every HEI) to ensure that its constitution, in whatever form prescribed by law, contains the mechanisms to neutralise or at least control these destructive elements.

Controls

3.14 Most of the essential constitutional safeguards against impropriety were identified at least as early as the 18th-century 'Enlightenment'. Unfortunately, we seem to have lost sight of the lessons taught by the political thinkers of that time. These are straightforward. First, to counter the abuse of power, there should be *a separation of powers*, that is to say, a system of checks and balances designed to safeguard against the concentration of power, especially (but not exclusively) in the executive (or in business parlance 'executive management'). This can be viewed as a system of mutual restraints, whereby responsibility for different but complementary functions in the decision-taking process is split between different persons so as to ensure a balance of power and authority. (See Siedentop (2000), on Federalism in the USA and Europe.) Secondly, to counter self-interest, there should be *a duty of good faith* and a well-developed rule against conflicts, so that persons charged with the governance of corporate enterprises should avoid putting themselves in a position where personal interests conflict with public duty. Thirdly, to counter secrecy, there should be *openness* and this should be articulated through policies of transparency and disclosure, particularly in the manner in which decisions are taken, recorded and made publicly known and in the financial reporting of an enterprise: 'The most powerful tool for ensuring that public business is transacted with propriety is openness' (Nolan (1996)).

3.15 In the context of the 18th-century Enlightenment, these controls could be said to produce the following equation: separation of powers + duty of good faith + openness = accountability and liberty. How can this theory then be applied to HEIs so as to promote more effective governance, rather than become so much chasing after the wind? How can the three main control mechanisms against impropriety be improved?

Improved controls

Checks and balances

3.16 Many of the recent governance problems in the higher and further education sectors can be traced to a breakdown in the system of checks and balances. Frequently, this occurs because the checks and balances are not clearly understood or respected by management or the board of governors.[1] The situation at the University of Portsmouth was clearly complex and, in his *Independent Inquiry Report* to the board of governors, Mr Jeremy Lever QC (Lever (1995)) acknowledged that, had the events occurred in any comparable organisation, they would have placed considerable strain on the direction and management of that organisation. Nevertheless, in respect of the Deputy Vice-Chancellor's agreed departure on payment of a severance package, the Chairman of the board of governors was criticised for imprudence for not having obtained board approval in advance for the course that he was proposing to follow. Similar criticism was levelled at the presentation to the board of governors as a *fait accompli* of the *de facto* abolition of the post of Deputy Vice-Chancellor and restructuring of the directorate without giving the board the opportunity to debate the relevant issues of principle.

3.17 The committee system of an HEI should also operate as part of a system of checks and balances. Thus, the role of the audit committee is to act independently and authoritatively in examining an institution's financial affairs (in particular the internal financial controls) more rigorously than the governing body as a whole.[2] Its conclusions should be reported formally to the board of governors so that any important matters can be debated. Similarly, the remuneration committee's function is to advise the governing body in relation to the remuneration packages of the Vice-Chancellor and other senior members of staff, including, where appropriate, severance payments, and this will also call for an approach which is both independent and robust. The Universities of Portsmouth and Huddersfield were criticised because certain committees did not appear to work effectively. Thus, at Huddersfield the original severance package proposed to the retiring Vice-Chancellor (totalling £411,493 plus a continuation of health insurance and car benefits) was plainly

---

1   With regard to the failure of boards to monitor overseas provision, see Swansea Institute (NAO (1997a)), Glasgow Caledonian (NAO (1998)), and Southampton Institute (PAC (1999)).
2   See the criticisms of the financial procedures and controls at Glasgow Caledonian University (NAO (1998)).

not subjected to the careful scrutiny of an independent remuneration committee which had access to appropriate professional advice. It was left to the HEFCE to be subsequently advised by leading counsel that the original package 'appeared to be excessive' and that accordingly, by agreeing to it, the University might have acted *ultra vires*. At the University of Portsmouth, it was the audit committee which was found wanting by the Lever Inquiry in one respect. In relation to its investigation into expense claims by the Vice-Chancellor, it made the mistake of communicating its conclusions to the governors informally, rather than by way of a formal report including the necessary supporting papers. The board was thereby deprived of an opportunity for formal discussion that could have led to further investigation.

3.18 Among FE colleges there is also evidence that roles and responsibilities have been misunderstood so as to result in the meddling of governors in management and by the principal in governance.[1] Two polarised viewpoints can often be detected. The first is that governors overreach themselves and meddle in management. Here, the mistaken view is that governors have a discretion over what management powers should be delegated to the principal and that governors should be using specialist skills and experience in the management of their college. It is also thought that they should exercise interventionist powers so as to manage a college directly when they think things are going wrong. Typically, in this situation the relationship between the chairman and principal will be poor, the principal may lack confidence, and management may be weak. The second viewpoint is that the principal usurps the governors' role. There is the mistaken view that the principal, as chief executive, should have a free rein to manage both the college and the governing body to achieve business goals. It is thought that, in the real world, 'lay' governors have insufficient understanding of the college, or have little time available, to determine strategy and that their role should be to ensure public acceptance of decisions which are in reality those of the principal and that active governors are an obstruction to effective governance. Typically, in this situation the relationship between the chairman and principal will be strong, and the principal will dominate the institution by force of personality. The experience of FE colleges is of direct relevance to those HEIs which are HECs. Their constitutional structures are very similar, for example, in the way in which the articles of government allocate responsibility for strategy and oversight to the governing body, and for executive day-to-day management to the head of the institution (that is to say, the college principal or university vice-chancellor).

3.19 Turning to the chartered universities, the constitutional drawing of checks and balances is much less clear. Thus, the University Council is often described as the 'executive governing body' responsible for the management

---

1   Hall (1994); and see the official reports and investigations into Derby: Wilmorton College, St Philip's Roman Catholic Sixth Form College, Matthew Bolton College, Stoke-on-Trent College, Wirral College, Bilston Community College, St Austell College, Gwent Tertiary College, Cricklade College, Halton College, Basildon College and Barnsley College.

and administration of revenue and property and the general control over the conduct of the university's affairs, and yet, in spite of the reduction in size of governing bodies in response to the recommendations of Dearing (1997), is often too unwieldy because of size to be able to carry out this function effectively without significant delegation to an inner 'cabinet'. In the post-1992 university sector, the dangers of the 'cabinet' metamorphosising into a small and powerful cadre of governors and staff were well illustrated by the PAC report into Southampton Institute (1999). The Vice-Chancellor is typically described as 'the principal academic and administrative officer', being generally responsible to the Council for maintaining and promoting the efficiency and good order of the university. Constitutionally, the Vice-Chancellor may lack the clearly defined responsibilities of his or her counterpart in a statutory university as 'chief executive'. The Vice-Chancellor's *de facto* role will thus frequently exceed the *de jure* specification. Doubtless the failure in many chartered universities to set out explicitly the respective roles and responsibilities of the Council, for strategy and oversight, and the Vice-Chancellor, for day-to-day executive management, flows from the historical separation of powers between the Council (for managing resources) and the Senate (as the supreme academic authority). The weakening of the Senate's powers post-Jarratt should prompt a reappraisal of the system of checks and balances, and the redrawing of responsibilities between Council and Vice-Chancellor.

3.20 There is plainly room for further improvement: 'Achievement of change is proving slow in some cases, and some Courts are loath to divest themselves of powers that have been made explicit to them', according to the Progress Report of CUC Working Party in 2000. With regard to the statutory universities, it is submitted that the existing corporate structure, with the different but complementary roles, provision for delegation of certain functions and the listing of other 'reserved' functions which may not be delegated, is a strong model which should be reinforced. Ways in which the model could be strengthened include:

–   developing the role of the secretary and clerk to the governing body to ensure that procedures are followed and that independent and authoritative constitutional advice is offered to the board, and particularly to the chairman and vice-chancellor, so that the interface between governors and management is harmonious and effective;[1]

–   the use of codes of conduct and ethics which have a very important role to play in promoting a better understanding of the responsibilities of governors, their accountability and duty to safeguard public funds, and the need to promote high standards of behaviour;

–   improved training for governors. There has perhaps been too ready an assumption in the higher education sector that governors sufficiently understand their role and responsibilities, and that the need for formal

---

1   'Independence should be achieved by a careful separation of the Clerk of Secretary's role from any senior administrative or managerial role within the HEI', *Guide for Members of Governing Bodies* (CUC (1998)).

training has been exaggerated. This is mistaken. Particularly at a time of financial crisis, HEIs need 'lay' governors who understand precisely what is expected of them. Better governor training should lead to a more effective operation of the constitutional checks and balances;[1]

– independent advice procedures. These should be adopted by governing bodies to enable governors to take independent professional advice where appropriate; and

– the careful review by boards of what responsibilities they are prepared to delegate, what responsibilities should be 'reserved' as non-delegable because of their significance, and the number, purpose and terms of reference of all standing committees (see CUC (2001)).

Safeguards against conflicts

3.21   In its Issues and Questions paper, Lord Nolan's Committee observed that the mechanisms operated by local public spending bodies for identifying and resolving conflicts of interest, 'do not appear to be as extensive as those employed by other branches of the public service, such as local government or non-departmental public bodies'. Considerable variety of practice was noted. Central to this issue is the need for HEIs to establish a coherent framework within which members of governing bodies are restricted or prohibited from participating in certain decisions in which they have some financial or other interest and which permits them to make a voluntary public disclosure of relevant interests. The articles of government of statutory universities and the standing orders of many of their chartered counterparts commonly require board members to declare any 'pecuniary, family or other personal interest in any matter under discussion' and to take no part in the consideration of, or voting upon, the matter. However, such rules often do not require a member who has an interest to withdraw (that is to say, physically) from that part of the meeting in which the interest is discussed, and there is commonly no provision which permits board members who have declared the nature and extent of any material interest and withdrawn from the meeting to be a party to the transaction or arrangement in which they have an interest.

3.22   Many HEIs have already adopted, or are in the process of adopting, a register of members' interests which is open to public inspection.[2] Various models exist, but a particular difficulty is how to define the 'relevant interests' which should voluntarily be disclosed. It is submitted that the guiding principle should be the voluntary disclosure of any interest, financial or otherwise, which is likely to interfere with the exercise of a board member's independent judgment or which, if publicly known, would be perceived as likely to influence that judgment. A secondary principle is that a board member should be invited to provide the same information, if known to him or her, in

---

1   See the training materials developed for FE College Governors by FEFC, and similarly commissioned by SCOP for HEI governors. This training of governors is also a role being undertaken by CUC.

2   Nolan (1996): 'all institutions should have publicly available registers of interests'.

respect of his or her spouse or partner, children, or other close relatives (for example, persons living in the same household or as a dependant). According to this test a board member should ask him or herself whether members of the public, knowing such information, would reasonably conclude that the relevant interest might influence his or her judgment. As a support for rules relating to non-participation and voluntary disclosure, codes of conduct, purchasing and procurement procedures and governance training programmes also have important parts to play in reminding board members and managers of the importance of demonstrating high personal standards of integrity and independence.

Openness, transparency and disclosure

3.23   Governing bodies in the higher education sector have, with some justification, been criticised as self-perpetuating and made in their own image and, therefore, at risk of appearing too inward-looking. The process whereby the composition of boards is reviewed and replenished by the filling of vacancies has prompted debate. Two recommendations made outside the education sector have particular significance. First, this is what the Cadbury Committee (1994) urged:

> 'Given the importance of their distinctive contribution, non-executive directors should be selected with the same impartiality and care as senior executives. We *recommend* that their appointment should be a matter for the board as a whole and that there should be a formal selection process, which will reinforce the independence of non-executive directors and make it evident that they have been appointed on merit and not through any form of patronage. We regard it as good practice for a nomination committee ... to carry out the selection process and to make proposals to the board.'

3.24   This theme was picked up by the Nolan Committee in its First Report (Nolan (1995)) which included a recommendation that appointments to non-departmental public bodies should be made 'on the basis of merit' with the aim of achieving 'a balance of relevant skills and backgrounds'. The Committee also recommended that all appointments should be made after advice from a panel committee 'which includes an independent element', and that the appointments process should be open and subject to external supervision. Adapted to meet the needs of HEIs, this seemed to suggest that governing bodies should establish search or nomination committees which include a significant non-governor element, and that the committee should trawl for candidates from a wide field by making appropriate use of advertising and executive search, by consultation with interested bodies, and by maintaining and using databases of interested and appropriate candidates. It was, therefore, not surprising that in its Second Report the Nolan Committee (1996) recommended that, 'appointments to the governing bodies of universities and colleges should be made on the basis of merit, subject to the need to achieve a balance of relevant skills and backgrounds on the board'. However, the report declined to recommend external scrutiny by the use of non-governor members on nomination committees, although such mechanisms were clearly favoured by the Nolan Committee and there is some evidence of an increasing use in higher and further education of non-governors in the selection of governing body members.

3.25   If HEIs are expected to operate openly and 'in the public gaze', so as to make it difficult for the dark forces of power and self-interest to take root, the lines of public accountability need to be examined. In the sense of 'giving a financial account', HEIs are subject to an upward accountability to the Government through the Funding Councils, and to Parliament through the PAC. The essential framework is that the PAC is responsible for scrutinising public expenditure. Under the National Audit Act 1983, the Controller and Auditor General is appointed by the Prime Minister with the agreement of the Chairman of the PAC. The Controller and Auditor General reports to the PAC and is head of the NAO. He has power to carry out investigations into the economy, efficiency and effectiveness of colleges. The head of institution of each university or college is its accounting officer and may be required to appear before the PAC, together with the chief officer of the relevant Funding Council. This framework, although commendable in establishing national lines of accountability upwards, does little to promote responsiveness in a horizontal direction to the local community. Although the constitutions of chartered universities provide for the establishment of the Court as a large representative forum for receiving a university's annual report and financial statement, the statutory universities lack an equivalent statutory mechanism for making their governing bodies more responsive to the local and regional communities which they serve. Middlesex University (one of the post-1992 universities) established its own Court with the purpose of supporting the University as an advisory body 'in the achievement of its stated objectives and to reflect upon its progress'. A growing number of further education corporations now hold annual public meetings for the purpose of presenting their annual reports and accounts and encouraging a dialogue with interested members of the public. It remains to be seen how effective such action will be in promoting genuine responsiveness of a horizontal nature.

3.26   The contents of the annual reports received particular attention in the Second Report of the Nolan Committee (1996) which encouraged greater openness in the way in which key information about the governing body, governance structure and policies, objectives, and performance criteria is made available to the public. The Nolan Committee also recommended that a standard of good practice should be developed to limit the extent to which FE and HEIs can withhold information from the public on grounds of commercial confidentiality, and emphasised the need to establish whistleblowing procedures and to publicise these to staff. When the Nolan Committee (1997) examined the progress which institutions had made in response to its earlier recommendations (Second Report (1996)), including governance in HE, it concluded that there was still much work to be done and singled out the introduction of 'whistleblowing' procedures as an urgent priority. HEIs have, in the main, taken up this particular challenge by disseminating good practices[1] and adapting policies and procedures which meet the requirements of the Public Interest Disclosures Act 1998 and, in some instances, go beyond these requirements (for example, by extending the right to protection from victimisation to 'whistleblowing' students in addition to staff and other 'workers' covered by the 1998 Act). However, examples of anonymous complaints to the Funding Councils being made by staff in higher education (see, for example, the trenchant conclusions of the NAO in its report on Glasgow Caledonian University (1998)) and FE (see Basildon College and Barnsley College (2000)), often because of an alleged climate of fear and intimidation, suggest that there is no room for complacency. Whistleblowing policies should not only be adapted by governing bodies but also actively promoted to staff, if HEIs are to operate in accordance with the principles of openness and accountability advocated by Nolan.

3.27   The proper role of staff and student 'representatives' on governing bodies has sparked some controversy among the statutory universities and colleges of FE and HE.[2] It is submitted that, although staff and student board members may play an important role by subjecting management to critical scrutiny, their primary function should not be that of 'watchdogs' or 'whistleblowers' (ie so as to make an institution more accountable upwards to the Government or its agencies), but as shapers of an institution's character and mission. By contributing to the decision-taking process, they are well placed to enhance the responsiveness of an institution to its staff and students as participants in a collegiate body. Accordingly, in the author's view, each HEI should be free to choose whether and, if so, to what extent, staff and student board members should be appointed and whether this should be by a process of election or co-option, and that such choice will be influenced by the tradition and needs of each institution. However, the Report of the Dearing Committee (Dearing (1997)) recommended that governing bodies should be 'required' to appoint staff and student members to ensure 'legitimacy' – and 'representation' of staff governors on the governing bodies of FE colleges has recently been strengthened by modifications made to the instrument of government of FECs by the Secretary of State (1999).

PERSONAL LIABILITY

3.28   This chapter concludes on an ironic note. Persons who offer their services voluntarily (that is to say, in an unpaid capacity) as members of HEIs' governing bodies are expected by the public to conduct themselves in accordance with standards which are open, clear and fair. They are entitled to expect similar treatment under the law. Instead, there has been some

1   See *Guide for Members of Governing Bodies*, Annex K (CUC (1999)).
2   Hall (1990) and see NATFE *Survey of Governance* in the post-1992 universities, 1999.

obfuscation in relation to the issue of potential personal liability. Concern has been expressed that this issue has been conveniently 'swept under the carpet', although there has recently been official recognition that a potential problem may exist and that board members of non-departmental public bodies should be indemnified as follows:

> 'The Government has indicated that an individual board member who has acted honestly, reasonably, in good faith and without negligence, will not have to meet out of his own personal resources any personal civil liability which is incurred in execution or purported execution of his board function.'[1]

3.29   In particular, unfavourable comparisons have been made about the relative positions of corporation members (of statutory and chartered bodies), company directors, and trustees. It is submitted that the law is most unsatisfactory in imposing a range of different standards, in relation to personal liability, in a haphazard and illogical manner (see especially Hambley, 1998). Thus, board members of HECs (comprising most of the post-1992 universities and colleges of HE) do not yet enjoy the right to claim relief from the court against personal liability in circumstances analogous to those which are available to trustees in the strict sense and those available to company directors.[2] This confusion is compounded by the fact that it can be argued with some force that trustees of those institutions which are unincorporated have greater personal risk (for example, in the event of an institution's insolvency) than company directors, who will have the benefit of limited liability unless wrongful or fraudulent trading can be proved.

Heads of potential liabilities

Statutory offences
3.30   There are many statutory offences which can be committed by corporations and which can result in criminal liability for both corporations and their members. Liability for corporation members is usually (but not exclusively) confined to the situation where the breach is attributable to some act or neglect on the part of the corporation member concerned. Examples include breaches of the legislation relating to health and safety at work, data protection, and environmental protection. Statutory offences can result in fines for members of corporations and, in the most extreme cases, imprisonment.

General criminal liability
3.31   Members of corporations are clearly potentially liable under the general criminal law for their activities in the course of their duties. Any fraudulent activity which is detected would be likely to lead to criminal charges. The common law offence of 'misconduct in a public office' could also be used in relation to any dishonest behaviour by corporation members.

---

1   Cabinet Office (1996), p 23.
2   See s 61 of the Trustee Act 1925 and s 727 of the Companies Act 1985; but see also the grant of a statutory right to relief against personal liability to governors of FECs under s 145 of the Learning and Skills Act 2000.

Joint civil liability

3.32 A person suing a corporation (for example, for personal injury caused by the negligence of the corporation) may seek to include individual board members in the action as joint defendants with the corporation. This would not be regarded as normal practice, but should be considered as a possibility, particularly in the context of arranging insurance cover.

Breach of duty

3.33 Members of corporations may find themselves the subject of proceedings for breach of duty. Board members have fiduciary and other duties to the corporation. These include the duties to act in the best interests of the corporation, not to allow personal interests to conflict with the interests of the corporation, and to exercise reasonable care, diligence and skill in carrying out their functions. With regard to the statutory HEIs, there are also the specific responsibilities conferred on corporation members by the articles of government, such as ensuring the solvency of the corporation and the safeguarding of its assets. There is a wide variety of situations in which breaches of duty could arise, but two specific examples will be used here to illustrate instances where personal liability may become an issue: misapplication of funds, and insolvency.

Liability in relation to misapplied funds

Higher education corporations

3.34 There are three main ways in which it may be argued that the governors of the statutory HEIs could be liable to the corporations of which they are members in respect of a misapplication of funds. These are: as quasi-trustees, as fiduciaries, and by analogy with the liability of directors of companies established under the Companies Acts. These three possible arguments will now be considered in turn, followed by some general comments on the situation.

3.35 *Liability as quasi-trustees*: since HECs are usually regarded as existing for exclusively charitable purposes, it seems clear that this type of corporation should be treated as an exempt charity. A court would view HECs as exempt charities only if it thought that their purposes were exclusively charitable. Schedule 2 to the Charities Act 1993 provides that HECs are exempt charities 'in so far as they are charities'. Paragraph 64 of Sch 12 to the ERA 1988 and para 69 of Sch 8 to the Further and Higher Education Reform Act 1992 (repealed by the Charities Act 1993) provided expressly and without qualification that the corporations were to be exempt charities. The corporation holds its property 'subject to a binding legal obligation to apply it for charitable purposes only'.[1] The authority on which this proposition is based is *Liverpool and District Hospital for Diseases of the Heart v Attorney-General,*[2]

1   *Tudor on Charities* (1995), p 159.
2   [1981] Ch 193.

and it fully bears it out. The somewhat fuller discussion in *The Law and Practice Relating to Charities*[1] is to the same effect. The safer view, however, is that it holds its property otherwise than as a trustee in the strict sense. On this basis it cannot be said that the managers or governors of the corporation are charity trustees as such, even though they are clearly charity trustees for the purposes of the Charities Act 1993.[2] It is at least arguable that they should be treated as if they were trustees, and, therefore, subject to the control of the High Court in the exercise of the court's jurisdiction with respect to charities.[3] This proposition is supported by the fact that, if there could be no personal liability on the part of governors in respect of a misuse of the property of a corporation, then there would in practice be nobody in relation to whom the jurisdiction of the court with respect to charities could be exercised.

3.36 Trustees in the strict sense can rely on s 61 of the Trustee Act 1925 to limit their liability for breach of trust. Section 61 of the Trustee Act 1925 provides that:

> 'If it appears to the court that a trustee, whether appointed by the court or otherwise, is or may be personally liable for any breach of trust, whether the transaction alleged to be a breach of trust occurred before or after the commencement of this Act, but has acted honestly and reasonably, and ought fairly to be excused for the breach of trust and for omitting to obtain the directions of the court in the matter in which he committed such breach, then the court may relieve him either wholly or partly from personal liability for the same.'

The problem is that, although governors might be regarded by the court as being in the same position as trustees, they will be unable to rely on s 61 if this section only applies to trustees proper.

3.37 *Liability as fiduciaries*: it seems clear that a governor is in the position of a fiduciary towards the corporation of which he or she is a governor. The position is well within the principles indicated in Underhill and Hayton's *Law of Trusts and Trustees*.[4] Furthermore, the case of *A-G v De Winton*,[5] where a borough treasurer was held to be in a fiduciary position towards the borough council of which he was the treasurer, supports the proposition that governors of HECs are in a fiduciary position as regards the corporations of which they are governors. However, that may not in itself mean that a governor would be liable in damages to the corporation if the governor participated in an *ultra vires* act. The principal obligation of a fiduciary is generally merely to return property or its equivalent value to that body from which the property was obtained by a breach of the fiduciary duty in question. It seems that, as a matter of principle, a

---

1   Picarda (1999), at pp 383–386.
2   Section 97(1) provides: 'In this Act, except in so far as the context otherwise requires ... "charity trustees" means the persons having the general control and management of the administration of the charity'.
3   *Harries v Church of England Commissioners* [1992] 1 WLR 1241. See also vol 5(2) of *Halsbury's Laws of England* (1993) at para 375, note 2. There is a fuller discussion of this question in an article by Hyams (1994) entitled 'The potential liabilities of governors of education institutions' in *Education and the Law*. See also Palfreyman (1998) (1998/99) (1999a) (2002a, forthcoming).
4   Underhill and Hayton (1995), p 16.
5   [1906] 2 Ch 106.

fiduciary is not liable to compensate the body in question for a loss caused as a result of his or her breach of fiduciary duty.[1] As a consequence, a governor who obtains property in breach of fiduciary duty, will have to return it or compensate the corporation for its loss – and no more.

3.38 *Liability by analogy with that of directors of companies established under the Companies Acts*: a director of a company established under the Companies Acts may be liable to the company of which he or she is a director, but such liability may be limited under s 727 of the Companies Act 1985, which applies not only to actions against directors for breach of trust but also to proceedings for negligence, default or breach of duty. Section 727 of the Companies Act 1985 provides as follows:

'(1)   If in any proceedings for negligence, default, breach of duty or breach of trust against an officer of a company or a person employed by a company as auditor (whether he is or is not an officer of the company) it appears to the court hearing the case that that officer or person is or may be liable in respect of the negligence, default, breach of duty or breach of trust, but that he has acted honestly and reasonably, and that having regard to all the circumstances of the case (including those connected with his appointment) he ought fairly to be excused for the negligence, default, breach of duty or breach of trust, that court may relieve him, either wholly or partly, from his liability on such terms as it thinks fit.

(2)   If any such officer or person as above-mentioned has reason to apprehend that any claim will or might be made against him in respect of any negligence, default, breach of duty or breach of trust, he may apply to the court for relief; and the court on the application has the same power to relieve him as under this section it would have had if it had been a court before which proceedings against that person for negligence, default, breach of duty or breach of trust had been brought.

(3)   Where a case to which subsection (1) applies is being tried by a judge with a jury, the judge, after hearing the evidence, may, if he is satisfied that the defendant or defender ought in pursuance of that subsection to be relieved either in whole or in part from the liability sought to be enforced against him, withdraw the case in whole or in part from the jury and forthwith direct judgment to be entered for the defendant or defender on such terms as to costs or otherwise as the judge may think proper.'

3.39   Section 727 does not have to be specifically pleaded by a director who is seeking statutory relief.[2] Relief is only available in respect of actions brought by or on behalf of the company.[3] The court is less disposed to grant relief to a director who is paid for his services rather than one who has been acting gratuitously.[4] There is substantial case-law regarding s 727, including a number of recent decisions, although each case tends to turn on the particular facts.[5] A failure to comply with the duty placed upon an HEC in its standard

---

1   See, in particular, Underhill and Hayton (1995), pp 826–829, in which strong disapproval of the case of *Re Leeds and Hanley Theatres of Varieties* [1902] 2 Ch 809, CA, is expressed.
2   See *Re Kirby's Coaches Ltd* [1991] BCLC 414.
3   See *Customs and Excise Commissioners v Hedon Alpha Ltd* [1981] QB 818.
4   See *National Trustees Co of Australasia v General Finance Co of Australasia* [1905] AC 373.
5   See *Re Claridge's Patent Asphalte Co Ltd* [1921] 1 Ch 543; *Re Duomatic Ltd* [1969] 2 Ch 365; *Re Welfab Engineers Ltd* [1990] BCLC 833; *Re Home Treat Ltd* [1991] BCLC 705; *Zemco Ltd v Jerrom-Pugh* [1993] BCC 275; *Bishopsgate Investment Management Ltd* (in liquidation) v *Maxwell (No 2)* [1994] 1 All ER 261; *Target Holdings Ltd v Redferns (a firm) and Another*

articles of government for 'the effective and efficient use of resources, the solvency of the institution and the corporation and for safeguarding their assets' could be regarded as giving rise to a personal liability on the part of the governors, if the court were to regard governors as analogous to directors. It is submitted, however, that it is inappropriate to equate the position of governors of HECs with that of company directors. This is not least because the duties of the two are fundamentally different. In addition, a company director can usually expect to be paid for his or her duties whereas, in contrast, the governors of HECs are unpaid volunteers.

3.40 *Generally*: in order to avoid the current uncertainty with regard to governor liability, it would be preferable for Parliament to make specific provision (probably in primary legislation) to regulate the situation. Such provision could simply apply s 61 of the Trustee Act 1925 to relevant governors. Alternatively, Parliament could enact that the governors of HECs (and FECs) have the right to apply to the court for relief from personal liability in terms similar to s 727 of the Companies Act 1985. As a result, governors would be entitled to no less protection than that which is presently available to company directors. It has been suggested that governors could become liable to an HEC in respect of an act which was *ultra vires* the corporation (ie beyond the corporation's statutory powers and therefore unenforceable) merely because they had caused the corporation to act *ultra vires*. Such a view is probably mistaken, despite what is said in *Halsbury's Laws of England*,[1] in reliance on the case of *Young v Naval, Military and Civil Service Co-operative Society of South Africa*.[2] In that case, the company directors whose liability was in issue acted *ultra vires* in voting that certain payments be made to themselves, with the result that the case is adequately explained by the principles governing fiduciary duties of directors. Before liability to the corporation can arise, there would have to be a breach of some duty owed to the corporation. Unless it were possible to establish liability as a fiduciary, a trustee or by analogy with company directors, or unless there were some other way in which a court might determine that governors could be held liable to the corporation, a decision by governors which causes the corporation to act *ultra vires* cannot properly be said, without more, to give rise to potential liability to the corporation. It has also been suggested that governors could be liable for a breach of warranty of authority to a third party with whom the corporation entered into a contract, where the corporation did not have the power to enter into the agreement, or alternatively, where some condition binding the corporation (such as Funding Council approval) had not been complied with. If the corporation had no

---

[1942] 2 All ER 337; *Coleman Taymar Ltd and Others v Oakes and Another* [2001] 2 BCLC 749; *In re Produce Marketing Consortium Ltd* [1989] 3 All ER 1; *Re D'Jan of London Ltd; Copp v D'Jan* [1994] BCLC 561; and *Framlington Group plc and Another v Anderson and Others* [1995] BCC 611.
1   (1974) vol 9, para 1344.
2   [1905] 1 KB 687.

power under its constitution to enter into the contract, then a person in the position of a governor could in theory be liable and such a claim is one against which it might be thought to be desirable to provide some measure of protection. It would be possible that the claim would fail on the basis that the warranty was a representation of law. If an alleged implied warranty is determined by a court to have been a representation with regard to the law, it will not give rise to liability on the part of the warrantor. If the warranty were one of fact, the claim would be successful. Liability could arise, for example, if the court held that a governor had impliedly warranted that a procedure required by the articles of government to be followed had indeed been followed, when in fact it had not. In contrast, where the warranty was that the corporation had the power to enter into a contract, when its statutory powers did not in fact allow it to do so, then it would, it seems, be a warranty with regard to the law.

Chartered corporations

3.41 The exposure of a governor of a university incorporated by Royal Charter to potential personal liability is at least similar to, if not the same as, that of a governor of a higher education corporation. This is subject to the *caveat* that the charter may make provision to the contrary.

Limited liability companies

3.42 The liability of a director of a limited liability company is well described elsewhere in the textbooks on company law (see also Chapter 15). However, it is helpful to examine the manner in which liability might arise for a director of a limited liability company which has the conduct of an HEI. As indicated above, the director of a company is not to be regarded as a trustee proper. However, according to *Gore-Browne on Companies* (Jordans): 'a director is answerable as a trustee for any misapplication of the company's property in which he participated and which he knew or ought to have known to be a misapplication'. On this basis, governors who are company directors are in the same position as trustees, albeit they are not trustees in the strict sense. In addition, it should be noted that a director can be liable to a company for negligence. In this sense a company director is exposed to a greater potential personal liability than a trustee proper.

Liability in the event of insolvency and dissolution

Higher education corporations

3.43 An HEC can only be dissolved by order of the Secretary of State for Education and Employment and, in that event, the Secretary of State may transfer the liabilities of the corporation to another educational body or one of the Funding Councils.[1] A failure to transfer relevant liabilities would be judicially reviewable. However, if it were held to be lawful to decline to transfer relevant outstanding liabilities, then it seems that the liabilities would remain

---

1   Statutory provisions which apply to the dissolution of an HEC are contained in s 128 of the ERA 1988.

outstanding, but that the members of the corporation would not be personally liable to third parties, such as creditors. According to *Halsbury's Laws of England*: 'If a man trusts a corporation, he trusts that legal person, and must look to its assets for payment; he can only call upon individual members to contribute if the Act or charter creating the corporation has so provided'.[1] In fact, none of the relevant statutes so provide. In addition, it seems clear that Part V of the Insolvency Act 1986 (which applies to the winding up of 'unregistered companies') would not apply. Thus, the best view is that the governors of an HEC would not be liable on dissolution of the corporation to meet the liabilities of the corporation. In addition, unless the Secretary of State transferred the right to enforce a breach of a governor's duties owed to the corporation (assuming there is such a right) under the relevant statutory provision, the governor's liability in respect of that breach would cease to be actionable. However, the position is unclear and untested in law where a corporation has become insolvent or where its assets have been seriously prejudiced as a result of mismanagement, and the Secretary of State declines to dissolve it. In such a situation, governors would be vulnerable to the argument that they had breached their duty under the articles of government to ensure solvency and safeguard the assets of the institution, and would be potentially liable to the corporation for the resultant financial loss. It is conceivable that, in such circumstances, a corporation might wish to take legal action against those governors who were regarded as wholly or mainly responsible for the insolvency.

Chartered corporations

3.44 In *The Law of Higher Education*, it is stated in relation to a university conducted by a chartered corporation that: 'Unless the charter provides otherwise, the members of the corporation are not liable for its debts'.[2] Although no authority is given in support of this proposition, it is consistent with the quotation from *Halsbury's Laws of England* set out above. In addition: 'Where a corporation has been dissolved, its members, in their natural capacities, can neither recover debts which are due to the corporation nor be charged with debts contracted by it'.[3] However, the authority is so old[4] that the proposition itself might be regarded as suspect. If the proposition is correct, then a governor's liability for the outstanding liabilities of a chartered corporation, in the event of dissolution, is likely to be the same as that of a governor of an HEC. It is unclear, however, what the position is with regard to a governor's liability *to* a chartered corporation in the event of its dissolution, but, if governors would remain liable in respect of a breach of their personal obligations owed to a chartered corporation, then an action to enforce such liability would require the joinder of the Attorney-General. This is because of the corporation's charitable status.

---

1   (1994) vol 9, para 1209.
2   Farrington (1994), para 2.84.
3   *Halsbury's Laws of England* (1994), vol 9, para 1398.
4   *Naylor v Cornish* (1684) 1 Vern 311n (1); *Edmunds v Brown and Tillard* (1688) 1 Lev 237.

Limited liability companies

3.45 The position of a board member of a limited liability company in the event of its dissolution is relatively clear – and well catered for in the textbooks on company law (see also Chapter 15). However, it is worth noting that, although third parties cannot sue the directors for debts of the company, in the event of its insolvency the liquidator of the company can pursue a director for compensation for a breach of a director's duties. In that event, the director may be able to rely on s 727 of the Companies Act 1985 for protection.

AVOIDANCE OF PERSONAL LIABILITY

Practical steps

3.46 There are a number of practical steps which board members can take to avoid suffering personal liability. These include:

– being aware of the limitations on the powers of the corporation and the terms of reference of all committees;
– being aware of the duties and responsibilities of board members;
– ensuring that sufficient information is available to the governing body;
– ensuring that all personal, financial and other interests are declared and are routinely recorded in a register;
– ensuring that the governing body takes professional advice wherever appropriate;
– ensuring that meetings are fully and properly minuted;
– in particular, making any dissenting views known and ensuring that they are minuted; and
– if things appear to be going seriously wrong, taking personal advice at an early stage.

3.47 The adoption of a well-drafted code of conduct (to which individual board members are required to subscribe) can be a useful means of achieving many of these steps. However, it should be noted that merely voting against a course of action will not necessarily absolve a member of liability. Similarly, resigning or threatening to resign may not be enough. For example, some positive action to safeguard the corporation's assets may be required in exceptional circumstances. (See Chapter 4 on the similar duties of care and diligence imposed upon charity trustees.)

Insurance

3.48 HEI constitutions normally allow corporations to insure their members against liabilities incurred arising out of membership and to pay the associated premiums. Indeed, the UUK recommends it. Insurance should very much be regarded as a safeguard of last resort, especially since it is not possible to insure against all liabilities. In particular, insurance against criminal liabilities (whether statutory or under the general criminal law) is not possible. In addition, insurance policies inevitably exclude various heads of liability. These vary from policy to policy and the exclusions should always be carefully scrutinised. Liability arising out of deliberate acts or where the person concerned knew that the act concerned was a breach of duty, or was reckless as to whether it was a breach of duty or not, may be excluded. This type of exclusion may mean that, in circumstances where advice should have been (but was not) taken in relation to whether a course of action was in breach of duty or not, the insurer may refuse cover. Liability for defamation is very often excluded, as is liability in connection with environmental pollution. There will invariably be a cap on the amount of cover provided by an insurance policy and there will frequently be an 'excess' provision, which means that below the level of the specified excess, there is no cover. The levels of excess in some local government insurance policies, for example, have been as high as £100,000 or more. Accordingly, board members should not allow the existence of an insurance policy to lull them into a false sense of security: an insurance policy will not assist with the inevitable trauma of a legal action, or with the possible damage to reputation.

CONCLUSION

3.49 An inescapable conclusion is that, in order for HEIs, schools and other bodies which provide public services to attract and retain volunteers of calibre for public service, legislation should be introduced which will clarify their potential liability and make available a similar range of protections to those which are available to company directors and trustees. Some progress has recently been made in the FE sector with the protection now offered to FE governors under s 145 of the Learning and Skills Act 2000 being similar to that available for company directors and trustees. Perhaps the next step will be for Government to extend this from the FE sector at least to the statutory HEIs? It would certainly be a valuable addition to the statute book for there to be a simple formulation which would define the limits of personal liability for *all* those persons who are charged with responsibility for conducting bodies which provide public services in an era when corporate governance occupies centre-stage. In the absence of appropriate legislation, however, only litigation will begin to clarify the extent of personal liability. Meanwhile, governors of statutory HEIs and members of Councils of chartered HEIs clearly need to ensure that they comply with good practice as set out in the various guides now emerging (CUC (2001); CEF (1995); AfC (1995)); in the well-trodden territory of charity law concerning the duties of trustees (Palfreyman (1995/96) and Chapter 4); in the area of company law concerning the fiduciary duty of directors (Chapter 14); and in relation to the proper conduct of meetings (Chapter 5). Certainly it should never be assumed that purchasing an insurance policy will compensate for ignorance and neglect.

Chapter 4

CHARITY TRUSTEESHIP AND PERSONAL LIABILITY

Emma Chamberlain (Barrister) and updated by David Palfreyman

EDITORS' INTRODUCTION

§4.1 This chapter links to Chapter 3 and explores the duties and powers of charity trustees. It will often not be appreciated that some individuals within an HEI are functioning as trustees, either by reason of the HEI itself being the trustee and hence its governors/members of council being quasi-trustees, or by certain individuals themselves being the trustees. There are more than 150,000 charities in England and Wales, with an annual income of approximately £15 billion, run by over one million trustees – of whom it is estimated that a third do not realise they are trustees, let alone properly understand the legal obligations of being a trustee. What is a charity? What is an exempt charity? What is the exemption from? Who/what is a trustee? What are the duties, powers and liabilities of a trustee? Does incorporation protect the trustees from personal liability? Are HEIs much different from other charities? Are those running the HEI also trustees with the same personal liabilities as for charity trustees in general? Who polices an exempt charity? Can trustees insure against their potential personal liability, in the same way that company directors can? Finally, for an interesting discussion of the Royal Holloway and Bedford New College sale of its Turners and other pictures, see Charity Commission (1993), Sheridan (1993/94), Phillips and Claricoat (1995), and, more generally, Palfreyman (1997).

§4.2 Where the HEI is the trustee, or where its individual officers or certain members of council or members of the board of governors are themselves the trustees of a specific trust (for example, a legacy provides money as a capital sum to be invested so that the income can be used for certain charitable purposes as required by the donor), the fiduciary duty will be similar to that set out in the extracts below from *The Trust Scheme of the Bedford Charity (The Harpur Trust)*, as recently revised and approved by the Charity Commission; in short, it will be one of prudence in managing the affairs of the charitable trust:

'35. DUTY OF CARE

(1) When carrying out any of the duties to which they are subject . . . each trustee must exercise such care and skill as is reasonable in all the circumstances, having regard in particular: (a) to any special knowledge or experience that he has or holds himself out as having . . .

36. POWER OF INVESTMENT

(1) The trustees may make any kind of investment which they could make if they were absolutely entitled to the assets of the charity.

(2) In exercising the power of investment conferred by this clause the trustees must have regard to the standard investment criteria . . .

38.   *STANDARD INVESTMENT CRITERIA*
The standard investment criteria . . . are:
(1) the suitability to the charity of [the proposed] investment . . .
(2) the need for diversification of investments . . .

39.   *ADVICE*
(1) Before exercising the power of investment conferred by this scheme the trustees must obtain and consider proper advice [from] . . .

(4) . . . a person who is reasonably believed by the trustees to be qualified to give it by his ability in and practical experience of financial and other matters relating to the proposed investment . . .

45.   *LIMITATION OF TRUSTEES' LIABILITY*
(1) A trustee is not liable for any act or default of an agent, nominee or custodian [to whom/which he has lawfully delegated certain tasks – for example, investment management] unless he has failed to comply with the duty of care applicable to him under clause 35 [in selecting, appointing and instructing the agent, etc] . . .'

§4.3   By analogy and by implication, the standard of care expected of HEI officers and members of council/members of boards of governors as fiduciaries in managing the HEI's assets as a charitable corporation which are not held on a specific trust as discussed above will be much the same, albeit *perhaps* not quite as onerous as for the trusteeship of a specific trust. However, the standard required will *probably* be more onerous than the levels of honesty, propriety, good faith, integrity, skill and care (currently) required of a company director having to operate in a more demanding, fast-moving and entrepreneurial commercial context where it is necessary to apply (in US legal terms) 'business judgment': see Chapters 3 and 15, Hambley (1998), and Palfreyman ((1998/99) (forthcoming)).

§4.4   As stated in Chapter 3 and as Hambley (1998) points out, the court can excuse a charity/trustee's honest misjudgment either in equity or (perhaps more readily) under s 61 of the Trustee Act 1925, and, similarly, the mistake of a company director made in good faith and within the normal range of commercial error may also be excused under s 727 of the Companies Act 1985. As yet, however, there is no such statutory provision for discretionary relief for the corporators of HEIs who make honest mistakes while managing the HEI general assets, as opposed to handling the business of any HEI specific charitable trust or any HEI trading company where the corporator is a trustee of the specific trust or a director of the trading company. That said, as noted in Chapter 3, recent legislation has extended to the governors of further education corporations the protection formerly available only to charity trustees and company directors, and such an approach will perhaps in due course be applied to HECs at least and maybe also chartered HEIs.

CHARITY TRUSTEESHIP

4.1 This chapter examines the following basic concepts of charity law. What is a charity? What is an exempt charity? Who or what are charity trustees? What are their general powers, duties and liabilities? These concepts are considered in the context of HEIs and we discuss some practical problems that can arise.

What is a charity?

4.2 The legal concept of charity has been developed by the courts over several centuries. There is still no statutory definition of charitable purposes, although the possibility of introducing one was discussed before the passage of the Charities Act 1992. In the end, it was decided that the benefit of flexibility, which allowed the scope of charitable activities to keep pace with changes in society, outweighed the advantages of certainty and clarity which a statutory definition might be expected to provide. To understand the words 'charitable', it is necessary, therefore, to fall back on an Elizabethan statute and case-law.[1] The famous Statute of Elizabeth I (preamble to the Charitable Uses Act 1601) contains a list of purposes which were at that time considered to be charitable. Some of the purposes sound odd to modern ears:

> 'The relief of aged, impotent and poor people; the maintenance of sick and maimed soldiers and mariners, schools of learning, free schools and scholars of universities; the repair of bridges, ports, havens, causeways, churches, sea banks and highways; the education and preferment of orphans, the relief, stock or maintenance of houses of correction; the marriages of poor maids; the supportation, aid and help of young tradesmen, handicraftsmen and persons decayed; the relief or redemption of prisoners or captives; and the aid or ease of any poor inhabitants concerning payments of fifteens, setting or of soldiers and other taxes.'

4.3 The Charitable Uses Act 1601 has now been repealed, but has been influential in developing the modern concept of charity. Subsequently, Lord MacNaughton gave an important definition of charitable purposes in the case of *Income Tax Special Purposes Commissioners v Pemsel*.[2] He said:

> 'Charity in its legal sense comprises four principal divisions: trusts for the relief of poverty; trusts for the advancement of education; trusts for the advancement of religion; and trusts for other purposes beneficial to the community not falling under any of the preceding heads.'

Education and charity

4.4 We are concerned here particularly with the second head of charity – that is, the advancement of education. The origins of this are found in the references in the preamble to the Elizabethan statute to 'schools of learning, free schools and scholars of universities'. HEIs broadly comprise universities and colleges

---

1   See also the annual *Decisions of the Charity Commissioners* (HMSO).
2   [1891] AC 531.

which may be established directly by Royal Charter (although they are not subject to Crown control) or by Act of Parliament. HEIs obviously come within the second head of charity – the advancement of education – although they may also become involved in other charitable purposes (for example, where they have been left a legacy in a will which is to be used for charitable but not primarily educational purposes). The problems of receiving such gifts are discussed later.

4.5   It is well established that education need not be provided free of charge in order to be charitable. Education is itself charitable whether the beneficiaries are rich or poor and whether or not fees are paid. Thus, schools in the private sector which charge fees may be charitable provided they are not run purely as profit-making ventures. Education is not confined to the provision of formal instruction. It is wide enough to cover the promotion of conferences devoted to academic subjects or to advance public knowledge of and interest in the arts. It is also not limited to instruction in academic subjects, so trusts to promote sport at schools and universities have been held to be charitable. The establishment and support of colleges, professorships, schools of learning and fellowships are all charitable.

4.6   An educational charity must be established for the benefit of the public or a sufficiently important section of the public, rather than for the benefit of individuals. In addition, if it is to be charitable, the subject matter of an educational charity must be of sufficient value to benefit the community. A leading case here is *Re Pinion*,[1] where the testator left his pictures, furniture and other objects to trustees to be maintained as a collection. Most of the items were of poor quality and the court decided that since there was no evidence that the gift would benefit the public it was not charitable. Generally, HEIs do not have to address the question of whether they, or their functions, are charitable. However, an HEI may on occasion receive a gift subject to a binding trust which is not actually charitable (for example, 'to the Master and Fellows of X college to use for research into the advantages of a revised alphabet and informing the public'). A similar bequest in *Re Shaw's Will Trusts*[2] was found to be non-charitable.

4.7   While individuals may derive benefits from an educational charity, the main purpose of the charity must be for the benefit of the public. The line can often be quite finely drawn here. Gifts for the education of limited classes of persons who constitute a sufficiently important part of the community have been upheld. Scholarship funds, for example, exist primarily to encourage high standards of learning which is clearly of public benefit, the advantage to the individual recipient being incidental to the primary purpose. However, a scholarship fund for the benefit of the descendants of certain individuals would not now be charitable, nor generally is an educational fund for the benefit of the

---

1   [1965] Ch 85.
2   [1952] 1 All ER 49.

children of employees. Trusts requiring only that a *preference* be given to the donor's descendants, however, are charitable.

Legacies from wills

4.8 HEIs may have to consider issues arising from the advancement of education in the context of legacies from wills. The following two issues arise here.

(1) Is the gift charitable at all? For example, does the gift *require* the HEI to use the money for too limited a class of beneficiaries to be charitable or is this a mere expression of wish ('precatory words')?

(2) If it is charitable, is it educational? An HEI may be left a legacy subject to a binding trust which is charitable within the terms of the *Pemsel* case but not in connection with any special purpose of the HEI. If the HEI accepts the legacy, it is obliged to follow its trusts; but, unless the HEI can broadly show that such a trust is established in connection with the purposes of the HEI, that legacy trust will not be an exempt charity within Sch 2 to the Charities Act 1993.

4.9 However, provided the gift itself is charitable, there do not seem to be any rules requiring the trust to be consistent with the original foundation, although some HEIs may not be able to accept gifts to their foundation without the consent of the Visitor. Conversely, an HEI is not bound to accept a gift to its foundation or property which is subject to a special condition. If it does so, the trust or condition must be performed whether the property given is adequate for the purpose or not. Care is needed, therefore, when deciding whether to accept legacies and lifetime gifts. The terms of any such gift should be examined to determine whether there is a binding trust or merely a wish, and whether the binding trust is sensible for the HEI to take on. Once the HEI accepts the gift, it has to carry out the obligation and cannot subsequently disclaim the benefit. The question of what constitutes acceptance of a trust is one of fact.

What are exempt charities and who regulates them?

4.10 The Charities Act 1993, s 96(1), defines charity as, 'any institution, corporate or not, which is established for charitable purposes and is subject to the control of the High Court in the exercise of the court's jurisdiction with respect to charities'. Note, therefore, that ecclesiastical corporations are excluded from s 96 (since the ordinary courts have no jurisdiction over their property), as is the corporate property of Oxford and Cambridge. Although the courts have jurisdiction over HEIs, the Visitor has exclusive jurisdiction to determine disputes arising under the domestic law of the HEI. Judicial review lies against the Visitor only if he acts outside his jurisdiction or abuses his powers in a manner wholly incompatible with natural justice. Thus, the courts have no jurisdiction to review the Visitor's construction of university statutes. (For more on the Visitor, see Chapters 8 and 30.)

4.11 Most charities are 'registered charities', which generally means that they are under the jurisdiction of the Charity Commission. However, HEIs are not registered but exempt charities under Sch 2 to the Charities Act 1993 in 'so far as they are charities'. The latter words take account of the fact that the Universities of Oxford and Cambridge, in so far as they are civil corporations, are the owners of corporate property which is not by its nature subject to any trust. (Individual colleges within Oxford and Cambridge *are* subject to s 96, like all other HEIs except Oxford and Cambridge.)

4.12 Under category (w) of Sch 2, any institution which is administered by or on behalf of an HE charity and is established for the general purposes of or for any special purpose of or in connection with the institution is also an exempt charity. The word 'institution' includes any trust or undertaking and, therefore, covers a wide variety of purposes subsidiary to the HEI itself such as scholarships, the endowment of lectureships or chairs in specific studies, libraries and funds for the provision of equipment and the maintenance of buildings. The words 'on behalf of' allow different types of educational bodies (for example, an FE corporation and an HE corporation, or a statutory corporation and a chartered corporation) to set up together an independent body established for the purposes of both institutions which, as such, would be an exempt charity.

4.13 As exempt charities, HEIs are generally not subject to the supervisory jurisdiction of the Charity Commission although they are subject to the jurisdiction of the court via the Attorney-General. The Charity Commission's powers to institute an inquiry (for example, to ensure that the property is being applied for the purposes of its trusts) under the Charities Act 1993, s 8, do not extend to an exempt charity. Consequently, the Charity Commission's powers under s 18 to act for the protection of charities (for example, by suspending trustees) are not available in respect of exempt charities. Similarly, the restrictions on sales, leases, mortgages and other disposals of land held in trust for a charity imposed by the Charities Act, ss 36 and 38 do not apply to exempt charities. As far as land is concerned, HEIs (whether created by statute or charter) can generally do anything that an individual can do – there is no need to give public notice or obtain a surveyor's report (although the latter may be sensible as 'good practice').

4.14 On the other hand, the enabling powers of the Charity Commission (for example, its power under the Charities Act 1993, s 26, to authorise a particular transaction with charity property which is expedient or to make schemes and orders under ss 13 and 16) *are* available to exempt charities on request of the charity or on an order of the court.[1] HEIs who hold old legacies subject to outdated trusts where the purposes cannot be carried out any longer may well want to make a *cy-près* application to the Charity Commission under ss 13 and 16 of the Charities Act 1993 to alter the original purposes.

4.15 The rationale for the exemption from Charity Commission supervision is that Parliament has been satisfied that acceptable and appropriate arrangements already exist for carrying out the objects of HEIs and safeguarding their property (for example, through the Secretary of State for Education). An exempt charity cannot, therefore, register with the Charity Commission, even voluntarily. Quite apart from the Secretary of State for Education, there were originally also quite extensive statutory controls exercised by the Ministry of Agriculture over the landowning aspects of college management – primarily Oxford and Cambridge colleges, but also including the University of Durham – although the extent of these controls was reduced by the Universities and Colleges Estates Act 1964. The educational aspects of HEIs – what courses they actually run and their content – are subject to direct controls (for example, in terms of funding and accreditation). The Policy Innovation Unit of the Cabinet Office is currently reviewing the concept of exempt charities, and indeed whether HEIs (and especially independent schools) should continue to enjoy charitable status, together with the financial benefits which charitable status brings by way of favourable tax treatment. The key issue is whether, in relation to exemption, HEIs can be trusted not to abuse charitable status and the proper management of charity assets (the investment of capital and the deployment of income arising from that capital only for charitable purposes). With respect to retaining charitable status at all, the key question is whether HEIs offer up sufficient public benefit, and especially if the criteria for the allocation of charitable status are narrowed to require also the relief of poverty (potentially a difficulty for independent schools, or at least those charging c £15K pa in fees; similarly, consider the variation in 'working-class' undergraduate intake and 'self-payers' in terms of academic fees between, say, Oxford and Durham or Bristol and Luton or East London and Humberside).

4.16 However, the controls on management of HEIs, at least until the passing of the ERA 1988, were generally less onerous than those imposed on non-exempt charities by the Charity Commission. Until then, control was exercised over HEIs through the power of the purse and in the giving of advice to the UGC. The ERA 1988 replaced the UGC with a Universities Funding Council (UFC), extending the legal controls exercised by the Secretary of State. In addition, University Commissioners were given substantial powers to change the nature of academic tenure and to amend the statutes of HEIs to enable redundancies and dismissals to be made. The Visitor in the chartered

---

1   Note that s 16(5), which gives power for the Charity Commission to make schemes on the application of one or more trustees or persons interested, does not apply to exempt charities. The application must be made by a majority of the governing body of the HEI itself or by court order.

HEIs also has a role in settling disputes between members of a corporation and inspecting and regulating the corporation.

4.17   The Inland Revenue acts as a controlling and supervisory body over exempt charities by examining claims for tax relief by charities and donors. In recent years, the Inland Revenue has examined the activities of HEIs closely to ensure that funds are being used for charitable objects and has looked at a number of trading activities of HEIs (for more on trading, see Chapter 15). The complexity of charitable status and the large sums involved by way of tax exemption can be seen in the recent case of *Oxford University Press v Commissioner of Income Tax*,[1] in which Oxford University Press (OUP) lost its exemption in India. Finally, the NAO has access to HEIs' books and any member of the public has the right to see an HEI's accounts on payment of a reasonable fee.[2] Note also that, although the requirements on accounts and annual reports imposed by the Charities Act 1993, ss 41–45, do not apply to exempt charities, under s 46 charity trustees of an exempt charity are required to keep 'proper books of account with respect to the affairs of the charity' which must be preserved for at least 6 years (something the HEI should be doing anyway for tax purposes).

CHARITY TRUSTEES

Who are charity trustees?

4.18   The term 'charity trustees' is defined in the Charities Act 1993, s 97, as 'the persons having the general control and management of the administration of a charity'. The expression is not, therefore, confined to trustees of charitable trusts, but includes the directors of charitable companies and members of committees of management of unincorporated charitable associations. If, as is argued later, members of governing bodies are charity trustees within s 97, then the restrictions in s 72 of the Charities Act 1993 would appear to apply to them in addition to any other conditions imposed on them by the particular charter of the HEI. Under s 72, certain people are disqualified from acting as charity trustees (for example, if they have been convicted of an offence involving dishonesty or deception, adjudged bankrupt or disqualified from acting as a director). It is generally accepted that, although a charitable corporation such as an HEI does not hold its property as trustee in the strict sense, it does hold it subject to a binding legal obligation to apply it for charitable purposes only and, therefore, its position is analogous to that of a trustee. But this would not make the HEI as such the charity trustee within the meaning of s 97. Although the managers or governors of the corporation are not strictly trustees, their role is similar to the boards of NHS trusts holding

---

1   2001 SOL Case No 053, Supreme Court of India (24 January 2001).
2   Charities Act 1993, s 47(2).

charitable trust funds. In this instance, the NHS trust is itself the sole corporate trustee of the charitable funds – the individuals who are responsible for the management of the funds are the directors of the NHS trust or other officers and are not themselves trustees of the charity. The duties, responsibilities and liabilities of the trusteeship lie with the body corporate. However, that body must act through individual persons in order to express its will. If the body corporate commits a breach of its duty as trustee, it will have done so only as a result of a breach by its directors or other individual officers of their duties towards the body corporate. The practical reality, therefore, is that the governors of an HEI are likely to be treated as if they were charity trustees and are subject to the control of the High Court. For example, in the case of *Harries v Church Commissioners for England*,[1] the governors of the Church Commissioners, a corporate charity, were nevertheless treated as charity trustees in respect of their powers of investment.

What are the duties of charity trustees?

4.19   In the most general sense, the duty of any charity trustee is to promote the interests of the charity and to ensure that its assets are applied only for its charitable purposes. The first duty of any charity trustee on appointment is to understand the terms of the governing instrument (whether the constitution is set up by charter or statute). The governing body must ensure that all the assets of the HEI are under its control and that all sums due to the HEI are recovered. This raises a number of practical issues common to all charities in relation to *ex gratia* payments. From time to time, the governing body may conclude that it is in the interests of the HEI to apply funds for furthering purposes which, strictly speaking, are not educational. For example, it might wish to add to the pension of a long-term employee on his or her retirement or give an extra redundancy payment. The governors are not legally required to make these payments, but wish to do so. These are *ex gratia* payments and not *prima facie* within the objects of the HEI (since, although an HEI may have the power to undertake such acts, those powers have to be exercised in furtherance of the objects). The governing body will only be able to make such payments and provision if it can justify that, in these particular circumstances, the long-term interests of the HEI will be well served and, therefore, the educational objects furthered. Wherever there are *ex gratia* payments, the question of personal interest must be closely watched, since there have been a number of cases in the HE and FE sectors (discussed in Chapter 3) in which conflicts arose in connection with severance pay to members of a corporation. Sometimes, HEIs may feel that there is a moral claim on them either to make a payment where there is no legal obligation to do so (for example, when they have inherited under a will, but the relatives of the deceased are in need) or to waive their entitlement to receive property. However, like any other charity, HEIs should not apply their funds for purposes outside their objects. Previously, a charity needed the authority of

---

1   [1992] 1 WLR 1241. See also *Cowan v Scargill* [1985] Ch 270, [1984] 2 All ER 750.

the Attorney-General to make an *ex gratia* payment. Now the Charity Commission also has the power (subject to the supervision of the Attorney-General) under the Charities Act 1993, s 27, to authorise charity trustees (including governing bodies of HEIs) to apply charity property or to waive a right to receive property in pursuit of a moral obligation. Applications must be made to the Charity Commission, setting out the circumstances and why the trustees feel they are under a moral obligation. If the Charity Commission refuses to give the necessary authority an application may then be made to the Attorney-General.[1]

4.20   The trustees must seek to preserve and maximise the assets of the charity. This includes taking professional advice on investment decisions and ensuring that the best possible price is obtained when charity assets are sold. An HEI must ensure that its investment policy maintains a reasonable balance between income and capital, and that the investments are not unduly hazardous. Investment should not be unduly influenced by non-financial or ethical considerations. Thus, a governing body must not allow its own personal opinions or moral judgements to affect investment decisions. *Harries v Church Commissioners for England* held that it is proper for the trustees to take non-financial considerations into account only where this still allows an adequate spread of investments. Problems have arisen for HEIs where students and members of the governing bodies have not wanted the HEI to invest in a particular company or accept money from a company with a bad labour record or with links to a poor human rights regime. If anything, the trend now is towards 'socially responsible investment' (*aka* 'ethical investment'): Leeds University has disinvested endowment held in tobacco shares (*The Times Higher Educational Supplement*, 16 November 2001, p 6), while other HEIs are ignoring similar campaigns led by their SUs.[2] HEIs have very wide powers to delegate administration to officers, committees or subcommittees and also to allow for delegation to external bodies. Indeed, the committee system can act as part of a system of checks and balances, but it must be properly supervised (see Chapter 5 on delegation of authority).

The liability of charity trustees of HEIs

4.21   Governing bodies of HEIs are usually interested in knowing the extent of their personal liability for breaches of trust. Unfortunately, this issue is not straightforward (see Chapter 3). There is no specific provision in the charters or statutes of HEIs for personal liability of a governing body and, therefore, no specific provision regarding the protection in certain circumstances of governors from such liability. Thus, there is nothing to relieve an individual governor of a corporation from liability along the lines of s 61 of the Trustee Act 1925, or s 727 of the Companies Act 1985 (and, more recently, FE governors via s 145 of the Learning and Skills Act 2000). Even if there is a general

---

1   Section 27(4).
2   See the useful discussion in Luxton (2001), paras 16.24–16.28 and 16.61–16.66 concerning SRI.

presumption against the personal liability of governors of HEIs on the basis that express words are needed to impose such liability, it does appear from cases that the courts may hold governing bodies accountable where there has been misuse of property on the basis that, if there can be no personal liability of the governors in respect of a misuse of property, then there would in practice be nobody in relation to whom the jurisdiction of the court could be exercised. However, the precise formulation of that personal liability is not straightforward. Although they might be regarded in the same position as trustees, it seems to have been accepted that governors of HEIs cannot rely upon the Trustee Act 1925, s 61, because that section only applies to trustees proper. (Section 61 empowers the High Court to excuse from personal liability a trustee who has acted in breach of trust, if the trustee has acted honestly and reasonably and ought fairly to be excused.) Governors of HEIs have fiduciary duties towards the HEI, ie they are under a duty to further the objects of the HEI and not to place themselves in a position where a conflict of interest may arise. If a governor has obtained property by breach of fiduciary duties (for example, a personal interest has not been declared), it is unclear whether that governor merely has to return the property or must go further and compensate the HEI for any loss caused by the breach of trust. It is likely that a court would decide that the governor should make some reparation for the loss. By analogy, a director of a company who acts in breach of his or her fiduciary duty (for example, by using the company's assets to procure a benefit) will be personally liable for any losses to the company which may result. The courts, therefore, may regard governors of HEIs in the same light as company directors on the basis that the governors of an HEI have a duty to safeguard the HEI's assets.

Ultra vires

4.22 A trustee commits a breach of trust if he or she acts in a way which is not authorised by the terms of the constitution. Whether this means that the governing body of an HEI could be personally liable if it had caused an HEI to act *ultra vires* is debatable. Unless there was some breach of fiduciary duty (for example, it had obtained some personal benefit from the *ultra vires* act), it is thought that the governing body does not have personal liability. Personal benefit is, however, likely to be widely construed.

Third parties

4.23 Governors of HEIs do not (*prima facie*) have personal liability to third parties, but can governors be liable to third parties with whom the corporation entered into a contract where the corporation did not have power to enter into such a contract? Again, there is some debate about this, but the third party might claim for breach of warranty of authority. If the warranty given by the governors was one of law (ie that the HEI did have power to enter into a contract, when in fact its statutory powers did not permit this), then no liability arises. However, if the warranty was one of fact (ie a governor had warranted that a procedure required by the articles of government had been followed, when in fact it had not), then the claim might well be successful.

Charity Commission advice

4.24 If individuals are concerned about a particular course of action, there seems no reason in principle why the governing body of an HEI could not apply under the Charities Act 1993, s 29, to the Charity Commission for advice or an opinion on any matter affecting the performance of duties. If the governors act in accordance with such advice, they will be protected against any allegation that they have not acted properly or have not complied with the terms of the governing instrument. However, the Charity Commission is empowered *but not obliged* to advise charity trustees and may refuse to do so if an HEI requests advice on a particular matter which the Charity Commission considers could be better dealt with elsewhere.

Criminal offences

4.25 There are a number of statutory offences which can be committed by corporations and which can result in criminal liability for both the corporations and their members. Liability is usually, but not exclusively, confined to the situation where the breach is attributable to some act or neglect on the part of the corporation member concerned (for example, breach of the legislation relating to health and safety at work and data protection: see Chapters 13 and 20).

Insurance

4.26 In the context of liability, insurance may be appropriate. Certainly, occupiers' liability and employers' insurance will always need to be taken out. But wider insurance against breach of trust should not be seen as a panacea and generally has quite a limited use. HEI constitutions normally allow corporations to insure their members against liabilities arising out of membership and to pay the associated premiums. However, insurance against criminal liabilities is not possible. Insurance policies also exclude various heads of liability, such as liability arising out of deliberate acts or where the person concerned knew the act was a breach of duty or was reckless as to whether it was a breach of duty or not. Taking advice from the Charity Commission on a particular point under s 29 of the Charities Act 1993, can, therefore, help to protect the trustees. In addition, some liabilities (such as liability for defamation or environmental pollution) are excluded from some policies. Quite apart from any exclusions, there is often a cap on the amount of cover provided by an insurance policy and there is frequently an excess provision. With reference to the discussion both in this chapter and in Chapter 3 concerning whether the governors of an HEI are to be judged by the court as effectively charity trustees or rather as company directors, and hence whether they may in certain circumstances incur personal liability, it is interesting to note the US experience as recounted in Kaplin and Lee (1995a), chapter II. They refer to the leading case of *Stern v Lucy Webb Hayes National Training School for Deaconesses and Missionaries*,[1] also known as the *Sibley Hospital* case, which reviews the obligations of the governors of charitable corporations, interpreting them in the context of corporate law rather than trust law with its higher level of fiduciary duties (see also *Corporation of Mercer University v Smith*,[2] which echoed the *Sibley Hospital* case in applying the laxer corporate law standards to the governors rather than trust law). This is on the basis that managing US HEIs is closer to running a broad-based business than administering a one-issue charity. The matter is yet to be tested in English law: if ever it were, the US case-law would be of interest (see also Evans and Evans (1998)). Palfreyman (1995/96) argues that at least for Oxbridge college Fellows, given their custody of permanently endowed, perpetual, eleemosynary institutions, a fiduciary duty closer to trusteeship rather than company directorship is appropriate. See also the OxCHEPS Occasional Paper, Proper Governance in the English Charted University (Palfreyman (2002, forthcoming)): access to the OxCHEPS website is detailed in para 1.39.

TRUSTEE ACT 2000

4.27 The Trustee Act 2000 effectively replaces the Trustee Investment Act 1961 in terms of setting the default powers of charity trustees where the trust deed does not exclude, widen, or otherwise modify these statutory powers. It also codifies the common-law duty of care required of trustees when they handle charity investments (they must act 'with such skill and care as is reasonable'), the level expected increasing if they have special expertise/ experience (*Re Speight; Speight v Gaunt*[3]). They are now automatically given a wider 'general power of investment' (including the power to buy land/property as an investment, rather than just for functional use as charity premises), but must always take into account 'standard investment criteria' (in effect, investment 'good practice': whether the particular investment or the broad investment strategy is appropriate for the charity, whether the range of investments is properly diverse, the taking of professional advice . . .) and must exercise appropriate skill and care in selecting, appointing and instructing a professional fund manager when delegating investment management. Finally, the archaic restrictions on insuring charity property are lifted. All in all, it amounts to a 'deregulation' of trusteeship. Thus, the way is opened for charity investment in hedge funds and in private equity funds, but not (yet) in such instruments as derivatives: charity investment can now be much less

---

1   381 F Supp 1003 (DDC 1974).
2   371 SE 2d 858 (Ga 1988).
3   (1883) 22 Ch D 727.

conservative, compared with the 'narrower' and 'wider' ranges of the 1961 Act. The enabling powers of the 2000 Act look very similar to those a brand new charity would try to award itself in drafting a scheme or what an old charity could achieve in seeking the approval of the Charity Commission to a revised 'state-of-the-art' scheme (see above concerning the Bedford Charity). For the latest guidance from the Charity Commissioner on its interpretation of the new Act, consult its website at www.charity-commission.gov.uk, and especially see *Investment of Charitable Funds: The Effects of the Trustee Act 2000*; *Appointing Nominees and Custodians: Guidance under s 19(4) of the Trustee Act 2000*; and *Interim Operational Guidance* all on the provisions of the Act. See also Luxton (2001), pp 853–858 for the text of the Trustee Act 2000: he also stresses (para 1.138) that the Trustee Act does *not* apply to charitable companies. The Charity Commission, however, is clear that the Trustee Act 2000 does automatically apply to a chartered charitable corporation (ie almost all the 'old', pre-1992 universities – except Oxford and Cambridge as civil, or perhaps statutory, corporations – and virtually all Oxbridge colleges), on the basis that such bodies hold their general corporate property on trust (unlike a statutory, 'new'/post-1992 university, as an HEC): this follows Hambley (1998); see also Palfreyman (1998/99) and (1999). Of course, there is not an issue of applying the Act if the chartered university or college has no general corporate assets to invest, nor any specific trusts of which it is the trustee. Thus a statutory university will be 'caught' by the Act only if it has become the trustee of a specific trust with investable endowment assets.

4.28   Going even further in investment terms is talk of the Charity Commission allowing charities to invest on a 'total-return' basis, rather than on the traditional income/yield: capital appreciation approach. Registered charities with permanent endowment as perpetual charitable corporations will be able to apply to the Charity Commission for much greater freedom to spend some part of their capital gains (while, of course, still protecting the long-term capital value of the endowment base).[1] An exempt charity would need Privy Council approval to change its investment statute (as one Oxford college has done). As a further example of a steadily more enlightened view of investment objectives and methodology on the part of the Charity Commission, the first pooled-fund Common Investment Fund (CIF) investing in commercial property has recently been approved for charities to use as a means of investing in this asset class, and one is probably in the pipe-line for a mixed equities/fixed interest portfolio.

4.29   Since the passing of the Trustee Act 2000 (together with the implementation of the new SORP for charities, and especially its emphasis on risk assessment and management), a veritable industry and army of consultants have sought to frighten charity trustees into thinking that the nature of the Act

---

1   See www.charity-commission.gov.uk; and for discussion of the legal niceties, Hill and Smith (2001), Dutton (2001).

is so burdensome that they absolutely need the services of such people at appropriate levels of fees: this is unlikely, assuming that the trustees collectively have a reasonable spread of experience and expertise, employ competent staff and professional advisers (auditors, solicitors), and apply common sense.

Chapter 5

THE LAW OF MEETINGS

David Palfreyman

EDITORS' INTRODUCTION

§5.1   The management of HEIs depends increasingly on the determination of issues in meetings of one kind or another. Therefore, it is essential for managers to understand the law governing meetings. The law of meetings is determined mainly by common law, but also by statute (for example, the legislation controlling limited companies which prescribes the format of annual general meetings (AGMs), meetings of boards of directors, etc). Procedure at, and the conduct of, meetings is often based on convention, which is sometimes not supported by common law – for example, common law does not require that a motion has a seconder before it can be put, but convention does. In the case of HEIs, the charter/statutes/ordinances/regulations/standing orders, or whatever, will often prescribe in detail the arrangements for meetings, covering areas on which the common law is silent. The HEI manager needs, first and foremost, to be familiar with the institution's governing instrument and what it says about the convening of meetings, the election of chairs, the quorum for a meeting, voting at meetings, etc, and, secondly, with the common law as applicable to meetings for circumstances where the HEI's rules are ambiguous or unhelpfully silent. The HEI manager needs also to be familiar with the legal concepts of power and authority, of delegation, of agency and of vicarious liability as also discussed in this chapter.

THE ESSENTIAL ELEMENTS

The role of the chair

5.1   The chair must conduct the meeting in an impartial, proper and orderly fashion, allowing fair opportunity for all members to contribute to discussion and ensuring that the meeting is clear about what is being voted on. The chair can propose a motion, and by convention will usually vacate the chair while doing so. In the HEI the threat of disorder in a meeting is remote, but still possible (for example, in meetings about student discipline, student accommodation charges, student academic fees or staff redundancies). The chair may use, or (more likely) permit porters/security staff to use, *reasonable* force (see Chapter 20) to remove a person from a meeting, *if* the meeting has first voted to exclude him because he is disrupting the meeting *and* after he has refused the option of going voluntarily. If the behaviour of that person is so blatant, the chair will probably adjourn the meeting for, say, 15 minutes and then, if circumstances are still chaotic, the chair may perhaps order the removal of the disruptive person without a proposal for exclusion being put to the meeting. In certain circumstances that person may find himself in breach of the peace and subject to criminal proceedings.

5.2   The chair can be removed by the will of the majority at a meeting (subject to the charter and statutes or similar), if there is reasonable evidence of corruption, gross partiality, or sheer incompetence. Indeed, the power to remove an incompetent or corrupt chair is judicially regarded as being crucial for the proper governance of a corporation,[1] but note that, if a chair is appointed by a superior/parent body, only that body can replace the chair. If the chair unilaterally departs, the meeting can legitimately continue after electing itself another chair – clearly anybody who is a candidate for the chair is not able to conduct the election (often the meeting is handed over to its secretary for election of chair). Subject to the charter and statutes stating that the chair of a given committee will be appointed by its 'parent' or senior committee, or shall automatically be a particular officer of the HEI, the chair is the creature of the meeting, not the other way around. The chair has a vote, simply as a member, but a casting vote as chair only if the charter/statutes specifically permit it – there is no casting vote in common law. If the chair has no casting vote, or decides not to use it, the *status quo* applies in that there will have been no majority reached for the proposal. A chair can vote one way using the personal vote, but another way using the casting vote: for example, some chairs might use the casting vote to maintain the *status quo*, after having personally voted for change, on the basis that change should come about only if there is significant support for it, not just by scraping through on a casting vote. Hence the lack of a casting vote under the common law is sensible: it means that the *status quo* prevails in the event of a tied vote, and is not to be altered by one member who happens to be chair and in effect has a chance to vote twice according to his personal views. The chair's action is (or should be) of only limited capacity. It may be necessary (especially during lengthy HE vacations), but the exercise of the chair's action must never be abused: it can be used only for matters which are urgent *and* minor *and* non-controversial. As discussed below, the committee is not able to delegate its routine or 'heavy' business to the chair, although it can give the chair formal authority to act on its behalf in relation to a specific matter which will predictably need attention between one meeting and the next. Any action by the chair needs, of course, to be fully minuted and properly reported to the next meeting of the committee.

Notice of meetings

5.3   In the unlikely event that *all* members qualified to attend were present and *all* agreed to an instant meeting, then at common law a legitimate meeting can take place, but the charter and statutes for an HEI will usually specify how to convene a meeting (even an urgent one) and common law requires

---

1   *Booth v Arnold* [1895] 1 QB 571, p 579.

reasonable notice to be given, unless *all* members agree to waive the notice period in the unlikely circumstances suggested above. Such notice must be 'a fair and candid and reasonable explanation of the purpose or purposes of the meeting'. Care is needed to ensure that nobody can argue that the notice given was 'a tricky notice'.[1] Similarly, in *Baillie v Oriental Telephone and Electric Co Ltd*,[2] Lord Cozens-Hardy MR said: 'The notice . . . seems to me to be not frank, not open, not clear, and not in any way satisfactory – it was tricky'. Care should also be taken over use of 'any other business', using this agenda item only for minor matters needing urgent attention; not for major matters, even if needing urgent attention – unless it is *really* safe to assume that the irregularity inevitably arising with regard to the lack of notice can be covered over by the fact that the majority of members will be present for the AOB item and will vote for it (see para **5.10**). Some statutes may specify that, for example, no proposal concerning the expenditure of money shall be considered at a meeting without notice of it having been explicitly given on the notice/agenda sheet. In counting the days in the period of notice required, the day on which the notice is served (actually reaches the members) and the day on which the meeting takes place will not count as 'clear days' in the sense of needing to give X days' notice. In addition, note that, where the notice is posted, the assumption is that delivery will take 2 days for first-class post (by analogy with the Interpretation Act 1978, s 7). It may be legitimate to assume that HEI internal post is faster and that email is instantaneous. It is likely that most HEIs contravene these minimum notice periods most of the time (see para **5.10**). The venue of the meeting must be of sufficient size for those attending, and configured so that all present can hear and see each other.

The quorum for meetings

5.4 Unless the charter/statutes specify a different arrangement, the common-law quorum is half plus one of the membership, and the quorum must be maintained throughout the meeting, not just at the beginning. The quorum is of voting members; non-voting members, observers, etc, do not count and nor, for specific items, would a voting member who is disbarred from voting on that particular matter because of having to declare a personal/financial interest in the item due to be discussed and voted upon, not least because convention requires that he should absent himself from the meeting while the item is discussed and voted upon (just as the HEI's standing orders may also specify withdrawal from the meeting once an interest has been declared). Unless the statutes, ordinances, etc, specify that meetings shall automatically terminate after a given period, a meeting can legally go on for as long as the members can bear it (or maintain a quorum, where relevant). The presence of a non-member at a meeting, whether officially as an observer or not, would perhaps be unusual (it may create issues of confidentiality and the risk of defamation –

---

1   *Kaye v Croydon Tramsways Co* [1898] 1 Ch 358, CA, pp 369 and 373 respectively; see also *R v Liverpool Corporation* (1759) 2 Burr 723, 97 ER 533.
2   [1915] 1 Ch 503, p 514.

see paras **5.13–5.17**), but it would *not* invalidate proceedings unless the individual participated in the business being conducted other than by invitation to address the meeting on a specific item.

Voting at meetings

5.5   At common law, voting is by show-of-hands of those entitled to vote (see above), unless a poll is called for by a member. A poll is a written vote, with members signing their names against a list or on a poll-slip. Thus, it is not the same as a secret ballot, which is a permissible variation of the show-of-hands. There is no provision at common law for a proxy vote, but it may be allowed for in the charter/statutes of a particular HEI. A recorded vote simply records in the minutes the names of the members who voted for or against, and who abstained, in a simple show-of-hands vote. A simple majority is required to decide a matter, unless the HEI's rules require, say, a two-thirds majority to change by-laws, amend standing orders, etc. Thus, a governing body of, say, 20 can function at common law with 11 present, and its own statutes or similar may require the 11 to be present *only at the start of the meeting*. In such a case, a matter can be decided not only by those among the 11 who actually vote on it (and several could abstain) but, later in the meeting as people leave, by a simple majority of, say, the five members who vote on it (while one other might abstain). Hence, three out of 20 can bind the rest, unless the chair suggests, and the meeting accepts that:

–   it is inappropriate to reach a decision at such an ill-attended stage of a meeting (perhaps leaving the opportunity for discussion to continue, but without the intention of reaching a vote/decision);
–   the rest may rescind at the next meeting any decision that is reached; and
–   the decision may be challengeable by the absentee majority on the limited grounds set out in para **5.10** (for example, because improper notice was given or because the decision was *ultra vires* or in breach of trust).

Discussion, debate, motions

5.6   There are conventions about how to conduct the debate, and sometimes the charter/statutes specify the procedures (often in the form of standing orders). If they do not, the common-law requirement is that matters be conducted in an orderly and reasonable way (for example, considering only one amendment at a time and recognising the hierarchy of the procedural motions which may be deployed in debating a substantive motion or item of business – see para **5.7**). It is to be noted that there is no requirement at common law for a motion to be seconded before it can be put, although the convention is that it should be – hence a chair would be safer to accept such a motion from an insistent proposer, even without a seconder, than to rule it out of order (presumably it would stand little chance of being approved, and a quick vote would dispatch the proposal into oblivion). Indeed, in *R v Flintshire*

CC *ex parte Armstrong-Braun*,[1] the court declared that a local council ought to think very hard before instituting a standing order that all proposed agenda items needed a seconder councillor, lest this new standing order might interfere with local democracy in terms of silencing individual councillors and stifling discussion (and especially since the county council had 'other ways of dealing with time wasters'). There will certainly be restrictions in the statutes, ordinances, etc, upon student members of particular committees being present for certain items ('Reserved Business', typically concerning individual students or members of staff and financial, legal or personnel matters). Similarly, any code of conduct for council members/governors will specify that individuals shall declare a personal or financial interest and withdraw from the meeting during the appropriate item of business (CUC (2001)): the same, at least by convention, applies to committee members all through the committee hierarchy.

Procedural motions

5.7 These procedural devices are merely recognised custom and practice. They include:

> *Closure*: or 'that the question now be put' is immediately voted upon when put, without any discussion;
> *Next business*: or 'that the meeting proceed to the next business' is an attempt to shelve an item of business and, again, the motion should be voted upon without debate;
> *That the matter lie on the table*: similar in effect to 'next business' and, yet again, to be voted on without debate;
> *Reference back*: is a somewhat more positive way of suspending discussion on a substantive motion; again to be voted on without further debate;
> *Adjournment of the meeting*: or 'that the chairman leave the chair' is also taken to the vote immediately;
> *Adjournment of the debate*: a vote on this procedural motion is taken only after the proposer of the substantive motion has had a chance to speak against adjourning any further discussion on his motion; and
> *Point of order*: a way to challenge procedure and invite the chair to rule on the alleged infringement of any standing orders, rules or regulations.

Minutes

5.8 The minutes are a record of who was present (ideally they should also record departures of members during a meeting) and of decisions taken as motions duly approved become resolutions. The minutes are the official record and can be relied on in civil proceedings; indeed, certified copies are often required by third parties as evidence of 'a proper decision' having been reached

---

1   [2001] LGR 344, CA.

concerning, say, a decision to borrow money or sell assets. There is no legal
duty to record discussion and to explain how and why a certain decision was
reached, unless the matter relates to an individual (discipline, grievance) and it
is appropriate to show that the requirements of natural justice (see para 5.11)
were complied with in reaching the decision. The 'house-style' as to the level of
detail included varies from HEI to HEI, but most HEIs use minutes to record
just the decisions (with reference to supporting papers) rather than the
nuances of debate. The decision is valid in law from the time it has been taken:
the approval/confirmation of minutes at the next meeting is merely recognition
that the minutes are accurate, and *not* a chance to debate again whether a
certain decision should have been reached. Where there is a controversial
matter, the chair will normally take care to make clear the exact wording of the
motion being voted on, and that wording will duly appear as the resolution in
the minutes. Convention will vary among HEIs as to whether the minutes need
to be signed at the meeting (or subsequently) once they have been confirmed:
there is no requirement at common law for signed minutes, although an HEI's
standing orders may require it.

Ultra vires and intra vires

5.9   Any decision or action reached by a committee has to be within its power
or authority (*intra vires*) and not beyond its remit (*ultra vires*). This means that
care needs to be taken that a decision is within the terms of reference for a
committee, or that there is an appropriate power under the charter/statutes for
the governing body of the HEI to do something (see Chapter 2). A committee
will typically have had certain powers and tasks (its remit, or terms of
reference) delegated to it by higher authority within the hierarchy of corporate
governance: it may not then further delegate those powers and duties
(*delegatus non potest delegare*), although a committee can create a sub-
committee of itself to undertake detailed work and report back. Similarly, the
Board of Directors in a company is not able to delegate unless express provision
is made for any such delegation in the company's Memorandum and Articles
(the company equivalent of a chartered corporation's charter/statutes and
by-laws/regulations).[1] The delegating, higher authority is essentially the
principal appointing an agent in terms of the law of agency (see para 5.19).

Dealing with irregularities

5.10   In the event of disputes as to whether a meeting was properly convened,
really reached a certain decision, was conducted badly, etc, the High Court will
issue an injunction prohibiting the consequence of the irregular proceeding
being put into operation only if a majority of the members seek it. A minority of
complainers will suffice only where the body concerned has *deliberately* tried
to exclude certain members from the decision-taking process, or is taking an

---

1   See Davies (1997), p 196.

ultra vires (see earlier) decision, or is in breach of trust (for more on trusteeship, see Chapter 4). As Shaw and Smith note:[1]

> 'If the majority at the meeting would be competent to do regularly that which has been irregularly achieved and they approve it, it would be futile for the minority to seek to impair the results of the proceedings; for the same results will ultimately be achieved by the will of the majority with due regard to the formal requirements of the [presumably, next] meeting. Accordingly the Courts will give no remedy upon the application of an individual member or even a number of members if they comprise only a minority of those present at the meeting.'

But, since a quorum might be only half plus one of the members, and since a decision may be reached by just a simple majority of those present *and voting* (ie many could abstain), an action *could* be approved by a very small section of the membership, and hence a judicious chair will ensure that potentially controversial matters are not decided when the number of members present has declined steadily as the meeting has progressed (see paras 5.3 and 5.4, especially in relation to any other business items). For some HEIs, of course, certain such disputes would be dealt with by the Visitor rather than the High Court, but the Visitor is likely to apply similar principles.

The rules of natural justice

5.11   Clearly, committee procedures, especially in relation to disciplinary and grievance processes dealing with the rights of the individual, need to follow the rules of natural justice – the *audi alteram partem* rule (need to provide a fair hearing) and the *nemo judex in causa sua* rule (a process which is impartial and free from bias: one should not be prosecutor, judge and jury on something one has already been involved in). Thus, decisions must be reached carefully and fairly, with procedures being followed consistently in all cases (and especially where an individual reasonably has 'a legitimate expectation' that a certain procedure will be applied in considering his case). In the USA all this would be called 'due process'. The objective is for justice both to be done and to be seen to have been done. It is depressingly easy to get all this wrong: even a Law Lord can fail to notice that his link with Amnesty might appear to compromise his involvement in the *Pinochet* case, while a Lord Chancellor in charge of promotion to and within the judiciary seemingly neglected to appreciate that for him personally to dispatch an invitation to a fund-raising dinner for New Labour 'champagne-socialist' lawyers might look bad. When HEIs lose student cases at judicial review (see Chapter 6), it is usually because they have fouled up over due process. (See Chapter 7 for further discussion of natural justice, Chapter 9 for discussion of judicial review, and Craig (1999) with de Smith (1999) for full details.)

---

1   (1979), p 179.

Company law relating to meetings

5.12   The HE manager of today is likely to be *de facto* and *de jure* the company secretary of the HEI's trading company, and possibly of the HEI's spin-off companies. Thus, he or she will need to be familiar with the legislation governing the conduct of meetings of boards of directors and the convening of AGMs, as based partly on the common law already discussed but mainly set out in relevant legislation. There are numerous standard texts on company law and on the role of the company secretary, including Davies (1997), chapter 21, Ferran (1999), pp 258–271, Impey (1999) and Shearman (1997), Part III. See also Birks (2000), chapter 3. (For more on nominee-directors, shadow-directors, and trading companies generally, see Chapter 15.)

DEFAMATION

5.13   Perhaps the nearest we can get to a definition of defamation is one offered in *Halsbury's Laws of England* (vol 28, para 100):

> 'A defamatory statement is a statement which tends to lower a person in the estimation of right-thinking members of society generally, or to cause him to be shunned or avoided or to expose him to hatred, contempt or ridicule, or to convey an imputation on him disparaging or injurious to him in his office, profession, calling, trade or business.'

The words concerned may not necessarily in themselves be defamatory, but there may be special circumstances whereby the ordinary recipients of them will infer a defamatory meaning about the subject of them: this is innuendo. Thus, the making in writing (libel) and, especially at meetings, orally (slander) of comments which, allegedly, damage an individual's reputation is clearly a risk in the committee process.

5.14   The speaker of such words at the committee meeting or the writer of the offending committee paper will be the obvious target of a writ for defamation (as may be the HEI itself if the speaker/writer was acting in the course of his employment: the HEI being vicariously liable for its employees), but so might the committee chair if he or she encourages the continuing repetition, and especially the reporting in the press, of what he or she should reasonably have appreciated were defamatory comments. The defence against a writ for defamation is likely to be that the comments made were indeed true (*justification*), or that they were reasonable observations on a matter of public interest (*fair comment*), or that the statements concerned were made in the context of a meeting where it was appropriate and legitimate to be discussing such a matter in that way in front of relevant interested parties (*qualified privilege*). A defence such as qualified privilege could be defeated if there was undue publication of the statement – for example, it was made orally before people who had no relevant interest in the matter and who just happened to be present, or it was circulated more widely in writing than it need to have been (except that dictating a letter to a secretary, or having a paper typed by a secretary, is not undue publication). Similarly, qualified privilege is no defence if it can be shown that the making of the statement had been motivated by malice and not on the basis of an honest belief that it was true and relevant to the matter concerned. Malice might encompass a reckless indifference to the truth, where a damaging statement was made or repeated without considering its validity. Malice would also defeat a defence of fair comment. Finally, a fourth defence is that of *unintentional defamation* under the Defamation Act 1996, ss 2–4: the person making the defamatory remarks will seek to make amends by publicising in writing a correction and apology, and, if appropriate, paying compensation. This particular defence will be defeated if it can be shown that the defamation was intentional in that the person knew that the remarks referred to the individual now complaining of defamation, and knew also that the remarks were both false and defamatory of that individual. Thus, a simple apology alone is no defence in a defamation action, but it may be seen at least as an attempt at mitigation of the damage done when it comes to the court awarding damages.

5.15 Shearman (1997), Part V, has a useful summary of the law relating to defamation, and texts on tort cover the topic – see, for example, Elliott and Quinn (2001b), plus Markesinis and Deakin (1999), chapter 7.1 and Birks (2000), chapter 14 E6. See also Farrington (1998), pp 127–128 and 131. The key case concerning employers giving potentially defamatory references is *Spring v Guardian Assurance plc.*[1]

5.16 HEI defamation cases in the USA are discussed in Kaplin and Lee (1995a), pp 111–112 and 543–549; (2000), pp 82–88 and in NACUA (1996). The latter stresses that the protection of qualified privilege can be maintained only if HEIs ensure that: 'Communications should be limited to persons who have an indisputable "need to know" or who have knowledge of facts essential to resolving the matter . . .' (p 12): and that, as far as references are concerned, they 'generally should not be provided by a person who has a history of interpersonal conflict with, or ill-will towards, the subject of the reference . . .' (p 15), while 'gratuitous, subjective evaluation of character or personality (as opposed to performance) should be avoided' (p 18). Kaplin and Lee (1995a), pp 543–549 consider the potential for libel within campus student publications: generally, providing the HEI exercises no control over the publication, it carries no likely liability (see Chapter 19 on the HEI–student union legal relationship).

5.17 Very recent US cases also demonstrate the HEI's ability to invoke qualified privilege as a defence against the alleged defamation in a student reference, or to argue that the alleged defamation has not been published in that circulation of the comments have been restricted to an internal group of relevant parties.[2] Some students, however, have been successful where the

---

1   [1993] 2 All ER 273.
2   *Ostasz v Medical College of Ohio* 691 NE 2d 371, Ct Cl Oh 1997; *Dean v Wissman* 996 SW 2d 631, Mo Ct App 1999.

academics have behaved unprofessionally.[1] Sometimes the academic sues the student, usually for making unsubstantiated allegations of sexual harassment.[2] Occasionally one academic sues another and/or the employing HEI over some squabble concerning tenure or research quality.[3]

A cautionary example

5.18   In the summer of 1999, a Board of Examiners discussed the possibility of plagiarism amongst a sizeable proportion of undergraduates in a given year on a particular degree course. To be declared a cheat in exams is clearly defamatory if not, in fact, true, but, whether true or not, discussion at a confidential meeting of the Board of Examiners is certainly covered by qualified privilege. However, when the Board resolved that there had indeed been cheating *and* when that decision became public (receiving much media attention), the University would probably be unable to raise a defence of qualified privilege if it had itself released the information, given the unnecessarily wide publication of the accusations. The Board's subsequent decision that mass cheating had not, after all, taken place would also negate the defence of justification (unless the Board's change of mind was, in the light of new information, that it could not, and should not, have reasonably been expected to have at the earlier meeting), arguably leaving the University with only the defence of unintentional defamation. Meanwhile, one particular student, having been accused and – apparently without being given a hearing or any opportunity to respond to the accusation (see para 5.11) – found guilty of cheating, publicly challenged the University's decision in the media. She complained of defamation, in that she had falsely been accused of cheating in such a way that she could be readily identified, from the media coverage, as one of the student cohort supposedly indulging in extensive collaboration and plagiarism.

DELEGATION, AGENCY, AND VICARIOUS LIABILITY

5.19   As already noted, the delegation of power from a senior committee (Council, Senate, the Board of Governors, the Academic Board) to a junior committee or sub-committee (Finance Committee, Buildings Committee, Planning Committee, Faculty Boards, etc) is an act of effectively appointing the lesser committee as the agent of the one above it in the hierarchy of governance. Similarly, an HEI Officer (Vice-Chancellor, Registrar, Dean, *et al*, and lay-members as Treasurer, Pro-Chancellor, etc) will also be the agents of the

---

1   *Smith v Atkins* 622 So 2d 795, La App 1993; *Ross v St Augustine College* 103 F 3d 338, 4th Cir 1996.
2   *Chiavarelli v Williams* 681 NY S 2d 276, NY Sup Ct App Div 1998.
3   *Henry v The Delaware Law School of Widener University Inc* 1998 Del Ch LEXIS 7, Ct Chan Del 1998, *affirmed* 718 A 2d 527, Del 1998; *Arroyo v Rosen* 648 A 2d 1074, Md App 1994; and *Abdelsayed v Narumanchi* 668 A 2d 378, Ct App 1995.

HEI, as well as usually its employees: thereby the concept of the employer's vicarious liability for the acts of its employees is introduced and overlaps with the concept of agency. This section briefly discusses the two concepts, which also crop up in later chapters (for example, on trading companies, on the students' union, in the HEI–student contractual relationship).

5.20 Farrington and Mattison (1990), pp 152–154 raise the question of whether the HEI will be bound contractually if a professor, without HEI knowledge or approval, takes on a research contract in his academic subject area from a company, or if the same unruly professor, again without HEI approval, orders a huge quantity of food for the HEI's catering operation from an outside supplier. Farrington (1998), pp 189–190 makes the same point: the latter action will probably not bind the HEI because the external supplier should have questioned such an order from such a strange source (unless he was a Professor of Catering Management); however, in the former case, there would be no obvious reason for a third party to believe that the professor may not be acting on behalf of the HEI and hence the HEI will be bound by the research contract.

5.21 Similarly, Kaplin and Lee (1995a), pp 87–101; and (2000), pp 45/46 and 72–76 give examples of several US cases in this area, illustrating the problems real HEIs have encountered.

– In *Blank v Board of Higher Education of the City of New York*,[1] the court rejected the HEI's claim that, since the Dean himself had not approved Blank's degree course special arrangements, it was not bound by (as the judgment put it) the student's 'obvious reliance upon the council and advice of [other] members of staff of the college administration to whom he was referred'. Blank had no reason to doubt that these other HEI staff had authority to agree to his requests and thus, the court gave judgment in his favour and he got his degree.

– In *Butler v Louisiana State Board of Education*,[2] the HEI was held vicariously liable for the negligence of a professor's supervision of a biology experiment.

– Moreover, the HEI may even pick up liability for the negligence of a 'gratuitous employee', as in *Foster v Board of Trustees of Butler County Community College*.[3] Here, a Butler basketball coach asked a student to collect a potential recruit from the airport; the student's poor driving injured the hapless visitor and killed himself and a taxi driver; the student had no driving licence and was uninsured while driving his unregistered car. A jury awarded $2.26m against Butler College and the student's estate; the College appealed but the Appeal Court simply noted that the College could and should have discovered the student driver's 'unfitness for the task had any investigation been conducted', especially since the

---

1   273 NYS 2d 796, NY Sup Ct 1966.
2   331 So 2d 192, La 1976.
3   771 F Supp 1122, D Kan 1991.

College had a practice of requiring student drivers to be licensed which clearly had not been applied.

- *Mozart v State* [of New York][1] concerned the HEI's liability for the tortious acts in the student newspaper at SUNY-Brighampton (see Kaplin and Lee (1995a), pp 544–548, for full details of the case). Was the student organisation the agent of the HEI? If not, did the HEI nonetheless have a duty to control the editing of the newspaper? The court answered both questions in the negative: the HEI did not have enough control to say it was a principal–agent relationship; and, anyway, the students were old enough not to need HEI control. Thus, those libelled got no damages: the 'deep pocket' of the HEI was closed to them and the student editors were 'men of straw' financially.

- In *Linkage Corporation v Trustees of Boston University*,[2] the court ruled that the University's vice-president for external programmes did indeed have apparent authority to renew a training contract with Linkage, and hence the latter was awarded $5.7m for the University's subsequent breach of contract when Boston University refused to recognise the contract. The University had tried to argue that only the *senior* vice-president could agree contracts over $5m: the court was not persuaded. Moreover, the court regarded the University as effectively having ratified the contract on the basis of 'informal acquiescence' in that it had not immediately refused to recognise the contract.

- In contrast, in *FDIC v Providence College*,[3] the court ruled that FDIC, as a bank providing two loans to a construction company, should have checked that the Trustees of Providence College had really authorised both its vice-president for business affairs and its director of physical plant to authorise the College to act as guarantor of these loans which, at more than $1m, exceeded the University's entire endowment.

- Again, in *Johns Hopkins University v Ritter*,[4] the court found it unreasonable of Professors Ritter and Snider to assume that a mere departmental chair really had authority to promise them tenure when he recruited them from tenured positions they already held elsewhere (Cornell and Duke Universities).

- At present, some New York restaurants are suing Columbia University because one of its academics, in the name of research, despatched 240 letters on University stationery complaining that he suffered food poisoning after eating at the restaurant.

5.22 A case closer to home is *Malcolm v Chancellor, Masters and Scholars of the University of Oxford (t/a Oxford University Press)*.[5] According to Mr

---

1   441 NYS 2d 600, NY Ct Cl 1981.
2   679 NE 2d 191, Mass 1997.
3   115 F 3d 136, 2d Cir 1997.
4   689 A 2d 91, Ct App Md 1996.
5   [1994] EMLR 17, CA; and see the understandably one-sided and polemical account by the plaintiff in *The Remedy*, privately published in 1999 by AKME Publications, 7 Southover Street, Brighton, BN2 2AU. The matter still rumbles on with Mr Malcolm recently trying (unsuccessfully) to get the High Court to enforce 'the gagging clause' contained in his 1991 settlement with the University (*The Times Higher Educational Supplement*, 22 February 2002, p 6).

Malcolm (pp 90–91), the University at one point attempted to argue that the actions of a commissioning editor at its OUP, a department of the University, were not its responsibility if he did not have formal higher approval to issue a contract to publish Mr Malcolm's proposed book, *Making Names*. The University supposedly then changed its approach, presumably soon after becoming acquainted with the basic principles of agency and vicarious liability (as, in fact, so clearly and authoritatively explained in such legal texts as Beatson (1998) covering contract/agency and Markesinis and Deakin (1999) covering tort/vicarious liability, and as indeed published by OUP itself!). The *Malcolm* case is more relevant, however, to the issue of certainty of agreement in a contract, to the calculation of damages for the loss of opportunity to enhance reputation by publishing a book, and to the question of specific performance as a remedy (ie the court would not order OUP to publish Mr Malcolm's book, since it could not closely supervise/enforce the co-operative working relationship needed between publisher and author), all as cited in Treitel.[1]

5.23 So, the *agent* acts and contracts on behalf of the *principal* – the HEI officer, employee or committee acting for the HEI as a corporation. The agent will usually be acting with *actual authority*, probably *express* and, in the case of an HEI, delegated. Sometimes authority will be *implied*, in that the agent will be tasked with doing something which inevitably requires a contract to be made. The difficult area is *apparent or ostensible authority*, where the third party reasonably believes, and relies on the belief, that the agent really has authority to act for the principal, because of the agent's job title, uniform, presence on the premises, the history of dealings between the third party and the agent as an employee, etc. Thus, as in the examples cited above, the external supplier should not reasonably have expected a professor to be ordering chips, but the student may well reasonably expect a lecturer to have authority to approve academic arrangements (unless the HEI has made it very clear to all students that only the Dean can do so) and a company may reasonably think that an academic can agree a research contract on behalf of his HEI: therefore, the HEI is bound by a contract about which it knew nothing in the last two instances.

5.24 The law of agency can operate, within a company structure, to bind the company where an innocent third party has dealt in good faith with a company officer or employee who, *reasonably* to the third party, appears to have authority to take a decision or place an order on behalf of the company (see Davies (1997), pp 224–228, Birks (2000), pp 168–170 of volume I and Ferran (1999), pp 101–111. The Companies Act 1989 now also gives greater protection to a third party when dealing in good faith with the Board of Directors itself or with somebody properly authorised by the Board to act on its behalf, where the hapless third party could have been caught by the old concepts of *ultra vires* and constructive notice (Davies (1997), chapter 10; Ferran (1999), pp 85–100). The general operation of the law of agency may

---

1   (1999), pp 47, 49, 52, 53, 923 and 960.

also be affected in the case of a company, to the potential benefit of the third party, by the rule in *Royal British Bank v Turquand*.[1]

5.25   Agency clearly overlaps with the concept that an employer is vicariously liable for the actions of employees, usually where the employee's actions lead to the injury of a third party. The employer may well also be personally liable for the wrong/tort, and the injured party can sue both employer and employee: in practice, the employer, or its insurers, will be the 'deep pocket' worth targeting. The employer may try to argue that the employee, in doing whatever led to the accident, loss or damage, was at that point 'not acting in the course of his/her employment' but was on 'a frolic of his/her own'. The employer would have to show that the employee was undertaking a task which clearly he or she had no authority to tackle, or that the employee was carrying out an authorised function, either in a way already expressly forbidden or in such a bizarre and dangerous way that no reasonably careful employer could have predicted an employee would behave like that (this latter line can be especially difficult to prove). An employer will not be responsible for an employee's act if it clearly has nothing to do with the job, even if the incident occurs at work and involves the employer's equipment – especially if the act is, say, an assault or theft: but note that in *Lister and Others v Hesley Hall Ltd*,[2] the sexual abuse of pupils on the premises by the warden of a boarding school provided a sufficiently 'close connection' between the tort and the employment for the House of Lords to hold the employer liable. In effect, *Lister* takes the test used to determine vicarious liability closer to the approach taken in discrimination cases (as in *Jones v Tower Boot Co Ltd*,[3] where Mr Jones had suffered serious verbal and physical racial harassment by work-mates 'in the course of employment'). If the employer is successfully sued by the third party and held vicariously liable, the employee, in theory, can then be sued by the employer in an attempt to recover some or all of the damages it has paid out: in practice, this rarely happens.

5.26   The issue of vicarious liability and the potential defence of the employee being 'on a frolic of his own' apply to the case of the US Government suing Harvard University for $120m.[4] It is alleged that two Harvard employees used for personal gain a development programme in Russia backed by the US Government. Harvard is reported as saying: '... no-one in a position of responsibility at the University had any knowledge of these alleged actions by the two individuals' (but should the University have monitored its staff more closely?)

5.27   In summary, the guidance Kaplin and Lee (1995a) provide for US HE managers applies equally to their UK counterparts concerning authority, delegation and agency:

---

1   (1856) 6 E&B 327, 119 ER 886, Exch Ch: see Davies (1997), pp 221–223, and Ferran (1999), p 98.
2   [2001] UKHL 22, [2001] 2 WLR 1311, *Education Law Journal* 2(3), pp 158–161.
3   [1997] 2 All ER 406, CA.
4   *The Times Higher Educational Supplement*, 6 October 2000, p 11.

(a) 'Trustees, officers, and administrators of post-secondary institutions – public or private – can take only those actions and make only those decisions that they have authority to take or make. Acting or deciding without authority to do so can have legal consequences, both for the responsible individual and for the institution. It is thus critical, from a legal standpoint, for administrators to understand and adhere to the scope and limits of their authority and that of other institutional functionaries with whom they deal. Such sensitivity to authority questions will also normally be good administrative practice, since it can contribute order and structure to institutional governance and make the governance system more understandable, accessible, and accountable to those who deal with it' (p 76).

(b) 'Miscalculations of the institution's authority, or the authority of particular officers or employees, can have various adverse legal consequences. For public institutions, unauthorised acts may be invalidated in courts or administrative agencies under the ultra vires doctrine of administrative law (a doctrine applied to acts that are beyond the delegated authority of a public body or official). For private institutions, a similar result occasionally can be reached under corporation law' (p 79).

(c) 'Similarly, administrators should understand the scope of their own authority and that of the officers, employees, and organisations with whom they deal. They should understand where their authority comes from and which higher-level administrators may review or modify their acts and decisions. They should attempt to resolve unnecessary gaps or ambiguities in their authority. They should consider what part of their authority may and should be sub-delegated to lower-level administrators or faculty and what checks or limitations should be placed on those delegations. And they should attempt to ensure that their authority is adequately understood by the members of the campus community with whom they deal' (p 80).

(d) 'Even when an institutional officer or administrator acts beyond the scope of his delegated power, so that the act is unauthorised, the board of trustees [governors, council] may subsequently "ratify" the act if that act was within the scope of the board's own authority. "Ratification" converts the initially unauthorised act into an authorised act' (p 88), and 'Even where an officer or administrator acts without authority and a higher officer or administrator or the board of trustees had not ratified the act, a court will occasionally estop the institution from denying the validity of the act. Under this doctrine of estoppel, courts may – in order to prevent injustice to persons who had justifiably relied on an authorised act – treat the unauthorised act as if it had been authorised' (p 89).

Cambridge and 'CAPSA': Another cautionary example

5.28   The recent governance and management problems experienced by the University of Cambridge when developing a major new financial/management accounting IT system ('CAPSA') well illustrate these issues of authority and delegation.

–   Which University committee(s) and/or officer(s) had the appropriate authority to initiate CAPSA?
–   To which other committee(s) and/or officer(s) and/or employee(s) was authority delegated for development and implementation of the project?
–   Who was meant to report to whom and who was supposed to monitor whom?
–   How could some £9m be spent and CAPSA still not be working?

See Palfreyman (forthcoming) for further discussion and for references to the impressive, incisive and interesting investigations instituted by Cambridge and undertaken by Professors Finkelstein and Shattock, whose Reports Cambridge bravely placed firmly in the public domain by posting them on its *Cambridge Reporter* (2 November, 2001; no 5861) website at www.admin.cam.ac.uk/reporter/2000-01/weekly/5861. Cambridge is not the first (for example, DHSS, DVLC, NHS) major organisation, and nor will it be the last, to find itself hugely embarrassed by an IT disaster, but it is perhaps unique in so openly (and willingly?) washing its dirty linen. It remains to be seen whether the concept of personal liability, as discussed in Chapters 3 and 4, will come into play in relation to clear weaknesses in the governance structure and in the management hierarchy at Cambridge (perhaps most notably in Cambridge allegedly neglecting to act on the warnings flagged *over several years* by *both* its internal *and* external auditors). Assuming CAPSA eventually works out at a final cost of, say, some £10m, and that, even if all had gone well, Cambridge would anyway have spent around £7m for a decent system, the £2m–£3m losses (plus legal costs) *might* be recovered from the directors' and officers' liability insurance cover which the members of the Cambridge council *should* have in place according to the advice given in CUC (originally 1994, now in a 2001 edn).

5.29   Yet, as also discussed in Chapters 3 and 4, just how competent and vigilant, pro-active and assertive should governors/members of council be in order to discharge their duty of skill and care towards the corporation: is it the high standard of the reasonably prudent and effective charity trustee (Chapter 4) or the less demanding expectations of the reasonably diligent company director (Chapter 15)? Is running the modern HEI closer to managing a business than governing a charity? As noted earlier, the US HEI is deemed to be more a business, but then the question would still remain as to whether the reasonably competent businessman could mess up an IT project as Cambridge did. If the Cambridge members of council and the key University Officers are to be judged by the fiduciary standards displayed by the boards of Barings, Equitable Life, Enron, Marconi and Independent Insurance (or indeed by, say, the incompetence displayed by Ministers and Government officials in handling BSE or FMD), then perhaps they will readily, fairly and easily escape personal liability.

5.30 All this assumes, of course, that there is anybody 'policing' Cambridge so as to even commence legal proceedings, given that clearly 'the corporation' itself as an artificial person needs to act through a natural person. Cambridge, as a civil corporation, does not have a Visitor, and hence in charity law terms the 'enforcer' would have to be the Attorney-General given also that the University is an exempt charity and so is beyond the reach of the Charity Commissioners' investigatory powers. Nor is the University a company and hence there are no shareholders or Companies House investigators to enforce the application of company law. The writ of the NAO and the PAC arguably applies only insofar as any of the seemingly wasted £2m–£3m can be shown to be public money as opposed to Cambridge's own corporate assets (which, since, as already noted, the University is a civil rather than an eleemosynary corporation, *may* not necessarily be charitable assets and hence within the remit of the Attorney-General as *parens patriae* and under the supervision of the High Court). That leaves the general law of corporations and one or more members of the council (or indeed of the University) attempting to 'defend' the interests of the corporation against the alleged mismanagement of the corporation's governors and officers. Given these difficulties concerning who has the necessary *locus* (and indeed incentive, stamina, or even money!) to commence legal proceedings, and let alone the problem of determining the objective standard of skill and diligence applicable and then proving negligence in meeting the required duty of care, it can pretty safely be predicted that, apart from the potential for a further wave of embarrassment if the NAO and PAC get involved, the Cambridge University CAPSA saga will not lead to any legal action to recover the losses to the corporation (even if, thanks to Cambridge's transparency in handling the matter, valuable lessons at least will have been learnt for the whole UK HE System: the Finkelstein and Shattock Reports will be required reading for all HEI managers for years to come).

Part 3

THE HIGHER EDUCATION INSTITUTION AND ITS STAFF AND STUDENTS

Chapter 6

THE HIGHER EDUCATION INSTITUTION–STUDENT CONTRACT

Nicola Hart, Joanna Forbes and Smita Jamdar (Martineau Johnson)

EDITORS' INTRODUCTION

§6.1   Within the HEI environment, the area which provides perhaps the greatest potential for legal confrontation is the relationship between the HEI and its students or potential students (applicants). This is not surprising since there are many students, who, as they are paying more and more towards their education, are likely, especially in an age of consumerism, to become increasingly demanding of 'value-for-money' and to resort to law if they feel thwarted: the undergraduate of yesteryear becomes 'the empowered consumer' of tomorrow. Could this be why, as the Oxford Proctor is quoted in Chapter 1, the majority of complaints originate from dissatisfied overseas students (they are likely to have paid out more of their own money than home students largely funded by the UK taxpayer, whose fees are lower anyway). Indeed, another factor might be the increasing maturity of the average student: a report[1] noted that nearly half of US college students are over 24, up from fewer than one-third in the 1970s – a trend which is 'changing the face of many campuses'. A US commentator is quoted as having remarked: 'This is a different population from your passive 18-year-old who comes in and is more accepting and less demanding' (the same process, of course, is happening in the UK). This chapter, closely linked to Chapters 7–10 and to 29 and 30, explores the HEI–student contractual relationship; while this (inevitably lengthy) Editors' Introduction also covers the HEI–student legal relationship in relation to tort (physical injury and educational malpractice).

The education experience

§6.2   Student–HEI confrontation used to be mainly in the context of discipline, especially in the late-1960s and early 1970s. Now it is about the appropriateness of 'the educational experience'. Can there be clear norms of what the reasonable HEI should supply by way of 'the educational experience' to the reasonable student? What is 'a reasonable student'? What happens if 'the product' falls below these normal standards, or the ones explicitly set by the HEI? What must the student do to prove that there is a duty of care in tort, or a contractual obligation to provide a reasonable educational package? How does the student show that the package is inadequate? Even if these two legal hurdles are overcome, what can be demonstrated as the damage suffered by the student? And, if there is damage, how can compensation be calculated? In short, will we see develop the concept of 'academic negligence' or

---

1   *The Times Higher Educational Supplement*, 31 May 1996.

'educational malpractice', as we have seen the evolution of medical negligence in recent decades? To what extent can the HEI rely on hiding behind the protective veil of expert academic judgement, whereby, providing there is no obvious neglect of the HEI's procedures, or of the basic rules of natural justice/due process, the court will not peer behind the veil to ask whether the academics were competent as examiners or teachers, or, in the case of applicants, in terms of how they decided to whom to offer places and whom to reject? How wide a definition of 'the educational experience' might the courts set? Is pastoral care covered? Should the HEI be expected to sort out personal problems amongst its students? Has it a greater duty of care while the student is under 18 (as a few might be, and as most applicants are)? If the 17-year-old applicants drink to excess in a campus bar when attending for interview, is the HEI liable if one chokes on his vomit during the night?

§6.3   Not even US courts assume that an HEI has an all-encompassing duty to supervise adult students in their private activities, as opposed to official organised games, field trips, laboratory practicals, etc. Kaplin and Lee (1995a) quote a case where 'the court held that the university's *power* to regulate student conduct on campus did not give rise to a *duty* to regulate student conduct on campus or to monitor the conduct of every student on campus . . . no duty to supervise social activity was found'.[1] However, perhaps where known risky fraternity rituals routinely take place the HEI should take steps to enforce its rules:

> 'The court determined that the university's own policy against hazing [apparently US students like to set each other on fire as some kind of male bonding rite!], and its repeated warnings to students against the hazards of hazing, "constituted an assumed duty" . . . amounted to an undertaking by the university to protect students from the dangers related to hazing, and created a duty to do so.'

§6.4   The Kaplin and Lee (2000) Supplement[2] notes that (bizarrely) hazing continues to be a major social problem at some US HEIs, in much the same way that excessively cruel bullying was part of the culture at the early nineteenth-century English public school (see Rutledge (1998)). They cite a case showing that the HEI gets into difficulty when a track record of incidents builds up, and especially once it tries (and usually fails) to regulate the conduct of student organisations such as the Greek fraternities (the sororities appear to be able to behave in a more civilised fashion): *Morrison v Kappa Alpha Psi Fraternity*[3] – involving damages of $312,000 to Mr Morrison; and *Knoll v Board of Regents of the University of Nebraska*[4] – involving abduction and injury. That said, in general terms the HEI is *not* usually liable for the drunken antics of its students in their private societies: *Lloyd v Alpha Phi Alpha and Cornell University*,[5] and *Rothbard v Colgate University*.[6]

§6.5   In general, however, the student doing stupid things, if aged 18 or over, will be assumed to appreciate the risks and the HEI is clear of liability (no longer being *in loco parentis*). In this way, an HEI cannot and has no strict duty to

---

1   At p 97, emphasis added.
2   At pp 59, 354–355, 360–370.
3   738 So 2d 1105, La Ct App 1999.
4   601 NW 2d 757, 1999.
5   1999 US Dist LEXIS 906, NDNY 26 January 1999.
6   652 NYS 2d 146, NY App Dist 1997.

protect students from the consequences of heavy drinking: 'The prevalence of alcohol consumption on the modern college campus would make compliance with such a duty almost impossible' (Kaplin and Lee (1995a), p 109). In 1997, there were three alcohol-related student deaths on two US campuses, while in 1996, eight members of one fraternity were charged with manslaughter in an alcohol poisoning case. Yet an HEI needs to be careful not to give itself a duty by virtue of making drinking 'a big issue' so that it seems that the HEI is assuming control. Indeed, a US case, *Hegel v Langsam*,[1] is noted with approval in a standard English law textbook, *Winfield and Jolowicz on Tort*[2] as confirming: 'A University incurs no liability for failing to control the private lives of its students, allowing them to be seduced, become associated with criminals, or become drug addicts'. Similarly, Kaplin and Lee (2000), pp 57–58 cite a case which found no duty on the HEI to prevent its adult students sledging in the snow.[3]

Protecting the HEI

§6.6   What can the HEI do to protect itself? Should its Regulations be as detailed as possible to legislate for anything and everything, or should they be general so as not to create hostages to fortune? What should be the procedure for dealing with student complaints, especially if the student starts to talk of going to law? There is no underestimating the management time likely to be taken up by such a case, and the potential cost not only in working through internal procedures but also of any court actions (especially if the complainant gets public funding). One case reported in 1996[4] had been dragging on since 1993, involved a claim for the refund of overseas fees amounting to £20,000, and had led to the NUS Scotland commenting: 'We do not believe the present procedure [at university X] constitutes an appeals procedure ... It does not conform to natural justice [in not allowing the appellant to appear in person before the Appeals Board]'. An article,[5] 'Complaints cost hard cash', referred to 'a rising tide of student complaints', dealing with which 'can cost an institution up to £50,000 a year', and to a report of the Higher Education Quality Council (HEQC) prepared by D Farrington which noted that many universities had no formal complaints procedure. Articles on the same page described an 8-year Visitor case at Birmingham University, and a threat of legal action from students at Westminster University over alleged course disruption caused by building work (the students were seeking public funding to sue for loss of earnings from part-time jobs which they would have taken but for needing to do extra academic work).

§6.7   Dearing (1997) largely echoes the report from the Nolan Committee on Standards in Public Life which recommended that: 'Students in higher education institutions should be able to appeal to an independent body, and this right should be reflected in the Higher Education Charters. The higher education funding councils, institutions, and representative bodies should consult on a system of independent review of disputes'.

---

1   [1971] 29 Ohio Misc 147, 237 NE 2d 351, 55 Ohio 2d 476.
2   (1994), p 103.
3   *Pitre v Louisiana Tech University* 655 So 2d 659, La Ct App 1995; *reversed* 673 So 2d 585, La 1996; see also *Apfel v Huddleston* 50 F Supp 2d 1129, D Utah 1999, concerning drunkenness at student society events.
4   *The Times Higher Educational Supplement*, 31 May 1996.
5   Ibid, 12 July 1996.

§6.8   It is not yet clear whether this simply means extending the Visitor chartered university model to all HEIs, or an enhanced version of the Visitor model, or binding arbitration, or an Ombudsman for each HEI, or even a completely new appeals quango of some kind for the whole HE system. (See also Chapters 8 and 9; and in Chapter 30 especially the section on 'The Visitor post-Nolan'; plus Farrington (1997) and CVCP (1997).)

§6.9   Yet it is not all a matter of the hapless student needing the protection of the law against the HEI which has the contractual advantage: a significant number of students seem to be in blatant breach of the HEI–student contract to educate (doubtless for what they and the NUS would see as good reasons – mainly, and allegedly, student poverty) in that, as the academic year ends, they have still not paid their academic tuition fees, while strangely their HEIs in several cases appear only rather belatedly to be trying to do something about it. It is difficult to think of any other area of life where 'the supplier' would (or indeed could in cash-flow terms) tolerate such mass refusal by 'the purchaser' to pay for 'the service'. Thus, it was reported[1] that bad debtors at Coventry amount to 600, at Luton 200, at UCE 200, and at Sheffield Hallam over 1000. Judging by the article's headline (*Indebted students lambast penalties*), at least some of these students expect not to have to pay.

The US perspective

§6.10   Kaplin and Lee in the 3rd edn (1995a) of *The Law of Higher Education* in the USA devote over 250 pages (one-quarter of the volume) to 'The college and the students' (see also Kaplin and Lee (2000), Part IV). They trace the evolution of the student as a person with enforceable Federal, State and contractual rights, rather than being on the receiving end of *in loco parentis* and the 'privilege' of being admitted to membership of the groves of academe. Even so, on the whole, 'courts have applied the contract theory to postsecondary institutions in a deferential manner ... Nor have institutions been subject to the rigours of contract law as it applies in the commercial world' (Kaplin and Lee (1995a), p 374; see also NACUA (1989)). Thus, HE used to be seen as:

> 'a unique enterprise that could regulate itself through reliance on tradition and consensual agreement ... The judiciary also was deferential to higher education ... courts accepted the proposition that attendance at a public postsecondary institution was a privilege and not a right ... The institution was given virtually unlimited power to dictate the contract terms, and the contract, once made, was construed heavily in the institution's favour' (Kaplin and Lee (1995a), p 374).

§6.11   All this has changed as the HE system, post-World War II, has moved from elite to mass in the USA (and, much more recently, in the UK). The new players in the game were not necessarily prepared to accept the cosy old rules: 'The notion that attendance was a privilege served as an irrelevant nicety in an increasingly credentialised society. To many students, higher education became an economic professional necessity ... One major trend is student (or educational) consumerism' (Kaplin and Lee (1995a), p 217). In the USA, students have sued after being 'accused' of plagiarism, after being barred from the campus computer network, after being dropped from sports teams,

---

1   *The Times Higher Educational Supplement*, 25 May 2001. Perhaps student debtors need to note the recent launch of the 'cyber court' where the HEI could sue, quickly and cheaply, on-line for unpaid fees (Money Claim Online, www.courtservice.gov.uk/mcol).

after suffering violence on campus as the result of alleged inadequate security, after being given low grades, and so on. Kaplin and Lee note that:

> 'Another potential source of tort liability, albeit a generally unsuccessful one for plaintiffs, is the doctrine of "educational malpractice" ... Although they often sympathise with students who claim that they have not learned what they should have learned, or that they, their professors, were negligent in teaching or supervising them, courts have been reluctant to create a course of action for educational malpractice ... The judge disagreed, ruling that the student was ultimately responsible for his academic success' (Kaplin and Lee (1995a), p 375).

§6.12 So, even in the USA, the land of the medical negligence suit and no win–no fee ambulance-chasing lawyers, the concept of 'educational malpractice' has not taken off. There is the difficulty of proving the damage (unlike, say, a patient with the wrong leg amputated as a result of medical negligence), let alone calculating the damages due: 'If I'd been allowed to get a First rather than a 2i, I'd be a rich City lawyer and not a poor university administrator ...'; or perhaps it should be, 'If I'd been allowed to get a Third rather than a First, I'd now be a Merchant Banker and not a University Professor ...'. The Kaplin and Lee 2000 Supplement, pp 67–69 stresses that students attempting educational malpractice claims continue to face the same 'judicial hostility' set by *Ross v Creighton University*,[1] citing the recent cases of:

– *Tolman v CenCor Career Colleges, Inc;*[2]
– *Ansari v New York University;*[3]
– *Andre v Pace University;*[4]
– *Sirohi v Lee.*[5]

§6.13 In terms of case-law, the latest cases emphasising the contractual nature of the HEI–student legal relationship are, in the USA, *Swartley v Hoffner*[6] and, in England, *Clark v University of Lincolnshire and Humberside.*[7] Kaplin and Lee (2000), p 229 conclude that the US courts are 'increasingly willing to hold colleges to express or implied promises to students under certain circumstances'. They will, for example, hold the student handbook to be contractually binding,[8] but also they continue to fight shy of second-guessing academic judgement. In *Mittra v University of Medicine and Dentistry of New Jersey,*[9] the court commented that 'Rigid application of contract principles to controversies concerning student academic performance would tend to intrude upon academic freedom and to generate precisely the kind of disputes that the courts should be hesitant to resolve'. Similarly, US students

---

1   957 2d 410, 7th Cir 1992.
2   851 P 2d 203, Cols App Ct 1992; *affirmed* 868 P 2d 396, Cols 1994.
3   1997 US Dist LEX15 6863, SDNY 1997.
4   618 NYS 2d 975, City Ct Yonkers 1994; *reversed* 655 NYS 2d 777, NY App Div 1996 – NB here the court specifically rejected educational malpractice 'as a matter of public policy'.
5   634 NYS 2d 119, Sup A Ct App Div 1995, re Columbia University.
6   734 A 2d 915, Pa Super 1999.
7   [2000] 3 All ER 752, CA. As cited in *Halsbury's Laws of England*, vol 15(2) on 'Education' (2001 reissue), para 838: 'it is now accepted that a student starts in a contractual relationship with a university whatever the nature [chartered or statutory 'old' or 'new'] of the institution he attends'.
8   *Fellheimer v Middlebury College* 869 F Supp 238, D Vt 1994.
9   719 A 2d 693, NJ Ct App 1998.

stand little chance of success in challenging their grades,[1] *unless* the HEI and/or its academic(s) have behaved in an arbitrary and capricious way in reaching the assessment.[2] In *Sylvester*, the court commented: 'While it is true that the assignment of a test grade is a purely academic evaluation, Sylvester is entitled to due process in that evaluation ... Between active manipulation and sullen intransigence, the faculty, embodying arbitrary government, have mistreated a student confided to their charge ...'.

§6.14 Much of the litigation focuses on the HEI's reservation (by way of using disclaimers) of the right to change course structures and the aggrieved student's attempt to 'get what he thought he signed up for'. As Kaplin and Lee state:[3]

> 'The contract theory is still developing. Debate continues on issues such as the process for identifying the terms and conditions of the student–institution contract, the extent to which the school catalogue [prospectus] constitutes part of the contract, and the extent to which the institution retains implied or inherent authority not expressed in any written regulation or policy.'

§6.15 There are aspects of 'unconscionable' (unduly harsh) contracts clearly unfair to the student, and 'contracts of adhesion' (take it or leave it) weighted in favour of the HEI. The moral is that:[4]

> 'administrators should be sensitive to the language used in all institutional rules and policies affecting students. Language suggestive of a commitment (or promise) to students should be used only when the institution is prepared to live up to its commitment ... should consider the adoption of an official policy, perhaps even a "code of good practice", or fair dealing with students.'

§6.16 Kaplin and Lee argue that: 'The judicial trend suggests that most rules and regulations will be upheld ... ', providing they are not arbitrary and capricious, they are reasonable, they are clear, and there is no malice or bad faith in their application in the case of student X. Even fewer legal constraints:[5]

> 'pertain to an institution's application of academic standards to students than to its application of behavioural standards. Courts are more deferential to academia when evaluation of academic work is the issue, believing that such evaluation resides in the expertise of the faculty rather than the court.'

§6.17 Thus, the US courts will not readily lift the veil of expert, academic judgement: 'The courts are not equipped to review academic records based upon academic standards within the particular knowledge, experience, and expertise of academicians' (from a 1975 case, Kaplin and Lee (1995a), p 467); 'Courts are particularly ill equipped to evaluate academic performance' (a 1978 case, Kaplin and Lee (1995a), p 467); 'judicial review of grading disputes would inappropriately involve the courts in the very core of academic and education decision making ... in the absence of demonstrated bad faith,

---

1   *Frabotta v Meridia Huron Hospital School* 657 NE 2d 816, Ohio Ct App 1995; *Altschuler v University of Pennsylvania Law School* 1997 US Dist LEXIS 3248, SDNY 21 March 1997; *affirmed* 201 F 3d 430, 3d Cir 1999.
2   *Sylvester v Texas Southern University* 957 F Supp 944, SD Tex 1997.
3   (1995a), p 375.
4   Ibid, pp 76–337.
5   Ibid, p 465.

arbitrariness, capriciousness, irrationality or a constitutional or statutory violation, a student's challenge ... is beyond the scope of judicial review' (a 1990 case, Kaplin and Lee (1995a), p 474). (Indeed, a 1997 English case follows this line, the court in *Thirunayagam v London Guildhall University*[1] refusing to supply the aggrieved student with an injunction instructing the University to award him a first class degree in law.) But an HEI must stick to the rules. One HEI in the USA lost a 1989 case for failing a student nurse who was deemed too fat to be an effective nurse, rather than being unable to pass the academic content of the exams.

§6.18   On the admissions process, Kaplin and Lee note that the benefit of the doubt also lies with the HEI, the applicant having to demonstrate that the HEI had been 'arbitrary and capricious' in decision-taking over his application – 'a formidable barrier for disappointed applicants to cross' (Kaplin and Lee (1995a), p 379). The HEI must, however, abide by any legislation concerning discrimination on grounds of race, age, sex, disability, and it must honour its published admission/selection criteria. Once an offer has been made and accepted, the HEI must honour the admission contract and have available the promised course for when the student arrives.

§6.19   As for the even wider duty of care, a recent US Federal Law (1990 and 1992) requires HEIs to provide data on the numbers and types of crime on and near the campus, especially in relation to sex offences. Such legislation was a response to the increasingly violent nature of US HEIs, not least arising from 'acquaintance rape' ('date rape' as it is also known) among students. Clearly, the collection and publication of such data puts the HEI on notice as to its security problems, and it then risks incurring liability if it fails to provide *reasonable* security measures and does not give 'timely warning' to its employees and students of growing security problems. But, as stated earlier, at least the HEI's duty of care does not, usually, extend to monitoring the student every hour of the day – they *are* adults.

Closer to home

§6.20   In *Tuttle v Edinburgh University*,[2] a student successfully sued his HEI for over £110,000 in relation to an accident when on a field-trip, whereby the University was negligent in not properly preparing its students for tree-climbing when specimen collecting. A St Andrew's University US student is currently suing the HEI for alleged negligence in not advising her that there was a high incidence of rape in Odessa where she was sent on a 'year-abroad' during her languages degree.[3] Her case is ongoing and she is seeking £100K in damages. Her then boyfriend, who was beaten up in the attack, is seeking £50K. St Andrew's no longer despatches its students to Odessa, but will be putting forward 'a robust defence'. According to another article:[4]

> 'A spate of high-profile expedition disasters has unleashed a wave of role-tightening across campuses and is endangering the future of a brave tradition ... These disasters highlight the fact that blame, and possibly litigation, may fall on a university if its name is associated with a botched expedition. A student at Queen's University in Belfast had an accident while

---

1   (1997) unreported, 14 March, CA (but see *Education Law Monitor* 4(8), August 1997).
2   1984 SLT 172.
3   *The Scotsman*, 9 October 1998; *Scotland on Sunday*, 4 October 1998 and *The Times*, 4 June 2001 and 15 October 2001. (See also Harbrugh and Britke (1998); Hoye (1999)).
4   *The Times Higher Educational Supplement*, 27 June 1999, 'Ill-starred treks'.

on a field trip a few years ago and sued the university, leading to an out-of-court settlement.'

§6.21   The issue is, of course, the duty of care by the HEI to its students, not just in relation to formal field-trips as part of the course but perhaps even to 'blessing' in some way a student organised and led expedition. That said, not even the victim-friendly US courts expect the HEI to be responsible for the quality of medical treatment received by a student on an overseas programme.[1] On the matter of student sport there is potential liability for the HEI if it is in breach of its duty of care to ensure that student sport is organised with safety in clear focus. There is a statutory (Health and Safety at Work etc Act 1974 (HSWA 1974) and Regulations, plus possibly the Occupiers' Liability Act 1984 (OLA 1984)) and common-law (the rules relating to negligence) matrix of responsibility falling upon the HEI to do all that is 'reasonably practicable' to put in place safe procedures and practices which are known about and used. It concentrates the mind to recall that health and safety legislation can bring criminal penalties to bear on individuals who have neglected safety issues, but that proposals concerning 'corporate killing' will make such prosecutions both easier and more likely (see Chapter 20). See the CVCP 1996 Report on *Sport in Higher Education* and also *Smoldon v Whitworth,*[2] concerning a 17-year-old seriously injured in a rugby scrum collapse and the negligence of the referee in failing to control the game: in an HEI context the referee might be a member of staff from the HEI's sports centre for whose negligence the HEI would be vicariously liable (although in *Smolden v Whitworth* it was of significance that the paralysed player was under 18 and it was a 'juniors' match). The case of *Watson v British Boxing Board of Control Ltd and Another*[3] illustrates how the boundary of tort can suddenly expand, when a brain-damaged boxer successfully sued the sport's governing body for not providing adequate ringside resuscitation arrangements. The Board had inadvertently assumed a duty of care towards its boxers by not merely *advising*, but *requiring*, a certain level of medical cover. Clearly, however, that level of cover was not sufficiently comprehensive to fulfil the responsibility it had taken upon itself. That said, student societies, *not* organised by and *not* involving HEI staff, are *probably not* the responsibility of the HEI, *unless* it steps in and begins to assume responsibility. Moreover, the student playing rugby or rowing assumes voluntarily a certain degree of risk of adult injury inherent in the sport: this is the line taken in a case cited by Kaplin and Lee (2000), pp 400/401, *Reagan v State,*[4] which concerned a broken neck in rugby.

§6.22   That said, the HEI *might* assume a duty of care by its employees intervening negligently to take responsibility for a very drunk student whom they fail to put in the recovery position and check frequently with the result that he inhales vomit and is brain-damaged: much as in *Barrett v Ministry of Defence,*[5] where the HEI became the Army and student became 'squaddie'; or (somewhat oddly, and rather worryingly in terms of 'stretching' the boundaries of tort – Atiyah (1997) as in *Jebson v Ministry of Defence,*[6] where the Army

---

1   See, concerning a broken ankle in Austria, *McNeil v Wagner College* 667 NYS 2d 397, Sup Ct App Div 1998. (See also Hoye (1999), and, more generally on tort liability for US HEIs, Bickel and Lake (1997) and (1999).)
2   [1997] ELR 249.
3   [2001] QB 1134, CA.
4   654 NYS 2d 488, NY App Div 1997.
5   [1995] 1 WLR 1217, CA.
6   [2000] 1 WLR 2055, CA.

thoughtfully provided transport in connection with a social evening out for its soldiers but, having thereby inadvertently assumed or impliedly undertaken a duty of care, then neglected to discharge that duty by supervising the inevitably drunken and rowdy soldiers as they returned to base at the end of the evening in the open-back lorry (Mr Jebson tried to clamber on to the roof and fell out). Moreover, just as US HEIs must provide data on the amount and type of crime on and around the campus, so Davies (2000) muses over a potential new source of a tortious claim against the UK HEI now that applicants are asked on Universities Central Admissions Service (UCAS) forms to indicate any criminal record: what then is the risk of an HEI thus on notice of the existence of a criminal record not making appropriate further enquiries and discovering that the record is for rape, but simply going ahead and admitting the applicant who next ends up in the HEI's mixed-sex residential accommodation? In this way, the boundaries of tort potentially stretch (while only occasionally contracting), as already noted above in relation to *Smoldon* and *Watson*, plus *Barrett* and *Jebson*. Thankfully, it still remains fanciful, even as tort expands to accommodate employers' liability for work-based stress-related psychiatric injury following *Walker v Northumberland County Council*,[1] to imagine an HEI being liable for stress-induced mental trauma to students taking unseen-paper examinations.

§6.23   There is also the issue of references for students (and indeed for staff) in which there may be statements which are difficult to sustain: a 1996 House of Lords' judgment led to an out-of-court £25,000 settlement from the HEI to an ex-student for lost wages after her prospective employee cancelled a job offer on receipt of a reference referring to her 'personal attitude and emotional stability'. So, who owes what duty of care to whom when supplying a reference?

Educational malpractice

§6.24   In connection with student complaints and grievances, discussed also in Chapters 7 and 29, it is noted that, while in theory the aggrieved student can pursue an action in tort or for breach of contract, the tort of educational malpractice has gained virtually no recognition in the USA and is merely at the fledgling stage in England despite *Phelps v Hillingdon London Borough Council*.[2] The reality is that the student will be very hard-pressed to demonstrate that the HEI and/or its academic(s) have failed to deliver a reasonable standard of professional care in the delivery of teaching, let alone that any such failure has really caused academic under-performance which in turn has led to measurable damage that can be compensated for appropriately in cash: as McManus

---

1   [1995] 1 All ER 737, [1995] ELR 231, HL: Mr Walker won £175K in damages and the county council was left with legal costs estimated at £500K; since then other local government employees have clocked up £200K, £203K and, the record to date, £254K. That said, the Court of Appeal (*Sutherland v Hatton* [2002] EWCA 76 Civ) has recently, to a degree, turned back the legal clock reducing the onus on employers to detect stressed employees. However, at the same time the HSE has drafted *more* demanding standards of employer care in relation to assessing and auditing the risk of stress (see Edworthy (2000) and Spiers (2002) on stress management). Closer to home, *The Times Higher Educational Supplement*, 16 November 2001 reported that 'the Health and Safety Executive is investigating high levels of stress-related illness among staff at Wolverhampton University', allegedly the result of a 'bullying' style of management within the HEI; the same article recounts a tale of the Visitor (not the HSE!) at Nottingham University being petitioned by a member of staff alleging stress-related illness arising from management bullying.

2   [2000] 3 WLR 776.

(2000) comments on *Phelps,* 'generalised allegations of educational malpractice are not likely to be viewed sympathetically' (as opposed to cases
concerning special educational needs, which was essentially what *Phelps* was
about). That said, in recent years even lawyers have lost their traditional
immunity from the unhappy client bringing a legal action against them for
negligent professional work in court (*Arthur JS Hall & Co v Simmons;*[1] House of
Lords' decision overturning *Rondel v Worsley,*[2] leaving them in the same
position as any other profession: they can be sued for professional negligence
in any aspect of their work. Moreover, in *Copeland v Smith and Another,*[3] it was
made clear that the duty of care of advocates includes keeping professionally
up to date through both the general law reports and the specialist ones
relevant to his/her area of practice: by analogy, perhaps academics need to
keep their 'scholarship' (and reading lists) up to speed in order to be effective
lecturers.

§6.25   In considering a student allegation of a breach of duty of care the court must
judge the allegedly incompetent HEI/academic by the standard of the
reasonably competent HEI/academic[4] providing professional services in the
sense of *Hedley Byrne & Co v Heller & Partners,*[5] where a special relationship
exists between the professional (HEI and individual academics) and the
person advised/guided (the student). It should not, however, be too
deferential to 'the professionals' and should still ask awkward and searching
questions and decide for itself whether the professional's or expert witnesses'
opinion was indeed reasonable in that it was rational and logical.[6] That said,
the standard applicable can be at the *lowest* level of the range of reasonably
and acceptably competent HEIs/academics, as in *Michael Hyde & Associates
Ltd v JD Williams & Co Ltd.*[7] All of this makes the chance of a success in an
educational malpractice case very small, other than where the failure in
teaching has been blatant (for example, teaching the wrong syllabus, lectures
being repeatedly cancelled, incompetent adding up of marks for examinations, substantially and demonstrably under-resourced laboratory or library
facilities, etc). The *Guardian Education* (16 January 2001) reported on the use
of a much-corrected and untidily handwritten Finals' paper at Liverpool John
Moores University, asserting that this fiasco was the culmination of problems
throughout the particular degree course: the report, if accurate, and the
reasoning/teaching deficiencies cited, if possible, would probably amount to
a failure in the duty of care so blatant as to amount to educational malpractice.
Moreover, *Merrett v Babb*[8] stresses that, potentially, the professional
employee is *personally* liable where the employer has no professional
insurance cover and also has gone into liquidation leaving no assets from
which to pay a professional negligence award of damages (here Mr Babb, a
surveyor employed by the firm appointed by Mr Merrett to carry out a
mortgage valuation, was negligent in reporting on the property concerned).
Fortunately for academic professionals, HEIs, while not always having

1   [2000] 3 WLR 543, [2000] 3 All ER 673.
2   [1969] 1 AC 191, HL.
3   [2000] 1 All ER 457, CA.
4   *Bolam v Friern Barnet Hospital Management Committee* [1957] 1 WLR 582.
5   [1964] AC 465.
6   *Bolitho (Deceased) v City & Hackney Health Authority* [1997] 3 WLR 1151, HL, and as applied
        in *Wisniewski v Central Manchester Health Authority* [1998] PIQR P324, CA.
7   (2000) *The Times,* August 4, CA. For further discussion of the *Bolam/Bolitho* test see *Adams
        and Another v Rhymay Valley DC* [2000] 39 EG 144, CA.
8   [2001] EWCA Civ 214, [2001] 3 WLR 1, CA.

professional indemnity insurance as part of their risk management (see Chapter 24), at least do not (so far) go into liquidation – they are, therefore, around to be sued as the 'deep-pocket'.

§6.26 The student, as already noted, can pursue a claim in tort or in contract, selecting whichever best suits him/her.[1] The two alternative routes offer different assessment of damages and have different limitation periods during which a claim can be brought (Birks (2000), chapter 18 B 1 and 2). The first major educational malpractice legal action post-*Phelps*[2] seems to be Ms Norfolk suing Hurstpierpoint College for £150K (*sic*) to cover loss of earnings, damage to career prospects, and personal distress allegedly caused by the school's supposed negligence in teaching 'A' level Latin, arguing that the E grade in Latin will reduce her chances of one day being a well-paid corporate lawyer. The court will clearly have fun with causation and remoteness of damage, and with assessing the amount of compensation: what linkage between an E grade at Latin rather than an A or a B, and success at university followed by passing the Legal Practice Course, getting articles with a top-notch law firm, survival as a young lawyer, becoming a partner and earning very big money? How much for distress, anxiety and upset? All this assumes that a breach of duty of care can be proved. Did the whole 'A' level group in Latin fare badly while doing well in other subjects, leaving inadequate teaching as the only common theme? If so, was the standard of teaching really below that of a reasonably competent 'A' level Latin teacher? Since Ms Norfolk was at a private school and hence paying tuition fees, she could have selected breach of contract: but how clear are the contractual terms concerning the school's obligation to provide a certain level of teaching quality? It is unlikely that any school warrants an A or B in every subject and, anyway, a partial refund of the, say, £10K pa tuition fees for a couple of years in the sixth form amounts to a lot less than £150K.

§6.27 Moreover, there are precedents being set by HEIs in terms of making compensation payments, perhaps as 'goodwill gestures' rather than as a formal admission of either breach of contract or educational negligence: in 1998 Anglia Polytechnic University compensated students at its Business School with £100 each for 'unacceptable management' after they complained of botched restructuring within the School which led to timetabling chaos, poor teaching and poor conditions. Similarly, at two Canadian universities (Dalhousie and York) students have threatened legal action, seeking compensation as damages for breach of contract when lectures at classes were disrupted by striking academics. The Dalhousie SU president believed that this added pressure, both on the Dalhousie management and its academic staff union, had led to a speedy settlement of the dispute. We may well see more such 'class actions', where groups of students collectively threaten legal action – see Chapter 29 and Hodges (2001); there is now a niche London law firm ('Class Law') specialising in such multi-party actions.

§6.28 On professional negligence generally, and hence by analogy educational malpractice, see Elliott and Quinn (2001b), chapter 2; Birks (2000), chapter 14B–14D; and Markesinis and Deakin (1999), Part 2. On negligence in an HE context see Davies (1996) and Palfreyman (1999b); with Boyd (1998), chapter 12 and Hyams (1998), pp 491–494 and 537–538 on education

---

1   *Henderson v Merrett Syndicates Ltd* [1995] 2 AC 145, HL.
2   (2001) *Sunday Times*, October 7.

within schools. See Appendix 1 to this chapter for a listing of key cases in relation to the HEI–student contract. On the significance, or otherwise, of *Phelps* for the development of the fledging tort of educational malpractice, see McManus (2000) as already cited, along with, in contrast, Greenwold (2000), Meredith (2000) and Berman *et al* (2001). For further discussion of the HEI–student relationship, concentrating on contract (including consumer law) and tort (including educational malpractice), see Palfreyman (2002, forthcoming), which is to be available as an OxCHEPS Occasional Paper at www.new.ox.ac.uk/oxcheps.

So what's new?

§6.29   However, in case one should think stroppy students are only a recent creation, consider fourteenth-century Europe:[1]

> 'Many of the southern [European] students were recruited from wealthy backgrounds, and a good number were of noble origin. A sizeable proportion of them were in their twenties or even older, and some came straight to university from holding positions of responsibility in society. Students of this type had a more legalistic, contractual view of university life than was prevalent in England. In the southern environment, students were accustomed to regard the universities and lecturing staffs as agencies to be used and hired so as best to serve the students' own convenience and future professional interests. This kind of thinking would have struck few chords in the English students, who accepted their role as academic apprentices.'

§6.30   See Chapter 24 concerning risk management in relation to the student context. See also Appendix 2 to this chapter for a specimen 'Student Complaints Procedure' and also the section on 'Complaints' in Chapter 7.

SCOPE OF THIS CHAPTER

6.1   This chapter deals with the legal nature of the relationship between the HEI and the student. Whether the relationship is equivalent to such a contract in legal terms will be the first question. The chapter then analyses the nature of the relationship, the status of the two parties and their obligations towards each other, the ways in which the relationship is entered into and may be terminated, and what consequences follow if one of the parties thinks they have been wronged. It is also concerned with the roles of the courts and the Visitor (see Chapter 8), and the extent of the regulation of the relationship through consumer law (see Chapter 27). Some preventive and remedial suggestions are offered, aimed at protecting the interests of the HEI by discouraging claims and minimising their chances of success if made.

6.2   Students are encouraged in today's individualistic culture to view themselves as consumers of the HEI's educational services. They are armed with charters setting out what many see as their rights. There are more mature students than ever before. They are more likely than the traditional school-leaver to have a financial stake in their degree qualification, possibly having

---

1   Cobban (1988), p 21.

given up employment to take up an HEI course. Students come from a wider variety of cultural and racial backgrounds, bringing different expectations and perceptions of the educational experience. HEIs are keen to encourage the growth of the market for their services overseas. Promises made in the sales drive abroad may turn out not to be matched by the reality of the UK student experience. Moreover, there are simply more students. This on its own is likely to result in a rise in the number of claims and complaints. Students have always complained. There is a long history of their challenges before the courts and the Visitor in the reported case-law. While it is true that more have been imaginative than successful, dealing with those claims and complaints is a significant drain on resources for the HEIs facing them, in terms of both expense and management time. New types of challenge develop as our culture and society's expectations change. 'Educational negligence' is now a common phrase. There is increasing statutory regulation of relationships between institutions as businesses and individuals, for their protection as consumers or visitors to premises, or on grounds of their race, sex or disability. HEIs, as institutions with a public role, have had their share of cases resulting from the rise in popularity of judicial review of administrative decisions in the High Court (see Chapter 9). Perceived unfairness is less likely than ever to go untested.

IS THERE A CONTRACT?

6.3 It is now generally accepted that the relationship between the HEI and the student is based on a contract.[1] The debate on the subject arose out of the need to label the relationship in order to decide what were the mutual obligations of the parties, or whether there were any obligations. The difficulty of categorising the relationship arose partly from the fact that it is not documented as a contract in the conventional way (ie in a single form of agreement). Nevertheless, the contractual analysis is the one which seems most closely to match the reality of the relationship. It provides a structure appropriate to the obligations of each side. Historically, it has not been seen as necessary or appropriate to document the relationship explicitly as a legal contract, which would require identifying the parties, the length of time the contract will last and what each party was to gain from it and required to perform under it. These elements are, however, present in various forms in the documentation which passes between the two parties and makes up the contract, without explicitly stating that there is a contract.

More than one contract?

6.4 Farrington (1998) and others consider that there are two contracts: the contract for admission and the contract of matriculation. The former covers the stage from pre-entry agreement up to registration and the latter from the point

---

1   *Moran v University College, Salford (No 2)* [1994] ELR 187, CA.

of registration onwards, when the student enters and becomes part of the HEI community. The reason for considering there may be two contracts is perhaps because the courts have generally analysed the obligations arising in one or other of these two phases – not crossing the boundary between them.

6.5   There are clearly different obligations and types of obligation at each stage of the relationship, but that does not necessarily lead to the conclusion that there must be two contracts. It may be more helpful and practical to consider the relationship as taking the form of a rolling contract which matures and changes shape in the course of its life. This analysis has the advantage of making more sense of the early phases of the relationship, where the weight of the obligations is otherwise very heavily on the HEI's side if the pre-entry stage is considered in isolation. It has the disadvantage that it is not easily reconciled with traditional contract theories, which require all the terms of a contract to be certain at the outset. However, it corresponds most closely to the reality of the HEI–student relationship and is, to that extent, a useful concept.

6.6   A partial analogy for this approach can be found in the employment relationship. An offer of employment on certain terms to start work on a certain future date is made by the employer and accepted by the prospective employee. Both sides are from that stage bound by the terms of the accepted offer, and if the employer seeks to withdraw from the arrangement before the employee starts work, he will be obliged to give due contractual notice of termination or else be liable for damages for breach of contract to the extent of paying the employee in lieu of notice.

Who are the parties?

6.7   Clearly, the HEI and the student are parties. The question arises whether there are any other parties to the arrangement. UCAS is involved as a broker in the early, pre-entry stages: what is its status and could it be claimed to have any contractual responsibilities? UCAS processes applications. That function does not make it an agent of the HEI in the relationship with the student. Therefore, the HEI is unlikely to be fixed with responsibility for a mistake made by UCAS, whereas it would be likely to be liable to the student for the consequences of a mistake in the information it disseminated or any offer it made through UCAS.[1]

How and when the contract is made

6.8   To form a binding legal contract the following elements are normally required:

- offer;
- acceptance;
- consideration;
- capacity; and
- intention to create legal relations.

---

1   See *Moran v University College, Salford (No 2)* [1994] ELR 187, CA.

6.9   In broad terms, the contract comes into existence between the HEI and the student when an offer is made and accepted; specifically, when the acceptance is transmitted to the HEI. That simple position is slightly complicated by the involvement of UCAS and by the fact that many offers are conditional. In the case of a conditional offer, the obligation to admit the student comes into effect at the point when the condition is fulfilled. Both parties are contractually bound from the moment of acceptance, but, if applicants fail to satisfy the conditions within the prescribed period, the HEI is not obliged to register them as students. From the HEI's point of view, it is clearly important to monitor the making of offers to avoid becoming bound to provide places in situations where it does not wish to be bound. The centralised admission service provided by UCAS goes some way towards standardising the application and admission process, thereby making it easier to monitor. There are, however, certain relatively common practices that may result in the HEI becoming contractually bound to provide places it may not have to students it may not wish to admit. For example, one of the points at which a contract may be formed is the stage where an informal offer is made to a prospective student. An informal offer may be made by a member of the HEI staff who has no authority to do so. Unless it can be shown that the student could not reasonably have believed that person had authority, the HEI may be bound by the offer (see paras 5.19 *et seq*).

6.10   Regulating the practice of making informal offers is difficult from the HEI's point of view. There are some practical steps which can be taken to ensure that the HEI does not become fully committed, in the legal sense, at too early a stage. One method would be to require that all prospective students who visit tutors or lecturers at the HEI should be sent a simple standard form of letter making clear that any discussions or offers made are informal, in principle only, and that the student will have to go through UCAS procedures before any binding commitment is made. The HEI should keep a record of all students who make contact in this way, noting whether they make a visit, who they see and that a standard letter is sent out.

6.11   As HEIs are increasingly seeking to recruit overseas students, the problems surrounding informal offers should especially be borne in mind in the context of international recruitment fairs. Members of staff attending such fairs may make statements to prospective students ranging from outright offers of a place to a guarantee of accommodation. These statements are capable of forming the terms of a legally binding contract, provided that the person making them has actual or ostensible authority to make such statements. In the case of prospective overseas students, it may be more difficult to arrange for the distribution of a standard form letter and it may be that the only practical way to prevent the formation of such contracts is to ensure that the members of staff concerned are fully aware of the risks.

6.12   Another situation in which the HEI may run the risk of becoming inadvertently bound to admit students is during the hectic 'clearing' period following the publication of examination results, when HEIs may have to process thousands of applications in the space of a few days. At present, the clearing period seems to be dealt with in a variety of ways by HEIs – some providing staff with formal training and procedures to deal with the applications, while others adopt a more *ad hoc* approach. Clearly, a more systematic approach is likely to facilitate control of the offers made during this period.

6.13 The procedures for postgraduate admissions may also have potential pitfalls from the HEI's point of view, particularly in the case of research degrees, where applications are usually made to individual supervisors. The fact that the decision to admit is made by individual academics may make the task of monitoring the number and quality of admissions more difficult. A number of HEIs, both in this country and abroad, have tried to tackle this by establishing committees who are charged with taking the final decision on whether to admit the applicant in question. The academic who has been approached by the student may submit his or her comments and recommendations to the committee. The committee will then consider these together with the likelihood of the applicant successfully achieving the qualification, and whether the HEI is able to make available to the student adequate and appropriate facilities. It is clearly easier for a body that is aware of all the applications that are being made to judge this last point than for an academic (who may only be aware of the applications that have been made to him or her personally).

6.14 A new set of regulations impose obligations on the HEI in relation to students as consumers where the contract is concluded by post, fax, e-mail or otherwise by means of distance communication (as is usually the case through UCAS). The Consumer Protection (Distance Selling) Regulations 2000[1] introduced two new rights for consumers: the right to receive certain specified information from a supplier of services, and the right to cancel the contract within a specified period. Students must, therefore, be given clear information about the service to be provided by the HEI before the offer of a place on a course is accepted and the HEI–student contract is concluded. This information includes details of the student's right to cancel the contract and the main characteristics of the course and related services, including fees. The information may be provided to students through the HEI's prospectus, though it would impose a heavy administrative burden to provide a copy to all students to whom the HEI makes an offer. The information could also be posted on the HEI's website, but it would be difficult to prove whether any particular student had gained access to it. In practice, many institutions may simply set out the required information in a letter sent to students at the time an offer is made to them. The student has the right to cancel the contract within 7 days of it being concluded by giving notice of cancellation to the HEI. This period is extended where the HEI does not provide the requisite information to the student on time. The effect of the student giving this notice is that the contract is treated as if it had never been made. The Regulations are enforced by the Director General

---

1   SI 2000/2334.

of Fair Trading (DGFT) and by Trading Standards Departments, which have the power to name and shame offending suppliers and to take proceedings for an injunction to prevent further breaches. It remains to be seen how, if at all, the Regulations will be enforced against HEIs.

6.15 Capacity to enter into a contract is generally no longer an issue. Capacity generally refers to age or mental capacity. Many students and prospective students of an HEI will be aged at least 18 and will, therefore, be legally capable of entering into a binding obligation. Any students who are under 18 will have the capacity to enter into a contract for education, as such contracts are considered to constitute 'contracts for necessaries', by which minors will be bound. The HEI no longer has to consider itself as being *in loco parentis* – an outdated analysis of the relationship now replaced by the contractual one (Lewis (1983), p 252). Both parties fairly clearly intend to be bound – the student expects the HEI to provide a place on a course in accordance with its commitment, and the HEI expects to honour its offers: it depends for funding on admitting students to courses, as well as depending for its reputation on complying with the terms of its offers. Consideration is more difficult to identify. There has been a debate on the question of what consideration the student provides. It is suggested that the correct analysis at the admission stage (according to *Moran v University College, Salford (No 2)*)[1] is that the student provides consideration at the point of transmitting his or her acceptance of the HEI's offer by giving up the opportunity, as required by UCAS rules, of negotiating with other HEIs. In other words, it is the opportunity cost of accepting an offer from one institution. At the post-registration stage, it is easier to identify the student's consideration, in a financial form by way of the tuition fee, whether it is paid personally or by some other party on the student's behalf.

How long does the contract last? How is it terminated?

6.16 The contract lasts until it reaches the end of its term (as agreed, whether expressly or impliedly) or is terminated earlier by agreement or breach. Termination will occur if one party commits a repudiatory breach which the other accepts as bringing the contract to an end (for example, if the HEI unilaterally withdraws a course and the student decides not to accept the alternative offered). Termination might also occur when the wronged party acts to bring the contract to an end as a result of the other's breach (for example, if the HEI expels a student for a disciplinary offence). Following termination for breach, the wronged party may have a right to claim damages or some other remedy, as discussed later.

The terms and conditions of the contract

6.17 There will be both express and implied terms of the HEI–student contract. The terms at the pre-registration stages are relatively easy to identify,

---

1   [1994] ELR 187, CA.

namely the obligation on the HEI to admit the student to the course on which he or she has been offered a place and the obligation on the student to turn up and register. It seems unlikely that an HEI would take action to force a student to comply with this obligation, but this does not mean that the obligation does not exist. When the student registers, the contract to teach comes into effect. The express obligations on the HEI and the student at the heart of the contract will be to provide the promised course and to pay the promised fees, respectively. In addition, the student will agree, usually expressly, to be bound by the terms of the HEI's rules and regulations.

6.18 The implied terms of the contract to teach are more elusive. They change and develop with the case-law, and with society's changing expectations and perceptions of HE. Continuous assessment, open book examinations, and even the more traditional supervision obligations in respect of postgraduate students could all be argued to require the HEI to take a more pro-active approach. Counselling and pastoral care, as well as academic feedback, could become part of the overall teaching contract obligations. There are also implied terms regarding quality. The HEI has an obligation to provide the student's education with a reasonable degree of care and skill.[1] If the student's course involves outplacement or practical experience, the quality of that experience is also likely ultimately to be the HEI's responsibility and will not be absolutely delegable. There will be implied terms that the HEI will provide appropriate and adequate facilities (such as library facilities, access to computers, science practicals and laboratory facilities) to give the student a proper opportunity of achieving the required standard to attain a degree.[2] Furthermore, the HEI is under a duty not to take any action, such as reducing ancillary facilities of this nature, which would have the effect of devaluing the resulting qualification in the market place.

6.19 As it is difficult to identify with certainty the precise nature and extent of the terms that the courts may be prepared to imply into the contract, there is a good argument for stating aspects that are of particular importance to the HEI as express terms of the contract. For example, many HEIs include express provisions in their registration documents to cover the question of a student's intellectual property (IP) rights. IP rights fall into the category of topics which should not be left as the subject of an implied term (see Chapter 11). HEI regulations, rules and procedures also have a place in the contractual nexus. The introduction of new rules and regulations during an individual student's course may be subject to challenge as a unilateral variation of the contract. The view of the Office of Fair Trading (OFT) is that, under the Unfair Terms in Consumer Contracts Regulations 1999 (UTCCR 1999),[3] HEIs may modify their regulations only at the beginning of each academic year. Moreover, in the OFT's view, such changes can take effect in respect of students already admitted to the institution only if they are for the students' benefit. Whilst the

---

1   See *D'Mello v Loughborough College of Technology* (1970) *The Times,* June 16.
2   *Sammy v Birkbeck College* (1964) *The Times,* November 3.
3   SI 1999/2083.

OFT's position has yet to be tested in the courts, it does appear correct in principle – except, perhaps, in the case of true emergencies. One HEI (South Bank) has already been 'persuaded' by the OFT to amend its procedures accordingly.

WHEN THINGS GO WRONG

6.20   At the admission stage, if the HEI refuses to admit the student to the promised course, or withdraws or makes changes to the course in circumstances where no effective disclaimer of liability applies, that will be a breach of contract. At the teaching stage, if the HEI fails to comply with any of the implied terms about teaching and its quality, that may be a breach of contract. Imposing unreasonable rules and regulations might also give rise to a claim.

External remedies

6.21   A student's complaint of breach of contract may go before the court or the Visitor. Since it is arguable that the Visitor does not comply with Art 6 of the European Convention on Human Rights, even students in chartered HEIs may be able to pursue any grievance in a court (see Chapters 8 and 30, plus Kaye (1999)). In court (usually the county court in contractual claims), students are entitled to represent themselves. Lack of legal representation on the student's part is not necessarily an advantage for the HEI. Some of the truly unmeritorious claims would be sifted out if the student claimants were better advised. In the absence of any advice, students often try to pursue non-existent or extremely weak claims to trial, which is an expensive process for the HEI. The only costs a student is likely to incur are for issuing proceedings and for photocopying and postage. Experience shows that many students who take a breach of contract claim before the courts have ample time to spend in preparing the case and are not unduly concerned about the hidden costs to them (in terms of lost earning time) of conducting the case. The fact that the student may have plenty of time to devote to preparation means that he or she will usually have an extremely thorough, if somewhat biased, understanding of the case. This can make such students tenacious and difficult opponents and can result in greater legal costs for the HEI as it tries to defend itself against the student's claim. Students conducting their own case are frequently incapable of, or unwilling to try, settling the action. It is small comfort for an HEI faced with a large legal bill to know that few cases of this nature have succeeded.

6.22   In breach of contract cases, the most likely remedy that students will seek in court is damages. They may seek a discretionary remedy (such as an injunction) to try to force the HEI, for example, to reinstate a course or part of a course. In practice, it is unlikely that a court would provide such a remedy where the withdrawal of the course had been as a result of circumstances outside the HEI's control, such as the death of a key lecturer. The same principle would apply in the case of a claimant who sought to force the HEI to comply with the terms of an offer made in error – generally, specific performance would not be appropriate. The Visitor makes a number of remedies available to the wronged student, including damages and a range of types of restitution (see Chapter 8). The jurisdiction of the Visitor in the chartered HEIs, and Oxford and Cambridge colleges, essentially covers all matters arising out of the HEI's internal laws. It is less clear that the Visitor's jurisdiction extends to the pre-offer stage to cover application and selection. Public law remedies may also be available to the student by way of judicial review (see Chapter 9). Students may seek this type of remedy where the claim cannot be brought within the boundaries of contract law. This could be, for example, a challenge by a student that the HEI's procedures are themselves unfair. Claims under the HRA 1998 would generally be brought by way of judicial review, and are discussed in Chapter 7.

6.23   A prospective student may use judicial review at the pre-contract stage. Applicants who consider that the decision to reject them has been taken on the basis of inappropriate selection criteria might consider a judicial review challenge. This type of complaint should be prevented by careful consideration of the way in which the reasons for rejecting an applicant are to be communicated, and indeed, whether any reasons should be given at all. As the publicity surrounding Laura Spence's rejection in 2000 by an Oxford College demonstrated, it is best to avoid giving detailed reasons in situations where there is scope for the rationale behind them to be misunderstood or challenged on grounds of inherent unfairness. Other complaints by applicants may be related to the manner in which any interview was conducted, where, for example, it was apparent that they were being interviewed by someone who had no knowledge of the subject area for which they were applying.

Damages

6.24   In order to obtain damages for breach of contract, the student must first establish that the contract has been breached. A causal link then has to be established between that breach and any loss which the student claims to have suffered. In many cases, this may be difficult, even where the breach is easy to prove. The causal link may be more easily established, for example, where a student resigns from a job, having accepted an offer of a place on a course which is subsequently withdrawn by the HEI. If the student can establish the necessary causal link, then the basic principles of compensation apply at both stages of the contract identified in this chapter. In the case of a breach of contract by the HEI in failing or refusing to register a student who has been offered a place and who has fulfilled any conditions attached to the offer, there will be two alternative methods of assessing damages – one based on the proposition that the contract should have been fully performed, the other on the basis that it was not made in the first place.

6.25   The first method will compensate the student by awarding damages – essentially on a future basis – calculated to meet the loss incurred as a result of not being in the position the student would have been in had the contract been performed. The measure of damages on a future basis may be quite difficult to calculate, because it will involve a number of imponderable factors such as the likelihood of the student surviving the course and passing the examinations at the end of it, as well as the prospects which may result from obtaining the degree. The nature of the breach of contract may be relevant. If the HEI made a clerical error and refused then to honour the offer to an unqualified candidate, it should be possible to argue that damages should be limited by the unlikelihood of the academically weak candidate succeeding in any event. The student will be under a duty to mitigate loss. In many cases this will mean attempting to find a suitable alternative course, or re-entering the system the following year or at the earliest opportunity. If this succeeds the loss may be minimal. The student must also give credit for the expense which would have been incurred if he or she had been admitted onto the course (for example, on course materials and books). The alternative method of calculating damages is to allow recovery of expenses incurred as a result of or in connection with the breach of contract. This may be expressed as the intention to place the student in the position, not as if the contract had been performed, but as if it had never been made. The student cannot recover both lost expenses and damages representing future loss.

6.26 In the case of a breach of the terms of the teaching phase of the contract, the same principles apply. Establishing a causal link between poor quality teaching or support and failure leading to loss is again likely to be a difficult exercise. It may be possible to use comparative material, drawing from the experience of other students on the same course, or from the claimant's results in other papers or examinations.

6.27 The emergence of the tort law concept of educational negligence has already been mentioned in this chapter. A claim of negligence would be brought alongside a claim for breach of contract, rather than instead of the contractual claim, because the parties involved will usually also have a contractual relationship. The courts have been reluctant, so far, to award damages in situations in which negligence on the part of the HEI has been alleged, usually because the causal link between the alleged negligence and the loss suffered is as difficult to prove as in the case of a breach of contract. However, the case of *Smoldon v Whitworth*,[1] where a referee was held liable for the injuries sustained by an amateur rugby player during the collapse of a scrum, may be an indication that the courts are not afraid to interpret the causation requirements liberally where the interests of justice are perceived to demand it. It is difficult to envisage a situation, other than one in which personal injury had been suffered, where the courts would be willing to adopt such a broad interpretation of causation. Personal injury nowadays is recognised as including (for example) the effects of nervous breakdowns and stress.[2] This point is reinforced by the recent case of *Phelps v Hillingdon London*

---

1   [1997] ELR 249.
2   *Walker v Northumberland County Council* [1995] ELR 231, concerning an employer's duty of care to an employee suffering from excessive stress by overwork: see also §6.22 above.

Borough Council.[1] The effect of this House of Lords' decision is that it is now possible for disgruntled current or former pupils to sue their teachers, school or local education authority (LEA) for alleged negligence in failing to diagnose a special need (in this case dyslexia) *and*, in theory, for poor teaching. Cases of alleged negligence in the education sphere will come down to whether the claimant can prove harm, causation and breach of the duty of care.

Consumer protection

6.28 In terms of pure contract law, the parties to the contract have freedom to define its terms by agreement between them. However, the legislative framework of consumer protection detracts from the HEI's freedom to set the terms, taking into account the disparity of bargaining power in relation to the student. The Unfair Contract Terms Act 1977 (UCTA 1977) deals with contract terms which attempt to exclude or restrict the potential liability of a business in relation to a consumer. The view is that UCTA 1977 does apply to HEIs. Liability for death or personal injury arising from negligence cannot be excluded, whilst the exclusion of other liability arising from negligence is subject to the requirement of reasonableness.

6.29 The UTCCR 1999 police unequal consumer bargains. Their effect is much wider than UCTA 1977 because they apply potentially to any express term of the contract falling within their scope. It is clear that the UTCCR 1999 do apply to the terms of the HEI–student contract, since they apply to any term of a contract, between a party acting for purposes relating to its business and a consumer, which has not been individually negotiated – that is, in all situations where the consumer is not able to influence the substance of that term. Students are inevitably regarded as consumers when courses, accommodation and materials are supplied to them by HEIs. Those standard terms which create or record a contractual relationship between the student and the HEI, ranging from course prospectuses to disciplinary rules, are a clear target. The consequence if the HEI's standard contract terms are unfair is that they will be declared void, with the effect that the HEI will be obliged to provide the agreed service without relying on the advantages conferred by the unfair terms. As indicated earlier, the OFT acts to enforce the UTCCR 1999 and has already stated that it considers education to be a 'problem sector'. The requirement of reasonableness essentially applies to both UCTA 1977 and the UTCCR 1999. Its application is not an exact science. The UTCCR 1999 contain an indicative and illustrative list of terms which may be regarded as unfair, helping to clarify the possible criteria which will be applied by the courts (see Sch 2). Reference may also be made to the OFT Bulletin, *Unfair Contract Terms*, which includes case studies of companies and institutions persuaded to amend the terms they include in their standard contracts. A potentially unfair term which is likely to be of particular relevance to HEIs is one which has the object or effect of enabling the seller or supplier to alter unilaterally, without a valid reason, any

---

1   [2000] 3 WLR 776.

characteristics of the product or service to be provided. Those terms which define the main subject matter of the contract or concern the price or remuneration are not subject to assessment for fairness, provided they are in plain, intelligible language.[1]

6.30 There is only a limited entitlement for people other than individual consumers to challenge unfair terms in court, since in UK law there is no general right of representative action on behalf of parties to a contract. This restriction currently means that SUs and other associations are unable to initiate proceedings in court. It is doubtful whether this satisfies EC Council Directive 93/13/EEC, Art 7.2, which provides that Member States must ensure that organisations which have a legitimate interest receive the right to take action. In addition, however, both individual students and student associations can make a complaint to the DGFT that a contract term is unfair.[2]

PRACTICAL PREVENTIVE OR REMEDIAL ACTION

Look at procedures

6.31 To avoid legal challenge, procedures must be fair in the way they apply to students and in the way in which they operate. Students may seek to challenge a procedure which denies them, for example, the right to put their side of the story, as being contrary to natural justice (see para 5.11). It is, therefore, important to look at procedures initially to ensure they are fair. The requirements of the HRA 1998 should also be taken into account (see Chapter 7). It is also vital to make sure that different sets of procedures – for example, HEI rules and course rules – are compatible, and not contradictory.

Follow procedures

6.32 Once procedures, policies and codes have been put in place by the HEI, those responsible for operating them must follow them, or risk legal challenge. Therefore, procedures need to be clear, unambiguous and workable in practice. If experience shows problems in any of these areas, the procedures should be reviewed and rewritten as a preventive exercise, although this is unlikely to be enough on its own. Those implementing the procedures must understand what they mean and how they work.

Know the policy

6.33 It is not sufficient, in cases of alleged discrimination and bias, to point to a documented policy. The courts expect those responsible for operating a policy to understand and be familiar with it. Again, this suggests that anti-discrimination policies should as far as possible be simply framed with

---

1   See UTCCR 1999, reg 6(3).
2   Ibid, reg 10. For further discussion of consumer law, see Chapter 29.

reasonably memorable requirements, avoiding excessive complexity. There is also an expectation that institutions of the scale of HEIs will invest considerably in training in equal opportunities, and monitoring and reviewing policies and procedures in operation.

Publication and information

6.34   The effect of the terms of the HEI–student contract, including disclaimers and exclusions of liability, will depend to a large extent on appropriate and timely publication. Disclaimers and exclusions will be ineffective if they are not drawn to the student's attention at or before the formation of the contract. Publications also need to be consistent. The HEI's prospectus should not be inconsistent with the terms, for example, of departmental literature or the HEI calendar. On arrival, the student should not receive a new set of literature in wholly different terms to that which was sent at the time the offer was made.

Clarity

6.35   Whatever preventive strategies are put in place, clarity as to what is expected of individuals who have a role to play in the relationship will greatly assist their effect. This applies not only to internal HEI procedures but also to the part played by outsiders (for example, employers who accept students on outplacements for a part of the degree course). Each party should clearly understand the scope and limit of their responsibilities and freedom to act. Clarity in the wording of procedures and regulations will also assist if those documents are challenged under the UTCCR 1999, which contain a general requirement of plain language.[1]

Effective complaints procedure

6.36   The QAA now requires every HEI to have a complaints procedure (see Chapter 7 and Appendix 2 to this chapter). If the procedure is operated effectively, it may be possible to prevent at least some of the complaints brought by students from reaching court. In some cases, sympathetic treatment of the complaint, a clear explanation of the HEI's position and a discussion of what, if anything, can be done to prevent a recurrence of the situation, may succeed in satisfying the complainant. This is in much the same way as complaints within the NHS are often effectively dealt with if handled speedily and openly, but tend to fester and become intractable if the complainant feels that ranks are being closed against him or her. It may be worth making a form of ADR available to a complainant before positions become entrenched at a formal disciplinary or grievance hearing (see Chapter 27). Institutions may also wish to consider the American option of setting up an in-house Ombudsman's office to whom any disgruntled member of the HEI community

---

1   See reg 6.

could turn for advice and assistance in the pursuit of a formal or informal remedy.

CONCLUSIONS

6.37   The HEI's actions and operations seem likely in future to come under increasing scrutiny by outsiders, and to be subject to a greater variety of challenges. Establishing and operating a strategy to deal with these challenges depends on individuals understanding, anticipating and taking avoiding action. Their ability to do so depends in turn on the framework within which they operate and, in particular, the clear understanding at all levels of the HEI of the essential and characteristic elements of the contract with the student, and of its challenges and opportunities.

A NOTE ON REFERENCES

6.38   A former student of the University of Glamorgan accepted £25,000 in settlement of a damages claim for a negligent reference. Staff giving references for students (or employees) should be aware of the basic principles and the possible liability of the institution (or, in some cases, even the individual). The key cases are *Spring v Guardian Assurance plc*[1] and *Bartholomew v London Borough of Hackney*.[2] According to the law, there is no obligation on an HEI to give a reference for a student. However, if a reference is given, then defamation, negligence and mis-representation are possible grounds for action, either by the subject of the reference or by the employer who relies on it. The institution will normally be liable for the consequences of a negligent/defamatory reference given by a member of its staff, unless (against the odds) it can establish that the reference was given outside the course of employment (or, as lawyers like to say, on a 'frolic' of the referee's/employee's own) – on defamation see paras **5.13–5.18**. Only *reasonable* exclusions of liability for negligent acts or omissions carried out in the course of a business will stand up in court. The question of what is 'reasonable' in this context has not yet been tested in court, but for now it seems sensible to include a disclaimer to the effect that neither the institution nor the referee can be held responsible for any error. The disclaimer should be backed up by following the good practice guidelines for staff:

–   tell students to seek in advance your agreement to give a reference;
–   if you are unable or unwilling to give a reference but you still receive a request for one from a potential employer, communicate your refusal carefully, without implying a negative reference;

---

1   [1995] 2 AC 296, HL.
2   [1999] IRLR 246; see also *Cox v Sun Alliance Life Ltd* [2001] EWCA Civ 649, [2001] IRLR 448.

- stick to facts and only give opinions within your professional competence (for example, no medical opinions);
- ensure that the reference does not give a misleading impression overall, even if the statements in it are factually correct. While a reference does not have to be full and comprehensive, it must be true, accurate and fair;
- include the institution's disclaimer;
- check there are no outstanding disciplinary proceedings/investigations (for example, cheating);
- mark all correspondence 'Private and Confidential – for the attention of addressee/committee/panel only' and state that the reference should not be disclosed to anyone without the referee's permission. However, you should note that the subject of the reference may have the right to obtain a copy of it from the recipient under the provisions of the Data Protection Act 1998 (DPA 1998); and
- if a reference is given orally, make a note of what was said.

(On the confidentiality of degree results, see Chapter 13.)

APPENDIX 1 TO CHAPTER 6

1. This Appendix provides a convenient analysis and tabulation of key cases concerning the HEI–student contract, as referred to in Chapters 6, 7 and 9. The well-managed HEI has little to fear from the law in relation to its relationship with students; the sloppy HEI is still managing to create case-law despite the guidance of Farrington since his 1994 first edition and of the first edition of this book in 1998.

2. From all this case-law it is, in summary, clear:

    (a) That there is indeed a contract to educate (*Clark*, 2000;[1] *Moran*, 1994;[2] the nineteenth-century cases of *Lyall*, 1863;[3] *Jex-Blake*, 1873;[4] *Cadells*, 1890;[5] and *Green*, 1896[6]).

    (b) That the Visitor has exclusive jurisdiction over student–chartered HEI disputes (*Thorne*, 1966;[7] *R v University of Nottingham ex parte K*, 1998;[8] *Cotran v Buckingham University*, 1998;[9] *Clark v University of Lincolnshire and Humberside*[10]).

    (c) That the courts will not act as an appeal tribunal in relation to the decision of university examiners, other than in the form of judicial review where, and only where, the statutory HEI's own regulations have not been complied with or fail to themselves comply with due process (*Thirunayagam*, 1997;[11] *R v University of Cambridge ex parte Persaud*, 2000;[12] *Queen on the application of Persaud v Cambridge University*, 2001;[13] *Seleh*, 1992;[14] *Carleton*, 1993;[15] *R v University of the West of England ex parte M*, 2001;[16] *Queen on the application of M v University of the West of England*, 2001;[17] and *Queen on the application of Ahmed v University of Oxford*, 2000[18]).

---

1   *Clark v University of Lincolnshire and Humberside* [2000] 1 WLR 1988: see also §6.13 and footnote 7 at p 105 above.
2   *Moran v University College, Salford (No 2)* [1994] ELR 187.
3   (1863) unreported.
4   [1873] 11 M 784.
5   (1890) unreported.
6   *Green v Peterhouse* (1896) *The Times*, February 10.
7   [1966] 2 QB 237.
8   [1998] ELR 184, CA.
9   (1998) unreported, 24 February, CA.
10 [2000] 1 WLR 1988, CA.
11 (1997) unreported, 14 March.
12 [2000] EdCR 635, QBD.
13 [2001] EWCA Civ 534, [2001] ELR 480, CA.
14 (1992) *The Times*, December 23.
15 (1993) unreported.
16 [2001] ELR 77.
17 [2001] ELR 458.
18 (2000) unreported, 7 November.

(d) That the HEI's own rules are the sole forum for dispute resolution in relation to such purely academic matters (*R v University of Aston Senate ex parte Roffey*, 1969;[1] *R v University of Humberside ex parte Cousens*, 1995;[2] *M v London Guidhall University*, 1998;[3] *R v University of Portsmouth ex parte Lakareber*, 1999;[4] *R v Cambridge University ex parte Beg*, 1999,[5] and *R v Cranfield University Senate ex parte Bashir*, 1999[6]). As with (c) above, the court will *not* second-guess academic judgment; but, as noted below, it *will* concern itself with procedural fairness (*Clark*, 2000).

(e) That there can be no question of judicial review as anticipated in (c) above concerning academic issues until the HEI's internal procedures have first been followed and exhausted (*R v Liverpool John Moores University ex parte Hayes*, 1998;[7] *M v London Guildhall University*, 1998[8]), while in any event judicial review is not to be used to resolve factual disputes (*Iqbal Sandhu v University of Central England*, 1999[9]).

(f) That, if there are procedural irregularities, then judicial review *will* bite (*R v Manchester Metropolitan University ex parte Nolan*, 1994[10]), unless they have resulted in no unfairness to the student (*R v de Montfort University ex parte Cottrell*, 1996[11]), and even if the procedural irregularity involves academic matters such as bias in the marking of examinations (*R v Leeds Metropolitan University ex parte Manders*, 1998;[12] *Flanagan v University College, Dublin*, 1988;[13] *R v South Bank University ex parte Coggeran*, 2000;[14] *R v South Bank University ex parte Burgess*, 2000;[15] *Queen on the application of Udemba v South Bank University*, 2000,[16] *R v Chelsea College of Art and Design ex parte Nash*, 2000,[17] and *Queen on the application of Isolyn Burgess v South Bank University*, 2001[18]).

(g) That similarly, in relation to social behaviour/misconduct, the internal procedures for student complaints/grievances or discipline again must have been exhausted before there can be access to the court in any breach of contract dispute, and there can be judicial review only if those internal procedures are misapplied or are

---

1   [1969] 2 QB 538.
2   [1995] CLY 1947, (1995) EdLM 2(6)11, CA.
3   [1998] ELR 149, CA.
4   [1999] ELR 135, CA.
5   [1999] ELR 404, QBD.
6   [1999] ELR 317, CA.
7   [1998] ELR 261, QBD
8   [1998] ELR 419, CA.
9   [1999] ELR 419.
10   [1994] ELR 380.
11   (1996), unreported.
12   [1998] ELR 502, QBD.
13   [1988] IR 724.
14   [2000] ICR 1342.
15   (2000), unreported.
16   (2000), unreported.
17   [2000] ELR 686, QBD.
18   [2001] ELR 300–310.

inherently faulty with respect to due process (*R v Sheffield Howlett University Board of Governors ex parte R*, 1994[1]).

(h) That judicial review of failed applications for admission is not appropriate (*R v University College London ex parte Idris*, 1999;[2] UCL is, of course, a chartered institution with a Visitor, but *probably* the jurisdiction of the Visitor does not extend to applicants).

(i) That the courts increasingly expect an appeal or grievance committee to give reasons for its decision, probably now to a greater degree of detail than in *R v University of Humberside ex parte Cousens*, 1995,[3] when the court was content with a fairly brief decision letter; and, furthermore, preferably to give such reasons reasonably soon after the decision: *Nash v Chelsea College of Art and Design*[4] (especially where the claimants had much at stake: for example, termination of degree course rather than, say, a quibble over second year marks as in the *Nash* case).

3. Arguably, however, for English law *Clark v University of Lincolnshire and Humberside*, 2000[5] now replaces *Moran*[6] as the leading case. The Court of Appeal comprised Lord Woolf MR, Ward LJ, and Sedley LJ, with the last giving the main judgment and declaring (without citing *Moran*!) that:

– the university–student legal relationship is essentially contractual;
– disputes concerning this contract are generally justiciable in the courts, unless the university has a Visitor;
– some aspects of the contract, however, may be 'unsuitable' for adjudication in the courts 'because these are issues of academic or pastoral judgement which the university is equipped to consider in breadth and depth, but on which any judgment of the courts would be jejune and inappropriate';
– there is a public law dimension in the case of the statutory HEIs and hence also scope for judicial review concerning due process; while Lord Woolf MR added . . .
– such student disputes should reach the courts only after the university's internal procedures have been exhausted;
– any such court involvement should preferably be by way of judicial review within its 3-month limitation period, but can also be by way of a claim in contract within its 6-year limitation period; and
– anyway the courts are 'far from being the ideal forum in which to resolve the great majority of disputes between a student and his or her university' (shades of the view referred to above that the courts really have rather better things to do than sort out the petty squabbles of academe!).

---

1   [1994] COD 470, QBD.
2   [1999] EdCR 462, QBD.
3   [1995] CLY 1947, (1995) EdLM 2(6)11, CA.
4   [2001] EWHC Admin 538, [2000] TLR 471, QBD.
5   [2000] 1 WLR 1988, CA
6   *Moran v University College, Salford (No 2)* [1994] ELR 187.

4.   Equally, from the above case-law it is not only clear but acutely depressing
      that UK HEIs still have some way to go in terms of:

      –   a preventative legal audit of the HEI's student contract so as to avoid
           creating problems;
      –   a sensible approach to case management once a problem develops so
           as to avoid fighting unwinnable cases (see Chapter 27); and
      –   a willingness to acknowledge the arrival of 'the empowered student
           consumer' so as to ensure that students are always treated just as one
           would personally like to be treated or would want one's own child
           treated if a student at that HEI (see Chapter 29).

5.   There are also some salutory cases from the USA and from Australia which
      indicate just how extravagant, drawn-out, expensive and bitter HEI–
      student legal disputes can become: no UK case has been so wild (so far).
      Three such cases give a feel for what happens when commonsense is the
      victim of an over-elaborate sense of grievance on the part of the student
      against the HEI. The students may not have had any chance of winning the
      litigation, but the cost of that litigation for the HEIs in terms of legal fees,
      management time and staff hassle will have been enormous. The cases are:

      (a)   The US case of *Napolitino v The Trustees of Princeton University*[1]
            which concerned plagarism and Ms Napolitino's reluctance to accept
            any punishment under the Princeton academic regulations (she
            alleged, *inter alia*, defamation, intentional afflication of emotional
            harm, invasion of privacy and malicious interferenc).
      (b)   The Australian case of *Fennell v Australia National University*[2]
            concerning Mr Fennell suing both the ANU and an individual
            academic personally over alleged misrepresentation at a recruitment
            interview for the degree of MBA.
      (c)   Another Australian case, *Dudzinksi v Kellow*,[3] where Mr Dudzinksi
            sued Griffith University and nine (*sic!*) of its academic and
            administrative staff personally for, *inter alia*, professional negligence,
            conspiracy, deceit, racial and sexual discrimination, intimidation,
            fraudulent misstatement, defamation, assault, injurious falsehood
            and contravention of the Trade Practices Act 1974.

6.   Finally, as with *Clark*, 2000, the Court of Appeal in *Cowl and Others v
      Plymouth City Council*, 2002[4] has stressed that litigation (including
      judicial review) should be a last resort, to be pursued only after any
      internal complaints procedures and then some form of alternative dispute
      resolution (see Chapter 27) have failed to resolve the dispute. Similarly,
      also as with *Clark*, the dividing line between public law judicial review
      remedies and private law contractual remedies is becoming increasingly

---

1   453 A 2d 263, NJ Sup Ct, App Div 1982.
2   [1999] FCA 989 (22 July 1999).
3   [1999] FCA 390 (8 April 1999).
4   (2002) *The Times*, January 8.

blurred: the court will not get over-concerned with the procedure under which a case is brought, but will want to get on and deliver justice (*Queen on the application of Oxford Study Centre Ltd v British Council*, 2001:[1] note the increasing emphasis on following due process in exercising contractual powers as with statutory powers).

---

1   [2001] EWHC Admin 207, [2001] ELR 803.

APPENDIX 2 TO CHAPTER 6

This is a specimen 'Student Complaints Procedure' based on one used at the University of Manchester (this document is reproduced by way of example and should not be adapted for local use without taking appropriate legal advice: see also the useful documents available at www.bristol.ac.uk/armed concerning 'student affairs' territory):

1. **General**

1.1 As part of its commitment to ensuring the standard and quality of its courses, services, and facilities, the University has established this Procedure to deal with complaints from students (which in this respect includes recent graduates). Every reasonable effort will be made to deal promptly and efficiently with all complaints, to investigate them thoroughly and objectively and to seek to resolve them satisfactorily.

1.2 Complaints will be dealt with positively and constructively. If a complaint is upheld the University will seek to provide a reasonable and appropriate response and will correct any mistakes or misunderstandings and will take any other action as appropriate. If a complaint is not upheld then reasons for the decision will be given.

1.3 All complaints will be dealt with in confidence with the proviso that an individual against whom a complaint is made has the right to be supplied with a copy of the complaint.

1.4 The University will treat all complaints seriously and will deal with them without recrimination. Where, however, a complaint is shown to be frivolous, vexatious or motivated by malice, disciplinary action may be taken against the complainant.

1.5 The time-limits set out in this Procedure will normally be followed. However, where, for good reason, this is not possible the complainant will be kept informed of progress.

1.6 The effectiveness of any complaints procedure depends on the University being able to collect appropriate information from the parties involved in order to investigate the matter properly. For this reason anonymous complaints will not be dealt with under this Procedure. It is at the discretion of the appropriate member of staff as to how an anonymous complaint is handled.

2. **Definition and Scope of the Procedure**

2.1 The University defines a complaint as **an expression of dissatisfaction which merits a response**.

2.2 The Procedure, which can be used by students for both individual and collective complaints, is designed for complaints relating to:

- courses, services or facilities provided by the University;
- actions or lack of actions by the University or its staff.

2.3 The Complaints Procedure does not cover the following:

- disciplinary issues (for which a separate procedure exists)
- matters where other separate procedures apply, for example:
  - Harassment.
  - Academic appeals relating to examinations or assessments.
  - Appeals against exclusion on academic grounds, or against refusal to be issued with a Certificate of Satisfactory Work and Attendance.
  - Complaints about the Students' Union.

2.4 This Procedure is available for students registered for programmes within the University, save that it is not available for students on recognised programmes of study, or on programmes of study approved or accredited for that purpose, in an affiliated institution or University College. These students should use the mechanisms and procedures for considering complaints which are in place within the affiliated institution or University College.

2.5 This Procedure comprises a number of stages, both informal and formal. It is hoped that most complaints can be resolved informally by students pursuing matters directly with the staff concerned. Only where the informal procedures have been pursued and the complainant remains dissatisfied should the formal stage be followed.

3. Informal Procedure

3.1 Most complaints can be resolved informally and where practical a complaint should be dealt with as close as possible to the point at which it arises. The complaint should therefore be made initially to an appropriate member of staff who seems best placed to deal with the matter.

3.2 Complaints should be made orally or in writing as soon as possible, and in any case within one month, after the events or actions (or lack of actions) which prompted the complaint.

3.3 The member of staff who receives the complaint shall look into the matter and shall give a response to the complainant normally within 10 working days following receipt of the complaint.

3.4 Where the subject of the complaint is of a general nature it might be more appropriate for the student to raise the matter with a student representative on the relevant departmental or service committee.

3.5 If the student is dissatisfied with the response, then he/she shall submit the complaint in writing to the Head of Department, Head of Service or Head of Residence as appropriate. If the complaint relates to action taken by any of these officers, the student should submit the written complaint to the Dean of the Faculty concerned (for academic-related matters) or to the Head of Student Administration (for all other matters).

3.6 The written complaint should set out briefly:

- the nature of the complaint;
- the informal steps already taken together with full details of the response received;

- and should include a statement setting out why the complainant remains dissatisfied.

3.7 The Head of Department/Service/Residence shall investigate the matter and notify the complainant in writing of the outcome, normally within 10 working days of the date of the receipt of the written complaint.

4.   Formal Procedure

4.1 If, having pursued the matter informally, the student is dissatisfied with the written response he/she should refer the matter formally in writing to the Registrar and Secretary together with copies of any correspondence exchanged during the informal procedure and any other relevant papers.

4.2 Receipt of the complaint will be acknowledged in writing within five working days by the Registrar and Secretary who, subject to being satisfied that the student has taken reasonable steps to follow the informal procedure set out in paragraphs 3.1 to 3.7 above, will specify a person or persons within the University independent of the source of the complaint to carry out an investigation.

4.3 The investigator(s) may seek to resolve the issue on the basis of the documentation, after having sought further information from the members of staff involved in the original complaint or may, at the investigator(s') discretion, call a hearing at which the student and any other persons involved may submit their respective cases. The complainant and any person who is the subject of the complaint may each be accompanied at any such hearing by another member of the University community.

4.4 After taking the steps set out in paragraph 4.3 above, the investigator(s) shall decide whether there is reasonable justification for the complaint or not and shall submit a report in writing to the Registrar and Secretary, containing such recommendations as deemed appropriate. The Registrar and Secretary shall decide on the action to be taken and this decision will be communicated in writing to the complainant and all other relevant parties normally within 20 working days of the date of acknowledging receipt of the formal complaint.

5.   Complaint Review

5.1 The stages of the Procedures set out above have been established to ensure a full and fair investigation of a student's complaint and that it is dealt with thoroughly and objectively. If, however, a student believes that his/her complaint has not been handled properly or fairly in accordance with this Procedure he/she may submit a letter of appeal to the Pro-Vice-Chancellor responsible for student matters requesting a review. The letter, giving reasons for requesting the review must be submitted to the Pro-Vice-Chancellor (c/o the Vice-Chancellor's Office) normally within 10 working days of the notification of the decision by the Registrar and Secretary, together with all previous correspondence and relevant papers.

Dissatisfaction with the outcome of the complaint shall not in itself constitute an acceptable reason for review.

5.2 The Pro-Vice-Chancellor shall consider the circumstances of the case on the basis of the documentation and, having taken such advice as he/she deems necessary, shall determine whether there is prima facie evidence to support the complainant's appeal that the case has not been handled properly or fairly. If he/she determines that no prima facie evidence exists then the appeal shall be dismissed and this decision shall be final. If, however, the Pro-Vice-Chancellor is satisfied that there is prima facie evidence to support the appeal then he/she may either review the case personally or request an independent person external to the University to do so. The Pro-Vice-Chancellor shall inform the complainant normally within 10 working days of the date on which the request for a review was received of the action to be taken.

5.3 The Pro-Vice-Chancellor, or the independent person, having reviewed the case, shall submit a report in writing to the Vice-Chancellor and the Registrar and Secretary containing such recommendations as he/she shall deem appropriate. The Vice-Chancellor (or Registrar and Secretary on his or her behalf) shall ensure that any appropriate action following the report and recommendations is taken and shall inform the complainant accordingly.

5.4 Following this review, there shall be no further opportunity for the complaint to be pursued within the University. [NB There is no mention of the possibility of appeal to the Visitor: see Chapters 8 and 29; or to some kind of 'independent body' as recommended by Dearing and Nolan.]

Chapter 7

THE REGULATION OF THE COMMUNITY: STUDENT DISCIPLINE, ACADEMIC APPEALS AND COMPLAINTS

Nicola Hart (Martineau Johnson)

EDITORS' INTRODUCTION

§7.1　As we said in Chapter 1, the generality of HEI employees are covered by the same basic employment law (the Employment Protection Act 1975 and similar legislation) as any other employee. This is the subject of many textbooks and hence we see no need to discuss employment law in this book (other than to note how things are to some degree different for one particular group of staff in many (but not all) HEIs: academic staff to whom the so-called Model Statutes imposed by the University Commissioners under the ERA 1988 apply, and some of whom still retain tenure: see Chapters 10 and 11). This chapter, therefore, concentrates on students, the disciplining of whom in the late 1960s and early 1970s was the main source of case-law involving HEIs and of references to the Visitor, but now which is of less prominence than conflicts about academic issues (say, the examination of a graduate thesis). The chapter also speculates on the likely impact of the HRA 1998, the arrival of which was much-heralded by many conferences and seminars: following the common-sense recent judgments of the House of Lords in three linked cases [1] concerning the compatibility of the planning appeals system with Art 6(1) of the European Convention on Human Rights – the right to a fair trial – *perhaps* some of the hype surrounding this Act will evaporate. Or perhaps all is now back in the judicial melting-pot concerning the possible conflict between English law judicial review and the Art 6(1) requirements. [2]

§7.2　Looking as far back as 1910 we find that Williams (1910), pp 182–183 comments:

> 'There is probably an implied contract that a university or college supplies efficient tuition. An action would lie by an undergraduate ... for breach of contract to educate ... [But] a member of a college is bound to conform to reasonable rules of discipline, and if we do not do so, the contract to educate is not broken. In a recent case, a Cambridge undergraduate was expelled for refusal to go to Chapel. He brought an action for breach of contract to educate ... On the trial at Herts Assizes, Wilts, J directed judgment for the college on the ground that the relation of an undergraduate to his college was in matters of discipline not a contractual one.' [3]

1　*R v Secretary of State for the Environment ex parte Holding and Barnes plc; R v S of S ex parte Alconbury Developments Ltd and Others; S of S v Legal and General Assurance Society Ltd* [2001] UKHL 23, [2001] 2 WLR 1399. See also *Ghosh v General Medical Council* [2001] UKPC 29, [2001] 1 WLR 1915, PC.

2　*Hutton v United Kingdom* (2001) ECHR, 2 October, concerning early morning flights at Heathrow.

3　*Green v Peterhouse* (1896) *The Times*, February 10.

§7.3   We are in complex legal territory, where contract law merges with the law of associations governing membership and where the student is voluntarily subjecting himself to the rules of the academic community.

§7.4   On the issue of harassment codes, note should be taken of the Protection from Harassment Act 1997 which is intended to deal with 'stalkers', and which may also strengthen the position of an employee facing harassment in the workplace by giving him or her the right to go to the police under the Act's two new criminal offences and to seek civil redress under the Act's new statutory tort of harassment. On the issue of 'stalking' see the book *Being Stalked* written by Robert Fine, a sociology lecturer at the University of Warwick, where Fine recounts his experience of being harassed by a mature student and his long legal battle, supported by the University, to obtain an injunction. Note that the Protection from Harassment Act 1997 makes harassment on two occasions a criminal offence and allows a criminal court or a civil court to make a restraining order/issue an injunction. The test is whether 'the reasonable man' would consider the behaviour and actions complained of to be harassment: this may include 'merely' causing fear of violence by using threatening language and, as mentioned, might apply to bullying within the workplace.[1]

§7.5   Griffiths (1977) argued that students do not get a sympathetic reaction from the judiciary, especially in the event of disputes about discipline reaching the courts when not automatically falling within the exclusive jurisdiction of the Visitor in the chartered HEIs. Later editions of his well known *The Politics of the Judiciary* do, however, somewhat soften the firmness of the view taken in the first edition, where Griffiths declared:

> 'Students are not one of the more popular minorities and Her Majesty's judges in recent times seem to have shared much of the prejudice shown by other, equally senior, members of society [167] ... the courts seek assiduously to find some ground on which to disregard breach of the rules of natural justice [on the part of the university/college authorities in disciplining students] [169] ... students are seen essentially as children and sometimes very unpleasant children – above all, as very undisciplined children. And universities and colleges are institutions of the State and so to be upheld [170] ... The student cases indeed are excellent examples of the judicial obsession with, as they see it, the necessity to protect and preserve the structures of constitutional authority without undue concern for the rights of those who wish to challenge that authority [197] ...'

§7.6   Some 25 years on, students are rather calmer in their group behaviour, except for the occasional protest over HE tuition fees. The result is that political protest, *cause célèbre* student discipline cases of the late 1960s and early 1970s have been replaced in the 1990s largely by disputes over academic matters: *Glynn*, the naked student sunbather of 1971, becomes *Clark* disputing examination board due process in 2000.

§7.7   See the Appendix to Chapter 6 for a Note on key cases concerning the HEI–student contract, and Chapter 24 concerning risk management in relation to the student contract. However, do not think that 'the regulation of the community' is confined to the HEI having to cope with difficult students: see Davis (1994) for an account of the bitter and lengthy dispute in the

---

1   See, generally, Infield and Platford (2000).

Department of Philosophy at Swansea; or note the recent furore at Oxford over allegedly non-collegial conduct among colleagues within (of all places) its Centre of Socio-Legal Studies (*The Times Higher Educational Supplement*, 1 June 2001, and 20 July 2001). Chapters 10 and 11 explore such disputes in the context of employment law, while Chapter 8 considers how the Visitor might handle such 'a domestic' (*not* involving the contract of employment) within a chartered HEI (see Davis (1994) and *Burrows v University of York*.)[1]

§7.8   Finally, see the relevant Units from the HEFCE-funded 'Active Risk Management in Education' project at www.bristol.ac.uk/armed. There are already Units available on 'Student Discipline' and 'Student Debt'.

SCOPE OF THIS CHAPTER

7.1   This chapter concerns the way HEIs regulate the relationship they have with their students in the key areas identified in the title. It identifies good practice and likely areas for challenge. It specifically examines the impact of the HRA 1998 and new grounds for complaint under HRA 1998, as well as under UK discrimination law.

GENERAL PRINCIPLES

7.2   As explained in Chapter 6, the HEI–student relationship is generally accepted to be based on a contract. The HEI's regulations form part of the contract's terms. On entering into the contract, the student agrees to be bound by the regulations, in particular disciplinary and related ones. The HEI is equally bound by the terms of the regulations. It must follow the procedures laid down in them. A contract is a matter of private law: an agreement made freely (in theory at least) between individual persons or bodies, and enforceable between the parties by the courts under the general law. But the HEI is generally also a public body. Public bodies are subject to additional obligations which do not apply to purely private sector organisations. These obligations can modify the strict regime of contract law. In some (but not all) circumstances, the individual is entitled to expect more of a public body than pure compliance with the terms of a contract. These expectations include that any rules and regulations which form part of the contractual matrix in the public sector context – disciplinary regulations, for example – will be fair in themselves and will be operated in a fair and reasonable way.

7.3   Public (or administrative) law is used to challenge the decisions or decision-taking processes of public bodies. It also provides remedies. Where damages would not suffice, a student can ask for a decision to be set aside or taken again (properly). The legal process for this challenge in a statutory HEI is judicial review (see Chapter 9). Chartered HEIs are generally also public

---

1   [1999] EdCR 586.

bodies but usually escape judicial review in relation to student challenges because these would be dealt with by the Visitor under the Visitor's exclusive jurisdiction (see Chapter 8). However, the Visitor would be expected to apply public law principles in his or her decision-taking. Judicial review regulates the exercise of statutory powers, which may or may not operate in a contractual framework. As a matter of public law, a wrong decision reached by a public body cannot be challenged as long as it was reached in a way that was unbiased and reasonable and within the terms of the body's own rules and jurisdiction. If the court finds that there was a failing in any of these areas, it will send the decision back to be taken again. It will not substitute its own judgment. The Visitor, in contrast, is fairly free to decide the case and substitute his or her own decision for that of the original body. The Visitor cannot be judicially reviewed except on very narrow grounds, essentially of exceeding his jurisdiction. This may change with the arrival of the HRA 1998, discussed further below.

7.4   There is an argument that judicial review is not an appropriate forum for dealing with student challenges arising out of what has come to be regarded as essentially a contractual relationship. Students should bring complaints about disciplinary decisions, or academic appeals, in the form of breach of contract actions in the county court, the argument goes. If they insist on starting actions for judicial review, these should be transferred out of the administrative courts. This argument seems unlikely to take off. Some claims by students are dealt with in the county courts. However, the process is exceedingly slow, and the county courts do not appear to be comfortable in handling disputes concerning higher education. Furthermore, in most cases students are not after the normal contractual remedy of damages. More often the student wants to be awarded his or her degree or qualification, or to have a disciplinary penalty lifted. The point about the appropriate forum has not been fully argued in any reported case concerning students, so far. Judges in the administrative courts have not shown themselves to be particularly amenable to throwing cases out of their division if, on the face of it, the case has been properly brought and is within the strict time-limits for judicial review.

7.5   Both HEIs and students are probably better served by the administrative courts in any event, even if the judges in those courts, who deal with public law issues all the time, sometimes appear to struggle to grapple with higher education, and normally avoid treading on any area to do with academic judgment. However, the procedure is much quicker, does not involve extensive witness evidence (at least in person) and does not result in damages being awarded. Given that as a general rule the longer litigious cases go on for, the more expensive they will be, judicial review is probably a better option also for HEIs from the point of view of cost. Complaints by students of discrimination (for example, in relation to supervision or examination marking) would normally be heard in the employment tribunal or county court. More detail on discrimination follows at the end of this chapter. Challenges under the HRA 1998 will normally be brought by way of judicial review.

HUMAN RIGHTS ACT 1998

7.6   A summary follows of the relevant provisions of the HRA 1998, which came into force on 2 October 2000, examining the way it may be expected to impact on HEIs in relation to the subject matter of this chapter. The views expressed here have to be qualified by the reservation that no cases determining these provisions in relation to HE have been heard under HRA 1998 at the time of writing, and there is considerable uncertainty and disagreement over the way in which it will be interpreted.

7.7   The HRA 1998 incorporates the rights set out in the European Convention on Human Rights into UK law, making them enforceable for the first time in the courts and tribunals of England and Wales. (The Scotland Act 1998 had the same effect in Scotland, with effect from April 2000.) The Act applies to public authorities. They must act compatibly with Convention rights, and may be challenged directly for breach of or failure to protect those rights. It is the author's view that HEIs will be classed as public authorities and, therefore, will be directly subject to challenge under HRA 1998.

7.8   In addition, courts and tribunals, as public authorities themselves, have to give effect to HRA 1998 in all cases before them – even those which do not involve public authorities. The ambit of HRA 1998, therefore, spreads much more widely, and potentially all organisations, and even individuals, will eventually feel its effects. Furthermore, all existing law and all previous cases now have to be interpreted or reinterpreted according to the requirements of the Convention, and taking into account (although not strictly bound by) 50 years of case-law from Strasbourg (where the European Court of Human Rights (ECHR) sits). The common-law principle of binding precedent in decisions of the higher courts, and our custom of interpreting statute law literally, have now effectively been removed.

7.9   The High Court will be able to declare that UK legislation is incompatible with Convention rights, giving Parliament the chance to amend it. Subordinate legislation may be overridden by the courts. In most cases, the courts are likely not to make such findings but to try to find a way of interpreting legislation which is compatible with Convention rights. Some of the Convention rights (for example, the prohibition on torture, inhuman or degrading treatment) are absolute. Others (for example, freedom of expression) are called 'defeasible rights': that is, the right may be defeated (as it were, trumped) in certain specific circumstances. In most cases, the first question to be asked will be whether a Convention right has been interfered with, and the second, which is often more pertinent (as interference with a right will commonly take place), is whether the interference is justified by the rule of law (ie statute), legitimate aims, or on grounds of proportionality.

7.10   So, which Convention rights will directly affect HEIs in the regulation of the student community discussed here?

Right to education

7.11 This is one of the absolute rights. However, there is no universal right to HE. Access to HE may legitimately be restricted to those who have the necessary qualifications or qualities to benefit from it. HEIs should have no difficulty with claims for breach of the right to education brought by students who have been expelled for disciplinary reasons, or not admitted to the institution on proper grounds. There is no right to education at a particular institution, and no right to education of a particular kind. The right is, therefore, quite limited on its own in relation to HE. It might be used to greater effect in combination with a discrimination claim.

Prohibition of discrimination

7.12 Article 14 states:

> 'The enjoyment of the rights and freedoms set forth in this Convention shall be secured without discrimination on any ground such as sex, race, colour, language, religion, political or other opinion, national or social origin, association with a national minority, property, birth or other status.'

This is another absolute right, but also rather limited. It is not a general prohibition, but a right to have the benefit of other Convention rights without discrimination. One has to show discrimination in relation to another right, not necessarily that that right was breached. 'Other status' is likely to be widely interpreted – in particular it will cover recent preoccupations of UK legislation, policy and case-law such as disability, trans-sexuality, sexual orientation and, probably, age. Even so, Art 14 does not add hugely to our existing discrimination law, which is fairly comprehensive, although somewhat scattered. Gaps which could be filled include the protection of disabled students in relation to their education. The Disability Discrimination Act 1995 (DDA 1995) at present (although amendments are promised) covers employees and conferees at HEIs, but not students themselves – see Chapter 22. Interestingly and conceivably, selecting students for favourable entry conditions according to postcode could be challenged as discrimination on grounds of social class.

Torture, inhuman or degrading treatment

7.13 While torture is unlikely to be relevant, complaints of degrading treatment are possible. The definition of 'degrading' is 'treatment which arouses in the victim a feeling of fear, anguish and inferiority capable of humiliating and debasing him . . .'. Exceptionally severe marking, disparaging comments made publicly about a student by a lecturer, or the imposition of a disproportionately severe disciplinary penalty, might provide grounds for a complaint. The threshold for a successful claim is likely to be set at a high level, as this is an absolute right. However, the degrading treatment would have to be exceptionally severe to persuade a court to uphold such a claim. Bullying could also be said to be degrading. An HEI's failure to take adequate steps to prevent bullying of a student could be used as a ground for complaint. The courts have recently started to allow claims based on failure to prevent bullying in schools, but so far based on the law of negligence rather than human rights.

Respect for private and family life, home and correspondence

7.14 This is likely to prove one of the most significant rights for HEIs. The rights concerned are broadly the protection of personal information, to a personal physical space, and to private communications. A wide range of issues and subjects could be covered, including for example: the interception of correspondence; telephone tapping; access to information about a person's identity; freedom to express one's sexuality; collection and use of information about an individual; the right to have and form social relationships; and the protection of a person's reputation. It is a qualified right, but exceptions will be narrowly construed, while the right itself will be interpreted broadly. The commentary here is restricted to those areas where the right may have an impact on student discipline, appeals or complaints. Enquiries about students may cause claims of interference with this right – for example, in the course of an investigation leading up to disciplinary proceedings, or if close circuit television (CCTV) or other monitoring is carried out secretly and used in evidence. As it is a qualified right, interference can be justified for legitimate reasons if it is necessary and proportionate: for example, searching a student's room in residential accommodation would require some kind of justification. Monitoring of use of the internet and e-mail should be covered by internet use policies which make clear what the HEI proposes to do, and preferably require the student's consent to necessary and proportionate monitoring for legitimate reasons (see Chapter 14).

Freedom of expression

7.15 The right may legitimately be interfered with in the interests of public safety, preventing crime, protection of health and morals, or the rights and freedoms of others, and prevention of defamation. It does not imply a freedom to express views in an abusive or harmful way, or that a student who does so will necessarily be protected from discipline. Complaints of interference with this right are likely to emanate from SU politics, but normally should be capable of justification.

Freedom of thought, conscience and religion

7.16 This is another qualified right, which will only impinge if a student's religious or conscientious persuasion was made known to the HEI from the beginning of the relationship. HEIs in most cases already go to considerable lengths to permit students to comply with requirements of their religion. The recommended course is to ascertain what those requirements are before the student commences a course and then to seek to accommodate them in a practical way in terms of the scheduling of examinations. Female students whose religion requires them to cover their face need special consideration: how will you identify them in examinations? The right overlaps with the Race Relations (Amendment) Act 2000, but extends protection to religious and other believers who do not fit into a racial category – for example, Christian groups and Rastafarians.

Right to a fair hearing

7.17 The rights contained in Art 6 of the European Convention are likely to be among the most heavily used and obviously have particular relevance in the context of this chapter. They are significant rights, which have been highly developed through Strasbourg case-law. Article 6 applies to the determination of civil rights and obligations (as well as to criminal charges, where additional safeguards apply). It clearly applies in all courts and tribunals. It has also been held to apply in disciplinary proceedings in the professions. The requirements are for a fair and public hearing, within a reasonable time, by an independent and impartial tribunal, with judgment in public.

7.18 Do these rights apply in internal HEI disciplinary (or other) hearings? This is a controversial area, further complicated by a decision of the ECHR reported in late 2000: *Lalu Hanuman v UK*.[1] The ECHR held (in an admissibility decision, with no reasoned judgment) that the proceedings of the university's academic appeals committee and the university's Visitor had *not* involved the determination of a civil right. There is a fine line between when a dispute is about contractual rights and when it arises from the exercise of a public law function. The ECHR regards legal disputes of an essentially public law nature as not involving civil rights and obligations. But we cannot rely on the UK courts necessarily taking the same view. The relationship between the student and the HEI, as noted at the beginning of this chapter, is governed by contract. Disciplinary and academic regulations form part of that contract. Therefore, civil (contractual) rights arguably are in question and potentially the Art 6 rights could apply, particularly if the disciplinary proceedings involve quasi-criminal charges – for example, offences involving cheating (fraud), drugs, theft or assault. In the case of an academic appeal, the issue could be whether a student achieves a professional qualification. Once again, because the conduct of an appeal will be a matter of contract, civil rights are arguably (and contrary to the ECHR decision just noted) in question.

7.19 The rights under Art 6 require access to a court or tribunal. One has to consider the whole process to decide whether the rights are satisfied. If the original decision is taken by an administrative body whose procedures do not satisfy Art 6, the requirements may still be met if the decision can be reviewed by a body that does satisfy them, either on appeal or by an external court or tribunal. The court or tribunal in that event would need to hear the full case –

---

1   [2000] ELR 685.

facts and evidence – and not just legal argument. There are doubts about whether the Visitor system in its present form complies with Art 6 (usually there is no hearing and it is not a public process). Doubt has also been expressed as to whether judicial review in its usual form would meet the criteria of Art 6.[1] Judicial review (limited as it is to points of law) may satisfy the fair trial requirements of Art 6 where the initial decision is taken by a quasi-judicial fact-finding body (in the *Bryan* case, a planning inspector). The House of Lords in the *Alconbury* case (referred to at para §7.1 of the Editors' Introduction) conferred that judicial review *was* a sufficient safeguard as a final result in planning appeals. The answer may depend on whether at some stage in the process a fully argued oral hearing on the facts is held. Judicial review is purely a review of the administrative decision-taking process, and does not go into the merits of the original case or the decision. This is in contrast to an employment tribunal, to which employees would usually have access if they are dismissed as a result of an internal disciplinary process, and which fairly clearly would satisfy Art 6.

7.20 Entitlement to a fair hearing was a requirement of public law even without the HRA 1998. The new provisions which may cause difficulty are the requirements for publicity, independence and impartiality, and the holding of oral hearings. Article 6 is most likely to be held to apply in serious disciplinary matters, or where an academic appeal will affect a student's ability to graduate or enter a profession. In theory, it could apply to the hearing of complaints, but only if what is at stake in the complaint is a question concerning the student's 'civil rights and obligations'. An example would be where a student complains of discrimination in the supervision of postgraduate research. In most cases, HEIs are prevented by their charters, or in the case of HECs by their statutory powers, from fully complying with the requirement of providing an independent tribunal to deal with these issues. In chartered institutions, the final resolution of student disciplinary or academic appeals, or complaints, is by the Visitor, with no general access to the courts after that: see Chapters 8 and 30. HECs do not have power to delegate the resolution of these matters to an outsider. Judicial review would be available to a student who was dissatisfied with the conduct of internal proceedings, but, as argued above, this would not provide a full hearing on the facts, and would probably only meet the requirements of Art 6 if there had already been a full oral hearing. HEI disciplinary procedures would almost invariably include provision for an oral hearing at some stage. Academic appeal procedures which do not provide for an oral hearing at any stage are the most likely to be vulnerable.

7.21 The idea of a public hearing in internal proceedings has also caused concern and doubt. In most cases, it is unlikely that a student will insist on a public hearing. Students are entitled to waive their rights. The HEI should offer the opportunity of a public hearing and give the student the option to choose. A public hearing does not need to be widely advertised or held in a large venue.

---

1   *Bryan v UK* (1996) 21 EHRR 342.

Notices of hearings posted on the usual bulletin boards dealing with administrative matters should suffice. Admission should then be granted to the hearing to anyone who is interested. Again, in most cases, this is unlikely to be a large number of people, although in some cases it may include the press.

7.22   Equality of arms is an important principle of Art 6. This means that procedures which specify that a student may not be accompanied by a legal representative are unlikely to stand up to challenge. Proportionality is also relevant here. If the procedures say that legal representation is allowed in certain circumstances, the HEI will have a discretion to refuse to allow it in minor or trivial cases where it would not appear to be necessary and would only have the effect of escalating the issue. This should be quite acceptable as a proportionate response.

7.23   Some pointers are offered below which may assist in improving compliance with the requirements of Art 6 in the procedures discussed here:

–   avoid delay: a hearing within a reasonable time is a specific requirement;
–   do not refuse a student the right to legal representation if, for example, he or she is facing serious disciplinary charges (response to this request should be proportionate);
–   include an oral hearing at some stage of the process; and
–   offer the opportunity of a hearing in public (which the student may waive).

7.24   The argument as to whether Art 6 applies directly to internal HEI hearings is still to be resolved. It is predicted that the courts in the UK will find that it does, in relation to certain types of hearing where serious issues are at stake for the student. Whether or not it is found to apply directly, its standards of fairness will start to permeate all formal disciplinary and appeal processes, as the courts develop its interpretation. For that reason alone, it is recommended that HEIs take steps towards compliance broadly with the criteria outlined above.

DISCIPLINE

7.25   What is the function of disciplinary proceedings and what gives HEIs the right to subject adult students to disciplinary proceedings and sanctions? As discussed in Chapter 2, the HEI is a community of quite a large number of people. Some offences committed by its members could lead to prosecution and possibly conviction in the criminal courts, or to one member of the community suing another in the civil courts for damages or an injunction (for example, for damage caused to property by negligence, or for the abatement of excessive noise). But in reality these legal remedies on their own do not provide sufficient coverage or protection, and would be unnecessarily impractical and expensive to enforce. So HEIs have developed their own internal disciplinary regimes, rules and procedures, to regulate the community and to protect members and property. The function of disciplinary proceedings is to enforce these rules.

7.26 As noted earlier, the basis of the disciplinary regime is the contract between the student and the HEI. The student signs up to a set of disciplinary regulations and agrees to abide by them. The HEI in turn is obliged to abide by the terms of its own disciplinary procedure, with the qualifications discussed below. Disciplinary procedures, which are usually found in general student regulations and enforced through the HEI's secretariat or registry, are distinguished in most HEIs from academic offences such as plagiarism and cheating, which are usually dealt with at least in the first instance through a separate set of academic regulations, enforced through academic boards, examination boards and the HEI's academic registry staff. The same general principles apply to both types of case, wherever what is, essentially, a disciplinary charge is being considered. Appeals against decisions taken on academic grounds are considered separately in the next section of this chapter.

7.27 If the function of disciplinary proceedings is to enforce the institution's rules, first of all it is necessary to define misconduct. The main grounds for bringing disciplinary proceedings are likely to be either misconduct, broadly described, or breach of the institution's rules. Conviction of a criminal offence could also be used either as a ground for discipline or as evidence of misconduct. For the purposes of the discussion that follows, it is assumed that disciplinary hearings will normally take a broadly adversarial, rather than inquisitorial approach. This is the approach adopted by most HEIs, at least for more serious types of discipline. Normally the student will be charged with an offence of misconduct, the case against him or her will be presented by a member of the HEI staff, and the student will respond to the charge by presenting a defence. A decision is then taken by a disciplinary committee hearing the case. Slightly different principles apply in purely investigatory hearings.

7.28 A useful summary is given by Brian Harris QC (1999) in his survey of disciplinary and regulatory proceedings.

> 'The proceedings of a disciplinary tribunal must be conducted in accordance with:
>
> – the tribunal's own rules except to the extent to which they may be inconsistent with
> – the rules of natural justice; and, in so far as they may be applicable,
> – the requirements of the European Convention.'

7.29 While it is very important for the HEI to follow its own procedures properly, disciplinary procedures should not be interpreted too strictly if that would lead to a result which would disadvantage the student. In the case of *Jones v Welsh Rugby Football Union; Jones v Pugh*,[1] a player charged with fighting had been refused the opportunity to challenge the factual basis of the allegation against him, and the disciplinary committee had refused without good reason

---

1   (1997) *The Times*, March 6.

to vary its procedures for viewing video evidence. The issues were whether the committee had applied its rules with undue rigidity and whether or not the rules were unfair. It was clearly arguable that the committee was wrong to refuse to vary its procedure for no other reason than that it did not do things that way. It was also arguable that a system which did not allow a party to challenge by question or evidence the factual basis of the evidence against him *prima facie* lacked basic fairness. The key concepts and principles in disciplinary proceedings are as follows.

Natural justice

7.30   The so-called rules of natural justice ('due process' in the USA) are not really rules, but broad principles of fairness, which underpin public law. These are not technical requirements, but embody a common-sense approach to ensure fair play. As applied to disciplinary hearings, the main points can be summarised as follows: no surprises, in that students should be told clearly and in advance the nature of the charges against them, or the case they will have to meet; and students must be given the chance to put their own case or side of the story, or version of events to an unbiased decision-taking tribunal. Failure to comply with these broad principles may be challenged by the student either by judicial review or in a petition to the Visitor. The HEI manager might usefully note that, broadly, these principles of due process apply also to employment law (see Further Reading generally, and Chapters 10 and 11).

No surprises

7.31   How specific should the terms of the charge be? They must be sufficient to enable the student to prepare his defence or answer to the complaint. As with a criminal charge, there should be 'a statement of the specific offence with which the [student] is charged describing the offence shortly, together with such particulars as may be necessary for giving reasonable information as to the nature of the charge'.[1] The charge must be provided to the student with sufficient notice to allow him or her time to prepare for the hearing. The student is entitled to be informed in advance if there is a fundamental change in the nature of the allegations.

7.32   While there is no strict rule that evidence needs to be disclosed in advance, if the student is taken by surprise by the presentation of evidence of which no notice has been given – whether in the form of documents or witness evidence – he would be entitled to ask for an adjournment in order to be able to prepare a defence in response. It is, therefore, best practice to disclose to the student, again sufficiently far in advance of the hearing to allow the material to be digested and a response prepared, all documentary evidence on which the HEI proposes to rely, and, in a serious or complex case, witness statements or at

---

1   Indictment Rules 1971, r 5(1), quoted by Harris (1999), p 262.

least a summary of the evidence which witnesses will be called to give. To some, this will seem an unduly legalistic approach. It should not necessarily be seen in this way. By disclosing evidence in advance, the HEI is simply providing information which will enable the subject of the disciplinary proceedings to prepare properly. Taking the opponent by surprise is no longer considered a fair or useful concept in litigation, and this principle can be usefully applied in disciplinary hearings too.

7.33　The same principle applies whether the HEI's procedures provide for an adversarial hearing, as generally contemplated here, or where there is a more inquisitorial approach. As long as the student is facing a disciplinary charge and/or penalty, he should not be denied access to evidence and information which will be used in determining the result. It should also be obvious that the committee hearing the case must not be given any information or evidence which the student does not also have access to, or of which he is unaware.

The hearing

7.34　The student must be given a fair chance to put his own case and version of events. What does this involve? While there is no general right to an oral hearing implied by law, the incorporation by the HRA 1998 of Art 6 of the European Convention has introduced this as a requirement on public authorities, as discussed earlier. Most disciplinary procedures in HEIs will allow for an oral hearing, or in smaller cases, a meeting or discussion, where the student has the chance to put his side of things. As the rights in Art 6 are not absolute, proportionality could be used as an argument against doing this in truly minor cases where there could be no real dispute over the evidence. It is generally accepted that a requirement of a fair hearing is that the student is not only allowed to present his own case, but to question witnesses giving evidence against him. Again, most disciplinary procedures should allow for this to happen, but if they do not, in the interests of fairness, questioning by the student should be allowed. The committee hearing the case will always retain a discretion to control and limit questioning to matters which are strictly relevant, and, of course, to prevent it from deteriorating into abuse or a series of statements.

7.35　Is the student entitled to be legally represented in internal disciplinary hearings? While there is no general implied right to legal representation in disciplinary proceedings, once again the HRA 1998 is likely to bring about a change in this respect. The principle of equality of arms means that the student should not be put at a disadvantage, particularly in serious or complex cases, by being denied access to an appropriately skilled and qualified representative. It would clearly be unacceptable for an HEI to claim the right to be legally advised and represented in putting its case against the student, while denying that right to the student. However, it is likely that a broader right to be legally represented in serious cases will start to be found by the courts following the 1998 Act.

Again, proportionality may be invoked to deny this right in cases where the seriousness or complexity does not justify it. This should be a matter for discretion by the committee. HEIs are quite entitled, and right in many cases, to say that lawyers should be kept out of internal domestic proceedings as far as possible. Lord Denning made this point in *Enderby Town Football Club Ltd v Football Association Ltd:*[1]

> 'In many cases it may be a good thing for the proceedings to be conducted informally without legal representation. Justice can often be done better in them by a good layman than by a bad lawyer … A domestic tribunal is not entitled to lay down an absolute rule: "We will never allow anyone to have a lawyer to appear for him".'

(The student's ability to find 'a good layman' to do the job may, however, be doubtful: unlike employees, students are unlikely to have ready access to trained non-legal advisers like trade union representatives.)

7.36 The factors which could be considered as relevant to the discretion to grant legal representation are summarised by Harris (1999), p 287:

– the seriousness of the charge and the potential penalty;
– whether any points of law are likely to arise;
– the capacity of the defendant to present his case;
– procedural difficulties, such as the need to interview and cross-examine witnesses;
– the need for reasonable speed in making the adjudication; and
– the need for fairness as between the parties.

7.37 The order of proceedings is usually laid down broadly in the HEI's disciplinary regulations, and mostly follows the model of a trial. The management case ('prosecution') is presented first, with witnesses being called by the HEI to give evidence and be questioned in turn by or on behalf of the student. The student will next call his witnesses, who can then be questioned in turn by the management representative. The committee will also normally ask questions of witnesses and the representatives on each side may ask further questions arising out of these questions. Both sides usually sum up. The student should have the final word before the committee retires to consider its decision. This basic framework does not require undue formality. The disciplinary committee does not have to behave like a court: this simply provides a sensible structure to allow both parties to present their own case and question the other's. It is important to maintain a separation of roles on the HEI's side. The person who is presenting the management case cannot also be a judge of it. In larger cases, the disciplinary committee may have a clerk or secretary to assist it. The clerk should not have been involved in the preparation of the management case or evidence. Failure to maintain this separation can lead to complaints of bias. In the case of *Flanagan v University College Dublin,*[2] the Registrar, who was acting as prosecutor in a disciplinary case of plagiarism, remained with the committee while it deliberated over

---

1   [1971] 1 All ER 215, at p 218 (as quoted by Harris (1999), p 286).
2   [1988] IR 724, [1990] CL 1808.

whether to submit the student's work for an expert opinion. This was found to be one of many (six) flaws which made the committee's ultimate decision unsound: see also *M v Secretary of State for Education.*[1]

7.38 What is the standard of proof in internal disciplinary hearings? The criminal standard of proof is 'beyond reasonable doubt', whereas the civil standard is 'on the balance of probabilities'. It is generally accepted that the criminal standard is too strict for internal disciplinary proceedings. However, it is also considered that the more serious the charge, the more satisfied the committee need to be that the offence has been committed. One way of expressing this is to say that there is a sliding scale and that for very serious offences, especially those involving honesty (for example, plagiarism or cheating), a higher standard, approaching that of criminal cases, should be applied. Another approach is to take the basic civil standard but to say that the more serious the offence, the less probable it is that it happened – therefore the committee needs to be more thoroughly convinced that it did happen, by stronger evidence. This does not strictly alter the standard of proof, but requires the committee to take more care to satisfy itself that a serious offence was actually committed, on the balance of probabilities.

Giving reasons

7.39 Are disciplinary committees required to give reasons for their decisions? This is a question which is mainly going to be of concern where the decision is adverse to the student. Although there is no general implied obligation in law for reasons to be given, the courts have developed this duty in more recent years, expressing disapproval of failures by public bodies to give proper reasons for their decisions. The HRA 1998 amplifies this and the trend is likely to be accelerated towards a presumption that, at least in serious cases, reasons will be given. The obligation to justify their decision should concentrate the minds of decision-takers on why they reached it, what factors they took into account and what they ignored. This should mean that the decision is more likely to be soundly based. The student is also more likely to be satisfied, even though the decision is adverse, if he can see that the relevant issues were considered properly and addressed in the reasoning. It may, therefore, prevent futile appeals. On the other hand, some people argue that giving reasons opens the decision up to easy challenge and appeal. The solution is perhaps to provide summary reasons. These should:

– state the facts found;
– identify the main issues, and the conclusion in relation to each of them;
– state whose evidence was preferred if there was a conflict;
– state if any evidence was discounted and why; and
– make clear the basis for the final decision.

---

1   [2001] 2 FCR 11, CA.

7.40   In many cases, this will mean no more than a straightforward summary of the facts found and the considerations which led the committee to reach its conclusion. In fairness to the student, the committee's decision and reasons should, of course, be given as soon as possible.[1] It should be within the committee's discretion to adjourn to consider their decision. It is good practice to deliver the decision in person to the student, at least in serious cases (to be followed up by written confirmation later).

Penalties and mitigation

7.41   If a punishment is imposed, it should be proportionate to the offence. Some disciplinary procedures will allow for separate representations to be made on the question of the appropriate punishment, after a finding of guilt has been made. As long as there is an opportunity for the student to present evidence in mitigation, this does not necessarily have to be at a separate stage. Mitigation might consist of extenuating circumstances or personal factors.

Conduct of proceedings

7.42   Subject to its rules, the disciplinary committee may conduct its proceedings as it thinks fit. It will have discretion to limit questioning of witnesses, or the number of witnesses, or to adjourn the hearing. The discretion must be exercised reasonably. A decision to refuse a request for an adjournment could be a breach of natural justice if the request is justified.

Related criminal charges

7.43   Should internal disciplinary hearings be deferred (or pursued at all) if the student is being prosecuted in the criminal courts on a related charge? It is often argued that pursuing internal proceedings could prejudice the student in the criminal case. There is no general rule that internal proceedings cannot be pursued and it will be up to the student to demonstrate that there is a real risk of prejudice. Similarly, it may be argued on behalf of a student who is being both disciplined and prosecuted that this is contrary to the double jeopardy rule. This is not correct. The rule prevents the trial of a person twice on the same charge in the same forum. An HEI is entitled to enforce its own disciplinary regulations internally, and is not obliged to have regard for the proceedings or outcome of any related criminal case.

7.44   These questions were considered in the *Report of the CVCP Task Force into Student Disciplinary Procedures,* commonly known as the Zellick Report (Zellick, 1994). The Report identified four situations where the HEI might have to consider whether to pursue internal discipline concurrently with criminal proceedings. The categories and recommendations were:

---

1   See *Nash v Chelsea College of Art and Design* [2001] EWHC Admin 538, [2001] All ER(D) 133 (Jul), [2001] TLR 471.

– where the conduct is closely related to the academic or other work of the HEI (for example, theft of library books) – proceed;
– where the conduct occurred on campus or other HEI property (for example, fighting between students on campus) – proceed;
– where the conduct involved other HEI members but was off campus (for example, student stalking a lecturer) – *prima facie* case to proceed; and
– where none of the above applied, but the conduct damaged the HEI's reputation (for example, student arrested for nude demonstrations in Trafalgar Square) or threatened the HEI community – possible to proceed, but with caution.

7.45   These categories are unexceptionable. The really difficult decisions are to do with whether to proceed with discipline in serious rape or assault cases. The basic rule is to remember that an HEI disciplinary committee is not a criminal court and does not have the equipment or expertise to try what amounts to a serious criminal offence such as rape, where forensic evidence, a high standard of proof, and extremely skilful and careful handling of witnesses are required. The HEI should generally not proceed in cases where the police or Crown Prosecution Service (CPS) have decided not to go to trial because of lack of evidence. In cases of this kind where the criminal case goes ahead, the HEI should not try to run a parallel trial, but if the student is found guilty in the criminal court, could consider instituting disciplinary proceedings subsequently, if this was thought to be necessary as a practical matter. It is unlikely to be necessary if the student is imprisoned, for example. In cases of this kind, an HEI will normally wish to suspend the student, pending the outcome of the trial or the disciplinary hearing. Disciplinary procedures should allow for a right on the part of the HEI to suspend, subject to the student's right to make representations about the proposed suspension. The suspension should also be reviewed at intervals. Suspension in these circumstances is not a punishment, but it is still quite a drastic action which can have major effects on a student's progression: hence these safeguards are suggested.

Appeals

7.46   HEI procedures usually provide for a right of appeal against a disciplinary committee's initial decision. There is no general right of appeal in law otherwise. The HEI will usually regulate the bringing of appeals by setting a time-limit and sometimes by limiting grounds for appeal. It is advisable not to be unduly restrictive in interpreting grounds for appeal: it is quite possible to spend more time (and expense) arguing about whether there are grounds than it would take to hear the appeal. There are two main types of appeal: either the case is reheard afresh by the appeal committee, or it is confined to a procedural review of the conduct of the initial hearing. There can be variations and combinations of these two themes and there are no rigid legal rules about which method should be used, nor are there rigid rules about who should sit on an appeal committee. However, it is obviously good practice to disqualify anyone who sat on the original decision-taking body from hearing an appeal from that decision.

Judicial review

7.47　If the student pursues the challenge further, it will normally be by means of judicial review (or petition to the Visitor in chartered institutions): see Chapters 8 and 9. Judicial review is not an appeal from a decision but a review of the manner in which the decision was made. It is concerned not with the decision but with the decision-taking process. It is normally only available when internal procedures have been exhausted. The normal remedy is for the decision challenged to be set aside, in which case the HEI will have to decide whether to try again or abandon the case.

ACADEMIC APPEALS

7.48　There is an overlap with disciplinary procedures where academic appeals concern findings of academic misconduct (cheating, plagiarism). These offences are normally dealt with through procedures set out in academic regulations rather than in the general disciplinary regulations, because the sanctions are academic ones. Academic regulations usually include a range of sanctions from progression decisions and re-sits, up to expulsion for academic failure or for academic offences. Some HEIs include academic offences in both sets of procedures – academic and general disciplinary. The rationale for doing so needs to be clear and duplication should be avoided. In academic hearings and appeals dealing with essentially misconduct issues, the general principles outlined above in relation to discipline should be applied. There is also a clear overlap between academic appeals and complaints by students about academic matters. Both areas are covered by the QAA in its *Code of Practice for academic appeals and student complaints on academic matters*, published in March 2000. HEIs were expected to have met the standards set out in the Code by May 2001. The Code sets out standards of good practice which will not be duplicated here.

7.49　The QAA Code usefully distinguishes between the nature of complaints and appeals, and bases its approach to the handling of the two on the distinction. A complaint is defined as 'any specific concern about the provision of a programme of study or related academic service', while an appeal is 'a request for a review of a decision of an academic body charged with making decisions on student progression, assessment and awards'.[1] The difference of approach is summarised at para 14:

> 'Because academic appeals are part of an institution's student assessment arrange-
> ments they are always likely to be dealt with in a formal way and their procedures
> and possible outcomes clearly framed in official regulations, Codes or guidance

---

1　　*Code of Practice*, para 12.

documents. They may also be subject to a system of precedents, to ensure consistency of treatment. Complaints, by contrast, can be raised about a very wide range of events or activities and may involve single or multiple complainants. Complaints procedures therefore need to be flexible and responsive to ensure that a fair and just outcome is assured in each case.'

The QAA Code emphasises the importance of dealing effectively with both complaints and appeals close to the point of origin. But what happens if things go wrong and the matter is pursued?

7.50 It should be noted first of all that the courts have proved most reluctant to involve themselves in questioning academic decision-taking. Michael Beloff QC (1999) notes that, while the courts recognise the importance to students of issues of academic progression, it is nevertheless a notable feature of the reported cases that 'either the treatment meted out was found to be fair – or, if it was not, discretionary reasons were somehow found to deny relief'. An example of the latter is the case of *R v University of Aston Senate ex parte Roffey*.[1] The student claimants had been expelled for failure in examinations. The course regulations provided: 'Students who . . . fail in a referred examination, may at the discretion of the examiners, re-sit the whole examination or may be required to withdraw from the course'. The students succeeded in showing that they had not been treated in accordance with natural justice because the examiners had taken into account extraneous factors as well as the exam marks, but had not allowed the students to be heard on these matters. However, the court refused to use its discretion to allow their claim because they had not acted promptly enough in bringing it.

7.51 More recently, in the case of *M v London Guildhall University*,[2] the Court of Appeal refused to intervene in the student's claim to be entitled to receive an honours degree rather than an ordinary degree on the grounds that the University had provision to determine disputes regarding the awarding of degrees, and that this was the proper vehicle for the determination and not the High Court. Despite the fact that the University had no Visitor, the judgment of Auld LJ referred to 'the primacy of the University authorities where proper machinery is provided for the regulation of issues between them and those making complaints about the performance of their university duties'. In another recent case, *R v University of Nottingham ex parte K*,[3] K failed the teaching practice element of the PGCE and sought judicial review of the University examiners' decision. Once again, the court declined to intervene, this time on the ground that the University Visitor had exclusive jurisdiction. The court was not deflected from this view by the existence of external (non-University) regulations on accreditation, the supporting ministerial circular, nor by the fact that responsibility for the teacher training part of the PGCE was shared with schools. None of these factors was considered to justify interfering with the Visitor's exclusive jurisdiction.

---

1   [1969] 2 QB 538.
2   [1998] ELR 149.
3   [1998] ELR 184.

7.52 The courts certainly seem to see the existence of the Visitorial jurisdiction as a convenient excuse to avoid intervening in reviewing academic matters, such as the application of university regulations relating to degrees and satisfaction of examiners. Even if the Visitorial jurisdiction is eventually modified or removed, it is suggested, based on the historical showing of reluctance, that the courts will be unlikely to wish to step into the breach in relation to issues of academic judgment. They have declined to do so even in cases where the university concerned has no Visitor – except where the university has departed from its own procedures. In his article 'The HEI– student legal relationship, with special reference to the USA experience', David Palfreyman (1999b) confirms that 'the US courts will not readily lift the veil of expert, academic judgement'. He quotes Kaplin and Lee (1995a):

> 'Courts are particularly ill equipped to evaluate academic performance ... judicial review of grading disputes would inappropriately involve the Courts in the very core of academic and education decision-making ... in the absence of demonstrated bad faith, arbitrariness, capriciousness, irrationality or a constitutional or statutory violation, a student's challenge ... is beyond the scope of judicial review.'

As Palfreyman notes, there is little need for timidity in dealing with academic/disciplinary matters, as long as the HEI's rules and regulations are applied accurately, consistently and fairly (ie avoiding bad faith, arbitrariness, capriciousness, etc).

7.53 If, however, the courts find procedural failings or breaches of natural justice, they will be much more ready to step in. The case of *R v Manchester Metropolitan University ex parte Nolan*[1] led the way here. The applicant had been found guilty by a disciplinary committee of attempting to secure an unfair academic advantage, but not guilty of cheating. The committee made no recommendation as to penalty to the board of examiners. The board treated the applicant as a cheat and imposed a severe penalty accordingly. The court granted the student's request for judicial review, quashing the board's decision and requiring it to consider the matter afresh in the light of all the relevant evidence which it had not taken into account the first time around. Sedley J noted in his judgment:

> 'It is, with respect, not easy to understand how a board of law examiners was able to conclude that, where the written procedure allocated fact-finding to a separate body which heard and evaluated evidence and then gave to the examiners the task of deciding on penalty, it was open to the latter body not only to substitute a different finding but to consider penalty under a different set of rules.'

One can sympathise with his impatience, and the courts have indeed in subsequent cases stepped in where there has been clear and obvious unfairness or departure from the HEI's regulations, while still refusing to take sides in disputes on matters of purely academic judgment. For example, in the case of *R v Cranfield University Senate ex parte Bashir*,[2] the student's doctoral thesis had been found not to meet the required standards. The court refused to interfere in

---

1   [1994] ELR 380.
2   [1999] ELR 317.

a disagreement between the student and the University about the competence of the examiners. In *R v University of Central England ex parte Iqbal Sandhu*,[1] the student handed in his dissertation one day late. As a consequence, he received zero marks and was prevented from being awarded an honours degree. The court held that it is for an examination board to consider the circumstances of each individual case, and awarding zero marks for late submission is not disproportionate or irrational. The board had made a decision which was within the bounds of its proper discretion and judgement.

7.54   It should be noted incidentally that the Visitor is just as unlikely as the courts to involve himself in matters of academic judgement. The offloading of responsibility onto the Visitor in this respect has little foundation in reality. As Beloff (1999) points out, the true reason is not the exclusive jurisdiction of the Visitor but perceived incompetence: 'The High Court does not act as a Court of Appeal from University examiners; and speaking for my own part, I am very glad that it declines jurisdiction'.[2] It seems likely that Visitors and the courts will continue to hold to this view.

COMPLAINTS

7.55   While student disciplinary and academic regulations have been accepted as part of the framework of universities for well over a century, procedures to deal with student complaints are not so traditional. Many HEIs have only recently introduced such procedures. What is the rationale (other than the requirements of the QAA) for having a complaints procedure? It will be seen from the previous section that the relatively few cases where students have succeeded in challenging HEIs in court are usually those where a decision-taking process was handled wrongly or the student was treated with blatant unfairness. As suggested in the QAA Code, referred to earlier, getting it right at the earliest stage is the best way of avoiding litigation. Complaints procedures fill a gap by allowing students to bring problems to do with their treatment outside the context of academic appeals and discipline to the attention of the HEI and have them dealt with properly in a structured way (see the Specimen Complaints Procedure set out in Chapter 6, Appendix 2). The alternative is usually to go to court or petition the Visitor to get a resolution of the problem – which is not likely to be in the interests of either party, compared with a speedy internal method which is capable of providing a satisfactory outcome. Avoiding litigation is not the only reason for having a complaints procedure. As the QAA points out in para 6:

'There is now a general and reasonable expectation that organisations providing services to the public should have effective systems for handling complaints. Students are entitled to no less effective a system to operate within higher education, than

---

1   [1999] ELR 121.
2   Diplock LJ in *Thorne v University of London* [1966] 2 QB 237.

operates in other public services they may use.' (See Chapter 29 concerning the student as 'the empowered consumer'.)

7.56 The ethos of a complaints system is different from both disciplinary and academic regulations. The purpose is to resolve a problem, not to punish offenders. The types of complaint brought by students cover a wide range. This section concentrates on those which, if not properly handled, or not handled at all, could lead to further problems and litigation. It may be difficult sometimes to tell where to draw the line between appeals and complaints, particularly at the postgraduate level of research or taught dissertations. For example, if the grounds of an academic appeal are the poor quality of supervision, or the choice of external examiners, or race discrimination, how should these apparent complaints be dealt with? If these issues only surface after the publication of results, they should most likely be dealt with as part of the academic appeals process, although investigations may need to be made in the same way as they would be in the case of a free-standing complaint. If a student complains before results have been produced about the standard of super-vision, or failure of supervisors to give adequate warning of problems with the work, these should fall within the HEI's complaints handling procedure. However, the appropriate outcome of a complaint might be the adjustment of a decision affecting academic progress or award. The HEI should define how and where these borderline cases will be dealt with in its procedures.

7.57   Other complaints commonly arise in relation to the terms of the student–HEI contract, particularly as a result of misinformation or misrep-resentations in prospectuses: for example, that a course is validated by a professional body, when it is not; that certain facilities or special equipment will be available, when they are not; that a course will be run, and it is cancelled at the last minute or halfway through. In most cases where the complaint is justified, the HEI will work with the student concerned (or commonly a group of students) to find a practical solution, often involving placing them at another institution – taking a practical approach to assist the students and mitigate their loss, rather than waiting for the claim to arrive. In cases where a complaint of this kind is clearly justified, there is much to be gained by apologising and taking practical steps to make amends as far as possible (an approach now being pioneered within the NHS in handling patient complaints).

7.58   A complaint may involve making accusations against another person within the HEI, and could lead to disciplinary action against that person – for example, for harassment, bullying, racist behaviour, even assault or sexual offences. If disciplinary action is taken, whether against another student or a member of staff, there needs to be a clear line drawn between that action and the handling of the complaint. The complainant should not be the prosecutor, or drive the disciplinary action, although he or she is likely to be a witness. Clearly disciplinary action cannot be pursued if the complainant is not willing to be identified, and as a practical matter it is unlikely to be pursued if he or she will not appear at a disciplinary hearing and give evidence. Any disciplinary action which follows on from a complaint must be in accordance with the usual disciplinary regulations and procedures, for students or staff as the case may be. If the HEI has separate procedures for harassment, it should be made clear in what circumstances those procedures rather than general complaints procedures would be invoked.

7.59   The HEI should provide in its procedures for spurious complaints to be the subject of disciplinary action. It may not be sensible to strike out such complaints as early on as the QAA Code seems to envisage, if it is implied that there should be no appeal from such a rejection. The QAA guidance is that an institution should: 'provide for applications judged to be frivolous or vexatious to be rejected, at the earliest possible time, with reasons given in writing to the student, as to why the application is an abuse of process'. While that has its obvious attractions, if the result is to deny a determined student access to the full procedure, the HEI may find itself facing more serious problems later on. Disciplinary action could, however, be taken at the end of the process against a student who brought and pursued such a complaint.

DISCRIMINATION

7.60   This chapter concludes with a brief review of the applicability of discrimination law in the UK to students in HE. Students can claim for discrimination on grounds of sex or race by education institutions under the Sex Discrimination Act 1975 and the Race Relations Act 1976 (RRA 1976) relating to:

−   the terms on which the institution offers to admit the student;
−   refusal or deliberate omission by the institution to accept the student's application for admission;
−   the way in which the institution affords access to the student to any of its benefits, facilities or services, or if it deliberately omits to do so;
−   exclusion of the student; or
−   any other detriment.

7.61   There are, however, certain exemptions from the general duty not to discriminate on the grounds of race covering 'positive discrimination' − for example, the provision of education for persons not ordinarily resident in Great Britain, or the special needs of racial groups in regard to education or training. Claims against HEIs are generally brought in the county court. Claims against other providers of vocational training can be brought in the employment tribunal. The time-limit for such claims is 6 months (3 months in the tribunal). Time can be extended by 2 months if the applicant applies for assistance from the Commission for Racial Equality (CRE), and generally at the court's discretion. In race discrimination cases, the county court judge must sit with two assessors appointed by the court, unless the parties agree otherwise. In sex discrimination cases, the parties can choose to have assessors. Successful applicants in race and sex discrimination cases can be awarded damages for compensation for injury to feelings, as well as the more usual damages for loss.

7.62   The Race Relations (Amendment) Act 2000 amends the RRA 1976 by extending the protection for individuals against the actions of public authorities. The main duty imposed by the new provisions is to make it unlawful for a public authority to discriminate on racial grounds in carrying out any of its functions. There is also a new general duty for certain bodies (HEI governing bodies are specifically included: Sch 1) to have due regard to the need to eliminate unlawful discrimination and to promote equal opportunities in the carrying out of their functions. This new duty will be enforceable both by the CRE and also by being made the subject of inspections by existing bodies such as the Office for Standards in Education (OFSTED). However, as HEIs have been covered by previous legislation, the only real difference is the new positive duty to promote racial equality and the fact that this duty can now be enforced by the CRE: in short, HEIs are now required to be pro-active in relation to avoiding unlawful racial discrimination (see the CRE website at www.cre.gov.uk).

7.63   There have been no reported cases in which a student has succeeded in showing discrimination on the grounds of either race or sex by an HEI.[1] However, this is a common ground of challenge by students, covering every aspect of student life, from allegations of bias in exam marking to sexual harassment.[2] HEIs should, therefore, seek to protect themselves from such claims by:

–   introducing and monitoring policies on equal opportunities and harassment;
–   providing training for staff in equal opportunities issues;
–   ensuring that, so far as possible, students' assessments and examinations are marked on an anonymous basis; and
–   monitoring the performance of ethnic minority students and taking steps to address any issues which arise.

7.64   At the time of writing, the protection afforded by the DDA 1995 does not extend to students engaged in education. However, the Special Educational Needs and Disability Act 2001 amends the DDA 1995 to bring students within the scope of the disability discrimination provisions for the first time. The new legislation, which will be brought into force in phases starting in October 2002, will make it unlawful for an HEI to treat a disabled student less favourably, without justification, than a student who is not disabled, and will require HEIs to make reasonable adjustments to ensure that disabled students are not put at a substantial disadvantage as compared to non-disabled students. These new duties do not mean that HEIs will immediately be required to ensure that all

---

1   There has, however, been much publicity about one research assistant's allegations of racism against the University of Oxford (*Anya v University of Oxford* [2001] EWCA Civ 405, [2001] ELR 711, (2001) ELJ 2(4) 227–228); and similarly, a Glasgow University academic is currently using race discrimination legislation, in an employment tribunal, to force Glasgow to reveal the names of the academic referees it relied on in deciding not to promote him to the personnel chair which, allegedly, was promised to him when he had initially been recruited.
2   See *Education Guardian*, 27 March 2001, p 15.

of their campus is accessible to wheelchair users; however, an HEI will be required to make reasonable adjustments to accommodate the needs of a particular student (for example, by moving that student's classes to ground floor rooms). Disability discrimination in relation to the right to education will in any event be covered by Art 14 of the European Convention on Human Rights, now incorporated into the HRA 1998. (See also Chapter 22.)

CONCLUSION

7.65 There are thus a variety of external legal forums which may be used by students to bring challenges against HEIs in relation to the operation of internal rules and regulations: the Visitor, judicial review, county court breach of contract claims, county court discrimination claims and employment tribunal discrimination claims. Would it be better if a more uniform system were to replace this diversity? Over the years since a proposal to this effect was first advanced in the original Nolan report, little progress has been made towards a consensus, although many ideas have been put forward by regulators, representative bodies and government-sponsored reports. The present favourite is an Ombudsman for HE. The disadvantages of this and of most of the other proposals are: first, that HE is a diverse sector resistant to the imposition of universal systems; and secondly, that these proposed dispute resolution systems would not necessarily exclude the jurisdiction of the courts and would only interpose another layer of dispute handling which will not put off the determined litigant.

7.66 The general principles to be followed in the proper handling of student discipline, academic appeals and complaints come down to some almost embarrassingly basic points, which are, however, surprisingly often forgotten. HEIs need to follow their own procedures; but also to bear in mind that, if rigidly doing so would lead to an unfair result, they should be prepared to vary them in the student's favour. If the rules in themselves are unfair, or are applied with undue rigidity, or both, the HEI's decision is likely to be struck down when judicially reviewed or subjected to a discrimination claim. The most fundamental principle is that students need to be treated in a fair way, as adults. A good test of this is to ask: would I like (or expect) to be treated like this if I were bringing a complaint / being disciplined / appealing against an important academic decision which affected my future? Standards of client care and service which are now expected of the professions may be more apt than the analogy of students as consumers, which seems too crude to encapsulate the complexities of relationships in HE. Students are not simply consumers of education, but have considerable responsibilities themselves, as well as rights.

Chapter 8

DISPUTES I: THE ROLE OF THE VISITOR IN CHARTERED INSTITUTIONS

David Isaac (Masons)

EDITORS' INTRODUCTION

§8.1   If the procedures within a chartered university – as opposed to a statutory university or a college of HE – fail to resolve a dispute between a member of the university (a student, an academic and certain senior managers and librarians, but not other employees) and the institution, then the role of the Visitor can be invoked for all disputes relating to the internal rules (except certain disputes concerning the contract of employment for academic staff and the senior managers or librarians referred to). But what is a Visitor? What jurisdiction and powers does he have? Is there an overlap between the jurisdiction and powers of the Visitor and the normal role of the courts in relation to the contract between the student and the chartered university? How does the university or, indeed, the aggrieved student, actually make contact with the Visitor? If the Visitor is the Queen (or some other great dignitary), who will actually handle the matter on her behalf? What does it cost to have the Visitor visit? Can the Visitor award damages? Is there any appeal against the decision of the Visitor? This chapter explores all these issues and notes the recommendation of the Nolan Committee (1996), p 28 that: 'Students in higher education institutions should be able to appeal to an independent body, and this right should be reflected in the Higher Education Charters. The higher education funding councils, institutions, and representative bodies should consult on a system of independent review of disputes'. The question arises whether a revised Visitor model would meet with approval from Nolan, both for continued use in the chartered HEIs and even for extending to the statutory HEIs.

§8.2   There are many Visitor cases from the eighteenth and nineteenth centuries, mainly in relation to Oxbridge colleges: but not in relation to the University of Oxford or the University of Cambridge, neither of which, unusually amongst the 'old' universities, have a Visitor (see Chapter 30, 'A Bibliographical Essay on the Visitor', for a discussion of whether Oxford and Cambridge do or do not have a Visitor). In addition, there are a few rather famous recent ones, including the only one which has ever been widely published (Davies (1994)). Here the Visitor, on behalf of the Queen, was Sir Michael Davies, a retired High Court judge, who produced a superb report which silenced 5 years of squabbling at University College, Swansea, and which superseded several earlier enquiries (and all at a cost of several hundred thousand pounds). As discussed in this chapter, there has been doubt whether the Visitor can award damages, but it is now clear that damages can be awarded[1] and perhaps aggrieved students will increasingly seek them in the content of becoming personally liable for tuition fees post-Dearing.

§8.3   The legal oddity of the visitorial function is interesting. It is an area of law left over from canon law and the Middle Ages (like a Consistory Court or a Court of Chivalry) and, as such, only in very limited circumstances does the ordinary court exercise a supervisory check on the Visitor via the mechanism of judicial review. The Visitor cannot be challenged on the ground of error of fact or even of law – only where he has acted outside the Visitor's jurisdiction (for example, no power under the university statutes to be involved, behaving contrary to the rules of natural justice or if refusing to act when clearly the Visitor should). Similarly, there is no appeal beyond the Visitor – the visitorial court is the *forum domesticum* of the university (Farrington (1998), quotes one case referring to the Visitor having 'untrammelled power to investigate and right wrongs arising from the application of the domestic laws of the chartered institution' and sums the role up as 'an Ombudsman with teeth'). Williams (1910) quotes Lord Camden, remarking of the Visitor function in an eighteenth-century case: 'a despotism uncontrolled and without appeal, the only one of the kind existing in the kingdom'.

§8.4   There is currently much talk of the Visitor *not* surviving a challenge under Art 6(1) of the European Convention (right to a fair and public hearing): most commentators are busily hammering nails into the Visitor's legal coffin (for example, Kaye (1999); Birtwistle (2000)), *but* Luxton (2001), paras 1.97– 1.105, and 12.06 provides a possible defence. Luxton argues that the Visitor can be shown to be an *independent* tribunal in line with *Campbell and Fell v United Kingdom*[2] concerning the Prison Board of Visitors (the ECHR decided that a Prison Board of Visitors when exercising a disciplinary function did *not* breach Art 6(1) and was *not* merely the creature of the Home Secretary who appoints the Board). Luxton notes that the HEI Visitor cannot be removed by the HEI itself and anyway the actual exercise of the visitorial jurisdiction is, in fact, usually performed by a member of the senior judiciary. Hence Luxton suggests that the HRA 1998 will 'not mark the end of this very useful jurisdiction'. That said, the weight of academic lawyer opinion will *not* put money on the Visitor surviving an Art 6(1) challenge; not least because, whether or not the Visitor is seen to be 'independent' of the HEI for the purposes of Art 6(1), he *may* not pass the test of being 'established by law' if, in the terms of Art 6(1), this means by legislation rather than being the creature of common law (and even if subsequent legislation has recognised or acknowledged the existence of the Visitor as a legal entity). Yet, so far, such Art 6(1) judicial review challenges seem not to have been very successful (*R v Visitor to University of East Anglia ex parte Hanuman;*[3] *R v University of Essex ex parte McPherson;*[4] *The Queen on the application of Jemchi v the Visitor of Brunel University*[5]).

---

1   See Chapter 30 and *Thomas v University of Bradford* [1987] 1 All ER 834.
2   (1984) 7 EHRR 165.
3   [1999] EdCR 781, [2000] Ed Law 232; and nor did Mr Hanuman get much further with the European Court: *Lalu Hanuman v UK* [2000] ELR 685 (see also paras 7.17–7.24 and 30.62).
4   (2001) unreported, 23 March, QED.
5   (2001) unreported, 23 April, QED.

§8.5   The author of this chapter updates the idea he put forward in the 1998 edition, an innovative elaboration of the visitorial system which could be used by all HEIs, statutory and chartered. This is still a matter for consideration and debate, and there is some doubt as to the virtues of extending the system, even in this modified form: the UUK consultation paper of July 2001 proposed to keep the Visitor, but to create a voluntary Ombudsman as the last level of the internal appeal system within the chartered HEI prior to the student invoking the Visitor jurisdiction. By early 2002, however, the UUK wind was blowing strongly *against* the survival at all of the Visitor's jurisdiction in relation to student complaints; while Scotland is now experimenting with a system-wide 'independent receiver'. Perhaps, eventually, some kind of unified system will emerge as a result of the Nolan Committee's interest in HE or as a follow-on from any future 'marketisation' of UK HE which leaves the Government feeling that the student needs consumer protection in a competitive marketplace. In the USA there exists at many HEIs an entity known as the 'Ombudsman of the University' to whom students and staff can complain. But, for now at least, the Visitor is alive and well in English and Welsh chartered HEIs, but is, of course, missing in the statutory HEIs, in Scotland's HEIs, and in the USA: where the Visitor is not to be found, there is usually discussion of whether something similar should be created. Chapter 30 reviews the literature and key cases.

INTRODUCTION

8.1   Since the first edition of this book there has been much discussion about the role of the Visitor and the determination of disputes within the education sector generally. Such increased awareness has arisen for a variety of reasons – the investigations of the Nolan Committee and responses to its report; the perceived litigiousness of students (and the corresponding debate amongst academics and practitioners about its impact) and, most importantly, the passing of the HRA 1988. These developments and awareness that students in different parts of the HE sector have access to different remedies and rights of redress (see Palfreyman (2000)) have resulted in a widening of the debate about dispute resolution within universities and to calls for the standardisation of remedies across the whole higher education sector. This chapter will examine the background to the establishment of the Visitor in chartered universities and will look at some of the advantages and disadvantages which have been identified in connection with the visitorial system. It will then move on to examine visitorial proceedings in the light of the HRA 1998 and the inevitability of challenges under that Act. In view of the perceived disadvantages of the present visitorial system, alternatives to the present model will be examined, but the chapter will conclude by suggesting that an updated and rejuvenated Visitor, who has jurisdiction across the whole HE sector, might provide the best solution to enable the speedy resolution of disputes within that sector.

BACKGROUND

8.2   The concept of the Visitor is an unusual one and has its origins in canon law (see Picarda (1999)). A Visitor is a person who has domestic judicial authority over 'eleemosynary, lay, and ecclesiastical corporations for the correction of the life and conduct of the members and the adjudication of disputes between them' (Mitcheson (1887)). In practice, Visitors have a role principally in religious and educational contexts. The theoretical justification for the appointment of a Visitor has always been that the founder of an institution should have the authority to determine disputes arising within that institution. The precise identity of the Visitor varies from institution to institution. It is frequently the case that the Visitor is the Queen or the Archbishop of Canterbury, or some other lay person, in which case a Commissary will be appointed to act in her or his place. Indeed, unless the Visitor is a lawyer, and one with sufficient time and inclination, a Commissary will almost invariably be appointed to undertake the task. Such a Commissary will usually be a QC or perhaps a retired judge. The precise role of each Visitor depends very much on the institution concerned and its instrument of government, which usually sets out the identity of the Visitor, the terms on which matters must be referred to him, and his visitorial rights.

8.3   Instruments of government usually provide that any domestic issue (ie one which relates to internal university management, abuses of management or other conduct concerning the government of the university) should be adjudicated by the Visitor. As a result, disputes about the running of the university and grievances raised by members of the university (from the Vice-Chancellor and lecturers to any student) must be referred to the Visitor. If an internal grievance procedure exists, a complainant must usually exhaust this route first. If a complaint is referred in this way, the Visitor will determine how the matter is to proceed and, if it cannot be settled, will be required to hear the case. Save in the area of employment (see the ERA 1988, s 206), where any dispute relating to the appointment, employment or termination of academic staff is deemed to be outside his or her jurisdiction, the courts have generally been keen not to become involved in the disputes which fall within the jurisdiction of the Visitor. This was especially the case in relation to matters of academic judgement in institutions with a Visitor, although the courts have been prepared to intervene in such matters in the statutory HEI sector (Chapter 6 and Kaye (1999)). However, as set out below, the implementation of the HRA 1998 is *likely* to change all that.

WHAT ARE THE BENEFITS OF THE VISITORIAL SYSTEM?

8.4   Sir Robert Megarry identified many of the advantages of visitorial proceedings in *Patel v University of Bradford Senate*.[1] Many of Sir Robert's

---

1   [1979] 1 WLR 1066, [1979] 2 All ER 582; *affirming* [1978] 1 WLR 1488, CA.

observations are still relevant today, although potential challenges under the HRA 1988 may shortly make many of these advantages irrelevant. The following are the principal benefits of the visitorial system which are still believed to be current.

Informality

8.5   A member of university who has exhausted any relevant internal grievance procedures can still ask that a matter be referred to the Visitor by lodging a complaint. It is unusual for a fixed procedure to exist. On the appointment of the Visitor, the complainant will be asked to set out his case in writing and the university will have an opportunity to respond. Rarely do further exchanges take place on paper. The next stage is for a hearing to be fixed and this usually takes place at the university. This relatively simple procedure tends to make for considerable informality, even if the involvement of lawyers does sometimes tend to encourage the production of increasingly formal pleadings. Every Visitor conducts cases differently, but proceedings are always held in private and are generally less formal than court hearings. The fact that complainants do sometimes appear in person encourages this approach.

Reduced cost

8.6   A direct consequence of the relative informality of the visitorial system is a reduction in costs for all concerned. This is due to the fact that cases tend to be heard faster than in legal proceedings and that preliminary hearings rarely take place. As a result, the risk of running up large legal and other costs is reduced – although it is not always avoided. This is usually good news for universities as they invariably meet the fees of the Visitor and all other costs attached to the hearing. The Visitor does have the power to award costs and damages against a party. Despite the rarity of this happening in practice, this fact can be a disincentive to staff or student complainants for whom such an award could result in financial disaster. Nevertheless, such a possibility may discourage frivolous claims.

Speed

8.7   It is undeniable that, if a matter can be brought to a hearing with fewer procedural requirements, it will inevitably be adjudicated faster. As a result, visitorial proceedings can be speedy when compared to the hearing of a non-urgent case in the High Court – even after the Woolf reforms. Delays, of course, sometimes occur even in visitorial proceedings. Depending on the identity of the Visitor or his Commissary, fixing a date can sometimes be far from easy. Demands on the time of a high-profile Visitor (or, indeed, a high-profile Commissary) often result in the deferment of cases. The complexity of a case, the volume of papers and a large number of witnesses can also make it difficult to fix an early date. Such difficulties, however, are minor compared to the fact that it may take at least one year before a case is brought to trial in the High Court. (For more on the litigation process, see Chapter 27.)

Privacy

8.8 There can be no doubt that the fact that visitorial hearings are held in private encourages greater self-confidence on the part of complainants. Not only is the risk of adverse publicity removed, but a complainant may feel that he can air grievances in a way which would not be possible in a public arena. The only drawback is that, since the results of Visitor hearings are rarely (if ever) published, there is potential for inconsistency between hearings – even in the same university. Hence, the noteworthy publication of the Visitor's report relating to an enquiry at University College, Swansea (Davies (1994)). However, as we shall see below, the very fact that visitorial hearings are held in camera now raises significant problems under the HRA 1998.

Impartiality

8.9 The fact that an internal hearing provides the opportunity for adjudication by someone completely removed from the running of a university is a unique feature of the visitorial system. This aspect, more than any other, generates great confidence in the forum provided by the Visitor. Although Visitors are sometimes criticised for being too partial to the administration of a university, such criticisms are usually unfounded as, in the author's experience, Visitors are all too keen not to be identified with the institution against which a complaint is being brought.

A useful resource

8.10 In addition to the points already mentioned, there is a further advantage which Visitorial proceedings present. This arises because a Visitor can provide a useful resource to a university by adjudicating informally on points of interpretation or areas of uncertainty – even if they are not central to a live dispute. A Visitor can be in an excellent position to determine uncertainties arising over the meaning of a statute. He can also be used as an arbitrator when members of a university (including the governing body) cannot agree on a particular issue of importance when all other avenues have failed.

DRAWBACKS TO THE VISITORIAL PROCESS

8.11 Notwithstanding the benefits described above, there are some significant problems in the way in which many visitorial proceedings are processed and heard. The most obvious are as follows.

Finality of the decision

8.12 In the first edition of this book it was indicated that the ability of the Visitor to make a final decision was a significant advantage to the determination of a complaint by the Visitor. Prior to the implementation of the HRA 1998, challenges to the decision of a Visitor were very limited save in the case where a Visitor is alleged to have exceeded his or her power or where judicial review proceedings are successfully brought because it can be argued that the Visitor is carrying out a 'public' function (see Chapter 9). As we shall see below, however, the provisions of the HRA 1998 now make visitorial decisions vulnerable to challenge.

Jurisdiction

8.13 Real problems can arise in identifying whether the Visitor actually has jurisdiction in a matter. Determining this issue alone can sometimes take a number of months, especially if it can be argued that the matter falls within areas that are now excluded under the ERA 1988. Other jurisdictional issues relate to whether or not a case falls squarely within those matters which are capable of being heard by the Visitor (which will depend on the instrument of government in question) or if an individual is eligible to bring a complaint. The latter issue has now been largely clarified as a result of 1980s' case-law. The reality, therefore, is that in some cases what will eventually be a very swift hearing can be delayed for some time until such jurisdictional matters are determined.

Procedural issues

8.14 Even if it has been agreed that the Visitor is to be involved in a complaint, important preliminary issues of procedure can often arise and must be determined. These usually relate to questions about the identity of the Visitor's Commissary (if the Visitor is not to sit himself), the form which the pleadings should take and whether or not there should be oral evidence. Frequently, the nature of a complaint is not entirely clear and it is essential that the Visitor or his advisers seek clarification from the complainant as to the precise nature of the matter in dispute. Such matters can cause delays, which will inevitably hold up an early hearing date. In some cases there are so many procedural issues in dispute that it is necessary to hold a preliminary hearing or for a written judgment to be delivered by the Visitor on these issues alone. Disputes of this kind also arise between parties in the context of legal proceedings, but, since legal procedures are more prescribed and well established, there is greater certainty as to the procedural requirements demanded of the parties. Further, more remedies exist when a party fails to heed directions.

Insufficient knowledge of the institution and HE

8.15 Although an historical connection often exists between a university and its Visitor, some Visitors do not have any particular knowledge of the institution in question or the wider HE context in which it operates. Such criticisms are perhaps made less frequently where a named individual is appointed to the post. Experience shows that these Visitors often build up an excellent knowledge of the institution, its personnel and its statutes. This is not always the experience of those universities which have Visitors appointed by virtue of their office, for invariably these Visitors appoint Commissaries who have no connection at all with the institution. As many issues within universities become more complex, some understanding of HE is an increasingly important requirement for a Visitor – particularly so when no other forum exists in which grievances can be aired. Indeed, one of the major criticisms made to the Nolan Committee by unions representing university teaching staff was that Visitors often lack an understanding of the increasingly commercial and pressurised academic world in which academics are now required to function.

Inconsistency of decisions

8.16 As each visitorial case begins without access to previous decisions, there is a great risk of inconsistency between cases or that an instrument of government may be interpreted differently from one occasion to another. Decided case-law relating to Visitors can provide some guidance, but the ultimate authority is always the Visitor, who has great potential to be subjective. The private nature of the proceedings also means that there is no opportunity for a Visitor to create precedents to be used by other HEIs.

Preferred rights

8.17 Some opponents of the visitorial system base their criticisms on the fact that the very concept of the Visitor affords preferred rights to academics and students. Such critics argue that the existence of a quasi-judicial forum within universities epitomises their unworldliness. They are therefore keen for universities to become as commercial as possible and believe that there should be no jurisdiction which governs the resolution of academic affairs other than the courts. To the extent that redress does not exist in law such critics argue that a hearing should be denied.

HUMAN RIGHTS ACT 1998

8.18 Many of the drawbacks of the visitorial system identified above have been thrown into even sharper focus by the passing and implementation of the

HRA 1998. This chapter cannot encompass a full discussion of the Act, but as will be obvious from the comments already made above, the HRA 1998 will inevitably lead to increased challenges to visitorial decisions. In simple terms, the HRA 1998 is concerned to establish that public authorities act in a lawful manner which is consistent with fundamental human rights as framed by the legislation. In advance of the passing of the HRA 1998 there was already some debate as to whether the legislation would extend to disputes in the HE sector. Yet, notwithstanding some questions over whether or not Oxbridge colleges are sufficiently funded by public money to make them public authorities, there now appears to be a measure of agreement which suggests that the HRA 1998 *will* apply to most chartered and HEIs, including perhaps the Oxbridge colleges. Debate now rages over whether legal challenges are likely to result from the new legislation. To consider this question in the context of the role of the Visitor we must examine the possible impact of Art 6 of the European Convention which sets out the 'right to a fair and public hearing'. Article 6(1) states:

> 'In the determination of his civil rights and obligations . . . everyone is entitled to a fair and public hearing within a reasonable time by an independent and impartial tribunal established by law. Judgment shall be pronounced publicly but the press and public may be excluded from all or part of the trial in the interests of morals, public order or national security in a democratic society, where the interests of juveniles or the protection of the private life of the parties so require, or to the extent strictly necessary in the opinion of the court in special circumstances where publicity would prejudice the interests of justice.'

8.19   The visitorial drawbacks identified above mean that it is difficult not to agree with Kaye (1999) that the determination of disputes by a Visitor does not 'pass muster' when measured against Art 6. Uncertainty as to the independence and impartiality of the Visitor raise particular concerns, as does the private nature of visitorial proceedings, for it is difficult to argue that any of the exceptions set out in Art 6 should apply. For these reasons alone, the author believes that there can be no doubt that the HRA 1998 identifies significant areas in which proceedings (as presently constituted) before a Visitor will be flawed. This must therefore be a significant concern for universities in view of their reputations and their financial management. It will also be of great interest to funding bodies. The real issue for universities is that the requirements of the HRA 1998 now mean that it is only a question of time before challenges to visitorial decisions will emerge. Indeed, such challenges may come from complainants wishing to leap-frog the visitorial system as well as those unhappy with the outcome of a particular decision. In the author's view, in the light of the HRA 1998, it will no longer be possible for the courts to issue a blanket refusal to intervene in visitorial matters. Nor will it be necessary (if the HRA 1998 is cited in the pleadings) to examine whether there are any legal arguments to establish whether a judicial review of a Visitor's decision is possible. In view of all of the drawbacks identified above and the probable challenges under the HRA 1998, it seems clear that the overhaul of the resolution of disputes within HE should be accelerated.

ALTERNATIVES

8.20 As mentioned in para **8.1**, there has been considerable recent discussion as to the manner in which disputes in higher education generally should be dealt with. One thing upon which all commentators appear to agree is the fact that some overhaul of the present system is necessary. To date there have been a variety of recommendations but these can broadly be categorised as follows (they are then considered in detail in turn):

- *The use of arbitration*: the Report of CVCP Working Party (1997) suggested, amongst other things, that to avoid recourse to the courts, to provide a more 'public forum' and to accelerate decision-taking, the parties to a disagreement should enter into a binding arbitration agreement.
- *A Code of Practice on student complaints*: this approach, which has been spearheaded by the QAA, seeks to establish a set of guidelines which would be of general application to the university sector and which would standardise approaches between institutions.
- *The creation of an HE Ombudsman*: calls have come from a number of academics and legal practitioners suggesting that an HE Ombudsman should be appointed. No specific brief has been set out by those demanding the creation of this office, but it is anticipated that the appointment would be by statute or statutory instrument. It is anticipated that the Ombudsman would be available to hear matters referred to him on appeal from HEIs. Subject to challenges under the HRA 1998 or by way of judicial review, he would be the final arbiter of decisions.
- *Updating the concept of the Visitor*: the first edition of this book called for a review and overhaul of the role of the Visitor. This call has been echoed by others who have demanded a better resourced and a reformed role for the Visitor, or even the appointment of an HE Commissioner. Such a person would be appointed across the whole of the HE sector and would be established without the necessity for statutory change.

Binding arbitration

8.21 While arbitration has much to commend itself when compared to litigation, the concept of a using a binding arbitration agreement in the context of disputes within HE does not, in the author's view, work even if the parties involved consent to the approach. The possibility of challenges under the HRA 1998 and the Arbitration Act 1996 (on matters of law) mean that there are good legal reasons which might frustrate the ability of the arbitrator to make a binding decision. However, from a practical point of view, there are also difficult issues relating to the manner in which student complainants are able to consent. These issues could be extremely fertile ground for challenges under the HRA 1998. In addition, it might also be sensible to consider mediation as a possible dispute resolution procedure. In terms of speed and cost, mediation can be attractive. The confidence of the parties in the mediation process is, of course, vital to the success of this approach and where such confidence exists it can be a useful method to resolve disputes. Experience has shown, however, that such confidence does not always exist and for this reason it would appear that mediation cannot generally be relied upon to resolve disputes in the university sector.

A Code of Practice

8.22   The call for a Code of Practice is intended to standardise the resolution of disputes across the whole of the HE sector and, in itself, is an excellent development. However, due to the differing types of redress available to complainants in different institutions, there is a strong chance that such a code would not be capable of general adoption across the whole university sector. In practice, it is useful to have general guidelines, but experience suggests that unless a financial or other requirement exists to compel observance there is little incentive for institutions to introduce change.

Ombudsman

8.23   As mentioned above, the establishment of an HE Ombudsman for the HE sector could only be achieved as a result of primary or secondary legislation. Even if sufficient political goodwill were to exist to achieve such change, financial and practical objections to the creation of this post are foreseeable. Certainly the cost of the creation of an Ombudsman (and accompanying administration) would depend upon the extent of the duties of such an office and the extent to which some of the functions (such as legal support) might be outsourced to private practitioners. These considerations aside, however, the creation of a quasi-judicial quango to resolve disputes which are internal to universities seems unnecessarily grandiose. Surely what universities and their staff and students require is a clear, robust and meaningful dispute resolution procedure – as consistent as possible with the HRA 1998 – which entitles them to have their disputes resolved quickly and efficaciously? As the concept of the Visitor already exists, is it not better to improve the established model rather than introduce another which is expensive and entirely untested?

A rejuvenated Visitor

8.24   Having considered all other options, it seems that the best way to improve dispute resolution in the university sector is to rejuvenate the existing concept of the Visitor. This approach would require that robust (and ideally standardised) internal disputes procedures should be adopted across the university sector generally. The role of the Visitor could therefore be retained by those institutions which already embrace the concept and could also be adopted by those which presently do not. In the event that disputes arise, having exhausted internal procedures, matters could be referred to a Visitor, whose procedures should be as compliant with the HRA 1998 as possible. The proposed new model for the Visitor is discussed in detail below. The major issue to be considered here is how such changes would be introduced across the sector as a whole? From a legal point of view, it does not appear that the changes would require statutory approval – although in the case of some institutions the consent of the Privy Council may be necessary. The greater question is whether any incentive – apart from a wish to avoid expensive litigation – exists to encourage governing bodies to introduce such a change. Funding bodies – mindful of the increasing cost to institutions of defending claims – should perhaps make it a condition of funding that such changes are introduced within a specified period of time.

8.25   A new visitorial model could have the following features:

(1)   The identification of a group of potential Visitors (possibly to be re-named 'HE Commissioners'). This could be a group of eminent men and women (including lawyers) with experience of the HE field and of dealing with disputes, from whom each HEI could appoint a Visitor when appropriate. Each institution could appoint their own named person – for example, Queen's University in Belfast amended its statutes in 1983 to establish a panel of four Visitors, including a lawyer and an academic – or there might be an approved panel from which an appointment might be made in the event of a referral of a matter to the Visitor. A Visitor would not be appointed for all time, since different Visitors would be experienced in different areas. Institutions could therefore take advantage of the different skills available and relevant to each case. It would be essential to appoint both male and female representatives. Training would also be a requirement.

(2)   All existing avenues of internal complaint within an institution should be exhausted before a referral to an external adjudicator is possible. If this route has been followed, the matter should always be within the jurisdiction of the Visitor, unless the issue does not relate to the university and its members and lies within the remit of another representative body.

(3)   Both the university and the complainant should have an opportunity to make representations on the appointment of a Visitor. However, in the event that the parties cannot agree the chair of the panel of Visitors should decide.

(4)   The Visitor should hear cases in public.

(5)   Visitors should follow an established procedure for hearing and determining cases. The system should cover cases of maladministration and malpractice and questions of academic standards and freedom. It should not relate to academic matters themselves. It might include employment matters, since an effective dispute resolution procedure outside

employment tribunals and the courts could deal adequately with most of these matters in universities and at considerably less cost.

(6) Standard forms might be used. The emphasis in these procedural steps should be on clarity, informality and speed. A Visitor should also have the right to dismiss frivolous or vexatious complaints.

(7) If appropriate, and by consent, the Visitor should act as a mediator and/or conciliator. The benefits of such a role were demonstrated by Sir Michael Davies when he acted as Visitor to the University College of Swansea (Davies, 1994). Nevertheless, it is clear from his report that no matter how hard a Visitor might try, it is sometimes impossible to achieve a negotiated settlement.

(8) The cost of the Visitor should be borne by the university. Depending on the time spent by the Visitor, this might be significant. However, to demand that a complainant should contribute or run the risk of paying all the costs is a considerable deterrent. The disadvantages of vexatious and frivolous claims are outweighed by the provision of an accessible system which ensures the smooth running and good health of the university. In addition, there would be no right to award damages. The only exception to this might be in the arena of employment matters.

(9) There should be an agreed timetable, specifying that issues in dispute should be determined quickly and, if possible, within 3 months of the complaint being lodged.

(10) There can be no guarantee that a challenge by way of judicial review or under the HRA 1998 would not materialise. However, to the extent that the above changes are introduced it would seem that except in the event of legal or other errors or omissions, the above structure will certainly minimise possible challenges.

CONCLUSION

8.26   Even in an age when it is acknowledged that universities have a contractual relationship with their students (Chapter 6), students pay large sums of money to be educated (Chapter 29), and academics are paid less than their peers in other professions (Chapter 10), it is suggested that disputes within universities should be dealt with in a manner which is as consistent with general legal requirements as possible. Nevertheless, in the author's view, special circumstances continue to exist within universities which warrant the continuation of visitorial proceedings wherever possible. An effective dispute resolution procedure is now essential to the success of any academic institution and the passing of the HRA 1998 firmly places a spotlight on the deficiencies of the present arrangements – including the visitorial system. Rather than becoming involved in piecemeal change (by responding to increasing inter-vention by the courts) or in wholesale change (through the introduction of an HE Ombudsman), the author believes that the rejuvenated visitorial model will provide a more effective method to reduce disputes and limit expensive legal challenges in universities. Whatever changes might be introduced, however, the passing of the HRA 1998 ensures that dispute resolution within universities will increasingly involve the courts.

Chapter 9

DISPUTES II: THE SCOPE FOR JUDICIAL REVIEW IN STATUTORY INSTITUTIONS

Paul Pharaoh (Martineau Johnson)

EDITORS' INTRODUCTION

§9.1   The statutory universities and colleges of HE do not have the Visitor as a means of dispute resolution (see Chapter 8). They rely on the courts to interpret the contract between the HEI and its students or its staff (whether academics or other employees): see Chapters 6, 7, 10 and 11. There are circumstances, however, when the law might be invoked by way of judicial review, in order to clarify whether the HEI has fair and proper procedures, whether it is applying them in a reasonable way, whether it might be exceeding its powers (acting *ultra vires*), etc. Or even to clarify whether any HEI, chartered or statutory, itself is getting fair treatment from, say, a funding body[1] or an accreditation agency.[2]

§9.2   Judicial review has become something of a growth industry in recent years, but, although more judicial review cases than ever before are being heard, many of them do not get the result the seeker hoped for, and many other seekers of judicial review do not even get past the first hurdle of an initial hearing to decide whether there really is a case to be pursued. Very few judicial review cases have yet involved HE disputes. The threat of judicial review is, therefore, like a dog's bark being worse than its bite. Yet judicial review is a 'heavy' and fast-moving legal process which can be used, or threatened, as an aid to concentrating the mind of an HEI as to whether it really does appreciate the legal position and feel secure in defending it.

§9.3   This chapter explores the circumstances where judicial review might be sought of an HEI's actions (or even of its inactivity), the likely defences for the HEI, the potential remedies if the seeker of judicial review succeeds in persuading the court that something is wrong, and the possible overlap with other kinds of court involvement. That said, as discussed in Appendix 1 to Chapter 6 and in Chapter 27, judicial review is litigation and the Court of Appeal has stressed that should be the last resort after any internal complaints procedures have been exhausted *and* after some form of ADR has been tried

---

1   *R v Higher Educational Funding Council ex parte Institute of Dental Surgery* [1994] 1 All ER 651.

2   *R v The Teacher Training Agency ex parte University of Exeter* [2001] EWHC Admin 264, unreported. See also *The Queen on the application of Oxford Study Centre Ltd v British Council* [2001] EWHC Admin 207, [2001] ELR 803, (2001) ELJ 2(4), pp 220–222, concerning the fine divide between public law remedies and private law contractual remedies, and, in either case, the importance of due process in exercising power (whether arising from statute as a public body or from the contract (as here) or as party to the contract).

(*Cowl and Others v Plymouth City Council*;[1] a similar case relating directly to HEIs is *Clark v University of Lincolnshire and Humberside*[2]).

§9.4   Note the Nolan Committee's recommendation that:[3]

'Students in higher education institutions should be able to appeal to an independent body, and this right should be reflected in the Higher Education Charters. The higher education funding councils, institutions, and representative bodies should consult on a system of independent review of disputes.'

This could theoretically have meant the Visitor model (or something similar) being extended to statutory HEIs (see Chapter 8), although in January 1997 a CVCP Working Group came up with the concept of binding arbitration as a last resort for dealing with student complaints and appeals (CVCP (1997)). The NUS' immediate response was to oppose the idea, its President commenting that: 'In no other sector are people expected to make the kind of investment they make in higher education without having the ability to take legal action if necessary'. The debate trundles on, with the Visitor looking like an increasingly endangered species but (as yet) with no final decision about binding arbitration or the latest idea of an HE Ombudsman (or, indeed, HERO – Higher Education Regulatory Officer). (See Palfreyman (2000) and the section on 'The Visitor post-Nolan' in Chapter 30; see also Chapter 7.)

§9.5   From a US perspective, Kaplin and Lee (1995a) note the difference in the USA between a *public* HEI (one that is substantially funded by the State) and a *private* HEI (one relying mainly on student fees and endowment income). The former is like a UK statutory HEI, its actions are 'State action', are subject to control under relevant public law legislation concerning 'due process' (the rules of natural justice). The latter is more like a chartered university in the UK (although, of course, a chartered university in the UK does receive significant public funding just like a UK statutory HEI). If, however, the US Government is so heavily involved in directly funding part of a private HEI's activities as perhaps to make the activity concerned *de facto* a publicly provided and funded operation, then the HEI may have to comply with relevant State law as if its actions were 'State action'. It has, in effect, become an extension of State bureaucracy for the purposes of providing State-subsidised academic programmes, or whatever, and hence is subject to public law via judicial review. Otherwise, the US courts seem broadly to follow the approach of the English courts: they will generally defer to the HEI's internal processes (unless they have been applied in an arbitrary and capricious way), and they will expect the HEI's internal disciplinary or appeal system to adhere to a 'substantial evidence' standard rather than to the more exacting 'clear and convincing' standard to be reached in a court of law.[4]

---

1   (2002) *The Times*, January 8.
2   [2000] 3 All ER 752, CA.
3   (1996), p 17.
4   *Reilly v Daly* 666 NE 2d 439, Ind 1996.

§9.6   Judicial review is not just about students challenging HEI disciplinary or academic decisions: it is also about academic staff challenging the HEI's promotion procedures;[1] and (as already noted) about HEIs themselves challenging the decisions of funding agencies or of academic validation agencies. This element of legal involvement in the relationship between HEIs and their inspecting agencies is entirely the norm in the USA.[2]

§9.7   Beloff (1999) analyses English cases concerning the disciplining and expulsion of students, noting the change in recent decades:

'For universities like other domestic or quasi-domestic institutions ... have been slow to realise that the wielding of arbitrary power, which has characterised their behaviour – in the case of Oxford and Cambridge and their colleges for several centuries – is no longer compatible with the development of natural justice – and renders them vulnerable to challenge in the new rights-based culture of our times ... .'

§9.8   He cites an early example of the courts requiring Cambridge to respect due process[3] and goes on to consider a range of relatively recent cases, as listed below,[4] before concluding:

'What then are the lessons to be learned?
First, that institutions should cause their constituent instruments to be reviewed by competent lawyers with a view to ensuring that they are both clear and fair ...
Secondly, that the basic rules of natural justice be observed ...
Thirdly (by way of qualification), no effort should mimic to the letter the procedures and practices of a court ...
Fourthly, where misconduct is alleged, reasons ought to be given for any punishment imposed: what the offence consisted of; how it was established [that Bloggs is guilty]; and why the particular punishment fits the crime. There is no legal need, however, for academic bodies to explain why a student's essay was not up to snuff.'[5]

§9.9   To Beloff's list in footnote 4, and to the cases cited elsewhere in this chapter, can be added *R v South Bank University ex parte Coggeran:*[6] first, a board of examiners and any appeal board must give due, proper, and careful consideration to circumstances allegedly mitigating academic failure *and* be seen to have done so by rigorously minuting the decision concerning the student; and, secondly, in the case of a pregnant student the case-law on

---

1   *R v University of Cambridge ex parte Evans* [1998] EdCR 151, [1998] ELR 515; see also *R v University of Cambridge ex parte Evans No 2* [1999] EdCR 556.
2   According to Geoffrey Alderman in *Education Guardian*, 6 March 2001.
3   *R v University of Cambridge (Dr Bentley's Case)* (1723) 1 Str 557.
4   *Herring v Templeman and Others* [1973] 3 All ER 569; *R v University of Aston Senate ex parte Roffey* [1969] 2 QB 538; *Ceylon University v Fernando* [1960] 1 WLR 223; *Ward v Bradford Corporation* (1972) 70 LGR 27; *Spruce v University of Hong Kong* [1993] 2 HKLR 65; *Brighton Corporation v Parry* (1971) 70 LGR 576; *Glynn v Keele University* [1971] 1 WLR 487; *Ex parte Forster, Re Sydney University* [1963] SR (NSW) 723; *R v Oxford University ex parte Bolchover* (1970) *The Times*, October 7; *Thorne v University of London* [1966] 2 QB 237; *M v London Guildhall University* [1998] ELR 149; and *R v Liverpool John Moores University ex parte Hayes* [1998] ELR 261.
5   Citing Sedley J in *R v Higher Education Funding Council ex parte Institute of Dental Surgery* [1994] 1 WLR 242: 'We would hold that where what is sought to be impugned is on the evidence no more than an informed exercise of academic judgement, fairness alone will not require reasons to be given ...'.
6   [2001] ELR 42, CA; see also [2001] Ed Law 38, at pp 40–42.

dismissal from employment under the Sex Discrimination Act 1975 and the EC Equal Treatment Directive did *not* apply by analogy to expulsion from a degree course. Similarly, the reluctance of the courts to second-guess academic judgment is reinforced by *R v University of the West of England ex parte M*[1] and by *The Queen on the application of Ahmad v University of Oxford;*[2] while, in contrast, the willingness of the courts firmly to require due process is emphasised not only in *Coggeran* (as above) but also in: *R v South Bank University ex parte Burgess,*[3] *The Queen on the application of Udemba v South Bank University,*[4] and *R v Chelsea College of Art and Design ex parte Nash.*[5] It is depressingly clear that, despite two editions of Farrington (1994, 1998) and one of Palfreyman and Warner (1998), some HEIs are in need of a comprehensive legal compliance audit and still have not understood the duty to apply their procedures carefully and consistently: see Appendix 1 to Chapter 6 for a handy summary of the key cases and principles; and see especially the section in this chapter on 'Reducing the risk of judicial review' at para **9.30**.

INTRODUCTION

9.1   This chapter gives an outline of the scope and application of judicial review, with examples in the context of education where possible. It considers the subject in relation to the statutory HEIs, which have no Visitor and are, therefore, accountable through the courts, at least until statutory provision is made for some alternative means of dispute resolution which parallels the role of the Visitor in the chartered universities. The chapter looks at the probable effect on judicial review of the HRA 1998, in relation to some general points which are worth bearing in mind when decisions are being made in order, so far as possible, to make them review-proof. The limited application of judicial review to the visitorial jurisdiction in the chartered universities is dealt with in Chapter 8. Although this chapter concentrates on judicial review in relation to HEIs established under the ERA 1988 as amended, the same principles, of course, apply to other parts of the educational system such as the funding councils or FEIs.

DEVELOPMENT OF JUDICIAL REVIEW

9.2   The role of the courts in reviewing the acts and decisions of public bodies has expanded very considerably during the last 35 years. The high profile of many judicial review cases ensures that it remains popular: with lawyers, as a burgeoning and glamorous area of work; with constitutionalists, or at least

1   [2001] ELR 77; see also *The Queen on the application of M v University of the West of England* [2001] ELR 458, [2001] Ed Law 156, pp 156–158.
2   (2000) unreported, 7 November.
3   (2000) unreported, 4 October.
4   (2000) unreported, 2 November.
5   [2000] ELR 686; see also *Nash v Chelsea College of Art and Design* [2001] EWHC Admin 538, (2001) *The Times,* July 25.

those who favour the judges' curbing of executive power; with academics, turning out a growing volume of books and papers; and with the public and parts of the press, as an effective method of enabling the little man to question or overturn acts of powerful and often faceless public bodies. Joshua Rozenberg's book *Trial of Strength*[1] is an intriguing account of what he sees as a contest between the judiciary and the Conservative government in its last years of office, fought out mainly in judicial reviews of ministerial decisions. These tensions have resurfaced since 11 September 2001, with allegations from the Home Secretary that the judiciary is becoming a threat to democracy and would be well-advised to leave law-making to elected MPs. The Lord Chief Justice, on the other hand, sees 'a basic duty of the courts to protect citizens against unlawful acts by the State and to act as an essential buttress to democracy' (Lord Woolf quoted in the *Guardian*, 1 December 2001).

9.3   Although all judicial review cases are dealt with by the High Court, the procedure is relatively straightforward. Oral evidence is not usually heard, and, although major points of principle may be at stake, both the pleadings and the judgments are often quite brief. Proceedings must be commenced promptly, and in any event within 3 months of the decision complained of, and may be concluded more swiftly than conventional litigation (see Chapter 27). There is an expeditious procedure for especially urgent cases. Frequent applications to the courts to review decisions of ministers (for example, on immigration or homelessness) or heavy commercial matters such as challenges to the award of television or lottery franchises, attract much publicity. This extends awareness of what judicial review can achieve and stimulates further recourse to the courts. They were braced in any event for a substantial increase in applications based on the incorporation of the European Convention on Human Rights into the domestic law of England and Wales via the coming into force in October 2000 of the HRA 1998. This rise in the volume of applications has not in the event materialised: 17 per cent of the applications for judicial review lodged since incorporation of the Convention have raised human rights issues.

9.4   There were only 160 applications for judicial review in 1974; by 2000 the number had increased to 4247: although only 1464 (about one-third) of these survived the first hurdle of gaining permission (formerly called leave) to proceed, and only a small proportion of those were ultimately successful. Another reason for the growth of judicial review is the expansion since 1979 of the number of public bodies whose decisions and procedures may be subject to it, as functions of central and local government have been transferred elsewhere. There are now over 3000 of these.

9.5   The impact of judicial review on HEIs should be kept in perspective, even in these days of directly enforceable human rights. Only a small percentage of all applications relate to the whole education sector, and of these the majority involve admissions to or exclusions from school, rather than anything to do

---

1   (Richard Cohen Books, 1997), sub-titled *The Battle between Ministers and Judges over Who Makes the Law*.

with HEIs. The number of HE cases where permission to proceed has been granted by the court is small, and the number where the claimant is ultimately successful is even smaller. However, education cases represent a growing proportion of the total judicial review caseload, as a result of increasing State regulation, the conflicts which have arisen from shifts of power in the sector, and the development of a competitive and consumer-led approach to educational provision.

NATURE OF JUDICIAL REVIEW

9.6 Hardly a news bulletin seems to appear without someone who is disappointed about something saying that they will be 'going for a judicial review', using the term for almost any referral of a non-criminal dispute to a court. The correct application is far more specific. Essentially, judicial review is a means of calling public bodies to account in the courts to show that they have acted lawfully, reasonably and fairly in reaching a decision. In conventional civil litigation, the courts are required to decide on the merits of the case, as between competing parties. In judicial review, the function of the courts is usually not to substitute their own judgement for that of the body which has made the decision. The judge has to ask only whether a lawful power exists to make the decision which has been made, whether that power has been abused, and whether it has been used unfairly. If none of these requirements for decision-taking by public bodies has been breached, the authority or institution concerned will be left to get on with its own business.

9.7 The courts have consistently refused to trespass on the particular expertise of the original decision-maker, or to apply a restrictive approach to construction of its specialist regulations. Lord Woolf MR said in *Clark v University of Lincolnshire and Humberside*:[1]

> 'A university is a public body ... Court proceedings would, therefore, normally be expected to be commenced [by means of judicial review]. If the university is subject to the supervision of a visitor there is little scope for those proceedings ... Where a claim is brought against a university by one of its students, if ... it does not have a visitor the role of the court will frequently amount to performing the reviewing role which would otherwise be performed by the visitor. The court ... will not involve itself with issues that involve making academic judgment.'

9.8 In the same case (not itself an application for judicial review) Sedley LJ explained the limits of the courts' involvement in university disputes by saying: '... there are issues of academic or pastoral judgment which the university is equipped to consider in breadth and detail, but on which any judgment of the courts would be jejune and inappropriate'.

9.9 In this case, the Court of Appeal has ruled that even in ordinary civil proceedings, which do not involve use of judicial discretion in the same way as

---

1　　[2000] ELR 345.

a judicial review (see below), the exercise of academic judgement by HEIs will not normally be questioned. This reluctance to trespass on areas of universities' special expertise is equally, or even more, present in judicial review. Whilst it will be welcomed by HEIs, this determination of the courts to steer clear of matters involving academic judgement is perhaps surprising, at a time when other areas previously immune from legal challenge (for example, liability in negligence of teachers and LEAs, or of advocates in court) are being newly held to account. A differently constituted Court of Appeal expressed itself more guardedly in *The Queen on the application of Persaud v Cambridge University*.[1] There was no principle of fairness which required, as a general rule, that a person should be entitled to challenge, or make representations with a view to changing a purely academic judgement. But each case must be examined on its facts. In this case, the applicant's appeal was partly successful. The university's error, however, lay in the process it had applied in determining academic judgement. That judgement itself was not directly impugned.

9.10   So the courts are not concerned to rewrite HEI's academic regulations or to take the interpretation of them out of their hands, provided that lawful powers are applied in a fair and reasonable way. In disputes involving disciplinary procedures, the courts regard themselves as having a wider role. They are especially resistant to acting as a Court of Appeal from university examiners.[2] In *R v Higher Education Funding Council ex parte Institute of Dental Surgery*,[3] the Higher Education Funding Council's (HEFC's) decision to re-assess the Institute's research was essentially a matter of academic judgement and not one for the courts, provided that the process of exercising that judgement was fair. In *R v University of Portsmouth ex parte Lakareber*,[4] the Court of Appeal said only the clearest and most obvious unfairness or departure from the university's own regulations would justify an attempt by judicial review to impugn an academic decision. In that case, the academic registrar and an independent member of the university's council had considered the student's appeal at a hearing which lasted over an hour; the court would not readily hold their decision to be erroneous in law. The courts are more ready to intervene where disciplinary or other procedural matters are at stake, rather than pure academic judgement – see *R v Leeds Metropolitan University ex parte Manders*,[5] where Collins J found that a student's allegations of bias and marking down in an examination were not questions of academic judgement.

9.11   Even if a claimant in judicial review is successful in challenging a decision in the courts, it may ultimately be unchanged. Once any defect in the original decision-taking process has been identified and remedied, a new decision taken by the correct route may still turn out to be the same or equally

---

1   [2001] EWCA Civ 534, [2001] ELR 480.
2   *Thorne v University of London* [1966] 2 QB 237.
3   [1994] 1 All ER 651.
4   [1999] ELR 135.
5   [1998] ELR 502.

adverse to the disappointed claimant. Judicial review is, therefore, a hollow victory in some cases, although public bodies are understandably averse to having their decisions queried or quashed in circumstances which often generate unfavourable publicity.

9.12 Judicial review is available only as a last resort as a means of challenge to decisions of public bodies, at least in the absence of exceptional circumstances. If alternative means of redress are available, such as an unexhausted internal or statutory right of appeal from the original decision, the claimant must be able to explain why review in the courts is appropriate – see *M v London Guildhall University*.[1] The lack of a visitorial jurisdiction in the statutory HEIs exposes them to judicial review, while the chartered universities have in the Visitor an additional level of appeal mechanism, which is not itself normally subject to review by the court. The Universities of Oxford and Cambridge may also be judicially reviewed because they, as civil corporations (unlike their constituent colleges as eleemosynary corporations), do not have a Visitor.

9.13 The judges have not precisely defined what 'exceptional circumstances' will justify intervention before internal remedies are exhausted. Review may be appropriate where the urgency of the situation requires faster action than the normal timetable of an internal appeals system permits – see *R v London Borough of Newham ex parte X*,[2] a school exclusion case, where 'bearing in mind how critically important every day and certainly every week was in the education of a child', interim relief was appropriate so the child went back to school 3 weeks before the normal statutory appeal was heard. In *R v Manchester Metropolitan University ex parte Nolan*,[3] a student successfully challenged disciplinary proceedings, without first having gone through the University's review procedure, because he could not obtain confidential minutes containing evidence of alleged irregularity without going to the courts. The judges are aware that it is often necessary to move quickly in education.[4]

9.14 In *R v Somerset County Council and ARC Southern Ltd ex parte Dixon*,[5] Sedley J, a judge who is willing to take an interventionist stance in many cases, nonetheless said: 'Public law is not about rights – even though abuses of power may ... invade private rights – it is about wrongs; that is, misuses of public power'. There is now an interesting process of integration as the existing jurisdiction is operated alongside the new jurisdiction in human rights.

---

1   [1998] ELR 149.
2   [1995] ELR 305.
3   [1994] ELR 380.
4   See Andrew Collins J writing on the new procedures in the Administrative Court [2001] EPLI 6(2), p 28.
5   [1997] COD 323.

GROUNDS AND REMEDIES

9.15 There are three principal sets of grounds for challenge by judicial review of decisions of public bodies. The first is **illegality**, including *ultra vires* (the exceeding of jurisdiction), error of law (for example, misinterpretation of regulations), and unlawful delegation of the decision-making function. The second is **the abuse of powers**, including irrationality, failing to take into account relevant facts or taking into account facts which are not relevant, bad faith, improper motive, and the fettering of discretion. The third set of grounds is **procedural unfairness** – bias, failure to provide a proper hearing, and material irregularity in the decision-making process. Some particular applications of each of these sets of grounds are considered later in this chapter, together with some probable effects of the HRA 1998.

9.16 Judicial review has its own category of remedies, in addition to the remedies generally available in litigation. All relief in judicial review proceedings (and some types of relief in other proceedings) are at the discretion of the court; no particular finding guarantees any particular result. The courts may decline to interfere, or do so minimally, if the wider public interest so requires, or if intervention would be futile or inappropriate. In *Moran v University College, Salford (No 2)*,[1] (not a judicial review case), the persistent Mr Moran established a contractual right to be admitted to a course, but had to be content with damages rather than a mandatory order enabling him to take it up. That was at the judge's discretion and was held to be inappropriate.

9.17 The court may make an order quashing an administrative decision or action by a public body, remitting the matter to the decision-maker, or directing it to reconsider the matter in accordance with the judgment of the court. If there is no purpose to be served in remitting the matter, the court may take the decision itself, unless statute requires it to be taken by the original decision-maker. The court may direct a public authority to comply with a particular obligation by doing something (a mandatory order); or prevent it from taking a decision which would be unlawful (a prohibiting order). The legal position may be clarified by declaration of the court. Injunctions to prevent unlawful action may be granted in judicial review, and there is now power under the HRA 1998 to make a declaration of incompatibility between UK legislation and European Convention rights. Damages for wrongful administrative action are available only where there is also some established cause of action in private law, for example negligence, or breach of statutory duty or human rights. The extent to which the courts will use their new powers to award damages for human rights violations in judicial review proceedings remains to be seen.

9.18 Judicial review is available only in respect of decisions made by public bodies, including government departments, the lower courts, local authorities,

---

1   [1994] ELR 187, CA.

financial services and utility regulators, competition and tax authorities, the Stock Exchange, and institutions forming part of the State education system, including the funding bodies. University Visitors are specifically excluded except on very limited grounds.[1] In *R v University of Nottingham ex parte K*,[2] an attempt to bring a chartered university within the scope of judicial review on the grounds, amongst others, that third parties were involved in accrediting the relevant course and that Visitors were an anachronism was unsuccessful.

9.19   The test which determines whether a decision-taking body is judicially reviewable, set out in *R v Panel on Takeovers and Mergers ex parte Datafin*,[3] is whether it operates in the public sphere or in pursuance of statutory powers. It was argued in that case that a statutory source of power was essential for making the decisions of an organisation liable to judicial review. The court disagreed, saying the nature as well as the source of the power had to be considered. If the body in question was exercising public functions, or if the exercise of its functions had consequences in terms of public and not just private law, that could be sufficient. Further widening of the scope of judicial review to include a sporting body was resisted by the Court of Appeal in *R v Disciplinary Committee of the Jockey Club ex parte Aga Khan*.[4] The courts have had no hesitation in identifying both the chartered and the statutory universities as public law bodies. In *Majid v London Guildhall University*,[5] the Court of Appeal agreed that the actions of a limited company which was running a university could be judicially reviewed. In *R v Thames Valley University Student Union ex parte Ogilvy*,[6] Sedley J held that the public law remedy of judicial review did not apply to an SU, despite arguments that statutory references to SUs gave them a public law dimension.

CONTRACTUAL ARRANGEMENTS

9.20   If a contract has been entered into between the applicant and the decision-taking body, the courts are likely to find this to be a private rather than public law relationship, which makes judicial review inappropriate. Thus, in *R v Fernhill Manor School ex parte A*,[7] a private school was held not to be a public law body, even though it operated within the statutory framework of control of the Education Acts. The relationship between a private school and its pupils was founded on the private contract between the school and those who paid for their education. Therefore, even though the rules of natural justice had not been followed when a pupil was excluded, the public law remedy of judicial

---

1   *R v Lord President of the Privy Council ex parte Page* [1993] AC 682, [1992] 3 WLR 112, see Chapter 8.
2   [1998] ELR 184.
3   [1987] 2 WLR 699.
4   [1993] 1 WLR 909.
5   *The Times Higher Educational Supplement*, 12 November 1993.
6   [1997] CLY 2149.
7   [1994] ELR 67.

review was not available. The position of maintained schools is different; see *R v Board of Governors of the London Oratory School ex parte Regis*.[1] Here, the school's articles and instrument of government had been made under powers contained in the Education Acts and no private contract had been involved. In *R v Governors of Haberdashers' Aske's Hatcham College Trust ex parte T*,[2] a City Technology College established under s 105 of the ERA 1988 was also held to be a public law body subject to judicial review. The judge in the *Fernhill Manor School* case quoted Professor Wade in the sixth edition of his textbook on *Administrative Law*:[3]

> 'Where a disciplinary body has no statutory powers its jurisdiction will normally be based upon contract. Members of trade unions, business associations, and social clubs and also students in universities and colleges have . . . contractual rights based on their contracts of membership, with implied terms which protect them from unfair expulsion. In these cases declaration and injunction are the appropriate remedies. [Quashing and prohibiting orders] are quite out of place, since the Crown's supervisory powers over public authorities are not concerned with private contracts.'[4]

As we have seen, declaration and injunction are remedies generally available in litigation, but quashing, mandatory and prohibiting orders are peculiar to judicial review.

9.21 It seems clear that, if the source of power of the decision-taking body is contractual, then judicial review is not available. The essential distinction is between the individual and consensual relations implied by a contract, and the general and involuntary liability to public law. Thus, attempts to secure judicial review by employees of a health authority in *R v East Berkshire Health Authority ex parte Walsh*[5] and of a county council in *R v Derbyshire County Council ex parte Noble*[6] were unsuccessful, even though these were undoubtedly public law bodies, because an employment contract is a private law matter.

9.22 The same reasoning was applied in *R v University College London ex parte Riniker*.[7] Mrs Riniker, who had already secured an admission of unfair dismissal and an offer of compensation from UCL in an industrial tribunal, asked the court for mandatory reinstatement and striking out of a condition of re-employment which banned her from entering or being involved with a language centre. She said this was a restriction on her right of free speech, confirmed by s 43 of the Education (No 2) Act 1986. The court accepted that s 43 was reviewable in an appropriate case.[8] UCL was a public law body, even though it is a non-statutory chartered institution. However, the restrictions

---

1   (1988) *The Times*, February 17.
2   (1994) *The Times*, October 19.
3   (Oxford University Press, 1988), p 425.
4   In *The Queen on the application of Oxford Study Centre Ltd v British Council* [2001] EWHC Admin 207, [2001] ELR 803, the British Council was held not to be amenable to judicial review of its decision not to give accreditation to a language school, as the exercise of voluntary function could not be seen to be 'woven into the system of government control'.
5   [1985] QB 152.
6   [1990] ICR 808.
7   [1995] ELT 213, (1995) EdLR 2(6)1.
8   For such a case see *R v University of Liverpool ex parte Caesar-Gordon* [1990] 3 WLR 667.

imposed by UCL on Mrs Riniker were found to be administrative matters linked to her private contract of employment, not an attempt to interfere with her public law right of free speech. Permission for judicial review was, therefore, refused. The same line was again followed in *R v University of Cambridge ex parte Evans (No 2)*.[1] The mere fact that certain functions of university government were public law matters 'did not mean that every dispute between a university and one of its employees could be resolved by resort to public law remedies'. In contrast, *R v City of Bath College Corporation ex parte Bashforth*[2] (a rare example of judicial review of an FE corporation) was a case brought by a lecturer whose appointment as a staff governor had been terminated by the corporation; here his employment as such was not an issue.

9.23   The courts are not keen on purely procedural contests, as between judicial review and ordinary litigation, when there are real issues to be resolved, usually (but not always) emphasising the need to retain flexibility between public and private law matters. Further, the position of private bodies which carry out some public functions will be affected by the HRA 1998, which will extend to such bodies the obligation to act in a way which is compatible with the European Convention when they exercise public law functions. Private bodies will be amenable to judicial review if they violate a Convention right while exercising public functions.

STUDENTS

9.24   If a contract of employment is a private law matter outside the scope of judicial review, what about relations between HEIs and their students, particularly the procedurally difficult areas of disciplinary and academic regulations, in the light of the contract of admission or matriculation? (See Chapters 6 and 7 for a detailed consideration of contractual issues.) Farrington (1998), p 241 says it is now clear that: 'when contemplating action against an institution which does not have a Visitor, and in the absence of any contractual dispute resolution procedure, a student has at least two possible alternatives: take action for breach of contract or apply for judicial review, depending on the nature of the dispute'.

9.25   There is a handful of early cases where chartered universities appeared in the courts, which pre-date both the establishment of the statutory HEIs and any recognition of the student contract, but they are now of interest only to show how the legal regime has changed. In *R v University of Aston Senate ex parte Roffey*,[3] where the Visitor's jurisdiction was (erroneously) not invoked, the court refused to become involved in procedural matters when students were excluded for failing exams, principally because of the applicants' delay, saying that insistence on the rules of natural justice would be 'a useless

---

1   [1999] CLY 1930, [1999] EdCR 556.
2   [1999] ELR 459.
3   [1969] 2 QB 538.

formality'. In *Glynn v Keele University*,[1] which concerned a student who sunbathed nude on campus, the court accepted jurisdiction and that there had been procedural unfairness, but again exercised its discretion against becoming involved in disciplinary proceedings. In *Herring v Templeman and Others*,[2] a case involving expulsion from a non-statutory teacher-training college, the Court of Appeal criticised the lower court's willingness in *ex parte Roffey* to entertain the application, and supported Professor Wade's view that the contractual nature of the relationship should have been considered. These rather quirky cases were exceptional in their time. The engagement of the courts in student disputes by means of judicial review is now more common, partly as a result of consumerist pressures. Student fees account for a large tranche of income within the HE sector. School leavers no longer constitute the student majority. Students no longer defer to title or status: respect for ability and quality of service has to be earned. (See also Chapter 29.)

9.26   The state of both student/institution relations and English administrative law has since moved on considerably. In *R v Manchester Metropolitan University ex parte Nolan*,[3] a Bar student had taken notes into a Common Professional Examination (CPE) examination, there had been procedural irregularities in the subsequent disciplinary proceedings, and also some confusion between the Faculty Disciplinary Committee and the CPE Examination Board. The case is described (Carroll (1994)) as the first occasion on which a student in the UK has been able to persuade a court of an abuse of academic disciplinary power sufficient to warrant judicial relief, and to establish that statutory universities without Visitors owe their students the full range of public law obligation, enforceable through applications for judicial review.

9.27   In fact the judge, Sedley J, dealt with the jurisdictional point very briefly. He said:

'[The defendant] is a body corporate by virtue of Chapter II of the Education Reform Act 1988. As a public institution discharging public functions, and having no Visitor, it is subject to judicial review of its decisions on conventional grounds. It is not disputed that [the claimant] has sufficient interest to bring the grounds upon which he relies before this court.'

The contractual/consensual argument for the basis of disciplinary rules appears not to have been considered.

9.28   Carroll (1994) concluded that the enforcement of student rights in academic and disciplinary matters remains within the law of contract for chartered institutions, whose powers are not underpinned by statute. He questioned, however, whether a student can be said freely to enter into a balanced contractual relationship with an HEI which admits him, and suggested that the limited application of judicial review to Visitors should be broadened, in order to provide the same degree of protection for students in

---

1   [1971] 1 WLR 487.
2   [1973] 3 All ER 569.
3   [1994] ELR 380.

chartered universities as is available in the statutory sector of HE. The QAA's Code of Practice on *Student Appeals and Complaints* (2000) has crystallised concerns about lack of uniformity across the sector, and non-compliance with the HRA 1998, which is likely to lead to a different approach to this long-standing problem.

9.29 Cases of judicial review involving statutory HEIs since *ex parte Nolan* illustrate many of the propositions discussed in the remainder of this chapter. In *R v University of Humberside ex parte Cousens*,[1] a student claimed that refusal to exercise a discretion to condone a part failure was irrational, in view of his otherwise satisfactory performance. The Court of Appeal did not agree. The question of contractual relationship does not seem to have been argued. In *R v Board of Governors of the Sheffield Hallam University ex parte Rowlett*,[2] a student was suspended for drug-taking after a University investigation, and expelled after a subsequent disciplinary hearing. She appealed unsuccessfully to the University governors and then applied for judicial review. Sedley J allowed the application because Ms Rowlett had not been given prior warning of all the charges against her. However, he rejected the arguments that there was a real danger of bias because of private knowledge of the chairman of the disciplinary committee, and that adequate notice of the evidence against Ms Rowlett had not been given. He found that the appeal panel had addressed irrelevant issues. Again, no reference to contract was made. The judges and lawyers in these cases tend to deal pragmatically with the issues, and not to be distracted by the jurisdictional question.

REDUCING THE RISK OF JUDICIAL REVIEW

9.30 As the possibility of judicial review is still a fact of life for statutory HEIs, how can they avoid falling foul of the courts? The following suggestions may assist.

The decision-taking body must be properly constituted

9.31 Clearly, the body which produces the decision must be correctly convened and made up according to the relevant constitutional provisions. In *R v Secretary of State for Education ex parte Prior*,[3] a maintained school got into a tangle over the respective roles and composition of its governing body, staff committee and appeals committee. It is vital to avoid a situation where an individual who may be involved at a later stage (for example, in hearing an appeal against a decision) becomes involved in the decision when it is first taken. But in *R v Liverpool John Moores University ex parte Hayes*,[4] the fact that

---

1   (1995) EdLM 2(6)11.
2   [1994] COD 470.
3   [1994] ELR 231.
4   [1998] ELR 261.

the same programme assessment board had reconsidered a student's case on two separate occasions during her course did not itself amount to procedural unfairness. Although there are few successful applications for judicial review of decisions by HEIs, they are often uncomfortably aware, when their process is examined in detail, that internal procedures (sometimes of quite unnecessary complexity) have not been correctly followed. This is not usually fatal, because of the extent of the judge's discretion, but may cause what should be a straightforward defence of a claim to become rather fraught.

The body responsible for making the decision must not delegate it without proper authority

9.32   The general rule is that a body to which decision-taking powers are formally delegated may not in turn delegate them further, unless there is an express power to do so. Particular care is needed if, as with many committees, certain powers are delegated to the chairman. It is wise to confine delegated decisions to minor or emergency matters, to ensure that major or permanent ones are decisions of the whole committee, and to set out clearly the scope of the chairman's delegated authority. In *R v University of Cambridge ex parte Evans*,[1] Sedley J found it was at least arguable that the University's statutes had been breached by the unauthorised delegation, to a committee, of the responsibility of the General Board of the University in making appointments to University office. (See Chapter 5.)

The decision must be within legal powers

9.33   A decision is *ultra vires* (outside legal powers) not only if there is no express power to make it in the constitution, statute or regulations concerned, but also if a decision-taking power is not used either in the way intended by Parliament or on the correct legal basis. If a decision is reached on a basis erroneous under the general law, then it is outside the parameters of permissible use and, therefore, *ultra vires*. The decision-maker's obligation to understand the law correctly and to give effect to it is extended by s 6 of the HRA 1998, which requires all public authorities to act compatibly with European Convention rights. There is an exception where the governing UK legislation requires the authority to act in a particular way, but even then, legislation must be interpreted so far as possible to be compatible with Convention rights. This applies to existing as well as new legislation, and overrules the doctrine of precedent as applied by the English courts.

The decision must exercise the mind of the decision-taking body

9.34   There must be an exercise of discretion which shows that the decision-maker's mind was not closed to the circumstances of the individual

---

1   [1998] ELR 515.

case. In *R v Warwickshire County Council ex parte Collymore*,[1] the council's decision to refuse a discretionary grant to a student on the postgraduate Legal Practice Course (LPC) was quashed because a blanket policy to refuse such applications had been applied without proper consideration of the individual circumstances.

The decision-taking body's discretion must not be fettered

9.35   This follows from the previous principle. A balance must be struck between the obvious desirability of achieving consistency and even-handedness in decision-taking, and following policy guidelines or precedents so slavishly that no discretion is exercised in the individual case or no allowance made for what might be the exceptional case. There have been a number of judicial reviews of schools' admissions policies on these grounds. There is no objection to the formulation or publication of guidelines, provided that discretion in applying them is not eliminated. Indeed, the rules of some public authorities require them to produce such non-binding statements of policy.

All relevant evidence must be considered

9.36   Reasonable enquiries to obtain the relevant evidence must be made before a decision is reached. Irrelevant considerations must not be taken into account. What is relevant or irrelevant may often not be defined in rules or regulations and, therefore, be open to interpretation by the decision-taking body and subsequently by the courts. If further relevant evidence emerges, the decision should be reconsidered. But judicial review is not a means of resolving factual disputes, provided the decision is within the proper discretion and judgment of the decision-maker – see *R v University of Central England ex parte Iqbal Sandhu*.[2] Although it is generally accepted that the courts will not intervene to correct an error of fact by a decision-maker (as opposed to an error of law), they have in some cases come close to doing so. This is an area where the law of judicial review is still developing. There may be challenges under the HRA 1998 as to whether a fair trial, an entitlement under Art 6 of the European Convention on Human Rights, is available when the court is limited to considering errors of law.

The decision must accord with the evidence

9.37   This is the famous test of '*Wednesbury* reasonableness'.[3] A decision is reviewable if it is manifestly absurd, irrational or perverse, one which no reasonable body properly directing itself could have reached. Recent cases tend to eschew use of dramatic words like 'perversity', and concentrate on

---

1   [1995] ELR 217.
2   [1999] ELR 419; *affirming* [1999] ELR 121, CA.
3   *Associated Provincial Picture Houses Ltd v Wednesbury Corporation* [1948] 1 KB 223.

straightforward reasonableness. Even on this test, unreasonableness sufficient to justify interference by the courts is difficult to prove; a partner in the city law firm Allen & Overy is quoted as saying: 'You have to establish that the decision-makers were on the verge of being carried off by the men in white coats'. The courts have resisted being drawn into considering the merits of a case under the guise of being asked to find a decision irrational. Decisions which interfere with human rights are certainly likely to be attacked as irrational, as well as illegal in their own rights. Public authorities will have to justify such decisions as a proportionate and reasonable response. This may well alter the burden of what has to be proved to establish irrationality.

9.38   In *R v A Local Authority and Police Authority in the Midlands ex parte LM*,[1] the claimant had a contract with the local authority to provide a school bus service, which was terminated when the authority received information suggesting, as a result of alleged misconduct 10 years earlier, he was not suitable for work involving children. He asked for assurances that the circumstances would not be disclosed to another local authority, with which he had a similar contract. The claimant argued that disclosure would be irrational and a breach of Art 8 of the European Convention on Human Rights – respect for private and family life. There were no recent allegations, and the original ones were never formally proved. The court found 'no pressing social need' for disclosure, which would justify a human rights breach in the wider interests of public policy, and hence the claimant was successful. But in *R v University of the West of England ex parte M*,[2] which also involved disclosure of prejudicial information by one public authority to another, the University's decision under academic regulations to remove M from a social work course, after concerns were expressed by a placement authority, was upheld. It had reasonably found that there was no likelihood of its being able to offer M another placement, so that she would not in any event be able to complete the course.

A decision must not be in pursuit of an improper purpose

9.39   Administrative powers may only be exercised for the purpose for which they are granted. Decisions which have an ulterior motive (seeking to achieve a certain result merely by using powers directed at other considerations) are liable to successful challenge.

The effects of a decision must be proportionate to the legitimate objectives of taking it

9.40   Proportionality is a European concept now required to be applied by the English courts, although it has been a feature of judicial review for some years. The courts have adopted proportionality as the benchmark for the degree of

---

1   [2000] 1 FLR 612, [2000] COD 41.
2   [2001] ELR 458, CA.

justification required to support a decision as reasonable. In *R v Manchester Metropolitan University ex parte Nolan*,[1] the judge held that failing a student permanently could be a proportionate response to the offence of seeking an unfair advantage by taking notes into an exam, even though this fell short of the more serious offence of cheating. In *R v Cambridge University ex parte Beg*,[2] a student was not allowed on judicial review to raise the question of whether his dismissal from the University was disproportionate to a finding of plagiarism, because he had failed to do so before the internal appellate body. In *R v Ministry of Agriculture, Fisheries and Food ex parte First City Trading*,[3] Laws J described 'Wednesbury unreasonableness' and European proportionality as 'different models of the same judicial concept, which is the imposition of compulsory standards on decision-makers so as to secure the repudiation of arbitrary power'. The increased significance of the principle of proportionality was emphasised in the light of the HRA 1998 by the House of Lords in *R v Secretary of State for the Home Department ex parte Daly*.[4]

The legitimate expectation of the individual who is the subject of a decision must be taken into account

9.41 This is the equivalent of estoppel in private law, and rests on the assumption that public law bodies will in the interests of fairness consistently apply known procedures in arriving at administrative decisions, particularly the practice of consultation before such rules are changed. In *R v Rochdale MBC ex parte Schemet*,[5] parents had a legitimate expectation that free bus passes would continue to be issued for travel to school until some rational grounds for changing the policy were given and they had an opportunity to comment. The court will ask whether the frustration of an individual's expectation is so unfair as to be a misuse of an authority's power. Courts have been wary of extending the principle of legitimate expectation too far. It was intended originally to protect the whole class of people potentially affected by a decision, not individuals in the sense of what was, or was not, said to them about their particular circumstances. However, in *R v North and East Devon Health Authority ex parte Coughlan*,[6] Sedley J found that a promise is capable of giving rise to an expectation of a benefit, if it has the character of a contract which cannot be frustrated, and if breach of the promise would amount to an abuse of power.

---

1   [1994] ELR 380.
2   [1999] ELR 404, (1999) 11 Admin LR 505.
3   [1997] 1 CMLR 250.
4   [2001] 2 WLR 1622.
5   [1994] ELR 89.
6   [2000] 2 WLR 622.

The individual who is the subject of a decision must first have the opportunity to put his case to an unbiased decision-taker

9.42 It is a fundamental requirement that the decision-taking body should hear both sides of the story, so that the individual's response to matters raised in respect of him or her is taken into account. This extends to the opportunity to comment on all the evidence against him (but not necessarily to a right to see in-house advice to the decision-taking body – see *R v Secretary of State for Education ex parte S*[1]). The requirement for advance disclosure is now reinforced by both human rights considerations and the DPA 1998. A properly adversarial procedure before an independent, impartial tribunal is one of the requirements of a fair trial under Art 6 of the European Convention on Human Rights. Difficult questions sometimes arise where the procedure for determining a dispute is set out in a statute or other regulation, but the abstract requirements of fairness seem to require additions to the procedure as so set out. The courts are increasingly willing to find that there has been procedural unfairness, even where the letter of the law has been followed, if a party has not been given every opportunity to answer allegations against him. See *The Queen on the application of Persaud v Cambridge University*,[2] where an application by a PhD student whose studies were terminated after 7 years was successful. Two academic reports on which the decision had been based were withheld from her, a process which 'failed to measure up to the standards of fairness required of the university'. See also para **9.9**, and note that in *The Queen on the application of McNally v Secretary of State for Education and Metropolitan Borough of Bury*,[3] Dyson LJ said the court is required, in certain cases, to construe general words contained in a statute as being impliedly limited by the ordinary rules and principles of the common law, including the principle of natural justice, unless Parliament had clearly indicated an intention to change the common law.

There must be a fair hearing

9.43 Provided that there is an adequate opportunity for the individual to put his case, the requirements of a fair hearing are not fixed. Under English law, there was no absolute requirement for an oral hearing if all the relevant evidence can be adequately considered in written form. Affected parties must have adequate notice of all the matters to be raised against them – see *R v Board of Governors of the Sheffield Hallam University ex parte Rowlett*.[4] The right to a fair hearing must now be considered in the light of Art 6 of the European Convention on Human Rights, which applies, as well as in criminal cases, to any determination of a civil right or obligation. It is now established that the

---

1   [1995] ELR 71.
2   [2001] EWCA Civ 534, [2001] ELR 480, CA.
3   [2001] ELR 772.
4   [1994] COD 470.

right to education in school is a public law right, not a civil right, so that Art 6 does not apply.[1] The hearing must be in public, before an independent and impartial tribunal established by law, and within a reasonable time. The ECHR has held that it is permissible for decisions to be made by bodies which do not comply with these requirements, provided there is a right of appeal to one which does, and has full jurisdiction to review all matters, whether of law or fact.[2] Although judgment must be given publicly, the press and public may be excluded from the hearing in certain circumstances. But, in *Lalu Hanuman v UK*,[3] the ECHR held that decisions taken by a university's academic appeals committee and the Visitor did not involve the determination of a civil right, so that Art 6 did not apply. No reasoning accompanied this decision. There is clearly scope for argument in the English courts. In *The Queen on the application of McNally v Secretary of State for Education and Metropolitan Borough of Bury*,[4] Kennedy LJ said it was doubtful whether Art 6 had any application to internal disciplinary proceedings, but it was unnecessary to decide the point in that case.

9.44   If a disciplinary hearing involves alleged conduct which also constitutes a criminal offence, particularly tight safeguards to ensure a fair trial will be required. Article 6 includes more guarantees of a fair trial for criminal cases than for civil rights. The determination of civil rights is not necessarily as all-embracing as it sounds – the Strasbourg court has held, for example, that immigration and nationality rights do not involve a civil right. It is probable, however, that some decisions of HEIs will be regarded despite *Lalu* as determining civil rights or obligations and will, therefore, be covered. It is not yet clear whether 'hearing' means the process of considering a case, however achieved, or whether at least the option of a public oral hearing followed by a published decision is now an absolute requirement. If the option is available, the parties may agree to dispense with a hearing altogether, or to hold it in private.

Reasons for a decision may be required

9.45   Failure to give reasons is still not necessarily a ground for judicial review, but a person affected by a decision must be able to rationalise it in order to determine whether to accept it, appeal, or apply to the court. If reasons are given they must be intelligible. The amount of detail which the courts require for the supporting of administrative decisions varies according to the gravity and frequency of the type of decision involved, and the severity of its effect on

---

1   *The Queen on the application of B v Head Teacher of Alperton Community School* [2001] EWHC Admin 229, [2001] ELR 359.
2   *Le Compte, Van Leuven and de Mayere v Belgium* (1980) 4 EHRR 1.
3   [2000] ELR 685.
4   [2001] ELR 772.

the person subject to it, but the requirements of the courts in the interests of public accountability are increasing in this respect. Five years ago, in *R v University of Humberside ex parte Cousens*,[1] the need for any more detailed reasons than were contained in the university's fairly brief decision letter was emphatically rejected. In *R v University College London ex parte Idriss*,[2] Sullivan J held first that it was very doubtful whether a straightforward decision by a university to refuse an application for entry to a course was susceptible to judicial review at all, and secondly, that there was no duty on the university to give reasons for refusing to admit an applicant; the university's statutes expressly stated there was no such requirement.

9.46   Ten useful principles on the extent of the obligation to give reasons were set out in *R v Ministry of Defence ex parte Murray*,[3] which recognised 'a perceptible trend towards an insistence on greater openness'. It is now likely to be suggested that failure to give reasons frustrates the rights contained in Art 6 of the European Convention on Human Rights (right to a fair trial) because people with a justifiable complaint, but no explanation of how a decision has been reached, will not be equipped to apply to a court at all. Article 6 in any event gives reasons as one of the characteristics of a fair hearing. Decision-makers in universities and elsewhere are sometimes tempted to say as little as possible about the reasons for their decision, on the grounds that this reduces the scope of challenge. Such an approach is to be discouraged. If a body is confident about its decisions, it should have no difficulty in explaining why it has reached them.

A decision involving human rights must not be discriminatory

9.47   Whenever a European Convention right is at issue in judicial review proceedings, a court will have to consider Art 14 – prohibition on discrimination. An otherwise reasonable act which affects a Convention right will be illegal if it is undertaken in a discriminatory way, unless the body which takes the decision can show this was a justifiable and proportionate act.

The decision-maker must be unbiased

9.48   An assessing person or body who is in some way linked with the proceedings may be disqualified from making a proper decision. In *R v Gough (Robert)*,[4] the House of Lords said that, where an adjudicator had a direct pecuniary interest in the outcome of the proceedings, the court would assume bias and disqualify him automatically. Otherwise, the test to be applied in all cases of apparent bias was whether there was a real danger of bias, in the sense

---

1   (1995) EdLM 2(6)11.
2   [1999] EdCR 462.
3   [1998] COD 134.
4   [1993] 2 All ER 724.

that a decision-maker might unfairly have regarded with favour or disfavour the case of any party to the dispute – see also *R v Board of Governors of the Sheffield Hallam University ex parte Rowlett*.[1] This became a highly topical area, following the embarrassment of the House of Lords in *R v Bow Street Metropolitan Stipendiary Magistrate ex parte Pinochet Ugarte (No 2)*,[2] where an appeal had to be reheard, before different Law Lords, when it became clear that one of the original judges had a connection with a party to the case. Public opinion, or at least press opinion, has become increasingly intolerant of any situation where the impartiality of a decision-maker seems to be compromised. In fact, it is often difficult convincingly to demonstrate such impartiality during an institution's internal proceedings, where the decision-maker is likely to be a professional colleague of the staff member who is in some way opposing the interests of the student.

PROCEDURE AND COSTS

9.49 The new pre-action protocol for judicial review provides helpful guidance on the form of communication which should take place between the prospective parties, before proceedings are commenced. Claimants should send a letter before claim, following a prescribed order, and setting out the decision under challenge, a summary of the facts and details of relevant information. A claim should not normally be made until after the proposed reply date, normally 14 days. The defendant's letter of response, also in a prescribed order, should make clear to what extent the claim is conceded, provide a fuller explanation of the decision (if appropriate), address points in dispute, and enclose relevant documentation. The protocol recognised that in urgent cases there may be good reason for not following it, although even in these cases it is good practice to fax the claim form to the defendant. The court may impose sanctions if parties fail to observe the protocol without good reason.

9.50 Judicial review proceedings are governed by Part 54 of the Civil Procedure Rules 1998 (CPR 1998). They confirm tight time-limits which cannot be extended by agreement between the parties. There has been a general updating of terminology: judicial review cases are now dealt with by the Administrative Court, no longer in the Crown Office List or the Divisional Court. The Latin tags learned by generations of law students – *mandamus* and *certiorari* – have been swept away (although the expression *ultra vires*, which of course does not appear in the Rules, seems to survive). English cases are heard in London, but there is power to hold hearings elsewhere, and Welsh cases are dealt with in Cardiff. The applicant completes a claim form, containing information prescribed by the Rules, and must serve it on all named parties.

---

1   [1994] COD 470.
2   [2000] 1 AC 119.

Anyone receiving a claim form must complete an acknowledgement of service within 21 days. The court may direct that the Crown be joined as a party if HRA 1998 issues are involved. Failure to file an acknowledgement, which sets out grounds for contesting the claim, bars a defendant from being involved at the permission stage, but not from the full hearing if permission is granted. If that happens, the defendant must file a full response and written evidence within a further 35 days. Applications for permission to seek judicial review are normally dealt with on paper and without an oral hearing. There is no appeal against this decision, but reconsideration at an oral hearing may be requested. Initially, it is up to the judge to decide whether the claimant's case has a reasonable chance of success. There are likely to be HRA 1998 challenges, under the fair trial requirements of Art 6, to refusal of permission on the basis of quick perusal of papers and consideration of limited evidence.

9.51 There is no tightly drawn definition of who can apply for judicial review. The applicant must have 'a sufficient interest in the matter' (Supreme Court Act 1981, s 31(3)). So busybodies with no legitimate interests may not apply, but an applicant does not necessarily have to have a personal stake in the outcome.[1] However, under the HRA 1988, only a victim of the alleged breach of a Convention right has sufficient interest to apply for judicial review on this ground alone. Although disclosure of documents and cross-examination of witnesses are now rare in judicial review, some commentators have suggested they will be required in order to provide the courts with the level of evidence they will need to make judgments as to proportionality on breaches of qualified European Convention rights. A high proportion of all applications are settled either before the application for permission is dealt with, or after it is granted. Negotiations leading to settlement may take many forms, but it is always worth considering whether a re-determination of the decision to which the claimant objects should be offered, without prejudice to the determination of the original challenge. This may short-circuit expensive and time-consuming proceedings, and may be useful later in relation to costs.

9.52 In most cases, costs are not awarded at the permission stage, even where the defendant successfully resists the application for permission. Institutions will therefore have to bear their own costs at this stage. If permission is granted, the question of costs will be reserved to the substantive hearing, and may be a factor in subsequent negotiations. Should a full hearing take place, costs will follow the event in the usual way subject to the overriding discretion of the court. If the claimant is receiving public funding, his or her liability to pay the other side's costs if the application is unsuccessful is limited by s 11 of the Access to Justice Act 1989. This means that, in practice, no order for costs will normally be made against a publicly funded claimant, leaving institutions to pay their own legal costs even when successful. However, the court still has a

---

1   See *R v Somerset County Council and ARC Southern Ltd ex parte Dixon* [1997] COD 323.

discretion to order costs against an unsuccessful publicly funded claimant, even though there may be no immediate prospect of their being paid. This is the so-called 'football pools' costs order, which could be enforced at some future time when the claimant's financial circumstances have improved. This might be especially relevant in the case of publicly funded student claimants who later move into employment.

Chapter 10

DISPUTES III: SELECTED EMPLOYMENT LAW ISSUES ('ACADEMIC FREEDOM', 'TENURE' AND 'GOOD CAUSE')

Oliver Hyams (Barrister)

EDITORS' INTRODUCTION

§10.1 This book does not cover employment law generally: the legal position for HEIs in relation to their contracts of employment with most staff is as for any other employer and is well-covered in the standard texts on employment law (for example, Birks (2000), chapter 12, Phillips and Scott (2001/02), and Selwyn (2000) for comprehensive coverage; and Duggan (1999) specifically on unfair dismissal). This also applies generally to race and sex discrimination disputes between HE employees (whether academics or not) and their HEI employers: the legal issues are the same as for similar disputes in other employment contexts and, sadly, the supposed ultra-rationality of the HEI environment does not make HEIs immune to these matters reaching a tribunal or court (for example, concerning racial discrimination, *Anya v University of Oxford*;[1] and concerning sex discrimination, see Suzanne Alexander's chapter 14 of Warner and Palfreyman (2001) *An Unsuitable Job for a Woman*). There are, however, particular areas where employment law and HE do come together in a way not applicable to other employee–employer relationships and hence not usually covered in the readily available standard texts. This chapter and the following chapter cover those areas, notably the protection given to academic staff under the label 'academic freedom', and the dismissal/redundancy of academic staff for 'good cause' in the context of 'tenure'; plus the complex interaction of the Model Statute and more recent legislation concerning short-term contracts. These topics are covered also in Farrington (1998), pp 128–131 and 405–412 respectively; and in Hyams (1998), pp 516–520 (plus 652) on the ERA 1988, ss 203–207, concerning tenure, redundancy and good cause: plus Hyams (1996). See also Brown (1997) for an interesting perspective. (By analogy see also Hyams (2000) on the school teacher–employer relationship.) Lewis (1997) discusses disciplinary dismissals and redundancy in HE and FE. Saunders (1999) considers academic freedom in the context of the HRA 1998, interacting with the ERA

---

1   [2001] EWCA Civ 405, [2001] ICR 847, [2001] ELR 711, (2001) ELJ 2(4) 227, at pp 227–228, CA; *The Times Higher Educational Supplement*, 15 February 2002, p 6: the matter continues, with Dr Anya losing at the employment tribunal subsequent to the Court of Appeal case but threatening to appeal (the tribunal did, however, find technical fault with Oxford's equal opportunities procedures). Note the 'Consultation Draft' for a *Statutory Code of Practice on the duty to promote race equality: A Guide for Institutions of Further and Higher Education* recently issued by the Commission for Racial Equality under the Race Relations (Amendment) Act 2000.

1988, s 202(2)(a). On the management of employees within HEIs see Chapter 7 of Warner and Palfreyman (1996; second edition due 2002/03), and the related volumes in the *Managing Universities and Colleges* series: *Managing Stress* (Edworthy (2000)) and *Managing People* (Hall, forthcoming); plus Warner and Crosthwaite (1995).

§10.2   For a US perspective on academic freedom, see Kaplin and Lee (1995a), pp 306–331, and notably concerning freedom to publish, the 1992 *Levin* case.[1] The US courts do not interpret 'academic freedom to be a licence for uncontrolled expression at variance with the established curricular contents and internally destructive of the proper functioning of the institution' (a 1972 case quoted in Kaplin and Lee (1995a)). In short, in terms of pedagogy, academics must co-operate within a management hierarchy. That element of their job is like any other (a 1991 case noted that 'The University's conclusions about course content must be allowed to hold sway over an individual professor's judgements'). Hence the management of an HEI is not able to tell an academic to increase or decrease a mark or grade awarded to a particular student. That would be violation of academic freedom, a challenge to the academic's professional judgement. However, the HEI's management can *itself* change the grade. Academic freedom in the context of research and publications, as opposed to curricular content and style, is a more clear-cut matter in US law: 'The classroom is the arena where institutional authority is greatest and courts are most hesitant to enter. Research and publication is the arena where the institution is likely to have least authority' (Kaplin and Lee (1995a), p 328).

§10.3   Kaplin and Lee in their Supplement (2000), pp 182–213 consider institutional academic freedom, quoting from *Feldman v Ho*:[2] US courts will defer to the genuine academic judgement of HEIs ('. . . the only way to preserve academic freedom is to keep claims of academic error out of the legal maw'). Similarly, in *Urofsky v Gilmore*,[3] the court even more strongly backed academic freedom. That said, institutional academic freedom, as it were, trumps that of the individual academic in terms of the latter being told by the former to teach class X using syllabus Y.[4] But in relation to detailed teaching methods and classroom behaviour (even where the students claim sexual harassment in the lecturer's speech) the courts tend to side with the faculty member.[5] It is, of course, different if the academic's complained of speech/behaviour is *not* pedagogically relevant or not germane to the academic context.[6] Finally, some US cases show the courts may be willing to back the academic against the HEI where the former speaks out in the name of academic freedom as a kind of whistleblowing (for example, *Bloch v Temple University*,[7] concerning health and safety issues in a physics laboratory).

1   *Levin v Harleston* 770 F Supp 895; *affirmed* 966 F 2d 85, 2d Cir 1992, at pp 312–315 of Kaplin and Lee.
2   171 F 3d 494, 7th Cir 1999.
3   167 F 3d 191, 4th Cir 1999, 2000 WL 806882, 4th Cir 23/06/2000.
4   *Webb v Board of Trustees of Ball State University* 167 F 3d 1146, 7th Cir 1999, and *Edwards v California University of Pennsylvania* 156 F 3d 488, 3rd Cir 1998.
5   *Blum v Schlegel* 18 F 3d 1005, 2nd Cir 1994; *Silva v University of New Hampshire* 888 F Supp 293, DNH 1994; and *Cohen v San Bernadino Valley College* 92 F 3d 969, 9th Cir 1996; *reversing* 883 F supp 1407, CD Cal 1995.
6   *Krakunas v Iona College* 119 F 3d 80, 2d Cir 1997.
7   934 F Supp 387, ED Pa 1996.

§10.4   On academic freedom in Canada, especially in relation to the exploitation of intellectual property arising from commercial contracts, see Nancy Olivieri's *Corporate Campus* (1999). In similar vein in relation to US HE, see Soley (1995) and Kennedy (1997). The case of *University of Nottingham v Fishel*[1] illustrates the potential for conflicts of interest over research activity and external consultancy when it comes to the fiduciary duty of academics towards their HEI employers: see paras **10.24** *et seq*, and also Chapters 12 and 14 for reference to similar 'split loyalties' cases in UK HEIs. Monbiot (2001) polemically explores 'the corporate takeover' of UK HE, with many (allegedly) 'naming and shaming' examples cited.

§10.5   On the confidentiality of academic research, see Kaplin and Lee (1995a), pp 337–343: '... judges are increasingly hostile to claims of a researcher's or scholar's privilege, especially when the information is sought for a criminal, rather than a civil, proceeding ... [hence] promises of absolute confidentiality to research subjects may not be enforceable' (p 341). The case of *Re Cusumano and Yoffie* [*US Government v Microsoft*][2] illustrates the reluctance of the courts to force academics to reveal their data and the identity of sources in a civil action; Microsoft wanted two academics from MIT and Harvard to provide information on their research interviews at its competitor Netscape in order to assist Microsoft's defence in antitrust litigation brought by the US Government. On tenure and redundancy for reasons of 'financial exigency', see Kaplin and Lee (1995a), pp 343–352 plus 369), and the leading cases of: *AAUP v Bloomfield College*;[3] *Pace v Hymas*;[4] *Krotkoff v Goucher College*;[5] and *Jimenez v Almodovar*.[6]

§10.6   On tenure, Kaplin and Lee (2000), pp 166–169 observe that, in assessing academics for tenure, besides the obvious issues of teaching competence and research productivity, US HEIs can require collegiality as 'institutional citizenship', and doing so has withstood legal challenges by those denied tenure.[7] See also Khan (1997) on Canadian courts not second-guessing academic decision-making in relation to the granting of tenure, unless there has been manifest or flagrant abuse of due process.

§10.7   Finally, as certain UK HEIs face major financial problems arising from general under-recruitment of students over the last year or so, and as even more highly-ranked HEIs have experienced under-recruitment in certain less popular subject areas, doubtless many HE managers will be checking the law on redundancy and some will need to be very clear on the applicability or otherwise to their institution of the concept of 'academic tenure'.

§10.8   The charity providing advice to concerned employees on 'whistleblowing' under the Public Interest Disclosure Act 1998 is *Public Concern at Work* (020 7404 6609; www.pcaw.co.uk). The current limit of £52,600 for employment

---

1   [2000] ICR 1462.
2   162 F 3d 708, 1st Cir 1998.
3   322 A 2d 846, NJ Super Ct Ch Div 1974; *affirmed* 346 A 2d 615, App Div 1975.
4   726 P 2d 693, Idaho 1986, at the University of Idaho.
5   585 F 2d 675, 4th Cir 1978.
6   650 F 2d 363, 1st Cir 1981, at the University of Puerto Rico.
7   For example, *Mayberry v Dees* 633 F 2d 502, 4th Cir 1981; *Stein v Kent State University Board of Trustees* 994 F Supp 898, ND Ohio 1998; *affirmed* 181 F 3d 103, SD NY 1994; *University of Baltimore v Peri Iz* 716 A 2d 1107, Md Ct Special App 1998; and especially *McGill v the Regents of the University of California* 52 Cal Reptr 2d 466, Ct App Cal, 4th Dist 1996.

tribunal damages/compensation does not apply to whistleblowing dismissals, and nor does the employee need to have been in employment for the
qualifying year usually required for access to other aspects of employment law
protection. Note Derby University's settlement with an academic whistle-
blower concerning the franchising of courses prior to the tribunal hearing its
defence of the case brought by the lecturer under the Act: the first such case in
UK HE;[1] see also the Unit on 'Public Interest Disclosure' available for HEIs at
www.bristol.ac.uk/armed, and for more on franchising see Chapter 17 below
and CUC (1997).

§10.9   The 'armed' website also has a Unit on 'Work Permits and Visas', and one on
'Research Misconduct'. Finally, as we go to press, the UUK is protesting about
terms in the Export Control Bill which *may* mean academics needing
government permission before 'exporting' their knowledge when collborat-
ing on international research projects, and hence be damaging for academic
freedom.

INTRODUCTION

10.1   This chapter considers some issues arising in relation to the staffing of
HEIs. In many ways, HEIs are no different from other employers. However, in
addition to the protection afforded to an employee of (say) a commercial
company, an employee of the body responsible in law for conducting a HE may
have a right to (for example) a hearing before a committee of that body before
being dismissed. The nature of this right may be regarded as a public law right,
or a right arising under the constitution of the body, which may be enforced by
means of an action otherwise than in the law of contract (ie usually via judicial
review – see also Chapter 9). Furthermore, a lecturer may be engaged under
terms which prevent the employer from dismissing him or her unless there is
'good cause'.

10.2   The major case concerning the exact contractual position of an
academic and dismissal for 'good cause' concerns a lecturer at the University of
Hull, with the key issue being whether redundancy was 'good cause'.[2] In that
case, the House of Lords decided that dismissal for redundancy could take
place because the University had a wide clause allowing dismissal for reasons
other than 'good cause' as defined in its statutes: Mr Page was duly made
redundant. Some HEIs did not have this wider clause; some have since
amended their statutes; and in any event all will now have had their statutes
amended by the Commissioners (as discussed below), to cover the redundancy
of academic staff *who have been appointed or promoted since 20 November 1987*.
It is argued that few HEIs have a gold-plated tenure protection in their statutes
and hence that, in fact, academics appointed or promoted prior to 20
November 1987 are mostly as vulnerable to being made redundant as their later
colleagues who are now 'protected' only by the amendments to statutes made

---

1   *The Times Higher Educational Supplement*, 12 January 2001, p 6.
2   *R v Lord President of the Privy Council ex parte Page* [1993] AC 682.

by the Commissioners via their 'Model Statute'. The HEI's only legal obligation in relation to redundancy for any employee where 'tenure' does not provide 'a job for life' is to pay the (fairly modest) statutory redundancy payment calculated by reference to years of service: in practice most employees (and especially academics) get rather more generous terms, usually under some special scheme financed by the funding council.

10.3   An academic is employed under a contract of employment, or service – not a contract *for services*, as when a tradesman is employed. However, the terms of this contract can prove difficult to ascertain from the raft of formal paperwork (further particulars, offer letter, acceptance letter, a signed contract, and the Statement of Terms required by employment legislation to be issued to all new employees concerning essential aspects of the full employment contract); the background paperwork (the HEI's statutes, its disciplinary regulations, IT policy, grievance procedures, harassment policy, etc); and any collective trade union agreements between the HEI and the AUT or NATFHE, as well as local or even industry-wide HE 'custom and practice'. This echoes the difficulties, noted in Chapter 6, of ascertaining the exact terms of the HEI–student contract. In addition, there will be implied terms such as mutual trust and confidence between HEI and academic employee in their dealings with each other, and a degree of fiduciary duty owed by employee to employer, while the employer has an obligation to provide appropriate support to an employee in performing his job (see any standard text on employment law for further detail: including Hyams (2000), for the analogy with the employment of teachers in schools). In the event of a merger of HEIs, as discussed in Chapter 16 and Palfreyman, Thomas and Warner (1998), very specific legal advice will be needed concerning the detailed legislation known as 'TUPE' (the Transfer of Undertakings (Protection of Employment) Regulations 1981[1]) protecting the existing employment rights when staff transfer from one employer to another.

10.4   In addition, lecturers in HE may well be engaged in research or, alternatively, in the provision of services which they could not supply unless they were employed at the institution in question. Issues may then arise in relation to the ownership of any intellectual property created during the course of the employment, or in relation to the propriety of the employee himself receiving payment for the relevant services. Intellectual property issues are dealt with in Chapter 12 of this book. The question whether an employee could lawfully receive payment personally for services provided as envisaged above is dealt with in this chapter. First, though, it is necessary to refer to the situation of HEIs which have a Visitor.

---

1   SI 1981/1794.

HEIs WHERE THERE IS A VISITOR

10.5 Employees in HEIs where there is a Visitor may be expected to take certain matters relating to their employment to the Visitor (although the jurisdiction of the Visitor is currently under attack as a result of two new pieces of legislation, referred to below: see also Chapters 7, 8, 9 and 30). This is so where the Visitor retains a role despite the provisions of the ERA 1988. The relevant provisions of that Act were passed to remove from the jurisdiction of the Visitor many matters which had previously been capable of being decided only by the Visitor, and not by the courts. Section 206(1) of the ERA 1988 prohibited the Visitor from determining 'any dispute relating to a member of the academic staff which concerns his appointment or employment or the termination of his appointment or employment'. This prohibition, however, is subject to s 206(3), which provides that the Visitor may nevertheless hear and determine appeals and hear and redress grievances in accordance with procedures established in pursuance of s 203(1)(d) and (e) of the Act. These new, 'Model Statute' provisions are:

> 'procedures ... for hearing and determining appeals by any members of the academic staff who are dismissed or under notice of dismissal ... or who are otherwise disciplined; and ... procedures ... for affording to any member of the academic staff opportunities for seeking redress for any grievances relating to his appointment or employment.'[1]

10.6 It is noted that this could be interpreted to mean that the Visitor may not act unless such procedures specifically enable him to do so. However, they could also be interpreted to mean that the Visitor may hear and determine appeals, and hear and redress grievances in accordance with procedures established in pursuance of s 203(1)(d) and (e) of the ERA 1988, even where they make no specific reference to the Visitor. The better interpretation appears to be the first, bearing in mind the clear words of s 206(1) of the Act. It is of note that Lord Irvine, the Lord Chancellor, acting on behalf of the Queen as Visitor to York University in *Burrows v University of York*,[2] said that he thought that s 206(1) did not preclude him from determining a complaint regarding the manner in which a grievance hearing was conducted. It is difficult to criticise that view.

10.7 The words 'a member of the academic staff' in s 206(1) are defined by s 203(4): s 206(4)(b). According to the Northern Ireland Court of Appeal, a probationary member of the academic staff is not included in this definition.[3]

---

1   ERA 1988, s 203(1)(d) and (e).
2   [1999] EdCR 586.
3   *D v Queen's University of Belfast* [1997] ELR 431, at pp 451F–G and 452F, per Hutton LCJ and MacDermott LJ respectively. Nicholson LJ's primary ground for his decision (which concurred with that of the other two judges) was that the contract of employment of a lecturer who was appointed subject to a period of probation, was conditional. The failure of the condition resulted in the lecturer never being a lecturer within the meaning of the relevant position in the University's statutes.

10.8 The prohibition in s 206(1) is subject to the qualification that the Visitor will retain jurisdiction in relation to a dispute if the dispute was referred to the Visitor before 'the relevant date' or the date when s 206 came into force (which was 29 July 1988). The relevant date for this purpose is defined by s 206(4)(a) to mean 'the date on which the statutes of the institution include such provision as is mentioned in section 203(1)(d) and (e) of this Act'.

10.9 Section 206(1) of the ERA 1988 appears not to exclude from the Visitor's jurisdiction any dispute which concerns the administration of a qualifying institution (a chartered HEI), but which also coincidentally concerns the rights of the institution as against a member of the academic staff. This is in part because ss 202–207 were addressed specifically at issues arising in relation to academic tenure. Thus, the Visitor can still act where the issue does not involve the potential termination of the employment of a member of academic staff; for instance, were there to be a dispute: (i) among academics concerning the interpretation of the HEI's charter or statutes over, say, where power lay to decide a particular matter; or (ii) within an academic department over how, say, the voting for the elected chair should be organised.

10.10 Whether the jurisdiction of the Visitor will survive the test of time is an interesting question. Traditionally, as far as the courts of England and Wales have been concerned (Scottish HEIs are not subject to the visitorial jurisdiction), the jurisdiction of the Visitor ousted any jurisdiction which the court would otherwise have had. Briefly, therefore, if a dispute arose concerning the manner in which a lecturer in a body which had a Visitor had been treated by that body, and the dispute was of a kind which, according to the constitution of the body, had to be referred to (and determined by) the Visitor, then a claim for breach of contract brought by the lecturer would not be decided by a court if the body in question raised the jurisdiction of the Visitor as a defence to the claim. (The same would be true in respect of a complaint by the body about the conduct of the lecturer.) That jurisdiction would be a complete defence, because the court would say that the Visitor was the only party who could determine the dispute. This exclusive jurisdiction in relation to the employment of academics was ended by the ERA 1988, but left intact in relation to student–HEI disputes. Now, the residual jurisdiction in relation to students may be challenged on the basis that it does not comply with Art 6(1) of the European Convention on Human Rights, which has been incorporated into the law of the UK by the HRA 1998. It may also be challenged on the basis that it contravenes the UTCCR 1999[1] and their predecessor regulations of 1994.[2] These matters are dealt with further in Chapters 7, 8, 9 and 30. It is interesting to note, however, that Tur (2001) argues that, paradoxically, the Visitor's former exclusive jurisdiction concerning academic dismissal within the chartered HEIs was probably more compliant with Art 6(1) of the European Convention on Human Rights and hence with the HRA 1998 than the 'Model

---

1   SI 1999/2083.
2   SI 1994/3159.

Statute' imposed by the University Commissioners under the ERA 1988, since the Visitor had been chosen for the HEI by, as it were, history, while the 'Model Statute' allows the HEI's Council or governing body to select its own external individual who will effectively constitute the appeal process. Tur sees a 'problem of institutionalised bias and structural unfairness generated by the Commissioner's Statute', the solution to which is 'the full restoration of the Visitorial jurisdiction', on the basis that: 'The procedures which obtain prior to the Commissioners' Statutes were intelligible, economic, effective, fair and (although the question did not actually [then] arise) Convention compliant. What we now have is a mess'. (See Chapters 7, 8 and 30 concerning the Visitor's compliance with Art 6 of the European Convention in relation to student grievance/discipline cases.)

Procedural protection under the constitution of an HEI

10.11   Certain (if not most) HEIs will be governed by constitutions under which employees have the right to a hearing by, for example, a committee before being dismissed. In many institutions, employees will have a right to more than one such hearing, the final one taking the form of an appeal hearing. The effect of a failure to afford an employee such a right is not always clear. The right could be seen simply as a private right, enforceable by an employee only in the law of contract. Alternatively, it could be seen as a public law right, enforceable in judicial review proceedings (as long as the court accepted that the matter was one which was properly to be regarded as subject to public law, the test for whether it was such falling to be determined under the principles in *R v Panel on Takeovers and Mergers, ex parte Datafin*[1]). The impact of a failure to afford the right in question would be affected greatly by the manner of the classification of the right: if it were a purely private law right, enforceable only in the law of contract, then a failure to afford the right would not make the dismissal invalid or void in any way, because of the line of cases culminating in *Boyo v Lambeth London Borough Council*.[2] Those cases make it clear that, in practice, if an employer breaches a procedural provision in a contract of employment, that may nevertheless bring about an ending of the contract (so a termination which is not in accordance with the terms of the contract may still be regarded by a court as having brought about an end to that contract), and the employer may have to pay damages to the ex-employee for breach of contract. In contrast, an act which does not comply with procedural provisions in the constitution of a body which may as a result give rise to a judicial review may be held to have had no effect and to be void, which could mean that the employee's job had not been terminated.

10.12   If the choice were between these two only, then as a matter of principle, it would normally be clear that the right was purely private (and, therefore, not capable of giving rise to a judicial review), with the result that an

---

1   [1987] QB 815.
2   [1994] ICR 727.

act of an employer which purported to terminate the contract of employment of an employee (and, therefore, the relationship between the employer and the employee), but which breached procedural requirements in the contract of employment, could nevertheless bring about a termination of the contract. This is clear from a number of cases, including *R v East Berkshire Health Authority ex parte Walsh*.[1] The only *caveat* to express here is that if the employee were also an office-holder, then it might well be that the High Court would be willing to accept that the principles of public law governed the termination of the office. If the office were closely related to, or even indistinguishable from, the employment relationship, then the employee would have the protection of public law in relation to the termination of the relationship.

10.13 However, there is a third possibility – that a procedural requirement in the contract of employment of an employee of an HEI may take effect as a right under the constitution of the body conducting that institution which, despite not being subject to public law, is capable of having the effect of a public law right. That possibility arises from several cases, including *Jenkin v Pharmaceutical Society of Great Britain*[2] and *Dickson v Pharmaceutical Society of Great Britain*.[3] The effect of those cases is that a member of a corporation may properly seek an injunction to prevent a breach of the corporation's constitution (in the cases themselves, the corporations were chartered, and the constitution was the charter, but the principle is clear). That said, it may be that that line of cases would not be applied to the employer–employee relationship, and the better view may be that it should not be so applied.

ACADEMIC FREEDOM

10.14 One of the purposes of ss 202–207 of the ERA 1988 was to remove from the jurisdiction of the Visitor most disputes between lecturers (and others whose employment was subject to that jurisdiction at the time of the passing of that Act) and the HEIs by which they were employed. The results are stated in paras **10.5** *et seq*. Another purpose of those sections was to regulate certain aspects of the employment of lecturers in HEIs. Section 202 established a body of persons, known as the University Commissioners (the Commissioners). In exercising their functions under ss 203–207 of the ERA 1988, the Commissioners were under a duty to have regard to the following needs (and it will be helpful to bear these in mind if any question of the proper meaning of any document produced by, or resulting from, the involvement of the Commissioners, arises):[4]

---

1   [1984] ICR 743.
2   [1921] 1 Ch 392.
3   [1970] AC 403.
4   ERA 1988, s 202(2).

'(a)   to ensure that academic staff have freedom within the law to question and test
       received wisdom, and to put forward new ideas and controversial or unpopular
       opinions, without placing themselves in jeopardy of losing their jobs or
       privileges they may have at their institutions;

(b)   to enable qualifying institutions to provide education, promote learning and
       engage in research efficiently and economically; and

(c)   to apply the principles of justice and fairness.'

10.15   It is the above guidance to the Commissioners which provides the only
formal protection for academic freedom within UK HE: this is in contrast to
many other countries, and notably the USA, where such protection is written
into the Constitution. As noted in the Editors' Introduction, academic freedom
is not only about freedom to teach and to research, but is also about freedom to
publish, and in this latter context there is some overlap with the issue of
intellectual property rights as discussed in Chapter 12. As Kennedy (1997)
notes, academic freedom may mean rights, but it also means obligations, and it
is not a licence simply to resist any aspects of working in an HEI which the
individual academic may find irritating. Similarly, 'within the law' clearly
means that it is not a licence to, say, download pornography in the name of
research or to teach in a racially discriminating way when both may be criminal
offences.

10.16   Saunders (1999) considers whether the HRA 1998 impacts on
academic freedom as it incorporates the European Convention on Human
Rights, and especially whether Art 10 of the Convention (freedom of
expression) gives new protections for researchers in publishing their results,
while perhaps Art 8 (right to private and family life) imposes restrictions
(along with the DPA 1998 – see Chapter 13) in their seeking out information
and processing it. Saunders notes that there is 'a complex mass of law',
including (in some European countries) formal legislative protection for
academic freedom, and hence he simply warns of the need to be conscious of
the HRA 1988 and the Convention rather than trying to provide a definitive
guide as to their potential impact.

POWERS AND DUTIES OF THE COMMISSIONERS: TENURE, REDUNDANCY, GOOD CAUSE

10.17   Sections 203 and 204 of the ERA 1988 contained the duties and powers
of the Commissioners respectively. The Commissioners were to have these
duties and powers initially for a period of only 3 years, subject to curtailment or
extension by an order made by the Secretary of State. That period was, in fact,
extended so as to end on 31 March 1996.[1] The effect of ss 203 and 204 will now
be felt in HEIs' governing instruments which were altered as a result of them.
For the purposes of exposition it is simplest, in order to explain what the
current position should be, to set out or describe the relevant parts of those

1   See the Education (University Commissioners) Order 1995, SI 1995/604.

sections. It will also be helpful to bear in mind those sections when considering whether to make an application to the Privy Council to amend any governing instrument which concerns the matters dealt with by those sections.

10.18 Section 203(1) required the Commissioners to exercise their powers with a view to securing that the statutes of each qualifying institution (defined in s 202(3)) included:

'(a) provision enabling an appropriate body, or any delegate of such a body, to dismiss any member of the academic staff by reason of redundancy;

(b) provision enabling an appropriate officer, or any delegate of such an officer, acting in accordance with procedures determined by the Commissioners, to dismiss any member of the academic staff for good cause;

(c) provision establishing disciplinary procedures determined by the Commissioners for dealing with any complaints made against any member of the academic staff relating to his appointment or employment;

(d) provision establishing procedures determined by the Commissioners for hearing and determining appeals by any members of the academic staff who are dismissed or under notice of dismissal (whether or not in pursuance of such provision as is mentioned in paragraph (a) or (b) above) or who are otherwise disciplined; and

(e) provision establishing procedures determined by the Commissioners for affording to any member of the academic staff opportunities for seeking redress for any grievances relating to his appointment or employment.'

10.19 Terms in s 203 are defined as follows:

– the word 'statutes' for the purposes of ss 204–206 includes 'any regulations, ordinances or other instruments which, in the opinion of the commissioners, serve as statutes for the purposes of [the] institution [in question] and are designated as such by the Commissioners': s 203(8);

– the word 'appropriate' in s 203 means in relation to a body or officer of a qualifying institution 'appearing to the Commissioners to be appropriate having regard to the nature and circumstances of the institution': s 203(7);

– dismissal includes removal from office, and in relation to a contract of employment is to be construed in accordance with Part X of the Employment Rights Act 1996 (ERA 1996): ERA 1988, s 203(7) (as amended);

– 'academic staff' for this purpose includes 'persons whose terms of appointment or contracts of employment are, in the opinion of the Commissioners, so similar to those of academic staff as to justify their being treated as academic staff for the purposes of [s 203]': s 203(4);

– the definition of 'redundancy' for this purpose is contained in s 203(5) of the ERA 1988, and is to the same effect as that contained in the ERA 1996;

– 'good cause' for the purposes of s 203 is defined in s 203(6) to mean in relation to a member of the academic staff of a qualifying institution: 'a reason which is related to his conduct or to his capability or qualifications for performing work of the kind which he was appointed or employed to do'; and

– capability and qualifications are defined by the same subsection to mean respectively 'capability assessed by reference to skill, aptitude, health or any other physical or mental quality' of the member of staff in question, and 'any degree, diploma or other academic, technical or professional qualification relevant to the office or position held' by the member of staff in question. This now has to be read as subject to the terms of the DDA 1995 (see Chapter 22).

10.20   The effect of s 203(2) is that no member of the academic staff of a qualifying institution may be dismissed by reason of any provision in the statutes made in order to give effect to the duties imposed upon the Commissioners by s 203(1)(a) or (b) 'unless the reason for his dismissal may in the circumstances (including the size and administrative resources of the institution) reasonably be treated as a sufficient reason for dismissing him'. This effect is achieved by the provision in s 203(2) that nothing included in the statutes of a relevant institution as a result of s 204 may provide otherwise. This wording is to the same effect as that contained in s 98(4)(a) of the ERA 1996 regarding unfair dismissal, and is likely to be construed by reference to at least some of the case-law relating to that section. This is subject to the qualification that there is no reference in s 203(2) to 'equity and the substantial merits of the case', as there is in s 98(4)(b) of the ERA 1996, as a result of which, it could be argued that the case-law regarding s 98(4) cannot apply. However, the better view appears to be that such case-law must provide at least some sort of guide. In any event, s 203(2) of the ERA 1988 gives a person who is not entitled to the protection of Part X of the ERA 1996 (conferring the right not to be unfairly dismissed on employees who have more than one year's continuous employment, and, in certain circumstances, on employees who do not have such continuous employment) – as well as one who is entitled to such protection – a right akin to that not to be unfairly dismissed for redundancy or 'good cause'.

10.21   The effect of a breach of that right is not easy to ascertain, for the reasons discussed above concerning the effect of a breach of a procedural provision governing the termination of employment (which will depend on whether it is regarded as governed by private law or by public law, or as enforceable by analogy with *Dickson v Pharmaceutical Society of Great Britain*[1]). If the relationship between the employee and the HEI in question is one which is properly to be regarded as contractual only, then a failure to comply with the right might give rise only to compensation. That compensation could, however, be significant, since a court could conclude that the employee would not have been dismissed for an indeterminate period, since there was not 'good cause' or redundancy in the circumstances. In that case, what the employee would have lost would be the income he would have received during the period of continued employment with the HEI in question, amounting, perhaps, to several years' salary. However, in deciding what damages should be awarded, the court would have to decide what the employee

---

1   [1970] 1 AC 403.

should have earned as a result of making reasonable efforts to mitigate his loss, and then deduct that amount from the damages to be awarded.

10.22 It should now be the case that no instrument may be made which modifies any provision of the sort referred to in s 203(1) in the statutes of a qualifying institution, unless it has been approved by the Privy Council. This is because s 203(3) states that, where any provision in the statutes of a relevant institution would have been capable of being modified without the approval of either the Privy Council or Her Majesty in Council, or without being laid before both Houses of Parliament, the Commissioners must exercise their functions in such a way that any instrument modifying the provision could have effect only if it had been approved by the Privy Council.

10.23 In order to give effect to their duties under s 203, the Commissioners were given power to 'make such modifications of the statutes of any qualifying institution as they consider[ed] necessary or expedient': s 204(1). The Commissioners were empowered also to make incidental, supplementary and transitional provisions: s 204(8). However, modifications made for the purpose of ensuring that the statutes comply with s 203(1)(a) (which concerns dismissal for redundancy) cannot apply to a person unless either: (i) his or her appointment is (or was) made, or his or her contract of employment is (or was) entered into, on or after 20 November 1987; or (ii) he or she is (or was) promoted on or after that date.[1] Section 204(3)–(6) makes extensive provision for determining whether a person was so promoted. Furthermore, modifications made for the purpose of securing that the statutes comply with s 203(1)(b) (concerning dismissal for good cause) do not apply 'in relation to anything done or omitted to be done before the date on which the instrument making the modifications' was approved by Her Majesty in Council.[2]

The impact of *University of Nottingham v Fishel*

10.24 The case of *University of Nottingham v Fishel*[3] concerned a lecturer (in Obstetrics and Gynaecology) who was a clinical embryologist, and an expert in relation to in vitro fertilisation (IVF). The case elucidated a number of matters concerning the position of employees of HEIs. The defendant, Dr Fishel, was originally a part-time lecturer, working at a hospital which funded his University post and paid him a further salary. He then became a full-time employee of the University. While he had been a part-time employee of the University, he had worked at private clinics for remuneration. These clinics were often situated abroad. Dr Fishel continued to do paid work for private clinics after he started to work for the University as a full-time employee. The University imposed clear requirements on employees in relation to carrying out work other than for the University during normal working hours. These

---

1   ERA 1988, s 204(2).
2   Ibid, s 204(7) and (9).
3   [2000] ICR 1462.

requirements included that employees obtained the permission of the University to do such work. Dr Fishel knew about these requirements, but did not comply with them. Dr Fishel also entered into agreements with private clinics for the provision of IVF services, and then supplied those services by paying staff in the University unit in which he worked to do work of the same sort as that which he himself did when working privately. In doing so, he made a profit. The other members of the University's staff carried out the services during their normal working hours. They, too, did not seek the permission of the University to do so.

10.25   The University eventually found out about the full extent of Dr Fishel's private income-generating activities, when he left its employment to set up a new clinic in conjunction with a commercial organisation. The University then sued Dr Fishel for breach of contract and breach of fiduciary duty. If Dr Fishel were a fiduciary, he would be obliged to pay over to the University any profits which he had made as a result of a breach of his duties as a fiduciary, ie he had a duty to act in the best interests of the University at the expense of his own interests. If, however, he had merely committed a breach of contract, then he would be obliged to compensate the University for the breach of contract only if the University had suffered any loss as a result of that breach. Among other things, Dr Fishel said in court that he believed that his line manager knew how much work he was doing for private clinics, and did not object. Dr Fishel therefore argued (on a number of bases) that the University could not now object to what had occurred.

10.26   Elias J, in a judgment of wide application, decided that Dr Fishel was not in a fiduciary position merely because of his employment. Furthermore, he decided, although Dr Fishel was in breach of his contract of employment when he worked for private clinics during his normal working hours, the University could recover no damages in respect of that work since, in the circumstances, the University had suffered no loss as a result of Dr Fishel doing such work. This was because the University would not have done the work itself if Dr Fishel had not done it, and because Elias J came to the conclusion that if he had not been paid for the work, Dr Fishel would not have done it. (Presumably, Elias J also thought that the University was unable to show that it had lost anything financially by reason of Dr Fishel's not devoting to the purposes of the University the whole of his working hours as an employee of the University.) However, Elias J decided that Dr Fishel became a fiduciary when he entered into contracts for the provision of work by other members of staff of the University, from which he himself benefited. He was therefore liable to account to the University for the profits which he made from those contracts. The rulings in the case are likely to be of assistance in connection with situations where employees are carrying out work for third parties which may be thought to be inconsistent with the employees' duties to the HEIs which employ them.

Chapter 11

TERMINATION OF EMPLOYMENT AND THE MODEL STATUTE: AND NOTABLY THE POSITION OF FIXED-TERM STAFF

Christopher Mordue (Pinsent Curtis Biddle)

EDITORS' INTRODUCTION

§11.1   This chapter complements the previous chapter. It is of crucial relevance to chartered HEIs operating within the context of the Model Statute, but it also provides a neat summary of employment law in relation to unfair dismissal which will be of interest to any HE manager and it alerts the managers of *all* HEIs to the impact of new legislation concerning fixed-term contracts.

INTRODUCTION

11.1   This chapter considers the often complex relationship between the provisions of the Model Statute in the chartered universities and Oxbridge colleges and the general legal consequences of termination of employment, both at common law and in respect of the law of unfair dismissal. It links to, expands on, and overlaps with Chapter 10. The contractual nature of the Model Statute is considered, in particular how it serves to control and restrict the university employer's ability to dismiss. The impact of the Model Statute on the traditional measure of damages for wrongful dismissal is also considered. In relation to unfair dismissal, the termination procedures contained in the Model Statute are considered against the standards of reasonableness by which employment tribunals assess the fairness of dismissals. Guidance is given on how the procedural requirements of the Model Statute should be augmented to minimise the risks of unfair dismissal liability. Finally, given the prevalence of fixed-term contracts within the HE sector, and the impact of recent changes to the unfair dismissal regime, particular issues arising on the termination of fixed-term contracts, including the application of the law on collective redundancy consultation, are considered.

THE CONTRACTUAL IMPORTANCE OF THE MODEL STATUTE

11.2   At common law, the right of the employer to terminate the contract of employment is governed by the contract itself. Typically, the contract will expressly provide for termination by employer or employee, for any reason, on the giving of a specified period of notice. In the case of fixed-term contracts, a specific expiry date will be contained in the contract, although it is common for there to be a contractual right to terminate the contract on notice during the course of the prescribed term.

11.3   The Model Statute is incorporated, usually expressly, within the contracts of employment of members of academic staff. The immediate effect of this is that, where the dismissal is by reason of 'redundancy' or 'good cause' as defined within the Model Statute, the procedural steps laid down within the Model Statute acquire contractual force. They must be complied with if the contract is to be terminated lawfully. However, the Model Statute has a more fundamental contractual significance than merely detailing the mechanics of termination. To the extent that it limits the employer's right of termination, it also operates to define and restrict the circumstances in which the contract can be lawfully terminated at all.

Overview of scheme of Model Statute

11.4   The implementation of the 'Model Statute' is not of course absolutely identical across all chartered universities. In some cases, the Model Statute procedures are amplified in the statutes or ordinances and regulations of a particular institution, particularly through the inclusion of specific time-limits for the procedural steps they prescribe. Further, there is no common definition of 'academic staff'. Nevertheless, the essential scheme of the Model Statute is uniform and can be summarised as follows:

–   it applies to 'academic staff' as defined by the university's council;
–   it contains provisions relating to the dismissal or removal of office of academic staff on the grounds of redundancy and good cause;
–   it confers the power to dismiss for these reasons to specified bodies or officers;
–   it sets out the procedural steps which must be followed for each ground for dismissal;
–   it provides that the decision to dismiss is subject to a requirement of reasonableness;
–   the provisions regarding dismissal for redundancy and good cause cannot be overridden by any provision of the contract of employment; and
–   it sets out certain overriding principles of interpretation.

11.5   Before considering the operation of the Model Statute in detail, it is appropriate briefly to consider the overriding principles of construction just referred to. These are as follows:

–   to ensure that academic staff have freedom within the law to question and test received wisdom, and to put forward new ideas and controversial or unpopular opinions, without placing themselves in jeopardy of losing their jobs and privileges ('academic freedom');
–   to enable the university to provide education, promote learning and engage in research sufficiently and economically; and
–   to apply the principles of justice and fairness.

11.6   Although these are described as 'guiding principles', their precise relevance to the Model Statute provisions is not entirely clear. First, it should be noted that these are principles of construction. While the Model Statute must be interpreted consistently with these provisions, the 'guiding principles' cannot actually override an express provision of the Model Statute. The concept of academic freedom is most relevant to the issue of dismissal for 'good cause', where the definition of 'good cause' must be read consistently with 'academic freedom' such that the exercise of academic freedom should not lead to disciplinary action. However, 'academic freedom' should not, it is submitted, be read as limiting the scope of the university to reorganise or implement redundancies. In any event, such an interpretation would contradict the second guiding principle, that of enabling the institution to 'provide education, promote learning and engage in research efficiently and economically'. The final 'guiding principle' – the requirement for justice and fairness – is clearly of more general application. In any event, the institution will need to take account of potential unfair dismissal liabilities, and this should also lead it to be conscious of the requirement for fairness during the application of any dismissal or disciplinary procedure.

When does the Model Statute apply? – (1) 'academic staff' and 'dismissal'

11.7   The first factor which governs the application of the Model Statute is the definition of 'academic staff'. While the term 'academic staff' is used in this chapter to refer to those covered by the provisions of the Model Statute, there is no universal definition within chartered universities of 'academic staff'. Indeed, in some universities, the Model Statute applies to 'academic and academic related staff'. The statutes of the particular chartered university in question must, therefore, be considered to determine whether they apply to the dismissal of a particular employee.

11.8   It should also be noted that the redundancy provisions of the Model Statute do not apply to academic staff whose contract of employment was entered into before 20 November 1987, unless they have been promoted on or after that date. In respect of such contracts, termination will be governed exclusively by the contract itself and the existence of an express or implied notice period therein. It is also possible that the provisions of pre-Education Reform Act statutes of the university concerned could also survive, through incorporation into the contract of employment. However, these statutes, with the notable exceptions of Oxford and Cambridge Universities, did not in any event restrain the contractual power to dismiss – see, for example, *R v Lord President of the Privy Council ex parte Page*.[1]

11.9   The second issue governing the scope of the Model Statute is the question of whether the member of academic staff concerned is being, or has been, removed from office or dismissed. It is vital to appreciate the width of the term 'dismissal'. This is not immediately apparent from the Model Statute itself, which simply provides that the term 'dismissal' is to be construed in accordance with s 55 of the Employment Protection (Consolidation) Act 1978 (EPCA 1978), which defined dismissal for the purposes of an entitlement to claim unfair dismissal and an entitlement to a statutory redundancy payment. The EPCA 1978 has now been replaced by the Employment Rights Act 1996 (ERA 1996), the corresponding provisions being s 95 of the ERA 1996.

11.10   Under the ERA 1996, and the EPCA 1978 (as was), 'dismissal' means:

–   an actual termination of the employment contract by the employer, whether on notice or otherwise;
–   the expiry of a fixed-term contract without renewal of the term under the same contract; and
–   a constructive dismissal, ie where the contract is terminated by the employee in response to a fundamental breach of contract by the employer.

11.11   For practical purposes, this last part of the definition can be ignored. It is difficult to see how a termination by the employee could ever fall within the provisions of the Model Statute, which control termination *by the employer*.

11.12   In the case of actual termination by the employer, it is vital to appreciate that the relevant issue is whether the *employment contract* has been terminated by the employer. It is possible for an employee to be 'dismissed', even though the employment relationship continues under a new contract. This is particularly relevant in cases involving redundancy or other re-structuring, where an existing employment contract is terminated and the employee takes up alternative employment.

11.13   As the original contract has been terminated by the employer, there has been a dismissal. Another scenario is where the employer, having failed to obtain a change to terms and conditions of employment by consent, forces through the change by terminating the contract of employment and offering alternative employment on new terms and conditions. Again, because the

---

1   [1993] AC 682, HL.

original contract of employment has been terminated by the employer, the statutory definition of 'dismissal' is satisfied.

11.14 A 'dismissal' will also arise under the Model Statute where the member of academic staff is employed on a fixed-term contract and the term expires without being renewed under the same contract. The potential application of the Model Statute to this type of dismissal is frequently overlooked. The term 'fixed-term contract' is not defined in any employment protection legislation, but case-law under the ERA 1996 and its predecessors identifies a fixed-term contract as one where the actual termination date of the contract is defined at its outset, either by reference to a particular duration for the contract (for example, 2 years) or by reference to expiry on a specified date. Note that it is not the expiry of the contract which triggers a 'dismissal' but rather whether the contract expires *without being renewed on the same terms*.

11.15 The requirement for the term of the contract to have been renewed 'under the same contract' can give rise to difficulty. The issue is the degree of difference between the old contract and the new contract. A mere difference in terms and conditions may not be sufficient to give rise to a dismissal in these cases. However, a fundamental difference in terms and conditions between the old and the new contract would give rise to a dismissal.

11.16 It is important to appreciate that the following types of contract are excluded from the definition of a fixed-term contract:

–   a contract for a defined task or job, when no time period for the completion of the task is specified (*Ryan v Shipboard Maintenance Ltd*[1]);
–   a contract which provides for termination on the occurrence of a specified future event rather than by reference to a fixed date (*Wiltshire County Council v National Association of Teachers in Further and Higher Education and Guy*[2]); or
–   a contract which continues only as long as a particular condition or state of affairs exists: for example, for as long as external funding is available (*Brown v Knowsley Borough Council*[3]).

11.17 In all of these cases, the contract will, as a matter of law, come to an end automatically when the specified event occurs, when the fixed task is completed or when the required state of affairs no longer exists. There is no 'dismissal' on termination of these types of contract, either under the ERA 1996 or the Model Statute. However, the Government is currently introducing legislation to implement the European Framework Directive on Fixed Term Work (Directive 99/70/EC). The Directive adopts a wider definition of 'fixed-term' contract than that currently included in domestic employment law and, consequently, the ERA 1996 provisions – and, it is suggested, those of the Model Statute – would have to take account of this legislative change.

---

1   [1980] IRLR 16.
2   [1978] IRLR 301.
3   [1986] IRLR 102.

11.18 Other situations in which there will be no 'dismissal' include circumstances where the employee resigns (other than in the constructive dismissal circumstances referred to above) or where the contract is terminated by mutual consent. Employment law also gives limited, and often grudging recognition to the contractual principle of frustration. In *Paal Wilson & Co A/S v Partenreederei Hannah Blumenthal*[1] Lord Brandon held that the two essential factors required in order to frustrate a contract were 'some outside or extraneous change or situation, not foreseen or provided for by the parties at the time of contracting which either makes it impossible for the contract to be performed at all, or at least renders its performance something radically different from what the parties contemplate when they entered into it'; and 'that the outside event or extraneous change of situation concerned, and the consequences of either in relation to the performance of the contract, must have occurred without the fault or default of either party to the contract'.

11.19 The typical grounds on which employment contracts are held to be frustrated are long-term ill-health incapacity and imprisonment. However, precisely when these situations may in fact operate to frustrate a contract remains difficult to predict, not least because of the reluctance of the courts and tribunals to recognise the concept under employment law. Some guidance is contained in the cases of *Marshall v Harland and Wolff Ltd*[2] (ill-health) and *FC Sheppard & Co Limited v Jerrom*[3] (imprisonment). Interestingly, while in the latter case the Court of Appeal held that the presence of a termination provision in the contract of employment should inhibit the courts from being too ready to find in favour of frustration, the Employment Appeal Tribunal held in the case of *Cambridgeshire County Council v Hogan*[4] that long-term incapacity had terminated the contract of employment by frustration, notwithstanding the presence within the contract of a procedure for termination on the grounds of ill-health.

Does the Model Statute apply? – (2) the reason for the dismissal

Redundancy
11.20 Under the Model Statute, a dismissal will be by reason of redundancy where:

– the university no longer carries on the activity for the purposes of which the member of the academic staff was appointed or employed by the university, either generally or at the place in which the member concerned worked; or

---

1   [1983] 1 AC 854.
2   [1972] IRLR 90.
3   [1986] IRLR 358.
4   (2001) unreported, EAT.

– the requirements of that activity (ie the activity for the purposes of which the member of academic staff was appointed or employed) for members of academic staff to carry out work of a particular kind have ceased or diminished, either generally or at a particular place of work.

11.21 This definition is very similar (but not identical – see below) to the statutory definition of redundancy under s 139 of the ERA 1996, in relation to unfair dismissal (where redundancy is a potentially fair reason for dismissal) and the entitlement of an employee to a statutory redundancy payment. The definition of redundancy under the ERA 1996 and its predecessors has essentially remained unchanged since its introduction in 1965. However, the proper interpretation of these statutory definitions has proved problematic and a number of competing interpretations have battled it out through the employment tribunals and the appellate courts. Given that the Model Statute essentially borrows its definition of redundancy from employment protection legislation, it is generally accepted that this case-law must also affect the interpretation of the concept of redundancy under the Model Statute.

11.22 Space does not permit a detailed review of the case-law on the interpretation of the redundancy definition contained in the ERA 1996 and its predecessor. However, the issue of when a dismissal arises because the employer's requirements 'for employees to carry out work of a particular kind' has ceased or diminished has proved particularly problematic. For many years, two competing tests dominated the case-law. Under one test, 'work of a particular kind' was judged by reference to the contract of employment of the dismissed employee, so that the dismissal would only be by reason of (this type of) redundancy if the employer's requirements for employees to carry out *work of the kind which the dismissed employee could be contractually required to undertake* had ceased or diminished. The competing test concentrated on the actual work which the dismissed employee was undertaking at the time of their dismissal. Only if the employer's requirements for *that* type of work had diminished or ceased was the redundancy definition met.

11.23 This confusion was ultimately resolved by the House of Lords in the case of *Murray v Foyle Meats Ltd.*[1] In this case, the House of Lords held that to determine whether an employee has been dismissed by reason of redundancy, due to a reduction in the employer's requirements for employees to carry out work of a particular kind, a two stage test applies. The first stage is to consider whether the requirements of the business for employees to carry out *work of a particular kind* has ceased or diminished. The answer to this question is established by looking at the requirements of that business generally, *not* the particular kind of work which the dismissed employee actually performed or could be required to perform under their contract. The second stage is to determine whether the employee has been dismissed and, if so, whether the reason, or principal reason, for that dismissal was the redundancy situation.

---

1   [1999] ICR 827.

While in most cases, the dismissed employee will have been performing the particular kind of work in respect of which the employer's requirements have reduced, this is not absolutely essential.

11.24   The position under the Model Statute is slightly more restrictive than that adopted in *Foyle Meats*. Under the ERA 1996 provisions, redundancy arises if the employer ceases to carry out 'the business for the purposes of which the employee is employed' or if the requirements of *that* business for employees to carry out work of a particular kind have ceased or diminished. The existence of a redundancy situation in both cases involves considering the position in relation to the *business* in which the employee is employed. However, the term ('business') is a wide one and can include the business of associated employers. It is not a concept which has occupied much of the case-law or which has operated to appreciably restrict the interpretation of redundancy. The tendency is to examine the employer's requirements generally.

11.25   Under the Model Statute, however, the term 'business' is replaced with the term 'activity'. Similarly to the ERA 1996 provisions, the 'activity for the purposes of which the member of academic staff is employed' is relevant to both types of redundancy situation under the Model Statute. It is only if the activity has ceased, or if the requirements of that activity for employees to carry out work of a particular kind have ceased or reduced, that redundancy arises. But what does 'activity' mean? The fact that it replaces the word 'business' in the ERA 1996 provisions indicates an interpretation based on the employer's organisational structure rather than the duties of the member of academic staff. But what is the 'activity' for the purposes of which the member of academic staff is employed? Does this relate to their school, faculty, department or, most narrowly, their individual specialism? In short, the word 'activity' is capable of being used to divide up the university's organisation in many more ways than the term 'business' would allow for a commercial employer's operations. It is, however, suggested that the term is to be given its widest interpretation since the identification of the redundancy situation is at the discretion of the employer and the second guiding principle of construction – the efficient and economical promotion of teaching and research – needs to be taken into account. However, even the most generous interpretation of the term 'activity' imposes some restriction on redundancy dismissals. Only if the redundancy affects 'the activity for the purpose of which the academic staff member is employed' can that individual member be dismissed for redundancy as defined in the Model Statute. The focus is therefore on the position in relation to the 'activity for the purposes of which the academic staff member was employed', not only in relation to redundancy cases arising where that activity ceases to be carried on but also those cases where there is a reduced requirement for employees to carry out work of a particular kind. The reduced requirement must relate to *that* activity, which serves to limit the pool from which redundancies can, under the contract, be made.

11.26 It is not, however, always immediately obvious whether there is a reduced requirement for members of academic staff 'to carry out work of a particular kind'. A particular problem arises where the overall number of employees remains the same but there is a change in the allocation of duties among the employees or a requirement for a 'different type' of employee to carry out the task, either in terms of their specific experience or qualifications or in the seniority of the employee carrying out the work. In such cases, if the redundancy definition is satisfied, then the dismissal will fall within the ambit of the Model Statute. If it is not, then the redundancy provisions of the Model Statute will not be triggered, leaving the issue – considered below – of whether the employer can legitimately dismiss at all.

11.27 The following offers some guidance as to when the redundancy definition will be satisfied in these cases.

– *Reallocation of duties*: where the employer redistributes the same amount of work among the same number of employees, it may be difficult to identify whether the requirements of the business for 'work of a particular kind' have ceased or diminished. For example, in *Murphy v Epsom College*,[1] Murphy was one of two plumbers employed by the college. Murphy also carried on some engineering work. He subsequently decided not to perform engineering tasks and was dismissed by the college, who employed an engineer who also undertook plumbing work. Murphy claimed unfair dismissal and the employers gave redundancy as the reason for termination. The college still needed two employees, one plumber and one plumbing/engineer. The requirements of the business for plumbers and plumbers/engineers remained the same and it appeared that there was no redundancy situation. However, the Court of Appeal considered that Murphy's dismissal *was* for redundancy. Prior to the change, the college required a plumber who did some engineering work. After the change, it required an engineeer who could do some plumbing. The Court of Appeal considered that a reorganisation creating a substantial change in the kind of work required by the employer could amount to a redundancy even though the overall requirements for work or employees remained the same. See also *British Broadcasting Corporation v Farnworth*.[2] Farnworth was employed as a radio producer 'mark 1' for a particular programme. The BBC decided that it required a more senior producer to work on this programme and appointed a 'mark 2' producer. Farnworth was dismissed. The Employment Appeal Tribunal upheld an employment tribunal's decision that the dismissal was by reason of redundancy. Farnworth's particular specialism was no longer required. The specialism of the new employee was sufficiently different from Farnworth's to amount to work of a different particular kind. His dismissal was, therefore, by reason of

---

1   [1985] ICR 80, CA.
2   [1998] ICR 1116.

redundancy, even though the overall numbers of employees required by the business remained the same.

–   *Where the same work is carried out under different terms and conditions*: a change in the terms and conditions upon which employees carry out work will not in itself amount to a change in the employer's requirements for work of a particular kind. The terms and conditions are not themselves definitive of the nature of the work being carried out. So, for example, where the employer abolishes a nightshift (but does not reduce the number of employees carrying out the particular work done on the nightshift, offering them positions on a dayshift) there will be no redundancy situation; the mere fact that the work is carried out at night is not sufficient to make it a different kind of work to work carried out during the day. Similarly, the Court of Appeal held in *Johnson v Nottinghamshire Combined Policy Authority; Dutton v Same*[1] that the introduction of a new shift system did not amount to a redundancy situation. A mere change in the hours over which work is carried out, without a change in the number of employees required to do the work, was not a reduction in the employer's requirements for employees to do work of a particular kind. Whether part-time work is a different particular kind of work to full-time work is not an issue which has been authoritatively decided. It is suggested that, if the number of full-time equivalent posts remains the same, there will be no redundancy situation if the employer replaces part-time employees with full-time employees or vice versa.

–   *Same work carried out by a different kind of employee*: as indicated above in respect of *British Broadcasting Corporation v Farnworth*, where the skills and qualifications of the new employee are such that the work they perform is a different kind of work to that performed by the old employee, the redundancy defintion will be relevant. However, it is important to recognise that personal attributes or qualifications are not relevant except insofar as they can be said to change the nature of the work being carried out.

–   *Redeployment*: in some cases, an employee's contract of employment may allow the employer some flexibility in the duties which the employee is required to perform. Therefore, although the employer's requirements for work of the particular kind of which the employee is performing have diminished, the employer may seek to overcome this situation by invoking such a 'job flexibility' clause and assigning the employee to other duties within the ambit of the contract of employment. In these circumstances, although there may well be a redundancy situation, the employer is not seeking to dismiss the employee – there is no question of the contract of employment being terminated simply by reason of the change in job duties. The change is expressly covered by the contract itself, which therefore continues. If the employee refused to perform the alternative duties, the employer may dismiss. In those circumstances, the

---

1   [1974] ICR 170, CA.

dismissal would not be by reason of redundancy – the employer would argue that the reason for the dismissal was the employee's refusal to obey a lawful instruction to carry out the alternative work, rather than the redundancy situation itself.

11.28 Particular problems in applying the redundancy procedure, in particular in relation to unfair dismissal law, are considered at paras **11.67–11.70**.

Dismissal for 'good cause'

11.29 The second reason for dismissal covered by the Model Statute is dismissal for 'good cause'. This is an umbrella term covering a number of different grounds for termination, namely misconduct, performance and medical incapacity. Conduct and performance issues are dealt with under the procedure for discipline dismissal and removal from office. Physical or mental incapacity is dealt with under a separate procedure regarding removal for incapacity on medical grounds.

11.30 Specifically, good cause is defined as 'a reason which is related to conduct or to capability or qualifications for performing work of the kind which the member of academic staff concerned was appointed or employed to do' and is defined further as meaning:

– conviction for an offence deemed by an internal tribunal (appointed under the statute) to be such as to render the person convicted unfit for the execution of the duties of the office or employment of the member of the academic staff; or
– conduct of an immoral, scandalous or disgraceful nature incompatible with the duties of the office or employment; or
– conduct constituting a failure or persistent refusal or neglect or inability to perform the duties or comply with the conditions of office; or
– physical or mental incapacity established under the statutory procedures for removal for incapacity on medical grounds.

11.31 Of these four elements of the good cause definition, the first two relate exclusively to misconduct. The third element could, depending on the facts, relate to issues of misconduct or poor performance. For the purposes of the Model Statute, this distinction is irrelevant. However, in the event of dismissal, and a claim of unfair dismissal by the dismissed member of academic staff, the employer will need to properly characterise the reason for the dismissal as either conduct or performance.

11.32 Note also that the disciplinary procedures envisage that performance or conduct matters are of two types — those falling short of possible good cause for dismissal and those matters which may constitute good cause for dismissal. Those issues falling short of good cause are dealt with through oral or written warning. If there is potentially good cause for dismissal, then separate procedural provisions apply under which a complaint is made against the member of academic staff which may result in the institution of charges to be heard by an internal tribunal appointed under the provisions of the statute. A complaint of misconduct is also envisaged under the statute where, despite a written warning having been given under the disciplinary procedures, there has been no satisfactory improvement in conduct or performance. This reflects the fact that the third element of the good cause definition outlined above covers a continuing state of affairs, rather than a single instance of misconduct or poor performance.

11.33 The fact that the first three parts of the definition are dealt with under the disciplinary provisions of the Model Statute gives rise to a subtle difference between the operation of the Model Statute in terms of dismissal for redundancy and dismissal for these types of 'good cause'. Under the redundancy provisions, it is the existence of a redundancy situation, as defined in the Model Statute, which triggers the application of the procedures for redundancy dismissal. In the case of good cause, the issue arises under the disciplinary procedure with a complaint of misconduct or poor performance which is alleged to constitute good cause for dismissal. The definition of good cause operates not only as a reason for dismissal, but also as a limitation on the university's power to dismiss. An internal Tribunal established under the Statute must determine whether the conduct or performance of the member of academic staff constitutes good cause for dismissal, or otherwise constitutes a serious complaint relating to the member's appointment or employment. The Vice-Chancellor or other appropriate officer can *only* dismiss the member of academic staff concerned where the charges are upheld *and* the Tribunal finds 'good cause' *and* the Tribunal recommends dismissal or removal from office.

11.34 Again, practical considerations in the implementation of the 'good cause' procedure are considered below, in the context of the relationship between the Model Statute and unfair dismissal law, see paras **11.71–11.78**.

The Model Statute and restrictions on ability to dismiss

Are the grounds for dismissal in the statute exhaustive?

11.35 As noted above, the usual position at common law is that the existence of a notice period in the contract of employment entitles either party to terminate the contract simply by giving notice. The Model Statute, however, constrains this power to dismiss in a number of respects. First of all, contractual procedures are imposed for the making of redundancy dismissals and for dismissals on the grounds of physical or mental incapacity. Contractual discipinary procedures must also be followed before the contract can be terminated for 'good cause'. Compliance with these procedures is a necessary precursor to the lawful exercise of the contractual power to dismiss.

11.36 This point is reinforced by the specific provision in the Model Statute that 'nothing in any appointment made, or contract entered into, shall be construed as overriding or excluding any provision made by the Statute, concerning the dismissal of a member of the academic staff by reason of redundancy or for good cause'. To this extent, any general contractual right to terminate on notice is constrained by the Model Statute and the specified procedures for redundancy and good cause dismissals must be satisfied before the contract can be terminated.

11.37 Equally, the fact that a contract is for a fixed term cannot exclude the operation of the Model Statute in respect of a termination which arises from the expiry of that fixed term without its renewal under the same contract. Consequently, the expiry date of the fixed-term contract must be read as being subject to compliance with the Model Statute at least where the dismissal is by reason of redundancy or good cause.

11.38 This restriction on the right of the university to terminate the contract of employment of a member of academic staff is often argued to prohibit dismissals on grounds other than those set out in the Model Statute, ie redundancy, good cause and capability. The argument is that a termination on some other ground – what might, in the unfair dismissal context be referred to as 'some other substantial reason' for dismissal – is not contemplated by the Statute at all. *It is submitted that this argument is incorrect.* The restriction mentioned above, properly considered, overrides any contractual provision *to the extent that* the dismissal is by reason of redundancy or good cause. It does not provide that the terms of the contract are overridden any further. Consequently, the Statute should not be taken as being an exhaustive list of the grounds on which the contract can be terminated. The fact that the Model Statute does not contain provisions relating to termination other than by good cause or redundancy does not prohibit such dismissals, but can be taken to indicate that these lie outside the scope of the Model Statute. This issue is particularly important where dismissal arises from a reorganisation which does not meet the definition of redundancy in the Model Statute. In such cases, it is submitted that the ability to terminate the contract is governed purely by the contract itself, and that the Model Statute is of no relevance. This may also be supported by the second 'guiding principle' for construing the Model Statute, namely 'to enable the university to provide education, promote learning and engage in research efficiently and economically'. There is, however, no authority on this point and it remains an issue of fundamental importance to the measure of damages for wrongful dismissal (see below).

Good cause and medical incapacity
11.39 The Model Statute procedure for dismissal by reason of medical incapacity envisages two scenarios. First, where the member of staff does not dispute removal on medical grounds. In these circumstances, although the Model Statute is silent on the point, it is assumed that termination will take place either by resignation, mutual consent or early retirement on medical grounds. In each case, the termination is unlikely to constitute a dismissal.

11.40 Where the member of staff contests the university's view that he or she should be removed on medical grounds, the issue is determined by a Board, established in accordance with the statute, which must include a medically qualified chairman. It should be noted that the issue for the Board is whether the member shall be required to 'retire' on medical grounds. This wording suggests not only that the staff member is unable to carry out the particular duties of employment, but also he is incapable (at least in the medium term) of working for the university at all. This, therefore, sets a relatively high contractual threshold for the termination of the particular employment contract.

11.41 One practical issue which may arise is the entitlement of the member of staff to take early retirement under the relevant pension scheme. This entitlement is obviously not within the discretion of the Board established under the statutes, resting entirely with the trustees of the pension fund. The two issues should not be confused, although it may be prudent to explore the possibility of early retirement under the pension scheme as part of the 'good cause' procedure (particularly as an academic staff member may be reluctant to agree to termination on medical grounds unless he knows that a pension will be received).

Requirement for reasonableness

11.42 The Model Statute does impose significant restrictions on the contractual ability to dismiss for redundancy or good cause. First, the power to dismiss for these reasons is expressly conferred only on the appropriate person or appropriate body authorised to effect that dismissal under the statute. More dramatically, any decision by these persons or bodies to dismiss *must be reasonable*: the Model Statutes provide that no provision in the statute relating to termination for redundancy or in relation to discipline, dismissal and removal from office 'shall enable the body or persons having the duty to reach a decision under the relevant Part to dismiss any member of the academic staff unless the reason for his dismissal may in the circumstances (including the size and administrative resources of the university) reasonably be treated as a sufficient reason for dismissing him'.

11.43 This requirement introduces into the employment contract considerations very similar to those which apply in unfair dismissal law. If the decision to dismiss is not reasonable (in this contractual sense), the dismissal will be unlawful. Even if all of the procedural requirements under the statute had been complied with, the employer would have fallen at the final contractual hurdle, namely whether or not the decision to dismiss was reasonable. Further, if the contractual standard of reasonableness is equivalent to the statutory concept of unfair dismissal under the ERA 1996, it follows that a finding of unfair dismissal should suggest that the employee had also been wrongfully dismissed.

11.44 To what extent will principles from unfair dismissal case-law be introduced to this contractual requirement for reasonableness? There is, as yet, no reported decision which explains how this provision is to be interpreted. The test would appear to be objective, and it is submitted that the appropriate test would be whether dismissal on the particular grounds and in the particular circumstances lay within the band of reasonable responses of a reasonable employer – in other words, dismissal will be unreasonable if no reasonable employer could have dismissed on those grounds.

11.45 However, if this contractual requirement for reasonableness is equivalent to the unfair dismissal test, it must be recognised that an employment tribunal determining a complaint of unfair dismissal would consider not just whether the decision to dismiss the employee for the identified reason was reasonable, but also whether that decision had been reached after a fair and proper procedure. The case-law on unfair dismissal shows very clearly that fairness is determined as much in relation to the procedure adopted by the employer as to the reasonableness of the decision to dismiss. If this approach is the standard against which reasonableness under the Model Statute must be assessed, then the dismissing body or officer must also ensure that the procedural standards usually required in the unfair dismissal context have been met. It is suggested below that the procedural requirements of the Model Statute itself will not necessarily be sufficient to meet the standards of reasonableness required under unfair dismissal legislation, particularly in the case of the redundancy provision.

11.46 While a comprehensive examination of the procedures recommended in respect of each reason for dismissal is outside the scope of this chapter, the essential principles are usefully summarised by Lord Bridge in *Polkey v AE Dayton Services Ltd*:[1]

> 'An employer having prima facie grounds to dismiss for one of [the potentially fair reasons] will in the great majority of cases not act reasonably in treating the reason as a sufficient reason for dismissal unless and until and he has taken the steps, conveniently classified by most of the authorities as "procedural", which are necessary in the circumstances of the case to justify that course of action. Thus, in the case of incapacity the employer will not normally act reasonably unless he gives the employee fair warning and an opportunity to mend his ways in showing that he can do the job; in cases of misconduct, the employer will not normally act reasonably unless he investigates a complaint of misconduct fully and fairly and hears whatever the employee wishes to say in his defence or in explanation or mitigation; in the case of redundancy, the employer will not normally act reasonably unless he warns and consults any employees affected or their representatives, adopts a fair basis on which to select for redundancy and takes such steps as may be reasonable to avoid or minimise redundancies by redeployment within his own organisation.'

11.47 It cannot be stressed enough that, although the requirements referred to above are expressed to be 'procedural', they do in fact go to the heart of the substantive issue of fairness. For this reason, in the unfair dismissal context, the employer can only rarely argue successfully that a failure to comply with these procedural standards does not make the dismissal unfair. The fact that additional procedural steps may not have affected the outcome is an argument relevant to compensation for unfair dismissal, but not usually to the reasonableness of the employer's actions. Again, *Polkey* is the lead authority:

---

1   [1987] IRLR 503.

'If an employer has failed to take the appropriate procedural steps in any particular case, one question the tribunal is not permitted to ask in applying the test of reasonableness imposed by section 98(4) is the hypothetical question of whether it would have made any difference to the outcome if the appropriate procedural steps had been taken. On the true construction of section 98(4) this question is simply irrelevant. It is quite a different matter if the tribunal is able to conclude that the employer himself, at the time of dismissal, acted reasonably in taking the view that in the exceptional circumstances of the particular case the procedural steps normally appropriate would have been futile, could not have altered the decision to dismiss and therefore could be dispensed with. In such a case a test of reasonableness under section 98(4) may be satisfied.'

A similar approach would, therefore, be taken to the concept of reasonableness under the Model Statute.

The Model Statute and damages for wrongful dismissal

11.48 At common law, there are two grounds on which a dismissed employee may claim financial compensation in respect of the dismissal, both of which are based on a breach of contract by the employer. First, an employee may claim damages for wrongful dismissal if the employer has breached the contractual requirements for terminating the contract. For example, in the case of a contract terminable on notice, an employee will be wrongfully dismissed if the requisite period of notice is not given, or if the employee has been summarily dismissed where the employee's conduct was not such as to entitle the employer to dismiss without notice. The second cause of action is constructive dismissal. In this scenario, it is the employee who brings the contract to an end, in response to a fundamental breach of contract on the part of the employer.

11.49 In both cases, the employee's claim will be for financial compensation for breach of contract. When calculating damages for breach of contract, the basic rule is that the court must consider what would have happened had the contract been performed in accordance with its terms: *Lavarack v Woods of Colchester Ltd.*[1] The employee should be placed in the same position as if the contract had been properly performed by the employer, while assuming that the employer would have operated the contract in the manner most favourable to him. In most cases, the traditional mesure of damages is confined to the net salary and benefits which the employee would have received during the period of contractual notice. The premise is that the employer had the contractual right to terminate on notice and that damages should be assessed on the basis that the employer would have terminated the contract on notice at the earliest date. In the case of a fixed-term contract not terminable on notice, the same principle would give an employee dismissed before the expiry of the fixed term a claim for net salary and benefits up to the expiry of the fixed term, that being the earliest date on which the contract could have been lawfully terminated.

---

1   [1967] 1 QB 278, CA.

11.50 In accordance with normal contractual principles, the wrongfully or constructively dismissed employee has an obligation to mitigate their loss. The employee must take reasonable steps to obtain alternative employment. Any earnings received in the alternative employment must be offset against any entitlement to damages from the employer.

11.51 However, the contractual nature of the Model Statute impacts on this traditional measure of damages in a number of ways.

11.52 First, the Model Statute imposes certain contractual termination procedures on the employer. If these procedures are not strictly complied with, the dismissal will be wrongful. Alternatively, a sufficiently serious breach of procedure on the part of the employer would entitle the employee to resign and claim constructive dismissal. In both cases, the period over which damages are awarded may be appreciably longer than the contractual notice period. The premise here is that before the employer could legitimately have terminated, either with or without notice, it would have to have complied in full with the relevant procedure. The court or tribunal would, therefore, assess damages by considering the earliest date on which these procedural requirements would have been satisfied and the employer could lawfully have dismissed. If this date is later than the actual date of termination, then the effect of the employer's breach has been to deprive the employee of an additional period of employment and the employee will, subjct to mitigation, be entitled to recover as damages the net salary and benefits which he or she would have earned during that additional period.

11.53 The measure of damages may be extended further if the employee can show that the additional period of employment denied to him or her by a failure to properly implement the procedure has deprived him or her of some additional benefit. For example, in *Raspin v United News Shops*,[1] the employer failed to comply with a contractually binding disciplinary procedure. At the date of termination, the employee had less than 2 years' service, which was then the qualifying period for the right to claim unfair dismissal. The employment tribunal concluded that had the contractual procedure been implemented properly, the date of termination would have been delayed by 3 weeks. The employee was, therefore, entitled to recover damages for lost earnings and benefits during this period. But additionally, if the date of termination had been delayed by 3 weeks, the employee would have had sufficient service to complain of unfair dismissal. The employer's breach of contract had, therefore, deprived her of the statutory right to bring this complaint and the Employment Appeal Tribunal held that the employee was entitled to recover common law damages reflecting her lost opportunity to complain of unfair dismissal.

11.54 While *Raspin* concerned a position where a premature and unlawful termination deprived the employee of a statutory right, the same principle would apply to contractual rights and benefits. See, for example, *Silvey v*

---

1   [1999] IRLR 9, EAT.

Pendragon plc,[1] where Mr Silvey was dismissed without proper contractual notice. The employer wrongfully dismissed by failing to give notice but made a full payment in lieu of notice which, prima facie, should have met the employee's claim for damages. However, had Mr Silvey remained in the company's employment for the full duration of the notice period, he would have received enhanced pension benefits. The wrongful dismissal, therefore, deprived him of this benefit. The Court of Appeal held that he could claim this amount from the employer in damages. It should also be noted that the enhanced pension payment was not, on the facts of this case, a payment which would have been due from the employer in any event – nevertheless the employee could recover it as contractual damages.

11.55 However, as observed above, the Model Statute not only lays down a contractual procedure which must be followed for a lawful termination on particular grounds, it also appears to restrict the contractual right of the employer to terminate at all. In particular, dismissals for good cause or redundancy will only be lawful if the contractual requirement of reasonableness is met (see above). If the decision to dismiss was found to be unreasonable, the employee would, as before, be entitled to recover damages to put him or her in the position as if the contract had been properly performed. But how would this principle be applied? Had the contract been lawfully performed the employee would not have been dismissed at all. Can an employee, therefore, argue that damages should be assessed on the basis that their employment would have continued until, for example, retirement?

11.56 There are two possible approaches. First, the employee should be entitled to recover damages based on the premise that his employment would have continued until some later date. But what later date would be chosen? While, prima facie, the employee might be able to argue that the employment would have continued until retirement, a court or tribunal assessing damages would also have to take into account the possibility of the employee leaving his employment (for example, to take up employment elsewhere, or as a result of a lawful dismissal at a later stage). Damages would also be reduced to reflect actual mitigation of loss by the employee obtaining alternative employment or else the probability of such alternative employment being obtained. Nevertheless, it can be seen that, on this approach, the assessment of damages is both rather speculative and potentially very expensive for the employer. For a comparable approach see *Barber v Manchester Regional Hospital Board*.[2] The plaintiff, a hospital consultant, was dismissed. His contract incorporated a procedure by which a consultant who considered his appointment was being unfairly terminated could submit his case to the Minister of Health, who was required to refer the case to a professional committee and, in the light of its advice, confirm the termination or direct reinstatement or some alternative course of action. The plaintiff was held to have been wrongfully dismissed. On

---

1   [2001] IRLR 685, CA.
2   [1958] 1 WLR 181, QBD.

the question of damages, the High Court ruled that the contract was subject to 3 months' notice only if the Minister of Health had taken the view that the contract was being fairly terminated. The judge considered that the Minister would have found the termination unfair. The judge considered that the plaintiff's employment would have continued and, therefore, awarded damages on this basis, holding a 5-year period of loss to be a fair assessment of damages. This is not a binding authority and it should be noted that the operative clause in this case applied to every dismissal, which, it is argued, the Model Statute does not. The fact that the case predates the introduction of the statutory right not to be unfairly dismissed may also be relevant.

11.57 The alternative approach would be based on the argument that the Model Statute is not exhaustive of the possible grounds for termination. While dismissal for good cause or redundancy is governed by the Statute, including the requirement that any decision to dismiss should be reasonable, the right to terminate on notice on grounds other than redundancy or good cause would remain. Damages would then be assessed on the basis that the employer would have performed the contract in a manner most favourable to it. The assessment of damages would, therefore, proceed on the basis that the employer could have exercised this more general power, existing outside the scope of the Model Statute, to terminate the employment contract at the earliest date. On this approach, the employer would argue that damages should be limited to the notice period because the employer would have exercised the right to terminate the contract on notice.

11.58 However, a further complication arises in the scenario where the employer is dismissed without the appropriate procedure under the Statutes having been initiated or completed. In such cases, if the employer was found to have acted in breach of contract, the court or tribunal must once again consider what would have happened had the contract been performed. Damages would be awarded for the period that would have been taken up by the proper performance of the contractual procedure. Additionally, the court or tribunal would have to consider whether, at the end of that procedure, the employer would have had sufficient grounds for termination, in order to give full effect to the contractual requirement for the dismissal to be reasonable. This would require the court or tribunal to assess damages by reference to their view of the likely outcome of the relevant procedure. This introduces a further level of speculation on the part of the court or tribunal. Of course, if the conclusion is that dismissal in the circumstances of the case would not have been reasonable, the issue just referred to will arise, ie whether damages should be assessed on the basis of a presumption that the employment would have continued into the future or whether damages should be limited to a notice period.

UNFAIR DISMISSAL AND THE MODEL STATUTE

11.59   The right to claim unfair dismissal is available to all employees provided (save in respect of certain categories of dismissal) that the employee has a minimum of one year's continuous employment with the employer.

11.60   The first issue in an unfair dismissal claim is whether the employee has been dismissed. For these purposes, 'dismissal' is defined in s 95 of the ERA 1996 as an actual dismissal (ie termination by the employer on notice or without notice), the expiry of a fixed-term contract without renewal or a constructive dismissal (ie where the employer has committed a fundamental breach of the employment contract, entitling the employee to resign with or without notice).

11.61   Once it has been established that there has been a dismissal, the next issue is whether that dismissal was fair. The first stage in this assessment is for the employer to show that the reason or principal reason for the dismissal is one of the potentially fair reasons under s 98 of the ERA 1996. These are as follows:

–   a reason relating to the capability or qualifications of the employee for performing work of a kind which he was employed by the employer to do;
–   a reason relating to the conduct of the employee;
–   that the employee was redundant;
–   that the employee could not continue to work in the position which he held without contravention (either on his part or that of his employer) of a duty or restriction imposed by or under an enactment; or
–   in the absence of any of the above reasons, that there was some other substantial reason of a kind such as to justify the dismissal of an employee holding the position which the employee held.

11.62   The onus is on the employer to satisfy the employment tribunal that the employee was dismissed for one of these potentially fair reasons. If the employer cannot overcome this hurdle, the dismissal will be unfair.

11.63   Provided that the employer shows a potentially fair reason for the dismissal, the next issue is whether, in dismissing that employee for that reason, the employer acted reasonably or unreasonably in treating the reason as a sufficient reason for dismissing the employee, in all the circumstanes of the case (including the size and administrative resources of the employer's undertaking) and having regard to equity and the substantial merits of the case.

11.64   In considering the reasonableness of the dismissal, the tribunal would consider not just whether the employer's decision to dismiss the employee for that reason was reasonable, but whether the employer reached that decision after a fair and proper procedure. In short, fairness is determined by reference to the procedure adopted by the employer as well as the reasonableness of the decision to dismiss.

General relationship between the Model Statute and unfair dismissal

11.65 As stated above, many of the concepts of unfair dismissal are incorporated into the Model Statute itself. The definition of dismissal is taken from the unfair dismissal provisions in the ERA 1996, the definition of redundancy is the same in both contexts, and the Model Statute raises a similar (although not identical) approach to whether the decision to dismiss was reasonable.

11.66 The incorporation of these terms into the Model Statute does not directly affect the application of the unfair dismissal legislation, in terms of identifying the potentially fair reasons for dismissal or in answering the substantive question of whether the employer acted reasonably in dismissing that employee for that reason. However, the provisions of the Model Statute may have *indirect* effect in the following ways.

– In considering the overall procedure adopted by the employer, the tribunal would take account of the procedural steps laid down in the Model Statute. Departure from these procedural steps would, in appropriate cases, render the dismissal unfair.
– The Model Statute may be taken as indicating what might amount to a sufficient reason for dismissal of an employee by a university. For example, as is discussed below, the 'conduct' element of the concept of 'good cause for dismissal' is rather narrow in scope. Conduct falling short of 'good cause' would appear not to give a sufficient basis on which a reasonable university employer could dismiss, because the right to terminate under the Model Statute arises only where the good cause definition is satisfied. And while 'some other substantial reason' is clearly a potentially fair reason under the ERA 1996, can its non-inclusion in the Model Statute be taken to indicate that this too would not provide a reasonable basis on which a university employer could dismiss a member of academic staff? This issue is unresolved, but it is submitted above that the Model Statute is not to be taken as being exhaustive of the grounds for dismissal of academic staff.

The Model Statute and the fairness of redundancy dismissal

11.67 Under the Model Statute, the first stage in the redundancy procedure is that the Council decides that it is desirable that there should be a reduction in the academic staff of the university as a whole or of any college, school, department or other similar area of the university by way of redundancy. The Council establishes a redundancy committee, with a prescribed composition, to give effect to its decision by a specified date and to select and recommend the requisite members of the academic staff for dismissal by reason of redundancy and to report their recommendations to the Council. The Council then either approves the selection recommendations made by the redundancy committee or remits the issue for further consideration. Once the Council has approved a selection recommendation, it authorises a university officer to dismiss a member of academic staff selected. The member of academic staff is then notified of the selection for redundancy, informed of the reasons for the selection (including an account of the selection process used by the redundancy committee), and given the opportunity to appeal against notice of termination of the employment.

11.68 These provisions are the primary example of how simple reliance on the provision of the Model Statute, and its procedural provisions, would give rise to unfair dismissal liability. The Model Statute redundancy provisions entirely neglect the general components of a fair redundancy dismissal, suggesting that the individual employee need only become involved in the process at a very late stage, after the decision to make redundancies has been taken, after the selection criteria have been applied and after notice of termination has been given.

11.69 Case-law on unfair dismissal in the redundancy context is diametrically opposed to the approach contained in the Model Statute. These cases address the need for early warning to employees generally that redundancies are required and the fundamental importance of consultation at each stage of the employer's decision-making process. The employer should warn affected employees that they are at risk of redundancy and consult with them and/or their representatives about whether there are any ways in which redundancies can be avoided. It may also be appropriate for the employer to consult with any relevant trade union over the selection criteria to be applied. The selection criteria used by the employer should be reasonable and as objective as possible. Again, it may be appropriate to consult employees prior to the application for selection criteria and in particular to obtain from them any information which should reasonably be taken into account when the selection criteria are to be applied. In any event, once the selection criteria have been applied, employees should be consulted about their assessments in advance of notice of termination being given. This involves providing the employee with a full explanation of how they have been assessed and how each of the selection criteria has been applied to them. The employee should next be given the opportunity to make representations about the scores which they have received. It would then typically be appropriate to seek alternative employment for the employee prior to notice of termination being made.

11.70 It is therefore suggested that, in any situation where it is contemplated that the redundancy provisions of the Model Statute may be triggered, there should be prior consultation with any relevant trade union or with the potentially affected employees directly as to whether or not redundancies are required and whether any alternatives to redundancy exist. This consultation should take place *before* the Council decides that it is necessary to make redundancies. If a redundancy committee is established, consultation with any relevant trade union and with the affected employees should also take place regarding the selection criteria to be applied. Before the redundancy committee reports back to the Council on selection recommendations, each individual employee should have been consulted over his assessment and given an opportunity to make representations about how the selection criteria have been applied to him. Alternative employment should also be considered before notice of termination is given.

Dismissal for good cause – misconduct

11.71 The general standards of fairness for misconduct dismissals are as follows:

- the employer must hold a genuine belief, on reasonable grounds after reasonable investigation, that the employee was guilty of misconduct; or
- the decision to dismiss the employee for that conduct must be within the range of reasonable responses open to the employer.

11.72 In addition, the ACAS Code of Practice on Disciplinary and Grievance Procedures (which is taken into account by employment tribunals in cases of unfair dismissal) indicates that in cases of misconduct, the following procedural safeguards and standards should be applied:

- workers should be informed of the complaints against them and, where possible, all relevant evidence before any hearing;
- workers should be provided with an opportunity to state their case before decisions are reached;
- workers should have the right to be accompanied at any disciplinary hearing;
- except in cases of gross misconduct, no worker should be dismissed for a first breach of discipline;
- disciplinary action should not be taken until the case has been fully investigated;
- workers should be given an explanation for any penalty imposed; and
- workers should be provided with the right of appeal against disciplinary sanctions.

11.73 On the whole, the provisions of the Model Statute meet these procedural requirements. Dismissal follows a hearing of charges of misconduct by an internal disciplinary tribunal. Provision is made for the member of academic staff to be advised of the nature of the complaint against him, both at the stage at which he is invited to comment on the complaint of misconduct or poor performance and again when charges of misconduct and poor performance are brought and presented to the internal disciplinary hearing. Furthermore, an opportunity is provided at the internal disciplinary hearing to meet the charges and put forward any information which he considers relevant to the case against him. The Model Statute also provides that the member of academic staff is entitled to be represented at the disciplinary hearing by a representative of his or her choice, including legal representation.

11.74 Nevertheless, the procedure for dealing with cases where conduct or performance constitutes possible good cause for dismissal is a lengthy and complex one, raising a number of practical problems. In particular, the procedure laid down by the Model Statutes is unwieldy and rather formalistic in nature. It can be time-consuming and resource-intensive to implement. Furthermore, the disciplinary hearing before the internal tribunal takes on an adversarial and quasi-judicial aspect, particularly as a result of the calling of witnesses and their cross-examination, and the entitlement of the academic staff member to be legally represented at the hearing.

11.75 Particular issues which should be considered when operating the procedure are as follows.

– In some cases a university's statutes, ordinances or regulations made thereunder require the various procedural steps to be carried out within relatively tight timescales. For example, they may provide that, once the Vice-Chancellor has received the member of academic staff's comments on a particular complaint of misconduct, he or she has only a matter of days to decide how the matter is to be taken forward, ie informal resolution, dismissal of the complaint, remitting the complaint to be heard under the procedure for conduct falling short of good cause, or by instituting charges of misconduct to be heard by a disciplinary tribunal. These procedural timescales must be complied with, given their contractual status. A degree of advance planning and consideration may be required. For example, under the ordinances of some chartered universities, the identity of the presenting offier and the witnesses who will be called to give evidence in support of the charges has to be given at the same time as the charges are provided to the member of staff.

– The power to suspend a member of academic staff on full pay pending the outcome of any disciplinary proceedings arises at a fairly late stage in the Model Statute procedure. The procedure commences with a complaint being presented which seeks the institution of charges against the member of academic staff. The Vice-Chancellor then has an opportunity to institute such investigations or enquiries, if any, as appear necessary. It is only once the Vice-Chancellor has completed these investigations and decided that the complaint should be dealt with under the good cause procedure – at least until after receipt of the written comments of the member of academic staff concerned – that the power to suspend on full pay arises. In some statutes, regulations or ordinances, the power of the suspension is constrained further, its exercise being limited to circumstances in which for example the 'well-being of staff or students is threatened'. There may also be an obligation to give written reasons for the suspension. The member of staff cannot be suspended at the preliminary stage of any investigation, ie before a complaint of misconduct is presented or before the Vice-Chancellor takes a preliminary view that the matter should be dealt with under the good cause procedure. Note also that the implication of the Model Statute provisions is that the power of suspension does not exist in disciplinary cases which are not considered to give rise to a potential dismissal for good cause.

- Charges of misconduct should be sufficiently detailed to enable the precise nature, and factual background, of the charges to be understood by the member of staff. The charges should cross-refer to relevant documentation or otherwise specify the supporting evidence. It is also particularly important, both for the benefit of the member of academic staff and the tribunal which will hear the charges, to identify why the conduct is said to amount to good cause, emphasising the particular gravity of the offence or the persistence and seriousness of the performance issues.

- The member of staff is not under any obligation to respond to the complaint of misconduct. If the member of staff makes no response then the case proceeds as if he or she had denied the substance or validity of the alleged case in its entirety. Nor is the member of academic staff obliged to provide any written comments once the charges of misconduct have been presented. While university regulations or ordinances made under the Model Statute may provide that the member of academic staff should provide in advance any documentary evidence on which he or she wishes to rely at the internal disciplinary hearing, this does not necessarily mean that the university will have a substantive response or full knowledge of the points which are likely to be raised by the member of academic staff during the hearing itself. This can lead to new matters arising during the hearing. Tribunals are typically given limited power to recall witnesses or the parties and it is advisable to remind the presenting officer and the staff member that they should ensure that the questioning of witnesses should anticipate matters which will be raised by subsequent witnesses to ensure that the issues are fully and properly explored. It is therefore suggested that, prior to a complaint being made or the presentation of charges, the matter is investigated as fully as possible to ensure that there are good prima facie grounds to support the charge and that the university is as fully aware as possible of the case that will be made by the member of academic staff concerned. Early and thorough investigation is also recommended, since the decision to institute charges has to be taken 'on the material then available' after the member of staff has commented on the complaint. Further investigation at this stage appears not to be contemplated at all by the Model Statute.

- It may be appropriate for the university to consider the use of written witness statements as a means of presenting the evidence against the individual at the internal hearing. The advantages of this approach are twofold. The use of statements in this way ensures that the case against the individual is presented in a clear and logical fashion. Complicated facts or detailed evidence can be more readily presented through written statements, as opposed to oral questions and answers. It is also usually a more time-efficient way of presenting evidence. Secondly, if these witness statements are prepared and disclosed to the individual member of academic staff before the hearing, this ensures that the member of academic staff has as much information available as possible before the disciplinary hearing and is given the fullest opportunity to understand in detail the nature of the university's case. There is, of course, no requirement on the part of the individual member of staff to prepare any written statements of his or her own witnesses. Inevitably, this means that the employer may be taken by surprise by some of the evidence.

–   The required composition of the disciplinary tribunal is set out in the Model Statutes. In the interests of transparency of appointments, it may be advisable for the university council and senate to nominate a number of members to serve on any disciplinary tribunals that may be required during that academic year. The particular member of staff may be given an opportunity to challenge the composition of the panel on reasonable grounds. It should go without saying that no one on the tribunal should be a member of the academic staff member's department or, ideally, faculty or school (see Chapters 5, 7 and 9 on natural justice/due process).

–   The disciplinary tribunal is charged with deciding whether the charges of misconduct against the member of academic staff have been made out. It must send to the Vice-Chancellor or appropriate officer its decision on the charge together with the findings of fact and the reasons for the decision regarding that charge and its recommendations, if any, as to the appropriate penalty to be applied. The Vice-Chancellor or other appropriate officer then has to consider, in a case where the tribunal has found good cause *and* recommended dismissal, whether or not the sanction of dismissal should be applied. This procedure places the Vice-Chancellor or appropriate officer in the difficult position of having to determine whether or not dismissal is warranted without having the opportunity to consider personally the evidence against the member of academic staff concerned. In particular, much rests on the quality and detail of the report produced by the tribunal. It is obviously preferable if this contains findings of fact which are sufficiently detailed to enable the Vice-Chancellor to understand the gravity of the misconduct involved and the basis on which the tribunal has considered that the good cause definition is satisifed. It must also be borne in mind that the Vice-Chancellor is only permitted, under the Model Statute, to dismiss if that decision is reasonable. The decision to dismiss will also be judged against the same standards that apply in terms of unfair dismissal legislation. This requires that the Vice-Chancellor, as the dismissing officer, should be satisfied that there has been a full investigation and that the tribunal has concluded, on reasonable grounds that misconduct has been made out. He should, therefore, expressly consider the tribunal's decision against the charges and ensure that all relevant issues have been explored and that the tribunal's findings are sufficient to support a conclusion of 'good cause'.

–   Before any employee is dismissed for misconduct, it is usually reasonable for any mitigating factors to be taken into account. There is no obvious stage during the good cause dismissal procedure for issues of mitigation to be raised. It is, therefore, strongly recommended that before any decision to dismiss is taken, the Vice-Chancellor, as the dismissing officer, should meet the member of academic staff concerned to allow him the opportunity to raise any issues of mitigation which he wishes to be taken into account before a decision on the dismissal is taken. The Vice-Chancellor should also specifically consider whether sanctions falling short of dismissal, such as a warning or disciplinary suspension or any other sanction, should be applied and, if the decision is still to dismiss, the Vice-Chancellor should in communicating the dismissal to the member of staff explain why such sanctions were not considered appropriate.

11.76 The appeals procedure against disciplinary action including dismissal is not dealt with specifically in this chapter. In practice, one of the key difficulties with the appeal procedure is the requirement for the appeal to be heard by persons who hold or have held judicial office or who are barristers or solicitors of at least 10 years' standing. This can lead to difficulties and delays (and possibly expense) in finding such a person willing and available to hear the appeal. ACAS may be of assistance in this respect. In connection with the recently introduced scheme for arbitration on unfair dismissal disputes, ACAS has a panel of trained arbitrators, a number of whom are experienced solicitors or barristers.

Incapacity

11.77 Incapacity through ill-health is a potentially fair reason for dismissal under the ERA 1996. The basic components of a fair termination procedure will involve the employer fully investigating the medical situation and, in particular, ascertaining the prognosis for the employee's return to work. The employer must also consider whether the employee could be given alternative duties or whether there are any further steps that it would be reasonable to take to aid the employee's return to work. The employer's decision to dismiss is judged not so much against the length of the absence but against the requirements of its business and, in particular, the extent to which it would be reasonable to hold open the employee's job. Length of service may also be relevant. It is also critical that the employer should consult fully with the employee before taking any decision to dismiss.

11.78 The Model Statute procedure for dismissal on the grounds of medical incapacity envisages two scenarios. The first is when the member of academic staff agrees that his or her removal on medical grounds would be justified. That scenario should not be problematic. Where removal is disputed, the Model Statute procedure contemplates that a decision will be taken in the light of medical evidence obtained from the member of staff's doctor and from any medical examination required by a Board established to determine whether the member of staff should be dismissed. In its deliberations, the Board should naturally take account of the standards required in the unfair dismissal case-law, referred to above. However, it is also vital to note the potential impact here of the DDA 1995 which will require any dismissal on the grounds of a disability related reason to be objectively justified (see also Chapter 22). This will also require that before deciding to dismiss, the employer has given full consideration to any reasonable adjustments that can be made to allow the member of staff to continue in employment.

PARTICULAR ISSUES IN RESPECT OF FIXED-TERM CONTRACTS

11.79   Fixed-term contracts are a prevalent feature of employment within the HE sector. Historically, those employed on fixed-term contracts have been in a less advantageous position under employment protection legislation than their counterparts on permanent contracts. This position arose largely from the employer's ability to include within the fixed-term contract a waiver of the employee's right to claim either a statutory redundancy payment or to make a claim of unfair dismissal on the expiry of the fixed-term contract without renewal. It was therefore possible to employ an individual on successive fixed-term contracts over a substantial period of time, while leaving the employee without any statutory protection on termination of the relationship. Further, as a result of the existence of waiver clauses, a degree of complacency has developed regarding the termination of fixed-term contracts. In particular, the expiry of these contracts has been viewed as a convenient way of dealing with issues of poor performance or misconduct or as an opportunity to replace the employee without necessarily having a fair statutory reason for doing so – the existence of the unfair dismissal waiver meant that the employer was safe from an unfair dismissal claim. Similarly, although expiry of a fixed-term contract without renewal has always been a dismissal under the Model Statute, the absence of an obvious contractual remedy for non-compliance with the statutes meant that the Model Statute has often not been applied to the expiry of such contracts.

11.80   This position has fundamentally changed, however, as a result of recent developments in employment law, which has seen the potential abuse of fixed-term contracts receiving greater legislative scrutiny. The first such domestic initiative was s 18 of the Employment Relations Act 1999, which removed the opportunity for fixed-term contracts to contain waivers of the right to claim unfair dismissal on the expiry of the fixed term, with effect from 25 October 1999. Fixed-term contracts which were in place or renewed before this date and which contain unfair dismissal waivers will continue to be valid, even where the fixed term is due to expire after 25 October 1999. Further, at the time of writing, the Government has proposed further legislation to implement the European Framework Directive on fixed-term work. In particular, this Directive requires Member States to implement legislation giving fixed-term contract workers the right not to be treated less favourably than permanent staff on the grounds that they are a fixed-term worker unless such treatment is objectively justified, and to regulate the successive use of fixed-term contracts.

11.81 Given the prevalence of fixed-term contracts within the higher education sector it is, therefore, useful to summarise the main employment law issues which employers should bear in mind in relation to these contracts.

Unfair dismissal

11.82 It is, of course, vital to note that expiry of a fixed-term contract without renewal is a dismissal, but not a reason for the dismissal. In other words, the employer must be able to show that the reason for the dismissal was one of the five potentially fair reasons listed earlier (see para **11.61**). In the past, many employers have not given much thought to attributing a reason to a dismissal which occurs by way of expiry of a fixed-term contract without renewal. The effect of the unfair dismissal waiver clause was that they did not need to do so. Employers will no longer be able to duck this issue. Furthermore, employers will not only have to justify the dismissal in terms of the reason for it, but will also have to establish that they have followed the appropriate procedures connected with that dismissal.

11.83 Furthermore, the existence of waiver clauses has meant that there is a relative dearth of authority about the circumstances in which an employee will be unfairly dismissed at the end of a fixed-term contract. It is likely that there will be an increasing amount of judicial guidance on this point when such unfair dismissal claims reach the employment appeal tribunal and the higher courts. In the meantime, it is recommended that employers should be able to identify the rationale behind the use of the fixed term, to consult with the employee before the fixed-term contract commences so that the employee knows the basis on which the fixed term has been arrived at and that, prior to the end of the fixed term, there is further consultation with the employee regarding the dismissal. Such consultation should explore whether the original basis of the fixed term remains valid, whether there is a continued need for the employee's service, and, if not, whether any alternative employment exists. In many cases, the expiry of the fixed term may be similar to a redundancy situation in which case issues of selection for redundancy might arise (and, in these cases, the Model Statute will also need to be applied).

11.84 It will also be important that issues such as conduct and capability are properly considered during the fixed term itself and dealt with under the appropriate procedures. It will no longer be sufficient to deal with these issues by waiting for the fixed term to expire.

11.85 Employers may now need to review their fixed-term contracts and ensure that appropriate procedures are put in place to limit exposure to unfair dismissal claims where such contracts expire without being renewed. For employees who are currently employed on valid waiver clauses, employers should be aware that the waiver clause will only be effective if the reason for the termination is the expiry of the fixed term. If the contract is brought to an end for any other reason (for example, if it is terminated early on notice, or where the employer's conduct entitles the employee to resign early and bring a constructive dismissal claim), the waiver clause cannot be relied on and the employee will be entitled to bring unfair dismissal and/or redundancy claims.

11.86   The removal of the waiver of the right to bring unfair dismissal claims is likely to make employers much more cautious about both the use of fixed-term contracts and the procedures adopted in relation to their termination. It has almost become a matter of routine for fixed-term contracts of the requisite length to include a waiver both of the right to a redundancy payment and the right to claim unfair dismissal on expiry of the fixed term. The rationale behind the use of these waivers was that the employee has the security of the fixed term and knows in advance that the contract will expire on a particular date. If the employee enters into that arrangement with 'his eyes open' then (it is argued) no compensation should be received when the arrangement comes to an end in the way envisaged by the parties. Now that the employees cannot waive their right to claim unfair dismissal on expiry of the fixed term, fixed-term contracts may become less attractive unless there are strong commercial reasons for their use.

11.87   The abolition of the waiver of unfair dismissal rights will necessitate a sea-change in the way in which universities approach the termination of fixed-term contracts. It will no longer be possible to avoid confronting performance issues by failing to renew fixed-term contracts. In respect of matters of conduct or performance, the university will have to take a more active role during the employment relationship, instituting proper performance reviews or disciplinary hearings to deal with issues of poor performance or conduct. Further, in redundancy cases, it is likely that universities will have to consider more extensively than before issues such as selection for redundancy.

The Model Statute

11.88   Under the Model Statute, the expiry of a fixed-term contract without renewal is a dismissal. The termination provisions of the Model Statute will therefore apply to the extent that the reason for the non-renewal of the contract falls within the definition of good cause or redundancy.

11.89   Whether or not the definition of redundancy under the statutes is satisfied is, as described above, not always clear. However, it is clearly possible that there could be a large number of redundancy dismissals in any academic year. The university will not wish to have to separately trigger the redundancy provisions of the Model Statute on each such occasion and it is therefore recommended that a standing committee of the redundancy committee should be established to regularly review the expiry of fixed-term contracts and report to the Council on these, in accordance with the Model Statute provisions.

Collective redundancy consultation

11.90   A further issue arising from the high use of fixed-term contracts within HEIs is the issue of collective redundancy consultation. The obligation to collectively consult under s 188 of the Trade Union and Labour Relations (Consolidation) Act 1992 is triggered where an employer proposes to dismiss as redundant 20 or more employees within a period of 90 days or less. For these purposes, the expiry of a fixed-term contract without renewal is once again a dismissal. Where a number of fixed-term contracts will expire without renewal within any 90-day period (particularly, for example, at the end of the academic year) there is a risk that the collective consultation obligation will arise. Failure to consult carries a significant financial penalty – a protective award of up to 90 days' pay, gross, without any statutory maximum, can be awarded to each affected employee. Consequently, this risk needs to be managed by ensuring that a standing committee is in place to consult relevant trade unions over these proposed redundancies. Care should be taken to ensure that consultation begins at least 30 or 90 days before the first dismissal, depending on whether the number of redundancies is between 20 and 100 or 100 or more.

11.91   Consultation begins by providing the appropriate representatives of affected employees with the following information:

– the reasons for his proposals;
– the numbers and descriptions of employees whom it is proposed to dismiss as redundant;
– the total number of employees of any such description employed by the employer at the establishment in question;
– the proposed method of selecting employees who may be dismissed;
– the proposed method of carrying out the dismissals, with due regard to any agreed procedure, including the period over which the dismissals are to take effect; and
– the proposed method of calculating the amount of any redundancy payments to be made (otherwise than in compliance with an obligation imposed by or by virtue of any enactment) to employees who may be dismissed.

11.92   Consultation must cover ways of:

– avoiding the dismissals;
– reducing the numbers of employees to be dismissed; and
– mitigating the consequences of the dismissals,

and must be undertaken by the employer with a view to reaching agreement with the appropriate representatives.

11.93 The process of consultation proceeds with the employee representatives responding to the information and proposals made by the employer. The employer has a duty to consider this response with an open mind and respond to any suggestions made. Although the consultation must be with a view to reaching agreement, there is no obligation on the employer to accept the proposals put forward by employee representatives. However, where these are not accepted, the employer must be seen to have given them genuine consideration and informed the employee representatives of the reasons for their rejection.

Part 4

THE HIGHER EDUCATION INSTITUTION
AND ITS ACADEMIC ACTIVITY

Chapter 12

INTELLECTUAL PROPERTY, COPYRIGHT AND TRADE MARKS

Alasdair Poore (Mills & Reeve)

EDITORS' INTRODUCTION

§12.1   Apart from company research and development activity, the software industry, parts of the media, and perhaps certain aspects of management consultancy, the issue of IP discussed in this chapter is largely otherwise only an issue in the world of HE. However, it is an increasingly important issue for HEIs and for individual academics (both nowadays in search of a patent fortune), and it is an area throwing up an increasing amount of legal activity, as shown in the survey of HEIs described in Chapter 1. This chapter also explains the basics of copyright (and see Chapter 14 re the potential copyright of websites), and Appendix 2 to this chapter explains the Copyright Licensing Agency (CLA)–HEI licensing arrangements for photocopying. IP is of growing significance in the contractual relationship between HEIs and their academics, but there is also the concept of trade marks. For example, the original University of Oxford shield was not a registered trade mark and it appears worldwide on T-shirts at no profit to the University, whereas the more elaborate 1980s' version is very definitely registered and clearly intended as a money-spinner (in fact, the University has opened its own shop: see also Chapter 15 on Trading Companies). There is also a link to Chapter 28 in that, as we go to press, the UUK is ready to protest about draft EU legislation which could restrict public sector bodies from fully exploiting the commercial value of their IP.

§12.2   For a US perspective on copyright, patents, and trade marks, see Kaplin and Lee (1995a), pp 748–762, and especially the *Kligman* case at pp 952–954,[1] concerning an academic at the University of Pennsylvania: 'universities engaged in collaborative research should be especially careful to develop and implement express patent agreements with faculty and staff and with all outside sponsors of research . . . All such arrangements should be spelled out explicitly and clearly in writing, to ensure that courts will recognise them in the event of disputes'.[2] On the terms in research contracts, see Kaplin and Lee (1995a), pp 945–952: 'The potentials and problems arising from universities' and faculty members' research relationships with industry have garnered more attention than almost any other higher education development of the past twenty years . . . complex combinations of legal, policy, and managerial issues. Perhaps most difficult are the potential conflicts of interest issues . . .'.

---

1   *University Patents Inc v Kligman* 762 F Supp 1212, ED Pa 1991.
2   At p 954.

This issue of 'split loyalties' is dealt with in depth at pp 959–963. At the time this book was being written there were media reports of a $10m lawsuit between a US drug manufacturer and two academics at major US HEIs, the former claiming that the latter's article in the *Journal of the American Medical Association* on a drug produced by the company had been inaccurate.[1]

§12.3   An example of a similar conflict of interest dispute in a UK HEI is *University of Nottingham v Fishel*:[2] see paras **10.24** *et seq.* Another dimension of sponsored/contract research is the potential for disputes when the sponsor does not like the research results and/or the HEI allegedly fails to produce research of the appropriate quality: see, for example, a report of a research contract row between LSE and its sponsor (the World Travel and Tourism Council).[3] (See also Editors' introduction to Chapter 15.)

§12.4   Note also the interesting case of *Ashdown v Telegraph Group Ltd*,[4] where Paddy Ashdown MP sued *The Sunday Telegraph* for its alleged infringement of his copyright in a minute he had made of a meeting with Prime Minister Blair. The newspaper invoked the right to freedom of expression in Art 10 of the European Convention on Human Rights, as now incorporated into English law by the HRA 1998, but the court was distinctly unimpressed and Ashdown got his legal remedies.

§12.5   Finally, the last word goes to the inimitable Laurie Taylor. The column set out below first appeared in *The Times Higher Educational Supplement* on 12 January 2001, and is reproduced with permission.

'*Corporate sponsor tries to block publication of academic research results that reflected unfavourably on product it paid to have tested – THES, Jan 5*

Do come in, Doctor Bunting.

Thank you, vice-chancellor.

Doctor Bunting, I believe you are in receipt of a research grant for Poppleton Pork Products.

That's right. They awarded me £45,000 to investigate the psychological benefits that might be derived from their new Jumbo Sizzler Sausage.

You've completed that research?

Yes indeed. I conducted a carefully controlled experiment in which 200 randomly selected subjects ate a pound of Jumbo Sizzlers every day for three months and then compared their results on a happiness index with 200 other randomly selected subjects whose diet was supplemented by normal sausages.

And the Jumbo Sizzlers produced more overall happiness?

Absolutely, 100 per cent of the Sizzler sample was "sausage happy" compared to only 63 per cent of the non-Sizzler sample. There was, though, one negative result that I thought I should include in the final report.

Doctor Bunting, I trust you are aware of the financial assistance provided to this university by PPP, assistance now formally acknowl-

---

1   *The Times Higher Educational Supplement*, 5 January 2001, p 44.
2   [2000] ICR 1462.
3   *The Times Higher Educational Supplement*, 12 January 2001, p 5.
4   [2001] Ch 685.

edged by the addition of a large pig to the university crest. And yet, I am now confronted by a letter from their managing director in which he claims that your inclusion of this negative result seriously detracts from the overall favourable nature of the findings. What exactly was this negative finding?

The tragic death of two of the Sizzler sample from gastric seizures.

Hardly a negative finding, Doctor Bunting. After all, your research clearly indicates that they would both have expired in a happy state. I can only ask you to withdraw that finding from your report.

You're suggesting that I lie?

Strong words, Doctor Bunting. Let's call it a little porkie.'

§12.6   See the 'Armed' Unit on 'Research Misconduct' at www.bristol.ac.uk/armed.

INTRODUCTION

12.1   IP is an area of very substantial importance in the business community. The accelerating pace of technological development, both in terms of articles and goods that are traded and the way in which individuals and businesses operate, means that the relevance of intellectual property will increase further. Examples are the use of the internet, of increasingly powerful computers and electronic communications, and the electronic distribution of information and publications. Innovation and new technology have risen to the top of the political agenda, so hardly a day passes without media reference to them. This development is one which is evidently crucial to HEIs. They are institutions at the heart of the development and dissemination of information and knowledge. Through research or teaching, they are involved in areas where IP is important; and, as pressure to look for further assets or marketing opportunities rises, intellectual property will be required to play a greater role. When looking at IP, however, one must not over-emphasise the prospect of a major development which may transform the finances of the institution. These arise rarely and usually unpredictably. Nevertheless, it is important to be aware that IP issues arise throughout the business of an HEI, and to ensure that, if the right framework exists, the HEI can support both small and great alike.

12.2   This chapter aims to give an overview of IP so that these issues can be addressed. IP consists of many of different types of rights, which are relevant to different aspects of the business of an institution. Here we give an overview of some general issues, a summary of the main IP rights which are relevant, a discussion of ownership and acquisition, transfer and exploitation, third party rights and the HEI's management of IP.

WHAT IS INTELLECTUAL PROPERTY AND WHY IS IT IMPORTANT?

12.3   Most people know in general terms what IP is. Patents, copyright, trade marks, rights in designs and confidential information are examples. They protect subject matter as different as drugs and computers, software, books, sculptures and musical performances, names such as Coca-Cola or the BBC, wallpaper, furniture and dress designs. Intellectual property is an umbrella term used to cover a very wide range of rights. Some of these rights have statutory origins, some arise from history; some must be registered, whereas others subsist without any formal steps being taken. Some relate to new technology, others to brand identity or image, and others to artistic expression. It is important to be aware of the diversity of IP. In detail, the rights are very different and must be handled in very different ways. However, they still often fit together to provide a broad umbrella of protection; and they also have common elements which mean that they are usually discussed together.

THREE GENERAL CONCEPTS

(1) Scope of protection

12.4   The essence of any IP right is that it can be used to stop other parties from carrying out an activity. It allows the owner to prevent others from:

–   using an invention which has been patented; or
–   making copies of a text or issuing those copies to the public; or
–   using the mark a trader has used or intends to use to identify its business.

However, the type of protection depends on the type of right.

'Reproduction' rights
12.5   Some rights can be used to prevent third parties copying the owner's work. They can be used to prevent the creation or distribution of copies or derivative works. In this way, they protect the investment in effort made by the owner. However, they do not act as a complete bar on making a similar product or one which satisfies the same need. If there is no copying, a third party cannot be restrained by this type of right, since these rights do not create a complete monopoly. If the owner identifies a market opportunity, others may still be able to take advantage of it, provided they do not copy. Rights which fall into this category are copyright, database extraction rights and unregistered design right.

Monopoly rights

12.6 These rights can be used to exclude others absolutely. It does not matter whether the third party obtained the idea from the owner or independently. An example is a patent, such as a patent on a drug. Here other parties can be prevented from making the drug even if they discovered it through indepen-dent research. There are two advantages: first, an absolute monopoly is much more valuable because the owner can ensure that only he, she or it benefits from the exploitation of the resulting product; and, secondly, it is much easier to prove infringement because it does not matter how the third party came to do the infringing activity.

Narrower rights

12.7 Protection for confidential information depends on the relationship between the 'owner' and the person using it. That relationship may be based on contract (such as a secrecy agreement), or on some implied duty of confidence.

(2) Registrability

12.8 The second general concept is registrability. Some IP rights arise automatically, or with no steps being taken by the owner. In other cases, some formal steps may be required to 'register' the right, usually with a national or trans-national authority. Usually, to obtain registration an application must be made, accompanied by an appropriate fee. In most cases the authority reviews ('examines') the application in order to see whether it meets the formal and substantive requirements. If it does, the application will be granted. Most registrable rights correspond to the monopoly rights. Examination of the applications sifts out those which *prima facie* do not justify a monopoly, and so prevents a person from obtaining an unfair advantage in the market. The main registered rights are patents, registered designs and registered trade marks.

(3) Intangibility

12.9 The third aspect of IP rights is that they are intangible. Unlike physical objects, they cannot be pinned down. A third party cannot be prevented from using the subject matter simply by keeping possession of it in the owner's heads. This is also what makes the rights so valuable. Once done, the work can be used again and again. For example, a piece of software, once written, can be duplicated many times for use by others. The value in the rights can be very considerable because it reflects the possibility of repeated use. Conversely, the possibility of replication makes IP relatively difficult to protect. In many cases, a third party can make the same use of IP as the owner. Moreover, the third party can change or even improve the subject matter. This mutability of subject matter often makes IP rights much more difficult to enforce.

NATIONAL CHARACTER

12.10   Almost all IP rights arise under national laws, which are specific to the country in question. However, in most cases now there are international Conventions which mean that the elements of the rights are very similar in each country. A few countries (such as Taiwan and some South American countries) are outside this international regime. National character does mean that, where registration is required, the right must be registered in each country, or occasionally, in each region.

TYPES OF INTELLECTUAL PROPERTY

12.11   The principal IP rights are patents, design rights, copyright, database rights, confidential information and trade marks. Design rights and trade marks can each be in two types, registered or unregistered. There are other significant rights in particular fields such as semiconductor topography rights, performers' protection and plant breeders' rights. Table 12.1 (see Appendix 1 to this chapter) summarises a selection of important rights with notes of their main characteristics and subject matter.

Patents

12.12   The criteria for a patentable invention in the UK are set out in the Patents Act 1977 (and the European Patent Convention), and case-law. The three principal criteria are as follows.

(1) Novelty
12.13   The invention must not have been described or used in public by the inventor or anyone else before the application is made. The most important consequence of this is that the inventor, and anyone else knowing of the invention, must not talk about it before obtaining protection, unless any disclosure is in confidence. Even confidential disclosures should be made only with care as confidentiality is rarely perfect. This is particularly significant in HEIs where students and researchers often have a primary aim of securing publication. In particular, in fast-moving fields where patent protection could be most important (such as genetic engineering) early publication is a prerequisite. Consequently, it is important to set up a framework for providing advice on such inventions and, if appropriate, authorising and obtaining protection, as rapidly as possible. Note that in the USA there is a one-year grace period, so that an application can be filed within one year of publication. This means that, *in extremis*, where publication has occurred, protection in the USA might still be possible.

(2) Not obvious

12.14   The invention must be inventive or not obvious. It is obvious if a person (or research group) of average skill working in the field would have thought of the invention (based on their knowledge and what similar people would be expected to know, and on publicly available information). In practice, this is quite an easy test to pass.

(3) Capable of industrial application and other policy exclusions

12.15   Essentially, this test has two functions: to separate out technical from aesthetic and similar innovations; and to avoid giving protection where, for policy reasons, this is thought inappropriate. Important examples are computer programs *per se*, and methods of surgery, therapy or diagnosis on humans or animals. In practice, the restriction on patentability can often be circumvented, and certainly in relation to much computer software and most methods practised on humans or animals, there are ways around it. Note also that the USA has a somewhat more favourable regime, so protection should be separately considered there.

Seeking protection

12.16   An application must be filed in respect of each country where protection is sought. It could be very difficult to file the large number of applications which might be required in a short time. Fortunately, international Conventions overcome this problem.

The Paris Convention

12.17   An applicant can file an application in one country. Provided other applications are filed within one year of the first application, they are deemed to be filed on the same date as the original application. A very large number of countries are party to this Convention.

Patent Cooperation Treaty

12.18   A single application can be made, designating a large number of countries (including most of those which are most economically important). This progresses as a single application for up to 2½ years, after which it is transformed into a number of national applications.

European Patent Convention

12.19   A single application to be made for a number of European countries, including all the EU countries. Again, this progresses and is granted as a single application, but then becomes separate national patents in each State.

Copyright

Criteria

12.20 Copyright protection is given to any original artistic, literary or dramatic work and to cinematographic and broadcast works. In the UK, 'original' means, broadly, that if effort has gone into making the work, copyright subsists in it. In practice, this is a very low threshold. Before copyright arises the work must be recorded in a material form. If it is recorded in writing or electronically (even transiently, such as in computer memory), the recording attracts copyright. There are also certain qualifying requirements which are rather technical (based on first publication and the nationality or residence of the author), but these are unlikely to be of significance for HEIs.

Seeking protection

12.21 In the UK, no steps are required to obtain protection. Copyright arises automatically when the relevant work is created. Copyright does not require to be registered. In many other jurisdictions, similar protection is obtained under two international Conventions – the Berne Convention and the Universal Copyright Convention. Copyright works are customarily marked with © or 'Copyright', the year of publication and the name of the copyright owner. In most cases this is no longer required, but is still valuable as an indication that the copyright owner claims rights. In the USA, copyright can be registered, and though doing so is not mandatory, it has some advantages in infringement proceedings.

Multiple rights

12.22 As a consequence of the simple manner in which copyright arises, many works may be subject to several different levels of copyright or similar protection. For example, each version of a piece of software may well fall within the scope of copyright in all the earlier versions of the software. This is of particular significance in relation to multimedia works, where there may be several different layers of protection available (and if a work is being prepared, several different consents required).

Related forms of protection

12.23 The following two additional rights also relate to copyright and should be mentioned briefly.

Moral rights

12.24 These arise under the Copyright Designs and Patents Act 1988. There are two important rights: the right to be named as author; and the right to prevent your work being subjected to derogatory treatment. As a result of the uncertainty about the problems which may arise with moral rights, it is common to require a waiver from authors. This prevents them asserting the right in the future against the person to whom the waiver is given. One such right, the right to be identified as the author, must be 'asserted' to be binding. It is easiest to assert this when an assignment is made or licence granted, and academic authors should be made aware of the desirability of doing so.

Database extraction right
12.25 This is a recent right introduced under EC law. It gives certain rights in relation to the extraction of information from a database, so that the owner of the database can prevent extraction of information from the database and further dissemination of that information. In the UK, it is similar in impact to copyright protection for databases. However, in most other countries copyright cannot be used to protect many databases. The right exists where information is collected into a database, and the obtaining, verifying or presenting the data involves substantial investment. The person making that investment is the owner, who is entitled to prevent third parties from re-using or extracting any substantial part of a database. Repeated small extractions can amount to a substantial part. There is an exception for use for the purpose of illustration in teaching and research and not for any commercial purpose. The right lasts for 15 years from completing the database.

Designs

12.26 Unregistered designs are very similar to copyright, except that the duration is only 10 years from first marketing or 15 years from creation, whichever is shorter. This right is valuable because (subject to some limitations) it can protect functional and non-aesthetic designs, such as machinery parts. Registered designs can be used to protect features of products such as the liners, contours, shape, texture, materials or ornamentation. The design must be new (ie not used or have been disclosed anywhere in the world within 12 months before the date of application) and have 'individual character'. A new Community Designs regime will come into force later this year enabling designs to be protected in all Member States of the EU by a single application process.

Trade marks

12.27 Trade marks are used to protect trading reputation. They are intended to identify goods and services and act as a sign that they come from the same source as other goods and services. Examples are the trading name or logo of an HEI. When used on textbooks, examination papers, in conferences or for consultancy, it suggests to the customer that the same quality of goods or services are to be expected as were previously provided. Trade marks can form the basis for identifying their source to third parties who have not encountered it before.

Unregistered trade marks
12.28 Protection arises from use of a name, logo or image. In due course, customers come to associate that name with a particular organisation or goods

or service. The courts will prevent a third party using the mark in a way which confuses or is likely to cause confusion. For example, use of the name 'de Montfort' in a way which suggested (incorrectly) an association with Demontfort University would be an infringement.

Registered trade marks
12.29 Registration permits a party to specify the trade mark in which it wishes to claim exclusive rights.

Distinctiveness
12.30 The trade mark must be something which can serve to distinguish products or services from each other. It must be a 'sign' and that sign must be capable of being used as a trade mark (ie it must be capable of acting as an indicator that goods or services come from one source as opposed to another). Protection will not be given for marks which are very descriptive until they have been used for a significant period of time. An example is the use of a geographical name or a surname, which might be used to describe the origin of goods. A leading case involved the name 'Yorkshire' for trailers; without use, it would not be registrable. In fact, the mark had been used for many years and was well recognised by those in the trade. This is clearly a common problem for HEIs which will often be called by geographical names. In order to secure registration, the mark must be shown to be distinctive or recognisable by potential consumers as that of the owner.

No conflict
12.31 No one else can have prior rights.

Foreign applications
12.32 There are several routes to foreign protection:

- the Paris Convention (as for patents, but the priority period is 6 months);
- the European Trade Mark Convention (a single application is effective through the whole EU);
- the Madrid Protocol and Madrid Agreement (these allow single 'umbrella' applications to be made in respect of certain countries).

The UK is not a member of the Madrid Agreement, but is a member of the Madrid Protocol. Under this arrangement, an application can now be made covering over 40 countries, although some major ones, in particular the USA, are not (yet) covered.

Domain Name

12.33 A domain name is that part of a web page address from the 'www' to the 'ac.uk' or other suffix; such names are becoming a problem area for academic institutions. Technically, they are not intellectual property rights, but the overlap is substantial, both because use of a domain name can conflict with other trade mark rights, and can establish trade mark rights. Whilst the academic community has some control over the allocation of academic internet addresses ending '.ac.uk' (they are managed by the United Kingdom Education & Research Networking Association, with strict rules about eligibility),[1] there are no restrictions on who can register domains with the more common '.co.uk' or '.com' suffixes. A number of HEIs are looking at registering '.co.uk' names and are finding that others have got there first. The courts on both sides of the Atlantic are coming down hard on opportunistic domain name registration, where an organisation or individual with no bona fide intention to use a name registers it and then offers it for sale to the relevant trade mark owner. There are also independent arbitration procedures for resolving domain name disputes which can provide a quicker and cheaper mechanism than the courts. Oxford University, for example, has taken successful action, via the World Intellectual Property Organisation, to recover its name from an Australian cyber-squatter.[2]

12.34 However, it is difficult to obtain an order for the transfer of a domain name where the owner can also claim legitimate use of the brand name in question. This could include, for example, a university society, affiliated body, or alumni association. The best advice is to register any names important to an institution as domain names first, in as many combinations as possible – '.com', '.co.uk', '.org.uk' and '.ac.uk', to name but a few. For these reasons, it may be worthwhile to register pertinent names as trade marks (possibly also as domain names). Trade mark registration may form a basis for securing cancellation or transfer of not only the same, but also similar domain names, or preventing their use in fields which impact on the HEIs.

CREATION AND ACQUISITION

12.35 Within HEIs, IP, or the subject matter of IP, is being created all the time. Staff who write lecture notes, or prepare texts for teaching, generate copyright works. Researchers create know-how directly as a result of their research; they also generate copyright works in the data that they collect and in the papers that they write. They might make inventions. It is widely recognised that often the most important issue in HEIs is recognising the IP which arises and identifying the elements which are valuable. This is important for two reasons. Clearly, for those rights which require registration, the essential ingredient must be spotted before registration is no longer possible. However, even for rights which do not require any formal steps to protection, unless they are recognised, it is unlikely any use will be made of them. The step of

---

1   See www.ja.net/documents/naming/ac.uk-naming-procedure.html for further details.
2   Including a variation which Oxford may not wish to make use of: www.university-of-f******-oxford.com.

identifying and recognising IP is discussed at greater length in 'Management of intellectual property' at paras **12.61** *et seq*.

OWNERSHIP

12.36   Ownership of IP arises either through its creation (or registration), or by transfer. The former is the most important for an HEI acquiring rights. Table 12.2 (see Appendix 1 to this chapter) identifies the 'original owner' in respect of a number of IP rights.

Variety of sources or creators

12.37   In HEIs there will usually be several different potential sources of IP rights, each with a different status: students of the HEI, lecturing and research staff, general staff, consultants, and outside contributors (such as external supervisors or industrial participants). Ownership issues will depend on who was the creator and in which circumstances the right was created. In some of these cases, an express contract will govern the relationship between the HEI and the creator (for example, the staff will be under a contract of employment and consultants may have specific consultancy agreements). In general, HEIs will wish to address the question of ownership expressly and in advance, therefore they will seek to set up some contractual arrangement.

Lecturing and research staff

12.38   In general, such staff will be employed under contracts of employment. If there are no express terms governing IP, the position will usually be governed by implied terms. Rights other than rights in inventions will belong to the employer if they were made by the employee in the course of his employment. Rights in inventions will generally be governed by the Patents Act 1977 (see Table 12.2 in Appendix 1 to this chapter). The question arises as to whether the IP was created in the course of employment when it was outside normal hours of work or at home. In practice, this will depend on whether it was part of work being carried out within the framework of the HEI and whether out-of-hours work is usual. A particularly pertinent example of this is illustrated in *Greater Glasgow Health Board's Application*.[1] A hospital registrar also acted as a lecturer and had the opportunity to carry out research. He made an invention at home, while studying for exams. In this case, the invention did not belong to the Health Board (or his associated University) because his duty was to treat patients, not to improve the facilities for doing so. The case emphasises the possibility that an invention (or copyright work) made at home *may* belong to the employer where it is part of the employee's job to solve such

---

1   [1996] RPC 207.

problems; on the other hand, it may not belong to the employer, even if done at work, if doing it was not part of the employee's duties.

12.39　In relation to patentable inventions, some staff (for example, administrative staff and arts research staff) are not in a position where inventions are likely to occur; as a result the inventions made by them belong to them. The argument has also been raised that lecturers in some HEIs are not 'paid to invent' on the grounds that they do not have a contractual obligation to do research. However, in most cases some element of research will form a part of their job; and if they carry out some research functions, those will probably be regarded as part of the job. The provisions normally implied by statute or general law can be varied (although, in relation to employee inventors, only in favour of them). Variation may be made by an express agreement or by an express intellectual property policy which is effectively incorporated into the contract of employment. However, variation can also arise by an established custom which has become part of the pattern of working. Although most HEIs will not have established such a pattern or convention in relation to inventions, there might be arrangements in relation to copyright works, such as books written by lecturers (most HEIs do *not* try to capture the lecturer's book royalties). Similarly, software written by lecturers and research staff may 'habitually' have been freely exploited by the staff. If there are such customs, then these may need to be addressed in a specific policy, taking care when the policy is introduced that it does not amount to a breach of the employee's contract of employment. In order to clarify the position, HEIs should adopt a general policy on IP which is applicable to all staff, and incorporated into the staff contracts.

Students

12.40　As discussed in Chapter 6, students are almost certainly subject to a special contract. Preferably, this should include provisions relating to IP. Alternatively, it may be possible to bind the student under a suitable IP policy. In the absence of a special arrangement, IP created by a student will usually belong to the student. In some cases, however, it will be important for the HEI to own the IP. Students may contribute an idea which is important to the results of the research and be patentable or produce copyright works of value (for example, software, datasets or written works). In other cases, such as music performed or written by students, it may be appropriate that the student retains ownership, although the HEI may wish to have rights, for example to use the work as teaching material or to publish it. One problem which frequently appears to arise in connection with students is that ownership rights are related to payment of grant moneys or sponsorship, and either the grant moneys or sponsorship are interrupted, or moneys from one source are applied to other projects. Ideally, a policy will implicitly address how such problems are handled.

Contract staff and consultants

12.41 There will often be a written contract under which such persons serve. However, unless this addresses intellectual property specifically, the HEI may still not acquire all relevant rights. The courts will imply the minimum necessary to give business efficacy to the contract. For example, if a contract author assists in writing teaching materials, the copyright in that work will remain with the author and there will be only a licence in favour of the person commissioning the work. If an invention is made, the invention will, in the absence of any express provision, belong to the consultant. Again, the court may imply a limited licence in favour of the HEI in order to use the results of the consultant's work.

Outside contributors

12.42 The general rule is that what they contribute will, in the absence of any agreement (possibly implied), belong to them.

Mixed sources

12.43 Another complication which may arise in HEIs is that a number of different people, with different positions, may create IP. It is particularly important to have a framework for resolving issues of ownership and use of the rights, otherwise disagreements over this may affect the whole project.

Creating an express contract in relation to intellectual property

12.44 The contract of employment, consultancy agreement, or research and development agreement can contain specific terms dealing with IP. This is likely to be the most common course where the arrangement is a reasonably formal one with an outside party, such as a consultant or research collaborator. Alternatively, the contract may make reference to an intellectual property policy. This would be quite common in relation to staff. A similar arrangement may be used in relation to students, if there is a contractual relationship between the students and the HEI (see Chapter 6). The advantage of such an arrangement is that, if properly implemented, it allows the HEI to change the detail of the policy without reaching agreement with each member of staff or student. For example, any share given to relevant staff of the revenues from the exploitation of IP generated by them might be changed from time to time, or the terms on which academic staff are permitted to publish might be altered. In addition, in considering what should be included in such contracts or rules it is clearly important to consider how to handle different forms of IP or rights which arise in different circumstances. The contribution made by a student acting as a research assistant on a scientific project might be treated very differently from that made by a musician recording music in conjunction with the HEI. The issue of IP may, perhaps, be addressed in a contract relating specifically to IP (for example, in a confidentiality agreement, or a specific agreement where a student is helping in a research project and there is no other policy arrangement which would apply).

Additional terms

12.45 At the same time, other relevant terms should be addressed; for example, the right of each party to use the IP and whether there is to be any reward or inventor compensation for the creator, assistance in securing protection, publication and confidentiality.

Assignments and transfers, exploitation and licensing

12.46 Exploitation is fundamental to the ownership of IP. If the rights are not exploited, there is little point in having them. Exploitation can be carried out in a number of ways. For businesses the main way is by carrying on, themselves, the activity protected by the rights. For a drug company, this will be manufacturing and marketing the drug. For a software company, it will be issuing copies of the software. In practice, HEIs are less likely to be involved in such direct exploitation. In most cases, exploitation will involve selling the rights to a third party or licensing a third party to use them.

Sale or licensing

12.47 These are two fundamentally different ways of giving others the right to use IP. The important difference is in control of the IP rights after the transactions. In a sale, the rights are transferred to the purchaser and, if there is a breach of the agreement or the purchaser becomes insolvent, the seller may have fairly limited recourse. Under a licence, the licensor may be able to terminate the agreement and find an alternative partner. There will usually be other substantial differences. For example, a licence is often subject to periodic payment of a royalty and issues such as maintaining and enforcing the rights will be in the hands of the licensor. Sale payments, however, will frequently be one-off or over a limited time, and enforcement will be in the hands of the purchaser. In addition, a purchaser might want some guarantees of the rights being purchased. However, these types of issue are not fundamental. There is considerable flexibility in the way in which they can be handled and often an agreement begins to look like a mixture of licensing and sale.

Spin-out companies

12.48 One particularly popular mechanism for exploitation at the moment is to set up a company which is licensed, or to which IP rights are transferred. Although technically more complicated, this can have a number of advantages. For example, it can (in principle) put the HEI in a position similar to that of a manufacturer, in which often the greatest return will be achieved from exploitation. A related issue is that it makes it easier to bring in outside investors, either by direct investment or by flotation. At the same time, the HEI can maintain an interest in the success of exploitation by retaining equity in the company. This process permits the HEI to maintain some level of influence in exploitation, and it can also provide a vehicle in which the academic inventors or collaborators can have an active interest. It can also be used as a method of isolating potential liabilities which might arise from direct exploitation or even licensing, and to overcome some of the issues involved in trading by HEIs.

12.49 There are evidently also disadvantages of this approach. The most fundamental is that it is more complicated and will not be suitable for small low-value opportunities; and is also unlikely to be suitable where the HEI does not have ready access to the skills for commercialising the relevant IP, either through its academics or others known to it. In addition, a usual corollary of obtaining greater upside return is that the HEI takes greater downside risk. In other words, if it does not work, the returns to the HEI are likely to be substantially less than those obtained by other exploitation routes. Returns may even be nil; and the HEI may lose the IP at the same time. A further practical complication of spin-out arrangements is that they often depend on involvement of the original inventors. Either the HEI will lose those academics, or their loyalties will be split between the HEI and their spin-out organisation. The latter can give rise to serious conflicts of interest, or behaviour which damages the HEI's interests. These potential conflicts of interest need to be managed carefully so as to benefit both parties, both by providing carefully drawn up contractual provisions, and by ensuring that active management of the relationship takes place.

12.50 There are a number of examples of situations where this has not occurred. One, not directly in the IP field, which illustrates the issues well is the case of a doctor who 'diverted' opportunities for foreign work to himself. The employer knew that this was taking place, and, although there was a specific provision that required the doctor to obtain prior consent to any such opportunities, his employer did not take steps to prevent it. The court held that the employer was not entitled to an account of profits made by the doctor from this activity because, although the doctor might have 'diverted' the opportunities from the employer, he did not have a specific obligation to offer the opportunities to the employer. A further action which showed how conflicts can arise was bolder. The doctor was found to have used the employer's staff for some of these opportunities. In this respect, his actions were regarded as a breach of his fiduciary duty to his employer. However, a finding of this nature is poor compensation for the breach occurring in the first place. (See also Chapters 10 and 11 re staff issues in HEIs, and Chapter 15 re trading companies.)

Formal requirements

12.51   There are relatively few formal constraints on how the licensing or sale of IP is carried out.

Content of the agreement

12.52   Most IP can be transferred or licensed without restriction. In practice, agreements for trade mark licensing should include certain requirements (relating to control of use of the mark and the quality of products or services to which it is applied). Failure to do so may lead, in due course, to the mark becoming unenforceable. In addition, any agreement must clearly comply with any competition law requirements. For example, there are specific provisions relating to tying supplies to patent licences. There are also more general requirements under UK and EC competition laws in respect of provisions restricting competition (such as price fixing or territorial limitations).

Formalities

12.53   Certain types of agreement or assignment must be in writing and might need to be signed by one or both parties. The main agreements covered are assignments and exclusive licences in respect of patents and applications (signed by both parties) and in respect of trade marks, copyright and design right (signed by the assignor).

Stamp duty

12.54   Stamp duty used to apply to written assignments and irrevocable exclusive licences of IP rights (other than know-how). A document which is not stamped cannot be used in evidence in a UK court and (subject to para 12.55) there is no other consequence. However, if it is necessary to rely on a document in court, and if the document is stamped late, penalties may be payable. The legislation has now been modified so that stamp duty does not apply to assignments of IP (or effectively to exclusive licences). There are some traps in this, so it is as well to be cautious. In particular, stamp duty still applies to the assignment of 'goodwill' and the Inland Revenue also takes the view that it applies to the assignment of domain names. This means, first that, if applicable, it is wise to include the 'certificate of value' which used to be included in assignments. (This is a statement in prescribed form that the consideration of this and related transactions does not exceed the relevant threshold – specific advice should be sought on this as it varies from time to time and the format is important.) Secondly, if the assignment is in exchange for shares, which is increasingly common, the transfer of shares may be subject to stamp duty.

Registration

12.55   Transactions relating to UK patents, registered designs and trade marks must be registered in the UK Patent Office. Failure to register means that a subsequent transaction may take priority over the earlier one. In addition, if the transaction is not registered within 6 months (without a proper reason) the ability to recover damages for infringement of the right may be impaired. The Patent Office is required not to register a transaction unless any appropriate stamp duty has been paid on it. HEIs will not usually be so concerned with stamp duty or registration issues, because they will usually be licensing or selling rights, rather than acquiring them. However, where they are building up a portfolio of rights for sale or licensing to a third party (for example, in an ongoing development project with other parties or through their exploitation companies), they will want to make sure those rights are effectively established.

Formal assignments

12.56   One other area of assignments and transfers should be mentioned. Often parties do not want full details of a licence or transfer to be available publicly. Registration of the transaction involves providing a copy of the document, which will usually be publicly available. In addition, if there is a need to rely in court on a transaction, this may receive wider attention. For these reasons, it is often the practice to execute a formal assignment or licence, which is in short form, confirming the rights granted, which can then be registered or shown to third parties. Inventors are commonly asked to execute an assignment, particularly as it might be required for US applications. Copyright is also important. Often copyright works are prepared under a consultancy arrangement in which copyright does not belong to the commissioning party. It is very desirable to obtain a short form of copyright assignment from all authors of any work which may be exploited, so that these can be relied on in any sale or dispute.

Infringement of third party rights

12.57   Businesses generally have to consider whether the products they manufacture or the name they use infringes third party rights. These issues are not, in most cases, so pertinent to HEIs. There are, however, areas of importance such as the conduct of research, the use of software or copyright works (for example, as texts in teaching or illustrations in books) and any business activities of an HEI. There is no exception for infringement of IP rights by HEIs. The fact that use is in an academic environment will not avoid infringement. In practice, owners of IP rights may take less interest in the activities of an HEI because these do not represent a competitive threat. In other cases, special arrangements have already been reached to address the needs of the academic community. However, where infringement represents a threat or loss of custom, action may be taken.

Exceptions

Experimental and research use

12.58   Generally, an HEI carrying out research is in the same position as other businesses. Consequently, if an HEI uses a patented technique for gene sequencing, it will usually need a licence. A body which is carrying out experimental work related to the subject matter of the invention does not infringe a patent covering that invention. Thus, where a research team is experimenting with a patented drug to examine how it acts, it would probably not infringe the patent by making the drug for that purpose. However, the exception has been applied narrowly in the UK. For example, carrying out clinical trials for a competing manufacturer would not be covered. This position is quite likely to change to a broader view in order to harmonise English law with that of other EU countries. In relation to a copyright work, fair dealing for the purpose of research or private study is not an infringement. In order to qualify as fair dealing, the copying which is carried out must not substitute significantly for original sales of the copyright work. Consequently, rules such as copying no more than 10 per cent of a journal and then only a single copy are sometimes applied. There are also specific exemptions in relation to teaching, examinations and other educational establishment functions which may apply.

Software/Database

12.59 Most use of software and copying databases will infringe copyright and the HEI or the relevant individual needs to be licensed. HEIs can benefit from some centrally negotiated licensing arrangements, which can significantly reduce the cost and administration associated with such activities.

Copyright licensing arrangements

12.60 In addition to arrangements relating to software, there are also general copyright licensing schemes in relation to copyright in literary and artistic works. Examples are the CLA and Newspaper Licensing Agency. Note that 'clippings' services, where copies are made of clippings, will usually be regarded as infringement by these two agencies. See Appendix 2 to this chapter concerning the CLA–HEI licensing agreement for photocopying. This agreement has been in dispute between the UUK and the CLA, with the Copyright Tribunal recently ruling in favour of the former: see the note to Appendix 2 to this chapter.

MANAGEMENT OF INTELLECTUAL PROPERTY

12.61 Understanding the issues involved is a small part of having a successful approach to IP in any organisation, including HEIs. The most important element is managing the IP. This falls into several areas:

–   creating awareness;
–   identifying and 'capturing' IP;
–   selecting viable IP;
–   protecting IP rights; and

–   creating a strategy for exploitation and managing exploitation.

In most instances, it is recognised that the first three of these are the most difficult.

Creating awareness

12.62   This can be achieved by a mixture of education and dissemination of success stories or disasters, usually combined with accessibility of advice.

Capturing intellectual property

12.63   There are a number of mechanisms used by HEIs for identifying IP rights and 'collecting' them under central control. These include carrying out IP audits, improving awareness by briefings or by inclusion of IP teaching on a wide range of courses and award schemes. In each case, these are likely to be fairly resource-intensive. The most effective method of capture is to have special staff dedicated to monitoring what is going on in the HEI, who discuss IP issues with academic staff of the HEI on a regular basis. Most HEIs are unlikely to have the resources to employ a person full-time in this role. In that case, a part-time research manager may be effective. Alternatively, outside bodies, including firms of patent agents, will be prepared to carry out the same job, in the expectation of obtaining some additional benefit. Implementation of a general policy relating to IP might also be effective. If effective and well publicised, this will reduce to some extent the necessity of searching for IP.

Selecting viable intellectual property

12.64   Decision-taking can be helped by knowledge of the potential for exploitation and the field in which it will be carried out. Many inventions can be sifted out on the basis that there is no commercial potential for them, but many others usually remain. Sometimes HEIs can be in a better position to assess these than outside businesses. Although HEIs do not necessarily have the exposure to the commercial market place, they often have much readier access to academic advice on the issues involved, and connections with possible commercial partners. If the HEI is not able to form a view, there are a number of outside exploitation organisations which have now established a reasonable reputation in identifying suitable partners.

SUMMARY

12.65   The principal element of managing IP is to be aware of it and to create awareness of it. In doing so, it may be desirable to adopt a policy specifically covering IP (including ownership, handling, rewards for innovators), and to implement that throughout the HEI. It will also probably be desirable to provide a focal point for information and advice as well as control (for example, of research and development contracts), by creating an IP responsibility or unit or by contracting with an outside party to provide such a service.

APPENDIX 1 TO CHAPTER 12: TABLES

Table 12.1   Summary Table of UK IP rights

Right	Registered/ Unregistered	Scope	Requirement	Exceptions	Term	Examples
Patent	Registered	Monopoly	New, not obvious, industrially applicable	*Application* of drugs or surgical techniques Plant and animal varieties Software *per se* Methods of doing business	20 years from application Renewal fees annually	*New articles*: corkscrew, computer equipment, biro, gear wheel, hovercraft, flow meter *New substances*: drugs, plastics, insecticides, toothpaste formulations, solvent mixtures *New methods*: polymer manufacture, cleaning method, opening a bottle, flying an aircraft, detecting an enemy ship
Registered Design	Registered	Monopoly	Features of lines, contours, shape, texture, ornament New and individual character	Functional or method of operation Must match Contrary to public policy or morality Certain emblems	25 years from application Renewal fees	Television monitor, arm-chair, telephone handset, perfume bottle, motor car, motor mower, electrical terminal, car hub cap, licence disc holder Fabric design, decorated teapot, jewellery, furniture, clothing design
Unregistered design	Unregistered	Not Copy	Shape or configuration, recorded, original work	Method of operation Must match, must fit	10/15 years; last 5 licensed	Car, steering wheel, book-end, gear wheel, electrical terminal, clothing design, circuit board
Copyright	Unregistered	Not copy	Recorded, original	(Fair use exceptions) Making articles to designs	70 years (after death of author in most cases)	Books, lists, tables, computer software Drawings, diagrams, pictures, sculpture, engraving, printed circuits, photographs, music, plays, films, buildings, broadcasts
Trade secret	Unregistered	Unconscionable or contract	Not known (relatively)	Employee issues	Indefinite, for ever	Customer lists, client preferences, pricing strategy, financial performance, secret formulae, product developments, research results
Passing off	Unregistered	Confusion	(*De facto*) distinctive)	(Descriptive)	Indefinite	Jif lemon, Macdonalds stores, Jaffa cakes, BCCI
Registered trade mark	Registered	Monopoly Confusion in some cases	Distinctive, not the same as another mark	(Descriptive) Honest use provisions Comparative advertising	Indefinite, forever Renewal every 10 years	Names: Coca Cola, Wranglers, Quaker, *The Times* Logos, packaging, shape of goods (coke bottle), jingles (Direct Line), smells (rose scented tyres, Chanel No 5), textures

Right	Registered/ Unregistered	Scope	Requirement	Exceptions	Term	Examples
Database rights	Unregistered	Not reuse/ extract	Substantial investment in selection, verification or presentation	Non-commercial use for illustration for teaching or research of publicly accessible and lawfully used database	15 years from completion (rolling)	Personnel records, customer list, property portfolio in formation, materials property in formation, weather information datasets
Others						Semiconductor topography rights, plant breeds rights, petty patents, geographical origins, (trade libel)

Table 12.2 Ownership of IP rights

Right	Original owner
Patent	Inventor, or inventor's employer if created in the course of special duties or normal duties and the circumstances of such duties would be expected to give rise to an invention
Copyright: Literary, artistic and dramatic works	Author or author's employer if created in the course of employment
Copyright: Sound recordings or films	The person/organisation making arrangements for the recording or film to be made
Copyright: Broadcasts	The person/organisation making the broadcast
Unregistered design rights	The author, the author's employer if made in the course of employment, or the person commissioning the design from the author or employer
Database rights	The person (or his/her employer) who makes the database: takes the initiative and assumes the risk
Registered design	The same as for unregistered design or a person who has acquired the right to apply the design
Unregistered trade mark	The person who or organisation which has generated the goodwill
Registered trade mark	The first applicant, unless the application is made in bad faith

APPENDIX 2 TO CHAPTER 12: HEI PHOTOCOPYING OF 'COPYRIGHTED' MATERIAL

The CLA has an agreement[1] ('The Higher Education Copying Accord') with UK HEIs to allow photocopying by them at a level which might otherwise leave the HEI, *and even* the person actually doing the copying, open to civil *and/or criminal* proceedings. Hence all HEI copiers should have a CLA Notice displayed near them setting out the rules. The *Blanket Licence* allows a lecturer to distribute copyright materials to students on an *ad hoc* basis, subject to the material not exceeding the greater of:

–   one chapter from a book; or
–   one article from a journal/periodical; or
–   one single case from a law report; or
–   5 per cent of a given work.

(NB A poem or short story can be copied whole, unless it exceeds 10 pages of the original text/printed format – *not* 10 A4 copier pages squeezing two or more printed pages onto each copier page.)

There is also provision for *Course Packs*, defined as:

> 'a compilation of materials (whether bound or loose-leaf) of four or more photocopied extracts from one or more sources, totalling over 25 pages of copyright material, designed to support a module or course of study, irrespective of whether the materials are copied at the start of the course, at intervals during the course, or are placed in a short loan reserve or equivalent for systematic copying at intervals throughout the course.'

The CLA's 'Rapid Clearance System' (CLARCS) will give written permission in advance for each Course Pack, charging around 5 pence per page and giving each Course Pack a specific CLARCS number.

The CLA agreement does not preclude copying allowed anyway by the Copyright, Designs and Patents Act 1988 (CDPA 1988), notably single copies for private research/study of an article or part of a book; and there are special limits for journalists, critics and libraries not of relevance here. These general rules will apply where the CLA Licence does not include certain publishers, or particular items published by those publishers within the CLA Licence, all as listed in the CLA *List of Excluded Categories and Excluded Works* to be found at www.cla.co.uk/have_licence/support/general-excluded.pdf or at www.cla.co.uk/have_licence/support/excluded.html. The electronic copying/scanning of copyright material *is*, of course, subject to the provisions of the 1988 Act.

---

1   This agreement is to be amended as a result of victory for the UUK over the CLA before the Copyright Tribunal. While the fee for the Blanket Licence will increase from £3.25 to £4 pa per student, the Course Pack system will be abolished: course pack copying is to be included within the £4 fee. In addition, the £4 will now cover artistic works. The CLA had originally sought a fee of £10.25, and *may* yet challenge this ruling of the Copyright Tribunal.

All of the above points concern only photocopying; *electronic copying/scanning* is a practice *not* covered by the CLA–HEI licensing agreement, nor is the copying of printed music, photographs and diagrams where they are free-standing artistic works and not, say, merely part of the support or illustrative material on the pages and within the text of an article or book.

Chapter 13

DATA PROTECTION AND FREEDOM OF INFORMATION

Gary Attle and Rufina Wong (Mills & Reeve)

EDITORS' INTRODUCTION

§13.1   In this chapter, the DPA 1998 is explored in terms of its impact upon HEIs. Here one may recall a flurry of headlines in September 2000,[1] when civil servants on behalf of Mr Blunkett, as Secretary of State for Education and Employment, requested the funding councils to get HEIs to release student telephone numbers so that the DfEE could commission MORI to verify HEIs' own figures on graduate employment. HEI managers politely reminded the Government that in 1998 it had passed an Act, the DPA 1998, giving ever greater protection to personal privacy. The funding councils cited legal advice that, *inter alia*, the University of Cambridge was wrong to reject the request; Cambridge quoted the Data Protection Commissioner as commenting that the scheme could operate only if ex-students gave their agreement in advance to the release of their telephone numbers for this purpose. Who won does not matter: the point is that HEI managers need to be up-to-speed on yet another legal issue.

§13.2   They also need to be aware that embarrassing e-mails can be obtained under the disclosure provisions of the DPA 1998, as used to powerful effect by the Channel 4 presenter and comedian Mark Thomas against the Department of Trade and Industry, whose Minister, according to one e-mail thus obtained, wanted allegedly 'to gather as much background dirt on him in order to rubbish him'.[2] Thus, data protection bumps up against freedom of information, as also explored in this chapter. Similarly, in the context of heightened national security following the terrorist attacks on Washington and New York in September 2001, HEIs encountering enquiries from the police (or Special Branch and similar) concerning students need to be aware that s 29 of the DPA 1998 gives exemption in terms of their complying with such requests for information in relation to the investigation of crime or the prevention of crime. In addition, s 28 provides for exemption in relation to 'safeguarding national security' but only when 'a certificate signed by the Minister of the Crown' has been issued.

§13.3   On the issue of the confidentiality of degree results, the key questions are:

(1)   Are degree results private and protected data as far as data protection legislation is concerned?

(2)   If so, has the recent legislation altered the former common law position?

---

1   For example, in *The Guardian*, 26 September 2000.
2   (2001) *The Times*, January 16.

(3)   While the marks in individual papers/modules are clearly confidential between the HEI and the graduate/student, can an HEI reveal to a third party the degree classification *without* the written permission of the graduate?

(4)   Should an HEI confirm degree results to selected 'official' enquirers with or without such permission: say, to other HEIs, to public bodies, to potential employers of the graduate (or only to the current employer)?

(5)   But, nevertheless, not confirm or reveal the degree result to, say, the parents of the graduate, or his/her former school?

(6)   If degree results are displayed on notice-boards within the HEI when first released, are they anyway from then on 'in the public domain'?

(7)   Could an individual student insist on his/her degree classification *not* being publicly displayed in this way?

(7)   In short, how does the HEI balance its duty of confidentiality towards the graduate with a wider public duty to maintain (publicly accessible?) reliable records on who has its degrees?

(9)   And what if the HEI knows graduate X is claiming to have degree Y, when in fact it is degree Z: should the HEI take the initiative in alerting the (potential) employer or other HEI?

(10) Has the HEI a broad duty of care towards the employer/potential employer which might override the duty of confidentiality towards the graduate?

§13.4   The answers to the above 10 questions *appear* to be as set out below (see Gledhill (1999), chapter 9, for a wider discussion of the confidentiality aspects of student records; see also Chapter 6 concerning references, and the Lancaster DP project website for up-to-date guidance on HE and data protection). Some HEIs will have slightly different interpretations, but almost all will be broadly aiming towards the same end result as follows:

(1)   Yes; although not (yet) tested in case-law: who anyway is likely to want to challenge an HEI being ultra careful about releasing data when, more likely, any challenge will be from a graduate annoyed that the HEI released data.

(2)   Yes, HEIs were more 'free and easy' about all this prior to the latest legislation which appies to *all* records (paper and electronic).

(3)   Yes, but see (4) below.

(4)   Yes, *providing*:
      (a)   the enquiry does indeed look 'official' (letter-head, etc – *not* merely a casual telephone call or e-mail);
      (b)   the graduate has been advised in the HEI's data protection statement issued to him/her while a student that the HEI will release data in this way, on the assumption that to do so is in his/her interests and that implicit permission has been given by the fact that he/she has cited the degree on an application form; and
      (c)   that the graduate has not subsequently told the HEI not to release degree results under any circumstances.

(5)   Yes; such enquiries would not be 'official' (as in (4) above).

(6)   No, it would be risky for the HEI to assume that thereby the degree results were now in the public domain, and anyway probably few HEIs are now 'publishing' degree results in that way and, even if they are, they will be offering students an opt-out from being named in the displayed

lists (or possibly, via a more cumbersome process, inviting them to opt-in).

(7) Yes, as in (6) above.

(8) With difficulty. The assumption being made within HE, and, insofar as the Lancaster project checks such assumptions with the Information Commissioner, is that HEIs in awarding degrees are *not* discharging a function where there is a legitimate public interest to override personal privacy. This is in contrast to the professional bodies (medicine, accounting, engineering, law, CORGI gas-fitters, etc) where we all need to know whether the person is indeed qualified/registered and hence lists are public. Perhaps the nearest an HEI gets is where it awards, say, BEd and PGCE qualifications, although it is unclear whether many HEIs will be altering their general policy about degree results to cover this analogy with professional qualifications/bodies.

(9) Probably not, unless the situation is grave: for example, a prominent political figure publicly and repeatedly making a misleading claim about his/her academic qualifications, or somebody making such a claim for clearly fraudulent purposes. Specific legal advice will be needed if this problem arises.

(10) No, the latter overrides the former *unless* the HEI (in *Hedley Byrne* fashion) is in direct contact with the employer and the employer will be relying on the HEI's response (or unless the circumstances are as in (9) above). As with (9), specific legal advice may be needed if a situation arises.

§13.5 Finally, the HEI manager probably needs to reconsider the protocols for job interviews, given that a proposed new code under the Freedom of Information Act 2000 gives not only employees a right of access (on payment of a £10 fee) to *all* employer records on them, but also gives job applicants the right of access to the employer's notes of interviews (this would include even those notes scribbled in the margin of a CV by the interviewer). The fear for the employer is, of course, that such notes will reveal potentially discriminatory comments that will in turn trigger claims and litigation – hitherto the aggrieved job applicant had to have commenced litigation before the process of 'discovery' (see Chapter 27) could be used to give access to interview notes. Moreover, the right of access will extend to those meant-to-be-helpful e-mails that often circulate after the interview itself amongst the interviewers and in which, as is so typical with e-mail, colleagues make unguarded comments as they might in casual unrecorded telephone conversations. The recruitment code, to be issued early in 2002 under the Act, runs in its current draft to over 50 pages, and is itself only one of four such codes to be issued during 2002 (others will cover employment records, monitoring at work, and medical testing). Some see all this as merely ensuring 'good practice' and hence posing no challenge to the organised employer; others see it as 'over-regulation' and a deluge of diktats.

INTRODUCTION

13.1 The day-to-day business of any HEI involves vast amounts of data being processed or used for one purpose or other. Since the 1960s and 1970s there has been an increased awareness of the need to protect information about individuals because the advent of computers has meant that large quantities of information can now be processed, transmitted or disclosed at the push of a button. The DPA 1998 came into force on 1 March 2000, replacing the DPA 1984 in its entirety. This new Act governs the way in which 'data controllers' such as HEIs can use or 'process' 'personal data' legally. The DPA 1998 imposes more stringent legal obligations upon 'data controllers' than its old counterpart, and some of the implications and applications of the DPA 1998 are considered below. It should be stressed, however, that the DPA 1998 itself is a lengthy piece of legislation and its implications and applications are complicated. Moreover, practice under the DPA 1998 is still being developed as this chapter is being written. This chapter merely skims the surface of this complicated yet pervasive area of law. See also Chapter 25 on data protection in relation to alumni activities.

SOME KEY DEFINITIONS

13.2   'Data Controller' – the DPA 1998 applies to 'data controllers' who 'process' 'personal data'. A data controller basically means an individual or individuals or organisation(s) who determine the purpose for which and the manner in which personal data are to be processed. A data controller need not have its own legal identity so, for example, a partnership can be a data controller as well as the more obvious examples of individuals and corporate entities such as limited companies.

13.3   'Personal Data' – is defined to mean data which relate to a living individual who can be identified either from those data or from those data and other information which is in the possession, or is likely to come into the possession, of the data controller. The important thing to note is that this means that the DPA 1998 only applies to information about a living individual and not to, for example, information about corporate entities. Of course, for HEIs there are obvious collections of personal data to which the DPA 1998 applies: students and applicants; other members of the HEI; staff; and alumni; as well as the categories that most businesses are likely to encounter.

13.4   'Processing' – is very widely defined and includes a whole range of activities concerned with personal data. Such activities include, among others, organising, holding, sending, storing, retrieving, consulting, disclosing, transmitting, and destroying personal data. Indeed, it is quite difficult to conceive of an activity involving data which does not amount to processing data.

Notification to the Information Commissioner

13.5   All data controllers such as HEIs have an obligation to notify the Data Information Commissioner of the purposes for which they process personal data (unless a limited number of exemptions apply). The register of notifications is accessible to the public. Failure to notify where appropriate can constitute an offence.

The data protection principles

13.6 There are eight data protection principles enshrined within the DPA 1998 and all data controllers must process personal data in accordance with these eight principles. In summary, these state that personal data shall:

- be processed fairly and lawfully, and shall not be processed unless certain specified fair processing conditions are met;
- be obtained for specified and lawful purposes, and shall not be processed in any manner incompatible with those purposes;
- be adequate, relevant and not excessive for those purposes;
- be accurate and kept up to date;
- not be kept for longer than is necessary for those purposes;
- be processed in accordance with the data subject's rights under the DPA 1998;
- be the subject of appropriate technical and organisational measures against unauthorised processing, accidental loss or destruction; and
- not to be transferred to a country outside the European Economic Area (EEA) unless that country has equivalent levels of protection for personal data.

'CATEGORIES' OF PERSONAL DATA

13.7 The DPA 1998 refers to two categories of personal data, namely that of 'personal data' and 'sensitive personal data'. 'Sensitive personal data' has a defined meaning under the Act and includes the following:

- the racial or ethnic origin of the data subject;
- his political opinions;
- his religious beliefs or other beliefs of a similar nature;
- whether he is a member of a trade union (within the meaning of the Trade Union and Labour Relations (Consolidation) Act 1992);
- his physical or mental health or condition;
- his sexual life;
- the commission or alleged commission by him of any offence; or
- any proceedings for any offence committed or alleged to have been committed by him, the disposal of such proceedings or the sentence of any court in such proceedings.

The legal criteria to process sensitive personal data fairly and lawfully are more stringent than for those personal data.

MANUAL RECORDS

13.8   While some differences between the DPA 1998 and the DPA 1984 are merely cosmetic in nature, there are also a number of substantive changes, one of the most notable probably being that the DPA 1998 also governs certain manual records, unlike the DPA 1984 which merely governed automated (largely computerised) personal data. The DPA 1998 will not apply to any miscellaneous collection of paper records but only those which are organised within a 'relevant filing system'. This is defined in the DPA 1998 as:

> '... any set of information relating to individuals to the extent that, although the information is not processed by means of equipment operating automatically in response to instructions given for that purpose, the set is structured, either by reference to individuals or by reference to criteria relating to individuals, in such a way that specific information relating to a particular individual is readily accessible.'

There has been some debate as to the exact meaning of this but it is generally understood that manual records such as staff and student records in a relevant filing system will therefore be caught.

TRANSITIONAL RELIEF

13.9   The DPA 1998 does allow for compliance with the Act to be implemented in stages. To qualify for this relief certain criteria must be fulfilled, but it is advisable for all data controllers to ensure full compliance with the DPA 1998 as soon as possible in any event. Subject to certain exceptions, new types of processing will need to comply as from 1 March 2000, most types of processing which was 'already underway' as at 23 October 1998 will need to comply as from 23 October 2001, and all specified processing of manual data which was *held* by the data controller as at 23 October 1998 must comply by 23 October 2007.

ACCESS BY DATA SUBJECTS: A DATA SUBJECT RIGHT

13.10   Data subjects such as staff and students have a statutory right of access to certain information held about them by a data controller if they make a request in an appropriate form. The data controller has 40 days from the time of receiving the valid request in which to comply with such instructions and it is, therefore, imperative that data controllers, and in particular large organisations such as HEIs, organise data banks and organisational structures so that any request can be dealt with swiftly and within the legal time-limit. Any HEI will hold a substantial amount of personal data and the information requested by a data subject may come from any or all of these. Typical examples of departments or areas holding personal data will include the academic registry, library, careers service, individual departments and the accommodation office.

Indeed it is quite likely that e-mails, if these are held under the control of the HEI, will be or include personal data. Not all personal data held by an HEI will be disclosable upon request by an individual and the DPA 1998 allows for certain exemptions, examples of which are set out below. Other data subjects' rights include the right to prevent processing likely to cause damage or distress, the right to prevent processing for the purposes of direct marketing, various rights in relation to automated decision-taking by the data controller and the right to compensation if the data controller fails to comply with certain requirements.

EXEMPTIONS

13.11 Exemptions under the DPA 1998 are rather complicated. This is because a particular exemption may apply to only one or other of the obligations or rights under the Act; while a different one may apply to all the rights and obligations; and they may apply based on the category of data or on other attributes, such as the identity of the controller or the proposed processing of the data. Certain exemptions in the DPA 1998 mean that data controllers need not comply with some or all of the obligations under the Act for certain categories of data. An example of such an exemption which is directly applicable to HEIs is that concerning examination marks and examination scripts. Personal data consisting of information recorded by candidates during an academic, professional or other examination are exempt from disclosure if such a request is made by the data subject, and data subjects are not allowed to know their examination mark in advance of their general release. Other important exemptions relate to confidential references provided by the data controller and personal data relating to third parties.

POWERS OF THE INFORMATION COMMISSIONER

13.12 The Office of the Information Commissioner (OIC) has various rights of enforcement against data controllers who do not comply with the DPA 1998. These include the right to serve enforcement and information notices, and a failure to comply with these is an offence (although the data controller in question has a right of appeal to a tribunal).[1]

APPLICATION OF THE DPA 1998

13.13 The DPA 1998 will require a review of all areas of data processing within an HEI to ensure compliance. Some of the areas to be considered include:

---

1   See para **13.16** re changes in nomenclature.

- the use of CCTV systems (see also Chapter 20);
- admissions forms;
- alumni records and activities (see also Chapter 25);
- use of the internet for personal data (see also Chapter 14);
- security measures for personal data;
- examiners' reports;
- research data (for which specific provisions apply);
- confidential references;
- institutional directories;
- monitoring of staff and student e-mails and internet access (note also the Regulation of Investigatory Powers Act 2000) (see Chapter 14);
- disclosure of data;
- record retention and archive policies;
- sensitive personal data (such as criminal records of students);
- the use of 'data processors' (to which additional obligations apply); and
- withholding examination marks.

FREEDOM OF INFORMATION ACT 2000

'Your right to know'

13.14   The Freedom of Information Act which received Royal Assent on 30 November 2000 must be read and interpreted in conjunction with the DPA 1998 since the thrust behind both pieces of legislation is for greater public awareness and openness. The Freedom of Information Act 2000 also introduces a number of important changes to the DPA 1998 and confers a general right of access to recorded information held by a 'public authority'.

Summary of key provisions

13.15   The Freedom of Information Act 2000 will apply to 'public authorities'. 'Public authorities' are defined and listed in the Act and will include most further and higher education institutions. The Act establishes a general right to information. This has two aspects:

- *the duty to confirm or deny*: any person, on making a request to a public authority for information, will be entitled to be informed whether the public authority holds that information; and
- *a right of access*: if the public authority holds the information, the person will have the right to have that information communicated to him. There are various exemptions to the right to information, some of which are absolute, but some still require the public authority to weigh whether the public interest in disclosure outweighs the public interest in maintaining the exemption.

13.16 Public authorities will be required to adopt a 'publication scheme' setting out how they intend to publish different classes of information which they hold. Codes of practice will be issued under the Freedom of Information Act 2000 and these will provide guidance to public authorities; for example, on how to respond to requests for information and associated matters and how to deal with record management for those public authorities whose records are subject to the Public Records Act 1958. The Information Commissioner will oversee both the existing regime under the DPA 1998 and the Freedom of Information Act 2000 (see para **13.12**). The Data Protection Tribunal will become known instead as the Information Tribunal. The Freedom of Information Act 2000 does not confer any civil right of action on an individual in respect of a failure of a public authority to comply with any duty imposed by the Act, in addition to the rights of action already contained in the DPA 1998, but does contain various enforcement measures which can be taken by the Information Commissioner. Many provisions have yet to come into force at the date of writing: for example, s 1 which confers 'the duty to confirm or deny' on 'public authorities' must come into force no later than 29 November 2005 or before this date as the Secretary of State may by order appoint.

Request for information

13.17 The Freedom of Information Act 2000 contains requirements for making a valid request and compliance by the public authority, including the following main points:

— *The request for information must:* be in writing; state the name of the applicant and an address for correspondence; and describe the information requested.
— *Mode of request and fee:* the Freedom of Information Act 2000 specifically states that a request made electronically is acceptable provided that it is received in legible form and is capable of being used for subsequent reference. A public authority may insist upon a fee to accompany the request.
— *Time for compliance with request:* once the public authority has received the request for information in the correct form together with the requisite fee, it will have to comply with the request promptly and in any event no later than the twentieth working day following the date of receipt. A 'working day' is defined as meaning any day other than a Saturday, a Sunday, Christmas Day, Good Friday or a day which is a bank holiday.
— *Communicating the reply to the request:* the applicant may express a preference for the mode of communication which the public authority should use. The public authority shall, insofar as is reasonably practicable, give effect to that preference and give reasons if it is not reasonably practicable to comply with any preference expressed.

– *Exemption where cost of compliance exceeds appropriate limit:* a public authority is not obliged to comply with a request for information if the authority estimates that the cost of complying with the request would exceed the appropriate limit (as yet to be prescribed).

– *Information must be 'held' by a public authority:* this does not extend to holding the information on behalf of another person but it does include information held elsewhere on behalf of a public authority.

What is a public authority?

13.18   In contrast to the HRA 1998, which applies to 'public authorities' but does not include a list of what amounts to a public authority, Sch 1 to the Freedom of Information Act 2000 defines and lists public authorities. The list is extensive and ranges from the Houses of Parliament to local government, river authorities, transport authorities, health authorities and health trusts, the Post Office, prison boards, the Pensions Ombudsman and the CRE. Of relevance to the education sector, the following bodies, among others, are specifically included:

– a maintained school within the meaning of the School Standards and Framework Act 1998;
– an institution within the FE sector;
– a university receiving financial support under s 65 of the Further and Higher Education Act 1992 (or any college, school, hall or other institution of such a university);
– an institution conducted by an HEC;
– a designated institution for the purposes of Part II of the 1992 Act (as defined by s 72(3) of the 1992 Act);
– the Central Council for Education and Training in Social Work;
– the HEFCE;
– the Qualifications Curriculum Authority.

(Certain 'publicly owned' companies are also regarded as public authorities for the purposes of the Act. Further designations may be made by the Secretary of State from time to time.)

Exemptions

13.19   In the Appendix to this chapter are listed the 24 broad categories of exemptions under the Freedom of Information Act 2000. Those marked with an asterisk are classified as 'absolute' exemptions. The others still require consideration about whether to make a disclosure in the public interest: the public authority must decide, given all the circumstances of the case and within a reasonable time, whether the public interest in complying with either aspects of the request for information outweighs the public interest in maintaining the exemption. If the public authority is claiming an exemption, it must give the applicant a notice within the 20-day period stating that fact and specify which exemption and why it applies. In respect of disclosures in the public interest, the public authority must state within the 20-day period if no decision has been made. Once a decision has been made, the public authority must give reasons for its decisions to the applicant.

Publication schemes

13.20 The Freedom of Information Act 2000 places a duty on every public authority to adopt and maintain a scheme relating to publication of information by the authority and this scheme must be approved by the Information Commissioner. The public authority may publish its scheme in such manner as it thinks fit, and must then publish information in accordance with its scheme and keep the scheme under review. The Information Commissioner may approve model publication schemes for public authorities within particular classes. The scheme must:

– specify the classes of information which the public authority publishes or intends to publish;
– specify the manner in which information of each class is intended to be published; and
– specify whether the information is, or is intended to be, available to the public free of charge or on payment.

Enforcement

13.21 The Freedom of Information Act 2000 does not confer any new civil right of action on an individual in respect of a failure of a public authority to comply with any duty imposed by the Act, but does contain various enforcement measures which can be taken by the Information Commissioner. The Information Commissioner has powers to investigate complaints and to serve 'a decision notice', 'an information notice' or 'an enforcement notice' as may be appropriate in the circumstances. If a public authority fails to comply with these notices, the Information Commissioner may certify in writing to a court that the public authority has failed to comply and the court may inquire into the matter. Witnesses may be produced against or on behalf of the public authority and after hearing any statement which may be offered in defence, the court may deal with the authority as if it had committed a contempt of court.

Relationship with the DPA 1998

General
13.22 It is important to note that a request for information will be exempt information under the Freedom of Information Act 2000 if the information constitutes 'personal data' as defined by the DPA 1998 and the applicant is the data subject. As noted above, the DPA 1998 defines 'personal data' as meaning

data relating to a living individual who can be identified from those data or from those data and other information which is in the possession of or is likely to come into the possession of the data controller. Such a request is dealt with as a data subject access request under the DPA 1998. The applicant does not need to specify the legislation on which he intends to rely. However, as will be seen below, the Freedom of Information Act 2000 does extend the scope of subject access rights under the DPA 1998.

Third party information

13.23   This is where the request for information constitutes personal data but the applicant is not the data subject. That information is also exempt if either of the two following conditions are satisfied:

–   the disclosure of the information would contravene one of the eight data protection principles or s 10 of the DPA 1998 (right to prevent processing likely to cause damage or distress); or

–   the person to whom it relates would not have a right of access by virtue of an exemption in Part IV of the DPA 1998 (for example, on grounds of national security, research and domestic purposes, etc).

Extended subject access rights

13.24   Part VII of the Freedom of Information Act 2000 (ss 67–72) has the effect that the rights of subject access and data accuracy under the DPA 1998 are extended to all personal information held by public authorities, with some modifications and exemptions. This is achieved by the provision in s 67 that all personal information held by public authorities counts as personal data for the purposes of the DPA 1998, which then cancels all the effects of that redefinition except those relating to subject access and accuracy (other than as regards personal information and non-designated functions of public authorities). Some modifications are made to the right of subject access as it relates to certain unstructured records. The DPA 1998 will, therefore, apply to *any* personal information held by a public authority, including non-automated records, even though they are not part of a 'relevant filing system' and not part of an 'accessible record' as defined in the Act. An example of that might be incidental personal information on a policy file, or in loose papers. But subject access will work in a slightly modified way in this new area, and s 68 introduces two important qualifications to the subject access right which are not found in the DPA 1998 as it stands, namely:

–   subject access need not be given to personal information which was not previously caught by the DPA 1998 unless the information is expressly described in the request. In other words, relatively unstructured personal information need only be provided in response to a subject access request if the data subject has expressly described it; and

– even where residual relatively unstructured personal information has been described, the authority will be able to rely on provisions to refuse a request *in so far as it relates to that information* where to do so would cost more than is provided for by a prescribed cost ceiling.

(Additionally, the *extended* subject access and data accuracy rights will not to apply to personnel information held by public authorities.)

Notification

13.25 The DPA 1998 is also amended so that a data controller which is a public authority for the purposes of the Freedom of Information Act 2000 is required to state this when making a notification under the DPA 1998. This information will then appear on the data protection public register.

13.26 Relevant websites on this topic are:

www.dataprotection.gov.uk
www.data-protection-act.co.uk
www.hmso.gov.uk/acts/acts1998/19980029.htm (the full text of the Act)
www.jisc.ac.uk
www.lancs.ac.uk/users/fdgmp (an HEFCE-funded project at Lancaster University on the impact upon HE of the DPA 1998, also accessible via www.hefce.ac.uk/goodprac/fdgmp/GMP154.htm).

APPENDIX TO CHAPTER 13: THE PART II EXEMPT INFORMATION

1   information accessible to the applicant by other means;*
2   information intended for future publication;
3   information supplied by or relating to bodies dealing with security matters;*
4   national security;
5   a certificate issued by a Minister under 3 or 4 above;
6   defence;
7   national relations;
8   relations within the UK;
9   the economy;
10 investigations and proceedings conducted by a public authority;
11 law enforcement;
12 court records;*
13 audit functions;
14 parliamentary privilege;*
15 formulation of Government policy;
16 prejudice to effective conduct of public affairs;*†
17 communications with Her Majesty, etc;
18 health and safety;
19 environmental information;
20 personal information;*‡
21 information provided in confidence;*
22 legal professional privilege;
23 commercial interests;
24 prohibition on disclosure.*

* Absolute exemptions.
† Insofar as the information relates to information held by the House of Commons or the House of Lords.
‡ Insofar as certain criteria are fulfilled.

Chapter 14

THE INTERNET: A MODERN PANDORA'S BOX?

David Palfreyman
(based on the text by Stephen Dooley,
Solicitor, contributed for the first edition)

INTRODUCTION

14.1 Extensive use of the internet is less than a decade old, but already in the USA and in the UK there have been libel actions for alleged defamation (between academics) – 'Cyber-libel'. In the UK, a Government Minister has 'invited' a Vice-Chancellor to 'deal with' a student allegedly disseminating defamatory material about the said Minister over the internet. HEIs have now posted appropriate warning notices by their e-mail terminals. The *Norwich Union*[1] case warns of the need to treat e-mail with great caution: here Norwich Union as the employer was required to pay damages of £450K to a rival insurance company about which Norwich Union employees had made defamatory statements on Norwich Union's internal e-mail system, leaving the Norwich Union vicariously liable for the actions of its employees (see Chapter 5 on both defamation and vicarious liability). The process of 'discovery' in litigation (see Chapter 27) means that embarrassing, defamatory or incriminating material can be retrieved from the recesses of the e-mail system even when the user thinks he or she has deleted the offending item.[2]

14.2 The ever-growing use of the internet raises other problems of copyright and data protection (see Chapters 12 and 13). What are the likely legal issues to do with the internet? What duty of care does an HEI have in terms of responsibility for attempting to control use of the internet by its students and

---

1   (1997) *The Times*, July 18.
2   In recent cases, the e-mails trawled from company back-up files were the smoking guns that won compensation for the aggrieved ex-employee: one referred to Mr X as 'a Machiavellian little sxxt and I want him out of my department'; another e-mailer (in a law Firm!) hoped that his next secretary would be 'a real fit busty blonde' and less 'trouble' than the one leaving; a third e-mail complained that a person 'behaved aggressively – these people always do'. The recent corporate disasters at Enron and the Allied Irish Bank will doubtless to some degree reveal their origins once forensic examination of back-up files gets underway, despite the hectic shredding (and presumably deleting) which took place at Enron's auditors. Similarly, 'cookies' can leave a trail revealing to the inquisitive employer just which websites the surfing employee has visited! Companies exist which specialise in, as it were, 'forensic computing': for example, Seattle-based Electronic Evidence Discovery (EED) is currently delving into Enron servers and PCs.

its staff? How can the HEI discharge that duty and avoid liability (if any)? What should it do if the Minister rings up, if thereby it is put on notice of a likely abuse of the campus internet? Are there any legal issues involved in, as the University of Oxford has done, cutting off the institution's users from accessing certain salacious areas of the Web? The disciplining of students for any misuse of the HEI's computing facilities links to Chapters 6 and 7.

14.3 Controversy at Cornell University, USA, over students disseminating politically incorrect statements over the internet, has led to a debate about free speech in cyberspace, about how much responsibility an HEI can be reasonably expected to take for such infringements, and about the HEI's duty to provide a non-threatening environment in which students can study and be protected from receiving offensive e-mail (the latter perhaps less a matter for the law and more about social conventions).

14.4 Since the 1998 edition of this book, several books on 'Law of the Internet' or 'Computer Law' (and even on, as it were, 'the law of e-mail') have emerged (see Further Reading). Farrington (1998) has little on the HEI and the internet (paras 6.77 and 6.89), but, doubtless, the next edition will have rather more. Similarly, Kaplin and Lee (1995a) had virtually nothing for the US context, but their 2000 Supplement has two new sections amounting to some 30 pages (para 4.18 on free speech within campus computer networks and para 7.2.18 on the regulation of computer network communications). John Marshall Law School has a website concerning cyberspace US privacy cases (www.jmls.edu/cyber/index/privacy), and the University of Maryland has a website concerning US campus computer use (www.inform.umd.edu/ CompRes/NEThics/). Essentially, the law is struggling both to keep up with technology and to balance the competing principles of freedom of information and expression on the one hand, and the regulation and protection of copyright and privacy on the other. See Thomas and Calder (2001) for further discussion of 'education on-line' in an HE context; see also Chapters 6 and 29 concerning HEI: student contracts for completion on-line/electronically and hence covered by the Consumer Protection (Distance Selling) Regulations 2000.

14.5 This chapter explores the legal interface between the HEI and the internet – a fast-developing area of law – and hence this chapter will inevitably 'date' faster than others in the book. Similarly, and as with employment law, no attempt is made here to provide an inevitably over-condensed version of a 500-page textbook on information technology/internet/computer law: instead, and again as with employment law in Chapters 10 and 11, we concentrate on very general legal principles and the special circumstances of the HEI in terms of the legal problems the HEI manager might encounter. This 'shelf-life' issue of 'internet law' and the fact that the extent of and type of internet use will vary from HEI to HEI means that we have deliberately *not* added to this chapter any suggested form of words whereby an HEI may attempt to limit its liability for breach of copyright, for defamation, for Data Protection Act problems, etc. We would urge each HEI to establish its own Code of Conduct or Acceptable Use Policy (AUP), and to keep the documentation under constant review. Such an AUP would cover, *inter alia*, copyright, the linking of websites, security of user ID and PIN numbers, logging out when leaving the terminal, trade marks and logos, the potential lack of privacy in relation to e-mail, defamation, the HEI's policy on monitoring computer usage, penalties for misuse, data protection, viruses, pornography and 'adult' websites, purchasing in the name of the HEI via e-commerce. Employees can be sacked for breaching such a policy, but preferably only where the HEI can show that they had been alerted to the AUP and were warned as to the possible consequences of serious misuse (for example, downloading pornography, originating or even just knowingly transferring defamatory material, excessive surfing for personal purposes, breach of data protection or commercial confidentiality rules).

14.6   Finally, for the HEI manager, all this is yet another area of legal risk management (see Chapter 24); as Stephen Dooley wrote in the Introduction to his 1998 version of this chapter:

> 'The internet appears to pervade throughout the academic community – many [surely now all] HEIs have webpages, some offer distance learning courses and give tutorials over the internet, colleagues discuss research projects by e-mail, and staff and students use internet search engines to gather information from any part of the world. A popular view amongst many of the internet's users is that because it is not located in any one country, it is an electronic wild frontier and not subject to any country's laws. In reality, however, the internet has a presence in almost every country in the world and all of these countries wish to regulate the use of the internet in accordance with their national laws. The internet is subject to more legal rules than any other structure on Earth. Consequently, an HEI manager needs to consider the risks to which the HEI, its employees and its students may be exposed through use of the internet, not only arising from UK laws but, potentially, from the laws of every country in the world. This chapter is designed to identify some of the risks which are most likely to arise and to suggest possible strategies to minimise these risks.'

DATA PROTECTION

14.7   The general principles of the DPA 1998 and related legislation are discussed in Chapter 13. Essentially, the DPA 1998 'catches' a wider range of activities than those covered by the DPA 1984. Thus, anyone holding data on anybody else needs to consider the potential impact of the combined legislation. As will be described below, perhaps the major problem for the HEI is 'policing' the IT activities of its students rather than those of its employees (although the HEI's academics may be less amenable to control than its administrative and clerical staff): just how pro-active and extensive can that policing be before the HEI is considered to be 'snooping' and itself invading personal privacy; and how energetic does the HEI's monitoring need to be so that, by demonstrating it has done all that reasonably can be expected of it, the HEI can escape liability for computer misuse by its students and (with perhaps more difficulty – see Chapter 5 on agency and vicarious liability) its employees? Certainly, the DPA 1998 imposes upon HEIs a duty to maintain IT security measures, and probably personal data on an employee or student will include that held on PCs and the HEI's server in the form of e-mail traffic.

'HACKING' AND COMPUTER MISUSE

14.8 HEIs can discipline employees and students for computer misuse, but there may also be offences committed under the general criminal law: especially, of course, where there is computer fraud, and particularly as reinforced by the Computer Misuse Act 1990 as hastily passed in the wake of *R v Gold; R v Schifreen*.[1] This created the offence of *unauthorised access* (s 1). Here the key element is showing that the unauthorised user both knew he/she was unauthorised (hence the HEI must make clear who has what access rights, and that they are not in turn able to authorise a friend), and that he/she really intended to 'hack' into the system (hence 'the system' might usefully warn 'visitors' of the consequences of illegal access). The unauthorised access offence also applies to an authorised user making unauthorised use of his/her access rights (see *R v Bow Street Magistrates Court ex parte Allison*[2]). A further offence is *unauthorised modification of data* (s 3): this covers logic bombs, viruses, etc (in *United States v Morris*,[3] a student at Cornell University infected 6000 computers at HEIs across the USA, and was fined $10K). In *R v Whiteley*,[4] the Criminal Damage Act 1971 was used against 'The Mad Hacker' who gained access to the HEI JANET network, but this was for activity before the passing of the Computer Misuse Act 1990. The problem of 'denial of service attacks', however, might be more difficult to fit into the offences available under either the Computer Misuse Act 1990 or the Criminal Damage Act 1971.

'THEFT' OF DATA

14.9 Essentially, information cannot be stolen; information and data are not property, although they may be IP and IP rights can be infringed: hence the exam paper can be stolen, as can the computer disc and the print-out; but the intangible, even if very valuable, data on the paper/disc/print-out cannot be stolen (*Oxford v Moss*[5] concerning the Liverpool University student and the 'removal' of an exam paper; see also *R v Absolam*[6]). The aggrieved party has to rely on the lesser crime of computer misuse, or pursue the culprit via the civil courts if the information is IP (see Chapter 12) and via the data protection legislation if the information involves personal data (see Chapter 13).

---

1   [1988] 1 AC 1063, HL.
2   [1999] 4 All ER 319.
3   (1991) 928 F 2d 504.
4   (1991) 93 Cr App Rep 25, CA.
5   (1978) 67 Cr App R 183.
6   (1989) 88 Cr App R 332.

Similarly, borrowing a disc and copying it is not the theft of the disc, assuming the disc is duly returned, even if it has been copied (*R v Lloyd (Sidney); R v Bhuee; R v Ali (Choukal)*[1]).

PORNOGRAPHY

14.10 While it is an offence to transmit 'grossly offensive' or 'indecent, obscene or menacing' matter 'by means of a public telecommunications system' (Telecommunications Act 1984, s 43), and while such agencies as UKERNA (responsible for JANET) close off access to certain specified sites, the main means of controlling the worst abuse of the internet by way of child pornography is a complex web of legislation (CJPOA 1994 which extends the ambit of the Criminal Justice Act 1988 and the Protection of Children Act 1978). Under relevant legislation, to 'make' an indecent photograph of a child also means to 'download' such a photograph (*R v Bowden*[2]), and being in 'possession' of such material also includes *knowingly* copying, storing or downloading it (*Atkins v DPP*[3]). Despite high profile prosecutions of former celebrities (and even of a Birmingham University academic (mis)using a university computer linked to the internet: *R v Fellows (Alban); R v Arnold (Stephen)*[4]), the criminal law is having difficulty not only keeping pace with technology (for example, 'pseudo photographs' and images recorded directly onto 'disc' rather than film), but also with the matter of jurisdiction (who enforces what against whom and where). The service provider unknowingly 'hosting' such material is probably not guilty of an offence unless and until it has reasonable cause to become aware of what lurks within its server *and* has cause to suspect that it is indecent material. In terms of detection and gathering evidence, the police may well use the controversial Regulation of Investigatory Powers Act 2000 to intercept e-mail at a server or to 'search' a server, and to oblige disclosure of any cryptographic key (as well as using the old-fashioned search warrant). An employer may monitor internal IT networks, checking for unauthorised use (Telecommunications Law (Businesses Practice) Regulations 2000[5]), but it remains unclear where the DPA 1998 fits in with respect to an employee's right to privacy. The Regulations require the employer to give general notice of monitoring, but the employee's consent is not needed. The employer's level of monitoring needs to be proportionate and applicable equally to *all* employees. Ideally, the employer might also take reasonable steps to alert the *recipients* of e-mails or phone calls from its employees that monitoring is taking place. The recording of phone calls should happen only in special cases when really needed. The employer might usefully provide a

---

1   [1985] 2 All ER 661.
2   [2000] 2 WLR 1083, CA.
3   [2000] 1 WLR 1247: hence, if unsolicited child pornography arrives as an attachment, or is accidentally downloaded, it needs to be immediately deleted, unless being kept only so as to alert the employer and/or report to the police.
4   [1997] 2 All ER 548.
5   SI 2000/2699.

separate and unmonitored phone, and perhaps an e-mail terminal, for the personal and private use of employees.

INTELLECTUAL PROPERTY: PATENTS, COPYRIGHT, DATABASES, TRADE MARKS

14.11 The law of IP is covered in Chapter 12: here we are concerned only with any special aspects relating to computer/internet use. Most obviously, copyrighted and even trade-marked (but hitherto less often patented) software is IP, and this IP is the main asset of 'the software industry': and the protection of that IP may now increasingly be patent-based following *IBM/Computer Programs* (T935/97)[1] (as the UK and EU catch up with US and Japanese law). In the UK, perhaps 25 per cent of software is pirated (cf allegedly 90 per cent in China). The HEI, of course, would never breach software copyright by purchasing pirated copies or by copying software itself (other than, usually, a back-up copy) or by breaching licensing terms re the number of users, but what if a student does so using the HEI kit? The internet service provider (ISP) is almost certainly not liable, in the sense that neither is the electricity company supplying power to the HEI computer system; the HEI might be in that its (supposed) control over student users of its IT facility is akin to the control it has over employees (even, in theory, academics): certainly, it should act immediately if copyright infringement is brought to its attention (perhaps most likely in relation to MP3 copying of music). In the case of databases, the legal protection comes from the Copyright and Rights in Databases Regulations 1997,[2] as well as (in some cases) the traditional copyright protection of 'compilations': the former is protected for 15 years; the latter for 70 years after the death of the author/compiler. A database is defined in the Regulations as: 'a collection of independent works, data or other materials which: (a) are arranged in a systematic or methodical way; and (b) are individually accessible by electronic or other means'. Hence it covers, say, the LEXIS law reports or a telephone directory. Finally, the issue of domain names as a trademark and the lengths some go to in order to protect them against 'domain name hijacking' and 'cybersquatting': for example, *British Telecommunications plc, Virgin Enterprises Ltd, J. Sainsbury plc, Marks & Spencer plc and Ladbroke Group plc v One in a Million Ltd;*[3] *Jeanette Winterston v Mark Hogarth*[4] (the latter being a Cambridge academic trying to register famous authors as domain names).

DEFAMATION

14.12 Defamation is discussed in Chapter 5. It is very easy to type something defamatory in an e-mail ('flame-mail'), and even easier to despatch that

---

1   [1999] RPC 861.
2   SI 1997/3032.
3   [1999] FSR 1, CA.
4   http://arbiter.wipo.int/domains/decisions/index.html; WIPO Case No D2000–0235, 22 May 2000.

message far and wide. The writer (student or employee) is liable for the statement, but could the HEI be liable if its computer/server was used? In the case of an employee, almost always for anything work-related (see vicarious liability in Chapter 5, and the *Norwich Union*[1] example). As for the student, much will depend on the degree to which the HEI has ensured that computer users are properly briefed concerning good practice, rules and penalties, and whether it takes appropriate and speedy action once it is put 'on notice' that there is computer/internet misuse (*Godfrey v Demon Internet Ltd*[2]): there is no need for the HEI to monitor student e-mail use (even if it were practical – and legal – to do so); but it might usefully remind all users that 'deleted' e-mails are usually retrievable from the recesses of the system (in *R v Scriba*[3] a doctor amended a patient record on his computer, but the disc still revealed all to the police and he was charged not only with the manslaughter of the patient but also with perverting the course of justice). Moreover, if the HEI decides to edit 'bulletin-boards' or 'chat-rooms' (assuming its system hosts any such), then it must do the job properly or not at all, since by putting itself in control of the content of the bulletin-board, it effectively becomes a publisher.

14.13   But is the HEI a publisher, whether it likes it or not, if it merely hosts student or staff websites on its server, besides the formal and official HEI central and departmental website, or if, as noted above, it allows users to run bulletin-boards on which others post notices/comments? By analogy with *Demon* above, in English law the answer at present seems to be 'yes' (in contrast to US law where liability could arise only if the HEI or ISP decided to exercise editorial control,[4] and in contrast to the protection which will be given to ISPs (as 'mere conduits' in 'catching' and 'hosting' third party data) when the European Directive on Electronic Commerce[5] (arts 12 and 15) is implemented in English law). As with other areas of 'internet law', there are also jurisdiction problems and enforcement difficulties (in terms of collecting damages) where, say, the defamatory statement is published in England and the 'victim' is in England, but the ISP and the authors of the words are in another country.

14.14   Leaving aside the international angle, there is a need to consider how an HEI may minimise its risks and those run by its staff and students in relation to a defamation action brought in England. It must be emphasised that what constitutes sensible and prudent action under English law may be viewed as an assumption of responsibility in another country. An HEI will have to consider what the most sensible approach is given its potential risks, but, as a rule, it is probably best to observe the law in this country before worrying about actions brought abroad. Parliament enacted the Defamation Act in 1996 which deals

---

1   (1997) *The Times*, July 18.
2   [1999] EMLR 542.
3   [1995] Crim LR 68.
4   See *Stratton Oakmont Inc v Prodigy Services Co* 1995, WL 323710 (NY Supp, 24 May 1995), giving rise to protective legislation (47 USC s 230, 1996) which may even protect the on-line computer service provider which knows of the defamatory material and still does nothing: *Zeran v America Online Inc* 129 F 3d 327 (4th Cir 1997), cert denied 118 S Ct 2341 (1998).
5   2000/31/EC, L178 [2000] OJ 17 July.

specifically with remarks put out across the internet. It does not, however, make the position of an HEI which hosts webpages or a bulletin-board any clearer. Traditionally, the law has provided that anyone involved in the publication of a defamatory remark may be sued, but it has distinguished between primary and secondary publishers. A primary publisher has no defence, even if it did not know the statement was defamatory. A secondary publisher, on the other hand, can escape liability if it can demonstrate that it did not know of the defamatory material, had no reason to suppose defamatory material might exist in the publication, and that this ignorance was not as a result of it failing to take reasonable and sensible precautions to avoid publishing defamatory material. If an HEI is responsible for deciding what appears on a bulletin-board or a website, it will clearly be at risk of being deemed to a primary publisher and be liable for any defamatory material originating from its internet connections. If, however, it does not control the content of the site then it may be able to claim to be a secondary publisher and to rely on the defence just described. Examples of sites where an HEI might be a secondary publisher include sites run by students or other individuals at an HEI or sites connected to the HEI's sites.

14.15   There is very little scope for claiming to be a secondary publisher in respect of sites which are maintained as the official HEI sites. If an HEI wants to plead the defence available to a secondary publisher it needs to show that it has behaved responsibly. At the very least, this will involve vetting postings on the computer systems about which it has cause to feel suspicious and, depending on the resources available to the HEI and the amount of traffic it has on its system, perhaps demanding some monitoring by those in charge of the bulletin-board. The HEI should also ensure that all users are aware that it reserves the right to edit material and even to disconnect users if that becomes necessary. At the same time, it should also make it very clear that individuals are responsible for the contents of their own websites and personal communications and cannot abrogate responsibility to the HEI. If this point is not made, the HEI may find itself liable for any defamatory remarks posted by any of its students or staff.

THREATENING E-MAILS

14.16   The sending of a threatening or malicious e-mail over a public telecommunications network is an offence under the Telecommunications Act 1984; it is also an offence under the Protection from Harassment Act 1997 (the 'stalking' legislation) if done on two or more repeated occasions. Irritating en masse e-mails ('spam'/'spamming') are seen by US courts as a form of trespass and the culprit sender can be injuncted; the English courts have yet to tackle this problem.

CONCLUSION

14.17 Thus, in essence, legislation to protect privacy or IP, to protect IT systems or children is attempting (and struggling) to keep up with fast-moving internet technology. The HEI as the operator and the supplier of a campus computer network is caught in the middle and must 'risk-manage' its way through a complex range of legislation and case-law. Sometimes the law of unintended consequences seems to apply: for example, the US Digital Millennium Act 2000, matched in the EU by the 2001 Digital Copyright Directive, could prevent the hitherto legal limited copying ('fair dealing') for personal use (for example, a back-up copy of software, a cassette tape for the Jaguar copied from one for the BMW Mini) by encouraging the development of 'digital rights management' (DRM) tools such as encryption and software keys while also legally preventing consumers from deploying other decryption technology to circumvent the protective devices. Certainly, in the USA at least, there is fierce debate about the balance between IP rights and creativity/ innovation in 'the information age', with the US Supreme Court about to consider the constitutionality of the 1998 law to extend the period of copyright by 20 years.

14.18 There are almost certainly ticking time-bomb e-mails hiding away in the HEI servers which one day will emerge in the discovery process of litigation or via the provisions of the Data Protection/Freedom of Information legislation: the HEI manager can only constantly remind colleagues that e-mail communication is not secure, confidential or private, and nor is it necessarily 'shredded' by pressing the 'delete' button.

Part 5

THE HIGHER EDUCATION INSTITUTION AS A BUSINESS

Chapter 15

TRADING COMPANIES

John Boardman (Eversheds)

EDITORS' INTRODUCTION

§15.1   A few HEIs have run all their commercial activities through a wholly owned subsidiary trading company for over 25 years. More have established such companies only recently and others have not (yet) seen the need to have a company at all. Some HEIs use such a company only for very specific trading activities. This chapter also explores the reasons (tax, commercial and legal) for creating a trading company. It looks at the structure of such a company as a corporation registered under the Companies Act 1985, and the degree to which it really can protect the 'parent' HEI as a statutory or a chartered corporation from liability if there were major problems and extensive damages to be paid. This chapter also explores the duties of the HEI staff, who will also be the directors of the company as nominee-directors, and whether they can be left, in certain circumstances, with personal liability or whether their personal position is always protected by their being employees of the HEI and by being directors only because they are required to be so by the HEI as part of their jobs; in which case, might not the HEI be vicariously liable for the actions and decisions of those employees via the well-established route of employer's liability (see paras **5.19** *et seq*), even when those employees are functioning as the supposedly independent directors of the trading company? Or perhaps the HEI will be deemed a shadow director and hence in this way pick up liability for any deficiencies in the management of the company? This chapter also deals with the routine demands of company law imposed on the running of the company, including the need to have AGMs, the need for meetings of the board of directors to follow a certain format, and the need to file company accounts annually.

§15.2   On the nature of 'corporate personality' and how it affords the crucial protection of 'limited liability', see the references to Birks (2000), Davies (1997) and Ferran (1999) as given in the Bibliography, together with the leading case of *Saloman (Aron) (Pauper) v Saloman (A) & Co Ltd; Saloman (A) & Co Ltd v Aron Saloman*,[1] which was more recently re-emphasised in *Lee v Lee's Air Farming Ltd*,[2] where the court firmly refused 'to lift the veil' and peek behind 'incorporation'. Similarly, *Adams v Cape Industries plc*[3] reviewed exhaustively the concept of lifting the veil and established that it will happen only in very exceptional circumstances on rare occasions, even when dealing with 'a parent company' and its 'wholly owned subsidiaries' which may effectively be functioning as 'a single economic unit' (as when an HEI owns

---

1   [1897] AC 22, HL.
2   [1961] AC 12, PC.
3   [1990] Ch 433, CA; [1990] 2 WLR 786, HL.

and operates its trading company). The shield of limited liability will remain in place unless the company is 'a mere façade' or 'a sham' involving fraud or wrongful trading (see, for example, *Gencor ACP Ltd v Dalby*[1]), and perhaps with the company being controlled by 'shadow directors'.[2] (This issue of shadow directors was, of course, much discussed in 2000/01 as the financial plight of the Millennium Dome worsened.) Moreover, as Ferran comments:[3]

> 'The plea "is it not time to know just when a company is a 'sham' and when the veil of incorporation *can* be 'torn aside?'" ... has gone unanswered [in terms of the House of Lords providing clear guidance], save that it can be gleaned from recent decisions that [even] the fraud category will be strictly confined.'

The court seems more likely to lift the veil for a State agency than for a company or its shareholders (Mitchell (1999)).

§15.3   Similarly, there is further comfort for HEI managers on two more issues as follows:

(a) *The HEI as the nominator of directors and HEI employees as its nominated directors* – Davies (1997), pp 609–610 states that nominee directors are required by law to ignore the interests of the nominator, citing *Boulting v ACTT*,[4] and *Kuwait Asia Bank EC v National Mutual Life Nominees Ltd.*[5] This latter case also clarifies that the nominator will *not* be vicariously liable for any breaches of duty to the company by the nominee director as its employee. So, the nominated HEI employee must be concerned *only* with the interests of the company to which he has been nominated as a director; while the nominator HEI, even if it cannot guarantee control of its nominee, at least need not worry that its employee will incur any liability for the HEI should he prove to be a negligent or corrupt director of the company. Yet, as Davies notes, the injunction that the nominee-director should ignore his nominating employer may not always be 'obeyed in practice'. (See also Ferran (1999), pp 159–160.) For the HEI employer, however, it is less comforting to note that the standard of the duty of skill and care expected of a company director, whether a nominee or not, has increased significantly in recent years and is now an objective test: has the individual performed as competently as the average director of a similar company?[6] Moreover, a director with special experience/expertise (perhaps the HEI Director of Finance as a nominee-director) may be expected to reach an even higher standard of competence. In addition, directors have, of course, always had a general fiduciary duty of honesty, good faith, and loyalty akin to the obligations of charity trusteeship in terms of avoiding conflicts of interest (see Chapter 4).

---

1   [2000] 2 BCLC 734.
2   *Re Lo-Line Electric Motors Ltd* [1988] Ch 477; *Re Euro Express* [2000] 2 WLR 907, CA.
3   Ferran (1999), p 16, n 71: citing *Ord v Belhaven Pubs Ltd* [1998] BCC 607, CA, and *Yukong Lines Ltd of Korea v Rendsburg Investment Corporation of Liberia (The Rialto) (No 2)* [1998] 1 WLR 294: see also *Trustor AB v Smallbone and Another* [2001] 1 WLR 1177.
4   [1963] 1 QB 606, CA at p 626 per Lord Denning MR.
5   [1991] 1 AC 187, PC.
6   For example, *Norman v Theodore Goddard (Quirk, Third Party)* [1992] BCC 14; *Re D'Jan of London Ltd* [1993] BCC 646; *Re Barings plc (No 5)* [1999] 1 BCLC 433; and *Re Simmon Box (Diamonds) Ltd* [2000] BCC 275.

(b) *The HEI as a shadow director of a subsidiary company* – Davies (1997), p 626 notes that s 741(3) of the Companies Act 1985 declares that for most of the purposes of Part X ('Enforcement of fair dealing by directors') 'a body corporate [ie our HEI] is *not to be treated as a shadow director of any of its subsidiary companies* by reason only that the directors of the subsidiary are accustomed to act in accordance with its directions or instructions' (emphasis added). So, the parent HEI will *probably* not be liable for the debts of its subsidiary company simply because, in effect, it controls the subsidiary through its nominated directors: again comforting for HEI managers, but perhaps not for the HEI's nominee-directors who could be said to have fettered their discretion and hence breached their fiduciary duty to the company by taking into account the HEI's interests. See, as a very recent case on just what a shadow director is, *Secretary of State for Trade and Industry v Deverell*.[1]

§15.4　From a US perspective, Kaplin and Lee noted in a new chapter to the third edition ('The College and the Business/Industrial Community') that: 'Entry into the world of business and industry exposes higher education institutions to a substantial dose of commercial law ... contract law is the foundation' (Kaplin and Lee (1995a), p 911). They comment that income-generating activities have increased significantly in recent years: 'With increasing frequency and vigour, post-secondary institutions have expanded the scope of "auxiliary" enterprises or operations that involve the sale of goods, services or leasehold (rental) interests in real estate' (Kaplin and Lee (1995a), p 929). As early as 1940, a US case concerned an HEI operating an airport to support its course in aeronautical engineering. A case in 1957 concerned the HEI running a TV station. Later cases concerned a laundry, a residential conference centre and the sale of hearing aids.

§15.5　Often the issue is allegedly unfair competition for local business arising from the use of State-subsidised HEI premises from which to run a similar operation. Some US States forbid publicly funded HEIs from engaging in certain competitive commercial transactions. There are also relevant Federal anti-trust laws (for example, the case of an HEI in an undergraduate textbook price war, the HEI bookshop and a local one being in fierce competition). The US laws are similar to those in the UK in relation to the taxing of profit-making trading activities. Also increasingly common are research collaboration projects, partnerships, joint ventures and sponsorship arrangements. As Kaplin and Lee (1995a) note (pp 947–948):

'Virtually all such arrangements, involving either institutional or faculty relationships with industry, have the potential for creating complex combinations of legal, policy, and managerial issues. Perhaps most difficult are the potential conflict-of-interest issues arising from arrangements that precipitate split loyalties, which could distract attention and drain resources from the academic enterprise.'

Hence great care and skill are needed to protect the HEI's interests. HEIs 'should make sure that they are served by legal counsel with expertise in the complex problems of technology transfer and the starting of commercial ventures' (Kaplin and Lee (1995a), p 948). For more on IP, see Chapter 12.

1　[2000] 2 BCLC 133, CA.

§15.6 On charities engaging in trading see the Charity Commissioners' booklet CC35 *Charities and Trading,* and the Inland Revenue's C52 *Trading by Charities – Guidelines on the tax treatment of trades carried on by charities.* The Charity Commissioners state in para 68 of their booklet that their guidance on good practice in relation to trading is based on 'our experience of cases, where substantial amounts of a charity's money have been lost as a result of ill-considered investments in subsidiary trading companies . . .'.

§15.7 Finally, note that the commercialisation of HEIs, in the UK, Australia, Canada and the USA, has led to strong arguments in favour of *and* against the trend – for example, see Clark (1998a, 1998b), Palfreyman (1989), Shattock (2000), Perlman (1988), Slaughter and Leslie (1997), and Sporn (1999) supporting 'the entrepreneurial university'; and in contrast see Considine and Marginson (2000), Nelson and Watt (1999), pp 84–98), Olivieri (1999) and Soley (1995), challenging the 'McDonaldisation' of the enterprise or corporate university. And certainly the debate over conflicts of interest, perceived or real, can be fierce: for instance, the furore at the University of Cambridge, whose then Vice-Chancellor was a non-executive director of Vodafone on a salary of (allegedly) some £35,000 per annum, over his being supposedly involved in a deal concluded by the University with Vodafone to distribute mobile phones amongst its students as a piece of corporate 'investment'.[1] On *Raising Standards and Upholding Integrity,* see *www.official-documents.co.uk* and Chapter 3 on HEI governance (plus Shattock, forthcoming).

INTRODUCTION

15.1 Trading companies are set up for a variety of reasons and can be a useful vehicle for an HEI to use. In 1996 the HEFCE produced a report on such companies. This was followed in December 2000 by a review and update. However, some questions remain. Why is the company being set up in the first place? Does the HEI have the power to set up the company? What continuing liability will the HEI and its officers have, and what are the responsibilities of the directors of the company? What are the disadvantages of having other shareholders in the company? Other models such as partnerships (including limited liability partnerships) are possible, but they are often unsatisfactory from a legal point of view and are seldom used.

The reasons for setting up a trading company

15.2 Essentially, trading through a separate trading company has a number of benefits, although sometimes the real purpose is not always clearly thought out and, in practice, it can often be difficult to know its true purpose. The benefits are listed below and are then discussed in detail.

---

1   *The Times Higher Educational Supplement,* 20 and 27 October 2000.

– *Charitable status and taxation*: it is encouraged, and may be necessary, under charity law; and it has tax advantages – profits derived from the activity may be taxable if carried on by the HEI. Although, in principle, taxable in the hands of the subsidiary, the extraction of the profits via Gift Aid eliminates the tax charges, and there may be VAT savings too.
– *Commercial*: the subsidiary company will be a separate entity from the HEI, with the benefit of limited liability and perhaps having a more entrepreneurial environment; and the powers of the HEI may not allow it to carry on the desired activity – companies can have much wider powers.
– *Tax/VAT schemes*: some companies are set up, not strictly for trading purposes, but for the purposes of tax or VAT saving schemes. However, most of the principles in this chapter would also apply to such companies, so they will be considered here.

Charitable status and taxation

15.3 HEIs usually possess charitable status either as an exempt charity or, exceptionally, as an excepted charity (see Chapters 2 and 4). The significance of their being exempt or excepted charities is that the Charity Commissioners have little jurisdiction over them and many of the regulatory provisions of the Charities Act 1993 do not apply. However, most of the information and guidance published by the Charity Commission expounds charity law in general (which does apply to exempt and excepted charities) and good practice, which all charities should generally follow. Some HEIs are charitable institutions and are subject to the direct control of the Charity Commissioners. The Charity Commissioners have stated that, where a charity wishes to benefit largely from permanent trading for the purpose of fund-raising, it should do so through a separate non-charitable trading company so that its charitable status is not endangered (see leaflet CC35, a Charity Commission publication on trading). If the HEI is not aware of the consequences of trading, it could, by such activity, be putting at risk its status as a charity for tax purposes. The purpose of trading is usually to generate income and profit, but the company must be extremely careful if it is to avoid paying tax on that profit. It is a common misconception that charities, and hence HEIs, are automatically exempt from tax. A charity is still, in principle, subject to tax on the profits of any trade activities. Although there are exceptions to this rule, they are restrictive and the conditions are often difficult to satisfy. Before an HEI establishes a subsidiary trading company for tax purposes, it should first consider whether this is actually necessary.

15.4 The activities which the HEI proposes to carry on may be covered by a statutory tax exemption contained in the Income and Corporation Taxes Act 1988 (ICTA 1988), s 505. Section 505(1)(e) provides that income from trading activity is exempt if the profits are applied for charitable purposes and:

–   the trade is exercised in the course of the actual carrying out of a primary
     purpose of the charity – as in the case of the provision of education
     training and research by an HEI; or
–   the work in connection with the trade is mainly carried out by
     beneficiaries of the charity (for example, in a workshop for the disabled).

15.5   The Inland Revenue leaflet C4 *Extra Statutory Concession* further states
that tax will not be charged on profits made at bazaars, jumble sales,
gymkhanas, carnivals, firework displays and similar activities arranged by
voluntary organisations or charities for the purpose of raising funds for
charities, subject to certain restrictions. The difficulty here is that all the
conditions of the concession must be met and there is no right of appeal if the
Inland Revenue refuses to grant the benefit of the concession. In any event, this
may not be of much help to an HEI. The Inland Revenue has also agreed to a
special *de minimis* exemption in cases where a primary purpose trading activity
which falls within s 505(1)(e) of the ICTA 1988 may include an element of
some non-exempt trading. However, the Revenue will establish first whether
the non-exempt activity can be assessed as a separate trade in its own right. It is
a difficult task to fall into these statutory exemptions. Charitable status confers
a number of tax benefits. It allows the HEI to be exempt from capital gains,
income and corporation taxes on income arising from the carrying on of the
HEI's primary purpose. Further, any receipt of money by way of inheritance is
exempt from inheritance tax, and the HEIs are eligible for other benefits (for
example, business rates relief), and are not liable to pay stamp duty. However,
by carrying out non-exempt trading directly, charitable status and its
consequent tax benefits may be lost.

Commercial
15.6   An HEI may want to devolve certain activities away from its core for
commercial reasons. This may be the case for certain money-making activities,
such as the exploitation of inventions and know-how. Setting up a trading
company could be to provide a focus for a commercial enterprise and for a
different culture from that which perhaps pervades the HEI itself. The
separation of 'pure' charitable activities from those which are essentially
commercial is sometimes seen as desirable. Using a trading company could also
facilitate the setting up of joint venture. A company structure is often a sensible
way to effect this. The establishment of a trading subsidiary will benefit the HEI
by providing it with limited liability. This allows for trading which is
considered more speculative or risky to be isolated from the assets of the HEI.
However, as we shall see, the HEI must be aware that this advantage might be
lost in certain circumstances.

Tax/VAT schemes
15.7   Many companies have been set up by HEIs as part of 'off the shelf' tax
schemes. These are established primarily to avoid tax and often have little or no
commercial justification. Many of these were set up to avoid substantial

amounts of VAT on building works, but some of the loopholes which they sought to exploit have now been blocked and the use of subsidiary companies for such a purpose is now less common.

TAXATION

15.8 As mentioned previously, taxation is one of the reasons trading companies are used. The establishment of trading subsidiaries for charities is a well-recognised practice, which is not classified as tax avoidance. There are a number of taxation consequences which are dealt with as follows.

Financing the trading company

15.9 One challenge is to provide adequate working capital without prejudicing the benefits of limited liability. However, this only becomes a real problem in the case of very substantial operations and is usually soluble. The important aims should be:

–   to make sure that all dealings between the HEI and the trading subsidiary are on an 'arm's length' basis and properly documented; and
–   to pay before the subsidiary's year end a generous estimate of its trading profit, less income tax at the basic rate, to the HEI.

Loans

15.10 Where there is a decision to establish a subsidiary, the charity will often own all the shares in the trading company. The trading company will require funding which could be made available by: borrowing from a commercial source; borrowing from the charity; or the issue of share capital. The Charity Commissioners have stated that capital required for the expansion, or even the survival, of a trading subsidiary should come from a commercial source and should not divert the charity's resources from its charitable activities. However, there are difficulties with this proposition. First, a commercial source will usually require a guarantee to repay any loan from the charity itself, so removing much of the protection of limited liability for the charity. Secondly, the subsidiary will usually have to pay a higher rate of interest on a loan obtained from a commercial source than would the charity. This will benefit neither the subsidiary nor the charity. Accordingly, the solution that most charities adopt is to provide the trading subsidiary with a secured loan at a market rate of interest. The provision of working capital to trading subsidiaries is a considerable practical difficulty, especially as they grow in turnover. All realised profits must be paid to the charity each year, so, if tax is to be avoided, they can only accumulate reserves by means of unrealised gains and frequently they have insignificant fixed assets. Sections 505 and 506 of the ICTA 1988 broadly state that the charity could lose a tax exemption already obtained if it uses the profits for non-qualifying purposes. A list of qualifying investments and qualifying loans is contained in Parts 1 and 2 of Sch 20 to the ICTA 1988. That list does not specifically include investment in, or loans to, subsidiary companies. However, a charity can make a claim to the Inland Revenue to ensure that it will treat such loans or investments as qualifying, on the basis that they are made for the benefit of the charity and not merely for the avoidance of tax. Both the Inland Revenue and the Charity Commissioners expect transactions with the trading subsidiary to be at 'arm's-length'. In other words, the investment must stand up to commercial scrutiny. This will be tested in the case of a loan by the rate of interest payable, the terms of the repayment and the security.

Extraction of profits

15.11 Once the subsidiary begins to make a profit, it needs to adopt an effective method of passing that profit onto the HEI without incurring any liability to tax. Previously, there were three different ways of passing profits made by subsidiaries onto HEIs without incurring any liability to tax:

– by deed of covenant;
– by Gift Aid; or
– by dividend.

15.12 However, changes made in the Finance Act 2000, which came into effect on 1 April 2000, ended tax relief on payments to charity under deeds of covenant and instead effected all relief on such payments through Gift Aid. The original Gift Aid scheme was introduced in 1990. It made provision for UK-resident individuals and companies to give single gifts of money to charity in a tax-effective manner,[1] but imposed the requirement that a minimum amount be given. The trading company would deduct basic rate income tax when it made a payment to the charity and pay the tax to the Inland Revenue. The charity could then reclaim the tax from the Inland Revenue, the gross amount of the payment being the charge on income. It was allowed as a deduction against the company's profits for corporation tax purposes for the accounting period during which the payment is made.[2] The Gift Aid scheme was amended by the Finance Act 2000 for donations made by individuals on or after 6 April 2000. The scheme has remained fundamentally the same as detailed above, but the following changes have been made in relation to Gift Aid for individuals:

– the £250 limit for Gift Aid donations has been abolished. Therefore, the scheme will apply to any size of donation;

---

1   ICTA 1988, s 339.
2   See Revenue Pamphlets IR 64 and IR 65 *Giving to Charity: How businesses/individuals can get tax relief*, IR 75 *Tax Reliefs for Charities* and IR 113 *Gift Aid – A Guide for Donors and Charities*. All of these publications are due to be updated as a result of the Finance Act 2000.

–   the separate tax relief for payments made under a Deed of Covenant has been abolished, and all relief for such payments is now given under the Gift Aid scheme; and

–   under the original Gift Aid scheme, whenever an individual or company made a donation to a charity net of basic rate tax they were required to present the charity with a certificate. Under the new scheme, this requirement has been substituted by the need for donors to give a Gift Aid declaration. The Gift Aid declaration can be given in writing or orally and provides for a much simpler system.

15.13   Transitional arrangements have been put into place in relation to deeds of covenant. Although from 6 April 2000, there is now no separate tax relief for payments made by an individual or company under a deed of covenant, charities will not have to get a Gift Aid declaration for payments under a deed of covenant that existed before then. The Guidance Notes for Charities issued by the Inland Revenue in November 2000 state that:[1] 'The abolition of a separate tax relief for payments made under a Deed of Covenant to a charity does not mean, of course, that such deeds will cease to exist. It does mean that they are no longer required so that a charity can reclaim tax on the donations'. In relation to Gift Aid for companies, any donations paid by companies to charities after 1 April 2000 must be paid without deduction of income tax. No declarations are necessary.

VAT

15.14   As charities, HEIs are subject to VAT administration that is extremely complex. It consists of aspects of standard-rated, zero-rated and exempt supplies, and involves questions of business and non-business activities. A detailed analysis of the nature of VAT can be found in *Halsbury's Laws of England*, 4th edn, vol 5(2), para 360. HEIs may apply for voluntary registration if their taxable supplies do not exceed the threshold, but those HEIs whose activities are either wholly non-business or wholly exempt, cannot register for VAT. This can be a disadvantage since inability to register means that input tax cannot be reclaimed. In practice, almost all HEIs' supplies are exempt and so they are able to recover input tax only on purchases for the purpose of non-exempt supplies which they are making. It is important that the trading subsidiary only carries out taxable activities, which means that it should carry on all activities for a profit. As such, all VAT charged to the trading company should be reclaimable, and it will account for output VAT on all its standard-rated supplies and on any zero-rated supplies also made by the trading company. Businesses which make only taxable supplies and recover all their VAT inputs will only have regard to the cost of an item excluding any applicable VAT. Education and training delivered by an HEI will be exempt

---

1   At para 3.16.3.

from VAT, but that supplied by its trading subsidiary will not. Equally, the HEI will not be able to recover VAT on its inputs for this activity, but the subsidiary will be able to do so. If, for a given course of education and training, there are significant inputs which are taxable for VAT purposes, it is possible (for the same net cost to the VAT-registered customer), to recover these inputs by delivering the training via the trading company. If the course is provided by the HEI, the VAT on the inputs will be irrecoverable.

POWERS OF THE HEI

15.15   As charities, HEIs must only apply property and income for their defined charitable purpose (see Chapter 4). In addition, the instruments which contain the constitution of the particular institution will need to be checked to ensure the HEI has the power to form and, if necessary, to fund the particular subsidiary (see Chapter 2), and also to ascertain which body within the HEI has the power to make the decisions in relation to it (see Chapter 5). For example, statutory HEIs will have their powers limited by the provisions of the ERA 1988. An HEI would have to consider carefully what it was allowed to do under its constitution before embarking on any such arrangement. Particularly difficult decisions will need to be taken in relation to companies formed as part of tax-saving schemes. The use of a subsidiary to avoid the problems is, as mentioned previously, encouraged by the Charity Commissioners and the Inland Revenue, but at the end of the day the subsidiary is doing something the charity often cannot. It will often be the case that there will be a fine line between what is *ultra vires* the institution and what is not. On the one hand, a training subsidiary will doubtless cause no concerns, whereas on the other hand, purely money making operations may be a problem. Particular problems will also occur with companies where the HEI does not have a 100 per cent stake. For example, guaranteeing the bank borrowing of such a company may be *ultra vires*.

RELATIONSHIP BETWEEN HEI AND TRADING COMPANY

15.16   There will often be an agreement between the HEI and its trading company dealing with the relationship between the two (see the HEFCE reports on related companies). The trading company may need to use various resources of the HEI. This can include the secondment of employees and management charges, and there may be a need for an agency or licensing agreement to allow the subsidiary to market the name and logo of the HEI, particularly if the company is not a 100 per cent subsidiary. Reporting structures from the trading company to the HEI are sometimes very unclear. It is important that these are defined so that clear lines of responsibility exist between the trading company and the appropriate body of the HEI.

LIABILITY

15.17 In theory, the establishing of a limited liability trading company has the potential to reduce the liability of the HEI. Establishing a trading company allows for trading which is more speculative, giving rise to the possibility of greater profit without risk to the assets of the HEI. If the trading company fails, the HEI can walk away. However, in practice, the position is often different and for legal and commercial reasons the HEI may still find itself liable.

Legal reasons

Three such reasons are given below – the latter two are then explained futher.

- If the HEI provides a guarantee, for example to the bank.
- Shadow directors and wrongful trading.
- Lifting the corporate veil.

Wrongful trading

15.18 If a company becomes insolvent, there is a potential liability for wrongful trading. The directors can be made personally liable for liabilities incurred by the company after the directors knew *or ought to have known* that an insolvent liquidation was inevitable.[1] For this purpose, 'directors' includes *de facto* directors (ie those who act as directors but are not formally recorded as such) and shadow directors. If an officer of an HEI regularly attends meetings or is involved in the strategic planning for the trading subsidiary and acts in a way which a director would, he may be a *de facto* director. All liabilities incurred by the other directors will thus be shared with any *de facto* directors as well. A shadow director is a person in accordance with whose instructions the actual directors of the company are accustomed to act. This may be the HEI itself or its officers – see *Re Hydrodam (Corby) Ltd (in Liquidation)*.[2] The effect of this is that in the event of insolvency, the HEI and its officers may be held liable as shadow directors for the debts of the company. The status of both *de facto* directors and shadow directors is, by its very nature, determined after the fact. Consequently, any HEI may be acting in such a manner without realising it. For this reason, great care is required to ensure that no person or body is acting in a way that could possibly be interpreted as incurring liability.

Lifting the corporate veil

15.19 The courts also have a general power to look behind the separate and independent nature of a subsidiary company in certain limited circumstances (for example, fraud). This is called 'lifting the corporate veil'.[3]

---

1   See the Insolvency Act 1986, ss 213 and 215.
2   [1994] 2 BCLC 180, [1994] BCC 161, (1994) *The Times*, February 19.
3   See *Halsbury's Laws of England*, 4th edn, vol 7(1), para 93.

Commercial reasons

15.20   In addition, HEIs may feel they simply cannot let a subsidiary of theirs fail and will support it in any event. If they let a subsidiary fail, it could damage their reputation.

STARTING THE COMPANY

General

15.21   The same practical considerations which would be required for any limited company will also usually apply to a trading subsidiary. A business plan should be prepared, which should contain details of the objectives of the company, the management structure, the requirement for financing, an assessment of risks and a discussion of the constraints which will or may be placed on the activities of the subsidiary. Consideration will need to be given to the effect which the establishment of a trading company will have on the charitable status of the HEI and whether a company is the correct vehicle for trade, rather than a partnership[1] or joint venture.

Incorporation

15.22   Every company will be different, although they will generally have the same basic aim which will be to trade. Companies can be incorporated as companies limited by guarantee or shares.[2] Companies are either purchased 'off the shelf' from a law stationers or can be newly incorporated. They are usually bought 'off the shelf' as it is often easier and quicker to purchase a ready-made company and adapt it than to incorporate a new company. Following incorporation, the company is given a unique company number which will never change, even though its name may. Once the company has been issued with the necessary constitution documents, it is ready to hold a board meeting of the directors. They should be appointed either at the first board meeting, or, if a company has been purchased 'off the shelf', directors will already have been appointed. At this meeting, a company secretary will also need to be appointed (although it is proposed to remove this requirement in the Company Law Consultation Document). The company secretary will act under the instruction of the company to file all documents required by the Registrar of Companies and keep the statutory books up to date. Failure to file these documents in time could result in a company being fined or struck off and can give rise to fines for the directors. Finally, a chairman should be appointed to run the meetings of the board. This should be one of the directors. The directors will have to decide on the company's accounting reference date, the address of its registered office and matters such as insurance and bank

---

1   For more on partnerships, see *Halsbury's Laws of England*, 4th edn, vol 35.
2   Ibid, vol 7(1), paras 103–110.

accounts, and appoint auditors (if needed).[1] The board will also need to grant service contracts to its directors and decide on their terms of employment, including remuneration. The service contracts can be awarded for a maximum of 5 years. The Company Law Consultation Document proposed to reduce this to one year, except that on first appointment the initial period can be up to 3 years. A longer term must be agreed by the members in a general meeting by ordinary resolution.

Types of company

Company limited by shares
15.23　If the HEI decides to set up a trading company limited by shares, it must decide who will have the shares and in what proportion. It may wish to take 100 per cent or it may wish to allow other bodies to be involved. The extent to which the HEI will be able to control the company will depend on the amount of shares it holds. If it holds over 75 per cent, it will have the power to pass special and extraordinary resolutions of the company and, with 51 per cent, ordinary resolutions. The effect of minority shareholdings will be dealt with later.[2] Where the HEI does not have a 100 per cent holding in the company, there will often be a shareholders' agreement. This is a contractual document signed by all the shareholders which details what agreements have been reached between the shareholders outside of, and in preference to, the memorandum and articles. This document should be used to protect the HEI's and other shareholders' positions within the company.

Company limited by guarantee
15.24　Companies limited by shares are commonly used where no profits are to be produced (for example, a charitable subsidiary or a non-profit making research association). A company limited by guarantee has no share capital. The members all agree that upon dissolution they will pay in an amount, commonly £1, by way of guarantee. They are generally a less flexible vehicle than a company limited by shares. Since 22 December 1980, the only companies limited by guarantee that can now be formed are private companies limited by guarantee with no share capital.[3] If a company limited by guarantee has no share capital, and is registered on or after 1 January 1901, any provision trying to give a person who is not a member of the company a right to participate in the divisible profits of the company is void.[4] Moreover: 'A company limited by guarantee may distribute profits to its members if there is nothing in the memorandum or articles prohibiting this. Every company has,

---

1　See *Tolley's Company Law Handbook,* 1997.
2　See the Companies Act 1985, ss 370, 378 and 379A.
3　Companies Act 1985, s 1(4).
4　Companies Act 1985, s 15(1) and Companies Consolidation (Consequential Provisions) Act 1985, s 10.

in the absence of an express provision, the implied power to distribute dividends'.[1]

Public Limited Company (PLC)

15.25   It is perfectly possible to form a subsidiary company as a PLC. This is sometimes done to give it greater credence and marketing appeal. There are downsides, such as the requirements for a greater share capital. There are also an increasing number of restrictions which apply to PLCs and not other companies which can make them traps for the unwary and reduce their flexibility.

Memorandum and articles of association

15.26   Companies have a memorandum and articles of association as their constitution. These are usually standard documents, tailored to meet the individual requirements. The memorandum states the main purpose of the company and its powers – what is and is not permitted. Although the company's memorandum could state it to be a 'general commercial company', the memorandum usually contains specific provisions defining the activities of the company. Where these provisions are not sufficiently thought out and do not enable the company to fulfil its aims, the efficient running of the company will be affected. If the company does something beyond its defined powers, this will be *ultra vires* and void. In particular, therefore, it will be vital that the memorandum provides the power to enable the company to pass its profits to the parent HEI. The articles state how the company is run, what its internal procedures are and, in particular, they will deal with members' and directors' rights and obligations. The usual changes from the standard articles will be in relation to companies with more than one shareholder and will deal with such matters as the allotment and transfer of shares, share rights and the appointment and removal of directors.

MEMBERS

15.27   Members of a company, called 'shareholders' in a company limited by shares, ultimately control the company. However, most of their powers are delegated to the directors and their real power lies in appointing and removing the directors,[2] although under the Company Law Consultation Document there are proposals to clarify the members' abilities to enforce compliance of the directors' duties. Meetings of members are called 'general meetings'. Any meeting other than an annual one (AGM) is called an extraordinary general meeting (EGM). The AGM usually consists of formal business such as receiving the accounts and appointment of auditors and directors. There are

---

1   West (2000), p 69, following at para 3.10.20.
2   See the Companies Act 1985, ss 292 and 303.

procedures for dealing with matters by written resolutions as opposed to formal meetings. If a formal members' meeting is held, the HEI will have to appoint a corporate representative to act on its behalf at the meeting. Although it is possible to have a private limited company with one shareholder,[1] it is still common for 100 per cent wholly owned subsidiaries to have two shareholders – the HEI and a nominee.

DIRECTORS

15.28 The board of directors will normally take the strategic management decisions in a company, with implementation being delegated from the managing director and the rest of the executive. There are two sources of directors' duties. Under statute, directors have certain liabilities (for example, in relation to health and safety legislation and environmental legislation). They will, therefore, be liable *directly* if things go wrong. Although it is possible to have insurance cover for negligent acts, it is not possible to get insurance cover for criminal penalties such as fines for a health and safety offence. Under the common law, directors are also under a duty to act in good faith in a fiduciary capacity. This means they should act above all in the best interests of the company. These duties are owed to the company and *not* to the nominating HEI. Difficult questions of conflicts of interest can arise in this way. The directors must also exercise reasonable skill and care in relation to the conduct of the company's affairs. Failure to do this could lead to the director being ordered to compensate the company for any loss incurred and account for any profit made. Directors have a duty to declare any interests they have in the company's contracts and property transactions.[2] The Cadbury Report (1994) gives guidelines on how directors should act, recommending divisions of responsibility among the directors and clearly laid down, effective procedures. It also recommends that all directors should be allowed to seek legal and financial advice at the expense of the company. Although not required by law, many private companies follow the Cadbury Code as guidelines of good practice. The Company Law Consultation Document proposes to include a statement contained within the new Companies Act setting out the director's duties, which a director would have to sign on appointment to confirm that he had read and understood it.

---

1   See the Companies (Single Member Private Limited Companies) Regulations 1992, SI 1992/1699.
2   See the Companies Act 1985, ss 317 and 320.

COMPANY SECRETARY

15.29 The company secretary is normally responsible for detailed compliance with the relevant legislation. This means that he must ensure notices of meetings are prepared and distributed correctly, the meetings themselves are conducted correctly and that resolutions passed by the company are filed if necessary. The minutes of all meetings must be entered in the statutory books, which must be kept accurate and up to date, particularly in relation to the Register of Directors and Secretaries, the Register of Members, the Register of Interests and the Registers relating to the allotments and transfers of shares. Failure to do this can result in fines.[1] As a board, the directors and company secretary must ensure that accounts and directors' reports are kept and filed when appropriate. The company will be required to make an annual return, stating the identity of the members and their shares in the company, together with a list of the directors' details. Further, the requirements relating to the publishing of the company name, registered office (a sign must also be displayed at that office) and company number on stationery must all be complied with. Failure to comply results in a fine.[2]

MINORITY SHAREHOLDINGS

15.30 Many companies owned by HEIs will be 100 per cent wholly owned subsidiaries. Some will have minority shareholdings held by other shareholders. This is often the case with companies beneath the main parent subsidiary. Sometimes, HEIs themselves may have a minority stake. Occasionally, the other shareholders may be staff at the HEI and this can give rise to difficult questions of conflicts of interest. It is important to understand the rights and obligations of other shareholders. Members of the company act by passing resolutions. There are four types of these – special, extraordinary, ordinary and elective. The special and extraordinary resolutions require 75 per cent of those present to be in favour. Ordinary resolutions require more than 50 per cent of those present to be in favour and elective resolutions must usually obtain unanimous consent. Ordinary resolutions are usually all that are needed, with special resolutions being reserved for more fundamental changes (for example, changes to the articles). However, as most decisions are in fact taken by directors or other executive staff, additional restrictions are commonly found in the articles or shareholders' agreement ensuring that certain decisions must have the agreement of all, or a specified percentage, of the shareholders. Minority shareholders have rights and remedies for the breach of those rights (for example, under the Companies Act 1985, s 459, they have the right not to be oppressed by the majority). This would mean, for example, that the majority shareholder is not entitled to pay out large salaries

---

1   Companies Act 1985, s 288.
2   See *Tolley's Company Law Handbook*, 1997.

to staff, thereby completely using up all the profits available for distribution by way of dividend. The articles will also deal with transfer of shares, usually with pre-emption rights giving the other shareholders the right to buy the shares of the transferor at an agreed price. Unfortunately, shareholders frequently fall out. The legal mechanisms in articles and shareholders' agreements will not make shareholders work together – at the most, they provide a mechanism for splitting up the company on a falling-out. Any structure which involves other shareholders, therefore, must be thought out very carefully.

Chapter 16

MERGERS AND ACQUISITIONS

Paul Pharaoh and Nicola Hart (Martineau Johnson)

EDITORS' INTRODUCTION

§16.1   The current system of FE and HE in the UK is one that has 'grown like Topsy'. It seems to owe nothing to rational planning and design, but everything to chance, politics and history. There is hardly a city in the country which does not have two or more HEIs and a sprinkling of FEIs. Sometimes those institutions have even grown up on adjacent sites, separated in one instance by only a low copper beech hedge and, in another, by grassed areas. It would seem extremely likely, therefore, that as financial pressures increase (as they surely will), there will be more and more mergers. These will not only take place between institutions from the same sector, but also between sectors, creating eventually the first 'regional' or 'community' universities in the UK, encompassing the complete spectrum of what is now designated as FE and HE work. It is important to note that during the last 20 years there have been many mergers. There is now hardly a single free-standing institution left from the hundred or so teacher education and art and design monotechnics of the early 1970s. They have all combined, been merged with larger institutions, or simply disappeared. This chapter is, therefore, most timely and the proposed list of questions for a due diligence report will, no doubt, be referred to on frequent occasions. The section 'Practical tips' is also extremely helpful. To it, we would like to add the following two points from our own experiences:

   –   If at all possible, do not use the term 'merger' in public and certainly not 'acquisition' or 'takeover' in public. Such words invariably cause low morale and even panic. Euphemisms such as 'partnership' are preferable.

   –   At an early stage in any discussions, agree the future of the two heads of institution involved.

§16.2   Illustrative of the gathering pace of 'co-operation' and 'collaboration' amongst HEIs (and indeed between HEIs and FEIs), all of which may lead to 'alliances', 'franchising', and 'partnerships' – if not to actual 'merger' – was a conference in January 2001, where there were case-studies given of: the Bradford/Leeds Metropolitan Alliance; the Universities of the North-East; Higher Education South-East; Springvale Education Village (Belfast Institute and the University of Ulster); the Peninsula Medical School (Plymouth and Exeter); the Worldwide Universities Network (Leeds, Sheffield, Southampton, York, with Penn State, Washington, and Wisconsin); the University of Surrey Roehampton Federal Partnership; the University of Glasgow and the Strathclyde University 'Preferred Partners' link-up; and the University of Sussex with Brighton University 'Sussex Academic Corridor'. There are also the various 'global partnerships' (UNext, Fathom, Scottish Knowledge, Universitas 21), the Oxford–Princeton agreement and the Cambridge–MIT alignment, although the much-heralded Aston–Birmingham merger to create a new HEI with a £300m turnover and 30,000 students has (for now) run into the sand: but there is now talk of a mega-merger between the University of Manchester and UMIST, of 'collaboration' between Royal Holloway and Brunel; and also of London Guildhall merging with the University of North London by September 2002 (and even of the University of East London joining in), although the LGU governors have expressed reservations concerning the financial liability of UNL and UEL. From the past, of course, there are memories of the happy union of Royal Holloway with Bedford to create RHBNC, and of the shotgun wedding of bankrupt University College Cardiff with its 'lean and mean' neighbour, the University of Wales Institute of Science and Technology, as well as many university–teacher training college mergers (at Warwick, Exeter, etc). Mergers need not always be HEI:HEI (or FEI); it can be one HEI's academic department with the relevant academic department in another HEI (for example, the recent 'merger' of geography departments at SOAS and at King's) – although is simply 'transfer' rather than 'merger' the correct term if all the academics and students end up at one site/HEI? Or it might be the merging of campuses in a town already served by two HEIs on subsidiary sites to their main sites (for example, Greenwich and Kent are thinking of merging their Medway activities).

§16.3   Illustrative of the crucial importance of the due diligence investigations is the Leeds University and Bretton Hall College merger now nearing completion, having been delayed while financial irregularities at the College exposed by the due diligence exercise were resolved.

§16.4   Finally, an example of an early alliance (which, however, has not – yet – led to merger over the following 550 years or so) is the *Amicabilis Concordia* of 1444 among New College, King's, Winchester, and Eton:

> 'Although the foundations over which they respectively preside are situate in different localities, yet they have one and the same object in view, and pursue it by the same means. It is, therefore, for the honour and advantage of all that they should support and defend one another in all causes, as well ecclesiastical as civil, in which any of them may be threatened.'

INTRODUCTION

16.1   Driven by various pressures – financial, funders, league tables, international competition, globalisation, diversification, and simply size – HEIs in the UK are looking for ways to raise their game by working more closely together, in collaboration, joint ventures or through full merger (or integration, the generally preferred description). There have been examples of a number of different types of merger and joint venture in the sector. These include HEI/FEI mergers (for a time off the agenda, but now restored, together with collaboration and consortia); mergers between chartered and statutory HEIs; the mergers of various colleges of the University of London and London hospital medical schools. There has been a proposal for a merger between two chartered universities, but this is not currently proceeding. However, a proposed merger between two statutory HEIs has been approved by the two

Boards of Governors and is set to proceed. In addition, there have been transfers of part of an institution's operation to another – for example, the transfer of its HE undertaking to a university by a college of FE and HE; or the integration into HEIs of NHS colleges of nursing and midwifery, hived off by the old Regional Health Authorities. Joint ventures take a variety of forms too: for example, a joint medical school set up between two universities; a new greenfield campus built and run via a joint venture agreement between a university and two FE colleges; a joint venture company owned between a UK university and an international partner to operate a campus of the university in the partner's country; or integration between HEIs using a joint venture charitable company to preserve the identity and status of the smaller one. In this chapter we examine the legal issues which arise in mergers and various types of joint venture involving HEIs. We explain the constitutional, statutory or contractual process by which mergers between different types of institution are brought about. We also explain the effect and implications of the TUPE, which automatically transfer contracts of employment and provide protection to transferring employees against dismissal or unfavourable changes to their terms and conditions or working lives. We explain why due diligence inquiries are worthwhile before any commitment to merger, and give some outline guidance on the content of those inquiries. Finally, we offer some practical tips for managers contemplating integration with another institution.

LEGAL FRAMEWORK

What happens in a merger?

16.2   There is a transfer of the activities and undertaking of one body to another. This will normally involve the transfer of assets, liabilities and staff. It will also normally, in the education sector, involve the disappearance of one or both of the parties as a legal entity, unless it is a transfer of only part of the undertaking. There is no direct equivalent, in the HE sector as it is presently conformed, of the purchase by a company of the share capital of another, which then becomes its subsidiary, keeping its status as a separate legal entity. However, the DfEE's guidance on flexibility in the instruments and articles of FEIs, issued in December 2000, with its consultation on changes to the instrument and articles, emphasises the availability, under s 22 of the Further and Higher Education Act 1992, of new governance models in FE, subject to the approval of the Secretary of State. These could include altering the standard categories or proportions of FEI members, so that a majority is appointed by a specified partner, such as an HEI. Similarly, the Chair and Vice-Chair could be appointed from a particular category of governor, and the quorum could require the presence of a certain number of members from that category. These new models could effectively make an FEI a subsidiary of an HEI. Such models present a means of control of an FEI by another body without, or prior to, a fully fledged merger. Securing control of an HEI by varying its instrument of government in the same way would be more difficult, requiring involvement of the Privy Council and compliance with Sch 7 to the ERA 1988 (see s 124A). But the Secretary of State has power to amend or repeal these provisions, so the same route could be available in future, with government support.

Constitutional mergers and contractual arrangements

How is the process of transfer achieved?

16.3   Depending on the nature of the institutions involved, it can be done either by contract (but only where there is a surviving body against which contractual terms can be enforced), or by statutory procedures which will dissolve the transferor and vest its assets and liabilities in the transferee. Staff transfer automatically with the undertaking in which they are employed, as described in more detail in below. There are two possible models of statutory/constitutional merger operating currently in the education sector. They are referred to in the former FEFC's Guidance on Mergers, Transfers and Incorporations as model A and model B. In model A, a new corporation is established, then the existing corporations dissolve and their property, rights and liabilities are transferred to the new corporation. In model B, a corporation dissolves and its property, rights and liabilities are transferred to an existing corporation.

16.4   In FE, the relevant statutory provisions are set out in the Further and Higher Education Act 1992 and supplemented by considerable further detail and extra guidance in FEFC Circular 98/36 (as now modified by LSC Circular 01/10). There have been a number of mergers in each category between FE colleges, sometimes involving three colleges, and more are anticipated under the regime now provided by the Learning and Skills Act 2000. In statutory and constitutional mergers in HE, the principles of model A and model B are equally applicable, although the statutory or constitutional framework will be different, as described below, and there is no equivalent of the prescriptive guidance on the merger process issued by the former FEFC.

16.5   In an out-and-out merger, both or all the parties become part of the same body which may be either an expanded version of one of the originals, or a new body created for the purpose. A merger is generally a final arrangement; de-merger is possible, but rare, as an ultimate admission of failure.

16.6   Confederation, which may be achieved by following a variety of models, brings partners together for certain purposes and functions only, so that the independent existence of each of them is preserved. By contract (or perhaps by the memorandum and articles of association of a limited company, which is a species of contract), they commit themselves to acting in common in certain respects. This represents a compromising of the power of each institution to act independently, but is not a final arrangement. Any contract should address what will happen if and when the contract comes to an end. For this reason, a contractual collaboration may be taken less seriously than a merger; and a so-called 'loose arrangement', not properly documented by a long-term contract at all, is of use only for as long as both the parties choose to maintain their interest in it. In a contractual joint venture, no new entity is created. The parties enter into an agreement saying who will do what and on what conditions. In a corporate joint venture, the parties become members of and usually are represented on the board of a new entity. As well as being bound by the company's constitution, they normally sign up to a contractual agreement. This is because operational details of the collaborative project are not appropriately set out in a company's memorandum and articles, a formal and public document, and because, under company law, the memorandum and articles may in some circumstances be changed contrary to the wishes of one or some of the members, without there being a breach of contract. As part of the terms of a contractual collaboration, the parties may agree to modify their own constitutional documents, in order to provide some mechanisms of governance which work in common. The result may be a system of federal committees or other groups, made up of representatives of both parties and having a formal standing in the governance structure of both. Their terms of reference will embrace the joint activities which form the collaboration. This can be a most effective way of making collaboration work; it will be carefully documented in a contract which may be called a federation agreement, or have some similar description.

16.7 In some cases, the existence of a new legal entity – a joint venture company – may be necessary as a condition of funding. If not, institutions should think hard about why a separate company is needed. If the members are to enter into a contract outside the company's constitution anyway, what will the company add? Some corporate joint ventures in the education sector have involved other stakeholders, such as community organisations, whose participation has been facilitated by membership of a limited company and the right to nominate one of its directors. But the construction of some such arrangements, based on commercial joint ventures, has involved daunting rafts of documentation: the company's own constitution, plus a central agreement and subsidiary contracts dealing with funding, cost-sharing and other aspects of the operation. While there is some truth in the common suggestion that the documents underpinning any collaboration are of no practical value until things go wrong, simple and concise documents should be capable of much more positive use. All the parties should feel comfortable with them, which is unlikely if the structures and the agreements which document them are over-complicated. The role of joint venture companies in the sector extends from umbrella organisations, designed for specific benefits such as joint purchasing schemes, marketing plans, or outreach premises used in common, to vehicles for the joint running of centres for the provision of education by one or more of the partners.

16.8 Many HEIs have entered into agreements or memoranda of co-operation with FE colleges for the delivery of HE courses. Such agreements should take into account the guidance issued by HEFCE and the quality assurance precepts of the QAA. The documents offered as examples of good practice on HEFCE's website are surprisingly diverse. A single university will commonly enter into a network of similar agreements with its associated colleges. But all collaborative agreements, whatever form they take, raise similar issues. Who is in control? Is the autonomy of the participating institutions compromised? How is accountability preserved and enforced? Are the proposed arrangements within the powers of the bodies concerned? Are there robust financial arrangements? Have regulatory requirements been complied with? The parties and their lawyers need to be able to give satisfactory replies to all these questions. Underlying them are some 'soft' issues which will not find full expression in the documentation. Do the parties trust each other? Do both, or all, feel that the opportunities and threats presented by the joint venture have been fairly apportioned? Lawyers cannot provide these essential components in education joint ventures, although they can preserve and enhance them by recognising the special characteristics of the sector, and avoiding the confrontational approach which is often taken in commercial transactions.

16.9   The pressure on HEIs to rationalise has already produced a number of disposals by one university, of parts of its undertakings, to another. These are contractual arrangements, probably evidenced by a disposal agreement based on documents used for the transfer of assets and personnel in the commercial sector. Particular problems may arise in relation to students of an institution who find that their surroundings have suddenly moved into different ownership. This may require transitional arrangements, under which the students of the disposing HEI complete their courses by means of resources and staff now the property of, or employed by, the acquiring HEI.

Powers

16.10   Does an HEI have power to merge with another institution? The answer will normally be yes (see Chapter 2). This chapter does not, however, deal with commercial (ie non-educational) partnering and joint venture arrangements, where the vires position is likely to be less straightforward. The power for statutory HEIs to dissolve and transfer assets and liabilities is contained in the ERA 1988. Under s 128 (headed 'dissolution of higher education corporations'), the Secretary of State may by order provide for the dissolution of any statutory HEI and the transfer of property, rights and liabilities of the corporation to:

–   any person appearing to the Secretary of State to be wholly or mainly engaged in the provision of educational facilities or services of any description;
–   any body corporate established for purposes which include the provision of such facilities or services;

- an HEFC; or
- an FEFC.

16.11 There can be no such transfer without the consent of the recipient, and, if it is not an educational charity, any property transferred must be held on trust, to be used for exclusively educational charitable purposes. Before making an order, the Secretary of State must consult with the HEI which is to be dissolved, and with the HEFCE. The Secretary of State's order may also provide for the transfer of staff, although TUPE will probably operate to transfer them automatically in any case. The Secretary of State's order under s 128 takes the form of a statutory instrument. Therefore, it has to be laid before Parliament for the requisite amount of time, and sufficient time must be allowed before that for the DfEE to ensure that the required consultation is carried out. In practice, the support of the relevant funding council will be critically important, as will timely liaison with the DfEE, but even so the formalities are considerably less onerous than for a merger in the FE sector.

16.12 A chartered institution will normally have power to merge with another institution, or to take over part of one, whether by contract or through a constitutional process. In a model B merger (where one institution is dissolved and its assets are transferred to the other), it will be relatively straightforward for the recipient to provide for the integration of the other into it. The charter may specifically provide for this (many include a power 'to enter into any agreement for the incorporation in the University of any other institution and for taking over its rights, property and liabilities and for any other purpose . . .'); but even if it does not, the powers of chartered institutions should be sufficiently wide (see Chapter 2) to allow the integration of another HEI. For the chartered institution which is to be dissolved, and its assets transferred to the other body, the process will be more complex, as dissolution will normally require Privy Council consent under the terms of the charter, and a local Act of Parliament to effect the transfer. A local Act is required because the general HE legislation provides for neither the creation of statutory HEIs (as opposed to designated institutions), nor for the transfer of the engagements between chartered bodies. A model A merger between two chartered institutions is likely to require, first, the agreement of the two bodies concerned; secondly, Privy Council consent to their dissolution, and creation of a new constitution for the successor body; and, thirdly, a local Act of Parliament to transfer the assets to the new institution and repeal legislation under which the original bodies were constituted. In both cases, all property, assets and liabilities will be transferred by the order or Act. The benefit of contracts, like the ownership of property, is, therefore, transferred by operation of law; there is no novation, or assignment requiring the approval of the other party to the contract. However, it is certain that security and financing will have to be renegotiated with lenders, as dissolution will be an act of default, as defined in the facilities letter or security document. Some other contracts may contain a similar provision.

Contractual mergers and joint ventures

16.13   Both chartered and statutory institutions will normally have the power
to enter into contractual mergers or joint venture arrangements. The charter
will normally enable the institution 'to enter into engagements and to accept
obligations and liabilities in all respects in the same manner as an individual
may manage his own affairs'. This would be sufficient to allow a chartered
institution to enter into a contractual merger (with the implications of
contractual obligations and liabilities) or a joint venture involving, for
example, the setting up of a jointly owned limited company, and entering into a
shareholders' agreement. Again, even in the absence of a specific power, the
very broad powers of chartered institutions to do anything, not expressly
forbidden by the charter, which an individual could do, would allow it to enter
into this kind of arrangement. Under s 124 of the ERA 1988, an HEI has power
to do anything which appears to it to be necessary or expedient in connection
with its principal powers (to provide HE, to provide FE and to carry out
research and publish the results of the research or related material), including
to enter into contracts[1] and to form or take part in forming a body corporate for
the purposes of carrying on activities undertaken in exercise of its principal
powers.[2] In a contractual merger, or joint venture, as noted above, two (or
more) bodies which are to survive the process will negotiate terms and
exchange warranties and indemnities, which will continue to be enforceable
after merger. A joint venture may be set up purely by agreement between the
parties, or by means of a jointly owned limited company, the management and
governance of which is laid down in a shareholders' agreement between the
parties. The memorandum and articles of association of a limited company
themselves constitute a contract between its members, but because this
information is in the public domain, and because of the statutory rules which
apply to amendment of the memorandum and articles, the parties often choose
to enter into a private contract as well, in the form of a shareholders' agreement.
In theory, a third legal means of establishing a joint venture would be by
establishment of a partnership, under the Partnership Act 1890. The various
disadvantages associated with this route (in particular the unlimited joint and
several liability of partners) mean that it is hardly ever used. The word
'partnership' is frequently encountered in the education sector, but rarely
carries its legal meaning.

16.14   In a contractual merger, the agreement between the parties will set out:

−   the basis on which the undertaking is to change hands;
−   when that will happen;
−   precisely what will be transferred in terms of assets, liabilities and staff;
−   what residual liabilities and claims (if any) can be fixed on the transferor;
    and

---

1   ERA 1988, s 124(2)(e).
2   Ibid, s 124(2)(f).

– if appropriate, the price to be paid (which could take the form of payment and/or assumption of liabilities of the undertaking, or some other consideration).

16.15 In a contractual merger or joint venture, the institutions will have the ability to pick and choose: to divide and select property, assets, liabilities and staff (subject to TUPE obligations and risks). Property will have to be formally conveyed, rather than transferring automatically, and contracts may have to be novated or assigned. A contractual relationship should be straightforward and flexible, defining the rights of the parties both as between themselves and with third parties. As no new legal entity is created, the agreement must make clear who is responsible for what, possibly adding cross-indemnities between the parties.

16.16 The joint venture company limited by shares is the most common vehicle for commercial operations. This route creates a separate legal entity, which can enter into arrangements with third parties in its own right. The participants can structure an appropriate arrangement between themselves by using ordinary, preference or non-voting shares, and loans of various types. Dealing with the shares presents a means of changing the ownership structure without necessarily altering the role of the company. The members are not themselves responsible for the liabilities of the company, unless required to give a personal guarantee, for example, by a lender or a landlord. However, this structure may not be appropriate in full in most education joint ventures, where the preservation of the charitable status of the participants, and their activity in common, will be an important factor. The appropriate structure for a company with charitable objects is a company limited by guarantee, not having a share capital. While still a distinct legal entity with limited liability, such a company has a simple membership structure, comprising the guarantors, which cannot be used to represent ownership in the same way as a share structure. A shareholders' agreement, or an agreement between the members of a guarantee company, will normally set out:

– the background to the project and the means of establishing it;
– whether the participants agree not to enter into similar arrangements elsewhere;
– how disagreements should be resolved;
– how directors will be appointed;
– quorum and voting arrangements; and
– what will happen when the joint venture comes to an end.

Making proper inquiries

16.17 HEIs proposing to enter into mergers will wish to commission a feasibility study at an early stage, followed by due diligence inquiries before the final commitment is made. Even in non-contractual mergers, where there is no structural legal consequence of due diligence and disclosure (since warranties could not be enforced later on), the governing bodies of both institutions will be under an obligation to satisfy themselves that the merger is well-founded and in the interests of their institution. Due diligence inquiries form part of this process, as described more fully in paras **16.21** *et seq.*

External approval

16.18   The final piece of the jigsaw to be included in constructing the basic legal framework is the regulatory overlay. In higher education there is very little, compared with the detail laid down in circulars issued by the former FEFC. In practice, before a merger takes place in the HE sector, funding council approval is likely to be needed and there will have to be consultation with the DfEE, and with the Privy Council in the case of chartered institutions. Consultation with trades unions or employee representatives, well in advance, is prescribed by TUPE. There is likely to be consultation with students and students' unions, and with community and partner bodies (such as NHS trusts). Consultation with other bodies, such as local councils, and with local Members of Parliament may be politic at least, even if it is not a formal regulatory requirement.

TUPE

16.19   TUPE is a statutory instrument which protects the employment rights of staff on the transfer of a business ('undertaking'). It applies to the transfer of a business or part of one as a going concern. Deciding whether TUPE applies in a given situation can be complex and requires expert advice.[1] TUPE:

 – is not limited to commercial operations;
 – will apply on a merger of two institutions;
 – can (but may not) apply on the contracting out (or contracting in) of services; and
 – is unlikely to apply to a simple transfer of assets.

16.20   Staff employed by the transferor of the business will automatically transfer to the transferee, with their continuity of employment, statutory rights, contract terms and general conditions of employment intact. All duties and liabilities of the transferor in connection with staff and their contracts and conditions transfer to the transferee. If an employee of either party is dismissed as a result of the transfer (whether before or after it), his dismissal will be treated as automatically unfair, unless it was for an 'economic, technical or organisational reason' entailing changes in the workforce of either party. Changes made to terms and conditions of employment after a transfer, even with an employee's agreement, may be ineffective and unenforceable. Current case-law suggests that this may be the case up to 12 months after the date of the

---

1   The case of *University of Oxford v Humphreys* (1999) unreported, 19 December was about how TUPE applied when Oxford transferred school examinations activities to Cambridge.

transfer. At some future date, yet to be announced, an amendment to TUPE will provide for the transfer of occupational pension schemes, which are presently excluded from protection. Collective agreements in force between the transferor and recognised trade unions in respect of transferring employees will transfer to the transferee, who may be deemed to recognise trade unions recognised by the transferor in respect of transferring employees. TUPE imposes obligations on employers to inform and consult, in advance of a transfer, representatives of recognised trade unions. Employment tribunals can award compensation for failure to comply with TUPE. It is not possible to contract out of the effects of TUPE by agreement, whether between transferor and transferee, or with staff.

16.21 TUPE will apply in the case of both model A and model B mergers, in transfers of part, and in joint ventures when employees are transferred into a new body – for example, a jointly owned limited company. In a model B merger, employees of the dissolving institution will transfer to the surviving (acquiring) institution. In contractual mergers, the employees engaged in the undertaking or part which is being transferred will move across with it to the transferee institution, once again with their contractual and statutory rights intact. However, unlike the situation in a statutory or constitutional merger, the two parties in a contractual merger may carve up between them the potential liabilities in respect of employment rights. The transferee may seek indemnities from the transferor against the costs of defending any unfair dismissals as a result of the transfer, for example. In a statutory or constitutional merger, there is no choice but for the acquiring institution to accept either the employees on their existing terms, or the liabilities associated with terminating employment or changing those terms.

Due diligence

16.22 Due diligence is a process of systematic inquiry into the activities of a proposed merger or acquisition partner. The governors of an institution are bound to exercise due diligence, or reasonable care, before committing it to the transaction. They must be satisfied that the merger is well founded. This does not necessarily mean that the merged institution will not have to face problems; but it does mean that risk should be identified in advance, and planned for, rather than taking anyone by surprise after the merger has become a commitment. Thorough due diligence absorbs a lot of expensive resources, and will only be undertaken once a clear understanding in principle has been reached between institutions. In a well-organised merger, due diligence will have been preceded by a detailed feasibility study, which is likely to flag up all or most of the areas to be inquired into at the due diligence stage. Usually, therefore, due diligence is undertaken more as a means of providing necessary reassurance, than in anticipation of dramatic new discoveries; but these are sometimes made. In a commercial transaction, due diligence is an integral part of the process leading to completion of a contract. The buyer will be seeking to protect its position by obtaining warranties and indemnities from the seller, which in turn will be seeking to minimise these commitments by disclosing its affairs in a way which prevents the buyer from complaining about them afterwards. The very purpose of due diligence is to bring problems up front, and to avoid unpleasant surprises later, but, if the worst comes to the worst, the buyer may have a claim against the seller for breach of indemnity or warranty. The process of due diligence may influence not only whether the transaction goes ahead at all, but the purchase price and other terms of the deal.

16.23 Much of this has no application in education mergers, which, as we have seen, are often undertaken on the basis of a constitutional or statutory process. In such cases there will be no contract, price, warranties or indemnities. One or both institutions will cease to exist, so there can be no redress against the other or either. While the absence of a contractual context does mean that due diligence in education mergers may operate in limbo, it also means that the advance identification of risk is even more important. Unanticipated loss, either direct or in terms of diversion of resources, will not be recoverable afterwards, and it is highly unlikely that the merger can be reversed. In a commercial transaction, there would be a clear conflict of interest preventing the same professional advisers from undertaking due diligence inquiries for, or about, more than one party to the same transaction, and in the relatively small number of HE mergers which have taken place so far, institutions have tended to follow this model. In FE mergers, however, it has become usual for the same advisers to undertake due diligence on behalf of both parties. This recognises the fact that, when institutions have identified sufficient common ground to agree a merger in principle, both governing bodies must exercise due diligence in justifying it. Their approach is not, or should not, be adversarial; both have a common interest in making the merger product successful. Most merger proposals which reach the due diligence stage are eventually completed. That is, of course, the beginning, not the end, of the very considerable task of establishing a successful combined institution. Due diligence reports should be useful at the beginning of the implementation stage in scoping the areas which require attention in the process of harmonisation or rationalisation. Even where a merger does not proceed after due diligence, the exercise will not have been entirely wasted. Few organisations would otherwise obtain such a comprehensive health check on all their activities, much of it quite different from the normal internal audit regime.

Legal due diligence

Constitution

16.24 Legal due diligence normally starts with an examination of constitutional documents: what kind of organisation is being looked at, and is it in compliance with its regulatory regime? So the presentation of information will vary according to whether the subject is a chartered body, a statutory corporation, a limited company or a trust. Many are likely to have charitable status, but to be exempt from registration with the Charity Commission. In the case of a company, extensive information is available from Companies House, and filing requirements will be checked. There may be associated trusts, or subsidiary companies. It is useful for lawyers undertaking due diligence to read minutes of the governing body, and its main committees, for at least the last two years. They will indicate what has been seen as matters of concern, and can often be helpfully cross-referenced to other information provided. Occasionally, they will prompt inquiries in areas where no information has at first been made available.

Property
16.25 As land and buildings are the major assets of most institutions, there will be a check on title documents, linked to inquiries with the Land Registry and other agencies. Lawyers should be encouraged not to produce a report which details every aspect of the title at equal length, but to concentrate on what may be of practical significance, particularly in terms of restrictions on use or disposal, and planning considerations. Sites originally provided by Victorian benefactors may be affected by reverter provisions if they cease to be used for educational purposes. If an institution has residential accommodation, the form of occupational licence should be checked. The report will also cover the terms of security over property granted to a bank or other lender, and the associated facility letter. For the reasons noted above, such arrangements are likely to require renegotiation if the merger involves dissolution of the borrower.

Employment
16.26 Because of the effect of TUPE, employees are likely to transfer subject to their existing terms of employment. It is, therefore, essential to establish what these are, and to identify early on differences between the basis of employment of the respective institutions. As explained in paras **16.18** *et seq*, harmonisation of terms must be treated as a separate and later process, if claims of unfair dismissal are to be avoided. Due diligence will also look at pension entitlement, and current or likely disputes between an institution and its employees.

Litigation and compliance with laws
16.27 An institution will certainly be interested if a potential merger partner is or has been involved in criminal prosecution or civil litigation of any type, or in circumstances which may result in such proceedings, whether involving its own students or third parties. Inquiries will also be made about registrations and regulatory regimes, extending from data protection requirements, through liquor licensing of restaurant or union premises, to registration of a children's nursery.

Contractual commitments

16.28 Management of educational institutions, when asked for evidence of its contractual commitments, can sometimes produce meticulously organised documentation immediately. Others struggle to assemble the information, and may then find that the institution itself does not have proper evidence of all its contractual arrangements. As with all other due diligence inquiries, a sense of proportion must be applied here. Small value contracts, terminable at any time or with a short duration, will not prejudice a successful merger, even if their terms are disadvantageous. On the other hand, a catering contract involving a capital commitment by the contractor may have a substantial value and a period of many years, and even a contract for the hire of photocopiers may have expensive provisions for early termination. A suitable formula for identifying and reporting on significant contracts needs to be agreed.

Insurance

16.29 A schedule of claims paid or pending will be required, and the schedule of cover and values insured will usually be included.

Intellectual property

16.30 Any institution involved in research is likely to have agreements with third parties as to the ownership of IP in the results, and registered or pending patents or trade marks. Ownership of IP rights as between an institution and its employees is usually covered by employment contracts. Teaching materials may be used under licence from a third party, or be licensed to others by the institution.

Environmental due diligence

16.31 The theory of current legislation on clean-up costs for contaminated land is that the polluter pays; but if the polluter cannot be found, or no longer exists, then the owner of land may end up paying instead. It has, therefore, become increasingly common for commercial property transactions to be preceded by the obtaining of a specialist report on geological and soil conditions. Even buildings which have been in educational use for more than a century may have been constructed on something nasty.

Accountancy due diligence

16.32 The first question to be asked in any HE merger should be whether the educational mission of the institutions involved will be enhanced by their combining together. The second, inevitably, is whether the figures add up. In FE mergers, this is sometimes the first question, where either or both of the participants is in acute financial difficulty. Clearly, putting together two cash-strapped organisations is likely to produce only a larger cash-strapped organisation, unless either substantial site rationalisation or other savings are identified, or more money will be available to the merged entity from external sources. Financial due diligence takes as its starting point publicly available statements and the results of audit procedures, and will comment on performance and forecasts in the light of the type of provision being made, the student base and the nature of competition. The accuracy of future forecasts will be critical, as affected by risks in the merger. The reasonableness of assumptions will be assessed, sometimes by reference to funding agencies. Capital expenditure forecasts and the basis of valuation of assets will be re-assessed. The real value of accountancy due diligence does not lie simply in a set of comments on published or forecast figures, but anchors consideration of a merger to what will really matter in making it work. Potential deal breakers should have been identified at feasibility stage. By the time of due diligence, one or more options for dealing with each of these should be apparent, providing governors with a checklist of conditions which must be met if a successful merger is to proceed.

BIG ISSUES TO WATCH OUT AND PREPARE FOR

Constitution and structure

16.33   The institutions must be able to reach agreement on the basic question of how the proposed merger is to be structured – particularly whether it is to be by a double dissolution and transfer of assets to a new institution, or by the dissolution of one and transfer of assets to the other. This can be controversial. So can the name of the merged institution.

Timescale

16.34   The constitutional process for achieving merger will have an impact on the overall timescale. In a statutory merger, time will have to be allowed for the Secretary of State's Order to lie before Parliament, which will require co-ordination with the parliamentary timetable. In a merger between chartered institutions involving a private Act of Parliament, a petition with a draft Bill (in a form approved by the Privy Council) has to be lodged with Parliament in November, before the Bill goes through three readings in each House, and committee stages. Again, the parliamentary timetable needs to be borne in mind. Achieving formal constitutional merger can take 2 to 3 years from start to finish.

Transitional issues

16.35   Because of the likely fairly lengthy timescale, institutions will have to think well ahead on matters such as the contents of prospectuses (which are printed a long time in advance of the courses, facilities and services they advertise). Whose degree will present and prospective students receive? Prospective students should be told if it is likely that it will be a degree of an institution other than of the institution they are applying to. If the institution's degrees are validated by a university other than the one with which it is proposed to merge, agreement will have to be reached between the current validating institution and the new partner institution to change the validating arrangements – unless the validating agreement has convenient termination provisions. Students may complain about changes of this kind being imposed unilaterally. The merging institutions may consider moving in together before the formal constitutional marriage is consecrated, in order to avoid merger blight over a long time period. This kind of arrangement should be properly documented by a formal agreement between the two institutions.

The top job

16.36   As in the corporate sector, mergers in the education sector can founder on failure to reach agreement about which of two principal officers will hold the top job in the new institution. Even where a smaller institution (for example, College of Health, HE College) merges into a large university, in theory the Principal/Chief Executive would be entitled under TUPE to transfer with his status (as Principal) intact. Equally, the Principal of the larger institution is fully entitled to retain his status. Agreement must be reached to resolve this situation. Negotiations can be like the irresistible force meeting the immoveable object. It is essential that this issue is identified and dealt with early on.

Redundancies and reorganisation

16.37   As noted, here TUPE imposes significant obligations, and limitations on the freedom of employers involved in a merger to dismiss or change terms and conditions. It is essential to have a properly planned structure in place to enable the merging institutions to reach, and justify, fair decisions on redundancies, or where two jobs will become one (for example, Finance Director).

Staff consultation

16.38   TUPE obliges the institutions involved in merger to commence consultation with recognised trades unions or staff representatives at an early stage. Information also has to be provided. Recognised unions in the education sector will expect to be involved. Failing to commence formal consultation soon enough, or failing to release sufficiently detailed information about what is planned in relation to employees (particularly in relation to redundancies and reorganisations) is likely to lead to an employment tribunal claim by the unions. This is not only potentially expensive in terms of possible compensation payable, but can mean a significant distraction from the merger process and a spanner in the works of smooth consultation/information.

Pensions

16.39 The transfer of occupational pension rights on merger is likely to be a major issue. Unions and employees will be concerned that individual rights are protected and transferred. Institutions will be concerned to identify the scale of liabilities they will be taking on – for example, is there any possibility that the pension scheme of a transferring institution will turn out to be in deficit to a significant sum? In contractual mergers, agreement may be reached between the parties for the transferor to indemnify the transferee against pension liabilities above a certain level. The wholesale transfer of pension schemes can take a long time and the issue should be addressed at the early stages of the process.

Banking and security issues

16.40 Loans and security held by lenders will almost certainly have to be renegotiated as a result of merger. They may be retendered from scratch. The terms may be less or more favourable. Both institutions need to understand the financial implications of any such renegotiation at an early stage.

Due diligence

16.41 A thorough due diligence exercise is recommended. It should not only expose potential liabilities, but it will also be of considerable assistance in smoothing the operational process of bringing two institutions together.

Feasibility

16.42 Due diligence work should not reveal any show-stoppers. Those issues should have been brought out at an earlier stage through a thorough feasibility review, which is not the same as due diligence. The institutions should begin by investigating both academic and financial feasibility at a fairly high level; and also answer the question 'Why merge?' It should be at this stage that potential show-stoppers are identified – such as a clash over who is to head the merged institution, or a pension fund on one side in severe deficit, or bank security which cannot be renegotiated except on extremely penal terms. Making the effort to produce a strategic analysis addressing the big issues at this stage will avoid unnecessary grief and wasted time later, especially if the answer to the question 'Why merge?' is negative.

Chapter 17

FRANCHISING

Nigel Sternberg and Stephen Roper (Eversheds)

EDITORS' INTRODUCTION

§17.1 At one time, the commercial concept of franchising was confined primarily to fast-food outlets; now we are seeing some HEIs allowing other HEIs and FEIs to deliver their academic courses (or parts of them) not only elsewhere in the UK but also in other countries. This process is as commercial as expanding the chain of fast-food outlets, but the delivery of the product is somewhat more complex, as is the measurement of the quality of the product. This chapter explores the legal relationship between the franchisor HEI and the franchisee institution. Just what is being franchised and under what terms and conditions? How does the franchisor control quality of delivery? In the event of dissatisfaction, against which institution might the unhappy student have legal redress? If there is such a complaint (or even a dispute between the two institutions), and the student and 'parent' HEI are in different countries, under the legal system of which country is the matter to be addressed? Indeed, is there a choice to be exercised by one party or another? If staff are being exchanged, which institution is responsible for the care and the good conduct of such staff when not in their employing HEI? It is quite probable that some of the franchising arrangements so far reached between institutions (especially between institutions in different countries) have not adequately dealt with these matters. It is also probable that they are based on the initial surge of enthusiasm and 'an exchange of letters'. What then happens in the event of the two institutions falling out?[1] What contractual terms might the law assume within ('imply' into) the non-existent formal contracts?

§17.2 *The Times Higher Educational Supplement* on 14 June 1996, contained the headline (concerning difficulties at Swansea Institute of Higher Education): 'Franchise row rages at Swansea'. The story concerned the problem of balancing entrepreneurial endeavour with the careful maintenance of quality control procedures, especially at a distance from the home HEI. Indeed, a Swansea MP referred the issue at the Swansea Institute to the NAO, and the principal of the Institute resigned over the matter (as did two of the governors). The PAC (1997) Report identified 'a breakdown in both governance and management', while at the same time an HEFCW audit report raised concern over a lack of control of overseas activities: for example, travel costs

---

1   See, for example, *East London College v University of East London* (2001) unreported, 15 February, QBD, re LLB teaching by ELC in Israel as franchised and 'verified' by UEL. ELC could not get an injunction forcing UEL to continue the 'co-operation' agreement which UEL was bringing to an end, leaving a problem in respect of a batch of students on a precursor course and not yet registered for the LLB.

for visits abroad as a substantial chunk of any fee income being achieved, and 'an unknown stock' of blank degree certificates being held by one of the Institute's foreign agents. The Report floats the concept of an HE Ombudsman. Recently there have also been problems at Derby University, involving NATFHE complaints about franchising standards and a QAA investigation. In the case of the University of Hull the NAO carried out an investigation into overseas operations, identifying 'clear weaknesses' in the control of finances within the School of Management, and 'an inadequate management response to the weaknesses', as well as there being 'weak' controls over the academic standards at overseas franchises (NAO (1999)). Also, the QAA has expressed concern about HEIs' academic activities in Spain, with the result that one has since pulled out of its collaboration with a Spanish college, while another acknowledged that its relationship with its Spanish collaborator had been too reliant on good faith and informality.

§17.3 Similarly, a further article[1] told of the franchising of an MBA from a UK university to a German private school. Despite careful vetting mechanisms and strong controls on the part of the UK HEI, the whole thing was an educational disaster. A *Financial Times* article, on 14 October 1996, explored the 'unfettered proliferation' of MBA courses in South-east Asia, offered by UK HEIs through partnerships and franchising which 'by common agreement are substandard'. The article talks of 'bad apples in the barrel [which] will rot the whole system', and notes that auditors from the HEQC had visited the region. The British Council was also concerned at the potential damage being done to the image of UK HE.

§17.4 In November 1995, the CVCP and the HEQC each published complementary codes of practice aimed at helping HEIs maintain and reinforce the standards of service they offer to international students (whether studying at the HEI itself or abroad under partnership/franchise operations). The CVCP's code (1995) concentrates on the HEI at home. The HEQC's code (1995) concentrates on collaboration with institutions abroad. Even so, the QAA very recently found fault with both Bournemouth University and, to a much lesser extent, Middlesex University, concerning their quality control arrangements within franchising packages in, respectively, Cyprus and Egypt.

WHAT IS FRANCHISING?

17.1 Franchising is a much-used term within education. It is also loosely used, embracing a variety of activities. It can mean franchising in the sense which retailers would understand, or something more akin to sub-contracting, or simply the transfer of IP in teaching materials. It can refer to operations within the UK, and also across the world. The essence of franchising within education is some form of collaboration or co-operation between two or more institutions, in order to facilitate the delivery of education or training to students. For ease of reference, two basic models of franchising will be used as

---

1   In *The Times Higher Educational Supplement*, 26 July 1996.

the basis for discussion in this chapter. These models are simplified, and the distinctions made between the two may not always be valid. Nevertheless, there is a practical value in identifying the following types of franchising.

UK based HE/FE franchise

17.2 Under an arrangement such as this,[1] an HEI (the franchisor) enrols a cohort of students as it would any other, but arranges for the delivery of teaching to those students to be performed by and at an FE College (the franchisee). The arrangement might not apply to all the teaching which the students are to receive under their arrangement with the HEI. Typically, the FE College may be responsible for the delivery of the first year of a 3-year course.

International franchise

17.3 In this model,[2] a UK HEI (the franchisor) enters into an arrangement with an institution in another country (the franchisee), whereby attendance by students at the overseas institution leads ultimately to an award of the UK HEI. The arrangement might involve little more than the validation of an existing delivery of education, or, at the other end of the spectrum, the wholesale transfer of know-how and course materials to the overseas institution (or grant of a licence to use such know-how and materials) specifically for the purposes of the franchise.

Figure 17.1 UK HE–FE franchise

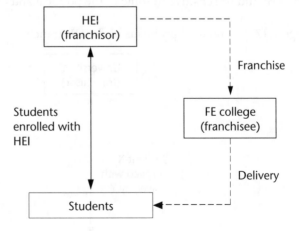

---

1   See Figure 17.1.
2   See Figure 17.2.

Figure 17.2   UK HE–FE franchise

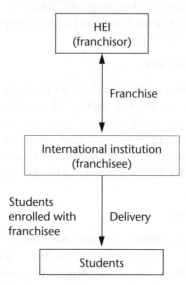

Approach of this chapter

17.4   Many of the points raised below will apply to other types of arrangement which may often be labelled franchises, such as pure validation agreements, accreditation agreements and education consultancy agreements. It is fair to say that franchising within the education sector generally has not always enjoyed the best of reputations over recent years. Arrangements have often been poorly documented, with the result that institutions on both sides of the equation have suffered. There has also been media attention, particularly in relation to overseas franchises in the Far East, where concerns have been voiced about the quality of delivery and lack of control by the franchisor. While HEIs should be sensitive to some of the political and other issues which have

Figure 17.3   Potential problems of the UK franchise relationship

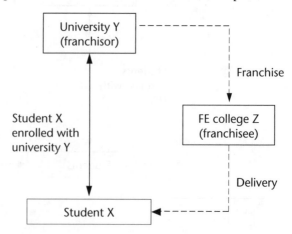

Figure 17.4 Potential problems of the overseas franchise relationship

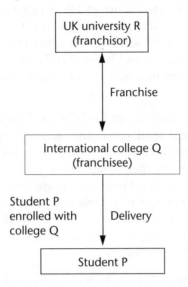

surrounded franchising, the most important legal consideration (and perhaps also the most important management issue) is the nature of the contracts which surround the franchise, and the terms of those contracts. If these issues can be addressed successfully, it is arguable that many potential problems will be prevented. This chapter, therefore, will focus very deliberately on points to be considered in negotiating and drafting franchise agreements.

THE CONTRACTUAL STRUCTURE

17.5 There are two distinct strands of the contractual structure which require analysis. First, there will be a contract between the HEI (the franchisor) and its partner institution (the franchisee). Some of the legal issues which arise from this are discussed in more detail later in the chapter. Secondly, the question of student contracts must be considered. The students to whom the franchised training or education is delivered will be in a contractual relationship with either the franchisor, or the franchisee, or possibly both.

The Student Contract

17.6 While there may have been for some considerable time a degree of uncertainty as to the nature of the relationship between students in HE and the institutions which they attend, it is now widely accepted that a contract forms the very heart of that relationship (see Chapter 6). The contract may come into existence at a very early stage, and forms the basis of the institution's authority to apply disciplinary regulations, academic procedures, and appeals

mechanisms. There may be additional, incidental contracts between institution and student: for example, in connection with the provision of
accommodation. A noticeable feature of HE over recent years has been an
increasing willingness on the part of students to assert themselves as
consumers of education, with legal rights against providers which they are
increasingly willing to enforce (see Chapter 29). The process has arguably been
accelerated by the introduction into HE of student charters, as part of the
Citizens Charter initiative.

17.7   This has serious implications for HEIs, both in terms of exposure to
compensation claims and legal costs, and in terms of management time.
Universities and colleges are rapidly having to reassess the management
arrangements which govern their relationship with their students, and to
overhaul these where necessary. These matters are brought sharply into focus
in a consideration of a franchise relationship. Consider, for example, some of
the questions which will arise in the context of a UK HE/FE franchise, where
Student X enrols with University Y for a 3-year course, the first year of which is
to be delivered at and by FE College Z:[1]

–   Does Student X register as a student of FE College Z as well as of
     University Y?
–   What happens if the student charter of University Y contains commit-
     ments (perhaps relating to residential accommodation or access to
     information technology) which FE College Z is simply unable to deliver?
–   If Student X behaves in a way in which is contrary to the disciplinary
     regulations of FE College Z but not to those of University Y (whether
     because of an oversight, or a different approach to such matters), does FE
     College Z have the necessary authority to instigate disciplinary
     proceedings?
–   Which institution is liable if Student X is dissatisfied with the quality of
     the education delivered, and threatens legal action?
–   How is the situation altered (if at all) if FE College Z has under-performed
     because of failures on the part of University Y (perhaps a failure to provide
     proper course materials)?

Privity of contract

17.8   In the three-way relationship between franchisor, franchisee and
student, it is necessary to pay some attention to the doctrine of privity of
contract. Until November 1999, a firmly entrenched principle of English law
was that only those who were parties to a contract could enforce its terms.[2] This
principle meant that if A agreed with B to provide services to C, C could not
take action against A for any failure by A to perform (as C was not a party to the
agreement between A and B for the provision of the services). In the context of

---

1   See Figure 17.3.
2   *Tweddle v Atkinson* (1861) 1 B&S 393.

HE franchising, the doctrine of privity of contract had a number of implications. For instance, in the example given in para 17.7, the contract for the delivery of education may exist solely between Student X and University Y. FE College Z, which is actually responsible for delivery, may find therefore that it has no contractual basis for attempting to enforce its disciplinary regulations against Student X. The matter needs to be addressed in the contract between University Y and FE College Z. For example, University Y might agree to take action against Student X if he or she were to infringe FE College Z's disciplinary code. On that basis, Student X might be required as a term of his contract with University Y to adhere to the disciplinary code of FE College Z. There were other implications if the contractual structure was different, for example, in an overseas franchise, in which Student P enrols as a student of overseas College Q, with education to be delivered under a franchise arrangement with UK University R.[1] If Student P is dissatisfied with the quality of education delivery, and wishes to take legal action, then, on the face of it, the rules of privity of contract suggested that Student P could take action only against College Q.

17.9 However, in November 1999, a new law (the Contracts (Rights of Third Parties) Act 1999) (the 1999 Act) came into force which significantly altered the doctrine of privity of contract. Now, a third party may have a right to enforce a term of a contract if the contract expressly provides that they may do so, or if a term purports to confer a benefit on the third party. The third party must be expressly identified in the contract either by name, as a member of a class or as answering a particular description, but need not actually be in existence at the time the contract was made. It is not possible to predict whether the effect of the principles of privity of contract or the exception created by the 1999 Act will be to the advantage of a franchisor or a franchisee in any given situation. Those involved in franchising should, therefore, not be complacent in assuming that either the doctrine will provide a shield against liability or that the 1999 Act will provide adequate redress (as the case may be), for the following reasons:

– the application of the 1999 Act has not yet been tested in the courts and there is some ambiguity as to the extent to which a third party need be identified in the contract and also as to when a term will purportedly confer a benefit on a third party;
– even before the 1999 Act, there was some evidence that the English courts have shown a willingness to introduce an element of flexibility into the doctrine of privity of contract;[2]
– the difficulties raised by privity of contract principles may be avoided by other means (for instance, through the application of the principles of

---

1   See Figure 17.4.
2   See, for example, *Jackson v Horizon Holidays* [1975] 3 All ER 92, and *Norwich City Council v Harvey (Paul Clarke)* [1989] 1 All ER 1180, CA.

negligence or of agency). Also, simply because the doctrine in certain scenarios may apparently operate to protect a franchisor against claims from students, it will not necessarily prevent claims being brought against the franchisor directly by the franchisee (particularly so where a student has already brought a claim against the franchisee);

– the doctrine may not operate as rigidly in foreign jurisdictions as it does in the UK and depending on the foreign jurisdiction in question, there may be other practical difficulties in relying on the new law (this chapter only focuses on the principles under English law); and

– it cannot be assumed that simply because Student P enrols with overseas College Q there will under no circumstances be a contract between Student P and UK University R. A contract is easily formed. A contract does not have to be reduced to writing, nor does the existence of one written contract (for example, the enrolment form between Student P and overseas College Q) preclude the creation of a further oral contract between other parties. Depending very much upon the terms of the franchise, and the circumstances which surround it, it may well be the case that a student of overseas College Q might overcome the apparent difficulties created by the privity of contract doctrine by establishing a direct contractual relationship with UK University R.

17.10 The practical lesson which emerges from these considerations is a principle which will be repeated. In order to avoid being drawn into some of the difficult technical arguments which might be thrown up by the privity of contract doctrine or the 1999 Act in the context of liability, and in order to find a route around some of the difficulties relating to enforcement of disciplinary regulations which the doctrine might create, the parties must deal clearly with all relevant matters in a written contract between themselves. Matters to be addressed will include the following:

– there should be terms which deal expressly with the application of student charters and disciplinary codes;

– there should be clear statements as to where the parties expect that liabilities towards students will lie. These may be entirely with one of the parties, or they may be divided between them. For example, the franchisee might accept responsibility for matters directly within its control (perhaps for the provision of accommodation). Similarly, the franchisor might retain responsibility for, say, the quality of the teaching materials, if the arrangement is that these will be produced by the franchisor and distributed to the franchisee. It is important that any division of liability be clearly expressed. Too often, agreements of this type refer to nebulous principles, rather than readily identifiable heads of liability;

– it may be appropriate for any apportionment of liability to be supported by contractual indemnities;

– where contractual indemnities are used, the parties should consider the inclusion of provisions allowing the party which will ultimately be responsible for accepting liability to have conduct of any claim. This is to avoid the situation in which the party against whom the claim is actually brought settles too quickly or too generously, safe in the knowledge that it has the protection of an indemnity; and

– there should be an express statement that the 1999 Act does not apply to the contract (if that is intended to be the case). The 1999 Act will apply to all contracts (with certain specific exceptions as set out in the Act) unless the contract itself expressly provides otherwise. Even so, if it is intended that any particular third party should be able to enforce a term of the contract, it is advisable to make express provision to that effect.

17.11 There are circumstances in which the contractual structures may be different from, and indeed more complex than, those set out above. For instance, it is not unknown for UK institutions to work jointly (through some joint venture or 'partnership' arrangement) to franchise an overseas institution. Whatever the practical arrangements, it is important that full consideration is given to the contractual structures. It is also important to consider carefully some of the individual key terms of the contract, which are dealt with below.

TERMS OF THE CONTRACT

Funding, payment and principal obligations

17.12 It is demonstrative of the wide range of arrangements which are caught by the term 'franchising' in HE that payment streams can operate in two entirely different directions, according to the nature of the arrangement. In a UK HE/FE franchise,[1] the HEI will make payments to the FE College in return for the FE College delivering educational services which would otherwise have been the responsibility of the HEI. In other types of franchise arrangement, the payment stream may be reversed. Where an HEI simply makes teaching materials available to another institution, whether in order to save development costs for the franchisee, or because the franchisee does not have the requisite time, knowledge or experience to develop the courses itself, the franchisee may make payments to the franchisor. This will generally apply in the case of overseas franchises, where the overseas institution will pay a franchise fee to the UK HEI in return for (perhaps) the provision of educational materials and endorsement of the final award. Whatever the structure adopted, is it important that the written agreement between franchisor and franchisee should record precisely the practical arrangements which the parties intend. The payment provisions should also make reference to a number of other matters:

---

1   See Figure 17.1.

–   a clear statement of the milestones against which payments are to be
     made, if there are to be staged payments;
–   reference to any external conditions which apply to payment, such as the
     receipt of funding from a third party;
–   the applicability of taxes, particularly (but not exclusively) in relation-
     ships with commercial providers and/or overseas institutions;
–   the treatment of students who drop out of courses part way through a year,
     and provisions to deal with increases in enrolment numbers; and
–   the fee payable where the arrangement runs for more than one year (for
     example, price review provisions or automatic price increases).

Intellectual property rights

17.13   Most franchise arrangements will involve some transfer of teaching
materials from franchisor to franchisee. The exception to this will include
arrangements which are in fact no more than validation arrangements and/or
where the yardstick for delivery is the achievement of a specific qualification,
for which the franchisee develops its own material. Where there is to be a
transfer of teaching materials, the question of IP rights needs to be considered
(see also Chapter 13). In particular, the franchisor will need to assess:

–   its own ability to make the necessary teaching materials available to the
     franchisee without infringing the IP rights of any third party; and
–   the use which the franchisee will be permitted to make of the teaching
     materials provided under the franchise arrangement.

Ownership of intellectual property rights
17.14   If an HEI, as franchisor, transfers to a franchisee materials which it
does not own, or which it is not otherwise entitled to transfer, it exposes itself
to the risk of actions for infringement of copyright or other IP rights. There are
two main areas of exposure: in relation to third party owned materials, and in
relation to the rights of academic staff.

Third party owned materials
17.15   Teaching materials have always drawn upon third party sources, such
as original text, photographs, and musical works. There has been statutory
recognition of this through the permitted acts set out in the CDPA 1988. These
provide some protection against actions for infringement of copyright for the
educational use of third party materials, including use for research and private
study, things done for the purposes of instruction or examination and
anthologies for educational use. However, it should be understood that these
exceptions are narrow in their scope, and that separate consideration will have
to be given to licensing schemes. If materials which are the copyright of third
parties are included in a teaching package without permission, and are not

within the scope of the permitted acts, their inclusion will constitute copyright infringement. The chances of the copyright owner taking action may be increased where the infringement is compounded by further dissemination of those materials to a franchisee under arrangements which may be to the financial benefit of the franchisor. Care should be taken, therefore, to ensure that unlawful use does not take place.

Intellectual property rights and academics within HE

17.16   The HEI will also need to consider the extent to which it can rightfully claim ownership (for the purposes of exploitation) of the materials which have been produced by its own teaching staff. Teaching materials are likely to attract copyright protection as literary works under the CDPA 1988. The first owner (and thus the person entitled to enjoy the benefits of copyright protection) of the copyright in a literary work made by an employee in the course of his employment will be his employer. Therefore, it would seem that teaching materials produced by an academic as part as his teaching duties will in fact be the property of his employer, the HEI. However, there are arguments to suggest that the situation is not so straightforward within HE. There is a long-standing custom and practice that lecturers are permitted to take their lecture notes with them as they transfer employment from one university or college to another. It is possible that this custom and practice may create some modification to the basic statutory principles of copyright.[1] It would seem, therefore, that an HEI cannot assume as a matter of course that it is entitled to make teaching materials produced by its academic staff available to its franchisees. How then should the HEI deal with this situation?

17.17   The situation may, of course, be clarified through contracts of employment. While policies vary from institution to institution, a number of universities and colleges have clauses in their employment contracts with lecturers which expressly reserve ownership of IP rights in teaching materials (and more widely) to the institution, sometimes in return for a share of the fruits of any exploitation. Such a policy may, however, raise other potential considerations which are outside the scope of this chapter.

17.18   In the absence of any express provision in the employment contract, the HEI will retain the ownership of the copyright in teaching materials created by lecturers (who are employees) during the course of their employment. However, if the HEI has been allowing the lecturers to use such teaching materials elsewhere when they transfer employment, it may be implied that the lecturers are granted a non-exclusive licence to do so.

17.19   Alternatively, the HEI might seek to clarify the position in its favour by ensuring that the copyright in all relevant materials does in fact vest with the HEI. This might be achieved by commissioning lecturers, as part of their employment duties, to produce teaching materials specifically for franchise packages. The individual lecturers will need to take the decision as to whether

---

1   *Noah v Shuba* [1991] FSR 14.

they produce new materials, or simply rely on their pre-existing material. Either way, if the situation is spelt out with clarity, the doubts as to ownership in copyright set out above are likely to be resolved.

Licence terms

17.20   One of the factors which may influence the discussions between the HEI and its staff with regard to teaching materials to be included in franchise packages is the purposes to which those materials are to be put. That in turn leads into a discussion of licence terms as they apply between franchisor and franchisee. For instance, if the intention of the franchisor is that materials are to be used by the franchisee only for its own internal purposes, and not for dissemination to other institutions, the franchisor will need to ensure that it has the ability to enforce any such restrictions through its agreement with the franchisee. That agreement will need to include a licence of IP rights or make suitable provision for a separate licence to be granted. Such a licence should deal (among other things) with the following matters:

–   the uses to which the materials can be put. There may be restrictions based on geography, types of student, types of course, or other factors;
–   use outside the agreed parameters should be prohibited, as should any copying or distribution to third parties other than that strictly required for the permitted uses;
–   clarification as to which of the parties will own the IP rights in any newly created materials;
–   there may be a need to deal with matters other than copyright. For instance, franchise arrangements may permit the franchisee to use the trade marks and logos of the franchisor, in which case the limits upon such use should be clearly stated. Also, there may be a need to refer to IP which does not enjoy any formal protection, such as know-how; and
–   the licence will also need to deal with what happens to the IP rights in the teaching materials, and the physical copies of those materials, when the franchise comes to an end.

17.21   The treatment of IP rights within universities has historically concentrated upon the exploitation of patentable inventions. There has generally been little examination of the IP rights in teaching and research materials. Consequently, there has often been a failure to deal adequately with IP in franchising and other related agreements.

Control over the quality of delivery

17.22   The very wide range of arrangements which fall within the generally understood meaning of franchising in HE means that there are also wide variations in the extent to which the franchisor will seek to control the delivery of teaching or training. In some cases, the only test may be the achievement of a specific award, as verified by external examiners. In other cases, there may be arrangements more akin to a retail franchise, where delivery has to take place strictly in accordance with a manual of instructions. The issues which flow from this go to the heart of much of the controversy which has surrounded franchising, both within the UK and overseas. Where franchising attracted adverse comment, it was often because of a perceived lack of control by the franchisor over delivery of teaching or training carried out in its name by the franchisee. This has particularly been an issue with regard to franchising in FE. The determination of what is an appropriate level of control by a franchisor over the activities of a franchisee is a management/academic issue. However, the legal documentation will need to capture accurately the respective obligations of the parties in this context, and there are at least three important issues which need to be considered by franchisors in putting together documentation.

Exposure to costs

17.23   It is a prerequisite of any properly regulated franchise arrangement that there be contact between the staff of the two institutions. However, the franchisor needs to be sure that the franchise agreement does not allow the franchisee to dictate how much contact there should be. The contract should define in precise terms the commitments of the franchisor, and should provide for an ability to levy additional charges and/or terminate the arrangement if demands are made in excess of those commitments.

Liability to students

17.24   While there are many good reasons why a franchisor should reserve the ability to exercise close control over delivery of materials by the franchisee, it should be noted that this may increase the exposure of the franchisor to liability towards students. If, by exercising close control, the franchisor is in effect accepting ultimate responsibility for determining how teaching or training is delivered, and delivery is unsatisfactory, the franchisor may find itself the target of legal action, either by students or by the franchisee. Depending upon the relative strength of bargaining positions, and the circumstances of the franchise, it may be possible for the franchisor to protect itself against this by way of contractual indemnity. However, there is a very fine balance to be struck between the need to achieve control, and possible exposure to liability. There is also a need to consider the issues relating to contractual structures discussed above.

Ultra vires – to provide or to procure?

17.25   In any consideration of franchising, it is worthwhile to make brief reference to developments which took place during 1996 in the FE sector. This, in turn, requires an understanding of the specific form of franchising in which FE colleges are widely involved as franchisors. Franchising within FE has generally involved a collaborative arrangement between FE colleges and other pre-existing training providers. These other providers include professional training organisations, the internal training departments of companies, and charitable organisations. Under the franchise arrangement, the training which those organisations delivered to their students was historically brought within the aegis of the FE College, so that it qualified for funding from the FEFC, and led to a College award. The FEFC increasingly sought to regulate such activities. This culminated in the publication of Council Circular 96/06 (followed later by Council Circulars 99/09 and 99/37) which questioned whether the type of franchise described above fell within the statutory powers of FEIs to 'provide further and higher education',[1] and suggested that, if the college did not in fact have sufficient control over the ultimate provision of training to students, it might be operating outside its statutory powers. These provisions do not translate unchanged into HE. A significant amount of franchising within HE is of a different type. Furthermore, the powers of HEIs, unlike those of FEIs, are not uniform. As well as the distinction between chartered HEIs and the statutory HEIs, there are many local variations in the constitutional documents of universities.

17.26 However, there are analogies to be drawn, and lessons to be learnt. In particular, the experience of the FE sector draws attention to the fact that all publicly funded education institutions have duties to ensure that quality of delivery is preserved, as well as legal obligations to act within their powers (statutory or otherwise), and to exercise a proper degree of care and control over their stewardship of public funds. These points should particularly be borne in mind in the context of innovative or speculative schemes. The whole area of the control over quality of delivery is difficult, and there are fine balances to be struck between potentially competing forces. Much will depend upon the practical arrangements which the parties envisage, and their relative bargaining strengths. However, it may be helpful to consider including within the franchise agreement provisions dealing with the following:

– clear indications as to the acceptable level of delivery under the franchise;
– a requirement that the franchisee should comply with any reasonable request which the franchisor may issue from time to time concerning the manner of delivery;
– provisions entitling the franchisor to inspect and audit the franchisor's records and to monitor the delivery under the franchise;
– an ability for the franchisor to have some input into the selection of staff who are to be responsible for the delivery and (if appropriate) the removal of staff from the franchised delivery; and
– provisions which deal fully with the ability of either party to terminate the arrangement (particularly in this context where performance is not up to standard), and the consequences of any such termination (see below).

---

1   Further and Higher Education Act 1992, s 18.

Termination and consequences of termination

17.27   Early termination of a franchise arrangement is likely to be harmful to both franchisor and franchisee; therefore, it is important, as with any commercial agreement, to ensure that the circumstances in which early termination may take place are properly documented. Particular care will be needed to ensure that the termination provisions tie in properly with the provisions relating to the quality of delivery or other appropriate aspects of the franchise arrangement. For instance, a franchisor may wish to be able to terminate the arrangement if the franchisee commits a significant number of relatively minor breaches of the applicable quality standards. The contract will need to provide expressly for this. There are also some consequences of early termination which are particular to an educational franchise.

Responsibility for completing delivery of training
17.28   If any agreement for the provision of education or training services is terminated early (whether it be a franchise agreement or some other form of agreement) there may be students left who have not completed their programme of study. For example, in a UK-based HE/FE franchise,[1] University Y may decide that part way through an academic year it has no option but to terminate its franchise arrangement with FE College Z. University Y will be left with a cohort of students to whom contractual promises have been made regarding the delivery of education, and will have to make alternative arrangements. This may be extremely difficult, and may lead to significant expense.

17.29   It is not suggested that wording in a contract can solve these problems. However, what the contract can do is to make provision for the franchisor to be reimbursed any additional expense which it suffers (whether by having to re-arrange the courses, or as a result of claims made against it by the students). There will also be merit in including clauses requiring the franchisee to co-operate fully with the franchisor in making alternative arrangements. Depending on the nature of the circumstances giving rise to termination, it may be appropriate to allow for termination following a period of notice, which may prove beneficial in allowing time to make alternative arrangements before the termination takes effect. The situation will be somewhat different with an overseas franchise, where the UK HEI would generally not expect to be in a direct contractual relationship with the students. However, the UK HEI should still seek to protect itself through the contract against any claims brought by students as a result of termination. It may prove difficult to bring any enforcement action against the overseas franchisee and the UK HEI would be well advised to consider taking some form of security from the overseas franchisee, such as a performance bond, at the outset.

---

1   See Figure 17.2.

Staff and the Transfer of Undertakings (Protection of Employment) Regulations 1981

17.30   It is possible to envisage circumstances which might arise on the termination (or indeed the expiry) of a franchise arrangement, in which TUPE would apply. TUPE gives effect to European Council Directive 77/187 (the Acquired Rights Directive). Where there is a relevant transfer of an undertaking (which may include the transfer of franchised activity from one franchisee to another, or from a franchisee back to the franchisor) TUPE will apply, with a number of consequences:

–   the transfer of the franchised activity will not operate so as to terminate the contract of employment of any person employed by the franchisee in that part of its undertaking. Any such contract of employment will be transferred to the party who takes over that undertaking (the transferee) together with all rights, powers, duties and liabilities under or in connection with that contract of employment;[1]

–   where any such employee of the franchisee or the transferee is dismissed, that dismissal will be treated as automatically unfair if the transfer or a reason connected with the transfer is the reason or the principal reason for the dismissal,[2] unless it can be established that the reason or the principal reason for the dismissal was an economic, technical or organisational reason entailing a change in the workforce.[3] Any dismissals prior to the transfer for a reason connected with the transfer (for example, an attempt to avoid the effects of TUPE by dismissing staff) will be automatically unfair without any exception; and

–   there will be duties to inform and consult employee representatives.[4] The maximum penalty for failure to comply is 13 weeks' pay per employee affected.

17.31   There has been (and continues to be) a significant volume of case-law relating to the interpretation of TUPE. Much of this has centred upon the definition of a 'relevant transfer' of an 'undertaking'. The approach in European cases has been to look at 'economic entities' rather than 'undertakings'. In a people-oriented operation, an economic entity may consist merely of the provision of services, and in such circumstances there is no requirement for there to be a transfer of assets or property. One of the key criteria is whether the economic entity retains its identity, so it is necessary to determine whether what has been transferred is an economic entity which is still in existence. This may be apparent where its operation is continued or renewed by a new employer with the same economic or similar activities.[5]

17.32   A related issue may be whether a particular individual is employed in the undertaking in question so as to fall within the scope of TUPE. Where a part

---

1   TUPE 1981, reg 5.
2   Ibid, reg 8(1).
3   Ibid, reg 8(2).
4   Ibid, reg 10.
5   *Spijkers v Gebroeders Benedik Abattoir CV* (C–24/85) [1986] 2 CMLR 296.

of an undertaking is transferred, TUPE applies to any employee who is 'assigned' to that part.[1] This means that, if employees are dedicated to a particular function and/or spend a substantial part of their time engaged in it, they are likely to be subject to TUPE. There is no precise guidance as to the meaning of a 'substantial part of their time', but a rule of thumb would seem to indicate something in the region of two-thirds.

17.33   If TUPE does apply to a franchised activity, then following termination or expiry of the franchise for any reason, the employees of the franchisee engaged in the delivery of education under the franchise might claim that their contracts of employment have been transferred if the franchised activity was transferred (whether to another franchisee or back to the franchisor). For this to be the case, the franchise would have to be arranged in such a way that those employed in connection with it formed a distinct and identifiable unit, devoting a substantial part of their time to the delivery of education under the franchise. Furthermore, it would require the franchised activity to be continued.

17.34   The potential effect of TUPE should not be overstated, but those involved in franchising should be aware that there are circumstances in which it can apply and it is advisable to include in the contract appropriate provisions dealing with TUPE. Such provisions might include:

–   an obligation on the franchisee to provide full details relating to all relevant employees and, generally, to co-operate with the franchisor or potential replacement prior to expiry or on termination of the contract;
–   a right of the franchisor to have some involvement in the selection (and deselection) of staff (on the ground that they may eventually become its own employees); and
–   indemnities from the franchisee relating to any TUPE transfer (particularly relating to any liabilities arising from a transferring employee's employment with the franchisee).

Dispute resolution, choice of law and jurisdiction

17.35   Even the most cordial and best documented relationship between two independent parties has the potential to lead to disagreement, and it is important that the parties should address how such disagreement should be resolved. In order to do this, it is necessary to consider two questions:

–   What is the preference of the parties with regard to the method of dispute resolution?
–   According to the laws of which country do they wish the contract to be governed and any dispute to be resolved?

---

1   *Botzen v Rotterdamsche Droogdok Maatschappij BV* (No 186/83) [1986] 2 CLMR 50.

Methods of dispute resolution

17.36   There are a variety of methods of dispute resolution from which the parties may select. These include a structured form of negotiated resolution, determination of certain matters by an expert, arbitration or mediation, and the jurisdiction of the courts. A favoured manner of dispute resolution within education franchises would seem to be a reference in the first instance to a structured negotiation, backed up by an arbitration clause. Other possibilities are, of course, available, and whatever method is chosen there are some critical drafting and practical points to consider (see Chapter 27).

Structured negotiation

17.37   A clause which provides for a structured negotiation will typically state that the parties will attempt to resolve any dispute under an escalated procedure, with discussions taking place, for instance, at first between course leaders, and then (if agreement is not reached at that level) moving up to be resolved between those at a more senior level of management. The clauses setting out such an arrangement should ideally contain the following provisions:

–   a statement that any negotiation will take place in good faith, with a *bona fide* attempt to resolve the dispute in question;
–   there may be circumstances in which it is quickly apparent to both parties that the problem in question is of a nature or a magnitude which renders resolution under this procedure unlikely. The procedure should, therefore, be capable of being abandoned by mutual consent;
–   as with any clause which provides for a matter to be referred initially to the parties, the clause should be checked carefully to ensure that it does not contain the possibility for deadlock. In particular, it should not require there to be mutual agreement before the next stage of the procedure is invoked, nor should it contain open-ended time periods; and
–   there may be occasions when one of the parties needs to take rapid action against the other, without being hindered by a negotiated dispute procedure. For instance, litigation relating to copyright infringement is often conducted through injunctive proceedings, where time is of the essence. The clause should, therefore, make provision for such steps to be taken without the need to go through the full discussion procedure first.

Expert determination

17.38   There are certain disputes which are most appropriately resolved by an expert (rather than an arbitrator). This may be particularly relevant where the dispute is of a technical nature. This method of determination may well have advantages in terms of time and cost, and may sometimes be appropriate in a franchise agreement (perhaps in connection with technical issues where a franchise is heavily dependent upon electronic teaching materials). If so, the following points should be addressed:

- the range of issues which may be referred to an expert must be clearly set out, and should be limited to matters within his expert knowledge;
- the way in which the expert is identified and appointed needs to be made clear, taking care once again to avoid any possibility of deadlock;
- the costs of employing the expert should be dealt with. A common provision is for the costs to be borne equally by the parties, unless the expert determines that the circumstances of the dispute or the conduct of one party has been such that that party should bear all (or a greater proportion) of the costs; and
- it should be stated that the decision of an expert will, in the normal course of events, be binding upon the parties (unless there has been a manifest error in the decision-taking process).

Arbitration

17.39   While there are undoubtedly some attractive reasons for using arbitration as the final method of determination, rather than jurisdiction of the court, there would seem to be a tendency to assume that arbitration is quick, cheap and easy. This is not necessarily so. Arbitration proceedings can turn out to be more time consuming and expensive than court proceedings. Any decision to include an arbitration clause should therefore be made carefully, with all relevant matters covered in the clause. In addition to the issues set out above concerning the appointment of the arbitrator, the costs of the proceedings and the availability of injunctive relief, an arbitration clause (particularly in an international contract) will need to deal, at the very least, with the following:

- the place in which the arbitration proceedings will take place should be specified, as well as the language of the proceedings. In this context, it may be helpful to remember the international reputation which London has for resolution of disputes;
- the rules governing the arbitration proceedings should be specified; and
- the parties should consider how any award of an arbitrator will be enforced. While for international contracts the New York Convention on the Recognition and Enforcement of Foreign Arbitral Awards 1958 may be of some assistance, it should be understood that difficulties may nevertheless arise if the party against whom the award has been made simply chooses to ignore it. In this scenario, arbitration proceedings may only lead to court proceedings by another route.

Jurisdiction/choice of law

17.40   While this is not the place to undertake a full and detailed examination of the complex provisions which apply to choice of law and jurisdiction clauses in international contracts, it is important to understand some of the basic principles, particularly in relation to overseas franchises.

Jurisdiction of the court

17.41 Even if it is decided that disputes will be dealt with by the courts, rather than by any other means, it is necessary in international contracts to seek to avoid any arguments concerning which country's court will have jurisdiction over the contract. It will generally be in the interests of a UK HEI for an international franchise agreement to be subject to the jurisdiction of the English courts, although in some cases it may be necessary or desirable for that jurisdiction not to be exclusive. Whether or not the parties will agree to the jurisdiction of the English courts will depend upon their relative bargaining strengths, but any English institution should be very wary about being drawn into a contract which is subject to the jurisdiction of the courts of the country in which the franchisee is located, or indeed of any neutral country. If this is unavoidable, the implications of a foreign jurisdiction should be clearly understood, with advice taken from foreign lawyers if necessary. Also, it is necessary to consider fully the enforceability of any award made by a foreign court.

Choice of law

17.42 Whatever method of dispute resolution is chosen, it will also be necessary to specify the law which will apply to the contract. This need not necessarily be that of the country whose courts will have jurisdiction. However, a UK HEI will generally wish the contract to be governed by English law, unless special factors apply. Again, if this is unavoidable, a full understanding of the implications of the foreign law is necessary. It should be noted that this chapter is based on the position of franchise arrangements under English law, and the position could be substantially different under the application of any foreign law. Whatever decision is made, it is important that it be recorded in the contract. Any failure to do so may lead the parties into very complex arguments concerning the governing law.

Further legal considerations

17.43 In addition to those matters explored in some detail above, there are a number of other legal questions which may need to be considered, according to the circumstances of the franchise arrangement. Some of these are listed below, merely in order to identify where further thought may be necessary. They are not treated in any detail in this chapter. Relevant areas would include:

– responsibility for health and safety;
– the effect of the Competition Act 1998 (the 1998 Act), and international competition law, where the franchise agreement attempts to place restrictions upon either or both parties (for instance, in terms of exclusivity);
– the impact of taxation, particularly VAT in UK franchise agreements, and the taxation regimes of other countries in international agreements;
– a careful consideration of what should properly constitute a 'force majeure' event under a franchise agreement;

– provisions governing insurance, particularly in order to support any contractual indemnities; and

– whether there should be any limitation of either party's liability (although any franchisor seeking to limit its own liability should note that, depending on the relative bargaining strengths of the parties, the franchisee is likely to require reciprocity which, on balance, could be less beneficial to the franchisor).

THE IMPACT OF RECENT DEVELOPMENTS

17.44 In recent years there have been rapid advances in multi-media and information highway technology. HEIs have been in the vanguard of the utilisation of such technology in the UK. As these developments become more fully integrated within education, it is likely that there will be a vast increase in the opportunities for franchised delivery of education, and for distance learning. The advent of the Learning and Skills Council and the drive to promote 'lifelong learning' will pose its own opportunities and threats for franchising in the HE sector. There are at least three important consequences of such developments for franchising within HE. First, written agreements need to be kept under review in order to ensure that they keep pace with changing methods of delivery. Secondly, as has been emphasised above, HEIs need to be sure that they are dealing with the IP rights in teaching materials in an organised and efficient way, and are protecting their interests when they make those teaching materials available to other parties. Thirdly, the ability of FE colleges to offer distance learning courses over the internet is already taking a stronghold in certain areas, and HEIs need to rise to the challenges created, both in terms of the competition for delivery by distance learning and also the opportunity to develop new and exciting franchise arrangements with FE colleges and other third parties.

CONCLUSION

17.45 The drafting of education franchise agreements is not, it is submitted, an area for the uninitiated. At the same time, it should not be thought that the complexities outlined in this chapter make the drafting of such agreements inordinately difficult. Many issues are capable of fairly rapid resolution, in order to achieve the level of protection for franchisors which are made necessary by good management, the requirements of quality control and commercial common sense.

Chapter 18

THE PRIVATE FINANCE INITIATIVE

Tim Costello (Eversheds)

EDITORS' INTRODUCTION

§18.1   The Private Finance Initiative (PFI), *aka* public-private partnerships (PPP) and perhaps also 'the Third Way', is no panacea; its track-record is patchy at best, and even obscure (little rigorous and credible work has been done to see whether PFI *really* has provided the taxpayer with value for money). Essentially, it is a mechanism which avoids the Government and the 'public sector' borrowing today for 25 or 30 years via gilts at a certain percentage per annum, and lets the private sector find the capital (at more than that percentage since nobody can borrow cheaper than HMG) in return for an income-stream at the expense of future taxpayers. This leaves the key question of whether the injection of private sector alleged expertise and efficiency compensates for the higher interest rate over the life of the PFI project. But whatever the politics of the PFI as a supposed panacea for raising capital, and whatever the economic and commercial realities of any particular PFI project, here we are concerned with the legal issues – with the contractual documentation drafted to structure the 'deal' and with the extent to which such documentation will try to address what are the duties of each party. It remains to be seen whether the *débâcle* of Railtrack's financial collapse will impede the onward march of PFI by making the private sector less willing to trust the Government, and even HEIs as the quasi-public sector. Certainly, PFI contractual documentation might get even longer as lawyers attempt to cover yet another set of eventualities.

§18.2   PFI attempts to procure an asset/service for an HEI at a lower cost and/or more quickly/efficiently than it alone could do in a traditional way and while also somewhat shifting the risk of failure away from the HEI towards the provider. The provider will clearly be influenced by the predictability of the HEI's income-flows: the introduction of tuition fees paid by students and the possible negative impact on demand for HE places will probably create extra uncertainty and make the putting together of a PFI jigsaw even more difficult. This chapter is also concerned with other more traditional ways of raising capital (for example, the mortgage), and with the possibility of an HEI or group of HEIs raising capital in the money markets by launching a bond (as is common among US HEIs, and as taken up recently by the University of Edinburgh).

§18.3   For an account of one of the few (but increasing number of) HE PFI projects, see McWilliam (1997) on student accommodation; for an accommodation PFI project of a somewhat different kind, see NAO (1997) on prisons! See also the HEFCE guidance on PFI and student accommodation (Circular 00/47) and *The Times Higher Educational Supplement*[1] for a review of the use of PFI in HE.

---

1   On 2 February 2001, at p 6.

§18.4   PFI mixed with VAT can be a minefield, through which a specialist guide is needed: see *Queen on the application of Greenwich Property Ltd v Commissioners of Customs and Excise,*[1] concerning zero-rating for the building of the University of Greenwich Avery Hill 'student village'.

§18.5   Finally, the EC Commission has expressed concern that the UK's approach to PFI/PPP conflicts with EU public procurement rules (see Chapter 28). The problem is that the Commission does not approve of the reliance within PFI/PPP on 'the negotiated procedure', allowed by the public procurement rules but not, according to the Commission, in these circumstances. This matter came to a head with the Commission challenging the Pimlico, London, schools' PFI project; the project was duly cancelled and hence the issue did not reach the ECJ for a conclusive decision. The Commission, scenting victory, has now issued a draft Directive which, *if adopted*, will make the preferred bidder route of PFI/PPP unlawful and introduce cumbersome procedures for the use of PFI/PPP which some believe would kill off PFI/PPP in the UK.

INTRODUCTION

18.1   This chapter is concerned with long-term contracts for the provision of services or serviced accommodation, where the contractor is obliged to make a capital investment which has no other purpose but the delivery of the service concerned. This includes a design, build, finance, operate and maintain contract but will also encompass other forms of PPP and externalisations and outsourcings. These contracts have in common the fact that the contractor needs the security of a long-term arrangement in order to recover the cost of providing the physical facilities involved.

WHAT IS A PFI TRANSACTION?

18.2   The PFI is a means by which private capital can be harnessed to deliver services required by the public sector. It is based on the concept that the public sector has duties to deliver services but it is immaterial whether it owns the assets through which those services are delivered. While traditionally the public sector has owned these assets, there is no reason why this should necessarily be so. In the case of services which require a substantial level of capital investment, if the assets concerned are owned and financed by the private sector, the demands on the Public Sector Borrowing Requirement (PSBR) will be commensurately reduced.

POSITION OF HEIs

18.3   HEIs are not part of the public sector. While they are largely funded from public sources, they are in fact independent of government and their

---

1   [2001] STC 618.

borrowings are not considered public borrowings for statistical purposes. In this respect they are different from NHS trusts and local authorities. Most will be able to borrow without being in breach of their constitutional documents (see Chapters 2 and 3). Their financial memoranda with the HEFCE, as a condition of funding, limit but do not prohibit borrowing. Unless they having already borrowed up to the limit imposed by HEFCE or for reasons of prudence do not wish to borrow, HEIs are in a real way able to make an assessment whether procuring facilities under the PFI or conventionally offers better value for money. Equally, HEIs may wish to transfer non-core activities, and the risks associated with carrying them out, to an outside party. An obvious example of this is the administrative IT function. There is no reason, however, why accounting, registry and personnel administrative functions could not also be the subject of an outsourcing.

RISK

18.4   Essentially, decision-taking in this area should be governed by an analysis of the risks involved (on risk management generally, see Chapter 24). It is a truism of PFI that the risks in a project should lie with the party best able to manage them, but this presupposes that there has been an exercise to identify those risks. One suspects that, in many cases, no real effort is made to catalogue the risks in a project before commencing the procurement process. If this were done and consideration given to whether some risks should be transferred to the supplier with others being retained, the outcome for the procuring body could be enhanced. Invariably, in the case of an accommo-dation project, the supplier will be a thinly capitalised single-purpose company. The bulk of the finance will be provided in the form of loans from a bank or other financier without the benefit of a guarantee from the equity holders of the company. Accordingly, the lenders' due diligence will consist of assessing the forecast cash flows of the company – *all* its expenses and *all* its income – over the life of the project. The obligations which the company undertakes in the project agreement will either need to be assumed by a subcontractor of substance, be insured or be covered by the cash available to the company at the time when they need to be paid. If the amount and date of occurrence of risks retained by the company is uncertain, lenders will normally insist on being covered by a standby borrowing facility. This has a cost, even if it is not used. Thus, PFI may properly be regarded as a form of procurement – not of assets, but of services. This is the fundamental concept, where the risk of ownership of the assets required for delivery of the service should remain with the provider.

18.5   Before current accounting conventions became applicable, leasing was a means by which finance for what was effectively the purchase of an asset could be kept off the balance sheet of the body acquiring the asset. It also used to be the case that, although a lessee became obliged to make payments of rent throughout the term of a lease, by accounting convention the aggregate of the rents due did not have to be recognised as a liability at the outset. The effect was that, although very significant liabilities were incurred, none showed on the balance sheet and nor did the asset. This was recognised as being misleading. Under the currently applicable accounting standard,[1] financial statements must reflect substance and not form. Where the lessor recovers, over the term of the lease, rents which in aggregate amortise the whole cost to the lessor of purchasing and financing the asset, the asset and the finance to purchase it must be shown on the balance sheet of the procurer. By contrast, if, for example, by the end of the term of the lease the lessor will only have recovered part of the cost of acquiring the asset (and will, in order to realise a profit on the transaction, be looking to sell the asset or let it for a further hire period), neither the asset nor the finance need appear on the balance sheet of the lessee.

18.6 In the purest form of PFI transaction, the procurer would never be the owner of the capital asset employed to deliver the services during or after the end of the contract. Normally, however, provided that there is a substantial transfer of the risks of ownership for a long period, neither the asset nor the finance required to pay for it need be recognised on the balance sheet of the procurer. One relevant concern is to look at which party bears the risk of the value of the asset at the end of the term of the lease. However, this is not the only test. It is a question of identifying who bears all the risks of ownership. In practice, the risks involved in responsibility for maintenance may be economically more significant than the residual value risk and, if that is the case, the asset will appear on the balance sheet of the party bearing the risk of maintenance. In examining where the various risks relating to the acquisition lie, the standard seeks to determine the substance of the transaction. It is not simply a question of ascertaining whether sufficient risk has transferred to, or remained with, the provider. The issue is whether the risks of *ownership* of the assets required to provide the service lie with the provider or the procurer. It might be thought that this must mean that the residual value risk is paramount, but this is not the case; the residual value may not be very significant in amount and it arises at the end of the contract term, so its present value is correspondingly lower. Suppose, under a PFI transaction, an HEI starts with a vacant plot and at the end of the contract period has a hall of residence standing on it, having paid the provider for the use of the building throughout the contract period and not being obliged to make any further payment to the provider after the end of the period. It is hard to avoid concluding that the HEI has 'bought' the hall of residence. This is so, even if the provider has borne every conceivable risk in the meantime. In practice, all the risks which apply in a particular case and which party bears them are examined and, provided that the procurer is sheltered from the majority of the risks of ownership (such as liabilities for maintenance of the fabric of the building), it is likely that the procurer will not be required to recognise the transaction in its accounts as the acquisition of an asset.

---

1   FRS 5, Accounting Standards Board Limited, 1994.

HOW IS A PFI TRANSACTION ACHIEVED?

18.7 Since central government is able to borrow at the finest rates available, if the capital required for a project is to be provided from private sources the cost of capital will inevitably be higher. Furthermore, the costs of setting up the transaction will be higher for the procurer, the successful bidder and those who are unsuccessful. These increased expenses will directly or indirectly increase the cost of the project. Accordingly, if PFI is to provide better value for money and given that the provider will be looking for a return on capital, the saving will need to be found in some other factor. For example, the provider may be able to deliver a given level of service by making a smaller capital investment, or by operating at lower running costs, than the conventional public sector solution. It might be able to use the assets at a time when they are not required to deliver services to the procurer. Buildings used for education are often not intensively used. A provider may be able to use them at times of the day or periods of the year when they are not required for their primary purpose. For this reason, it is important for the procurer to specify the services it requires and not the asset through which they will be delivered. This allows the provider maximum freedom in which to decide the nature and extent of its capital investment – reducing the cost to the procurer and maximising the provider's return. A comparison can be made between the recurrent cost of conventional procurement and the charges which will be made for the services by the provider. In this way, one can determine whether PFI offers value for money.

ASSETS OR SERVICES?

18.8 To some extent, the argument that the use of premises can be seen as the delivery of a service rather than the acquisition of an asset is specious. In the case of a pure service (such as a payroll computer bureau), the employer can use another bureau and the bureau can find another customer. Where there is use of a particular building, it is not the same. It is likely that the HEI will want to continue to use the building (even if dissatisfied with the service) and the provider may not readily find another user of the building. To the extent that it can be done without prejudicing the accounting treatment of the transaction, it is as well if the form of the transaction reflects this. The subject of the services might not be the use of a building, but might instead concern equipment (for example, a computer network). In this case, although it may be impractical for the physical assets to be used elsewhere, the cost of the equipment is relatively small compared to the cost of delivering a computer service. Accordingly, it is possible to disregard the fact that part of the regular payments to the provider are, in fact, for the hardware. The substance of the transaction will not be the sale of the equipment but the provision of services, of which use of the equipment is only a part.

PFI IN HIGHER EDUCATION

18.9 Since 1988, all HEIs have been outside the public sector, so one might ask why PFI has any relevance to them. The answer is partly for reasons of political expediency and partly because it is thought that the benefits which PFI can deliver to the public sector will also be applicable to a sector which is largely paid for by the taxpayer. Indeed, because HEIs are private bodies they are not able to borrow ('cost of funds') as cheaply as the government, and hence a PFI project may well for an HEI begin to look financially attractive. HEIs are charities. Those who are responsible for their governance and management have a fiduciary responsibility to achieve best value for money. Central government, local authorities and the national health service are required to establish whether PFI offers better value for money by use of the so-called 'public sector comparator'. This compares the net present cost of procuring the services concerned by conventional means over the life of the project with the net present cost of the PFI solution. PFI is only used if it offers better value for money. The fact that there have been so many concluded PFI projects is evidence that they offer better value for money on numerous occasions. An HEI would be unwise to ignore the possibility of making use of PFI.

Regulatory framework

18.10 HEIs are not currently required to consider using PFI as a means of procuring new projects. The HEFCE has said that in the future HEIs might need to show that they have explored opportunities for involvement of the private sector, but currently they do not need to.[1] The financial memorandum between the HEFCE and an HEI may, however, encourage the HEI to consider PFI. Some of the newer HEIs inherited liabilities from the LEAs of which they were once part. This means that borrowing to make capital investments is difficult, because they do not have strong balance sheets (even though HEFCE reimburses them for debt service costs on these loans). For such institutions, PFI can have a great benefit, provided that they have the income to support the recurring charges for the service provided.

Other factors

18.11 There is, nevertheless, political pressure on government departments to demonstrate a flow of PFI transactions in the sector for which they are responsible. The Department for Education and Skills (DfES) is no exception to this and the unit within it charged with this responsibility is actively promoting PFI in HE as elsewhere. The capital funds at the disposal of the HEFCE are now so paltry in relation to the size of the sector that new developments are likely to have to be funded from other sources. Some HEIs might be in the position of not having the capital available and not being

---

1   See HEFCE Circular 17/95.

willing or able to carry the debt required to fund development on their balance sheets. This will mean that for their own reasons they will be driven down the PFI route.

Conventional procurement

18.12   Figure 18.1 shows diagrammatically the various different parties who will be concerned in a building project. This might concern the construction of a new teaching facility on a site already owned by the HEI. The HEI will have direct contractual relationships with all the principal providers of finance, goods and services and will have the opportunity of structuring the transaction and choosing the various firms and companies involved as it wishes (within the confines of the public procurement rules and consistent with demonstrating value for money).

Figure 18.1

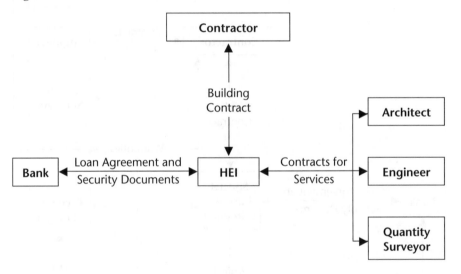

Procurement under PFI

18.13   If, instead of obtaining a building, the HEI procures services (consisting of making available fully serviced teaching space), there will be one basic contractual relationship to which the HEI will be party together with the provider of the services. The provider will have a multiplicity of relationships with the various entities contributing to the provision of the services. Figure 18.2 shows a simple arrangement which illustrates this. Customarily, in bidding for the contract, the provider will specify the names of the other firms and companies which will be providing goods or services, but the HEI will not have the opportunity of choosing them individually.

Special-purpose companies

18.14   PFI has been embraced more or less enthusiastically by the building contractors. However, in the UK such companies normally need to devote their available resources to the core business. They cannot be expected to be long-term holders of shares in a series of special-purpose companies set up for the various projects which they have built. In due course, there will be a need for the initial holders of the shares of the special-purpose companies to sell their shares. Indeed, the aggregation of these companies is likely to be the method by which specialist PFI providers emerge as a distinct business sector. Equally, the HEI may be concerned about the timing of any sales of shares and perhaps the identity of any future shareholders.

Figure 18.2

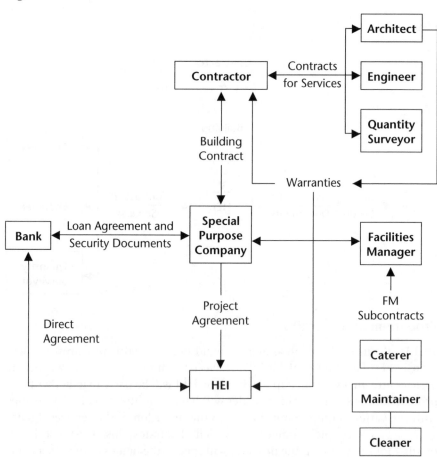

ANATOMY OF A PFI TRANSACTION

18.15   As with any procurement, the initial issues are value for money and affordability. It hardly needs saying that the concept of value for money requires competitive tendering. Even if this were not the case, it would be required by the public procurement rules.

Payment mechanism

18.16   Under PFI, the procuring body only pays for the service it receives. This is achieved by a contractual payment mechanism which normally allows deductions from the unitary payment on the basis of unavailability and failure of service standards. The whole of the unitary charge will be at risk in this way. Normally, the whole of the new facilities is divided into discrete areas; each of these is assessed against availability standards daily or even twice a day. Service shortfalls may be assessed by area or globally. The principle is that (apart from some indemnity provisions) this is the only means of financial adjustment between the parties during the contract period.

Public procurement regime

18.17   As part of the completion of the single market, the Council of the EU has adopted a series of measures regulating the procurement of goods, services and construction works, not only by public sector bodies, but by bodies which, while having a private character, exist for the purpose of meeting needs in the general interest with respect to education and are financed mainly from public sources. This definition includes almost all HEIs. The underlying purpose of the rules is to ensure that all enterprises within the EEA (the 15 members of the EU, Iceland, Liechtenstein and Norway) have the opportunity of bidding for publicly financed projects in whatever country the project may be taking place. The public procurement rules may seem to be bureaucratic and mechanical regulations which are of comparatively little significance. However, they impose a procedure that underlies the whole procurement process. The regime only applies if the cost of procurement exceeds certain limits – €5,000,000 for works and €200,000 for services and supplies. The value in national currencies is fixed biennially by the EC Commission. A substantial new facility for an HEI will be covered either by (works) Directive 93/37/EEC and the Public Works Contracts Regulations 1991[1] or by (services) Directive 92/50/EEC and the Public Services Contracts Regulations 1993.[2] Both sets of regulations have been amended by the Public Contracts (Works, Services and Supply) (Amendment) Regulations 2000:[3] see Chapter 28.

---

1   SI 1991/2680.
2   SI 1993/3228.
3   SI 2000/2009.

18.18   If the facility is to be obtained under PFI, it is a matter of debate which Directive applies. With the exception of the differing threshold this issue is of no practical consequence. One of three award procedures must be followed:

–   the *open procedure*, under which contract documents must be prepared and issued to all those who request them for the purpose of submitting a tender;
–   the *restricted procedure*, under which interested suppliers apply to be included on a shortlist of those invited to bid on the basis of contract documents supplied only to them with the invitation; or
–   the *negotiated procedure*, under which selected applicants are invited to negotiate the terms of the proposed contract until the contract is let to the one of them with which the most satisfactory agreement can be reached.

18.19   The negotiated procedure can be used only in limited circumstances. One of these is where prior overall pricing is not possible.[1] There are two difficulties with this exception to the rule that the open or restricted procedures must be used rather than the negotiated procedure:

–   the provision commences with the word 'exceptionally', at least implying that the negotiated procedure may not be used in all cases where the nature of the services or assessment of risks makes overall pricing impossible; and
–   the output specification giving details of the services required, produced at the beginning of the procurement process, will in all cases be very precise and the risks will not be obscure.

18.20   Nevertheless, the Treasury, responsible for enforcing the public procurement regime, is convinced that the negotiated procedure can be used in PFI. This is, however, being challenged by the EC Commission in relation to a school being procured by Westminster City Council. The reason why one seeks to use the negotiated procedure is in order to permit the provider to be as free as possible in configuring the physical environment in which the services will be delivered and to tailor the documentation to the actual proposals put forward by the provider. It is this process in which the provider can make suggestions which improve value for money. Post-tender negotiations are not permitted under the open and restricted procedures.

Mechanics

18.21   An HEI intending to use the negotiated procedure for a project would send a notice for publication in the *Official Journal of the European Communities* (OJEC). The notice, in the form specified in the Public Services Contract Regulations 1993, Sch 2, Pt D, invites requests to be selected to negotiate. The

---

1   See the Public Services Contracts Regulations 1993, reg 10(2)(b): 'exceptionally, where the nature of the services to be provided, or the risks attaching thereto, are such as not to permit prior overall pricing'.

notice must allow at least 37 days from the date of dispatch of the notice to the OJEC for interested parties to submit their requests. The HEI may exclude from those to be invited to negotiate only those who fail to satisfy the standards of economic and financial standing and ability and technical capacity required by the contracting authority. The evaluation will be made in accordance with paras 14, 15, 16 and 17 of the Regulations. Once the invitation to negotiate has been issued, regs 14, 15, 16 and 17 will no longer have any bearing in choosing the eventual provider. Selection can only be made in respect of the respondent and, if it is a consortium, all the members of the consortium. The experience of those to whom work would be subcontracted should not be taken into account. Invariably, architects are not members of consortia, but they are very important in choosing the eventual provider. The Public Services Contract Regulations 1993, regs 14–20 contain detailed provisions dealing with the selection of those to be invited to negotiate. Conventionally, having received these requests, the procuring body would send a questionnaire to all applicants by way of reply. Replies to the questionnaire would be examined and suitable respondents would be invited to make an oral presentation. After this, a final selection would be made and an invitation to negotiate sent to those chosen. At least three applicants must be invited to negotiate (or all the applicants if requests are received from fewer than three people).

18.22 This procedure is open to a number of objections. The tests of economic and financial standing and ability and technical capacity are meant to be threshold tests which applicants either pass or fail. They should not be used to rank applicants and they can only be historic, not prospective. In practice, it will be important to make the selection based on the proposed designer, who is unlikely to be a consortium member and therefore cannot be evaluated. Finally, because the invitation to negotiate must be issued simultaneously to all invitees, if someone drops out they cannot be replaced. The solution is to issue to all those who qualify under the tests of economic and financial standing, and ability and technical capacity, an invitation to submit outline proposals; this amounts to a formal invitation to negotiate. The responses coming back can be ranked. Some may be excluded without interview. Interviews can then be held and a shortlist of three or four identified.

18.23 The procuring body would then invite priced bids by the issue of a document (commonly called an 'ITN') containing a detailed output specification of the project and a draft of a proposed contract. The objective of the HEI must be to obtain bids which offer a genuine choice and which are priced on the basis of the proposed contract terms, including the payment mechanism. Those to whom it is issued are required to submit detailed proposals by a fixed date. Following receipt of these proposals and an oral presentation, the preferred supplier would be chosen. Detailed negotiations then follow. Frequently, there will be an interim, best and final offer (BAFO), stage where some or all of the bidders are asked to make final proposals on the basis of the procuring body's requirements as they have been clarified as a result of the bidding process. While bidders are in competition with each other, they have an incentive to concede commercial points. The procuring body must, therefore, seek to ensure that it obtains agreement on all important issues before naming the preferred bidder.

Form of the transaction

18.24   The exact relationship of the procurer and the provider will naturally vary according to the nature of the services. Suppose the subject matter of the arrangement is a hall of residence which will be made available to students during term time but used for purposes unconnected with the HEI at other times of year. In this case, the transaction might well not give the HEI any interest in the building. It could essentially:

– oblige the provider to make the accommodation available during term time to students nominated by the HEI; and
– oblige the HEI to nominate students to occupy 95 per cent of the available space or pay for the unused rooms.

It would doubtless deal with other matters (for example, the risk of students failing to pay their lodging charges), but there would be no question of the building being an asset of the HEI. (See McWilliam (1997) and NAO (1997).) Another typical example might be a laboratory building which would be required for research and teaching purposes 24 hours a day throughout the year. The HEI would want to make sure that only its staff and students, contractors and other visitors authorised by the HEI had access. In this case, the HEI itself would be the occupier of the building with exclusive possession and, however the agreement between the provider and the HEI is described, it will take effect as a lease, if the HEI is not already the owner of the freehold.

18.25   How the provider acquires the property in order to be able to make it available will normally depend on where the site is and what the parties want to happen at the end of the contract term. Where the site is already owned by the HEI and/or where the HEI wishes to be sure of retaining the property at the end of the contract period, it makes sense for the HEI to have an interest in the property superior to that of the provider (either the freehold or a superior lease) and to grant a lease to the provider. The provider would then grant an underlease to the HEI so that it can occupy the building. For the transaction to be regarded as qualifying under PFI, it will be essential for the provider to bear all the risks of ownership. Accordingly, the underlease to the HEI will not contain any of the tenant's obligations to repair and insure normally found in an occupational lease (see Sparkes (2001)).

Ancillary services

18.26 As mentioned earlier, PFI is concerned with services, not assets. Accordingly, where the subject matter is occupation of a building, it will be much more credible as a PFI project if as many of the services as are required for use of the building are bundled together and delivered under the PFI contract. These services could include maintenance, energy supply, cleaning, telecommunications, catering, security, porterage and possibly even office services (for example, photocopying and secretarial help). This raises the following difficulties:

– normally, contracts for these services would run for a much shorter period than the 25 or 35 years common for a PFI contract. The discipline in such relationships is exerted by the fact that the contractor knows that, if standards fall, the HEI will simply fail to renew the contract. This means that there is no need to satisfy any objective test before replacing the contractor. If, however, the service declines during the life of the contract, the HEI will be obliged to prove that the contractor has not complied with the terms of the contract. This is not necessarily easy, even in simple cases such as frequent breakdowns of equipment. It is even more difficult if, for example, the food provided tastes bad or if cleaning is inadequate. This is the case however well the output specification is drawn;

– neither party may want to agree a price for such a long period. Indexation may be an adequate adjustment tool for up to 5 years, but after that either the increase in the cost of delivery or the market price for such services, or both, will diverge from the index; and

– the needs of the HEI are likely to change over the period of the contract.

18.27 The first problem can only be fully addressed by having the period of the ancillary service contract shorter than the main PFI contract term. The pricing issue can be solved by a benchmarking process. Effectively, this is done by comparing prices for equivalent services on the review date and adjusting the contract price to the cheapest. However, the nature of services under a PFI contract for occupation of buildings is that they will be bespoke to that building. It will not be easy to ascertain comparable prices without asking other suppliers to tender. They are not likely to be prepared to do so unless they have a chance of being awarded the contract. So, again, it may be a question of having shorter-term contract periods for the services. Logically, this calls into question the wisdom of bundling everything up together at the outset. The key element is building maintenance ('hard FM' in the jargon). This must be within the PFI contract in order to secure the required balance sheet treatment. A service like catering has little relationship to the risks of ownership of the building and may best be let as an independent contract. Then there are services such as caretaking and porterage which, because they include some minor reactive maintenance, may provide economies if they are included within the PFI project agreement. Change can be addressed by a mechanism in the contract which allows either party to propose changes in the contract, obliges the provider to quote a variation in the price and permits the HEI to decide whether to proceed with the change. This should work well for increases in service, but may be less robust in the case of reductions where the provider quotes a reduction in the price which the HEI considers too small. This final difficulty can probably be overcome by reference to an independent expert for a decision.

Timetable

18.28 Figure 18.3 gives the typical timetable for a project involving a new building.

Figure 18.3

	Month 1	Month 2	Month 3	Month 4	Month 5	Month 6	Month 7	Month 8	Month 9	Month 10	Month 11	Month 12	Month 13	Month 14	Month 15	Month 16
Prepare and issue OJEC Notice	■															
Prepare outputs specification and bidding material		■														
Prequalify respondents Invite bids			■													
Shortlist bidders Invite priced bids				■												
Clarify requirements as bidders develop their bids					■											
Receive and evaluate bids Invite BAFO								■								
Bidders prepare their BAFO									■							
Evaluate BAFO											■					
Name preferred bidder												■				
Obtain detailed planning permission Find negotiations														■		
Contract close																■

CONCLUSIONS ON PFI AND PRACTICAL CONSIDERATIONS

18.29   There are a number of reasons why an HEI might want to procure a new project by PFI:

–   the recurrent cost might be cheaper because of the skill of the provider in specifying the assets required to deliver the required service;
–   the provider might have an alternative use for those assets when they would otherwise be idle and be prepared to reduce the charge to the HEI accordingly;
–   it might be good politics to support the initiative which the Government is promoting; and
–   the HEI might need to avoid borrowing the money required to fund the capital costs of the project because its balance sheet would not be strong enough.

18.30   If either or both of the first two motives are applicable, the HEI need not be concerned whether the transaction actually qualifies under the PFI. If the third motive is dominant, it may be possible to come sufficiently close to a PFI transaction to satisfy those who are concerned to promote the PFI without fully conforming to the strictest requirements. It is only in the case of the fourth motive that strict compliance will be necessary; otherwise FRS 5 may require the facility concerned to be considered an asset of the HEI and the obligations under the contract to be recognised as a loan.

18.31   Unless PFI is likely to be a significantly cheaper option in net present cost terms, an HEI will be wise to choose conventional procurement. The transaction costs are cheaper and the process will be quicker. Where PFI might offer benefits, it will be well to test the opportunities. Given the constraints imposed by the public procurement rules, it will usually be possible to test whether the market can produce a solution under PFI which is more cost-effective than conventional procurement. If this turns out not to be the case, it will be possible to switch to conventional procurement at that stage. It is important that the original notice to the OJEC allows for this. Otherwise, the need to issue a fresh notice may cause cost and delay.

18.32   If the PFI route is started, the key issues are:

–   establishing an investment appraisal including the net present cost of conventionally procuring the same result;
–   formulation of the output specification; and
–   dealing with the legal requirements for properly authorising the transaction, compliance with the public procurement rules, and establishing the contractual documentation.

18.33   The HEI will require advice from surveyors (if the subject matter is the occupation of buildings), accountants and solicitors. There could be a significant cost saving if the professional advisers are used only as required, rather than all of them attending every meeting of the project team. Legal advice will be required at every stage and solicitors can usefully be appointed as lead advisers.

OTHER PRIVATE SOURCES OF FINANCE

18.34   If PFI does not seem worth considering in detail or has been rejected, HEIs are usually able to obtain finance by way of loans from banks. Debt finance would also be available from the bond market. Leasing should be considered for plant and machinery. The regulatory framework is that, under HEFCE Circular 5/96, HEIs are required to obtain the consent of the HEFCE for borrowing, if the annualised servicing costs of borrowing exceed 4 per cent of total income as reported in the latest audited financial statements. Annualised servicing costs are the cost of capital repayments and interest spread evenly over the period of the borrowing. (The annualised servicing costs of debt inherited from LEAs is excluded from the calculation.) For this purpose, 'borrowing' includes finance leasing and other schemes where borrowing is the substance of the transaction.

Borrowing

18.35   As well as borrowing from banks – for which there is ample oppor-tunity – HEIs can consider raising finance in the long-term bond market. One university has done this directly. The cost can be high, as this involves giving a great deal of information about the activities, assets, liabilities and financial state of the HEI. Financiers have also suggested a co-operative approach to the market. This would involve a specially incorporated company issuing the bonds which would have the benefit of the guarantee of an insurance company. The funds raised would be on-lent to the participating institutions. Because of the credit enhancement provided by the guarantee, minimal information about the participating HEIs would be required. The advantage of using the bond market is that a rate of interest is fixed for a period up to 25 years. A complicating factor is that investors like the whole amount of the face value of the bond to be repaid by one instalment on the due date of the bond. The HEI using the money raised, however, will need to provide for repayment out of its income throughout the period of the bond. There is bound to be a difference between the interest rate payable on the bond and the interest which can be earned on the amounts set aside to make repayment. Nevertheless, the bond market offers a form of finance which HEIs should probably use for part of their borrowing requirements. It is a very well-established process for US HEIs, museums and other not-for-profit organisations.

Leasing

18.36   Because HEIs are charities they do not usually have income which is taxable for corporation tax purposes. Accordingly, when they make an investment in plant and machinery for which a commercial entity would be able to obtain capital allowances, they cannot obtain the benefit because they have no tax liability in the first place. If, however, they are able to lease the plant and machinery from a leasing company which can obtain the capital allowances and, as is normal, pass on part of the benefit to the lessee, the financing cost of obtaining the use of the plant and machinery will be less than if the money to purchase it had been borrowed by the HEI.

CONCLUSIONS

18.37 For the foreseeable future, the Government will not be providing significant funding for capital projects. HEIs will be forced to find the capital required from private sources. Since they are private bodies their borrowings do not form part of the national debt and they are not required to use PFI rather than conventional procurement. HEFCE does not oblige HEIs to consider PFI for their capital projects, whereas FE colleges were obliged by the FEFC to evaluate the PFI option.[1] Nevertheless, in some cases, PFI will be the preferred option. In some ways, HE has the best of all worlds: it is able to take advantage of the fact that PFI is being developed as an innovative way of providing services more economically in some cases than conventional procurement; on the other hand, it is not forced to use PFI or even to incur the expense of evaluating it in depth where it is unlikely to be more cost effective.

---

1   See FEFC Circular 95/25.

Chapter 19

THE LEGAL STATUS OF THE STUDENTS' UNION

Anthony Jones (Shakespeares)

EDITORS' INTRODUCTION

§19.1   What is the legal status of the SU? Who is in charge of it – the community of students or the HEI itself? If not the latter, what legal responsibilities does it have for the proper management of the SU, and what powers (if any) to ensure the proper management of the SU? Who owns the SU building and the land on which it stands? What happens if something goes wrong – if the SU becomes bankrupt, or is sued for breach of contract and has to pay substantial damages, or if there is a death arising from neglect of health and safety matters? Who clears up the financial mess, who pays the financial penalty and who faces the criminal prosecution brought by the Health and Safety Executive? If things became difficult in this way, can the HEI, which earlier might have wanted to be in control of the SU, now try to distance itself from all responsibility, especially in terms of being a financially deeper pocket for the payment of those damages? Is the gap between the SU and the HEI sufficiently wide for no liability of the former ever to transfer to the latter? Can the gap be made wider? This chapter deals with all these questions and more issues besides, including the relevant legislation under which SUs exist, their extensive trading activities and their governance. Clearly, there are links to Chapter 3 (Governance), Chapter 4 (Trusteeship), and Chapter 15 (Trading Companies).

§19.2   These are very real issues . . . In a case in 1996 four students were expelled from the SU for alleged financial and procedural impropriety by South Bank University and were refused leave by the Court of Appeal for judicial review. They were reported[1] to be considering an appeal to the European Court. The case highlighted whether the University had the power to take over the running of the SU, to install a caretaker manager and to impose an interim constitution on the SU. In *R v Thames Valley University Student Union ex parte Ogilvy*,[2] an SU was found to be a private, voluntary association and hence *not* subject to judicial review (as opposed, of course, to the HEI itself) in respect of the Education Act 1994 (EA 1994), s 22: the TVU SU is, unusually, completely free-standing from the HEI and is not part of the HEI's corporate structure (and hence, presumably, the HEI will not become liable for its bad debts, negligence, breach of contract, etc). The issue in *Commissioners of*

---

1   In *The Times Higher Educational Supplement*, 26 July 1996; see (2001) ELJ 2(4) 228–229 for the continuing saga, reaching the House of Lords in *Anyanwu and Another v South Bank Student Union and Another and Commission for Racial Equality* [2001] UKHL 14, [2001] ELR 511; see also para **19.24**.

2   [1997] CLY 2149, (1997) 4(8) ELM 6, QBD.

Customs and Excise v University of Leicester Students' Union[1] was exemption from VAT for sales by the SU to its members: the High Court held that, for VAT purposes, the SU is *not* part of the HEI and hence unable to shelter within any VAT exemption which the HEI may have. Thus, the *Anyansu*, *Ogilvy*, and *Leicester* cases all point towards the SU not being part of, nor as it were a department of, the HEI; it is an unincorporated association linked to the HEI in terms of sheltering within the HEI's charitable status (but not its VAT exemptions) and in terms of the HEI having some supervision duties imposed by the EA 1994 concerning freedom of speech, elections, affiliations, etc. The HEI is therefore probably already reasonably well insulated from the liabilities of the SU, but this chapter ends by considering incorporation of the SU as a way of 'thickening the veil' between the SU and the HEI.

§19.3   As an historical footnote, it is interesting to note that collectively stroppy students in need of firm handling by the HEI is nothing new. From the archives of New College, Oxford, Item 678 tells the story of a power-struggle between the Junior Members (students) and the Fellows (Governing Body). The archives document is an Opinion given by Sir William Erle in 1868 on the legal status of the Junior Common Room (JCR, an Oxbridge college SU) and the ownership of 'its' property: this property duly reflected time-honoured student priorities in consisting of 'eleven Pipes of Port . . . Plate . . . Furniture . . . a few Books'. The Fellows wanted to be more assertive in controlling the JCR; the JCR had promptly resolved either to dissolve itself and divide this property among its Members or to go 'off-shore' by transferring the property to rooms beyond the College walls and hence 'beyond the authority of the College'. The Bursar dutifully sought legal advice, as recorded in copper-plate in Item 678: 'Right of property in the Realty and Personalty used by Members of the Junior Common Room' lies with the College, and that the 'interest' of the Members of the JCR 'arises only by a licence from the College' for them to make use of these facilities. Hence the Junior Members had no 'right or any colourable [credible, plausible] claim over these items', and College could take whatever action it sees fit 'to secure the property legally, if necessary, for the future use of its Undergraduate Members in perpetuity': such 'action' might include, should College 'deem it necessary or expedient', the closure of the JCR for a time. The Opinion usefully added that, if the pipes of port were 'perishable commodities', these could, during this period of closure, be sold and 'the proceeds kept with the Plate and the like according to the occasion'. (Exactly the legal advice which the Fellows hoped for. It would, of course, be unduly cynical to note that Sir William had once been a Fellow of New College.) Today the HEI can simply threaten the SU with a reduction in budget: UCL SU recently called off a planned non-payment of tuition fees protest when UCL declared it would cut £60,000 from the SU funding.[2] Otherwise, injunctions can, of course, be obtained to constrain the SU or to recover possession of occupied HEI buildings.[3]

---

1   [2001] STC 550; subsequently confirmed by the Court of Appeal (2002) *The Times*, January 25.
2   Reported in the *The Times Higher Educational Supplement*, 8 June, p 3.
3   *University of Warwick v De Graaf and Others* [1975] 3 All ER 284; *University of Essex v Djemal and Others* [1980] 2 All ER 742.

DEFINITION

19.1 Prior to the EA 1994, the term 'students' union' was a generic term which did not require further definition. The EA 1994, which came into force on 1 April 1995, made significant changes to the law regarding SUs and imposed certain onerous obligations on HEIs and FEIs in relation to their SUs. The EA 1994, s 20(1), defines an SU as being:

> 'an association of the generality of students at an establishment ... whose principal purposes include promoting the general interests of its members as students; or a representative body (whether an association or not) whose principal purposes include representing the generality of students at an establishment ... in academic, disciplinary or other matters relating to the government of the establishment.'

19.2 This is a wide definition and its purpose is to encapsulate the spectrum of the many differing types of SUs that exist. In fact, to emphasise this, s 20 of the EA 1994 goes further to highlight that the definition of an SU extends to include bodies or societies which represent undergraduates or postgraduates, committees, and halls of residence and colleges within a university (for example, Oxford and Cambridge Universities). The 'association' referred to does not require a majority of students to be classed as 'a generality of students'. It is doubtful that the definition extends to include specific subject societies (for example, the Electrical Engineering Society), but it may cover a more general organisation (for example, the Faculty of Engineering Society), depending upon the objects of the organisation. The provisions of the EA 1994 do not apply to organisations whose principal purposes are the organisation of social activities (for example, Friends of the University, sports clubs, social committees, etc), since these organisations are not promoting the general interests of their members or representing them in disciplinary matters.

19.3 Any affiliated associations or bodies are classed as SUs under the EA 1994, which have a 'branch' at another establishment, must comply with the provisions of the EA 1994, s 20(4) at both establishments. However, this requirement does not extend to include nationwide or worldwide organisations such as the NUS. Organisations such as the NUS are excluded from complying with the EA 1994. Another recognised exclusion is that part-time students may be excluded from SU membership, if an HEI determines that they are not eligible for SU membership. Therefore, if the HEI decides, the EA 1994 may apply only to SUs which represent the 'generality' of full-time students. It is important to remember that, for the obligations under the EA 1994 to apply, the organisation must come within the definition of an SU, not merely have that title. The basic premise being that an HEI which has an association which promotes the general interests of students or which represents students in relation to academic or disciplinary matters would have to comply with the requirements under the EA 1994.

THE REQUIREMENTS OF THE EA 1994

19.4   The intention of the EA 1994 is to provide a framework to ensure that an SU operates in a fair and democratic manner within its constitution and accounts for its finances. However, the EA 1994 does not regulate all the activities of SUs. It is the responsibility of the governing body of HEIs to ensure that the specific provisions in s 22 of the EA 1994 are followed. An HEI is 'to take such steps as are reasonably practical to secure' compliance of the SU with all the more specific requirements under s 22. These are as follows:

–   the SU should have a written constitution, which should be made freely available to all students;

–   the constitution should be approved by the governing body and subject to review at least once every 5 years;

–   a student has the right not to be a member of the SU and a person who chooses not to be a member of the SU should not be unfairly disadvantaged in respect of the provision of services which members receive. This provision allows membership to be voluntary, students having the opportunity to 'opt out' of the SU. The aim is to allow greater choice and democracy in SUs. Students and prospective students must be notified at least once a year of their right to 'opt out' of the SU. To ensure that students are not unfairly disadvantaged in respect of the availability and provisions of facilities and services, the governing body can make an agreement with the SU to continue to provide these facilities to students who have 'opted out' or provide separate parallel facilities. The EA 1994 does not detail exactly what facilities and services should be provided for students who have 'opted out' and the Parliamentary Under Secretary of State stated that:[1] 'It is not for the Government to say what services should be available; that is quite properly a matter for the Institution to decide. I emphasised that in initiating the measures, we are leaving matters to local decision wherever possible and not seeking to prescribe in concrete the exact procedures to be followed'. It has been suggested that 'opted out' students should have equal services in relation to welfare, catering and sport. Obviously voting rights in relation to the SU would not be open to non-members. Again, HEIs must ensure that at least once a year 'opted out' students are informed of the alternative services available to them;

–   secret ballots should be held for elections to major SU offices (for example, President and Vice-President). It is up to the HEI to determine which are the major officers as no further guidance is given. However, Baroness Blatch said that she would: 'expect the requirement to apply to the Union President and others with a significant role in running the Union'.[2] Normally, the 'major offices' of the SU subject to a secret ballot would include the President, Vice-President, Secretary and Treasurer. The

---

1   *Hansard*, Standing Committee, col 386, 21 June 1994.
2   *Hansard*, House of Lords, vol 553, col 167.

requirement of a secret ballot does not apply to the Open University or any distance learning colleges;[1]

–   the SU elections should be 'fairly and properly conducted', and HEIs should ensure that the SU's constitution contains appropriate provisions for the conduct of elections;

–   a person should not hold sabbatical union office or paid elected union office for more than 2 years;

–   the financial affairs of the SU should be properly conducted and scrutinised. Arrangements should be made for the approval of the SU's budget and the monitoring of expenditure by the governing body. The turnover of some SUs is larger than many businesses. The EA 1994 requires the governing body to ensure that the SU is 'accountable' for its finances, that its financial affairs are 'properly conducted', and that its budget is approved and spending monitored. How a governing body addresses this monitoring and approval is again left to the HEI's discretion. Although an HEI will wish to ensure that it does not become liable for the finances of the SU, it may wish to enter into a formal financial memorandum with the SU including these requirements;

–   the financial reports of the SU should be published annually and copies made available to the governing body and all students. These reports should contain a list of all external organisations to which the SU is affiliated or to which it has made grants or donations. The purpose of this requirement is to prevent SUs making donations which are contrary to charity law. External relations and affiliations should be in furtherance of the objectives for which the SU was established and within its objects and powers. This requirement follows a line of legal actions brought by students with regard to the donation of funds to external, political or non-charitable organisations by their SU;

–   the allocation of resources to groups or clubs should be fair and there should be a detailed written procedure available for examination by all students. This requirement is essentially a codification of what has already been common practice within most HEIs;

–   if the SU decides to affiliate to a new external organisation, then a notice should be published detailing the cost of this affiliation or the donation which the SU will be making along with its application. This notice should be bought to the attention of the governing body and all students;

–   the annual reports should contain a list of the external organisations to which the SU has made donations in the period and the amount of those individual donations;

–   there should be a procedure for the review of affiliations to external organisations. Every year, the current list of affiliations should be approved by the members. The EA 1994 does not provide specific details of how this review should be conducted, but this requirement would be best dealt with at an annual general meeting. A proportion of SU members

---

1   See the EA 1994, s 22(2)(a).

(not exceeding 5 per cent) may requisition a ballot to question the continued affiliation to a particular organisation. The decision upon continued affiliation is conducted by secret ballot of all SU members;

– a complaints procedure should be implemented to allow students who are dissatisfied with their dealings with the SU, or who claim to be unfairly disadvantaged by reason of opting out of the SU, to air their grievances. The written complaints procedure should be brought to the attention of the students by the governing body. The complaints procedure must provide for an independent person to investigate and report to the governing body. This independent person has not been defined within the EA 1994, but it was envisaged that he would be appointed by the governing body, and not be connected with the HEI. The complaints procedure is intended to provide an independent and impartial review procedure. It is left to the governing body to decide whether to accept the independent person's report but it has to ensure that, where a complaint is upheld, that there is an effective remedy available;

– all complaints should be dealt with promptly and fairly. The HEI must provide an effective remedy when a complaint is upheld following investigation; and

– the governing body of an HEI should prepare and issue a code of practice detailing how each of those requirements are secured and observed. This code of practice should be brought to the attention of all students at least once a year, along with instructions as to the restrictions imposed on SUs by charity law and the rights of students to freedom of speech. This is, of course, in addition to the SU's written constitution and the complaints procedure.

19.5 The governing body of the HEI has some discretion how to implement, observe and monitor these requirements within the HEI. This increases the burden of the task and leaves sufficient scope for varying methods of implementation and infringement. The legal responsibility for ensuring compliance with these requirements rests with the governing body of the HEI, and failure to comply could result in judicial review proceedings or even claims under the Human Rights Act 1998.

FREEDOM OF SPEECH

19.6 Under s 22(4) of the EA 1994, HEIs must outline the provisions of the Education (No 2) Act 1986, s 43, regarding the freedom of speech in HEIs and issue students with a copy of any code of practice relating to it. Section 43 requires the HEI to 'take such steps as are reasonably practicable to ensure freedom of speech for students and employees of the HEI and for visiting speakers'. This duty includes the use of any HEI premises, so far as possible. The use of the premises cannot be denied on the grounds of the beliefs, views, policies or objectives of the individual or organisation requesting the use of the venue. The HEI should issue and keep up to date a code of practice outlining the procedures to be followed by students or employees with regard to meetings or other activities involving speeches or debates. The conduct required of any students or employees organising or arranging such meeting may also be outlined in the HEI's code of practice along with disciplinary measures to ensure compliance.

19.7 There is very little guidance upon what is 'reasonably practicable' in relation to this obligation. However, the case of *R v University of Liverpool ex parte Caesar-Gordon*[1] has helped to clarify the position. The case concerned a proposed meeting of the University of Liverpool Conservative Association, at which members of the South African Embassy in London had been invited to give a speech. The University gave provisional permission for the meeting, subject to the co-operation of the local police. After consultation with the local police, the meeting was cancelled because the University was not satisfied 'that adequate arrangements could be made to maintain good order'. It was feared that public violence would break out in neighbouring areas, which had a large black and Asian population. There was an internal appeal in accordance with the University's code of practice. On appeal, the University agreed to allow the meeting to be held on certain special conditions, but later cancelled the meeting again following further consultation with the police. The Chairman of the University of Liverpool Conservative Association brought judicial review proceedings against the University on the grounds that the University's decision was *ultra vires* and in breach of the Education (No 2) Act 1986, s 43. The court held that 'good order' could only relate to 'good order' within the precincts of the university. The University, in discharging its duty under s 43(1), was not entitled to take into account threats of 'public disorder' outside the confines of the University by persons not within its control. Police concerns of public disorder in the surrounding area were not sufficient reason for the University to refuse permission for the meeting to be held. It would be for the police, with the University, to consider whether a breach of the peace would occur and to forbid or cancel the meeting on the grounds of public interest. An interesting point was that the court decided that the University was acting reasonably by imposing conditions. The special conditions that the University imposed were that:

–   attendance at the meeting would be confined to a limited number of staff and students;
–   there would be no publicity of any kind for the meeting; and
–   entrance to the meeting was to be granted only on production of a valid university identity card.

19.8 This case is useful in establishing that an HEI can concern itself with disruption on its premises but not in the surrounding areas, and that it is perfectly within an HEI's authority to impose special conditions (provided that

1   [1990] 3 All ER 821.

these are reasonable). This case also demonstrates the effectiveness of having a good code of practice.

STATUS

19.9 SUs are usually unincorporated associations separate from the HEI, although some are now considering acquiring corporate status. The majority of the SUs are established either by charter, by statute or by the articles of government of the HEI itself. The only real exceptions are Cambridge, Essex and York Universities where their SUs are established by an 'ordinance'. The difference between an ordinance and a charter, statute or articles of government is that an ordinance may be terminated by the institution without the consent of the Privy Council. The various charters, statutes, articles of government and ordinances vary considerably in their definition and regulation of an HEI's SU. Before proposing any major change to the status, organisation or constitution of the SU, it is advisable to examine the HEI's own constitutional documents for any provisions regarding the SU. It is also necessary to examine the 'objects' within the constitution of an SU, as these differ in their detail and comprehensiveness from institution to institution. An SU should have clearly defined objects, which are in accordance with the HEI's own objects and, as far as possible, able to be construed as charitable. The objects should certainly not be broader than those of the HEI.

Unincorporated association

19.10 The majority of SUs are unincorporated associations which was defined in *Conservative Central Office v Burrell*[1] as:

> 'two or more persons bound together for one or more common purposes, not being business purposes, by mutual undertakings each having mutual duties and obligations, in an organisation which has rules which identify on whom control of it and its funds rests and upon what terms and which can be joined or left at will.'

An unincorporated association is governed by its own constitution which acts essentially as a legally binding contract between its members. It must have identifiable rules and an identifiable membership (which should be sufficient to satisfy the provisions for a written constitution).[2] An unincorporated association itself has no separate legal existence, unlike a company, and is seen in law as a group of individuals who have duties and liabilities to one another. There are no statutes dealing directly with unincorporated associations, and so the law applies to unincorporated associations in the same way as it does to individuals. Therefore, a member of an unincorporated association who enters into a contract on its behalf is personally liable on that contract, although the

---

1   [1982] 1 WLR 522, [1982] 2 All ER 1, CA.
2   See the EA 1994, s 22(2)(a).

member may be entitled to be indemnified out of the association's funds under its rules.

THE SU AND CHARITY LAW

19.11 HEIs are charitable institutions in accordance with the ERA 1988, s 125A. They are classed as 'exempt charities' (for more detail see Chapter 4). Under the Charities Act 1993, Sch 2, all institutions or colleges connected with an HEI or any institution which is administered by or on behalf of an HEI and 'is established for the general purposes of, or for any special purpose of or in connection with' the HEI is also an exempt charity. Accordingly, so long as there is congruence of administration and purpose, the SU will have exempt status.

Advantage of charitable classification

19.12 The advantages of being an exempt or registered charity is that the rules relating to certainty of a trust and perpetuity are no longer applicable. However, the biggest benefit, of course, is in relation to tax advantages, exemption from capital gains tax, income tax, corporation tax (other than trading income), and business rates reduction. HEIs are also normally exempt from VAT on the supply of education and research. However, VAT is payable in relation to trading activities. The advantage of exempt status is that the SU does not have to comply with so many statutory requirements as a registered charity, making its administration easier. However, it is important to remember that the rules regarding trustees acting 'reasonably and prudently' in all matters, and careful application of funds in accordance with the charitable objects and powers of investment, still apply.

Charitable status and donations

19.13 Basically, the SU exists to further the educational purposes of the HEI, to promote the general welfare of the students, and to advance the interests of the HEI. Any non-charitable activities should be supplemental or incidental to the overall development of scientific, artistic, cultural, athletic, political, religious and social activities amongst students. Any expenditure or donation by an SU should be made only to further these objects. The subject of charitable status and donations by SUs has been raised in court on a number of occasions where it was questioned whether funds were being correctly applied in donating money to charitable (but non-educational) organisations and political organisations.

19.14 In 1972, the University of Sussex SU intended to make donations to War on Want and to a campaign protesting against the abolition of free school

milk. The matter came before the courts in *Baldry v Feintuck*,[1] and Brightman J
said that:

> 'it is not open to the Union ... to authorise the use of the Union's funds for the purpose
> of promoting any object which may happen to interest the members of the Union
> regardless of whether such object is charitable and educational or not ... If the
> members of the Union wish to express their views financially that money should come
> from their own personal funds and not from trust money. Admittedly, part of the
> educational business is research, discussion, debate and reaching a corporate
> conclusion on social and economic problems, but, in my view the provision of money
> to finance the adoption outside the University of that corporate conclusion does not
> form any part of the educational process.'

It was held that the payments to War on Want, despite being a charity, were not
educational, and that: 'it is not open to one charity to subscribe to the funds of
another charity unless the recipient charity has expressly or by implication a
purpose or object of the donor charity'. As for the campaign against abolition of
school milk, it was held that this was a non-charitable purpose and, therefore,
'charitable funds cannot be lawfully used for setting up such a fund'.

19.15   In 1985 another case came before the court.[2] North London Polytechnic proposed making a substantial payment towards the striking miners and in
aid of victims of the Ethiopian famine. The Attorney-General took the view that
these payments were outside the scope of the SU's objects and were *ultra vires*.
The SU argued in this case that, while some of its objects were charitable,
others (such as its affiliation with the NUS and other outside bodies)
demonstrated that its main purpose was not charitable. Therefore, the SU
should not have charitable status and should be free to make any donations it
wanted. Scott J disagreed and, in holding that the SU did have charitable status,
said:

> 'There is, in my view, no reason in principle why a students' union being a charity
> should not affiliate itself to the NUS, a non-charity and pay the subscriptions or fees.
> The NUS is the leading National Student Organisation. I do not, therefore, accept
> Counsel's argument that affiliation to the NUS and payment of affiliation fees is
> inconsistent with the SU having a charitable status.'

Therefore, if the SU's constitution as well as expressing charitable objects,
allows certain non-charitable activities to be carried on, provided these
non-charitable activities are regarded as being merely ancillary or supplementary to the SU's main objects, it is not fatal to charitable status (which, anyway,
should be well worth preserving for tax reasons).

19.16   Another interesting case considering the more detached relationship
the SU had with its HEI is *London Hospital Medical College v Inland Revenue
Commissioners and Others*,[3] concerning a medical college attached to a hospital.
The SU had been formed with the objects of promoting, encouraging and

---

1   [1972] 1 WLR 552.
2   *A-G v Ross* [1986] 1 WLR 252, [1985] 3 All ER 345.
3   [1976] 2 All ER 113.

co-ordinating 'social, cultural and athletic activities amongst the members so as to add to the general comfort and enjoyment of the students', but qualified hospital staff could also be members of the SU. The SU was reliant upon the college for a proportion of its funding and regarded itself as under the control of the college. However, the Inspector of Taxes challenged the SU's charitable status on the grounds that its activities solely benefited its members. The court decided that the SU did exist solely to further educational purposes and it achieved this aim. The SU was heavily dependent upon the college and the benefits given to members were for the purpose of encouraging and carrying out the main educational purpose of the college. Brightman J took into account that, if the college removed its support, the SU would close and that the main object of the SU was furthering the purposes of the college and not for private benefit. The SU was, therefore, charitable: see also *Harrison v Hearn*,[1] concerning the Students' Council at Macquarie University.

19.17   In the light of the above cases, the provision in s 22 of the EA 1994, regarding the publication of external organisations to which the SU is affiliated or wishes to be affiliated or donate funds, can now be appreciated. Furthermore, the requirements under the EA 1994 to bring to the attention of all students the restrictions imposed on the activities of the SU by charity law also becomes evident.

RISK AND LIABILITY

19.18   The activities of SUs are frequently the subject of media attention. The SU undertakes a variety of events, entertainments and sports which can often lead to publicity and legal actions. Governing bodies of HEIs are obviously concerned about being held liable for the actions, omissions or debts of the SU. The question whether an HEI could be held liable for the SU will depend on the nature of the claim that has been brought and the status of the SU.

Health and safety aspects

19.19   Injury or damage caused by defects in buildings or health and safety prosecutions will usually remain the responsibility of the HEI as the owner of the building. Health and safety regulations are extensive and leave few grounds for a defence in relation to occupiers' liability. An HEI could transfer ownership of the SU building to the SU to reduce its potential liability, but this then creates difficulties in that the SU may mortgage the property, sell it, lease or licence parts of it to third parties. Furthermore, if the students were to go into 'occupation', the HEI would have few or no powers to intervene. There is also no guarantee that the SU would keep the building in adequate repair or satisfactory condition. HEIs could consider the possibility of leasing or

---

1   [1972] 1 NSWLR 428.

licensing the SU premises to the SU itself. A lease or licence may provide for repair and upkeep of the building and for its general safety and security, which again should reduce the potential liability of an HEI.

Employment and staff disputes

19.20   In an unincorporated association, the person who is liable to an employee is the person who actually engaged or appointed the employee (for example, the SU President or the SU Executive Committee). This obviously creates difficulties should a member of staff bring an action against the SU in relation to any employment rights.[1] More recently, Swansea University SU has publicly apologised for dismissing its general manager and has paid him substantial damages.

Contractual and tortious liability and the unincorporated association

19.21   Perhaps more of a concern for an HEI is the possibility of liability for debts, breaches of contract, injuries or damage caused by negligence, which result from the activities of the SU. An unincorporated association enters into a contract through individuals, who may remain personally liable for the debts or breach of contract resulting from that agreement. If authority to enter into a contract was given by a committee, then the committee members would be liable for breach of the contract. An ordinary member of the SU (ie a full-time student) or the HEI itself would not usually be liable for the debts or breach of contract by the SU, because they have not been given any implied authority to make that contract, nor contracted personally. Liability under a contract is for the full amount of the claim and not limited to the funds which the unincorporated association holds. However, liability may be limited by a specific provision in the contract to the funds of the association, provided such a provision is considered reasonable under the UCTA 1977. In cases of negligence and other torts, some or all of the members of the SU may be liable depending upon the extent to which they held overall control of the activities concerned. As there is little existing case-law, it is difficult to establish or predict a court's approach or conclusions. However, it is important for the SU to maintain adequate insurance for all types of public liability which, in the case of an unincorporated association, will need to be taken out by an officer or the committee of the SU, who then holds it on behalf of all the members of the SU. This insurance must be capable of indemnifying individual members.

---

1   See *Hadden v University of Dundee Students' Association* [1985] IRLR 449; *Leicester University Students' Union v Mahomed* [1995] ICR 270.

POTENTIAL HEI LIABILITY

19.22   HEIs have always recognised that SUs are a potential risk in terms of liability and have tried to emphasise to the parents, students and others that the HEI itself is not responsible for the SU and is not liable for its activities. Normally, an HEI will not be liable for breach of contract by the SU as it is not a party to the contract and, therefore, cannot be held liable upon it. However, liability could arise if the HEI has given a guarantee in relation to the contract. The issue of whether an HEI could be liable for the negligent activities of its SU is an interesting question. A plaintiff (say, a student) bringing a claim for negligence has to show that there was duty of care owed by the defendant and that this duty of care has been breached (say, lack of safety equipment, slippery floors, inadequate facilities) which has caused damage to the plaintiff and was foreseeable in the circumstances. This is a very simplistic view of the tort of negligence; it is not possible here to discuss the variety of circumstances in which a duty of care may arise. In the absence of any substantive case-law, it is difficult to predict quite how far a court would go in determining the extent to which an HEI owes a duty of care to members of the SU.

19.23   The HEI has a duty of care to ensure, for example, that the buildings in which students study and work are safe (see Chapter 20), and that examination papers are marked fairly and correctly (see Chapter 6). The HEI is also vicariously liable for the negligent actions of its staff in the course of their employment (see Chapter 5). However, whether an HEI's duty of care extends to activities which are not part of a students course (for example, climbing or diving) is an interesting discussion point. The courts have held that social and sports activities are part of HEI objects and that this is the reason why SUs maintain exempt charitable status, so it is arguable that injuries may be foreseeable as a result of students engaging in social or sporting activities organised by the SU, or a particular section of it, and that the HEI has a duty of care to ensure such activities are conducted properly. On the other hand, the HEI is certainly not any longer *in loco parentis* and is not obliged to supervise student social activities. But, when an individual has been severely injured or killed as a result of negligence, the courts are often anxious to compensate the plaintiff for the damage they have suffered and a duty of care may be constructed all too easily for the HEI as a 'deep pocket' (and almost certainly carrying insurance: see Chapter 24) in those cases where the SU itself is unable to meet the liability.

19.24   An HEI may be held liable for knowingly aiding the SU to commit an unlawful act under the RRA 1976. In the recent case of *Anyanwu and Others v South Bank Student Union and Others*,[1] the House of Lords has decided that the expulsion of two students, who were elected officers of the SU, from the HEI and their exclusion from any University building, including the SU, which effectively prevented them from carrying out their offices, could amount to

---

1   [2001] 2 All ER 353.

aiding the termination of their employment by the SU within the RRA 1976, s 33(1).

REDUCING THE RISKS BY INCORPORATION

19.25   An HEI can reduce the risks associated with its SU, by ensuring that the SU is well organised and managed, with proper procedures in place and that the officers and staff are accountable for the running of the SU. The tendency of the courts is to put ever greater responsibility onto the HEI for the activities of its SU, and so HEIs will have to respond by managing the risks concerned. This must be a better strategy than suddenly being faced with defending a potentially high profile court action with its media publicity and financial consequences. The incorporation of SU is now seen as one way for the HEI to reduce its risks and liabilities associated with the everyday running of the SU. Incorporation of the SU does not guarantee exemption from liability, but it *may* improve the chances of successfully avoiding liability should it arise. The use of trading companies by HEIs has become more common (see Chapter 15). These companies are used for structural, commercial and tax reasons. With the substantial turnover of some SUs, it may soon become essential as opposed to desirable, for SU bars to be run through trading companies to avoid difficulties with their charitable status. The following brief outline of some of the difficulties which may be experienced if full incorporation of the SU were envisaged is accompanied by some possible suggested solutions. Incorporating SUs is not a simple task and there are many issues to be considered. The success of incorporating the SU, its continued development and efficient governance would depend upon the objects and powers which are given by the memorandum and articles of association. An HEI should consider exactly how much influence or control it wishes to have over its SU.

Format

19.26   The SU would probably be incorporated by means of a company limited by guarantee which has independent status, but which differs from a company limited by shares in that:

–   it has no shares;
–   each member of the company agrees to contribute to the assets of the company to a specified amount (say, 5p) should the company be wound up for any reason;
–   the members of the company are the original subscribers, along with any other persons who agree to become members in accordance with its articles of association; and
–   it may operate without using the word 'Limited' after its name, provided the company's objects are the promotion of commerce, art, science, or education, and that any profits are spent promoting these objects.

Memorandum and articles of association

19.27 A company limited by guarantee must have a memorandum and articles of association setting out the objects and powers of the company, the directors' powers and members' rights and voting powers. These documents are the governing document of the SU and should satisfy the requirement for a written constitution. These documents have to be carefully drafted so that the administration procedures they lay down are workable and capable of compliance.

Running an incorporated SU

19.28 The SU (as a company) must comply with the various provisions of the legislation concerning companies. The obligations placed on a company by this are too numerous and extensive to discuss in detail here. However, briefly, the company's day-to-day obligations are that it must:

- print the company name, registration number and registered office on all notepaper and invoices;
- keep statutory books with details of directors, members, debentures and charges and directors' interests;
- file an annual return with Companies House;
- file annual audited accounts with Companies House;
- register with Companies House and keep Companies House notified of any changes of director;
- hold an annual general meeting;
- make any changes to the constitution of the company by holding an extraordinary general meeting and have the resolution approved by 75 per cent of the members present; and
- comply with the provisions in the Companies Act with regard to the calling and holding of meetings.

The requirements are extensive. There are 80 circumstances in which documents are to be submitted to Companies House. The task of ensuring that an incorporated SU complies would not be a simple one. Failure to file returns or accounts will result in substantial fines, or even criminal liability being imposed on directors and officers. It may be wise for the company secretary to be a permanent member of staff of the HEI in order to ensure compliance and provide continuity.

Directors and members

19.29 An important issue to consider is who will be the directors and members of a company. One approach would be to appoint the sabbatical officers as the directors of the company and all students (except those who have expressed a wish to 'opt out' of the SU) as members of the SU. The register of members could be maintained by keeping a list of all students attending at the

HEI. If this list is kept or printed from a database kept on the computer, then both the HEI and the SU should consider compliance with the DPA 1998 before any information is transferred (see Chapter 13). If this approach is adopted the HEI will lose all direct control over the governance and conduct of the SU, although it may retain some considerable indirect influence if it is the main provider of financial support. The students may enter into contracts, change the constitution, change the name, secure finance and alter the membership provisions, without the consent or approval of the HEI. This would be a dangerous situation, particularly considering the legal obligations of an HEI's governing body under the EA 1994, which they may be unable to carry out if the SU was completely self-governed. HEIs may, therefore, wish to consider the following ways of maintaining some control over the company:

–   appoint members of the HEI staff as directors of the company. This carries some risk of personal liability for those directors, particularly if the company were to become insolvent (see Chapter 15); or, as a charitable trustee, should the directors act imprudently or unlawfully in relation to the memorandum and articles of association (see Chapter 4). An HEI may consider it sensible to invest in directors' and trustee liability insurance. It is also important to remember that appointing a director does not give the HEI control of the company and that control is ultimately given by membership voting rights; or

–   give the HEI enhanced voting rights either in all situations or only in specified situations. Alternatively, the HEI may be given a right of veto in certain circumstances.

Incorporation and charitable status

19.30   On incorporation, the SU will become a separate legal entity from the HEI, but should be able to maintain exempt charitable status by its association with the HEI.[1] As we have seen earlier, in order to obtain exempt charitable status, the SU must have congruence of administration and of purpose with the HEI. The congruence of administration should be satisfied by the requirement in the HEI's constitution, charter, or articles for the establishment and funding of the SU and the requirement for the SU to account for its funds to the HEI. The congruence of purpose should be satisfied by the objects of the SU being educational, charitable and compatible with those of the HEI. It is advisable to submit copies of the articles and memorandum of association in draft to the Charity Commissioners for their examination and comments to avoid possible difficulties later. There is also the issue of remunerating the sabbatical officers who would normally be directors of the SU. Remuneration of charitable trustees is normally only allowed in 'special circumstances' and, although this should be possible, clearance with the Charity Commissioners is again highly advisable.

---

1   Charities Act 1993, Sch 2(w).

Shadow directors

19.31 A 'shadow director' is a person in accordance with whose directions or instructions the directors of a company are accustomed to act.[1] However, a person is not deemed to be a 'shadow director' by reason only that the directors 'act on advice given by him in a professional capacity'. Therefore, if the directors of an SU are 'accustomed to act' in accordance with the instructions of the HEI, the HEI is likely to be a shadow director. All the directors, or at least a governing majority of them, must be accustomed to act upon the directions of the shadow director. In order to establish that the directors are 'accustomed to act' there must be examples of more than one act to establish a course of conduct. It is not essential for any element of compulsion to be proved in the relationship between the shadow director and the board of directors. The HEI may be regarded as a 'shadow director' by reason of a director being employed by it; or by reason of its enhanced, special or majority voting rights as a member of the company which results in the directors being accustomed to act in accordance with the HEI's instructions. If an HEI is deemed to be a shadow director it will be liable in the same way as an ordinary director and may become liable for the actions of the company. This could be of particular concern should the company become insolvent. The shadow director route might be used also as a method of lifting the corporate veil in an instance involving tortious liability.

Incorporation and drink

19.32 The SU will need to consider the nature of any licence to sell intoxicating liquor. If it is a club requiring a registration certificate under the Licensing Act 1964, Sch 7, then the use of enhanced or reduced voting rights for members may not be permissible. This problem could be circumvented by making an application for a Justices' Licence.

CONCLUSIONS

19.33 Of all the matters discussed in this chapter, incorporation is perhaps the most complex, interesting and important. Incorporation will not necessarily guarantee the HEI protection from tortious liability in particular, but it might help by thickening the veil between the SU and HEI (depending on the exact balance of distance between, control of, and involvement within, the SU by officers of the HEI). It might also at least ensure a clearer regime for the routine management of the SU by invoking the procedures of the legislation concerning companies – the key element probably being the competence of the SU permanent secretary acting as the company secretary. At least one HEI is known to have incorporated its SU.

---

1   Companies Act 1985, s 288.

Part 6

THE HIGHER EDUCATION INSTITUTION
AND ITS PROPERTY

Chapter 20

SECURITY: SURVEILLANCE, TRESPASS, 'REASONABLE FORCE' AND 'CLAMPING'

Lisa Robotham (Shakespeares)

EDITORS' INTRODUCTION

§20.1   Some HEIs in the USA have their own police forces and some of those forces are armed. Oxford University has had its Proctors and the University Marshall, backed up by 'bulldogs' (porters in bowler hats) for many centuries (but they are not – yet – armed). All HEIs have security problems and all have security cover (usually from directly employed porters and security officers, but sometimes by way of a contract with a private security firm). This chapter explores the power these security forces have in law when trying to maintain good order on the campus. Just how much force can security personnel reasonably use in removing a protestor from the animal house or in restraining a car thief? When does 'reasonable force' become unreasonable and excessive force, leaving the porter open to being charged with assault and his employer, the HEI, being held vicariously liable for the porter's actions if the aggrieved protestor or car thief should sue in tort? What is the legal position as regards the clamping of cars? When does a non-member of the HEI cease to be a welcome member of the public, entitled by implicit invitation to enjoy certain campus facilities (for example to stroll around the lake, to browse in the bookshop or to buy a loaf in the Student Union shop) or by explicit invitation to join the sports centre, to watch a play in the theatre, or to attend a public lecture, and become a trespasser whom the HEI can order off the campus? Linking back to the disciplining of students in Chapter 7, this chapter examines the options open to the HEI authorities in dealing with student protest in the form of the threatened occupation of HEI buildings or their actual occupation. What is the law concerning the reasonable use of force to prevent the building being occupied? Once occupied, what are the steps in the legal process to repossess it? This chapter also explores the legal issues surrounding the use of surveillance cameras and what happens to the CCTV footage, as well as the vexed issue of 'clamping'. There is, of course, nothing unusual in the management of safety, parking and security for HEI premises that will not be covered in any general texts on 'facilities management' covering health and safety and relevant aspects of criminal law, several of which are listed in Further Reading: hence, we provide a mere outline and, where possible, refer to cases concerning HEIs.

§20.2   It is not only a matter of students potentially being in conflict with the HEI's security personnel: Oxford University has been forced to establish 'an external inquiry into the forced ejection of a scholar ["a junior colleague"] from university premises'.[1] Allegedly, the University Proctors should have carefully considered whether it was really necessary for the Head of Department to call upon University security to escort the employee from the building, rather than merely 'rubber-stamping' the request. There is no suggestion that individual members of the Oxford seats staff behaved inappropriately, rather that the institution itself had inadequate safeguards to avoid any abuse of the employer's right to secure HEI premises and to remove employees who threaten HEI stability.

§20.3   The concept of 'reasonable force' when security personnel are either defending themselves or restraining and detaining an intruder is a vexed issue. The campus security manager in advising his team can only keep up with the material under 'Public and private defence' in the chapter on 'General defences' in the latest edition of Smith and Hogan (currently 1999). The level of force causing personnel injury may be justified if it was a reasonable reaction in all the circumstances, and the test of quite what is reasonable is whether the security officer honestly believed it was necessary: *it is irrelevant whether this belief was mistaken or even unreasonable* as long as he at the time genuinely felt he was doing only what was necessary to defend himself, his colleagues, HEI property, etc.[2] The magistrate or jury will decide on the evidence whether the belief, no matter how mistaken or unreasonable, was genuine.

§20.4   Clearly, the jury will have to consider whether the amount of force used was proportionate and such that the security officer was properly convinced he had no choice in deploying it: as Smith and Hogan express it, 'Is it reasonable to kill or cause serious bodily harm in order to prevent rape? Or robbery, when the property involved is very valuable, and when it is of small value? How much force may be used to prevent the destruction of a great work of art?' But the jury will be guided not to be too finicky, as one judge put it: 'In the circumstances one did not use jeweller's scales to measure reasonable force ...'.[3]

§20.5   Thus, four HEI security personnel using heavy torches as truncheons to quell a 70-year-old running amok at a University of the Third Age Summer School may be unreasonable and disproportionate force; while one patrolman grabbing a heavy wrench to defend himself against, or to protect a female student being attacked by, four hefty youths, may be justified. Of course, proper training will anyway emphasise the sense of, wherever possible, avoiding violent situations, of trying to calm things down, of summoning back-up speedily, of retreating if that would not leave colleagues/students exposed, and perhaps of not risking life and limb merely for HEI property (even the Vice-Chancellor's Jaguar!). A jury may be unimpressed by the use of deadly force solely for the protection of property rather than people, and perhaps especially of HEI property rather than, say, the person's home: all this is the stuff of media attention, just as when a pensioner uses an antique rifle to defend his allotment from repeated vandalism, or a farmer uses a shotgun to protect his isolated house from yet another break-in.

---

1   *The Times Higher Educational Supplement*, 29 June 2001, p 6; see also 7 December 2001, also at p 6: the High Court rejected an attempt by the Head of Department to block such an inquiry happening and a retired High Court judge will now undertake the inquiry.
2   See *R v Williams (Gladstone)* (1984) 78 Cr App Rep 276.
3   *Reed v Wastie* [1972] Crim LR 221.

§20.6   The following quotes from relevant cases will give a feel for how the jury is guided by the judge in assessing the use of reasonable force:

> 'If there has been an attack so that defence is reasonably necessary it will be recognised that a person defending himself cannot weigh to a nicety the exact measure of his necessary defensive action. If a jury thought that in a moment of unexpected anguish a person attacked had only done what he honestly and instinctively thought was necessary that would be most potent evidence that only reasonable defensive action had been taken. A jury will be told that the defence of self-defence, where the evidence makes its raising possible, will only fail if the prosecution shows beyond doubt that what the accused did was not by way of self-defence.'[1]

> '... Are we satisfied that no reasonable man (a) with knowledge of such facts as were known to the accused or believed by him to exist (b) in the circumstances and time available to him for reflection (c) could be of the opinion that the prevention of the risk of harm to which others might be exposed if the suspect were allowed to escape, justified exposing the suspect to the risk of harm to him that might result from the kind of force that the accused contemplated using.'[2]

§20.7   And thus the Criminal Law Review Committee has recommended:[3] 'The common law of self-defence should be replaced by a statutory defence providing that a person may use such force as is reasonable in the circumstances as he believes them to be in the defence of himself or an other person'. Similarly, for the related issue of provocation, see *R v Smith (Morgan James)*.[4]

§20.8   More broadly, it is necessary to remember the need to get a licence for certain activities: the University of Cambridge neglected to do so in respect of its Kettle's Yard arts centre which was operating as a commercial entertainment venue, forcing it to cancel some events while it belatedly regularised the position. On lost property and bailment, see Chapter 26. HEI managers need to watch out for the detailed implementation in statutory instruments of the Private Security Industry Act 2001, especially in relation to any impact on the HEI's contract with a security or wheel-clamping firm. Finally, what about the security of examination papers? In *Oxford v Moss*,[5] Oxford being the Chief Constable of Merseyside and Moss being an engineering student at Liverpool University, the court held that Mr Moss was not guilty of the criminal offence of stealing intangible property in the form of confidential information (a civil engineering paper due to be sat by Mr Moss that June). Mr Moss had no intention of removing the paper; he wanted to look at the questions. Such confidential information is not property for the purposes of the Theft Act 1968 and hence cannot be stolen. Such a student would need to be dealt with under the HEI's cheating regulations (see Chapter 7) unless he/she damages HEI property while forcing open an office door or filing cabinet or actually removes the piece of paper itself.

---

1   *Palmer v R* [1971] 1 All ER 1077, at p 1078.
2   *Reference under s 48A of the Civil Appeal (Northern Ireland) Act 1968 (No 1 of 1975)* [1976] 2 All ER 937, at p 947.
3   In its Fourteenth Report, Cmnd 7844 at para 72a.
4   [2000] 4 All ER 289, HL.
5   (1978) 68 Cr App Rep 183.

INTRODUCTION

20.1   Regardless of the size or locality of the HEI, some system of security will already exist. However, given ever-increasing petty crime in educational establishments, there is an even greater demand for increased levels of security no matter where the property is situated. Although security must now be regarded as a necessity, it is essential to create a balance among the following:

–   the necessity to protect the safety of students and staff at the HEI but in such a manner to enable them to move on and off campus freely at various times;
–   the need to maintain the security of the HEI's property; and
–   the benefit in allowing members of the public access to campus facilities (such as bookshops, theatres and sports centres), which the HEI may encourage the public to use.

Achieving that balance may not be easy, particularly with pressures from various action groups attempting to promote civil liberties and the individual's right of freedom. However, the lack of proper security systems may result in claims of negligence against the HEI. Security systems in operation in HEIs at present range from flood lighting and surveillance cameras to guard dogs and security patrols. Further attempts have been made by many HEIs to protect the individual's security (for example, by issuing personal alarms to staff and students – male and female).

OCCUPIERS' LIABILITY

20.2   Whether the HEI is an owner or merely an occupant of the property, it owes a duty of care to anyone who may come on to that property under the OLAs 1957 and 1984. This duty relates to the state and condition of the property, and to things done or omitted to be done on them. To consider whether the HEI is an occupier for the purposes of the duties imposed by law, the test to be applied is whether the HEI has some degree of control associated with its use of the property – see *Wheat v Lacon*.[1] Where there is a sufficient degree of control, the HEI will be considered an occupier and obligations will, therefore, be imposed on it.

20.3   The duty imposed on HEIs for *visitors* and those entering the property lawfully differs from those who enter as trespassers – a higher level of care being required for the visitors and those entering the property lawfully. In practice, however, since the OLA 1984, there will be little difference between the duty imposed in respect of a lawful visitor and that owed to a child who is a trespasser. The duty imposed by law on the occupier in respect of lawful visitors is to take such care as is reasonable in the circumstances to ensure that the visitor will be reasonably safe in using the property for the purposes for

---

1   [1966] AC 552.

which that visitor is invited or permitted to be there (OLA 1957). Therefore, one would expect property to be free from obstacles and hazards, particularly those areas being used by staff and students. Routes should be kept clear and the fabric of the building itself should be in a safe state so as to avoid injury to any visitors. Warnings of potential hazards on the property should be given. Section 2 of the OLA 1984 specifically states that the occupier must be prepared for children to exercise less care than adults, which means that greater effort will be required where children have access to the property (which will even be the case where a child trespasses onto the land): in *Jolley v London Borough of Sutton*,[1] the judge at first instance perceptively referred to the danger in question as a trap or allurement to children, and to the accident that subsequently resulted as reasonably foreseeable. If an HEI offers crèche facilities or play groups for children, it must exercise extra care to ensure that the property is safe and specially designed for such purposes.

20.4 Liability to those who are not the HEI's visitors and who are on the land without authority (ie *trespassers*) arises under the OLA 1984 only:

– if the HEI is aware of the danger or has reasonable grounds to believe that a danger exists;

– if the HEI knows or has reasonable grounds to believe that a person is in the vicinity of the danger or may come into that vicinity (whether or not it is lawful for that person to be in the vicinity); and

– the risk is one against which the HEI may reasonably be expected to offer some protection.

20.5 The HEI's duty is to take such care as is reasonable in the circumstances to see that the person on the land does not suffer injury on the property resulting from the danger contemplated. This will apply to trespassers as well as authorised visitors. The HEI should be aware that old security methods (such as fixing glass in cement on top of walls) may create such a danger and, should injury result, are likely to be a breach of the duty owed by the HEI. Although the HEI does have a duty to the trespassers, this extends only to the person and not to the personal property of the trespasser. The HEI may, depending on the individual circumstances, discharge its duty by giving warning and notice of the danger in order to discourage any person from taking the risk. For example, in *Ratcliffe v McConnell*,[2] Mr Ratcliffe, a student at an agricultural college, suffered tetraplegic injuries after diving at night into the shallow end of an open air swimming pool (despite warning notices against this) when closed for the winter. The nature and extent of the duty owed was discussed by the Court of Appeal and it was agreed that such duty would depend on a variety of factors, including the age of the trespasser and consequent appreciation of the nature of the risk involved. The Court decided that pursuant to the OLA 1984, s 1(6), Mr Ratcliffe was aware of and had

---

1   [2000] 1 WLR 1082.
2   [1999] 1 WLR 670, CA.

willingly the risk involved and hence the college had discharged its duty in all the circumstances. Such warning notices, if provided, should be especially clear for any property where children are likely to be enticed onto the property, although any signs or other attempts to exclude liability will be subject to the UCTA Act 1977, under which death and personal injury due to negligence cannot be excluded. In the case of damage or loss, the exclusion must be shown to be reasonable.

20.6 The case of *Swain v Natui Ram Puri*[1] helps to provide further understanding of the working of the OLAs in practice, particularly given the fact that there have been few (and in some cases, apparently conflicting) decisions on the subject.[2] And note that the HEI's duty of care is not limited only to the buildings. It extends to all parts of the property belonging to or used by the HEI. The public often have rights of access to cross HEIs' land by means of footpaths or roadways. These routes should be adequately maintained and, if any hazard does arise, an appropriate warning in a prominent place should be given. The HEI must exercise a duty of care in these circumstances in order to avoid negligence claims which may arise if, for example, pathways are uneven and a pedestrian is injured when tripping. In fact, *Darby v National Trust*[3] provides some comfort to HEIs fearful of 'a compensation culture' in terms of the court taking a common-sense approach to life's natural hazards: swimming in lakes and ponds is obviously risky and the landowner need not plaster the area with warning signs (*Darby*); cliff-path walking can be dangerous (*Cotton*); strolling on the unfenced Cobb at Lyme Regis is scary in a storm (*Staples*); and external sixteenth-century steps are patently slippy in the wet (*Hogg*). The duty of care, of course, increases if the HEI lake is used by school-children for environmental studies and hence the HEI is inviting on to its land those less likely to appreciate the natural hazards of the campus.

HEALTH AND SAFETY

20.7 Although occupiers' liability places some control on HEIs for the standard of their properties, HEIs are also subject to stringent health and safety legislation. The HSWA 1974 places a duty on employers and those responsible for places of work to ensure that employees, visiting staff and other individuals are protected from risks arising out of work activities. This will include protection for students, members of the public and contractors. Specific duties regarding high-risk areas (such as radiation and genetics) have been introduced by various regulations following HSWA 1974, and the EU has called for

---

1   [1996] PIQR P442, CA.
2   See *Greenaway v Tesco* [1998] and *Jacob v Tesco* (unreported) 5 November 1998, CA.
3   [2001] PLSCS 24, CA – building on *Hogg v Historic Building and Monuments Commission for England* [1989] CLY 2573, on *Cotton v Derbyshire Dales District Council* (1994) *The Times*, June 20, and on *Staples v West Dorset DC* (1995) 93 LGR 536.

the implementation of further directives to ensure the health and safety of the workforce. These have been implemented in the Health and Safety Regulations 1992. It is suggested by the CUC in their *Guide for Members of Governing Bodies of Universities and Colleges in England and Wales* (CUC, 1995) that HEIs and other organisations should make sure that:

– a health and safety statement in which management responsibility for health and safety issues is clearly designated;

– those with designated responsibility are aware of and have access to regulations, advice and training;

– the institution plans the implementation of its policy and sets health and safety standards which it expects to be achieved;

– the institution has structures and arrangements for implementing its safety policy (for example, safety officers and appropriate committees); and

– the institution monitors its activities to ensure that the agreed standards are being met.

20.8   A large range of requirements is set out in legislation governing such matters. This chapter is focused merely on security and, hence, does not discuss this aspect in detail: in any event, it is territory well covered in many texts aimed generally at managers, whether of HEI premises or of hospitals, offices, shops and factories (see Further Reading). Suffice to say here that health and safety, although concerned with hazards, also places great emphasis on the existence of reporting procedures and constant review by employers and occupiers. HEIs are probably most at risk in relation to their labs working with potentially lethal genetically modified viruses: an *Observer* headline (19 August 2001, at p 9) screamed: 'Threat from fatal bugs breach statutory rules' and cited alleged infringements at Imperial College, Birmingham University, the London School of Hygiene and Tropical Medicine, and Edinburgh University. It is no defence for an HEI to argue lack of money to refurbish aging laboratory infrastructure. A good health and safety policy, however, will aid in a defence against any negligence claim – and the health and safety burden upon employers is ever-increasing (and can arise under strange circumstances – see *Lewis v University of Bristol and Ultra Violet Light Properties (Third Party)*).[1] For example, the Government proposes new offences of 'corporate killing' which could leave a 'controlling mind' (the Vice-Chancellor, the Director of Estates) within the HEI, along with any employee tasked with specific health and safety duties which may have been neglected, facing up to life imprisonment in certain dire circumstances.[2] In the meanwhile, if imprisonment is not yet likely, the fines can be huge: £750K and £400K in respect of deaths at a supermarket warehouse and in council offices. In *Stark v Post Office*,[3] the Court

---

1   (2001) unreported, 15 June, CA.

2   Welham (2001); and see *A-G's Reference (No 2 of 1999)* [2000] 3 All ER 182, 2 BCLC 257, CA, as to just how difficult it currently is, pending the passing of this proposed legislation, to secure the conviction of a company/corporation on a charge of manslaughter by gross (corporate) negligence.

3   [2000] ICR 1013.

of Appeal interpreted reg 6(1) of the Provision and Use of Work Equipment Regulations 1992[1] as imposing an absolute requirement upon employers to maintain work equipment (here a postperson's bicycle) 'in an efficient state, in efficient working order and in good repair', hence leaving the HEI (by analogy) with strict liability for any injury to an employee even if the defect in the equipment could not have been discovered by any amount of frequent and rigorous inspection and testing. Moreover, an equally interesting US case in 2001 awarded some $2m to an employee who was 'working at home' on the day he was injured while clearing his drive of snow ready for a delivery of business papers for him to work on: his home was temporarily his place of work. Where does this leave the employer in terms of a health and safety responsibility for 'teleworkers', or indeed the HEI in relation to academics 'working at home'? Should the HEI be carrying out a risk assessment of the academic's study ('office'), or of the kitchen ('staff cafeteria'), or of the family Aga ('work equipment'), and be testing the safety of the family electric kettle and toaster? Or simply banning academics from working at home as too risky?

Controls on parking and wheel-clamping

20.9   Parking arrangements on private property can often be problematic and solutions for easing parking problems may cause controversy. [*Editors' note:* remember the jocular definition of a university: 'A collective of academics united only by a common grievance over car-parking'!] It is often necessary to implement constraints or restrictions on parking, thereby easing congestion and keeping emergency access ways clear. Pay-and-display machines, barrier systems, parking attendants, individual parking passes and wheel-clamping are a few methods which may be considered. Some methods of control will prove effective only where the number of access routes onto the property are limited. Unauthorised parking can amount to trespass on the property and wheel-clamping may be considered as a solution. However, where wheel-clamping is operated on private land, various conditions must be satisfied – otherwise, the clamping may be illegal. HEIs in Scotland should be aware that wheel-clamping is clearly illegal and it is taken to fall within the limits of extortion (depriving a motorist of his vehicle by detaining it against his will can amount to theft). The conditions necessary to ensure legality in England and Wales apply even where the person parking the car clearly enters the land as a trespasser. The following conditions need to be satisfied:

–   there must be a clear and unambiguous notice in an obvious place stating that wheel-clamping is in operation. If no notice is given, the motorist may not realise that he is trespassing on the land. If a motorist then parks his car on the land where notices are clearly placed, he consents to or willingly assumes the risk that the car will be clamped.[2] If the motorist did not realise there was a risk of clamping, he could claim trespass and (perhaps) conversion amounting to wrongful interference with goods

---

1   SI 1992/2932.
2   See *Vine v Waltham Forest London Borough Council* [2000] 4 All ER 169.

under the Tort (Interference with Goods) Act 1977 (see also Chapter 26, plus Birks (2000), p 502, n 496);

– once the motorist does park, he then accepts that a fee will need to be paid to release the car, although any release fee must be reasonable. If a sum is excessively high, it may be held to be unwarranted. The Theft Act 1968, s 21, provides that the unwarranted demand for revenues with a view to gain or with an intent to cause loss can amount to the offence of blackmail. The law does not establish what sum of money would be deemed reasonable for a release fee and the amount may vary according to the circumstances of the case. The court would probably look unfavourably on the use of a release fee to make a profit, as opposed to deterring illegal parking or at most covering costs;

– the vehicle must be released without delay once the motorist offers to pay the fee. If the vehicle is not then released, an intention permanently to deprive the motorist of the vehicle could be inferred. This could give rise to an accusation of theft; and

– there should be a means by which the motorist can communicate an offer of payment. The notice should state a telephone number or contact point, and it is necessary for someone always to be available to release the car.[1]

20.10 The practicalities of operating such a system reliably may be difficult to meet, particularly if no one is available at certain hours to release the car. If a private firm is employed to take on the responsibility of clamping, then the individuals concerned should be easily identifiable (by means of a uniform or identification badge). It is *not* considered illegal for a motorist to remove a wheel-clamp provided he does not damage the clamp.[2]

SECURITY GUARDS: POWERS OF ARREST AND USE OF REASONABLE FORCE

20.11 Although private policing may be considered an expensive security arrangement, it does have its advantages – most noticeably, the fact that someone is physically available on site to deal with issues as and when they arise. Further, the mere presence of security guards may prevent incidents from arising. It must be remembered, however, that private security guards do not have the same powers as the police, particularly in respect of arrest and detention. Section 24 of the Police and Criminal Evidence Act 1984 authorises an arrest without a warrant by any person in certain limited circumstances. Any person may arrest anyone in the act of committing an 'arrestable' offence, or arrest anyone that person has reasonable grounds for suspecting is committing such an offence. Where an 'arrestable' offence has been committed, a person may arrest someone guilty of the offence or someone the person has reasonable grounds for suspecting is guilty of it. However, the reason for the

---

1   *Arthur v Anker* [1995] NPC 187.
2   *Lloyd v Director of Public Prosecutions* [1992] 1 All ER 982.

arrest must be given at the time or as soon as reasonably practicable thereafter. The courts have also decided that if the person arrested is subsequently acquitted of the arrestable offence, then the original arrest will be rendered unlawful.[1]

20.12 Common law (as opposed to statute) vests certain powers of arrest in the ordinary citizen where:

– an arrestable offence is being committed or there are reasonable grounds to suspect that such an offence is being committed;
– an arrestable offence has been committed and there are reasonable grounds to suspect that the person is guilty;
– a breach of the peace is committed in the presence of the person making the arrest;
– the arrestor reasonably believes that such breach will be committed in the immediate future by the person arrested; or
– a breach has been committed and there is reasonable belief that renewal of it is threatened – see *Albert v Lavin*.[2]

20.13 Every citizen in whose presence a breach of the peace is being, or reasonably appears about to be, committed has the right under the Criminal Law Act 1967 to take *reasonable* steps to prevent that breach. There is a duty for the arrestor to hand over the arrested person to the police as soon as is reasonably possible. If the person arrested claims that the arrest has been made falsely, then he can claim damages for trespass to the person, including a claim of false imprisonment if the individual is detained. If security guards are employed at the HEI, they are not permitted to use unreasonable violence or force on a trespasser, even if that individual is engaging in a criminal activity – see *Revill v Newbury*.[3]

20.14 As the use of security firms is becoming more widespread, it is important that the security staff do not invade the private rights of students and staff. Concerns may arise since the background of hired security staff is often unknown, particularly as to whether they have criminal records. It should be the case that any member of security staff can be easily identifiable by means of a uniform and/or badge, particularly where a private firm is contracted to take on this role. The HEI must consider the risk that they will be held vicariously liable for the actions of any security guards they employ or hire. It is, therefore, sensible for the HEI to consider insuring for such liability, or, if a security firm is instructed to provide such service, checking to see that it has insurance cover for wrongful or unlawful arrest, or even for false imprisonment. Damages for trespass against the person may still be given even if there is no proof of damage. If the security personnel are employees of the HEI, then clearly the HEI would be wise to check the records of prospective employees.

---

1 *R v Self* [1992] 1 WLR 657.
2 [1981] 3 All ER 878.
3 [1996] QB 567, and Editors' Introduction above.

20.15 The reasonable use of force to defend the property or to eject a trespasser is lawful. The trespasser must first be asked to depart before any attempts to physically eject him or her. Excessive force must not be used – for example, a security guard using a cosh or truncheon on an unarmed drunken student would constitute excessive force, as could four guards being 'over-zealous' with just one trespasser. The force should be matching – that is, only if the guard is attacked or really believes himself to be about to be attacked, should he resort to violence, using something to hand as a *defensive* weapon only if the assailant has an *offensive* weapon. If it is a matter of removing a trespasser, the guards should take care not to inadvertently cause injury by using certain risky arm-locks or neck-holds. Clearly, self-defence training provided by the HEI for its security force will help establish that it had not only discharged its duty of care as an employer to its employed security staff, but that it had also attempted to ensure that they were less likely to render the HEI vicariously liable for damages. Where any staff are employed on the premises for promoting security, the landowner should be aware that it is responsible not only for those employed (employer–employee relationship), but also for the actions of those so employed (vicarious liability) – see paras **5.19** *et seq* on vicarious liability.

SECURITY OF PROPERTY

20.16 As well as the safety and security of the people using the HEI's buildings, the security of the buildings themselves must be considered. Floodlighting, for example, can help to improve safety and security on campus, but HEI managers should be aware that the erection of floodlights may require planning permission. As for the security of an individual's property and belongings, the HEI will not wish to accept responsibility for these. Disclaimers stating that the property is left at the owner's risk could go some way towards avoiding responsibility, particularly with cars parked on campus. It might be worth considering putting notices disclaiming responsibility for loss on any tickets needed to park. Ideally, such notices should be brought to the attention of the individual prior to the purchase of any tickets. Responsibility for death or personal injury cannot, however, be contracted out of under the UCTA 1977. Furthermore, the implementation of the UTCCR 1994 (and as amended 1999) means there is now an even greater requirement for clarity and reasonableness in notices and contracts directed at 'the consumer'.

Occupation of HEI property by students

20.17 Security of HEI property may be put into question by some form of sit-in or protest by the students, or even just by the threat of such action. Where this occurs the HEI can commence proceedings in the High Court either for an injunction to restrain students from occupying or for an order for possession once they have done so. The HEI need not identify every individual involved, as long as reasonable steps to identify individuals have been made. It will, in any event, often be impracticable to obtain the names of everyone concerned. Usually the injunction or order names officers of the SU as the representatives of the student community. Orders for possession under the Rules of the Supreme Court, Ord 113, can now be made even when all occupying students cannot be identified – see *University of Warwick v De Graaf and Others.*[1] Courts have made possession orders not only for those parts of the property adversely occupied, but also in situations where there has been a threat that the students might occupy other parts of the HEI's premises. So, the order may be extended by the court to cover the whole of the HEI – see *University of Essex v Djemal and Others.*[2] There are also criminal repercussions if damage or injury to persons is caused as a result of the occupation. The SU, however, will often be required by the HEI to pay for damage to the premises of the HEI from its grant or budget allocated from the HEI. When areas of HEI property have been invaded as part of a demonstration, the fact that an individual is not motivated by the desire for personal gain will be taken into account in sentencing. In circumstances where criminal welfare campaigners entered and destroyed property in a university department and removed slides showing rodents being injected, it was decided that, whilst the law cannot be taken into the hands of campaigners even if they believed they were morally justified, such behaviour should result in a custodial sentence but that such a sentence should be suspended – see *R v Adams.*[3]

20.18 It remains to be seen whether the CJPOA 1994 may yet be used by the police in the context of a student occupation. This makes trespass a criminal offence under certain circumstances (for example, 'raves', the Stonehenge summer solstice gathering, and 'squatters' in private houses), giving, for once, some force to the old 'wooden lie' of 'Trespassers will be prosecuted'. Section 69 of the CJPOA 1994 creates the offence of 'aggravated trespass', whereby a person who intimidates others so as to deter them from following a lawful activity or who obstructs or disrupts that activity may be liable to up to 3 months' imprisonment. This is really aimed at 'hunt saboteurs' and relates to an offence 'on land in the open air'. Hence, even if the police were willing to act under s 69, they could do so only if the trespassers were 'occupying', say, a playing field or a car park, rather than the Animal House or Registry. (See Chapter 23 concerning eviction of students from HEI residential accommodation.)

FREEDOM OF SPEECH

20.19 There is a duty on the HEI to take reasonable steps to ensure freedom of speech for its members, students, employees and visiting speakers under the

---

1   [1975] 1 WLR 1126, [1975] 3 All ER 284.
2   [1980] 2 All ER 742.
3   (1985) 7 C App R (S) 97, CA.

Education (No 2) Act 1986, s 43. Such 'steps as are reasonably practicable' includes an obligatory code of practice to be prepared by the HEI concerning the organisation of meetings, invitation of speakers, etc. The HEI is not, however, under any duty to take into consideration persons and places outside its control, but the premises of the SU will normally be deemed part of the HEI premises and under its control – see the Education (No 2) Act 1986, s 43(8), and *R v University of Liverpool ex parte Caesar Gordon.*[1] Any HEI, *whether statutory or chartered*, could be subject to judicial review (see Chapter 9) over its implementation or non-implementation of s 43. (See also Chapter 19 on SUs.)

CLOSE CIRCUIT TELEVISION

20.20   CCTV is being used very widely for security purposes. It can also help promote a sense of security in that perception may matter more than reality. Use of CCTV systems is now governed by the DPA 1998, together with the *Code of Practice for Users of Close Circuit Television*, which sets out a comprehensive legal framework. In addition, two categories of CCTV surveillance, 'directed' and 'intrusive' covert surveillance are also subject to the provisions of the Regulation of Investigatory Powers Act 2000. The DPA 1988 regulates the use of 'personal data', or data which relates to a living individual who can be identified:

–   from those data; or
–   from those data and other information which is in the possession of, or likely to come in to the possession of the data controller.

20.21   Any image from which it is possible to distinguish an individual will be covered. The HEI, as the 'data controller', will be required to comply with the requirements of the DPA 1998 even if another is engaged to undertake the processing. Eight principles are set out which must be complied with; these include a requirement for fair and lawful processing, that data be obtained only for one or more specified and lawful purpose, that the data be adequate, relevant and not excessive for the purpose for which it is processed, and that it should not be held longer than is necessary for the purpose for which it is processed. The individual or 'data subject' also has certain rights in connection with the obtaining, processing and use of the data. Specified exemptions from compliance with the principles may be relevant to CCTV schemes. For example, processing for prevention or detection of crime or apprehension or prosecution of offenders will provide an exemption from the first principle for fair and lawful processing. The HEI should carefully consider who will assume responsibility for monitoring the screens and who should be permitted access to the film footage. Appropriate signs advising of the use of CCTV surveillance should be installed and can often help as a deterrent in themselves.

---

1   [1990] 3 WLR 667, [1990] 3 All ER 821, [1991] 1 QB 124.

20.22   The HEI should also bear in mind in particular the provisions of the HRA 1998. While CCTV may be installed for the purpose of monitoring car theft and vandalism, the HEI will need to ensure that the cameras do not also look over neighbouring private residences. Quite apart from being in danger of breaching the DPA 1998, the HEI may find itself breaching Art 8 of the European Convention on Human Rights, which contains the right to respect for private and family life, home and correspondence. The attitude of the student population should also be considered but, if the benefits of CCTV are made clear, and it is stressed that the recordings will be closely controlled and that cameras will not be placed in areas which might reasonably be considered private by the students (such as common rooms as opposed to entrance lobbies), hopefully, there will be no objection to their presence.

Chapter 21

HOUSES IN MULTIPLE OCCUPATION AND WHAT IS A 'HOUSE'?

Beverley Firth (Mills & Reeve)

EDITORS' INTRODUCTION

§21.1   Is a hall of residence a house in the terms of the relevant legislation governing fire safety, sanitation, overcrowding, etc, in HMOs? Even if such a structure can be a house in law (whatever the man on the Clapham omnibus may see it as in common sense and architectural terms), is it actually in multiple occupation? Is an HEI hall of residence an HMO? Is an Oxford college quadrangle or a Cambridge college court a hall of residence or even a house? If the relevant legislation is applicable, what impact might it have in terms of the need to meet the standards set for HMOs? Are grants available for the costs of meeting those standards? What powers of enforcement are there? Where an HEI operates a property leasing scheme, whereby it rents whole houses from landlords and in turn acts as a landlord in renting the house or a room within it to students, what are its responsibilities to these students under HMO legislation?

INTRODUCTION

21.1   With the ever-increasing demand for HEI places and particularly as a result of the changes which were required for certain HEIs to achieve their status as statutory universities, the requirement for accommodation in HEI towns has reached an all time high. The legislation governing HMOs was introduced primarily to deal with problems encountered by local authorities faced with irresponsible landlords (both in the student market and the other sectors of the private rental market) who failed to make adequate provision for the prevention of fire, but it is now being looked to as legislation which might counter the perceived social 'problems' which have arisen as a result of a growing student population. With local authorities being required by members of the public to look closely at both existing and new cases involving potential HMOs, the HEIs and their managers will no doubt find themselves increasingly involved in ensuring compliance with the legislation itself and with the particular requirements of each individual local authority. Typically, however, a good number of the houses occupied by students will not at present be classified in law as HMOs. Even if this is the case, the HEI managers are still likely to incur costs – in money and time – in establishing the position. They may also encounter difficulties when planning new developments within the local community or when considering further or new head tenancy leasing schemes. There is also the possibility of more stringent regulation if the Government proceeds with planned HMO legislation.

21.2   This chapter provides an overview of the law and its sanctions and looks at the approach which has been taken by some local authorities and government guidance with the aim of providing an understanding of the issues which arise. Taking the law itself as a starting point, it is necessary to consider how the law has been interpreted, how the interpretation will affect HEIs and what action may be required as a result. This chapter then goes on to cover proposed changes to the law, as set out in the Consultation Paper on the Licensing of Houses in Multiple Occupation, published in April 1999 (DETR).

WHAT IS AN HMO?

21.3   The legal definition of an HMO can be found in the housing legislation and not, as one might expect, in planning law. An HMO is defined in the Housing Act 1985, s 345(1) as 'a house which is occupied by persons who do not form a single household'. It is clear that the legislation will include much more than the traditional 'picture book' house. Decided cases have defined a 'house' as 'a place fitted and used and adapted for human habitation'.[1] Flats in multiple occupation are also HMOs – see the Housing Act 1985, s 345(2). The definition is a wide one from which individual local authorities can derive differing interpretations of what does and does not constitute an HMO.

21.4   HEIs will be primarily concerned with two types of student accommodation and whether or not that accommodation constitutes an HMO. These are:

– shared student houses; and
– halls of residence (and similar types of accommodation within the HEI itself, such as the Cambridge college courts or Oxford quadrangles).

Shared houses

21.5   The all-important factor in determining whether or not a shared house is also an HMO appears to turn on whether, as a matter of fact, the sharers live together as a single household. Does a shared house operate as a home? Ministerial guidance has been issued to local authorities on this point (and generally, in relation to what does and does not constitute an HMO). However, the final decision is particular to each case which is looked at by a local authority and turns on the individual facts of that case.[2]

---

1   Per Lord Harman in *Reed v Hastings Corporation* (1964) 62 LGR 588, CA.
2   See Department of the Environment (DoE) Circulars 12/86 and 12/93.

21.6   The guidelines suggest a set of relevant questions to be looked at in each case, including:

– whether the student occupiers share cooking, washing and cleaning;
– whether they occupy on separate contracts;
– whether the individual rooms can be locked;
– the extent of the shared rooms and facilities; and
– whether the landlord is entitled to fill a vacancy at the property should one arise.

21.7   In *Barnes v Sheffield City Council*,[1] it was decided that a small house which was let by a private landlord to students was not an HMO. The court found that the students were occupying the house as a single household and stated that it is inherent in student life that groups vary in their habits and that different students come and go at different times.

21.8   In *Islington LBC v Rogers*,[2] the Court of Appeal held that, where it was clear that there was no relationship (ie family and long-standing relationships) between the occupants, there could not be a single household and that the property was an HMO. In this case, Mr Rogers let a 10-bedroom house to young adults who were not students. They shared the bathrooms, living room and kitchen. Applying *Barnes*, the Court of Appeal held that cases involving students were distinguishable from this case because, between students, there were sufficient degrees of comradeship and a common aim to minimise the expenses of university life to constitute a household. They further held that their decision was reinforced by the fact that Mr Rogers' tenants were a disparate and changing group without a common bond, as opposed to the four or five tenants in *Barnes* who took up occupation for a set period as a pre-existing group.

21.9   In most cases, local authorities have found it helpful to identify categories of potential HMOs. Where lists have been drawn up, these include a category for the 'traditional' HMO (ie a house divided into bedsits with shared kitchen or bathroom facilities), a category for houses converted into flats with a shared access but no shared living or dining facilities, and a category for a house shared by a number of individual people. It is this third category into which the typical shared student house will fall. What is very clear, however, is that individual local authorities take different approaches (notwithstanding the ministerial guidance) to determine whether or not a house shared by a number of individuals does or does not constitute an HMO.

21.10   In a report to the Development Control Subcommittee (27 January 1995) the director of development of Newcastle-upon-Tyne City Council considered whether there should be a strict application of the requirement to occupy as a single household failing which the property would be classified as an HMO. The director concluded that making a distinction between

---

1   (1995) 27 HLR 719, CA.
2   [2000] EHLR 3.

occupation as a single family or occupation as a single household was difficult to establish both on a practical and factual level, pointing out that changes can be effected easily beforehand to ensure that, on inspection, the house appears to be in single household occupation. Reference was made to a decision by one housing inspector on appeal who accepted that the use of a property by students was a communal one, on the basis that there was joint decision-taking and sharing of facilities and services, and notwithstanding the fact that the bedrooms were lockable or that desks, chairs and kettles were kept in each individual's room.

21.11   This approach can be contrasted with that of Hart District Council (from its guide *Standard for Houses in Multiple Occupation*) which made a clear statement that one of its categories of HMOs comprised: 'Houses occupied on a shared basis where occupants may belong to a specific group or have a common background, for example students. Tenants normally have an individual room and share the kitchen and bathroom, together with a communal living area'. Most authorities seem to take the view that a household with a degree of shared use of facilities (such as kitchen and sanitary accommodation) will *not* fall within one of the categories of HMO and will, therefore, be outside the regulations. Arguably, it is these shared households which fall outside the ambit of the HMO regulations (and the provisions of planning law which regulate change of use) which can give rise to some of the greatest problems. This is discussed later in relation to planning control.

Halls of residence

21.12   Although, using a wide interpretation, halls of residence could be brought within the meaning of an HMO for the purposes of the Housing Act 1985, it is arguable that, in drawing up their categories, local authorities have impliedly excluded halls of residence. There can be no doubt that a hall of residence is 'a place fitted and used and adapted for human habitation'. However, given that the categories listed by the various local authorities expressly include hostels, hotels (where a reasonable proportion of the guests are occupying as their principal place of abode) and residential homes involving an element of care, then it is arguable that halls of residence are not intended to be caught.

21.13   In practice, the housing authorities may be unlikely to take steps to investigate the condition and status of a hall of residence unless a complaint is received. In all probability, if the HEI and its managers are maintaining the halls to a reasonable standard, then the issue is unlikely to arise. In practice, it is far more likely that students with complaints about HEI halls of residence will take the matter up with HEI accommodation officers directly or bring pressure to bear through the SU. If the local authority is thought of at all in such cases, it will most likely be as the very last resort.

Does planning law have any impact?

21.14   In planning law, there is no definition of what constitutes an HMO. A dwelling house is defined, however, and includes occupation by not more than six unrelated residents living together as a single household as well as occupation by a single person or by people living together as a family.[1] No planning permission is required to change the use of a property from use as a dwelling house in the occupation of an individual or in the occupation of a single family to use by six or fewer sharers. Thus, there is no opportunity at the planning stage for local authorities to 'catch' houses which may or may not become HMOs and to seek to regulate them. Certain changes to properties would require planning consent, including dividing a house into self-contained flats or bedsits, or changing the use of a property to use it as a hostel or residential home. As most halls of residence are purpose-built, planning consent will be required for any new halls in any event before the commencement of the development. Similarly, any new development of HMOs will require planning consent and planning authorities have separate factors which will be taken into account. For example, in Newcastle-upon-Tyne the Development Control Subcommittee takes account of:

–   the nature of the locality and the impact on the area of HMOs;
–   the size and suitability of the premises;
–   the privacy of prospective occupiers;
–   the impact of any necessary fire escapes;
–   availability of car parking; and
–   provision for refuse storage.

However, in the majority of cases, there will be no recourse to planning law where, for example, disaffected local residents wish to complain about noisy student parties, unkempt gardens, traffic congestion, car-parking problems or problems with refuse.

EFFECT OF A STUDENT RESIDENCE BEING AN HMO

21.15   Having established that a certain property (either within the HEI's own portfolio or forming part of a property leasing scheme) is an HMO, it is necessary to consider what action might be needed as a result. The relevant housing authority has various means of control in the form of registration schemes, associated 'control provisions', and the imposition of management regulations and control orders. In using their powers, local authorities should use a risk-based approach, as set out in the DETR's *Houses in Multiple Occupation Guidance on Standards* (issued to local authorities on 28 April 1999). Brief details of each of these controls are set out here, but for more comprehensive information the reader is referred to the bibliography.

---

1   See the Town and Country Planning (Use Classes) Order 1987, SI 1987/764, Class C3.

Registration schemes

21.16 The purpose of the schemes is to allow the local housing authorities to gather and record information. Authorities should be approached on an individual basis to ascertain whether or not a registration scheme has been put in place, and whether the scheme affects the area in which the particular property is situated and the type of HMO concerned. A local authority search should reveal this information when a property is purchased. The law in relation to registration schemes is governed by the Housing Act 1996. Any schemes made before this Act came into force will now have ceased to have effect. If the HEI is renting a property to students which it believes may be an HMO, or indeed if the HEI is operating a head tenancy leasing scheme involving such properties, it will be under a duty to register the property if a registration scheme is in operation (unless the HEI is excluded from the registration scheme, as to which see below).

21.17 The local authority has power to require owners or occupiers or any other person (which would include HEIs operating head tenancy leasing schemes) to inform the authority if a house is registrable and to provide information to enable the authority to establish the particulars which are to be registered. It is an offence punishable by a fine not to provide information if requested to do so or to make a deliberate misstatement.[1]

Control provisions

21.18 The registration scheme usually incorporates control provisions. The inclusion of these provisions will make it an offence to permit occupation of a property which is not registered or to allow occupation of the property by more people than the registration permits. The local housing authority can also prohibit the owner or manager of the property from allowing any more people into occupation. The offences are punishable by fines of up to either £4000 or £5000. In addition, the control provisions usually allow the local housing authority to refuse to register an HMO if the house is unsuitable for use as an HMO and cannot be adequately altered. Alternatively, requirements could be imposed as a prerequisite to registration of the property as an HMO. Control provisions can also be included to allow the authority powers to intervene after the house has been registered as an HMO. Registration can be revoked at any time either for breach or because the manager of the HMO is not a fit and proper person. There are rights of appeal.

21.19 Following the Housing Act 1996 the DoE issued Circular 3/97 dealing with registration schemes and setting out two models, one being a simple scheme and the other containing control provisions. Local authorities have the choice whether to adopt one of these schemes or to devise their own. However, any scheme which does not follow the models requires confirmation by the Secretary of State. The model schemes specifically exclude HEIs from the

---

1   See the Housing Act 1985, s 350.

requirement to register. A particular local authority could seek to vary the excluded categories, but would have to convince the Secretary of State that the proposed HMOs to be included (which would otherwise be excluded) constituted a serious health and safety risk to their occupants and that the problems could not adequately or effectively be dealt with using the authority's discretionary powers to take enforcement action against any of its HMOs.

21.20 Under the Housing Act 1996, s 65(1), landlords will have to apply for re-registration every 5 years. This allows the local housing authority an opportunity to re-assess the landlord and the relevant properties. The Houses in Multiple Occupation (Fees for Registration Schemes) Order 1997[1] provides the maximum fees that may be charged by a local housing authority for first registration of an HMO under a registration scheme. Where the registration scheme has no control provisions, the maximum charge is £80. Where it does have control provisions, the maximum fee is £60 per habitable room (ie a room normally used in the locality as a living room or bedroom).

21.21 A further element of the Housing Act 1996 is the introduction of special control provisions. These are aimed at protecting the neighbourhood from particular types of tenant rather than protecting the tenants from adverse conditions in the HMO. Special control provisions are not included within the model schemes and local housing authorities will need to make out a strong case for specific approval. The bodies and organisations (such as HEIs) excluded from the model schemes will also enjoy exclusion from the special control provisions. Therefore, such special control provisions will not necessarily assist disgruntled local residents who are at odds with the student population and who are seeking to prohibit HMOs being set up in their neighbourhood.

21.22 Although the registration schemes and associated control schemes allow the local housing authorities an opportunity to deal with HMOs, HEIs are excluded by the model schemes from the duty to register, and, even if they do have to register, there will be many student properties which 'escape' registration and the requirements which can be imposed thereafter. Birmingham City Council has implemented an Owners' Charter, which allows responsible landlords an opportunity to apply voluntarily for chartered status in respect of their rented property. The charter sets out standards of repair, safety measures and amenities which should be provided, and sets out legal and other guidelines for landlords to follow in managing their properties. The benefit to landlords of working to achieve chartered status is that their properties will be more likely to be included on lists of approved accommodation which are held by the HEIs in the city and perhaps afford them the opportunity to be included by the HEIs as part of an HEI head tenancy leasing scheme.

---

1   SI 1997/229, as amended by SI 1998/1813.

Power to require works

21.23   The provisions contained in the Housing Act 1985 relating to houses unfit for occupation or in serious disrepair will apply equally to HMOs as to other properties. In addition, the Housing Act 1985, s 352, gives the housing authority power to serve notice on the person having control of the house or managing it. This clearly catches HEIs operating head tenancy leasing schemes. The notice can require works to be carried out to ensure that there are:

–   satisfactory facilities for the storage, preparation and cooking of food (to include adequate sinks with hot and cold water);
–   adequate toilet, bath, shower and wash-basin facilities; and
–   adequate means of escape from fire and other fire precautions.

21.24   The notice will set out a reasonable period within which the work must be carried out. Failure to comply is a criminal offence punishable by fine and, if works have not been carried out, the local housing authority can undertake them and pass on the cost (both of the works and of any administrative and other expenses) to the owner or the manager.

21.25   It is important to note that s 73 of the Housing Act 1996 (although not yet in force) will impose a duty on landlords to keep HMOs up to the standard of fitness required for the number of occupants. This will not depend on service of a notice by the local housing authority. Breach is punishable by a fine and landlords may also face civil action by their tenants. This will be unique in relation to HMO provisions.

Power to stop overcrowding

21.26   The local authority has power to serve an overcrowding notice if the number of people occupying the premises or likely to be occupying the premises is thought to be excessive. Alternatively, a direction to reduce overcrowding could be issued with a limit being placed on the number of people who may be accommodated at the property. This could have an impact on some HEIs, particularly at the beginning of a new HEI year, when students arrive to enrol without accommodation and need to be temporarily housed in rooms shared with other students until alternative accommodation is available. Again, offences are punishable by fines.

Imposition of management regulations

21.27   There are a number of matters required by statute and certain matters which can be required by the local authority exercising its discretion, all of which seek to ensure that the property is kept in good repair and good order. The management regulations are enforced by service of a notice on the manager of the property requiring the works to be carried out within a reasonable time. The local authority has power to carry out the works in default and to recover the expenses from the manager, as is the case with repair notices.

Control orders

21.28 If all else fails, the local authority can take possession of the property (subject to the rights of the existing occupiers) by making a control order and by assuming responsibility for the management of that property. The local authority acts as manager and has very wide powers (including the power to collect the rents and to discharge the expenses of management from those rents). In addition, removal expenses and rehousing expenses for those who may need to move out in order to allow works to be carried out may be claimed, together with the cost of the works themselves. The owner or manager from whom the local authority has taken over control is generally entitled to receive one half of the rental value of the property, by way of compensation, for the duration of the control order.

Control provisions – summary

21.29 Clearly, any of the control provisions, if invoked, will have a considerable costs impact on the owner or manager of the property. The onus is, therefore, on the owners and managers to ensure that their properties are 'up to scratch' without the need for the local authority to rely on the control provisions. With ever-decreasing funds available to HEIs, the requirements in respect of HMOs are likely to leave a further damaging hole in the annual budget.

AVAILABILITY OF GRANTS

21.30 Grants are now governed by the Housing Grants, Construction and Regeneration Act 1996. This provides for various types of (mainly discretionary) grant, including 'renovation grants' for the improvement or repair of a dwelling or the provision of dwellings by the conversion of a house or other building, and the 'HMO grant' which can be made for the improvement or repair of an HMO and for the provision of HMOs by the conversion of a house or other building.

21.31 Generally, applications can only be made in respect of properties that are at least 10 years old, although there are exceptions to this. Grant applications will only be approved if they are for purposes eligible for a grant. These are specified in the Act, which sets out conditions that attach to the various types of grant; no further conditions can be imposed unless the Secretary of State consents. Certain public authorities are listed in the Act as not being eligible for a grant and the list can be added to by regulation. HEIs do not appear on the list. It should be noted, however, that since most of the available grants are discretionary, it is likely that local housing authorities will inject an element of means-testing into the approval process and that grants will be reduced accordingly. HEIs will need to approach their individual local housing authorities to determine whether or not proposed works will attract any of the available grants.

FUTURE DEVELOPMENTS

21.32   In April 1999, the DETR published a consultation paper seeking views on strategic issues on the scope and operation of HMO licensing. The proposals are to introduce a national mandatory licensing scheme for HMOs. Licences would specify a maximum number of occupants, to reflect the condition of the premises and the standards of management. The existing scheme would be repealed. The favoured proposal for defining an HMO is to extend local housing authorities' powers to *all* houses which are occupied by persons who are not all members either of the same family or of one or other of two families. The consultation paper discusses the fact that most student shared houses would be included within this definition, and concludes that this is in the Government's view the most appropriate way to deal with these houses. These proposals would, therefore, unequivocally bring student shared houses within the scope of any new HMO legislation. The consultation paper leaves open the question of whether student halls of residence should be included in the proposed licensing scheme. There has as yet been no further action in terms of new legislation. New legislation in this potentially controversial area could, of course, be in a significantly different form from that proposed in the consultation paper.

CONCLUSIONS

21.33   In looking at the housing available, whether it is already in the HEI's portfolio or being considered for purchase or for inclusion in a head tenancy leasing scheme, the distinction between houses which are HMOs and fall within the legislation and those which are not will clearly be of great importance. The primary impact will be the cost of ensuring that, if the property is an HMO, all the necessary regulations are complied with. For those who have not already done so, HEI managers would be well advised to establish good working relationships with the officers at the local housing authorities in order to establish a spirit of co-operation in the management of all the HEI's properties, whether or not these are HMOs. Although the law in relation to housing has been radically overhauled with the passing of the Housing Act 1996, it is not inconceivable that further legislation could follow in the wake of public criticism about those areas of towns and cities which are being given over to student housing. In the shorter term, and in the face of complaints from local residents about noise, anti-social hours, poor standards of maintenance and increased crime (particularly during student holidays), the local housing and planning authorities will be increasingly looked to as the powers able to tighten up local plans and restrict future development of what would otherwise be properly regulated HMOs. In such cases, it will undoubtedly be easier for the HEI to plan for the future if it is working with the co-operation of its local housing authority. (Note: a pilot scheme exists in Canterbury to improve control of rowdy students, and Leeds is looking at a similar scheme.)

21.34   In summary, for the average HEI involved in three main types of student residential accommodation the position is as follows:

–   for *halls of residence*, there are likely to be no HMO implications unless students bring in the local authority by making complaints and the local authority finds the premises to be seriously defective;
–   for *houses owned and run directly by the HEI*, again they are probably *not* to be defined as HMOs, and, even if they are, there will be no requirement to register them under the model registration schemes which were established under the Housing Act 1996. However, an authority could seek to alter the excluded categories in the model or seek a property out and label it an HMO, if it really wanted to be persistent; and
–   for *head tenancy schemes*, there is probably a duty to register under the model schemes (unless the HEI's involvement means that the properties are excluded from the registration scheme), but at least the liability for meeting HMO standards will lie with the owner, not the HEI.

21.35   That said, any HEI directly running (or involved via head tenancy schemes in) overcrowded and ill-maintained property with inadequate fire precautions, whether a hall of residence or a house, is subject to stringent local authority controls should student complaints bring the property to the attention of the local authority whether or not the property is deemed an HMO. But, if the property is an HMO, the HEI has a clear duty under the Housing Act 1996 to keep the property up to standard and should not simply be waiting around to be 'caught' by the local authority. Being found in control of defective residential premises is not only a criminal offence by the HEI under the Housing Act 1996, but, in the event of injury to occupants, a likely source of an expensive and time-consuming action in tort (fire precautions and means of escape, plus the potential for carbon monoxide poisoning from gas appliances, are the areas of most risk to HEIs in terms of tortious liability).

Chapter 22

THE IMPLICATIONS FOR HIGHER EDUCATION INSTITUTIONS OF THE DISABILITY DISCRIMINATION ACT 1995

Daff Richardson (Manches)

EDITORS' INTRODUCTION

§22.1   The DDA 1995 is an example of the kind of increasingly complex and ever-encroaching legislation which tends to creep up on the unsuspecting manager of an HEI. Another problem is the over-enthusiastic interpretation and application of legislation on HMOs by some local authorities (see Chapter 21). Before a luckless HEI knows where it is, there is a technical breach of the law and a potential bill for civil damages or for minor works and improvements of one kind or another. In some cases there can also be scope for criminal prosecution of the HEI (and even of individual officers within it). Sometimes the pressure for an increasingly stringent legislative regime is EC-driven (see Chapter 28). The particular piece of legislation described in this chapter is not only relatively new, complex and wide-ranging (hence, potentially expensive) in its applicability to HEIs, but also it involves matters of some moral force (if not also ones of great sensitivity in terms of 'political correctness') and is evolving further. The HEI manager needs to tread carefully.

§22.2   In the case of ill and incapacitated employees, there is clearly a general need for employers to be 'reasonable' about obtaining proper and competent medical opinion, about *sympathetically* exploring part-time or an alternative type of work, and now also about determining whether the particular employee might be covered by the DDA 1995. For example, an illness could be an *impairment* which has a *substantial, long-term* and *adverse* impact on the employee's ability to carry out day-to-day activities, and hence the individual employee has become 'disabled' for the purposes of the Act. Many employers would have a much more simplistic view of what constitutes a disability, and few would agree with a US court which ruled that persistent lateness in an employee's arrival at work was, in the special circumstances of that case, a disability under the Americans with Disabilities Act 1990. Reasonable employers should have nothing to fear; but those managers who fire first, and only belatedly when under legal pressure bother to ask questions, will need to be rational.

§22.3   From a US perspective, Kaplin and Lee (1995a) comment on the 'Section 504' comprehensive legislation, dating back to the Rehabilitation Act 1973 and reinforced by the Americans with Disabilities Act 1990, outlawing any discrimination against disabled students and employees. A survey in the USA estimated a $9 billion price-tag if all US HEIs were to comply with the 1990 legislation. In 1993/94 alone, $300 million was spent on appropriate modifications. A UK survey estimated that new lifts cost about £150,000 each, an automatic door about £6000 and a disabled lavatory conversion about £1000. The CVCP called for £50 million; HEFCE allocated £6 million to cover the three academic years 1996/97 to 1998/99. Similarly, 'Universities UK' has calculated the potential cost at £250 million for UK HEIs complying with the Special Educational Needs and Disability Act 2001 (SEND 2001).

§22.4   As Kaplin and Lee (2000), pp 133–139 note, the Americans with Disabilities Act can get especially complicated in relation to academics claiming psychiatric disorders as a defence against dismissal for, as the HEI sees it, a distinct lack of 'collegiality' in their working relationships with other colleagues (*Neberry v East Texas State University*[1]): the court was unsympathetic to Professor Newberry; cf the award of $137,500 plus reinstatement to Professor Nedder dismissed for obesity (a widespread US health problem) in *Nedder v Rivier College.*[2]

§22.5   Similarly, in the USA litigation by disabled students challenging the denial of admission 'is expanding rapidly', leaving HEIs with the challenge of acting 'within the ADA [Americans with Disabilities Act]'s requirements while maintaining the academic integrity of their programms' (Kaplin and Lee (2000), pp 239 and 317). One case concerned a blind applicant to a medical school;[3] her challenge was unsuccessful, as was Mr Gill's claim that the HEI had been put on notice that he suffered from a post-traumatic disorder simply by the fact that he had stated on his application form that he was the child of an alcoholic parent (*Gill v Franklin Pierce Law Center*[4]). In *McGuinness v University of New Mexico School of Medicine*,[5] the court ruled that 'test anxiety in math and chemistry' was *not* a disability for ADA purposes.

§22.6   Back here in the UK, there has been a report[6] on the needs of a disabled student and just what is a reasonable level of educational support: one student wanted videotapes of all his lectures and audio transcripts of books. How do academic standards and academic merit fit with special provision and fair treatment? This chapter provides guidance to HEIs on the implications of SEND 2001 extending disability discrimination to the contract to educate and hence giving students the protection currently offered by the DDA 1995, but hitherto confined to employees of HEIs and to consumers of non-education services provided by HEIs. But, of course, staff too enjoy the protection of the DDA 1995: South Bank University had to pay Mr Brown, a lecturer with MS whom it dismissed, £46K for loss of earnings and £8K for injury to feelings (at that time a record under the DDA 1995 where such compensation had not exceeded £3K).[7]

---

1   161 F 3d 276, 5th Cir 1998.

2   908 F Supp 66, DNH 1995, 944 F Supp 111, DNH 1996. See the *Enforcement Guidance on the Americans with Disabilities Act and Psychiatric Disabilities* (25 March 1997) at www.eeoc.gov>. for a flavour of what is likely to happen here in the UK.

3   *Ohio Civil Rights Commission v Cane Western Reserve University* 666 NE 2d 1376, Ohio 1996.

4   899 F Supp 850, DNH 1995.

5   170 F 3d 974, 10th Cir 1998.

6   In *The Times Higher Educational Supplement*, 23 March 2001, p 6.

7   *Brown v South Bank University* (1999) Case No 2305234/97, 86 EOR 15, 22, 23, EAT. See also, for example, *Hanlan v University of Huddersfield* [1999] Disc LR 82, EAT: in this case the university won.

§22.7   Some estimates put the number of disabled students as high as 10 per cent, although less than 5 per cent are actually registered as such with their HEIs. The higher figure will include 'hidden disabilities' (for example, epilepsy, asthma, diabetes, ME, Asperger's syndrome, dyslexia). Sometimes such hidden disabilities become very visible on the field-trips so essential for certain subjects – see, for example, the Geography Discipline Network (draft) guides on field-work learning support for students with disabilities at www.chelt.ac.uk/gdn/disabil/index.htm.[1]

§22.8   The website for the Disability Rights Commission is at www.drc.gov.uk.

INTRODUCTION

22.1   Legal protection in respect of discrimination against disabled people was introduced at the end of 1996 by the DDA 1995. The DDA 1995 gives disabled people a range of rights and remedies aimed, particularly, at combating discrimination in employment and by the providers of goods and services. As originally drafted, the DDA 1995 expressly excluded the provision of education from the scope of the Act. That position is likely to change. In December 1999, the Disability Rights Task Force published its report *From Exclusion to Inclusion* which, inter alia, made recommendations about the provision of education, including higher education. These recommendations are being implemented in the form of the SEND 2001. It is anticipated that the provisions relating to higher education will come into force in September 2002, 2003 and 2005. Furthermore, the HRA 1988 came into force in October 2000. The HRA 1998 states that 'no person shall be denied the right to education'. It also provides that the rights enshrined in the Act shall be secured without discrimination; while disability discrimination is not expressly mentioned in the HRA 1998, it is almost certainly included in this provision. The implications of the HRA 1998 in relation to the provision of education to disabled students will be considered briefly below.

MULTI-FACETED HEIs

22.2   HEIs need to be aware of their existing and prospective duties under the DDA 1995 from a number of perspectives:

---

1   Other employer–employee cases include: *Jones v The Post Office* [2001] IRLR 384, CA (need for a careful risk assessment as to whether an insulin-dependent diabetic could safely drive Post Office vehicles; the employer can discriminate if to do so is not irrational or unreasonable); *Heinz (HJ) Co Ltd v Kenrick* [2000] IRLR 144, EAT (employer must check on reason for long-term sickness absence: the employee may have a disability); *London Borough of Hammersmith and Fulham v Farnsworth* [2000] IRLR 691 (employer may reasonably be expected to know of employee's disability even if employer claims ignorance); *British Gas v McCaull* [2001] IRLR 60, EAT, with *Quinn v Schwartzkopf Ltd* [2001] IRLR 67, EAT and *Bradley v Greater Manchester Fire and Civil Defence Authority* EAT/253/00 (what level of adjustment it is reasonable to expect the employer to make for the disabled employee).

–   HEIs employ a significant number of staff. The employment provisions in
    Part II of the DDA 1995 apply to HEIs;
–   most, if not all, HEIs provide non-education services to members of the
    public, typically conferences, accommodation, and catering facilities.
    They may also provide certain types of consultancy service. Part III of the
    DDA 1995 applies in such cases, making discrimination in the provision
    of goods and services unlawful; and
–   HEIs provide education. As originally enacted, the DDA 1995 essentially
    provided that HEIs had to submit a disability statement to their funding
    council. Under the SEND 2001 this requirement will be repealed when the
    relevant provisions come into force, but HEIs will be under a duty not to
    discriminate against disabled students in the access they have to education
    and to student services provided by HEIs.

22.3   The DDA 1995 is a complex piece of legislation, especially as now
amended by the SEND 2001. Many of its provisions are supplemented and
qualified by Regulations. There is a great deal of case-law already in existence
in relation to the DDA 1995 (and, in particular, to the employment provisions).
It is proposed to refer only to a few key cases in this chapter.

THE DEFINITION OF DISABILITY

22.4   The definition of disability is one of the most complex areas of the DDA
1995. If litigation ensues because of an alleged breach of the DDA 1995, then
determining whether an individual is a disabled person as defined in the DDA
1995 can be of critical importance. That said, in employment cases, for
example, it is often prudent for an employer to consider the same matters and
steps in relation to an employee, whether or not the employee is in fact disabled
as defined in the DDA 1995, in view of potential liability for unfair dismissal.
Under s 1 of the DDA 1995, a person has a disability if they have a physical or
mental impairment which has a substantial and long-term adverse effect on
their ability to carry out normal day-to-day activities. Schedule 1 to the DDA
1995 sets out, *inter alia*, the meaning of 'impairment', 'long-term adverse effect'
and 'day-to-day activities', and further guidance is provided in the Disability
Discrimination (Meaning of Disability) Regulations 1996 and in non-statutory
guidance published by the Secretary of State for Education and Employment
under s 3 of the DDA 1995 (*Guidance on matters to be taken into account in
determining questions relating to the definition of disability*). There is also now a
body of helpful case-law adding to the statutory provisions.[1]

22.5   It should be noted that in considering whether an individual may be
disabled for the purpose of the DDA 1995, the effects of treatment (including
medical treatment, the use of a prosthesis and therapy) are discounted (with
the exception of the use of glasses and contact lenses). Thus an individual with

---

1   See, especially, *Goodwin v Patent Office* [1999] IRLR 4.

a condition which is wholly controlled by medication will be deemed to be disabled if, without their medication, their impairment would have a substantial and long-term adverse effect on their ability to carry out normal day-to-day activities. Finally, at the time of writing, it has been proposed to extend the definition of disability in the DDA 1995, to provide more protection, for example, to people with cancer and asymptomatic progressive conditions.

EMPLOYMENT

22.6 HEIs are, of course, large-scale employers of academic, academic-related and non-academic staff. The employment provisions of the DDA 1995 apply to all employers who have 15 or more employees. This threshold can be reduced, but not increased, by regulations; and indeed it has recently been announced that the small employer exemption will be completely abolished by October 2004. Whilst no HEI will itself be affected by the small employer provisions, according to current case-law the number of employees of subsidiary and associated companies are not aggregated with those of the rest of the group. Thus if an HEI owns a trading company which directly employs fewer than 15 members of staff, those staff would not, at present, be protected by the DDA 1995. As a matter of good practice, however, an HEI's subsidiaries might wish to comply with the DDA 1995 in any event. The DDA 1995 outlaws discrimination against disabled people at every stage of the employment process, from the advertisement of a vacancy to dismissal. Discrimination can thus occur in the arrangements for interview, the decision whether to offer a candidate a post, the terms offered to a prospective employee, opportunities for promotion, transfer, training or other benefits, and dismissal or the subjection of the employee to any other detriment.

Discrimination

22.7 There are two key aspects to disability discrimination in the field of employment. First, discrimination can occur where the employer, for a reason which relates to the disabled person's disability, treats that person less favourably than he treats or would treat others to whom that reason would not apply. The employment provisions of the DDA 1995 focus on individual employees and their specific disabilities: the HE provisions contained in the SEND 2001 operate somewhat differently (see paras **22.21** *et seq*). It should be noted that the DDA 1995 does not outlaw all detrimental treatment of a disabled person but only that detrimental treatment which is related to their disability. Thus, if a disabled person's job is genuinely redundant, or if they are disciplined for misconduct, the employer is unlikely to face liability for discrimination, unless the employer has based its decision partly or wholly on the fact of the employee's disability, or has perhaps failed to take the effect of his disability fully into account. Secondly, an employer may also discriminate against a disabled person if he fails to take reasonable steps to prevent work arrangements (such as procedures for the selection of employees, or terms and conditions on which employment, promotion, transfer, training or any other benefit is offered) or physical features of the workplace placing the disabled person at a substantial disadvantage in comparison with persons who are not disabled. This is often referred to as 'the duty to make reasonable adjustments'.

Justification

22.8   In both of the above cases, the employer will not be liable for unlawful discrimination if the detrimental treatment of the disabled person in question can be justified. Justification is permitted only where the reason for the detrimental treatment is material to the circumstances of the particular case and is substantial. It should be noted that, in this respect, the DDA 1995 differs significantly from race and sex discrimination legislation.

Reasonable adjustments

22.9   The DDA 1995 gives a non-exhaustive list of examples of reasonable adjustments, including making adjustments to the premises or training, altering working hours and providing a reader or interpreter. Again, the Secretary of State has published detailed guidance (*Code of Practice for the elimination of discrimination in the field of employment against disabled persons or persons who have had a disability*). Further helpful guidance on how to approach the issue of reasonable adjustments can be found in *Morse v Wiltshire County Council.*[1]

Practical steps

22.10   There are many practical steps which employers can take to combat potential disability discrimination problems before they become a reality, including:

–   devising *and implementing* a detailed disability policy, complementing the institution's equal opportunities policy;
–   instituting disability awareness training as part of staff development programmes;
–   integrating employment policies relating to disabled employees and candidates with those policies which relate to disabled 'customers' (for example, members of the public attending conferences or other functions) and students; and
–   monitoring candidates and existing staff (perhaps by the use of confidential questionnaires) to establish whether any of them have disabilities (and then considering whether any adjustments might need to be made).

---

1   [1998] IRLR 352.

Consultation

22.11   It is good practice, where an employer has a disabled candidate for a post or has an existing employee who is or who becomes disabled, for the employer to consult the candidate or employee to discuss ways in which potential problems faced at work by the disabled person can be alleviated. There are numerous sources of advice, and in some cases financial assistance, on which employees and institutions can call, including the Employment Service, charities concerned with disabled people and commercial disability consultants. Advice from such sources can be invaluable – in consultation with the individual in question – in determining what adjustments might be appropriate.

Leased premises

22.12   Where the HEI's premises are leased and it appears that physical adjustments are necessary to accommodate the needs of a disabled employee, then, if the terms of the lease prohibit alterations or impose conditions, the employer should contact the lessor in writing and seek consent for the alterations. The lessor is obliged not to withhold its consent unreasonably to the request. This provision will, of course, affect both HEIs which rent property in which their staff work, and HEIs which themselves are the landlords of commercial premises. The duty to make physical adjustments to premises will not come into force until 2004.

Victimisation

22.13   The DDA 1995 also outlaws victimisation of any person, whether or not they are disabled, if they have complained that discrimination has taken place against a disabled person, or given evidence in the course of such a complaint.

Vicarious liability

22.14   If an employee of an HEI commits an act of unlawful discrimination in the course of his or her employment, the HEI may be vicariously liable for that act. The HEI may, however, have a defence if it can prove that it took reasonably practicable steps to prevent the discrimination. A key element to such a defence would be having and using an appropriate disability policy.

Remedies

22.15   Employment complaints under the DDA 1995 are dealt with by the employment tribunals. There were 1743 complaints of disability discrimination made to the tribunals between 1 April 1999 and 31 March 2000. The majority of these were settled or withdrawn. There is no qualifying period of service which a complainant must accrue before bringing a claim. As with sex and race discrimination complaints, there are no limits on the amount of compensation which may be awarded. It should be noted that compensation for disability discrimination which involves the dismissal of a disabled person can be significant: many disabled people are at a disadvantage in the job market and may have difficulties in mitigating their losses. Damages can also be awarded for injury to feelings. The employment tribunal can also make a declaration as to the rights of the employer and the employee, and can recommend that the employer takes action to alleviate the problem about which the complaint has been received.

PROVISION OF SERVICES

22.16   Since 2 December 1996, the DDA 1995 has made it unlawful for providers of goods, services and facilities to the general public ('service providers') to discriminate against disabled people by:

–   refusing to serve a disabled person;
–   failing to comply with the duty to make reasonable adjustments if that failure makes it impossible or unreasonably difficult for the disabled person to use the service;
–   discrimination in the standard of service provided to the disabled person; or
–   discrimination in the terms on which the service is provided.

22.17   In this context, 'discrimination' means treating a disabled person less favourably for a reason relating to the disabled person's disability than the service provider would treat people without the disability in question, where the treatment cannot be justified. Since October 1999, service providers have been under a duty to make reasonable adjustments: in the case of a service provision this means that if the service provider has a practice, policy or procedure which makes it impossible or unreasonably difficult for disabled persons to make use of that service, the service provider must take such steps as are reasonable to change the practice, policy or procedure. Failure to make reasonable adjustments is discriminatory, unless it can be justified. Also since 1 October 1999, service providers are obliged to take reasonable steps to provide a reasonable alternative method of providing the service where there are physical features (for example, building design) which make it impossible or unreasonably difficult for disabled persons to use the service. From October 2004, this duty will extend to altering or removing the physical features. The rules about leased premises apply to service providers as well as to employers. Service providers must provide 'auxiliary aids' (for example, audio information, large-print menus and so on), where to do so will enable disabled people to make use of the services. There is extensive guidance on the obligations of service providers (*Code of Practice: rights of access to goods, facilities, services, and premises*).

22.18   Discrimination in the provision of services may be justified if:

- the differential treatment is necessary so as not to endanger the health and safety of any person (including the disabled person);
- the disabled person is incapable of entering into the contract or giving informed consent (where relevant);
- the detrimental treatment is necessary to enable the services to be provided to the disabled person or to members of the public;
- otherwise the service could not be provided to the public;
- in some cases, where there is a cost differential in the provision of the service to a disabled person.

22.19   The rules relating to provision of services, as originally drafted, do *not* apply to the provision of publicly funded education, including education funded by the HEFCs. It should be noted, however, that the legislation does not define 'education'. The status of services to students which are ancillary to the provision of education (such as catering, accommodation and leisure facilities) is currently unclear, and HEIs would be prudent to assume that the DDA 1995 applies to such services. (It will be seen that the SEND 2001 expressly includes student services within its provisions.) In any event, HEIs (or their trading subsidiaries) will be service providers for the purposes of the DDA 1995 if they provide:

- conferences;
- public dining facilities;
- out-of-term accommodation to non-students;
- public access to sports and leisure facilities; or
- public access to entertainment (for example, plays and concerts), which are held on the HEI's premises.

(Note: this is not an exhaustive list).

22.20   Given that HEIs need to comply with the DDA 1995 in respect of these 'public services', the possibility that ancillary student services may be caught by the DDA 1995 may not be too significant. Furthermore, depending on the subject matter of the courses, provision of commercial summer schools or evening classes might not count as 'education' and might, therefore, be included within the provision of services for the purposes of the DDA 1995. Hence, HEIs should consider all areas of their activities where they provide non-educational services to the general public, including 'indirect' provision of such services (for example, by letting conference facilities to commercial organisers). The HEIs should then explore whether there are any particular problems in relation to those services for disabled people at large who might wish to take advantage of them. They should consider whether any changes ought to be made to the arrangements for the provision of the services, including the physical features of buildings. They also need to ensure that any staff who will be dealing with members of the public understand that they must not discriminate against disabled people. A person who has a complaint against a service provider may claim damages, including damages for injury to feelings.

Surprisingly, at the time of writing there is little case-law on the duties of service providers, but it has very recently been reported that damages of £500 have been awarded to a person with visual impairment who was refused entry to a restaurant with his guide-dog.

EDUCATION: IMPACT OF THE SEND 2001

22.21   The DDA 1995 obliges the funding councils to have regard to the requirements of disabled people in exercising their functions and to make the publication of a disability statement by each HEI one of the conditions for grant. The thrust of the DDA 1995 as originally drafted, therefore, was not to impose any direct duties on HEIs with regard to their selection of students, the courses they offer or the arrangements for the provision of those courses, but to encourage HEIs to have regard to the needs of disabled students. The phrase 'to have regard to' is not an uncommon one in legislation; it is also a woolly one. Moreover, whether or not an HEI is being 'reasonable' within the law, for example, in not making extensive and costly changes to certain parts of its premises in order to provide access to disabled employees and conference trade users (having paid due regard to the DDA 1995), the question will remain of what the funding council should reasonably expect of HEIs in relation to disabled students and of what political pressures there are within the HEI for action even if it is not strictly required by the law. Thus, the individual disabled student or disabled applicant may not have direct access to the courts in relation to a dispute with a given HEI, but he might be able to exert a degree of moral or political pressure and may raise the matter with the funding council. He might also encourage the HEI to fund improvements reasonably required by virtue of its being an employer and/or it using the premises to provide services to non-students.

22.22   The SEND 2001 was enacted in May 2001. Chapter 2 of the SEND 2001, dealing with discrimination by FEIs and HEIs in the provision of education and student services to disabled people, is not yet in force, but is expected to amend the DDA 1995 from September 2002. First, the SEND 2001 will insert a new s 28R into the DDA 1995, which will provide that it is unlawful for the governing body of an HEI to discriminate against a disabled person (as, of course, defined in the DDA 1995):

−   in the arrangements it makes for determining admissions to the HEI;
−   in the terms of admission; or
−   by refusing or deliberately omitting to accept an application for admission.

22.23   The SEND 2001 goes on to provide that it will be unlawful for the governing body of an HEI to:

−   discriminate against a disabled student in the student services it provides or offers to provide; or

–   discriminate against a disabled student by excluding him permanently or temporarily from the HEI.

22.24   As is usual, victimisation is outlawed, and 'student services' means services of any description which are provided wholly or mainly for students: besides the provision of education itself; these might include accommodation and sporting and leisure facilities. For clarity, regulations can be made to provide which services are, and are not, 'student services'.

Meaning of 'discrimination'

22.25   The definition of discrimination under the SEND 2001 is similar to the employment provisions of the DDA 1995, although there are notable differences in the provisions relating to reasonable adjustments. Under the SEND 2001, the governing body of an HEI will discriminate against a disabled person if, for a reason relating to that person's disability, the HEI treats the disabled person less favourably than it treats, or would treat, others to whom that reason does not or would not apply, unless the treatment in question is justified. The governing body of the HEI will also be under a duty to take reasonable steps to ensure that disabled people are not put at a substantial disadvantage, when compared with people who are not disabled, in relation to admissions to the HEI, and that disabled people are not disadvantaged in relation to student services. There will be a code of practice. It should be noted that the duty to make reasonable adjustments under the SEND 2001 is a duty to disabled people 'at large', rather than in relation to specific disabled persons. This differs from the employment provisions of the DDA 1995 and means that HEIs will need to consider the provisions they make for disabled students generally. Given that HEIs are already under a duty to disabled employees and users of non-education services, it is likely that the biggest impact of the SEND 2001 will be in relation to the provision of education and any other student service which is unlikely to be offered to the public as well, and no doubt students may already have benefited from policies and procedures designed to address the HEI's existing general duties under the DDA 1995. The SEND 2001 indicates that if a disabled person has made a 'confidential request', asking for the nature or existence of their disability to be kept confidential, then in considering whether reasonable adjustments have been made, regard must be had to compliance with that request. This regime is new, and there is no corresponding provision in the parts of the DDA 1995 dealing with employment or services.

Justification

22.26   It may be possible for an HEI to justify acts of discrimination. Less favourable treatment can be justified if the reason for the treatment is material to the circumstances of the particular case and substantial. Less favourable treatment can also be justified if it is necessary to maintain academic standards (and other standards to be prescribed by regulations). It may also be justified in other specific circumstances spelt out in regulations. It is anticipated that this defence of justification will be one of the more important and controversial aspects of the SEND 2001. Discrimination will not occur in relation to failure to take a particular step where the HEI does not know, and could not reasonably have been expected to know, that an individual was disabled and the failure to act was attributable to the lack of knowledge; nor will taking a particular step amount to less favourable treatment if at the time in question the HEI did not know, and could not reasonably be expected to know, that an individual was disabled.

An example

22.27   The explanatory notes to the SEND 2001 give an example of the provisions in practice. To comply with the duty to make reasonable adjustments, it would be advisable for HEIs to have a policy for students with dyslexia. This might include giving such students extra time to complete examinations. If an HEI did not know (and could not reasonably be expected to know) that a particular student had dyslexia, then the HEI would not discriminate against that student by not applying the policy to him.

Premises

22.28   Similar provisions relating to alterations to leasehold premises will apply under the SEND 2001 as are contained in the other parts of the DDA 1995.

Remedies

22.29   A disabled person who believes that they have been discriminated against by an HEI under the new provisions will have the right to bring a claim in the county court. Students who are also employees may bring any employment-related disability claim in the Employment Tribunal in the usual way. The Disability Rights Commission (DRC) (which has now replaced the Disability Rights Task Force) has an extensive role in enforcement of the DDA 1995, including the ability to provide conciliation services in relation to the parts of the DDA 1995 relating to service providers (this will include the amendments affecting HEIs introduced by the SEND 2001). Thus it is entirely possible – and to be hoped – that litigation will be minimal, as HEIs will undoubtedly have their own student grievance procedures, and there may be recourse to DRC conciliation before the courts need to be involved.[1]

1　　For example, the University of Central Lancashire has settled out of court a claim from a blind diploma student that it failed to provide adequate learning support given his special needs (*The Times Higher Educational Supplement*, 7 December 2001, p 6).

Timetable

22.30   At the time of writing, it is understood that the duty not to treat disabled students less favourably and the duty to make reasonable adjustments to non-physical arrangements (for example, policies and procedures) will come into force in September 2002; the duty relating to the provision of auxiliary aids and services not requiring physical adjustments to buildings will come into force in September 2003; and the duty relating to physical adjustments to buildings will come into force in September 2005. Draft Codes of Practice relating to the SEND 2001 can be seen at www.drc-gb.org/drc/InformationAndLegislation/Page34A.asp.

HUMAN RIGHTS ACT 1998

22.31   The HRA 1998 brings the rights set out in the European Convention on Human Rights under the protection of UK law. It came into force in England on 2 October 2000. (A detailed analysis of the HRA 1998 and its effect on HEIs is set out in Chapter 7.) It should be noted that the HRA 1998 is directly enforceable against public authorities and quasi-public authorities, which include HEIs. The key convention right with which we are concerned in this chapter is the right to education, contained in Art 2 of Protocol 1 to the Convention:

> 'No person shall be denied the right to education. In the exercise of any functions which it assumes in relation to education and to teaching, the State shall respect the right of parents to ensure such education and teaching is in conformity with their own religious and philosophical convictions.'

The UK has a formal reservation in relation to this right, which reads: '. . . the principle affirmed in the second sentence of Protocol 1, art 2 is accepted by the United Kingdom only so far as it is compatible with the provision of efficient instruction and training and the avoidance of unreasonable public expenditure'. Note, however, that the reservation relates only to the rights of parents to choose the type of education they desire for their children, and not to education generally. In so far as the Convention right relates to higher education, the reservation appears unlikely to apply.

22.32   Article 14 of the Convention establishes that Convention rights shall be secured without discrimination on any ground. While disability is not specifically listed in the non-exhaustive examples of discriminatory grounds set out in Art 14, there is little doubt that it is covered. Taken together, Art 2 of Protocol 1 and Art 14 give disabled individuals the right not be denied an education. There has been some debate, however, as to whether HE is education for the purposes of the HRA 1998. It is true that most of the cases in the ECHR relating to the Convention right to education have centred on primary or secondary education and often on parental wishes. From cases such

X v United Kingdom[1] and *Glazewska v Sweden*,[2] we can extract the principle that where certain, limited, HE facilities are provided by a State, it is not incompatible with the Convention to restrict access to such facilities to those students who have attained the academic level required to benefit from the courses offered. Although it does not have a specific bearing on the interpretation of the HRA 1998, it is also worth considering that the right to education as set out in the United Nations Convention on the Rights of the Child recognises, *inter alia*, the accessibility of HE. It would follow, therefore, that under the HRA 1998, disabled students who will benefit from HE should not be denied access to apply to HEIs; and, once accepted, should not be treated detrimentally in the HEI's provision of education. It is suggested that the provisions of the SEND 2001 will address these issues, although it should be remembered that the HRA 1998 does give individuals free-standing rights against public authorities, irrespective of the amended provisions of the DDA 1995.

1   (1980) 23 DR 228.
2   (1985) 45 DR 300.

Chapter 23

STUDENT ACCOMMODATION: LEASE OR LICENCE, EVICTION OR QUIET ENJOYMENT?

Simon Arrowsmith, Clive Read, Angela Pearson and Martin Edwards (Martineau Johnson)

EDITORS' INTRODUCTION

§23.1   Is the student who is renting HEI accommodation a tenant with a degree of security of tenure, or merely a licensee? If the latter, how easily can he be evicted: is a court order needed? What if the HEI refurbishes the residence block around the resident students: how much 'quiet enjoyment' can they expect and will the court enforce their rights? This chapter provides the answers: probably a licensee; the HEI would be wise to get a court order rather than attempt a DIY eviction; and even students as licensees have rights (for example, to peace and quiet during examination time, and hence they could sue Trent Polytechnic to prevent it undertaking building work in the residences).[1]

§23.2   Moreover, this chapter also discusses the HEI–student residential contract in relation to the UTCCR 1999,[2] as recently invoked by the OFT[3] in reproaching Keele, Derby and Writtle College concerning unspecified hidden charges, the unreasonable retention of deposits, attempts to exclude without any appeal mechanism, and high and/or unspecified penalties for late payment of rent. Perhaps it is not surprising that some HEIs are looking hard at outsourcing the management of their halls, at sale or lease-back deals, and effectively at privatisation of the residence function (see Chapter 10 re TUPE and Chapter 18 re PFI).

§23.3   Finally, can the HEI withhold examination marks and degree results, or even the degree transcript or certificate if there is debt, arising from non-payment of tuition fees or accommodation charges? As this chapter explains, the answer is probably not. Examination results can be obtained anyway via the DPA 1998 (see Chapter 13), while it would be unwise of the HEI to confound an academic sanction (withholding the degree certificate/transcript) relating to the contract-to-educate (see Chapter 6) with the entirely separate accommodation contract, and, moreover, the European Convention on Human Rights includes the right to have educational achievement recognised (see Chapter 7). Such debts need to be pursued via the Small Claims procedure in the county court (Simmons, 1999), although the sanction

---

1   *Smith and Others v Nottinghamshire County Council* (1981) *The Times*, November 13.
2   SI 1999/2083.
3   Bulletin No 13 at www.oft.gov.uk.

of not allowing a debtor to attend a degree ceremony may be effective (perhaps the proud parents will pay up on behalf of their impecunious graduand offspring!). See the 'Armed' Unit on 'Student Debt' at www.bristol.ac.uk/armed.

INTRODUCTION

23.1 Student accommodation is operated by two main types of agreement, the lease (or tenancy agreement) and the licence. This chapter examines the nature of both types of agreements and discusses the ways in which they can be terminated. The main difference between the grant of a lease and the grant of a licence is that the grant of a lease of a property creates an interest in the land on the part of the tenant, while granting a licence merely gives the occupier permission to use or enter a property. The permission prevents the occupier being a trespasser. As Vaughan CJ said in *Thomas v Sorrell*: 'a dispensation or licence properly passeth no interest, nor alters or transfers property in any thing, but only makes an action lawful, without which it would have been unlawful'.[1] The significance of tenants having an interest in the land is that it is more difficult to remove a tenant from a property than to remove a mere licensee. For many years, owners granting the right to occupy land called the agreements establishing rights of occupation 'licences' purely to avoid giving occupiers the full rights of a tenant. Over the past two decades, the law has been refined in this area and it is no longer possible for a landlord to evade responsibilities to a tenant.

LEASE OR LICENCE

23.2 There are now specific rules to indicate whether an arrangement is that of a lease or a licence. The definition of a lease was clarified in the House of Lords' decision in the case of *Street v Mountford*.[2] In this case, Lord Templeman outlined a three-point test that should be used when trying to determine whether an agreement is a lease or a licence. This test applies regardless of what the parties call the arrangement. If the legal effect of the terms of the agreement is to create the rights and obligations of a tenancy then a tenancy is created:

> 'If the agreement satisfied all the requirements of a tenancy, then the agreement produced a tenancy and the parties cannot alter the effect of the agreement by insisting that they only created a licence. The manufacture of a five-pronged implement for manual digging results in a fork even if the manufacturer, unfamiliar with the English language, insists that he intended to make and has made a spade.'[3]

---

1   (1673) Vaugh 330 at p 351.
2   [1985] AC 809, HL.
3   Ibid, at p 819F.

23.3   Lord Templeman stated that the test for establishing whether or not a lease or a licence was in place was to look at the circumstances of the arrangement:

> 'To constitute a tenancy the occupier must be granted exclusive possession for a fixed or periodic term certain in consideration of a premium or periodical payments. The grant may be express or may be inferred where the owner accepts weekly or other periodical payments from the occupier.'[1]

This approach has been confirmed by the Court of Appeal in *National Car Parks Limited v The Trinity Development Company (Banbury) Ltd.*[2] Arden LJ, in delivering the leading judgment said:

> 'so the Court must look to the substance and not to the form. But it may help, in determining what the substance was, to consider whether the parties express themselves in a particular way ... It would in my judgment be a strong thing for the law to disregard totally the parties' choice of wording and to do so would be inconsistent with the general principle of freedom of contract and the principle documents should be interpreted as a whole. On the other hand ... it does not give rise to any presumptions. At most it is relevant as a pointer.'[3]

23.4   Thus, for an agreement to constitute a lease there must be:

- exclusive possession;
- for a term;
- at a rent. (Note Fox LJ's observations in *Ashburn Anstalt v Arnold (WJ & Co) and Another*[4] that, where rent was not payable, you could still have a lease, but this case has since been overruled by the House of Lords in *Prudential Assurance Co Ltd v London Residuary Body and Others*,[5] for which see Lord Templeman at p 395G.)

23.5   Despite the fact that *Street v Mountford* is still the leading authority, the case of *Mehta v Royal Bank of Scotland plc*[6] has thrown this area of law back into a state of some confusion. In this case the courts looked back to the days before *Street v Mountford*, when the intention of the parties was the overriding consideration. However, this decision is not considered to be a good authority (Pawloski (1999)). Indeed, the House of Lords case of *Bruton v London and Quadrant Housing Trust*[7] looked solely at the three-point test in *Street v Mountford*, and ignored the intention of the parties and the fact that the owner was legally unable to grant a lease to the occupier. This chapter continues on the basis that the strict test in *Street v Mountford* is the only test that applies. In applying the test, the requirement for exclusive possession causes most uncertainty.

---

1   Ibid, at p 818E.
2   (2001) unreported, CA.
3   Case transcript, para 28.
4   [1988] 2 All ER 147, at pp 154E–155A.
5   [1992] 3 WLR 279.
6   [1999] L&TR 340.
7   [1999] 3 All ER 481.

Exclusive possession

23.6   Where a person is given exclusive possession of a property (and the two other requirements are satisfied) a tenancy is created regardless of the intention behind the agreement. In *Street v Mountford*, Lord Templeman identified the following exceptions to this rule[1] and these exceptions are called possessory licences:

–   where there is no intention to create legal relations;
–   where the relationship is one of seller and buyer;
–   where there is occupation by an employee as a service occupier; or
–   where there is incapacity on the part of the grantor to grant a new tenancy. (But contrast this with *Bruton v London and Quadrant Housing Trust*[2] and the council's inability to grant a lease to the housing trust under s 32(3) of the Housing Act 1985.)

23.7   Exclusive possession is the right to exclude other people, including the landlord, from entering the premises:

'The tenant possessing exclusive possession is able to exercise the rights of an owner of land, which is in the real sense his land albeit temporarily and subject to certain restrictions. A tenant armed with exclusive possession can keep out strangers and keep out the landlord unless the landlord is exercising limited rights reserved to him by the tenancy agreement to enter and view and repair.'[3]

23.8   In *Street v Mountford*, Mr Street granted Ms Mountford the right to occupy two rooms in a house for £37 per week. The agreement was entitled 'licence agreement' and contained a declaration signed by Ms Mountford stating that she understood that she had no right to claim protection under the Rent Acts. Notwithstanding this, the agreement was held to be a tenancy. It was held that the accommodation had been granted for a term, at a rent and with exclusive possession.

Services

23.9   One significant factor in determining the existence of exclusive possession is the extent to which services are supplied to the occupier:

'The occupier is a lodger if the landlord provides attendance or services which require the landlord or his servants to exercise unrestricted access to and use of the premises. A lodger is entitled to live in the premises but he cannot call the place his own.'[4]

In *Abbeyfield (Harpenden) Society Ltd v Woods*,[5] the occupation of a room in an old people's home was held to constitute a licence rather than a lease because services (including meals, heating, lighting and even a resident housekeeper) were included in the 'rent'. *Marchant v Charters*[6] was another case where occupation of a furnished room was held to be under licence as the room was

---

1   [1985] AC 809, at p 821B.
2   [1999] 3 All ER 481.
3   Per Lord Templeman in *Street v Mountford* [1985] AC 809, HL at p 816C.
4   Ibid, at p 818A.
5   [1968] 1 WLR 374.
6   [1977] 1 WLR 1181.

cleaned daily and the bed sheets changed weekly. Similarly, in *Westminster City Council v Clarke*,[1] it was held that warden-controlled single rooms with a bed and limited cooking facilities were occupied by people as licensees not as tenants. This case highlights not only the fact that where services are provided to an occupier the agreement may stand as a licence, but also that the extent to which the grantor retains control over the property is an important factor.

Control

23.10   The property in *Westminster City Council v Clarke* was occupied by single, homeless men with personality disorders, drug or alcohol addiction, or those who had been discharged from hospital or prison. They were given occupation of the rooms until they found permanent accommodation. The terms of the licence stated that a representative from the council should be entitled to enter the accommodation at any time. It also required the occupants to be in their rooms at 11 pm, and visitors to have left by this time. Due to the degree of close supervision, the agreement was held to constitute a licence. In *Esso Petroleum Co Ltd v Fumegrange Ltd*,[2] the occupier of an Esso service station agreed in a licence agreement not to 'impede in any way the officers, employees, agents or contractors of Esso in the exercise by them of Esso's rights of possession and control of the service station'. Again, the degree of control exercised over the conduct of the business was held to be a significant indicator of the nature of the occupation.[3] The recent case of *National Car Parks v The Trinity Development Company (Banbury) Ltd*[4] contained a similar provision to the one above, but it did not refer to the owner's right of control. The agreement was still held to be a licence although the approach to the decision may have been misguided. In reconciling the case with *Shell-Mex & BP Ltd v Manchester Garages Ltd*, Judge Rich QC stated that the absence of a reference to the owner's right of control did not mean that the case should not follow *Shell-Mex*. He accepted that the owner's right to control the premises could be indicative of whether there was a licence or a lease, but also said that it was not necessary to have the control of the property if you had the possession of it, as the control element came from having possession. In his view, the issue was 'whether the grantor [has] retained possession rather than merely reserving rights of entry over premises in respect of which he has granted exclusive possession to the grantee'. The focus of the judgment looked to the intention of the parties in a similar way to cases predating *Street v Mountford*, and did not use a strict application of Lord Templeman's three-point test. However, the Court of Appeal has revisited the applicability of *Shell-Mex*.

23.11   The Court of Appeal upheld the decision in *National Car Parks v The Trinity Development Company (Banbury) Limited*.[5] Helpfully, there was clarified

1   [1992] 1 All ER 695, HL.
2   [1994] 46 EG 199.
3   See also *Shell-Mex & BP Ltd v Manchester Garages Ltd* [1971] 1 All ER 841: the facts of the case and the 'not to impede' clause are very similar.
4   [2000] EGCS 128. For commentary on the first instance judgment, see Roger Cohen: 'Licence or Tenancy? The Make-or-Break question', *Property Law Journal*, 22 January 2001.
5   (2001) unreported, CA.

the parties' intention to create the licence and not a lease. The key issues related to the extent to which the owner retained control of the car parking and whether, on the wording of the licence, the owner reserved to itself rights in a manner which would be more appropriate in a lease. The licence was subject to the use by the owner of 40 car parking spaces which were to be available free of charge and there was also included a 'not to impede' clause. It was stated that National Car Parks 'shall give all reasonable assistance and facilities to afford the Licensor and its agents occupation of the Licensed Premises on a temporary basis for the re-surfacing thereof'.[1] It was asserted by National Car Parks that the provision of 40 free car parking spaces and the reference to the re-surfacing of the car park were reservations of rights which, taken in the whole, were inconsistent with having possession as a licensor and were more akin to the grant of a lease. Arden LJ discussed these assertions and upheld the decision by Judge Rich QC at first instance. The right to control provisions were felt not to be so substantial as to affect the true interpretation of the document. There were a number of pointers which indicated a licence rather than a tenancy. There was no dispute that the document did not include covenants for quiet enjoyment and no express right of re-entry (forfeiture). So far as the provision of car parking spaces was concerned, Arden LJ concluded that:

> 'on the true construction of the agreement as a whole, the landlord is only to have 40 car parking spaces free of charge and will then be charged the same rate as the general public for the rest. The number of free car parking spaces is relevant to the calculation of net profit under ... the agreement ... There is nothing ... which would stop the landlord entering upon the premises for other purposes ...'[2]

So far as the reference to re-surfacing was concerned, their Lordships decided that this did not indicate the grant of exclusive possession subject to which the landlord would then have to retain rights of access. Instead, re-surfacing was only ever likely to arise in exceptional circumstances; to carry out such work would only occur on a temporary basis; and, crucially in their Lordship's opinion, the owners would require assistance from the licensee to ensure access to parking spaces in order to re-surface the car park at the most opportune time:

> 'the function of [the not to impede clause] ... is to ensure the occpier's co-operation ... [it] is not in substance of right of re-entry reserved to the landlord. It is in truth a perfectly understandable provision for the protection of the landlord and not a provision which indicated that NCP has a right to exclusive possession.'[3]

---

1   Case transcript, para 5.
2   Case transcript, para 33.
3   Case transcript, para 35.

Dwellings

23.12 The case heard by the House of Lords of *Uratemp Ventures Ltd v Collins*[1] clarified the definition of 'dwelling' within the meaning of the Housing Act 1988. It has added an interesting gloss for owners everywhere who might believe that providing use of a room by itself without further facilities precludes the grant of a lease. This case reinforces the fact that courts will always look at the facts. The Lords decided that in order to claim an assured tenancy had been granted to him of 'a dwelling-house … let as a separate dwelling' within the 1988 Act, it was not necessary for Mr Collins to have access to cooking facilities.[2] Mr Collins had been a longstanding resident of a room at the Viscount Hotel, Kensington. The Act makes clear[3] that part of a house may be a dwelling-house and the case indicates that it was common ground that a bed sitting room may be a dwelling-house.[4] Following a change in ownership of the hotel, the new owners sought possession of the room which Mr Collins occupied. He asserted that he was entitled to an assured tenancy under the 1988 Act. This was upheld following an appeal to the House of Lords. They decided that the definition of 'dwelling' was not to be restricted by the precondition that cooking facilities were available. Lord Irvine of Lairg LC summarised the position:

> ' "Dwelling" is not a term of art, but a familiar word in the English language, which in my judgment in this context connotes a place where one lives, regarding and treating it as home. Such a place does not cease to be a "dwelling" merely because one takes all or some of one's meals out; or brings takeaway food in to the exclusion of home cooking; or at times prepares some food for consumption on heating devices falling short of a full cooking facility.'[5]

23.13 The facts of occupation remain important to denote whether a property or any part of it occupied by a person is enough to establish a tenancy, along the lines already established in *Street v Mountford*. Lord Millett, in giving the leading judgment indicated that if exclusive possession could be demonstrated the question is then whether the premises are occupied as the tenant's home. If that could be answered positively, Lord Millet concluded it would be a dwelling. There would be a separate hurdle to be overcome that the premises should be occupied as the only or principal home[6] but that was not an issue on the facts. In reaching his decision, Lord Millett noted:

---

1   [2000] L&TR 369, CA; [2001] UKHL 43, [2001] 3 WLR 806, HL: lack of cooking facilities in a hostel bed-sit does not alone mean that the long-term occupant is not living in the room as his 'dwelling' (Housing Act 1988, s 1(1)) and hence he can indeed be a tenant with an assured tenancy under the Housing Act 1988. See also [2001] PLSCS 213, [2001] 17 EG, 176; also *Carroll v Manek* (1999) *The Times*, August 18.
2   Housing Act 1988, s 1(1) lists, too, the subsidiary hurdles that have to be overcome in order for an assured tenancy to have been granted, namely: the tenant must be an individual; the dwelling is occupied as his only or principal home; and the tenancy does not otherwise fall within the list contained in Sch 1.
3   Housing Act 1988, s 45(1).
4   Per Lord Steyn in *Uratemp Ventures Ltd v Collins* [2001] UKHL 43, [2001] 3 WLR 806, para [14].
5   Per the Lord Chancellor ibid, para [3].
6   Housing Act 1988, s 1(1)(b).

'If the tenancy agreement grants in addition, the right to the shared use of other rooms, the question is whether the room or rooms of which he has exclusive possession are his dwelling place or only part of it. This depends on the nature and extent of the right and the character of the other rooms. The right to occupy a living room in common with and at the same time as the landlord is such an invasion of his privacy that Parliament cannot be taken to have intended that the tenant should enjoy security of tenure ... a right to occupy a kitchen (as distinct from the right to some limited use of its facilities) in common with the landlord will take the tenancy out of the Acts. The presence or absence of cooking facilities in the part of the premises in which the tenant has exclusive occupation is not relevant.'[1]

23.14 The interest that this has for HEIs largely revolves around ensuring that the terms upon which a student is granted rights to use accommodation mirror the factual position. Any confusion is likely to be treated unfavourably by the OFT. Notwithstanding that leases granted to students cannot be protected within the Housing Act 1988,[2] ensuring that the document which has been entered into is either clearly a licence or clearly a lease carries with it important ramifications in terms of an HEI seeking repossession of the property, which is covered in paras **2.24–2.26**.

Terms of the agreement

23.15 Other indicators as to whether an agreement is a lease or a licence can be found in the written document itself. There are certain general clauses that point to the existence of a tenancy and others that would be more appropriate in a licence. This is because certain terms are inconsistent with the idea of a lease and the argument that exclusive possession has been granted. The following terms point to the existence of a lease:

–   a right to enter and inspect the property; and
–   a provision for quiet enjoyment.

23.16 Such terms would be inconsistent with the concept of a licence. This is because, if the owner were entitled to enter the property at any time (as he would be under a licence), he would not need to reserve expressly the right of re-entry. Where a right of entry is reserved, the full extent of the landlord's right would be expressed in the agreement, leaving the tenant with exclusive possession qualified by the landlord's express reserved rights. Similarly, the concept of giving the licensee/occupier a guarantee of quiet enjoyment has traditionally been unnecessary, as a licensee would not be entitled to it in any event.

Quiet enjoyment and building works
23.17 However, the case of *Smith and Others v Nottinghamshire County Council*[3] put this longstanding principle into some doubt. In this case, the Court of Appeal held that students holding a contractual licence to occupy a room in a hall of residence were granted an implied term that the HEI (Trent

---

1   Per Lord Millett in *Uratemp Ventures Ltd v Collins* [2001] UKHL 43, 3 WLR 806, para [58].
2   Housing Act 1988, Sch 1, para 8 as amended by the Housing Act 1996.
3   (1981) *The Times*, November 13.

Polytechnic as it then was, legal ownership before the ERA 1988 being with Nottinghamshire County Council) would not do anything without reasonable excuse that would interfere with the purposes of the students' occupation. In implying this term the courts, in effect, put licensors under an obligation not to 'derogate from the grant', an obligation normally only associated with the rights of tenants. Lord Denning, in *Moulton Builders Ltd v City of Westminister LBC*[1] summarised the principle of derogation of grant:

> 'If one man agrees to confer a particular benefit on another he must not do anything which substantially deprives the other of the enjoyment or benefit because that would be to take away with one hand what is given with the other.'

23.18   The students occupied the property during the academic year for the purposes of their studies, to sleep and study there and anything the owner did which interfered with this would breach the implied terms of quiet enjoyment. The Master of the Rolls stated that the case turned on its own particular facts and conceded there was no doubt the students were only contractual licensees and not tenants. However, in this case, replacing the windows in one hall of residence amounted to such a breach. It is easy to have sympathy with the students: the county council decided to replace dangerous window frames; scaffolding went up in March 1981 and work which should have been completed over the Easter vacation continued until June after the windows had to be redesigned; and the disturbance created by the work caused great distress to students who were due to take exams at the end of May and during June. As the case report indicated: 'it seemed clear as a matter of good sense and implication that the Council should do nothing without just cause to disturb students from getting on with their studies in their rooms in reasonable quietude'.

23.19   It is clear that universities will be more vulnerable to students enforcing rights of this nature during exam periods and *Smith* did turn on its particular circumstances. However, universities even if they grant licences rather than leases should be aware that, in effect, an implied term of quiet enjoyment could well apply all year round. What scope, then, is there for universities to carry out necessary remedial work and when can they do it? *Smith* refers to the owner having 'just cause'. As can be seen even carrying out remedial work of some dangerous window frames is no guarantee of having such a just cause. Universities are generally sensitive to the needs of students, especially during exams. *Smith* suggests that all but the most urgent and necessary work should wait until vacations or other periods when students are less likely to be using the Halls of Residence (but, of course, this might then clash with using halls for conference trade earnings, and also many HEIs rent out student rooms on a 50/52 week basis anyway). Clearly, the need to remedy a dangerous situation (gas leakage, latent defects) requires a university to act swiftly but the lesson of *Smith* is that such swiftness must not overly interrupt students' use of premises, especially just before or during exams. *Smith* does

---

1   (1976) 30 P&CR 182.

not mean universities can never carry out works and universities can take some comfort from the fact that temporary inconvenience is not a breach of an express covenant for quiet enjoyment in a lease.[1] *Smith* can perhaps best be seen as an example of prolonged and physical interference with use.

Quiet enjoyment generally

23.20   Is there an overall duty of quiet enjoyment placed on the universities, for the benefit of licensees or tenants concerning the quality or soundproofing in halls of residence? The two cases of *Southwark LBC v Mills* and *Baxter v Camden LBC*[2] heard by the House of Lords suggests not. In these cases, tenants living in blocks of flats owned by two London borough councils asserted that the lack of sound insulation allowed them to hear the sounds of even normal day-to-day activities made by adjoining occupiers. Claims for breach of quiet enjoyment and nuisance were dismissed: a breach of quiet enjoyment would only arise after the grant of a lease because the tenants took the premises as they stood and there was no implied warranty that the premises were fit for their purpose; and the ordinary use by neighbours of adjoining premises was not a nuisance. Lord Clyde stated: 'Neither landlord and none of the occupiers of adjoining properties has done ... anything since the tenancy agreements were entered into which was not contemplated by everyone concerned' (at p 449E) and Lord Hoffmann concurred: 'I don't think that the normal use of residential flats can possibly be a nuisance to the neighbours' (at p 459J). The result might have been different for excessive noise (parties) but that could generally be expected to be covered by the normal principle of nuisance.

University obligations

23.21   The OFT is becoming more and more involved with the regulation and terms of accommodation agreements. It has traditionally been the case that accommodation agreements contained many restrictions on how student licensees had to conduct themselves during the term of their licences, but rarely did agreements contain detailed requirements as to how the university was to be restricted (if at all), nor did they provide great detail as to the specific services that were to be provided. As we have shown above this may, historically, have been due to the fact that students only occupied property as licensees and the university could exert as much control over the licensees as it wished to and it did not need to describe the services that it was to provide. However, times are changing and there is a growing expectation that universities, whether as licensors or landlords, will have to commit themselves in writing to providing minimum levels of accommodation and services. Students are consumers and they have increased awareness and recognition of their rights and the consideration of payment of academic and accommodation fees raise expectations of what the university will provide – how universities manage and deliver on those expectations is just another aspect of being able to

---

1   See *Romulus Trading Co Ltd v Comet Properties Ltd* [1996] 2 EGLR 70.
2   [1999] 4 All ER 449.

attract and retain students in today's competitive markets. Universities should recognise that exercising control over students needs to be balanced with universities providing these consumers with attractive student accommodation governed by a reasonable and balanced agreement.

23.22   The following terms point to the existence of a licence and we have already seen the effect of these above:

– anything retaining control and dominion over the property (*Shell-Mex v Manchester Garages Ltd*);
– terms of a personal nature that show the parties have a different relationship to that usually seen between a landlord and a tenant (for example, terms stipulating that only one particular brand of a product can be sold from the property: *Shell-Mex v Manchester Garages Ltd*); and
– terms whereby a landowner provides services in the property (*Street v Mountford*).

23.23   It may well be, therefore, that students in halls of residence will be licensees due to the amount of control that is exercised over them, but there can be no absolute guarantee that a judge would not interpret a 'licence agreement' as a lease. It all depends on the facts of each case which can and should be reinforced by drafting the document so that the indications of a licence are prominently displayed. Terms similar to those described here as being characteristic of a licence should be included in the written agreement and consideration should be given to the underlying operational issues. The more control seen to be exercised, the more likely it is that an agreement will be held to be a licence.

Repossession

23.24   What are the potential benefits to an HEI of granting a student a licence and not a lease? There are important differences with regard to terminating and recovering possession of the property depending on whether it is licensed or let. The principal differences are listed below.

Licence
23.25   This is a contractual right to occupy the premises which should be recorded in writing. A licensee is entitled to remain in occupation until his contractual licence has come to an end. The licence itself should specify the events which will trigger termination, and must be terminated in accordance with the terms of the written agreement. In the event that there is no specific agreement as to termination, the licensee must be given reasonable notice. Assuming the licence period is expressed to be for a fixed term (for example, the academic year), no other form of prescribed notice to terminate is required. However, in the event that the licence is granted on a periodic basis, then 4 weeks' minimum notice in a prescribed form will be required.[1] Once the licence

---

1   Protection from Eviction Act 1977, s 5(1A).

has come to an end, the licensee becomes a trespasser. However, the owner cannot simply evict the former licensee/trespasser without first obtaining an order from the county court, as he would otherwise be in danger of falling foul of the criminal sanctions contained in various statutes which protect occupiers of residential accommodation from unlawful eviction.[1] There is a short-form (summary) procedure for obtaining such a court order in these circumstances[2] which is relatively speedy (ie the claim will normally be heard by the court within a week or two from the start of the proceedings). With effect from 15 October 2001, the procedure is under CPR 1998, Part 55. Application for a summary Possession Order will normally have to be made to the local county court and will only be entertained in the High Court in exceptional circumstances. Once the court order has been granted, the owner must then obtain a warrant for possession, which must be executed by court bailiffs.

Lease

23.26 Although a letting by a 'specified educational institution'[3] is excluded from qualifying as an assured tenancy,[4] it still remains a lease (although unprotected) and a different regime applies for termination and recovery of possession. Proper notice to quit must be given to terminate the lease and the length of notice will vary according to the circumstances. In any event, the owner must ensure that he complies with the provisions of the Protection from Eviction Act 1977, s 5(1A), by giving at least 4 weeks' notice in the prescribed form. Following the termination of the lease in this way, the owner cannot invoke the summary court procedure mentioned above. Following the termination of the lease in this way, the owner cannot invoke the summary court procedure mentioned above. A 'standard' possession procedure will apply with effect from 15 October 2001 – and again pursuant to CPR 1998, Part 55. This means that it will take longer for the owner to obtain an Order for Possession – the standard period between issue of the proceedings and hearing (when the owner's claim for possession will be heard) is likely to be 8 weeks. This procedure potentially entails more work and, therefore, increased costs in preparing for and attending at the formal hearing, as compared to the summary procedure for licences. The owner is still required to obtain a warrant for possession and can only recover possession through the county court bailiffs.

Unfair Terms in Consumer Contracts Regulations 1999

23.27 The provisions for terminating a student's lease or licence must be fair in the light of the UTCCR 1999. Unlike the UCTA 1977, these Regulations apply to contracts relating to land and this should be remembered when

---

1   Protection from Eviction Act 1977; Criminal Law Act 1977; Powers of Criminal Courts Act 1973.
2   Summary Proceedings under Part 8B of the CPR 1998 (CCR Ord 24, r 1(1)).
3   Assured and Protected Tenancies (Lettings to Students) Regulations 1998, SI 1998/1967, reg 3.
4   Under the Housing Act 1988, Sch 1, para 8, as amended by the Housing Act 1996.

drafting any lease or licence. The UTCCR 1999 define an unfair term as follows:

> 'A contractual term which has not been individually negotiated shall be regarded as unfair if, contrary to the requirement of good faith, it causes a significant imbalance in the parties' rights and obligations arising under the contract, to the detriment of the consumer.'[1]

23.28 It will invariably be the case that student leases/licences will not be individually negotiated, and students are generally accepted to be consumers (see Chapters 6 and 29). The OFT has the power to investigate any allegation of an unfair contract term and, if the DGFT decides the term is fair, then he or she must give reasons.[2] If a term is found to be unfair, it will not be enforceable, although the remainder of the agreement will still bind the parties.[3] *Camden LBC v McBride*[4] revolved around the inclusion of a term in a lease which required the tenant not to do anything which could be a nuisance to others. The question of whether something constituted a nuisance was to be determined by the landlord in its sole discretion. The court held that the term was too favourable to the landlord, and was, therefore, unfair under reg 4 of what was then the UTCCR 1994.

23.29 The DGFT does investigate allegations of unfair contract terms and examples of unfair terms before and after his intervention are listed in the regularly published *Unfair Contract Terms Bulletin*. For example, an educational institution whose accommodation agreement permitted the institution to retain the deposit where a student failed to take up the place had to be altered so that the institution would only retain the deposit if the room could not be re-let. Another common clause of university accommodation agreements stipulates that there is collective responsibility for any damage caused, often without making provisions for an appeal. After investigation into clauses of this nature contained in one college's accommodation regulations the DGFT stated that the college could not hold students collectively responsible for damage and students would only be liable for damage for which they or their agents were responsible. (See *Unfair Contract Terms Bulletin* (13 April 2001) produced by the OFT for examples of the DGFT's interventions and the changes made.)

23.30 HEIs often enquire as to whether it is permissible to withhold a student's degree certificate in circumstances where there has been a breach of the terms of occupation of a lease or a licence (for example, non-payment of the licence fee, or a fine imposed for misconduct). There will usually be a provision in the HEI's general student regulations entitling it to withhold a degree certificate for non-payment of any debts. Whilst the fairness of such a provision has not yet been tested, we suggest that HEIs tread carefully, as the courts are

---

1   Unfair Terms in Consumer Contracts Regulations 1999, SI 1999/2083, reg 5(1).
2   Ibid, reg 10.
3   Ibid, reg 8.
4   [1999] CLY 3737.

likely to be sympathetic to students. In particular, it is unlikely to be fair to withhold a certificate if the amount of the outstanding debt is relatively small. With the advent of student loans and the erosion of student grants, the scale of this problem is growing ever larger and it is one that neither universities nor students can ignore. In addition, it is thought that withholding degrees may fall foul of the HRA 1998 and, therefore, be unlawful (see Crook (1999)).

Bruton v London and Quadrant Housing Trust

23.31   Another interesting point to raise in relation to the lease/licence debate arises in the case of *Bruton v London and Quadrant Housing Trust*.[1] Mr Bruton was given a 'licence agreement' by the London and Quadrant Housing Trust to occupy a flat contained in a block for £18 per week. The block of flats was to be demolished. The actual owners of the block of flats were Lambeth Council and they had granted the Housing Trust a licence (as they were not empowered to grant a lease[2]) in order to further the Trust's charitable object – that of providing temporary accommodation for the homeless. The essence of the claim against the Housing Trust was that they had breached their repairing obligations as a landlord under s 11 of the Landlord and Tenant Act 1985. In order to claim this, Mr Bruton had to prove that he had a tenancy and not just a licence. On the facts the House of Lords held that Mr Bruton did have a tenancy: he had exclusive possession of the property, for a term, at a rent. The significance of this case is that it was held possible for the Housing Trust with no proprietary interest (freehold or leasehold ownership) to grant a proprietary interest to another. The reasoning behind this was that where the facts denote that a tenancy exists, the rights of the tenant should not be denied solely by reason of the lack of authority of the person who is granting the right to occupy to do so (although this is hard to reconcile with the idea that a person can only grant a tenancy for a period of time equal to or less than the remainder of his interest in the land).[3]

23.32   The significance of the lease/licence distinction as we have discussed it in this chapter is that a lease provides the tenant with an interest in the land itself which is binding against third parties. However, we can see from *Bruton* that a tenancy can be purely contractual in nature and that, although it can bind the lessor, it would not be able to bind third parties as no legal interest in the land in the conventional sense would have been created. In *Bruton*, the Housing Trust was unable to prevent the Council from entering the property, and was also unable on behalf of Mr Bruton to exclude the Council from entering the property, as it had no authority to do so. Mr Bruton held a personal 'tenancy' and this could only bind his immediate 'landlord', and not those with

---

1   [1999] 3 All ER 481.
2   See s 32(3) of the Housing Act 1985.
3   See *Milmo v Carreras* [1946] KB 306 and M Pawlowski and J Brown 'Bruton: A New Species of Tenancy?' (2000) 4 L&T Rev, Issue No 6.

a superior title. Where students are occupying halls of residence, *Bruton* may not have any significant impact as there is usually a very high degree of control exercised over the students. Where the outcome of the case may have some effect is in the area of head tenancy agreements.

23.33 A head tenancy agreement is used in situations where a private owner of property grants a lease of property to an HEI, which in turn leases the property out to students. The agreement governs the contractual relationship between the private owner and the HEI. The head tenancy may stipulate terms that are to be included in the sub-lease to the student (such as the length of any sub-lease term) and forfeiture provisions for future action by the private owner in the event that these are not included in the sub-lease or those terms are breached in any way. The application of *Bruton* to head tenancy agreements may be limited as the private owner will usually grant a lease to the HEI, and not a licence. However, it appears that the courts are moving towards a system of landlord and tenant law based on contractual entitlement, and we shall have to await the outcome of future cases to see if the ambit of *Bruton* will be widened.

DISCIPLINE IN STUDENT ACCOMMODATION

23.34 Another important area which often causes difficulties is the issue of discipline in student accommodation. HEIs often include rules of behaviour in their accommodation agreements, but do not set out any proper procedure for dealing with disciplinary incidents. A student who is alleged to have misbehaved in accommodation is entitled to a 'fair hearing' in the same way as a student charged with any other disciplinary offence, and should be given a proper opportunity to put forward his or her defence, and a right of appeal against any penalty imposed. This can be done by way of a procedure set out in the accommodation agreement, or through the HEI's ordinary student disciplinary regulations (Chapter 7). One sanction commonly imposed on students living in HEI-owned accommodation is a requirement that all of the students living in a particular flat or on a particular floor contribute towards the costs of any damage. This is often known as a 'communal damage provision'. HEIs should note that such provisions are likely to be found to be unfair under the UTCCR 1999, unless they include some degree of flexibility such as a right of appeal by an individual student. Other provisions, such as the right for an HEI to terminate an occupational licence if a student breached one or more of the obligations in detailed 'Student Duties', were amended at some HEIs by the DGFT following his intervention so that the licence could only be terminated if the student was in serious breach: see *Unfair Contract Terms Bulletin* 13 April 2001, p 16. That intervention and the recommended change sits more easily with human rights legislation and existing domestic law and the means of enforcing it through the courts.

CONCLUSION

23.35　Although it is clear that it is beneficial for an HEI to grant students licences rather than leases, the agreements must be drafted with care. There can be no guarantee that a judge will interpret an arrangement as a licence rather than a lease. It is suggested that all student accommodation agreements should be revisited periodically to ensure that the *terms* of the agreement display prominently the badges of a licence, but the HEI must also remember that the *factual circumstances* of the relationship must support the title or description of the agreement. An agreement will not be interpreted as a licence if the facts behind the agreement do not support the idea of one. It is, therefore, vital that there is a sufficient degree of control over the property being licensed, even to the extent that services are supplied to the occupants, and that the details of these are recorded in the agreement. It is also clearly the case that the onward march of consumerism and balancing the rights and obligations between a university and its students will continue to exert a growing influence on the way in which students use residential accommodation. The courts are keen contractually to protect residential occupiers of all kinds: the *Smith* and *Bruton* cases are two examples of this. Universities need to be more conscious than ever of the need to produce fairly drafted and evenly balanced agreements with their students if those arrangements are to withstand the rigours of our legislative and judicial systems.

Chapter 24

RISK MANAGEMENT AND INSURANCE

Sally Pelham (Eversheds)

EDITORS' INTRODUCTION

§24.1   The HEI manager is ultimately a manager of risk on a daily basis, from the routine to the strategic, from petty problem to grand vision. The results of an HEI's mismanagement of risk may not be as dramatic or expensive as the effects of management incompetence at Equitable Life, BT, Marconi, Enron, Independent Insurance and Barings; nor as dangerous as the tragic medical failings at the Bristol Royal Infirmary; and certainly not both dangerous and expensive as with the BSE disaster or the gross negligence of Railtrack. Yet HEI corporate blunders *do* matter to staff, students and their families, potential employers, and politicians; they inevitably damage institutional morale, and even threaten institutional survival (Thames Valley, University College Cardiff; see the *Managing Crisis* volume forthcoming in the *Managing Universities and Colleges* series, Open University Press). The key elements of good management practice within HEIs are explored in Warner and Palfreyman (1996, second edition due 2003) and in their 20-volume series referred to above).

§24.2   This chapter explores the assessment and management of risk, and the interaction of risk assessment and type/level of insurance cover needed: insurance being a process by which certain risks can be managed by paying a premium to an insurance company to take them on under a policy. Now, admittedly, insurance law is not exactly a riveting subject, but the HEI clearly needs the optimum scope of insurance cover to protect against its carefully assessed range of risks. Insurance manages those risks by a neat balancing of the cost for insurance premiums against the risk of potential losses in an incident (calculated by multiplying the maximum likely loss by the probability of such a loss). The first edition of this book did not cover this area, but a reviewer of that edition helpfully highlighted it as a deficiency (Harvey (1999)). We are pleased in the second edition to remedy this defect by discussing insurance as a means of risk management within HE alongside the mechanisms for identifying and managing risk. Perhaps the first risk that should ever be insured against is fire, and fire probably still remains the *prime* insurable risk (especially since, even if the fire is contained, the water damage arising from fighting the fire can be rather more extensive: the May 2001 fire at City University raged at level 5, but water damage also affected several floors below). Another important insurable risk is 'business interruption': what will it cost City University to 'reoffice' all those staff and find alternative teaching space for the students? Moreover, City has had to spend £60K on adverts to tell the world-at-large that, despite the £6m fire, it really still is 'business as usual'. Could an HEI invoke *force majeure* and justify breach of the student–HEI contract to educate if a Hall of Residence is put out of commission (see Chapter 6) or even to terminate the student accommodation licence (see Chapter 23)?

§24.3   The HEI manager must be ever-vigilant for new kinds of legal risk thrown up as legislation is passed or as the common law evolves via case precedent: for example, increasingly stringent legislation on environmental pollution may impact on the waste-disposal procedures of the chemistry department, or the case of *Walker v Northumberland County Council*[1] may ring alarm-bells for the HEI as an employer in relation to work-induced stress-related psychiatric injury to employees; similarly, the implications of compliance with the DPA 1998 or for the giving of references arising from *Spring v Guardian Assurance plc.*[2] A further example could be a Court of Appeal case reported in 2000: in *Ribee v Norie*,[3] the landlord of premises in which his bedsit tenants negligently started a fire was held responsible for fire and smoke damage to adjoining property on the basis that the landlord could and should have laid down rules preventing the tenants/licensees smoking in the communal areas; the landlord had, in theory, power to control the premises (even if, in practice, he did not actually exercise much control) and should have anticipated that an occupant would eventually drop a smouldering cigarette on to the settee. So, should the HEI's property leasing scheme ban students from smoking in the kitchen/dining areas, or just take out extra insurance cover for when the students at 23 Acacia Road burn it down along with 21 and 25?

§24.4   The HEI manager needs to keep pace not only with case-law and with new legislation, but also with how people use that legislation via various legal mechanisms: for example, the issue of work-related stress noted above links to the development of the common law via *Walker*, and may lead also to legislation[4] being used by employees or students to pursue claims against the HEI at tribunals rather than in the courts. The former are seen to be faster and cheaper to access than the latter, and can now provide unlimited compensation in relation to disability, sex and race; while, in relation to unfair dismissal disputes not involving such issues, the maximum compensation has been increased to £52,600. That said, only a very few discrimination cases have involved big pay-outs, as in *Kirker v British Sugar plc*,[5] concerning disability discrimination (see Chapter 22); most cases involve awards of less than £6000 (Fredman (2002), p 173).

§24.5   Finally, and linking to Chapter 18 concerning PFI, the HEI manager, tempted to 'outsource' as many activities as possible while concentrating on the 'core' business, needs to be mindful of the legal risk in managing complex service contracts with suppliers, including (like Railtrack) losing sight of issues such as safety amidst a morrass of loosely linked and poorly co-ordinated parties servicing the groves of academe.

§24.6   The HEI manager should make use of the HEFCE-funded 'Active Risk Management in Education' project at www.bristol.ac.uk/armed, where there are Units on many aspects of the law as it impacts on HEIs.

---

1   [1995] 1 All ER 737.
2   [1994] 3 All ER 138.
3   [2000] NPC 116.
4   The Working Time Regulations 1998, the Disability Discrimination Act 1995, and the Sex Discrimination Act 1975 or the Race Relations Act 1976, for example.
5   [1998] IRLR 513.

INTRODUCTION

24.1 'Avoiding the danger of life is no safer in the long run than outright exposure . . . life is either a daring adventure or nothing . . .' (Helen Keller). This may be a philosophy by which some of us would like to live our lives, but it is hardly one by which we expect our HEIs to be governed. Yet the HE sector is going through a period of change. Technological developments mean that the virtual university, if not yet in our living room, is just around the corner. The globalisation of education is resulting in our HEIs facing increasing competition from existing and new sources. The university where the teaching of students and research are bedfellows, albeit sometimes uneasy ones, may not be the blueprint for the future. HEIs are going to have to adapt to these changes if they going to retain their world-class status and national reputation, and this is inevitably going to involve an element of risk. As the private sector has long realised, 'nothing ventured, nothing gained'. The greater the risk, often the greater the award.

24.2 Thus, on the one hand, we expect a greater degree of entrepreneurialism from our universities than in days of old, and, on the other, we expect increasing accountability and control of the use of both public and private funds. Can risk management help with this? The answer is yes, it can. It has a central role to play in the effective governance of every HEI and the fulfilment of its objectives. It is not about the elimination or avoidance of all risk: '[i]t is about facing risk deliberately and systematically, avoiding taking unnecessary risks, and carefully managing risks which you have decided to take' (Caron Murphy). There are many definitions of risk but in essence it is an occurrence which, if it happens, will have an adverse effect on the institution and affect its ability to achieve its objectives. The potential risks facing HEIs are numerous – from the risk of fire and theft, failing to meet student targets, overrunning on a campus redevelopment, and the clawback of European Regional Development Funding on a particular project, to the departure of key staff. The likelihood of some of these risks occurring, and the impact on the institution if they do, will vary considerably. A risk management review will take these factors into account.

24.3 What exactly is risk management? This question prompts a variety of responses from 'It's nothing new. We have been doing this successfully for years – we just had a different name for it – common sense!', to those who think that it something best left to those with PhDs in statistics. Risk management is neither rocket science nor common sense such as that attributed to the ordinary man on the Clapham omnibus. It is more a systematic, planned and informed review of the risks facing the institution. It is a concept which is not new to the sector:

> 'Higher Education institutions have for a long time managed risk successfully, pursuing greater entrepreneurialism and exploiting new opportunities whilst at the same protecting their reputation and long term financial liability.'[1]

---

1   Sir Brian Fender *Risk Management: A Guide to Good Practice* (HEFCE).

24.4   If it has been around for a while, why has risk management become such a buzz word? Over the last decade there have been a number of reports following a series of well-publicised cases of business collapse or fraud in the public and private sectors. These reports culminated in 1998 in the publication of the *Combined Code on Corporate Governance*, produced by the Institute of Chartered Accountants in England and Wales (known as the Turnbull Report). The main principle emerging from the Turnbull Report is that '[a] company's system of internal control has a key role in the management of risks that are significant to the fulfilment of its business objectives'. The report was, of course, directed at publicly quoted companies. There are, however, lessons on corporate governance to be learned by HEIs, and many have recognised the advantages to be gained from following the Turnbull approach in managing their internal procedures. Risk management can be a tool which is cost-effective in protecting the reputation of the institution and, by helping to ensure its financial liability is controlled, in building the confidence of its stakeholders. The awareness of risk management in the HE sector has been increased by the changes introduced in HEFCE's *Accounts Direction to Higher Education Institutions for 2000/01*.[1] As part of the revised policy on corporate governance, institutions are now required to adopt a risk-based approach to internal controls covering business, operations, compliance and finance. Every institution should be in a position to make a full compliance statement covering all aspects of internal control for the year-end 31 July 2003. This, together with the publication of HEFCE's *Risk Management: A Guide to Good Practice*, will ensure that risk management stays firmly on the HE agenda.

THE RISK MANAGEMENT PROCESS

24.5   In one sense risk management occurs, and has done for many many years, on an *ad hoc* basis: for example, weighing up the risks and rewards of entering into a joint venture with another university and taking advice on the appropriate legal structure for the venture. Often it is considered in terms of disaster recovery or insurable risks. What Circular 24/00 and the HEFCE guidance envisage, however, is a more systematic review of all risks facing the institution, including 'governance, management, quality, reputation and finance' as concentrating on the most significant risks to the institution. There are numerous guides on how to implement a risk management review, some of them aimed at the education sector; others more general. In particular, the Chartered Institute of Public Finance and Accountancy (CIPFA) *An Introductory Guide to Risk Management in Further and Higher Education* and the HEFCE *Risk Management: A Guide to Good Practice* explain how such a review could be implemented. It is not the purpose of this chapter to look at this process in detail, but, in summary, a risk management review should contain the following stages.

---

1   Circular 24/00.

Identifying the scope of the review

24.6 Is it to be a comprehensive review of all the risks facing the institution or will it be limited to a particular area (such as human resources issues)? Who will be involved in the process? Who will have overall responsibility for the review?

Identifying the risks

24.7 This is a crucial stage. After all, an unidentified risk is an unmanaged risk. There are a number of ways in which this can be done from reviewing relevant documentation, self-assessment questionnaires, and facilitated workshops, to one-to-one interviews with relevant staff.

Measuring the risks

24.8 The risk must be assessed both in terms of the likelihood of occurrence and the potential magnitude of its impact. Quantifying risk can be a straightforward exercise in certain circumstances, using actuarial formulae. In other areas it is not so straightforward, given the variables involved, hence measuring the risk is not an exact science. It is essential that at this stage risks are assessed against the institution's objectives so that they can be prioritised. No institution, after all, has the resources to address all risks, nor would this be desirable.

Reviewing the options for reduction and control of risks

24.9 There are four main recognised ways of doing this:

- *risk avoidance*: for example, a university is considering entering into a franchise agreement with a south-east Asian institution. After considering the proposition in detail and preparing a business plan, the university concludes that the risks involved are so high that, despite the potential rewards, it decides not to proceed;
- *risk reduction*: this consists of putting controls in place, such as policies and procedures, to reduce the likelihood of the risk occurring and/or its impact if it does. For example, revising the institution's financial regulations and carrying out comprehensive staff training to improve contract management;
- *risk transfer*: passing the risk onto another party. An obvious example, which we will look at in more detail below, is insurance. An unforeseen risk is swapped for a present fixed cost. Another form of risk transfer often used by the sector is outsourcing. For example, many institutions are adopting this practice in relation to their catering operations, where there is a vast amount of legislation relating to hygiene which must be complied with; and

–   *risk retention*: the risk may be so unlikely to occur or its consequences if it does so minimal that the institution decides to take no action. Risk retention should, however, be a positive decision rather than something which arises by default.

Formulating, communicating and implementing of the risk management plan

24.10   This is essential if risk management is going to work. The plan should identify who will 'own' various risks. It is important that the commitment to the plan emanates from the top of the institution and permeates down to all relevant managers and staff. Risk awareness and other relevant training will have an important role to play. This may be an individual, a group of individuals, or a committee: 'Acknowledging ownership is not the same as shouldering the entire burden of the risk. The owner should see himself or herself as the person in the best position to oversee the management of the risk'.[1]

Monitoring its effectiveness

24.11   Like many management tools, risk management is not a one-off or once-a-year activity. It should be a continuous process. Where a formal plan has been drawn up it should identify how, by whom and when a particular risk will be monitored. The governing body will want to ensure that procedures are in place to keep it regularly appraised of risk management issues. There are advantages to linking in the risk management process with existing management practice (for example, by incorporating a risk management review as part of the annual business planning exercise, or by effective use of internal audit to monitor the institution's management of risk).

24.12   For a systematic risk management review, it is useful to think of these as six processes, but they can be grouped together as three fundamental stages: risk identification (paras **24.6–24.7**), risk measurement (para **24.8**), and risk control (paras **24.9–24.11**). These elements will need to be addressed whenever risks are considered – be it in a formal review of the type discussed above, or when deciding how to deal with a specific risk or, indeed, when considering the options available to the institution before embarking on a particular project such as capital building works. We may never be able to eliminate the human element, but for risk management to be wholly successful it needs to become embedded in the culture of the institution.

---

1   HEFCE *Risk Management: A Guide to Good Practice*.

LEGAL RISK MANAGEMENT

24.13 The law often gets overlooked when it comes to carrying out a risk management review; or it is considered only in terms of claims-handling or ensuring compliance with an institution's statutory obligations (such as those in relation to health and safety, data protection and the vast array of discrimination and employment legislation). Legal issues, however, have a far more fundamental role than this to play in risk management. After all, the law governs practically every relationship an institution has: those with its staff, students, the funding council, contractors, collaborative partners, suppliers, and subsidiary companies. The institution may even have legal responsibilities towards somebody with whom it has no contractual or other formal legal relationship: for example, its responsibility under the OLAs 1957 and 1984 to members of the public coming onto its property (see Chapter 20). The law sets the parameters within which the institution operates. Legal issues, therefore, need to be at the heart of every risk management review. The essential elements of legal risk include:

– compliance with all relevant regulations and legislation. Failure to do so may in certain circumstances lead to criminal prosecution or lead to civil claims based on the institution's failure to comply;
– invoking contractual and/or other legal claims; and
– defending or containing contractual and other legal claims brought against the institution.

24.14 Legal risks have the potential to cause wide-ranging damage to the institution. On the financial side there may be compensation to be paid (ie financial loss) and legal fees, but also there will be the hidden costs of damage to reputation, a negative impact on the morale of staff and students, and unwanted attention from the media and other bodies such as the funding councils, the QAA, the OFT. In many circumstances, the unseen costs can have a greater impact on the institution than any financial damages awarded by the courts. The elements of legal risk listed above are seen, not surprisingly, as the traditional stamping ground of lawyers. Those institutions which are in the fortunate position of rarely having been in the courts should not, however, rest on their laurels. We are becoming an increasingly litigious society: employee claims increased dramatically over the last decade; student claims may follow in their footsteps. Even if formal legal proceedings have not been commenced, think of the management time spent in dealing with student complaints, staff grievances or, for example, trying to resolve a dispute in relation to a long-term supply arrangement which was entered into several years earlier and where no one can recall whether a written contract was in fact signed (a not uncommon occurrence). Consider the loss of revenue to the institution if it cannot recover certain charges from students because these were not drawn to the students' attention before they accepted a place. These are real cost implications for institutions which do not adequately address legal risks and have no policies and procedures for controlling such risks, even if disputes do not involve lawyers or the courts.

24.15   All HEIs will have procedures for handling certain kinds of disputes – such as student complaints, academic appeals and staff grievances (see Chapter 7). It is important that these procedures are as effective as possible. It is not just a question of getting the procedure right on paper; the procedures must be followed in letter and in spirit. This will benefit both the institution and the complainant, and reduce the likelihood of the complaint being taken any further. If the institution does not follow its own procedures or pays them lip service only, it is more likely to exacerbate the complainant's frustration and in certain circumstances may make litigation more likely. By no means will all disputes be covered by such a procedure, particularly those involving external parties (for example, disputes with suppliers). Institutions need to consider how such disputes are handled at an early stage. If they are not promptly and efficiently dealt with, seeking legal advice where necessary, they may well escalate. HEIs are not in the same business as retailers, but many people will have been in a situation where the courteous, prompt, efficient resolution of some problem in relation to a service received or something bought leaves them with a better impression of the organisations involved than if there had been no problem in the first place.

24.16   In an increasingly litigious world, however, it is inevitable that institutions will find themselves either issuing or, probably more often, at the receiving end of legal proceedings. Litigation is always risky and is likely to be a very expensive route to follow. Consequently, it is not a road which should be embarked upon lightly, although sometimes the institution will have no choice in the matter. Once litigation is commenced, specialist advice will be required either from within the institution or from its external legal advisers to ensure that the process is managed effectively (see Chapter 27). An increasing number of institutions are handling certain disputes in-house, such as industrial tribunal claims or those brought before the small claims court. Litigation is now about active case management and it is important to consider alternative methods of dispute resolution in order that the conflict can be settled promptly and with as little expense as possible.

Legal insurance

24.17   As we have discussed, insurance is one method of controlling risk and many institutions will have insurance policies in place to protect them from some of the legal risks discussed above. It is compulsory for HEIs to have employer's liability insurance to cover their legal duties to prevent personal injury and disease to employees arising in the course of their employment. They will also have public liability insurance in place to protect against claims by members of the public for personal injury or damage to property arising from defects in the premises or negligence of their employees. Many institutions will also have professional indemnity cover to protect them against claims if they fail to exercise the degree of skill and care legally expected of them. It is also possible to take out legal expenses insurance specifically to cover their legal fees in the event of certain types of litigation. In light of such protection, do institutions need to worry unduly about legal risks? The answer has to be yes: '[I]nsurance is never a substitute for the proper management of risk'.[1] The following limitations on the effectiveness of the use of such 'legal insurance' should be borne in mind:

– such policies are usually not comprehensive, even if the institution has all the types of cover mentioned above. Each policy may differ but, for example, claims for breach of contract or racial discrimination will often not be covered. Insurance will not cover fraud or deliberate wrong-doing. When taking out a policy it is difficult to envisage exactly what claims the institution may face and no policy will cover every eventuality;

– even if the policy covers the claim in question, not all the risks associated with the claim can be transferred to the insurance company. Where, for example, a member of staff sues for sexual discrimination, the damages and legal fees may be paid for by the insurer, but the management time involved in the case, the adverse publicity, the damage to the institution's reputation, and the effect on staff morale will be keenly felt by the institution;

– an insured claim is a claim over which the institution does not have full control. Insurers are likely to view the claim mainly in commercial terms. This may not be the primary concern of the institution: the defence of its reputation or the avoidance of setting a precedent may be equally or, in some cases, more important. The insurer's and the insured's interests are not always the same, but the insurer will be handling the claim and probably driving any legal action (via a process known as 'subrogation': it acts in the name of the HEI). Many insurers will require the use of their solicitors rather than those of the institution;

– insurance can be expensive. Making a claim can have a dramatic effect on the premiums paid by the institution. It should not be forgetten that insurers are in the business to make a profit; and

– insurance, therefore, has a valid but a limited role to play when it comes to controlling legal risks. More and more institutions are deciding to self-insure certain legal risks and to take out insurance which they are legally obliged to do (employer's liability cover) or to deal only with catastrophic legal risks rather than 'slips and trips'.

Controlling legal risk

24.18 Risks must be identified, measured and managed. An institution *could* carry out a comprehensive review of all the legal risks it faces; however, few have the resources to carry out such a review. It is also questionable how

---

1   CIPFA Guide.

beneficial or cost-effective it would be. It is far better if an analysis of the legal risks is an integral part of every institution's risk management review. The most effective review would be one that looks at the full picture and is, therefore, able to prioritise risks against the institution's objectives. In carrying out a comprehensive risk management review, there are a number of ways in which an institution can seek to ensure that legal issues are adequately addressed. If the institution has an in-house lawyer, he could be a key member of the risk management review team. Those institutions with no in-house lawyer may wish to bring in their external lawyers to assist them with the process, although this may prove expensive. An alternative is to seek the comments of an external lawyer, who knows and understands how the institution operates, on the draft risk management plan. Such a lawyer may be able to identify not only areas of legal risk which may have been overlooked, but also suggest valuable methods of controlling these risks. The identification of legal risks is important, but so too is their management. Having appropriate policies and procedures in place to minimise legal risks is crucial (such as policies dealing with equal opportunities, the use of e-mail and the internet, and financial regulations). Many (perhaps the majority of) student and staff complaints could be avoided if effective policies and procedures were in place and properly implemented. The risk management review may also identify particular areas on which the institution wants legal advice, such as reviewing a particular policy, specific advice on an issue or a legal audit in an area such as governance, the institution's procurement process, or, as discussed in some detail below, the student contract.

Using lawyers

24.19   The control of legal risks is not just about formal risk management reviews. It has to be a continual process. There are two tools, which are closely linked, and the importance of which cannot be overestimated when it comes to managing such risks: the effective use of lawyers, and training. One of the best ways of reducing an institution's legal risk would be for it to do nothing without consulting its lawyers: enter into no agreements; issue no rules or regulations; employ, dismiss or exclude no one without picking up the phone. But at what cost? This would involve a great deal of expense and operational difficulties – perhaps even to the detriment of the achievement of the institution's main objectives. Legal risk management is not about legal perfection. There is a need, however, to move away from the way lawyers are traditionally used. Sometimes lawyers are brought in as a form of crisis management. Institutions need to move away from this reactive use of lawyers towards a more proactive use. Prevention, after all, is better than cure. When an institution has found itself in legal difficulties, both it and its lawyers (if they have been involved) should automatically be considering what steps should be taken to prevent the problem arising again. This may often be done when a large legal bill has brought the costs of such risks home, but in how many cases are those discussions actually followed through, implemented and monitored? With major projects, such as campus redevelopment works or collaboration agreements, it is better to get lawyers involved earlier rather than later. The greater the risk, the more important it is to have the correct documentation in place. It is not always the case that lawyers can be brought in at the last minute just to dot the 'i's and cross the 't's of the deal agreed. The legal implications should be considered at the start of a project, as they may determine the way it is structured or, in certain circumstances, whether the institution should proceed at all. Consideration of legal risks earlier rather than later is usually more cost-effective. For any risk management plan to be effective it must be communicated, understood and 'lived' by the institution's staff. This is no easy matter. Plans, policies and regulations have a tendency to gather dust on shelves or to lurk in the most seldom visited areas of the internet. When it comes to legal risk, training is crucial if the internal controls put in place to deal with those risks are to work. Staff need to understand the policies and procedures which affect their work, why it is important that they are followed, and what could happen if they are not followed, so that they become relevant and alive rather than mere bureaucracy. This may well involve training on legal topics – such as the student contract for those in the finance department charged with recovering student debt, or the legal issues involved in disciplining students for all those sitting on the institution's disciplinary committees. Certain managers will have the day-to-day management of legal risks and it may be worth considering linking legal training to their appraisal, or in some cases making knowledge of the law part of their job description.

An example of a legal risk management review – the student contract

24.20 Students are the life blood of HEIs. When considering the risks facing such institutions, it is likely that students will be at the forefront of people's minds. Usually, however, this view of risks will be in terms of failing to meet student targets and the resultant claw-back of funding, or failure to recruit an adequate number of overseas students. Failure to have in place an appropriate or adequate 'contract' with the students is unlikely to leap to mind as a serious risk. Yet students are rapidly becoming a more demanding body in terms of their expectations from the sector and the likelihood of their complaining if those expectations are not met is increasing (see Chapters 6, 7 and 29). It is the terms of 'the student contract' which determine so much of the relationship between the institution and its students. Many complaints can be avoided by setting out clearly the obligations of the institution and the students in the student contract and having appropriate procedures and policies in place.

Learnitwell University's review of its student contract
24.21 As part of a more comprehensive risk management review, Learnitwell University identified the student contract as an area which needed detailed

examination. Concerns about the contract had been brought to a head by a general increase in the number of student complaints and by two incidents in particular. One student claimed that she had been unfairly excluded following an incident which involved another student but which took place outside the University campus. The disciplinary code and procedure gives the University authority to take disciplinary action in such instances, but the student in question claimed that she had never in fact seen a copy of the code or the disciplinary procedure and hence that the University had no right, contractual or otherwise, to exclude her. The other incident involved students on the art and design course who refused to pay the fee of £30 per term for field trips to galleries and museums, claiming that such trips were described in the prospectus and course literature as an integral part of the course, and that no mention was made anywhere of additional charges being made for them. The potential loss of revenue to the University is in the region of £8000 for this year of this course. However, the SU has become involved and it is likely that similar problems may arise in relation to payment for field trips on other courses.

Scope of the review
24.22   The review focused on the contract between the University and its undergraduate students. Its aims were to ensure that the contract reflects the University's intentions, that all its key terms are incorporated into the contract, that its terms are enforceable, that all the relevant regulations, policies and procedures comply with relevant legislation, and that full information is given to prospective students about all charges. The key members in the review team were the newly appointed in-house lawyer who works closely with the Secretary's Department, the Academic Registrar, the Head of Student Services and the Head of Admissions. Various other members of staff and students were involved at different stages of the review.

The methodology
24.23   A number of methods were used to identify the risks:

–   *a desktop review of documentation*: the in-house lawyer reviewed all documentation from which contractual terms could be drawn, including the student charter, the University prospectus, open-day literature, the admissions policy and procedures, offer of acceptance letters, enrolment forms, the disciplinary code and procedure, the academic appeals procedure, the student complaints procedure, the student handbook, and the student accommodation agreement;
–   *a self-assessment questionnaire*: using a list of best characteristics in the sector, the in-house lawyer prepared a self-assessment questionnaire covering six areas, extracts from which are set out below:
    (a)   **determination of terms**: questions included 'Are documents forming contract terms dated and are redundant documents then removed from circulation?';

(b) **incorporation of terms**: questions included 'Are staff responsible for marketing and admissions aware of how the contract is formed?', and 'Are the contract terms, including the right to cancel the contract by written notice within seven days drawn to the attention of the students in writing, at least to the extent required by the Consumer Protection (Distance Selling) Regulations 2000?';

(c) **implementation**: questions included 'Are responsibilities within the management for implementing the contract terms clearly allocated and reflected in job descriptions?' and 'Are all staff aware of the contract terms which relate to their work?';

(d) **resolution of disputes**: questions included 'Does the University's complaints procedure comply with the charter of Higher Education and the QAA code of practice?', 'Is it widely understood by students and staff and operated consistently?' and 'In the application of the University's disciplinary procedures are the "rules of natural justice" observed and in particular are students given details of the charges against them provided with a fair hearing and their decisions not taken by those who may be or who may recently be perceived to be biased?';

(e) **evaluation**: questions included 'Does the University regularly monitor its performance in carrying out its contractual obligations?' and 'Does the University regularly collect and evaluate information on levels of student satisfaction?'; and

(f) **discrimination**: questions included 'Does the University have an equal opportunities policy which recognises its obligations under the Sex Discrimination Act 1975, the Race Relations Act 1976, the Disability Discrimination Act 1995 and the Human Rights Act 1998?', 'Is such a policy review of intervals not less than three years in light of both the changes to the law as the experience of the University?' and 'Is it appropriate for staff training to be undertaken on equal opportunity and discrimination issues?'; and

– *interviews*: the in-house lawyer carried out face-to-face interviews with a selection of staff involved in student admissions and student services, various academic departments and of groups of students across the full spectrum of courses offered by the University to assess how the contract was formed and implemented in practice.

Measuring risks

24.24 As a result of the exercises discussed above, the team identified 20 areas of risk to the University. Each risk was then given a value from A to E representing the likelihood of its occurrence, where A is extremely likely and E is unlikely. It was also given a further value from 1 to 5 representing the likely consequence of that event should it materialise: 1 being disastrous and 5 insignificant. Each member of the review team measured the risks individually.

Not all members of the team felt in a position to measure all the risks as some of them required specialist legal knowledge. The list of risks was discussed with and separately measured by the University's external lawyers who have considerable expertise within the sector. The individual risk assessment, including that by the external lawyers, was then considered by the group as a whole and a final agreed valuation given for each risk.

Controlling the risk

24.25 A further meeting was arranged at which the University's external lawyers were present, in which the team discussed in some detail how to address and control the identified risks. It was agreed that at this stage priority would be given to the top five risks. The in-house lawyer went away and prepared a risk management report for the senior management team, explaining what had been done, what the main findings of the team were, and what action should be taken. Attached to the report was the risk management review plan identifying the risk, the action to be taken if any, the person responsible for the action, and the date when the action should be taken. An extract from this plan is set out in the table below.

Table 24.1 An extract from Learnitwell University's student contract risk management plan

Risk	Action	Responsibility	Date	Monitor
Formation of Contract				
It is not possible to clearly identify the terms of the contract.	Review and identify what terms the University wants to be included.	In-house lawyer/ Head of Admissions	Feb 2001	Academic Registry
Necessary steps have not been taken to ensure that they have been properly incorporated into the contract. This includes the disciplinary code.	Produce a single document referring to all main terms: – refer to and summarise in prospectus; – put on website; – where possible, send to all applicants, before an offer of a place is made.	In-house lawyer/ Head of Admissions Head of Admissions	March 2001 Intake Sept 2001	Academic Registry
	Make clear to applicants in all communications (including prospectus and on website) that acceptance of place is subject to acceptance of these terms.	Head of Admissions	Intake Sept 2001	Academic Registry
	Make full copies of any rules, regulations and policies referred to freely available.	Head of Admissions	Intake Sept 2001	Academic Registry
Fees				
Inadequate information is given to prospective students about fees.	Include as much information as possible in prospectus/course literature.	Head of Admissions	March 2001	Academic Registry
	Refer students to website where exact details of fees will be published as soon as finalised.			

Risk	Action	Responsibility	Date	Monitor
	Send full details to all students as soon as possible.			
Overseas Students				
Potential breaches of the Education (Fees and Awards) Regulations. Non-EU students are charged tuition fees in full without a proper assessment of their fee status.	Review method by which the fee status of prospective students is determined to ensure compliance with relevant regulations.	Student Services/ Finance Department	March 2001	Academic Registrar
Unenforceable terms				
Various terms which should form part of the contract may be unenforceable under relevant legislation.	Review all contract terms.	In-house lawyer/ Head of Admissions	Feb 2001	Academic Terms

CONCLUSION

24.26   There is no doubt that risk management has arrived in the HE sector and that it is here to stay. It is something that the senior management and governors are going to have to embrace if they have not done so already. The funding council is leaving them with little choice in the matter. Institutions should, however, welcome this impetus. Risk management can be a beneficial management tool in that it identifies potential problems and risks: it allows procedures to be put in place to deal with these problems, to limit the risk occurring in the first place and its consequences if it does; this then minimises the risks and the costs that the institution is exposed to; and it helps protect the institution's reputation and the confidence of its stakeholders. The proactive control of legal risk needs to pay a pivotal role in any institution's risk management strategy and the day-to-day conduct of its affairs. Insurance will have a role to play, but it is no substitute for the proactive management of legal risk.

24.27   So, if it is such a powerful management tool, where are all the success stories of risk management? It is probably true to say that you do not hear about risk management when it is going well. The opposite, however, is often true. With the benefit of hindsight we can see how effective risk management may have prevented a number of *cause célèbres* – from the space shuttle disaster on the one hand, or the downfall of Barings as Britain's oldest bank and the *débâcle* at Equitable Life as Britain's oldest mutual, to the problems experienced within the sector (such as those at Lancaster University). The University of Lancaster's fortunes suffered a rapid turn around between 1994 and 1996:

> '[I]n the summer of the University's 13th birthday, the future for the University seemed very bright, especially in the excellence of its teaching and research as evidenced by the external reviews. Eighteen months later, however, the University was in deep financial difficulty and facing a set of problems, many of which related to a perilous financial situation and the inevitable unpleasantness of the cutbacks that ensued.'[1]

What caused this sudden reversal? A huge, complex and costly programme of capital works funded by debenture stock, the acquisition of a college, and two programmes of premature retirement and voluntary severance; all embarked upon, it is probably be fair to say, without a thorough appraisal of all the options available to the University of the risks involved and the implementation of appropriate controls to manage the risks. The University even appears to have failed to learn from its own mistakes in relation to capital development:

> '[A]n Internal Audit Report of 1994 on Chancellor's Wharf presaged many of the problems encountered in 1995/96. Had this report not been ignored, and if lessons had been drawn from it, matters might have been quite different. Instead it remained unimplemented until 1996.'

24.28   A salutary lesson for us all. (See also paras **5.28–5.30** concerning the mismanagement of the CAPSA IT project at the University of Cambridge.) Risk management is about systematic planning for the future. It was Edmund Burke who said 'You cannot plan the future from the past'. Institutions can, however, learn from the mistakes that they and others have made (after all, the idea is that we get wiser as we get older), and bring these lessons to bear when dealing with the management of risks facing them and the attainment of their objectives.

---

1   Peter Rowe *The University of Lancaster: Review of Institutional Lessons to be learned, 1994– 1996.*

Chapter 25

ALUMNI: FRIEND-RAISING TO FUND-RAISING

Derek Elsey and Joss Saunders (Linnells)

EDITORS' INTRODUCTION

§25.1 The first edition of this book did not cover alumni, but clearly the attitude of HEIs towards their alumni is becoming increasingly sophisticated, prompted by an ever-more desperate search for funding, encouraged by the US fund-raising model, and stimulated by a more generous UK tax regime for charity giving. This chapter will help HEIs think through the legal aspects of managing the HEI–alumni relationship. More generally, on the HEI's interaction with its alumni, see the relevant chapter in Albrighton and Thomas *Managing External Relations* (2001, in the 20-volume *Managing Universities and Colleges*, Open University Press, 1999 onwards).

ALUMNI

25.1 It is clear that having an active association of alumni can be a great benefit to an HEI, not only because of the financial advantages which alumni can bestow on the HEI, but also because of the role models they provide to students and aspiring students, their ambassadorial function, the research and consultancy contacts which they can provide and the opportunities for alumni to continue their learning. By involving alumni in the ongoing life of the HEI, it encourages them to act as stakeholders in a continuing enterprise.

ALUMNI ASSOCIATIONS

25.2 The usual ways in which HEIs go about attracting and maintaining continuing contact with their alumni is through the establishment of an Alumni Association serviced by a section of the HEI's administration, which provides information to students who have completed their courses, programmes of study and research degrees about joining the association and maintaining records of membership and the services provided to alumni.

Power to form and administer an Alumni Association

25.3   Power to form and administer an Alumni Association will be derived from the Charter of the pre-1992 HEIs and from s 124 of the ERA 1988 in the case of post-1992 HEIs. Under s 124, a post-1992 HEI is empowered to provide higher education, to provide further education, to carry out research and to publish the results thereof. It may do anything which appears to it to be necessary or expedient for the purpose of or in connection with these powers or which is incidental to the conduct of an educational establishment providing higher or further education. *Blacks Law Dictionary* defines 'incidental' as 'something of lesser importance; having a minor role' and the *Oxford English Dictionary* as 'occurring as something casual, of secondary importance; not directly relevant to; following upon as a subordinate circumstance'. The only judicial authority on the term 'incidental to' is *Fahy's Will Trusts; Mcknight v Fahy*,[1] where it was held that the phrase 'costs of and incidental to the negotiations' meant 'costs of and consequent upon negotiations'. However, in that case these words were, and had to be, construed narrowly. That view would be too restrictive with an interpretation of the provisions of the ERA 1988, and hence the dictionary definitions are to be preferred. It is, therefore, clearly arguable that the establishment and administration of an Alumni Association is incidental to the conduct of an HEI providing higher and further education. In general, the charters and statutes of pre-1992 HEIs do not contain any provisions setting out powers of the HEI, which appear to derive merely from the description of the HEI in its title. By implication, therefore, an HEI which is described as a 'university' is empowered to undertake all the normal functions of a university including the establishment and operation of an Alumni Association. (See Chapters 2, 3 and 5 concerning HEIs' powers.)

Benefits to alumni

25.4   The following sorts of benefits are commonly provided to alumni by the HEI's Alumni Association:

−   *lifelong membership*: automatic lifelong membership of the HEI which is usually free of charge and which may entitle the alumni to enter certain premises of the HEI, in particular, its library, possibly via the issue of a pass card. In the case of issue of a pass card, the HEI needs to ensure that the system is set up whereby cards are delivered to the correct address or issued to alumni personally upon proof of identity and completion of the relevant qualification. HEIs may also wish to consider the position of spouses of alumni. The HEI may be prepared to allow alumni to use its student computer facilities and e-mail system and/or the internet via JANET, but in this case each alumnus should be required to undertake to

---

1   [1962] 1 All ER 73, per Plowman J at p 75.

comply with the HEI's computer use regulations and any regulations relating to the use of e-mail and the internet (see Chapter 14);

– *magazines and newsletters*: the provision of magazines and newsletters informing alumni of current developments in the HEI and containing articles on the activities of various alumni since completing their qualifications. Letter and contact pages may also be included. HEIs will need to bear in mind the laws relating to publishing in producing such a publication, particularly, if they accept articles and letters from alumni (for example, infringement of another's copyright, breach of duty of confidentiality, infringement of privacy (to the extent that such a right exists), defamation, obscene or blasphemous publications, publications which offend the Public Order Act 1986 (for example, incitement to racial hatred and causing harassment by a threatening, abusive or insulting display to a person likely to be caused harassment, alarm or distress thereby), contempt of court and breach of the Official Secrets Acts) (see Chapters 5, 12, 13 and 14). HEIs will note that it may not be possible to absolve themselves from liability in a publication by the use of a prominent disclaimer, but this may be of help, particularly in a borderline case;

– *research awards and scholarships*: certain research awards and scholarships may be restricted to alumni. Any such restriction needs to be clearly spelt out in the trust deed or regulations which establish the award and must comply with the relevant anti-discrimination legislation (see Chapter 3).

– *alumni meetings and activities*: alumni meetings, dinners, balls, weekends and even an alumni travel programme may be provided whereby alumni can undertake 'educational' holidays. It is advisable that the HEI arranges for a commercial service such as a travel programme to be provided by a subsidiary company of the HEI or by an independent contractor in return for a commission or royalty, since it is doubtful that this activity would fall within the charitable objects of the HEI (see Chapter 15);

– *continuing education opportunities*: details of continuing education and lifelong learning opportunities may be more easily provided to alumni through a magazine, on alumni web pages on the HEI website and by direct mailing (see data protection below). Membership of special interest groups of alumni, HEI staff and all students may also be made available to alumni enabling them to maintain and develop contacts with the HEI and with other like-minded individuals;

– *alumni tracing service*: the Alumni Office may offer a 'finding of contemporaries service' to enable alumni to trace former colleagues. The HEI will need to bear in mind its express or implied duty of confidentiality to alumni and students and its obligations under the DPA 1998 (see below) and should only offer to forward inquiries to the last known address of the person sought and not to disclose their personal details (such as change of name or address) to the inquirer; and

–   *affinity and credit cards and discounts on goods and services*: it is possible for
    an Alumni Association to offer affinity and credit cards and discounts on
    goods and services provided to members, an example of the latter being
    the University of Cambridge's telephone discount service which provides
    discounted telephone call charges to members and royalties to the
    University. The contents of contracts with the providers of such affinity
    and credit cards and goods and services need to be considered carefully
    and are referred to in greater detail below.

Benefits of an Alumni Association

25.5   The prime examples of universities which obtain a sizeable proportion
of their income from trusts and endowments, the funds for which were
provided initially or mainly by alumni, are to be found in the USA. Harvard
University has an endowment fund of some $19.2 billion including the sum of
$5 billion raised in investment income in 1999. The University of Texas came
next with an endowment fund of more than $8 billion in 1999. It was followed
by Yale (more than $7 billion), Princeton and Stanford (more than $6 billion);
in the UK only Oxford and Cambridge compete at around £2.5 billion each
(mostly 'locked' within the colleges: Tapper and Palfreyman (2000), pp 158–
159; Warner and Palfreyman (2001), chapter 2). The tradition of alumni giving
is more firmly entrenched in the USA than in the UK, but the indications are
that UK HEIs will need to maximise their use of this resource to obtain
additional funding.

CHARITABLE GIVING

25.6   UK HEIs are exempt charities for the purposes of Sch 2 to the Charities
Act 1993. Donations made to UK HEIs or to charitable trusts established by
them to raise funds for a particular purpose or for the benefit of the HEI
generally may, therefore, qualify for tax relief if they are made in the correct
way. The principal tax reliefs are:

–   relief from inheritance tax for transfers of value;
–   relief from capital gains tax or corporation tax on chargeable gains on
    disposals by way of gift;
–   relief from income tax for:
    (a) gift aid payments of cash by individuals;
    (b) payroll giving schemes;
    (c) covenanted payments (now replaced with gift aid); and
–   relief from corporation tax for:
    (a) gift aid payments of cash by companies;
    (b) covenanted payments (now replaced with gift aid).

Inheritance tax relief

25.7 Under the Inheritance Tax Act 1984, s 23 (as amended), a transfer of value is an exempt transfer if takes effect in favour of a particular charity, provided that the transfer is not exempt if:

- it takes effect subject to a prior life or other interest;
- it is subject to a condition precedent which is not satisfied within 12 months of the transfer; or
- it is capable of being defeated or becoming applicable for non-charitable purposes.

There are, however, ways of satisfying some of these provisos by partitioning the residue.

Capital gains tax relief

25.8 Under the Taxation of Charitable Gains Act 1992, ss 2 and 8 (as amended), a disposal of an asset which would otherwise give rise to a chargeable gain will not do so if made in favour of a charity otherwise than under a bargain at arm's length (ie by way of gift or at cost). A bargain at arm's length is deemed to have been a disposal at market value.

Gift aid

25.9 Under the Finance Act 1990, s 25 (as amended), from October 1990 individuals have been able to make single cash donations to charity attracting income tax relief both at the basic rate and at any higher rate. This provided a considerable extension of the ways in which a person could undertake tax-efficient charitable giving and is of major significance for the raising of funds from alumni, particularly now that the upper and lower donation limits have been removed (the lower limit was £250 until 6 April 2000). The conditions which apply to gift aid are as follows:

- the gift must be a payment of a sum of the donor's own money;
- the gift must not be repayable or made under the payroll giving scheme (see below);
- the donor and any connected person (as defined in the ICTA 1988, s 389 (as amended)) must not receive a benefit in consequence of the gift which exceeds any of the following:
  (a) where the gift does not exceed £100: 25 per cent of the gift;
  (b) where the gift exceeds £100 but is less than £1000: £25; or
  (c) where the gift exceeds £1000: 2.5 per cent of the amount of the gift,

subject to adjustment if the benefit is received over a period of time up to an overall maximum of £250. In addition, the gift must not be connected with an arrangement under which the charity acquires property from the donor (or a connected person) except by way of gift; and the donor must be resident (or deemed to be resident) in the UK at the date of the gift, or the gift must be made by a Crown servant or a member of the UK armed forces serving overseas, or the grossed up amount of the gift must be paid out of profits or gains chargeable to tax in the UK; and the donor must give a declaration containing the information prescribed in regulations.

Tax treatment

25.10   Donors have to pay an amount of income tax and all capital gains tax or have received non-repayable tax credits on dividends paid by UK companies or have had tax deducted from bank and building society interest which is not repaid equal to the tax deducted from their donations (which tax is claimed from the Inland Revenue by the charity). Donors should be warned about this because if there is a shortfall the Inland Revenue will pay the charity the tax and claim reimbursement from the donor. It is not necessary to send a separate letter to each potential donor; a notice in, for example, a newsletter may be sufficient. If an HEI is doing a funding mailshot, it would be advisable to insert this warning relating to gift aid. From 6 April 2000, donors will be able to claim higher rate tax relief on their donations against both income tax and capital gains tax.

Declarations

25.11   Declarations have replaced the more cumbersome gift aid certificate which was required before 6 April 2000. The declaration can be given in writing whether or not by electronic means or orally. The declaration must contain: the name of charity, the name and address of the donor, details of the donation(s) and a confirmation that the charity is to treat the donation(s) (enclosed, past or to be made in the future) as gift aid donation(s). A written declaration must contain a notice relating to the implications of gift aid donations (see above). It also advisable to include a DPA 1998 notice of processing (see below) and a note that the HEI is an exempt charity. An oral declaration will not be effective unless the charity sends the donor a written record of the declaration containing the information set out above (with the tax warning notice) and also explaining the donor's right to cancel the declaration retrospectively within 30 days, and setting out the date of the oral declaration and a date on which the charity sent the written record to the donor. The written record may be sent electronically provided that an adequate record is maintained for audit purposes.

Cancellation

25.12   Any declaration can be cancelled at any time by notification to the charity, but, except in the case of cancellation of an oral declaration referred to above, a cancellation only applies to donations received after the date of cancellation.

Particular types of declaration
25.13

– **Joint declarations**

Joint declarations on the same form may be made by spouses or persons living together but they will need to identify how a joint donation is to be split between them for the purposes of the charity's records;

– **Partnership declarations**

It is possible for one partner to make a gift aid declaration on behalf of all the partners in a partnership provided that he has power to do so under the terms of the partnership agreement. The partners can then enter their share of the donation on their tax returns; and

– **Sponsored events**

The money raised from a sponsored event does not belong to the individual who raised it. He needs to ask each sponsor to make a separate declaration to the charity. Alternatively, it is possible to create a sponsorship form as a joint declaration form if it contains the following information:

(a) the name of the charity;

(b) each sponsor's full name, address and postcode;

(c) the amount pledged;

(d) the amount collected and the date of collection;

(e) a tick box confirming that the sponsor wishes to have the amount treated as a gift aid donation;

(f) the tax warning notice; and

(g) the date when the amounts collected were handed over to the charity.

Deeds of covenant

25.14   From 6 April 2000, there is no longer a separate tax relief for payments made by an individual or company under a deed of covenant. To qualify for tax relief payments must be made under the gift aid scheme. Transitional relief applies in respect of covenants existing prior to 6 April 2000, whereby the charity does not need to obtain a separate gift aid declaration and payments made under those deeds of covenants will be automatically treated as gift aid payments. Covenants have the advantage of providing an income stream over a period of years, so charities who wish to continue to receive payments under deeds of covenant may do so, provided that in order to qualify for tax relief the deed contains all the information required in a gift aid declaration.

Deposit or loan covenants

25.15   Prior to 6 April 2000, if a donor wished to make a donation of a large sum but to spread the tax relief over a period of years, this could be achieved by entering into a deed of covenant for at least the minimum period allowed (which was more than 3 whole years) and paying to the charity the first annual instalment under the deed together with a loan or deposit of a sum equal to the balance of the payments due under the deed with a provision that the loan deposit would be discharged by payments made under the deed of covenant as they fell due. It should still be possible to make provision for such an arrangement under the gift aid scheme provided that it is made clear that the payments made under the deed of covenant are gift aid payments (despite conflicting advice from the Inland Revenue).

Gift aid for companies

25.16 Companies may make gift aid donations to charities from 1 April 2000 without deduction of income tax. No declaration or certificate is required and the £250 minimum limit has been abolished. Payments made under a pre-existing deed of covenant will be converted into gift aid payments which means that if they were expressed to be payable after deduction of tax, from 1 April 2000 the company must pay the grossed up amount of such payment and reclaim tax relief on this amount when calculating its profits for corporation tax purposes. Charities need to monitor payments received and remind companies of the new rule if they continue to pay covenant donations net of tax. Companies which are owned by charities have nine months from the end of their accounting periods in which to determine the amount which they wish to give or are obliged to pay to the charity under a deed of covenant which is designed to shed profit from the company to the charity. They can claim the deduction against corporation tax on profits made in that accounting period.

Benefits received by donors

25.17 HEIs need to be aware that if the benefits received by donors exceed the limits identified above, then the donation cannot qualify under the gift aid scheme. A benefit is any item or service provided by the charity or a third party to the donor or a connected person in consequence of making the donation. The mere acknowledgement of a donor's generosity in the charity's literature or on a plaque will not normally be a benefit unless it amounts to an advertisement of the donor's business. The provision of literature relating to the work of the charity will not normally amount to a benefit even if it has a cover price and is on sale to the public. Where an item is purchased at an auction the sale price is normally taken to be its value but in the case of charity auctions the Inland Revenue recognises that people often pay much more than an item is worth to benefit the charity. If it can be shown that the market value of such a purchase is less than the sale price, the lower value can be taken as the value of the lot if the item has a clear and recognisable value. Where the value of the item has been enhanced (for example, through ownership by a celebrity) the market value will be taken to be the sale price paid at the auction. In the former case, if the lower value of the lot falls below the donor benefit limits, then the whole payment for the lot can qualify for gift aid. If the value of the lot is greater than the donor benefit limits, then the donor can split the payment so that part is specified to cover the actual value of the lot and the remainder is a qualifying gift aid payment. Evidence should be maintained of how the payment was split and the reasons for the calculation.

Payroll giving

25.18 The payroll giving scheme is provided for in s 205 of the ICTA 1988 (as amended). It is based on a US model and is designed to encourage employees to give regular donations to charity via deductions from their pay which thereby qualifies for tax relief. A payroll giving scheme is set up by the employer (whether of its own volition in order to motivate staff and to demonstrate a commitment to its local community, or as a result of a request by its employees). The Government recognises that payroll giving is a valuable source of funding for charities and to encourage the setting up of more schemes, from 6 April 2000 to 5 April 2003 it will add 10 per cent to all payroll giving donations. Employees are free to decide whether or not they wish to join a payroll giving scheme, which charities they wish to support (ie they do not have to support the employer's preferred charity or charities) and how much they wish to give by way of deductions from their gross pay. National Insurance contributions remain payable on the sums deducted. The employee thereby receives tax relief straight away at the highest rate. Employees can stop giving at any time on notice to the employer and can increase or decrease their donations on notice, but the employer can limit the number of changes to one or two per year. Employers who wish to set up a payroll giving scheme must make the necessary arrangements with an agency approved by the Inland Revenue. This agency will receive all pay deductions made by the employer and will pay the requisite sum to the charities specified by the employees. Agencies can charge administration fees of up to 4 per cent of the donations received or 25 pence per donation, whichever is the greater, but some charge less. Agencies may also provide campaign support as part of their service.

Fund-raising

25.19 Following the Charities Act 1992, it is unlawful for a professional fund-raiser to solicit money or property or for a commercial participator to represent that charitable contributions are to be given to, or applied for the benefit of, a charity unless done so under an agreement with the charity which satisfies the prescribed requirements. A 'professional fund-raiser' is a person who carries out fund-raising business and who is not a charity or company connected with a charity, or a person who for more than £5 per day or £500 per year or £500 per fund-raising venture, solicits funds for a charity (Charities Act 1992, s 58 (as amended)). A 'commercial participator' is a person other than a company connected with a charity who carries on business for gain (other than fund-raising business) in the course of which it engages in a promotional venture which is stated to be for the benefit of a charity. The prescribed requirements for the agreement are set out in the Charitable Institutions (Fundraising) Regulations 1994[1] and include a requirement for professional fund-raisers and commercial participators to make available to the charity any

---

1   SI 1994/3025.

relevant books, documents or records and to transfer funds to the charity without deduction. Professional fund-raisers and commercial participators are required to comply with the provisions of the Charities Act 1992 relating to the information to be supplied to those who are solicited for money or property, including details of the right to a refund in the event that any payment of £50 or more is made. If this statement is made orally but not directly to or in the presence of the person to whom it is addressed, a written statement containing the requisite information and details of the right to a refund must be given to any donor of £50 or more. Failure to comply with these requirements is a criminal offence.[1] A court may grant injunctive relief to a charity if a person solicits money or property or represents that charitable contributions are to be given to that charity in breach of the above requirements, or if he uses methods of fund-raising to which the charity objects, or is not a fit and proper person to raise funds, or where the conduct complained of involves making representations which the charity does not wish to be associated with. The charity is first obliged to serve on that person a 28-day notice to cease soliciting or making representations. Under s 63(1) of the Charities Act 1992, it is an offence falsely to represent that the institution for which money is being raised is a charity.

DATA PROTECTION

25.20   Under the provisions of the DPA 1998, in order to process personal data relating to individuals, the alumni officer of the HEI needs to satisfy one of the conditions set out in Sch 2 to the Act. Of these conditions, the most likely to be applicable to the processing of data relating to alumni will be:

– that the individual has given consent to the processing;
– that the processing is necessary for the performance of a contract with the individual; or
– that the processing is necessary in order to pursue the legitimate interests of the business (unless prejudicial to the interest of the individual).

25.21   If the Alumni Office wishes to process sensitive personal data (ie racial or ethnic origin, political opinions, religion or other belief, trade union membership, health, sex life and criminal convictions), it needs to comply also with one of the conditions set out in Sch 3 to the Act of which only para 1 would appear to be applicable; ie explicit consent to processing of sensitive personal data. In most cases, the HEI will wish to copy the relevant data from its student administration system to its Alumni Office and to collect further information from its alumni as to addresses, their work and possibly information obtained from questionnaires. The question is whether the HEI requires actual consent to this processing or whether it might be argued that if, under their contracts

---

1   Charities Act 1992, s 60(7).

with the HEI, students are automatically entitled to become members of the Alumni Association on successful completion of their course or research degree, then this and subsequent processing of their personal information by the Alumni Office is 'necessary for the performance of a contract' with the students/alumni for the purposes of para 2 of Sch 2 to the Act, or that the processing is necessary in order to pursue the legitimate interest of the HEI under para 6. Whilst it might be preferable for the students/alumni to give consent to all processing in their original application to the HEI and/or upon invitation to join the Alumni Association (see the rights of the data subject to require cessation of processing of his data for any or any special purpose below), the OIC has given some guidelines to HEIs on this issue at its meeting with representatives of the Council for the Advancement of Support of Education on 25 January 2000.

25.22 The OIC has indicated that alumni might 'reasonably expect' Alumni Offices to process their data for the following purposes, which do not, therefore, require explicit 'positive' consent:

– sending HEI mailings (for example, alumni magazines, newsletters, annual reports, etc);
– sending HEI mailings to offer benefits, services and affinity products to alumni;
– HEI related fund-raising initiatives;
– seeking non-financial alumni support (for example, careers advice to students, help with student recruitment, ambassadorial function);
– contacting alumni regarding events and reunions which are relevant to them;
– use of mailing houses for large scale mailings (with confidentiality agreements in place);
– forwarding of messages from other alumni (without disclosing data); and
– including information on products and services which may be of interest to alumni within HEI mailings (for example, affinity card materials).

25.23 Although explicit positive consent may not be required for these purposes, the OIC has advised that data controllers need to inform alumni that they have certain rights relating to the data processed on them, and they have the right to object to use of their data for direct marketing purposes. As long as these rights are communicated to the alumni, consent for the above purposes could be considered to be ongoing. Best practice suggests the inclusion of 'opt out' statements when alumni data is used or collected for a particular purpose. For example, if the HEI forwards a message on behalf of another alumnus, the OIC has advised that it should enclose with that message a statement explaining that it has forwarded the message without disclosing the address of the alumnus, but that if the recipient would prefer the HEI not to forward similar messages in future, he has the right to request this.

25.24 The OIC has indicated that positive notification of consent would be required in the following circumstances: sharing data with branches of Alumni

Associations and other affiliated bodies, hosting mailings for third parties, sharing data with third parties for affinity products and services, processing sensitive data (see above), making unsolicited telephone calls and especially where an alumus has registered with the Telephone Preference Service (TPS) and transferring data outside the EEA except in certain circumstances. (These are explored in greater detail below.) Ideally, if consent is sought it should be in writing signed by the student/alumnus and worded to include a reference to sending the individual information about the Alumni Association and its events, future study opportunities and other services and products and contacting him in connection with the HEI's fund-raising activities and any of the other matters which the OIC has indicated will need specific consent. The OIC has said that positive consent may be inferred by an individual not ticking an 'opt out' box on a form or questionnaire, where mention is made of the purpose(s) for which consent is required, provided that the form is actually returned. Thus, it would be acceptable to ask students to sign and return a form in order to receive their qualification, but to include on that form an 'opt out' box for them to tick if they do not wish their data to be used for specified alumni purposes. If they return the form with the box unticked, this will be adequate consent for the Alumni Office to process their data for those purposes, as it would be also with a questionnaire.

25.25 A further difficulty arises in connection with alumni who became students or alumni prior to the implementation of the DPA 1998 and who may not have signed any consent to use their data for alumni purposes but, by implication, have accepted such use of their data until now. The first transitional relief provisions of the Act (until 23 October 2001) covered the use of automated data such as mailing lists processed by the data controller only for the purposes of distributing or recording the distribution of articles or information to the alumni and consisting of their names, addresses and other information necessary for effecting such distribution and exempted such use from the data protection principles and Parts II and III of the Act until then. However, it is questionable whether information relating to their award, other courses and research and jobs, etc, would be covered by this exemption, in which event the HEI would need to satisfy one of the grounds in Sch 2. Obtaining retrospective consent could prove to be difficult. There is also the question of whether, and if so at what stage, a student/alumnus should be given the option of opting out of Alumni Association membership and/or the use of his data for specific alumni purposes. The preferred view is that a right of opt out should be given in respect of each such circumstance, in which event the student's data must not be used for the purposes of the Alumni Association or for the specific purposes for which he has withdrawn his consent (as the case may be).

25.26 The HEI should check that its data protection notification/registration covers all the purposes for which it may wish to process the alumni data. In the event that alumni matters are dealt with by a separate legal entity from the HEI (for example, by a separate trust or HEI company), that legal entity will need to register its own notification with the Information Commissioner and the provisions of the seventh data protection principle will apply (see below). In theory, it would be possible to require a candidate for a place on a course/research degree at the HEI to be required to sign a consent which could extend to allowing the HEI to provide his personal data to third parties for all purposes for which positive consent is required. Acceptance of such a consent notice could be made a requirement of enrolment. However, such consent might be said to have been obtained involuntarily through duress. It also flies in the face of an HEI's express or implied obligation of confidentiality to its students/alumni and it may transgress the provisions of Art 8 (right to respect for private and family life) and/or Art 14 (prohibition of discrimination) of the European Convention on Human Rights which is now directly enforceable against an HEI (as a public body) under the provisions of the HRA 1998. The OIC has frowned on the proposed practice of linking consent to enrolment unless the individual is given the opportunity at any time without penalty to object to the use of his data for any purpose and, if such objection is made, it is acted upon forthwith. The power to withdraw consent must relate to the sorts of third party disclosure referred to above and not to processing which the HEI has to undertake in order perform its obligations and duties. Such a power to withdraw consent would enable the HEI to defeat any objection that the consent obtained on enrolment was tainted by duress, because the individual could withdraw it at any time.

Processing which may require consent

25.27 Sharing data with branches of Alumni Associations and other recognised affiliated bodies may require consent, although the OIC is reasonably comfortable with sharing of data with such groups for alumni purposes, on four conditions:

- that data protection statements circulated to alumni (such as on questionnaires and mailing cover sheets) make mention of this generic type of purpose;
- that alumni are given the opportunity to object to the disclosure of their data for this type of purpose;
- that confidentiality agreements are in place, whereby those receiving data guarantee not to disclose them to third parties; and
- that where an agent (for example, a publishing company acting on behalf of an HEI to prepare an alumni directory) is involved, a contract is in place that stipulates that the company is acting as a data processor for the HEI, and that where the company makes direct contact with alumni, any material sent out make it clear that it is acting as an agent of the HEI (see also comments on the seventh data protection principle set out below).

'Host' mailings for third party companies

25.28 'Host' mailings are distributions of advertising materials to a group of alumni which have been put together by a third party commercial company but which are mailed in the name of the HEI and they may also contain information prepared by the HEI. The HEI may or may not receive a fee for undertaking the host mailing. Alumni data is not provided to the third party company which delivers the pack of material to the HEI for mailing to its alumni and covers the cost of mailing and administration. There is a clear distinction between host mailing and merely inserting advertising inserts in, for example, the alumni magazine for distribution to alumni (where positive consent will not be necessary). Notwithstanding that no personal data are actually transferred to the third party company, the OIC regards host mailing as 'trading in personal information' such that positive consent is required before it is undertaken. Even if consent is obtained (say, at enrolment), it is advisable to include in each host mailing an opt out provision entitling individuals to object to any future host mailings. Since no data are transferred, it is debatable whether the view of the OIC is correct in law, but in the event that an HEI pursues host mailing without the consent of its alumni and it is challenged by an aggrieved alumnus, it is clear how the OIC will react and a court decision will be necessary to resolve the issue. In addition, when proposing to undertake host mailing, HEIs will need to ensure that their contracts with the host mailing companies allow them to object to the inclusion of certain types and contents of advertising material which might bring the name of the HEI into disrepute. HEIs may have a checklist of advertisements or companies which they would not be prepared to include for objective reasons. It is preferable for HEIs to have power to approve in advance all materials to be supplied to alumni and to reject any that they do not approve of. The contract should also include standard indemnities relating to publishing of material, compliance with the Advertising Standards Authority requirements and any regulatory or statutory requirements including the provisions of any regulations made under the Consumer Credit Act 1974 concerning the content of advertisements and ss 20 and 21 of the Consumer Protection Act 1987 (CPA 1987) concerning misleading price indications.

Sharing data with commercial third parties for affinity products and services

25.29 Not unnaturally, the OIC has ruled that positive consent is required before any data relating to alumni is provided to such third parties. An HEI is, however, able to include advertising and information from such third parties in its magazines and newsletters, etc, inviting alumni to apply for products and services on their own initiative. HEIs will wish to carry out stringent vetting procedures to ensure that suppliers of affinity products and services are reliable, offer a good quality service or product with adequate after-sales service, product guarantees, access to complaints procedures etc, do not hold themselves out as the agent or partner of the HEI and provide full indemnities to the HEI in respect of their provision of services and products to alumni, in addition to the indemnities indicated above relating to host mailings. In the case of provision of products, it is particularly important to ensure that the supplier holds adequate insurance in respect of any claims for damage caused by defective goods and that it indemnifies the HEI against any such claims. It is unlikely that an HEI would allow its trade mark or logo to be placed on a product, but if it does so it will have joint and several liability for any claim under the CPA 1987. Victims no longer need to prove negligence in bringing such a claim. If an HEI is prepared to license an affinity service provider to use its trade mark, logo and/or coat of arms, it will need to include provisions relating to goodwill in the mark(s) and requiring the supplier not to do anything that may damage the distinctiveness or reputation in the mark(s). The HEI may also require power to approve in advance the contents of any materials supplied to alumni by the supplier.

Unsolicited telephone calls

25.30 The OIC's view is that telephone calls made in the ordinary course of the Alumni Association's dealings with its alumni (for example, to confirm the booking of a weekend course) falls within the implied consent category, but unsolicited calls in connection with, for example, fund-raising will require specific consent. In addition, where an individual has signed up to the TPS the OIC takes this to be a withdrawal of consent for all purposes unless the call has been specifically requested irrespective of any ongoing relationship between the individual and the organisation, or unless the individual has indicated to the HEI that he is content to continue to receive calls notwithstanding his TPS registration. The OIC has confirmed that provided an HEI undertakes to review this situation in the event of any complaints, it can infer consent to telephone an alumnus if he completes a questionnaire with his telephone number when the questionnaire clearly refers to fund-raising and/or marketing activities.

Location-based advertising

25.31 A related issue to unsolicited telephone calls is location-based advertising (which is likely to be of lesser significance to HEIs but is noted here for completeness). Location-based advertising is advertising directed at a mobile phone in a particular location, for example, offering a person a cheap holiday as he passes a travel agent's premises or, perhaps, marketing an HEI to school leavers as they collect their 'A' level results from school or college. Such advertising is currently prohibited under the Telecommunications (Data Protection and Privacy) Regulations 1999,[1] unless the individual has previously notified the caller that for the time being he consents to such communications being sent by the caller on that line. This consent can be withdrawn at any time. Calls have to contain certain specified information

---

1   SI 1999/2093.

including the caller's name and address or a freephone telephone number on which it can be contacted. Similar rules apply to faxes.

Transfer of data outside the EEA

25.32 Personal information may only be transferred outside the EEA if the country or territory of the recipient ensures an adequate level of protection for the rights and freedom of data subjects in relation to the processing of personal data unless the data subject has consented to the transfer or the transfer is necessary for the performance of a contract between the data subject and the data controller. Transitional relief is available until 23 October 2001 for processing of such data which is already underway. The EC Commission is currently considering the data protection laws of a number of non-EEA countries to ascertain whether those countries provide adequate protection for personal data transferred from the EU. Countries which are considered to do so will be subject to a 'Community finding' allowing open transfer of data to those countries without further consideration as to the adequacy of their data protection laws. At the time of writing, the EC Commission has agreed that Switzerland and Hungary provide adequate protection and Canada is currently being considered. The Commission has also approved the 'US safe harbour' arrangement whereby organisations in the USA commit themselves to comply with a set of data protection principles backed up by guidance provided by a set of Frequently Asked Questions issued by the US Department of Commerce. Such commitment would provide an adequate level of protection for transfer of personal data to that organisation from EU Member States.

Internet publication

25.33 In general, any publication of information relating to alumni or students on the internet will require their express consent because such publication will be worldwide. However, the OIC has indicated that it would be acceptable to publish a list of names, academic departments and years of graduation of alumni on the internet as a way of contacting 'lost' alumni, but no other information should be provided without consent.

Right to object to direct marketing

25.34 Under s 11 of the DPA 1998, an individual is entitled by notice to the data controller to require it to cease, or not to begin processing his personal data for the purposes of direct marketing, which means communication, by whatever means, of advertising or marketing material which is directed to particular individuals.[1] If the data controller fails to comply with the notice, application may be made to the courts for an injunction.[2]

Right to object to processing of personal data

25.35   If the individual has not consented to the processing and none of the other conditions in paras 1 to 4 of Sch 2 is met, under s 10 of the DPA 1998 an individual is entitled by written notice to the data controller to require it to cease, or not to begin, processing or processing for a specified purpose or in a specified manner his personal data on the ground that the processing is likely to cause substantial damage or substantial distress to him or to another and such damage or distress is or would be unwarranted. Again, application may be made to the courts for relief if the data controller fails to comply.

Outsourcing

25.36   In the event that an HEI wishes to outsource any part of its operation relating to alumni such that it wishes to provide a copy of or extracts from its alumni database to the third party provider, it will need to ensure that it complies with the seventh data protection principle.[3] Examples of such outsourcing may relate to employment of a professional fund-raiser or commercial participator (see para **25.19**) or outsourcing printing and mailing of the Alumni Magazine or other information from the Alumni Association to the alumni.

25.37   The seventh data protection principle requires that, where processing of personal data is carried out by a data processor (for example, the fund-raiser/printer) on behalf of a data controller (the HEI), then the data controller must:

- choose a data processor providing sufficient guarantees in respect of technical and organisational security measures governing the processing to be carried out;
- take necessary steps to ensure compliance with those measures;
- ensure that the processing is carried out under a contract evidenced in writing under which the data processor is to act only on instructions from the data controller; and
- ensure that the contract requires the data processor to comply with obligations equivalent to those imposed on the data controller by the seventh data protection principle (ie implementing appropriate technical and technological measures to ensure an appropriate level of security and taking reasonable steps to ensure the reliability of employees who have access to the data).

---

1   DPA 1998, s 11(3).
2   Ibid, s 11(2).
3   Ibid, Sch 1, paras 11 and 12.

25.38   It is sensible to provide in such contracts for the HEI or its agents to have powers to inspect and verify the data processor's data protection practice from time to time, together with an obligation on the data processor to indemnify the HEI in the event of any claim arising by reason of its breach of the provisions of the DPA 1998 and/or the contract.

CONFIDENTIALITY

25.39   Allied to the issues of data protection is that of confidentiality of personal information relating to students and alumni. It is well established throughout the HE sector that HEIs have an implied duty of confidentiality to their students and alumni. The limits of this obligation are, nevertheless, somewhat vague and as a result of this and the increased involvement of, for instance, parents and employers in the education of their children and employees, many HEIs have taken the step of defining exactly what are the limits of their obligations of confidentiality to their students and alumni. The following issues are apparent:

–   To what extent does the HEI require the consent (oral or written?) of its students/alumni before it can disclose all or any of their personal information to a parent, guardian, spouse or employer?

–   If consent is required in all instances, can it be implied if the student/ alumnus is:
   (a)   ill;
   (b)   seriously ill;
   (c)   in a coma;
   (d)   dead;
   (e)   in debt to the HEI;
   (f)   in debt to a third party;
   (g)   found guilty of misconduct;
   (h)   found guilty of misconduct resulting in his expulsion or suspension;
   (i)   suspended as a result of incapability (physical or mental);
   (j)   subject to investigation relating to any of the above?

–   In what circumstances can assessment results and attendance details be disclosed to others, particularly sponsoring employers?

–   To what extent can consent be implied for the HEI to supply information to the student's/alumnus's:
   (a)   solicitors;
   (b)   Member of Parliament;
   (c)   doctor;
   (d)   advice worker;
   (e)   the SU?

It is recommended that each HEI should codify its position and make sure that steps are taken to allow candidates, students and alumni to be informed of that position.

CONCLUSION

25.40   All of the above issues will not necessarily apply to all HEIs, but most of the issues will apply to most HEIs. HEIs may derive considerable benefit from their alumni, but in order to do so they need to ensure that they meet the requirements on their side of the equation, providing the infrastructure for a vibrant and effective Alumni Association which, in turn, meets its legal obligations as outlined above.

Chapter 26

A NOTE ON PERSONAL PROPERTY WITHIN THE LAW OF PROPERTY: LOST PROPERTY, TREASURE TROVE, BAILMENT

David Palfreyman

26.1   We are concerned here with complex legal terms (see Figure 26.1) and essentially with *personal property* (also known as *personalty*), rather than with *real property* as land and the buildings sitting on it (*realty*): although *chattels real* as *leasehold interests* in land are technically part of *personalty* along with *chattels personal*. The latter divides into *choses in possession* as tangible, corporeal things such as computers, cars and carpets; and *choses in action* which includes intangible, incorporeal concepts or abstract personalty such as business goodwill, shares, and IP (patents, copyright, trade-marks, know-how, etc). In fact, choses in action sub-divide into *pure intangibles* (a debt, goodwill, copyright) and *documentary intangibles* (a bill of exchange or promissory note, an insurance policy, shares). The general principles of real property or land law are the same for any individual or organisation and hence are not covered in this book (see Birks (2000), chapter 4; Sparkes (1999) and (2001)), while intellectual property is covered in relation to HEIs in Chapter 12. This chapter concentrates on things or chattels insofar as HEIs may encounter legal problems relating to them.

26.2   Chattels can be possessed or owned, the latter being the strongest possible version of the former. If the employee of an HEI finds lost property on its premises, the HEI thereby comes into possession of that property, but it is not the legal owner unless the previous possessor/owner has clearly abandoned the item, or until a reasonable time has gone by without the true owner reclaiming it and during which the HEI ought to take reasonable steps to locate the true owner. If, however, a non-employee of the HEI finds the lost property on HEI premises, then he is the possessor even if he hands it in at the HEI's reception as lost property. Thus, if the item is never claimed by its true owner and the HEI sells it, the sale proceeds belong to the finder – see *Parker v British Airways Board*,[1] concerning Mr Parker as a passenger finding a valuable gold bracelet lying on the floor in the executive lounge of Heathrow Airport. Where the chattel is attached to or embedded in the land, however, it is already in possession of the land-owner (the HEI) even if found by someone who is not an

---

1   [1982] QB 1004.

Figure 26.1   The complex legal terms relating to property

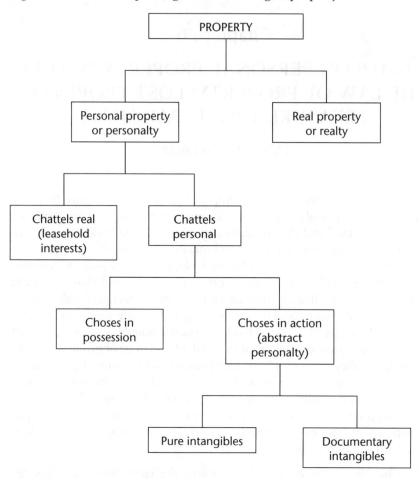

HEI employee (*South Staffordshire Water Co v Sharman*;[1] and also *Waverley Borough Council v Fletcher*[2] re a medieval broach – maybe Henry VIII's hat pin! – worth £35K and uncovered by a Mr Fletcher using a metal-detector in a Waverley Borough Council park). Moreover, should the finder be a trespasser on HEI land, rather than, say, a student or conferee, then the HEI will again be deemed the possessor of the item.

26.3   All of this is overridden where the thing found is, in fact, treasure trove (defined in the Treasure Act 1996 broadly as old coins, gold, silver and archaeologically/historically significant objects more than 200 years old): here the finder would get a reward from the public purse, as might the HEI as land-owner, while the British Museum or similar gets to keep the treasure. The items need no longer necessarily have been hidden by an unknown owner: they

---

1   [1896] 2 QB 44.
2   [1996] QB 334.

are still 'treasure' under the Treasure Act 1996, even if not actually 'trove' as under the previous law (see Sparkes (1999), pp 562–563).

26.4 However, what if Rich Student graduates and leaves behind his smart new BMW Mini in the campus car-park? The HEI is the possessor, and also the owner if Rich Student can be shown to have abandoned it (unlikely!), or given it to the HEI in gratitude (even more unlikely!), or really cannot be contacted, or consistently fails to respond to repeated letters. The HEI is not liable for the care of the vehicle: the HEI is initially an *unconscious bailee*; then (once aware of the situation) an *involuntary bailee*, and liable to Rich Student only if it intentionally damages or destroys the car before it can be said to have become the owner after trying and failing to contact its alumnus. If, however, drunken Rich Student has handed car and keys to HEI security at their request and then staggered off into the darkness, the HEI is the *gratuitous bailee* and Rich Student the *bailor* of the Mini now in *bailment*, and the HEI must exercise reasonable care to keep the car safe until Rich Student returns for it (the same applies if a waitress offers to take a diner's coat in a restaurant, as opposed to the diner personally hanging it up). If Rich Student duly returns and for, say, disciplinary reasons the HEI unwisely refuses to hand over the Mini, the HEI's duty to take care of the car increases to the level of effectively being the all-risks insurer of this valuable chattel and with strict liability to compensate Rich Student if anything should now happen to it.

26.5 A similar potential gratuitous bailment legal problem could arise where an HEI packs up the contents of a student's bedroom and stores these items as a helpful gesture where the student has, say, been in an accident and is in hospital, or where the HEI offers to store the belongings of overseas students during the summer-long vacation. If a legal dispute then arose, the aggrieved student bailor may sue the HEI bailee if the contents are damaged, destroyed or lost through its negligence in minding them. The HEI will not, however, commit the tort of conversion, involving *detinue*, unless it is refusing to hand back the room contents and, say, holding (or detaining) them against unpaid rent (Markesinis and Deakin (1999), pp 409–410). Of course, in the BMW Mini example above, the HEI will probably be committing the tort of conversion once it is requested to return the keys and refuses (see also Chapter 20 on wheel-clamping). Moreover, if the HEI charges the student to store belongings, there is a contract and the HEI becomes a *rewarded bailee* with an even higher liability properly to care for the possessions: like a theatre cloak-room charging for items deposited.

26.6 That said, at common law an innkeeper may detain the luggage of a guest who fails to pay his bill; in effect the innkeeper may exercise a lien over the guest's chattels, but not his vehicle (Hotel Proprietors Act 1956). An HEI in providing student residential accommodation (or even conference trade 'B & B') is not covered by this special legal recognition of the 'common calling' of the medieval innkeeper.

Part 7
CONSEQUENCES

Chapter 27

A GUIDE TO LITIGATION

Jonathan Leslie (Travers Smith Braithwaite)

EDITORS' INTRODUCTION

§27.1 Standard texts on litigation will normally run to over 500 pages. We recognise, therefore, that the author of this chapter was set a near impossible task in being asked to summarise litigation in only a few thousand words. Yet it has been achieved *and* made relevant to HEIs in terms of the particular potential problems of handling litigation within, and on behalf of, an HEI. Litigation and even arbitration is not territory for the DIY legal enthusiast within HEI management, unless the HEI does not mind losing a case and running the risk of having to pick up the legal costs of the opponent. The process of litigation – the tactics – is the same for any person or organisation. Hence, one should not need to address such an issue here in great detail since the ground is covered in any standard text on litigation. However, for an HEI, during litigation, there can be confusion about who has authority to speak for it, and, especially in the chartered universities, there may well be a distinct lack of corporate spirit and responsibility (reflecting the relatively weak management structure as compared with most organisations and even as compared with 'managerially minded' statutory HEIs).

§27.2 Kaplin and Lee (1995a), pp 131–132 devote several pages from the US perspective to exploring the degree to which a member of staff not directly authorised to do a particular thing can be seen to act as an agent and bind the HEI on the basis that to a third party he or she has 'apparent authority' to act and that it was reasonable of the third party to rely on the words of the member of staff or agent: see also paras **5.19** *et seq*. They also comment on the demands of litigation:

> 'administrators should never trivialise the prospect of litigation. Involvement in a lawsuit is a serious and often complex business that can create internal campus friction, drain institutional resources, and affect an institution's public image ... Particularly for administrators, sound understanding of the litigation process is predicate to both constructive litigation planning and constructive preventive planning.'[1]

§27.3 They refer to 'campus common law' in the form of 'academic custom and usage' (p 17) which the courts may review in terms of the student:HEI contract, or even the academic's employment contract. Finally, Kaplin and Lee stress that sometimes a claimant may be prevented (or at least delayed) from bringing a court suit by the *'exhaustion of remedies* doctrine' (p 27): ie the internal appeal mechanism must be fully utilised before resorting to litigation

---

1   Kaplin and Lee (1995a), pp 20–21 and 22.

(as discussed in relation to students in Chapters 6, 7 and 9 above, and in Palfreyman (1999)).

§27.4   This chapter also explores ADR as an option besides full litigation in the courts. Indeed, the court can now stay proceedings to give time for the parties to pursue ADR as recommended/encouraged (if not quite 'instructed') by the court (as in *Clark v University of Lincolnshire and Humberside*[1]: see Appendix 1 to Chapter 6). Similarly, in *Cowl and Others v Plymouth City Council*[2] the Court of Appeal again stressed the use of internal complaints procedures and then if necessary ADR, with litigation only as a last resort. There are, of course, always the concepts of negotiation or even mediation, as attempts to avoid legal costs, but care must be taken that exploration of informal routes does not create hostages to fortune if and when matters escalate. In certain circumstances, of course, the litigation will anyway effectively be beyond the control of the HEI. The HEI's insurance company may be in charge, albeit the action is still in the name of the HEI ('subrogation'): the insurance company meeting the legal fees and eventually picking up the tab for any damages awarded against the HEI will be paying the piper and hence will be calling the tune (see Chapter 24). Finally, the HEI should be aware of how easy it is to lose control of legal costs, which can easily spiral once litigation commences: one UK university has spent probably almost £1m on three *unsuccessful* legal disputes in the past decade.

§27.5   Chapter 1 and Further Reading refer to the three series of education case reports which include reports of HE cases, a few of which are also reported in the *Times Law Reports*. An HEI manager tangled up in litigation concerning, say, the student contract would do well to read the relevant cases referred to elsewhere in this book in order to get a feel for how the court approaches such cases and hence in order to be better able to discuss management of the case with the HEI's lawyers.

INTRODUCTION

27.1   Recent years have witnessed an escalation of contentious legal disputes. These have affected all areas of life, both commercial and private, as legislation and the judgments of the courts in the UK and the EU have assertively extended government controls and the involvement of the common law into new areas. This trend, coupled with what is perhaps a modern cultural tendency to take disputes to the law, have greatly increased the volume of contentious issues that proceed through the courts.

27.2   HEIs may be involved in contentious legal disputes as much as bodies in other walks of life. Except, perhaps, in the case of those chartered bodies that remain subject to the exclusive jurisdiction of the Visitor (see Chapters 8 and 30) when that jurisdiction is properly exercised and is not excluded by statute, HEIs are subject to the jurisdiction of the courts both in relation to their internal operations and in respect of their relations with the outside world. They are also free to submit those disputes to arbitration or to assisted methods

---

1   [2000] 1 WLR 1988.
2   (2002) *The Times*, January 8.

of resolution. Students and staff aside, HEIs are as likely to end up in dispute over a building contract as any other 'employer' of the services of the UK construction industry.

27.3   This chapter aims to:

–   describe briefly the types of dispute in which HEIs may become involved;
–   explain the practices and procedures most typically followed in the resolution of disputes if any internal methods of resolution fail;
–   describe in outline the chief remedies available at law and how they can be enforced; and
–   give some examples of practical safeguards that may be followed to protect the interests of the parties should a dispute need to be resolved at law.

TYPES OF DISPUTE

27.4   Disputes affecting HEIs may be characterised (for present purposes, very broadly) as either internal or external disputes. Internal disputes are those that affect the relationships between members of the institution – among themselves, or between individuals or groups and the HEI. External disputes are those that arise among the institution or members of the institution and the outside world. The former may be easier to contain than the latter, and may, in many cases, be dealt with by internal procedures and by reference to codes of practice (see Chapter 7). It will only be if those *ad hoc* methods fail that the more formal steps referred to later may have to be invoked (see Chapter 9). In some cases, the internal procedures may be subject to the exclusive jurisdiction of the Visitor (see Chapter 8). The courts generally decline to adjudicate on legal challenges to decisions of the Visitor provided that the jurisdiction has been properly exercised. Exceptionally, the jurisdiction of the Visitor to determine employment disputes has been removed by statute (see Chapter 10). In cases where the Visitor has no jurisdiction, the internal procedures of the institution will generally be subject to the jurisdiction of the courts or to arbitration. External disputes will always be subject to the jurisdiction of the courts or to arbitration.

27.5   Examples of internal disputes are those involving:

–   employment;
–   sexual harassment;
–   internal discipline;
–   the quality and nature of tuition;
–   property rights (for example, student accommodation); and
–   conflict between the HEI and the students' union.

27.6   External disputes may typically involve the following areas of law:

–   IP (for example, disputes concerning copyright, trade marks and patents);
–   the construction industry;

- real property (ie those concerning the ownership and use of land);
- the management of investments of the institution; and
- commercial contracts.

27.7 Although each type of problem may be different, there are broad similarities of approach in relation to each of them and they are all generally subject to the same procedures for their resolution.

THE RESOLUTION OF DISPUTES

27.8 If internal procedures have failed, there are three principal ways in which legal disputes may be resolved: litigation, arbitration and ADR. 'Litigation' is the name given to the process of the compulsory determination of legal disputes through the courts. 'Arbitration' is the determination of such disputes through a process which is agreed by the parties either as a part of an agreement entered into before any dispute concerning it has arisen or, alternatively, once a dispute has developed. While the process is consensual, an arbitration agreement may be enforced by the courts. These two procedures have dominated the procedural landscape for generations. Their efficiency has come under increasing scrutiny. As a result, recent movements have led to extensive reforms of both systems, and these are described later. Outside the area of formal dispute resolution, one of the most popular responses to problems associated with litigation and arbitration has been ADR, which is the term used to describe a range of consensual methods of mediation intended to by-pass contentious processes. Most typically, this is pursued on the private initiative of the parties in dispute but, as is explained later, the courts now encourage mediation in most cases.

27.9 Litigation in England is conducted under procedural rules that are derived from a mixture of statute, common law and what is called 'the inherent jurisdiction of the court', which is the power of the court to regulate its own procedures, subject to statute and common law precedents. The rules are updated frequently to reflect changes in the substantive law. 'Substantive law' is the term for the general system of law that creates rights and liabilities (for example, the law of contract, trusts and tort). 'Procedural law' governs the system by which those rights and liabilities are adjudicated by the courts. It is equally important, for without it there is no means of giving effect to the substantive law. In addition to the rules themselves, there have always been certain underlying principles and objectives. Some of these have now been formally identified and embodied in the rules of court and are explained below.

27.10 The system of litigation in England has undergone a process of fundamental reform and rejuvenation following the introduction, in April 1999, of the CPR 1998. These rules made significant changes in both the philosophy underlying the conduct of litigation, and to the rules that govern the process. To some extent, even before the new rules were introduced, the judges, especially those in the higher courts, had begun gradually to modify their approach to the process of litigation and to adopt an attitude that was more interventionist than had traditionally been taken; but the CPR 1998 radically accelerated the process. The new regime is described later, but to set it in context and to show how the system has changed it is first necessary to outline how litigation was previously conducted.

27.11 There is a broad dichotomy between what is called adversarial litigation and inquisitorial litigation. The first prevailed in England before the CPR 1998, and still exists in a somewhat modified form. It is characteristic of litigation in the common-law jurisdictions. The second is inquisitorial and is largely adopted in the civil law countries, especially those in continental Europe. In such systems, the court plays an active role in the course of the litigation and frequently takes the initiative in identifying the facts in dispute and the legal issues that arise, and generally controls the conduct of the case.

27.12 'Adversarial litigation' is a process that allows the parties to determine the conduct of court proceedings very largely on their own initiative. Although the dispute is governed by the procedural rules that apply in all cases, the courts themselves do not take an active role in the conduct of the litigation and instead most frequently respond to calls by the parties for rulings at any stage of the process. The court sits impartially to determine disputes among a number of hostile participants each of whom has a case to assert or to defend. The court plays little part in the process of identifying the facts in dispute or the legal issues to be tried. To a large extent, the participants dictate the pace of the case and the general way in which it is conducted, and decide on the evidence to be adduced. The court will not normally interfere of its own volition with the way in which the case is put in law, the way in which it is presented at trial, or with the pre-action preparations. It is for the parties and not the court to ensure that all relevant evidence is adduced.

27.13 The adversarial system has much to commend it, but it is also susceptible to abuse. The conduct of court cases in adversarial litigation is often likened to a game, in which tactics enable the participants to take advantage of the weakness of their opponent. Thus, a claimant's lawyers will usually try to use every rule to force the defendant to face trial as quickly as possible, whilst the defence team will strive to create tactical delays in the hope that the claim will lose impetus or that the claimant will run out of money or lose interest. Oppressive demands for disclosure of documents are routinely made. To a very large extent, the courts under this system permit the parties to fight as they will and seldom intervene to assist someone whose lawyers or resources put him or her at a disadvantage to a better organised or more powerful opponent. It is a system in which the parties must look after themselves and within the procedural rules 'no holds are barred'. The courts will not police the day-to-day conduct of the case to see if time-limits are being obeyed or if an abuse is being practised behind the scenes, although they will, if called upon, give procedural directions where appropriate.

27.14 This was the system that applied in England before April 1999. For some years before then, there had been a movement towards a system that was fairer to the parties, more expeditious and which made the courts more responsible for the overall conduct of a case. In addition, there was seen to be an unfortunate degree of complexity in the practices and procedures of different courts. Thus, the rules in the county court were different from those in the High Court; and the High Court was in turn divided into branches that had their own separate rules and conventions. These were thought to fetter the efficient running of litigation and to offer opportunities to recalcitrant parties to circumvent the spirit and letter of the rules, and to confuse the lay clients whose interests it was the duty of the courts to promote.

27.15 Under the auspices of Lord Woolf, the present Lord Chief Justice, a new system – *the Woolf reforms* – was introduced following a process of public and professional consultation. This system is still fundamentally adversarial in nature, but incorporates some features of the inquisitorial process. The reforms operate at a number of levels. Thus, the language of the rules is simplified (some would say, over-simplified) so that parties may better understand what is required of them at any time. Next, the structure of the courts was overhauled so that the old distinctions between the rules in the county court and the High Court have been removed, and rules of the separate divisions within the High Court are reconciled and made uniform.

27.16 The rules themselves have been completely rewritten so that not only is new language employed but also the substance of the rules has changed so as to impose new obligations, time-limits and objectives. The court will now take a more interventionist approach as a case progresses and may overrule the parties' wishes if it considers that they are inconsistent with the proper conduct of the case. Above all, the underlying philosophy of the conduct of litigation has been redefined. All litigation is now subject to what is described as the 'overriding objective', which is to deal with cases justly. This means that courts must deal with a case so as to ensure, so far as possible, that parties are on an equal footing; that expense is saved; that procedures are applied in a way that is proportionate to the amounts in issue, the importance of the case, the complexity of the issues and the financial position of each party; and that it is dealt with expeditiously and fairly and with an appropriate allocation of the court's resources.

27.17 Another feature of the philosophy underlying the new regime is that litigation should be regarded as a last resort. Parties should now attempt to settle a dispute before an action is begun, and, in addition, the parties are encouraged to give in advance full details of their claims and defences, together with supporting evidence and documents. This process is reinforced by the introduction of pre-action protocols in the cases of certain types of litigation which will be more widely used in the future. Only once those preliminary steps have been taken should litigation start. This so-called 'front-end loading' of cases, whereby careful early preparation is carried out before litigation starts, can, however, run counter to the overriding objective of reducing costs.

27.18 These features of the new system are brought to bear partly by the obligation of the parties to respect them but, more importantly, by the process of active case management by the courts. In the past, as has been seen, the courts played a somewhat passive role in the system, and that offered opportunities for abuse. Now the courts play a more active role, and their presence is felt in litigation to a much greater degree than before. This approach finds expression in a number of different ways. It may include encouraging the parties to co-operate in the conduct of proceedings; identifying quickly which issues need full investigation, and disposing of other issues summarily; imposing timetables and directions that the court considers appropriate and even where the parties have otherwise agreed; and, perhaps most importantly, urging, and even in some cases requiring, the parties to consider ADR.

27.19 The court's intervention may come at virtually any stage of the process. Thus, at the beginning of an action, a case will be allocated to one of the management tracks and, at the same time, given timetables for the immediate steps in the litigation. A single judge will frequently be appointed to oversee a complex case from the outset, whereas before a case might have come before a number of different judges in its course, leading to expense and confusion. In all cases, judges take an active part in case management conferences and at other significant applications, so as to ensure that the case is made ready for trial at the earliest possible date and without unnecessary expense. The court can also supervise the type of evidence that the parties adduce at trial, and in particular the court may stipulate that the expert evidence relied upon be given by a single witness.

27.20 In the final section of this chapter, an assessment is offered of the extent to which the Woolf reforms have made a significant difference to the conduct of litigation in England. Attention will be drawn to some of the drawbacks and inconsistencies in the rules, and especially to the unfortunate and almost immediate development of individual codes of practice adopted by some of the specialist courts. That process is inconsistent with the philosophy of the reforms, which included, as a fundamental objective, the adoption of uniform rules of practice throughout the court system. First, however, the following section outlines the main features of the procedures that apply in accordance with the new rules, but, given space constraints, cannot take into account any variations adopted by individual courts.

THE STRUCTURE AND JURISDICTION OF THE COURTS

27.21 The term *structure* is intended to refer to the hierarchy of the courts and their organisation. By *jurisdiction* is meant the powers and authority of any court to determine a given type of case.

27.22 Civil cases in England are dealt with by the following courts: magistrates' courts, county courts, the High Court, the Court of Appeal and the

Judicial Committee of the House of Lords. In addition, various tribunals may hear a variety of what are typically claims brought under statutes. This chapter deals with the county court and High Court procedures. Following the introduction of the CPR 1998, the rules of the High Court and the county court are now the same. As a general rule, the jurisdiction of both courts is concurrent, but there are certain exceptions. These reflect mainly the amounts of money that are claimed and the complexity of the issues involved.

27.23   For example, only the High Court may hear applications for judicial review and defamation. Alternatively, only the county court has jurisdiction to hear claims to enforce certain regulated agreements under the Consumer Credit Act 1974 and certain actions to redress unlawful sex discrimination. Some claims under statute may be heard by the High Court but only provided that no costs are awarded to the applicant. Sometimes a claim in respect of which there is concurrent jurisdiction may be brought in the High Court only if it exceeds certain money limits. These include claims for sums less than £5000 or claims over estate or trust property valued at less than £30,000. However, claims valued at less than £25,000 are usually tried in the county court, while claims over £50,000 should be tried in the High Court. There are also special provisions for personal injury claims. Where the claimant does not expect to recover more than £50,000, the case should be brought in the county court. Penalties involving the payment of legal costs may be applied in cases where claims have been begun in the wrong or inappropriate court, and in extreme cases where the error was wilful, the case may be struck out. The jurisdiction of county courts also relates to their location. Any case may be begun in any county court, subject to the limits just mentioned, but if a case is defended it may either automatically or in the exercise of the court's discretion be transferred to the court for the area in which the defendant resides or carries on business, or where the claim arose.

27.24   The High Court also sits in geographical locations throughout the country but has its centre in the Royal Courts of Justice in London. It is divided into three main divisions: the Queen's Bench Division, which deals with general matters including personal injury, defamation and commercial claims, and judicial review; the Chancery Division, which deals with issues concerning land, trusts and estates, IP and company cases, as well as complex commercial disputes involving equity law; and the Family Division, which handles divorces and issues concerning the welfare of children. There are, in addition, certain specialist courts which handle cases that involve particular trade and industry practices. These include the Admiralty Court, the Technology and Construction Court, the Commercial Court and the Patents Court.

27.25   Above the High Court is the Court of Appeal, which hears only appeals and has almost no original jurisdiction. Permission to appeal is now almost invariably required either from the court of first instance or, with increasing frequency, the Court of Appeal itself. Finally, the Judicial Committee of the

House of Lords is the last appellate court of England and Wales, Scotland and Northern Ireland.

LITIGATION PROCEDURES: OVERVIEW

27.26 Some cases are subject to unique procedures. For example, an application for judicial review must follow special rules that apply to no other process. The majority of cases, however, follow the same broad procedures. Not every step that is catered for in the CPR 1998, of course, will be invoked in every case, as some will not be appropriate. The following steps are nevertheless frequently taken in most civil actions.

27.27 To begin with, it is now necessary to refrain from issuing proceedings in court until full details of the claim have been put to the other side in writing and an opportunity has been given to answer the claim and to settle. Where pre-action protocols apply (see below), there are clear guidelines for what steps should be taken to meet these requirements, but even where the action is one for which no protocols have yet been prepared, it is still incumbent on the parties to follow these general principles. If no settlement can be reached, a claim form is issued and served. There follow the delivery of more detailed statements of the claim and of a defence, the allocation of the claim to one of the case management tracks, and thereafter disclosure of documents, service of witness statements and experts' reports, and finally the trial. Throughout this time, the court exercises a supervisory capacity and is involved in case management conferences as may be appropriate.

LITIGATION PROCEDURES: STEP BY STEP

Pre-action protocols

27.28 These are intended to set out what procedures should be followed before an action is begun. It is intended that in due course such protocols will be drafted to cover all types of claim, but at the time of writing only a limited number have been drafted. These include personal injury, defamation and construction cases. It is nonetheless expected that the spirit of these protocols is to be followed in every case. In earlier times, litigation could be started without any notice at all, although it was more usual for a letter before action to be sent first. Such letters were usually threatening in tone and somewhat uninformative, and strict and oppressively short periods for compliance were set. Now in some urgent cases, for example those involving applications for an injunction, an action can be begun without notice, but in the ordinary course of events, compliance with the protocols involves sending a detailed written demand setting out the case in full and providing the critical documents to be relied upon. In personal injury cases, a further copy must be provided for the insurer. A reasonable period of time must be given for a response. The defendant must in turn give a responsible reply along similar lines. It is expected that a genuine attempt to settle will be made at this stage; and if that is not possible, the defendant may protect his position by making what is called a Part 36 offer (see para **27.36**). Sanctions, including penalties involving legal costs, may follow an infringement of these requirements.

Starting proceedings

27.29   If it is not possible to settle the claim, the action may begin. This is by the presentation to the court of a claim form and, upon the payment of a fee, the issue of proceedings. This registers the case in court and is the operative date for the purposes of any relevant limitation period for the bringing of a valid claim.

Serving proceedings

27.30   The claim and a 'response pack', which is also prepared by the claimant or his solicitor and which contains the forms referred to below, must then be served, normally within 4 months, upon the defendant. Although service may be effected by the court, usually the claimant deals with this. Service is most typically undertaken by first-class post but can also be effected personally. Within 14 days, the defendant must deliver to the court an acknowledgement of service showing if he intends to defend the case or if he admits it in whole or in part.

Particulars of claim and defence

27.31   Either at the same time as serving the claim form or within 14 days from service of it, the claimant must serve a statement of case. This is done by the service of 'particulars of claim'. A defence and, where appropriate, a counterclaim are served 14 days thereafter. Further statements may be served later where amplification is necessary, and there is also provision for requests for the provision of information to be answered.

Track allocation

27.32   Once a defence has been filed, the court will send the parties an allocation questionnaire so that it may (on the basis of the information returned) allocate the case to one of three tracks. The small claims track is for claims of less than £5000. The fast track is for claims from £5000 to £10,000. Both are intended to provide a quick and uncomplicated process leading to an early result. The multi-track is for more complex cases.

Disclosure of documents

27.33   In cases allocated to the fast and the multi-track, there is an automatic obligation on the parties to prepare and serve a list of documents which are in their control on which they rely and also those which adversely affect their or another party's case, or support another party's case. This is called 'standard disclosure'. All documents have to be disclosed but may be divided into categories according to whether the parties are prepared to produce them for inspection, or claim privilege over them, or do not have them in their possession. (Privilege is, broadly, protection given to certain types of document, usually those prepared by a party's lawyer in the course of preparations for litigation; or for giving general legal advice.) Disclosure of documents may be subject to abuse, either by a failure to make a genuine attempt to reveal documents or by attempts to demand the production of documents that are not strictly necessary for the case but are presumed to be difficult to organise. For this reason, the courts are astute to ensure that the process should be conducted in a way that is fair and proportionate to what is involved in the action. Genuine and adequate efforts must be made to search for such documents, and more extensive disclosure may be ordered if appropriate.

Preparation of evidence

27.34   The parties are under an obligation before the trial to give full and open disclosure of all the evidence on which they propose to rely. This includes all the documents referred to in para **27.33**, and their statements of witnesses of fact. Where it is intended to rely on hearsay evidence, notice to that effect must also be given. In addition, their experts' reports must be disclosed. The courts are particularly concerned that expert evidence is properly monitored, so that such evidence is only called when necessary and in reasonable numbers. Usually, each party may call his or her own expert witness for any discipline, but in some cases such evidence is limited to one expert, who is appointed by the court.

Case management conference

27.35   As part of the court's supervisory process, a case management conference will usually be called to allow the court to take stock of any outstanding issues and to make directions and rulings appropriate to the proper conduct of the trial. In complex cases, there will be more than one such conference in the life of the action.

Part 36 offers and payments

27.36   A Part 36 (CPR 1998) offer is an offer to settle a claim by making or accepting a sum of money in settlement. It must satisfy certain specific requirements and therefore must be carefully drafted. A Part 36 payment is a payment into court of a sum of money in satisfaction of the claim. Except where made before the action is begun, an offer may be effective only if the claim is for relief other than a payment of money. Where the claim is for money, a payment into court should be made. The purpose of the procedure is to promote the reasonable settlement of claims. The sanction is that if the offer or payment is not accepted, the party in whose favour the offer or payment was made proceeds further with the case at risk for the costs thereafter. If he fails to obtain an order for more that the offer or payment, he is exposed to the risk of paying the whole or a substantial part of his opponent's costs incurred thereafter. A Part 36 offer may be made by either party.

Listing the case for trial

27.37 The courts' policy is to list cases for trial as soon as possible. This is done at the time of allocation in the case of small claims, and generally not later than 30 weeks after allocation in the case of the fast track. No time-limits apply to multi-track cases, but the position in such cases is still monitored, for example, at the case management conferences. In the case of the fast track and the multi-track, the court may either fix a date or give a 'window' within which the case is likely to come on for trial.

Trial

27.38 The trial is conducted usually by a single judge sitting in open court. The procedure is that cases are presented orally, usually by counsel but sometimes by solicitors if they have the relevant rights of audience in the higher courts, by reference to the documents disclosed and the testimony of the witnesses of fact and experts. Judgment may be given orally immediately after the trial, or at a later time in writing.

Costs

27.39 Costs may be awarded at different stages of the action. Usually, an order for costs is made for and against one of the parties for every occasion on which an attendance at court is made. In some cases, usually those where the application is short, the court may give an immediate assessment of costs, but in a complex application, and invariably at trial, the order is for costs to be assessed at a later stage. The usual rule as to the liability for costs is that the party who has succeeded on the application is entitled to be paid a proportion of his costs by the losing party, but the jurisdiction to award costs is discretionary and may vary with the circumstances.

27.40 The procedures referred to above are the most frequently invoked. In the space available, there is only room for a brief mention of other *special* procedures. One of the most important of these is an application for summary judgment. This is sought where the claimant or defendant contends that there is no triable issue on the case and, therefore, that a full trial is unnecessary. Such a case may be dealt with without trial and evidence is given in writing rather than orally. Another important procedure concerns claims for an injunction. Here, special rules apply that enable an injured party to claim immediate interim relief either by itself or ancillary to another claim, again on the basis of written evidence. It is invariably necessary in such cases to proceed thereafter to a full trial when a final result is determined. Other special procedures include applications for security for the costs of the litigation, and for an interim award of damages.

ARBITRATION

27.41   Arbitration is an alternative method of dispute resolution that largely avoids recourse to the courts. The object of arbitration is to enable the parties to have their dispute resolved in a binding and enforceable way by a tribunal of their own choice and pursuant to procedures to which they have expressly agreed. It is a popular means of dispute resolution where privacy is important or in areas that habitually involve specialist commercial customs and practices (for example, in shipping, commodity, insurance, commercial leases and partnership disputes). Historically, arbitrations in England have tended to follow the practices and procedures of litigation, with complex pleadings and discovery culminating in an oral hearing involving counsel. Owing to a number of factors, including the need to pay the fees of the arbitrator (which could be considerable), the fact that the arbitrator had fewer powers than a judge to enforce rulings against recalcitrant parties, and the comparative freedom of the parties to refer issues of procedure or substance to the courts over the head of the arbitrator, a system that was intended to be flexible, cost-effective and quick had become discredited as a less efficient and costlier surrogate of litigation. In response to this concern, the Arbitration Act 1996 was enacted. Arbitration is consensual – that is, except in certain limited cases when arbitration is imposed by statute, a party will only be able to instigate an arbitration if his opponent agrees. The agreement will either be entered into as part of a larger contract at the time of reaching an agreement on other matters, for example in a charterparty or a building contract, and before any dispute has actually arisen, or at the time when the dispute arises. The main features of modern arbitration under the new legislation are as follows.

The autonomy of the parties

27.42   Arbitration recognises the freedom of the parties to have their dispute resolved outside the courts of law if that is their wish. This involves the freedom to apply whatever procedures they choose, subject to the duty of the arbitrator to adopt procedures that will avoid unnecessary delay and expense.

The supportive role of the courts

27.43   The courts are now given a less interventionist role in arbitration and are confined to supporting the process of arbitration, if the process has broken down in any particular case. Appeals to the court from the decision of the arbitrator will be confined to important points of law where the arbitrator has made a serious mistake.

Flexibility of procedure

27.44 Litigation involves a prescribed procedure. In arbitration, there is no set procedure and the parties may adopt whatever rules they consider to be appropriate. Sometimes, they may choose to adopt the rules of one of the recognised arbitral bodies. In other cases, they may, for example, agree to dispense with all formality and have the dispute adjudicated without an oral hearing, or even on general principles of 'equity and fairness' rather than in accordance with the substantive law of the land.

Increased powers of the arbitrator

27.45 Under the new system, the arbitrator is given enhanced powers to compel compliance with interim orders and to make more far-reaching final orders such as injunctions and specific performance.

The advantages

27.46 The advantages of arbitration can be summarised as follows:

- *privacy:* an arbitration takes place in private and not in open court. This makes it suitable for disputes that concern confidential commercial matters that the parties do not want to be aired in public;
- *simplicity:* in many cases (for example, in disputes arising out of commodities markets), arbitration can be dealt with purely 'on paper' (ie a submission of essential contractual documents to an arbitrator who determines the dispute without hearing oral evidence). Other, more complex cases, can often be more protracted;
- *expense:* it is likely that an arbitration will be less costly and speedier than litigation;
- *specialisation:* an arbitrator is an adjudicator chosen by the parties rather than imposed by the court and may be selected because of knowledge and experience of the commercial transactions and issues; and
- *enforceability:* in some cases involving international disputes it is easier to enforce abroad the award of an arbitrator than a judgment of the court, owing to the sophisticated system of international enforcement treaties that apply to most arbitrations.

The disadvantages

27.47 A disadvantage of arbitration is that it is not possible to force parties other than those who have agreed to participate in the arbitration, and this makes the procedure inappropriate in cases where, in the same proceedings, a respondent wishes to seek redress from a stranger to the arbitration agreement.

As a result of the changes brought about by the new legislation, it may be expected that arbitration will be restored to the position it once occupied as a genuine and popular alternative to litigation.

ALTERNATIVE DISPUTE RESOLUTION

27.48   ADR has only recently emerged and become recognised in England as a useful technique for resolving disputes outside traditional litigation or arbitration methods. It has, however, been widely used in one form or another in other countries, particularly in the USA, and it is fast gaining ground in England as lawyers and their clients have embraced it as a means of achieving a cost-effective solution that promotes the clients' real objectives. ADR bears no real comparison to litigation or arbitration – its function is not to *impose* the resolution of a dispute on the parties, but to help them to agree a resolution between themselves.

27.49   The overriding purpose of ADR is to help parties who have been unable to settle their dispute by traditional negotiation to find an amicable solution without the need for (further) intervention by the courts. It may be seen as an alternative to litigation or arbitration in the sense that it may precede the commencement of proceedings. Alternatively, it may be seen as complementary to those processes by assisting the resolution of disputes once they have developed into legal action. These purposes are achieved by a variety of somewhat different but flexible means, the most typical of which is a structured meeting or series of meetings between the parties and a neutral mediator or adviser whose job it is to:

–   help each party conduct a realistic assessment of his or her opponent's case;
–   facilitate common-sense dialogue;
–   assist in solving problems or breaking deadlocks; and
–   encourage a settlement that is agreed as opposed to a resolution that is ultimately imposed by the court or arbitrator.

27.50   ADR is a wholly consensual process. ADR is generally conducted on a 'without prejudice' and confidential basis. In England, almost all ADR procedures can loosely be described as either 'mediation' or as 'mini-trials'. Mediation is by far the most common form of ADR in use in England. This involves a neutral mediator acting as a facilitator of settlement by a process of 'shuttle diplomacy' during a continuous series of meetings held over a number of days. Mini-trials are more formalised settlement conferences involving the abbreviated presentation of evidence by representatives of the parties to a panel usually consisting of one neutral member and one senior executive of each disputant who, ideally, has no detailed knowledge of the dispute. Mini-trials can be more appropriate than mediation in large commercial cases involving particularly difficult questions of fact or law.

27.51   ADR provides the following benefits that are usually not available with other methods of resolving disputes: cheaper, quicker, more flexible and more private. Apart from the inevitable fact that the process is not mandatory, there are few disadvantages to ADR. It is sometimes said that ADR involves an unfortunate show of 'weakness' and denotes lack of resolve to fight and the need to show one's hand. This may be true, up to a point; but if settlement can be achieved nevertheless, no harm has been done. If settlement cannot be achieved, images can be restored soon enough. Further, as has been shown, litigation itself is conducted on the basis of full disclosure, so whatever is revealed in ADR processes will usually have to be disclosed in court proceedings in any event.

REMEDIES

27.52   The following are the main awards that a court (or arbitrator) may make.

Damages

27.53   Damages are the pecuniary compensation paid by a defendant to a claimant to compensate, insofar as money can, for the wrong which the defendant has committed. The object of an award of damages is to give the claimant compensation for a loss or injury suffered. It is the principal and most frequently sought remedy.

Specific performance

27.54   In some cases, damages will not be adequate to compensate the claimant. When the subject matter of a contract has special value or unique features which make damages an inadequate remedy, the court may order a defendant to perform the contract rather than pay damages for its breach.

Rectification

27.55   The court may order that a contract that does not properly record the agreement between the parties should be rectified to reflect the true agreement.

Injunction

27.56   In certain circumstances, damages will not be adequate to compensate the claimant because he needs to restrain the defendant from starting or continuing a wrongful course of conduct or to force him to do certain things in the claimant's interest, and not merely to compensate the claimant for continuing losses. The court may, in certain circumstances and on conditions, grant an injunction to restrain the defendant from acting wrongfully or require him to do things in the claimant's interests. In many cases, a claim for an injunction is coupled with a claim for damages.

Declarations

27.57 In some cases, the claimant seeks to have rights determined by the court by means of a declaration. This may be coupled with a claim for damages or other forms of relief. This may be appropriate, for example, in cases involving rights over land or in respect of contracts or the interpretation of legal documents that will affect rights in the future.

Restitution and tracing orders

27.58 Where it is alleged that the defendant has acquired property of the claimant, for example, unlawfully or for no consideration and in circumstances where he has been unjustly enriched, the claimant is entitled to reclaim the property or an equivalent sum from the defendant. Such claims are often linked to a separate claim for a tracing order in which property of the claimant which has fallen into the hands of the defendant can be traced and recovered.

Possession of land

27.59 In an action under a lease or in respect of real property, the court can order that the land, or the right to possession of it, be returned to the claimant.

Action for an account

27.60 In certain cases, the court will order the defendant to provide to the claimant an account of profits arising from use or misuse of the claimant's property and to give to the claimant the money so accounted for. This frequently arises in cases involving breach of copyright or trade mark, where it is proved that a defendant is accountable to the claimant for earnings from the infringement.

Judicial review

27.61 In addition to those awards referred to earlier, the court may also quash unlawful decisions of public bodies (which may include HEIs – see Chapter 9), restrain them from acting unlawfully or order them to take certain steps (by a process known as 'judicial review').

ENFORCEMENT OF ORDERS

27.62 It is outside the scope of this chapter to describe in detail the ways in which orders of the court or arbitrators may be enforced. The principal means available include:

- insolvency proceedings;
- attachment of assets and bank accounts; and
- seizure of goods.

SAFEGUARDS FOR THE HEI

27.63 Litigation and arbitration in England are, by nature, hostile and involve contested evidence. Cases are frequently won or lost as much because of the weight and type of evidence adduced as because of their underlying strengths and weaknesses in law. It frequently happens that cases are lost before a dispute develops by making unguarded statements or writing ill-advised letters or documents, or even simply by a failure to realise that a dispute is likely to become serious and needs to be dealt with professionally. Disputes involving HEIs could possibly give rise to serious problems of this nature because of a relatively informal and unstructured student–tutor relationship, and a generally individualistic approach within organisations which are, in management terms, relatively unhierarchical (especially in some chartered HEIs). The following account sets out in summary some of the safeguards that can be taken at an early stage in litigation to prevent such mistakes from being made. The safeguards may also help with internal procedures of dispute resolution and disciplinary hearings.

Identifying the dispute

27.64 It often happens that a dispute becomes litigious without its having previously been considered to be genuine or serious – too relaxed an initial approach may cause difficulties later. The ability to recognise when a dispute may become litigious, apart from enabling the problem to be controlled, can give an immediate advantage. For example, an admission may be obtained on a point that might later be contested or the imprudent disclosure of documents may be provoked. Equally, notes of conversations can be made and records kept that may help later if someone's word is doubted. Realising that a problem may develop into a legal dispute will also alert those involved as to the potential damages and generate a more cautious and disciplined approach. It is only when the dispute has been identified that the basic precautions outlined below can be taken in order to ensure that nothing is done before lawyers are instructed which may make their job more difficult or prejudice the prospects of success in ensuing litigation.

Time-limits

27.65 One of the most important threshold issues in any contested action is the time within which the claim must be brought. Great care should be taken over such issues as sometimes it is not clear that a dispute has arisen and the other party may not voice tacit concerns, hoping the time-limits for claiming will pass unnoticed. Limitation periods, which are mainly governed by contract or statute, usually start to run, in contract cases, from the date when the contract is breached or, in the case of most other wrongful acts, from the date when loss or damage is suffered. In most cases, the relevant period is 6 years from the applicable starting date, but it may be longer or shorter depending on the circumstances and the precise nature of the claim. It is especially important to note that there are cases where untypically short limits are imposed (such as in contracts of employment or where a contract requires litigation or arbitration to be started within a shorter than usual time from the accrual of a cause of action or the arising of a dispute). If the remedy sought is the recovery of a debt or damages, the only timing issue will be the statutory or contractual date beyond which no claim is to be brought. If, however, the aim is to obtain certain remedies such as an injunction or specific performance of a contract, proceedings should be brought as soon as possible after the existence of the claim has become known. This is because if the court finds that the claimant has unduly delayed the issue of proceedings and that the opponent has been prejudiced as a result, the remedies may be refused solely on the basis of delay.

Effective delegation

27.66 Where there are a number of points of contact between the parties, consideration should be given to who should handle the case and who ought to conduct any negotiations. This may be particularly relevant for HEIs where disputes may arise, for example, between students and staff. In such cases, it should be made clear at the outset whether a member of staff who becomes involved in a dispute has authority to act on behalf of the institution and is equipped to make statements and representations on its behalf. A student, who will inevitably be regarded as being in a subordinate position, may claim to be entitled to rely on what is said by a member of the academic staff even where that person has no actual authority (see paras 5.19 *et seq*). It is generally wise to delegate the handling of a dispute to one person who (subject to reporting to whomever is appropriate) is in charge of deciding whether the individual most closely associated with the dispute or the one who has the closest relationships with the opponent's personnel should be responsible for negotiating a settlement. Those who are the most obvious individuals to negotiate a settlement may often be the best choices, but they may be so closely connected to the problem and the people involved that it will be difficult for them to negotiate effectively, or for continuing relationships or existing contacts to continue undamaged. Appointing an independent person may, therefore, be the most appropriate response. It may also be prudent to suggest that someone who might be regarded as being in a subordinate position should be independently advised or represented by another person. It would also be wise to ensure that discussions take place in the presence of an independent witness.

When to involve lawyers

27.67 If the dispute is limited to fact or if the chosen negotiator is experienced, the instruction of lawyers may be delayed. However, it may be considered expedient to instruct lawyers at once if legal issues are involved or if the opponent has instructed lawyers. This is particularly true in those areas where complex legal issues are involved and where time-limits are short.

Admissions and the 'without prejudice' rule

27.68 Where a dispute arises, it is important that no admissions are made during negotiations which the opponent might later exploit. Admissions on a point of law or fact may be admissible in later proceedings and could be damaging. To overcome this problem and to encourage parties to settle disputes, a general rule has been developed whereby it is not possible to use in evidence admissions made at meetings or in letters the purpose of which is to try to achieve a settlement of a dispute. It is important that all such meetings and communications are expressed to be 'without prejudice', in case the dispute is not settled. It should be noted that the mere use of the words 'without prejudice' at meetings or in correspondence will not automatically prevent admissions from being deployed in court. The rule only applies to a communication, the genuine purpose of which is to advance the settlement of a dispute. If in doubt, it is probably sensible to stipulate that all such negotiations are without prejudice, but beware of using the term loosely in any circumstances that may appear to have a legal effect. Meetings or communications that are intended to be part of a formal record should be 'open' (ie without prejudice).

Documents and discovery

27.69 Litigation in England is increasingly document-oriented and cases can be won or lost by documents that evidence material facts. It is therefore sensible to be cautious about what is put in writing at this (or, indeed, at any) stage of the process. An essential safeguard is to avoid the creation of documents that may be damaging and that may need to be shown to an opponent if proceedings are commenced at a later stage. Particular care should be taken of manuscript notes made on documents, whether originals or copies. If a manuscript is added to a letter or document, this would have to be disclosed and may then materially damage the case and prejudice a possible settlement. Equally, documents should not be destroyed or lost if they are likely to be required for litigation. It is, nevertheless, sensible to make a careful contemporaneous record of what is said and done in the course of a dispute or its attempted resolution so that any misleading evidence given later may be challenged.

THE FUTURE OF DISPUTE RESOLUTION

27.70   It is too early to form a considered view as to how the litigation process will respond to the Woolf reforms, and possibly also too early to assess the future of arbitration under the ERA 1996. Initially, there would seem to have been a downturn in the volume of litigation, but it is difficult to judge if that has been as a result of the intention that more disputes should be settled before litigation or arbitration begins, or of a shift in cultural or economic conditions. The conduct of litigation has certainly changed in response to the new rules, with their greater emphasis on speed and simplicity, early preparations, and the courts' more pronounced supervisory role. But it remains to be seen whether this will prove to be a long-term development. The fact that various divisions of the High Court and the specialist courts devised their own rules of practice almost immediately following the introduction of the CPR 1998 is hard to reconcile with the drive towards uniformity and certainty that underpins the CPR 1998.

27.71   Perhaps the most obvious benefit of the CPR 1998 has been the development of mediation as a means of reaching a settlement. Relatively few years ago, mediation was regarded with some suspicion, but now it is seen as a natural adjunct to the litigation process and one that is invoked with increasing frequency and success. This process is likely to continue, and will be as relevant to HEIs as to all other institutions.

Chapter 28

THE IMPACT OF EUROPEAN LAW

Derek Elsey and Joss Saunders

EDITORS' INTRODUCTION

§28.1 The aim of this chapter is to review the impact so far of European law on English law in relation to HEIs and to contemplate what *might* happen as European law evolves. Some of the relevant ground has been covered earlier. Other areas, not mentioned elsewhere, are covered in detail in this chapter – notably:

– the definition of EU nationals and their entitlement to UK Government financial support as students at UK HEIs;
– the residence rights of EU nationals (and their families) as students in UK HEIs;
– the recognition of qualifications within the EU;
– the EU public procurement rules; and
– the EU rules to regulate anti-competitive practices.

§28.2 The chapter ends by predicting that the development of European law will continue to have a profound effect on English law and hence our HEIs.[1] The 1996 ruling of the European Court on the 48-hour working week (leading to the Working Time Regulations 1998) may prove significant if AUT and NATFHE surveys of the long working hours of HEI academics and administrators are to be believed. Similarly, the experimentation with 2-year courses needs to be considered in the context of the EU arrangements for the mutual recognition of degrees and qualifications which envisage post-secondary courses of *at least* 3 years in duration: it has to be remembered that the English and Welsh 3-year single honours degree is not only unusually specialised by international comparison, but also unusually short, even compared to the 4-year norm in Scotland. This chapter also addresses the issue of EU-driven changes in competition law and their possible inpact on HE.

§28.3 Moreover, the big impact on UK HEIs will surely be the move towards the European Higher Education Area by 2010, as the Bologna (1999) and Prague (2001) Declarations of, as it were, good intent become the internationalisation or at least Europeanisation of HE, including perhaps a Europe-wide version of QAA: the 'Euro-degree' to match the 'Euro-sausage'. Not, happily,

---

1 For example, *R v HM Treasury ex parte University of Cambridge* Case (C-380/98) [2000] CMLR 1359, [2000] All ER (EC) 920, [2001] CEC 30, [2000] 1 WLR 2514, has recently clarified when a university is a public body for purposes of the public procurement directives. See also *Agorà Srl v Ente Autonoma Fiera Internazionale di Milano* (C-223/99); *Excelsior Snc de Pedrotti Bruna and C v Ente Autonoma Fiera Internazionale di Milano* (C-260/99) [2001] TLR 412, concerning the definition of a body governed by public law as *not* including an entity having an industrial or commercial character. At the time of going to press, there is awaited a European Court judgment on whether VAT should be imposed on the university research commissioned by 'eligible' bodies which is currently VAT exempt.

a process of potentially undue bureaucratisation that the world's most successful HE system has to contend with, despite the USA also being a federal structure (Siedentop (2000)).

INTRODUCTION

28.1   According to Lord Denning in *Bulmer (HP) v Bollinger (J) SA:*[1]

'When we come to matters with a European element, the Treaty is like an incoming tide. It flows into the estuaries and up the rivers. It cannot be held back.'

28.2   The EU is probably the most highly developed example in the modern world of political and economic integration amongst independent nations. Its 15 Member States occupy most of the land mass of Western Europe and by the end of the decade it is likely to encompass much of Central Europe. Its current population now greatly exceeds that of the USA and Japan, and its combined gross domestic product (GDP) is now approaching that of the USA. The Treaty of Rome 1957 contained no express reference to education. The first major revision of the Treaty by the Single European Act 1986 introduced new provisions on social policy and on research, but still contained no express reference to education. Only in 1992, in the Treaty of European Union at Maastricht, was education included as one of the policies of the Community, in order to help it meet its newly amended and extended objectives. Article 3(q) provides that the activities of the EU shall include a 'contribution to education and training of quality'. New Arts 149 and 150 on education, vocational training and youth were introduced by the Treaty on European Union 1992 (The Maastricht Treaty). Article 149 relates to the development of quality education by encouraging co-operation between Member States and the development of a European dimension in education, particularly through language teaching, mobility of students and teachers, recognition of study abroad, youth exchanges and distance learning; while Art 150 relates to vocational training and the development of a vocational training policy.

28.3   Even before the Maastricht Treaty, HEIs were affected by the growing body of European law in their capacity as employers, providers of services, purchasers, managers of a property portfolio, and in many other aspects of their activities both in the public sector and in their business dealings. Education has become a key area of EU activity. HEIs are affected by rules governing both public and private institutions. The rules are found partly in legislation and partly in case-law, particularly the decisions of the ECJ in Luxembourg. The rules affect public procurement, employment law, IP licensing, data protection, financial services, research and development agreements and other joint ventures, health and safety at work, the recognition of degrees in Europe, environmental issues, the employment and residence of

---

1   [1974] Ch 401, [1974] 3 WLR 202.

both academics and students, and the burgeoning programmes for research grants and international educational links.

28.4 European law applies to the Member States of the EU and is not to be confused with the rules of the Council of Europe in the European Convention on Human Rights, which is a measure of the Council of Europe, not of the EU, although that too has an impact on HEIs and will have an increasing impact as a result of the direct application of Convention rights into UK law by the coming into force of the HRA 1998 in October 2000. Much European law also involves other States. Norway and Iceland are partners of the EU through the EEA Agreement, which came into effect on 1 January 1994. As is seen at airports, special immigration rules apply. Less visible, but equally important, are the EEA rules on public procurement and employment.

28.5 The EU also has Association Agreements with a number of countries, and such agreements can give rise to enforceable rights by nationals of those countries when in the UK and when in other Member States. Thus, for example, some EU rules on free movement can be relied upon by Turkish nationals. There are also Association Agreements in place with many of the countries of Central and Eastern Europe. While such agreements do not give rise to the same generous treatment of nationals, they do contain important rights and obligations. Furthermore, there are currently discussions between the EU and the 'first phase' applicants from Central and Eastern Europe (the Czech Republic, Estonia, Hungary, Poland, Slovenia) and with Cyprus, which are intended to facilitate their entry in about 2002 provided that they can demonstrate democratic and economic credentials.

28.6 In this chapter, three categories of people are referred to:

- EU nationals;
- EEA nationals, which expression includes EU nationals and nationals of Norway and Iceland; and
- nationals of other States who have enforceable rights under certain EU Treaties. As this category is subject to ongoing change, the up-to-date position should always be checked.

THE MAIN LAWS

Articles, Regulations and Directives

28.7 The foundations of European law are contained in the Treaty of Rome 1957, the Single European Act 1986, the Treaty of European Union 1992 (Maastricht Treaty) (which came into force on 1 November 1993), and the Treaty of Amsterdam 1997 which amended, repealed and renumbered many of the articles in the previous Treaties and under which a consolidated version of the Treaty Establishing the European Community 1997 was produced.

Articles

28.8   References to articles usually means the clauses of the European Treaty or clauses of Regulations or Directives. Practical expression of the principles laid down in the articles of the European Treaty is largely contained in Regulations or Directives (issued by the European Council), and in Decisions of the European Commission in Brussels and judgments of the ECJ. The most significant articles for HEIs are:

– Art 12 (which prohibits discrimination on the grounds of nationality);
– Arts 23–31 (which require free movement of goods);
– Arts 39–42 (which require free movement of persons);
– Arts 43–48 (which require freedom of establishment);
– Art 49 (which requires free movement of services);
– Arts 81 and 82 (which ban certain anti-competitive practices); and
– Arts 149 and 150 (on education, vocational training and youth).

Regulations

28.9   These are binding and directly applicable in all Member States of the EU. Assuming they are sufficiently clear and unconditional, the Regulations themselves create direct legal rights and obligations for individuals and companies, which are specifically effective from the date of issue and do not need prior parliamentary approval. Such Regulations have 'direct effect' and override any conflicting provisions in English law. They are enforceable in the English courts and tribunals.

Directives

28.10   These are binding on the Member States of the EU as regards the result to be achieved (usually expressed in great detail) but leave it to each country to implement the directive by bringing into force national legislation (often by statutory instrument) within the time period allowed, which is often 2 years from the date the directive is made. Since a directive is addressed to Member Governments, it was thought not to create directly effective rights which can be enforced against private persons or companies, but it can be enforced by the Commission against the country if the date set for implementation passes without it being implemented by that country. Moreover, as a result of ECJ case-law, directives may have legal effect if they have not been implemented by the deadline date, or if they have been implemented incorrectly. In some cases, the governments of EU Member States can be sued by individuals or organisations who have suffered as a result of non or faulty implementation – for example, the Joined Cases C-6 and C-9/90 *Francovich and Bonifaci v Republic of Italy*.[1]

---

1   [1991] ECR I–5357, [1993] 2 CMLR 66, ECJ.

Discussions, Recommendations and Opinions

28.11   Commission Decisions are binding on the organisations to whom they are addressed, while Recommendations and Opinions are not legally binding but may have some persuasive legal effect.

European Union or the European Community

28.12   Since most of the law affecting businesses is based on the provisions of the Treaty of Rome 1957, which have been gathered into a consolidated version following the Treaty of Amsterdam 1997, it is correct to continue to refer in that connection to European Community law. Law arising from the provisions of the Maastricht Treaty 1992, relating to education, common foreign security policy and co-operation in justice and home affairs, is properly called EU law, but both are referred to in this chapter as forming part of European law.

PUBLIC PROCUREMENT

28.13   A frequently quoted estimate is that the public sector in the EU generates about 14 per cent of the EU's GDP. Although not all of this vast amount is amenable to public procurement procedures, the European Commission estimates that a total of between 240 and 340 billion Euros of public sector annual purchasing power can be opened to competition. This is a formidable amount of purchasing power. As most of it in the past was purchased domestically, it had shut out potential cross-border providers. The 'public procurement' directives are intended to open up this public spending to wider tendering competition. For the purposes of European law, public procurement means the procurement by central, regional and local government, other bodies governed by public law, and utilities of goods, construction works (works) and services. These bodies are called 'contracting authorities' in the directives.[1] In the UK, these directives have been implemented by secondary legislation.[2]

Do the public procurement directives and regulations apply to HEIs?

28.14   There have been doubts expressed as to whether the public procurement directives and regulations apply to HEIs. It is necessary to refer to Directive 93/37, the relevant part of which is set out as follows:

---

1   Council Directive (EC) 92/50, as amended (Public Service Contracts); Council Directive (EC) 93/96, as amended (Public Supply Contracts); Council Directive (EC) 93/97, as amended (Public Works Contracts).
2   Public Works Contracts Regulations 1991, as amended, SI 1991/2680; Public Services Contracts Regulations 1993, as amended, SI 1993/3228; and Public Supply Contracts Regulations 1995, as amended, SI 1995/201.

'*contracting authorities* shall be the State, regional or local authorities, bodies governed by public law, associations formed by one or several of such authorities or bodies governed by public law; *a body governed by public law* means any body:

– established for the specific purpose of meeting needs in the general interest, not having an industrial or commercial character, and
– having legal personality, and
– financed, for the most part, by the State, or regional or local authorities, or other bodies governed by public law, or subject to management supervision by those bodies, or having an administrative, managerial or supervisory board, more than half of whose members are appointed by the State, regional or local authorities or by other bodies governed by public law.'

28.15 In *EC Commission v Spain (Madrid University)*,[1] the European Commission instituted proceedings in response to the award by the University of Madrid of a works contract without advertising it in the OJ. The Spanish Government argued that it was exempt because of conditions of 'extreme urgency'. This was the need to complete the work before the start of the next academic year. The ECJ rejected this argument, finding that the exemption should be interpreted strictly and applied only where there was 'extreme urgency brought about by events unforeseen by the contracting authority'. Student numbers had been increasing steadily over a period of years and the influx due at the start of the next academic year was neither unforeseeable nor would it cause any greater overcrowding than in previous years. In addition, the ECJ considered that, had the accelerated time-limits provided for in the directive been applied, there would have been sufficient time (around 6 weeks) to advertise the contract and organise a proper selection procedure, while still achieving completion of the work before the start of the academic year. The Opinion of Advocate-General Lenz in that case stated that a 'State University, even if independent from an organisational point of view, is as a rule a State Institution'. He added that 'No doubts have been raised in the course of the action, either as to the status of the University as a legal person governed by public law, or as to the applicability of the Directive'. The Court found that Spain had not complied with the public procurement rules. Moreover, Annex 1 to Directive 93/37 includes as one of the categories to which public procurement rules apply: 'universities and polytechnics, maintained schools and colleges, Research Councils'.

28.16 In *R v HM Treasury ex parte University of Cambridge*,[2] the ECJ held, however, that, whether an HEI is subject to the public procurement regulations crucially depends on more than half of its annual income being publicly financed. Public finance includes HEFCE 'block grants', awards or grants paid by one or more contracting authorities (for example, the Research Councils) for the support of research, student tuition fees paid by the Student Loans Company or local education authorities directly to HEIs; but it did not include endowment income nor payments made in the context of contracts for services such as research, consultancy or the organisation of conferences, nor students personally paying tuition fees. Therefore, the decision as to whether an HEI is a

1   (Case 24/91) [1992] ECR I–1989, [1994] 2 CMLR 621.
2   (Case C-380/98) [2000] 1 WLR 2514.

'contracting authority' must be made annually and the budgetary year in which the procurement procedure commences is the appropriate period for calculating the way in which the HEI is financed so that the calculation must be made on the basis of the figures which are available at the beginning of that budgetary year, even if they are provisional. An HEI which constitutes a 'contracting authority' when the procurement procedure commences, remains subject to the requirements of the directives and regulations until the procedure is completed. Under this decision, therefore, most UK HEIs will be 'contracting authorities' subject to the directives and regulations, but some will have to carry out the annual calculation indicated above to determine whether they are a 'contracting authority' in a given year. A few HEIs (including most Oxbridge colleges) will never exceed the 50 per cent public funding test and hence might be able to ignore the public procurement rules.

28.17 The decision of the ECJ is, however, subject to criticism in that it signally failed to address the issue of the second limb of the third indent of Directive 93/97: ie whether a UK HEI was: (1) 'subject to management supervision by the state, regional or local authorities or other bodies governed by public law'; or (2) 'having an administrative, management or supervisory board more than half of whose members are appointed by [the above bodies]'. The second part of this formulation is a matter of arithmetic (ie if the governing body of an HEI has a majority of members appointed by these bodies it would be a 'contracting authority', but the first part relating to 'management supervision' by the State is more problematic. Whether this could be said to extend to, for example, the HEFC's supervision of HEIs is debatable. HEIs are increasingly monitored and to some extent 'controlled' by the HEFC, but whether this monitoring and control could be said to amount to management supervision by the State or its emanations is ultimately a question for the ECJ to resolve. There is currently no ECJ case-law on this issue, but in *Gebroeders Beentjes BV v The Netherlands*,[1] the Court, in holding that the Public Works Directive applied to a land consolidation committee, said that the function of the body was of greater significance than its form. This case does not appear to have been considered in the *Cambridge* case and it is open for the ECJ to take this line in a later case. Furthermore, if the UK Government were to consider that, as a matter of good practice or policy, all UK HEIs should comply with the UK public procurement regulations (notwithstanding that they may not be 'contracting authorities' for the purposes of the EU directives), then the government could pass legislation to make compliance mandatory. Given its current priorities, the government is unlikely to do so in the short term.

Thresholds

28.18 The directives (and resultant UK regulations) only apply to procurements above certain threshold values quoted in Euros. For this purpose only, an exchange rate is fixed every 2 years, so that money market fluctuations do

---

1   (Case 31/87) [1990] 1 CMLR 287.

not bring contracting authorities arbitrarily in and out of the net. Until January 2002, the sterling currency conversions for the thresholds are set out below:

Currency conversions for the thresholds of contracts (to 31 January 2002)

Public Works contracts	5 million Euros	£3,370,000
Public Services contracts	200,000 Euros	£134,800
Public Supply contracts	200,000 Euros	£134,800

28.19   The aim of the legislation is to harmonise all national public procurement rules and to increase transparency of procedures and practices. It introduces a minimum body of common rules for contracts above the defined threshold. The rules set down a detailed code of strict procedures which apply from the time when contracting authorities start to consider buying in goods, works or services. These procedures continue to apply until after the contract is awarded. There are many types of action which can deliberately or unwittingly contribute to the infringement of the rules – such as the artificial fragmentation of what is, effectively, one big contract into several small ones so that individual contracts fall below the threshold, the failure to provide full information to potential tenderers, and the use of discriminatory terms in contracts. An example of the latter might be the specification of products of a specific make, where this is not permitted under a derogation or dispensation.

28.20   There may be a need to aggregate two or more connected contracts for threshold purposes. The aggregation of works contracts does not apply, however, if the value of each connected contract (net of VAT) is less than 1 million Euros (which, at the time of writing, equals £674,000), provided that the total estimated value of these contracts worth less than 1 million Euros does not exceed 20 per cent of the total estimated value of all the contracts relating to those services. With public supply contracts (subject to one exception where there is a single requirement for goods and it is proposed to enter into a number of contracts to fulfil that requirement), the estimated value of each must be aggregated for the purpose of establishing whether the contracts must be dealt with under the Public Supply Contracts Regulations (ie there is no lower limit on each contract). Similar aggregation rules apply if goods are to be acquired over a period of time, and there are special rules for calculating the estimated value of such contracts by reference to the aggregate value of consideration given during the preceding period of 12 months taking into account expected changes in the quantity and cost of the goods. The exception to the above is where both the goods are to be acquired for the sole purposes of a discrete operational unit within the organisation and also the decision whether to purchase or hire the goods has been devolved to such a unit independently of any other part of the contracting authority in respect of those goods. In each case (works, services and supplies), attempts to evade the regulations by splitting up contracts is prohibited.

28.21   The technical specifications must be non-discriminatory and refer to European standards whenever possible. They should be defined by reference to:

–   national standards implementing European standards; or

- European technical approvals; or
- common technical specifications; *unless*
    - (a) such standards, etc do not exist; or
    - (b) these standards would oblige the contracting authority to use products or materials incompatible with equipment already in use or would entail disproportionate costs or disproportionate technical difficulties; or
    - (c) the project is genuinely innovative and common standards, etc would not be appropriate; or
    - (d) in the case of services and supplies contracts only, special rules (EC Directive 86/361 and Council Directive 87/95/EEC relating to information technology and telecommunications) apply in relation to telecommunications equipment.

Third party claims and complaints

28.22 A complaint could be made to the national courts by disgruntled would-be tenderers in respect of 'unlawful decisions' taken by contracting authorities. Failure to comply with the procedures could lead to a claim for damages or to prevent the tendering process from continuing. After a contract has been awarded, the courts cannot cancel the contract but may award damages. Particular problem areas are:

- which set of regulations apply (supplies, works or services);
- which thresholds apply and whether there is a need to aggregate contracts;
- filing the correct notices in the OJ, at the right time and in the right form;
- using the correct contract award procedure (there are several), and complying with specific time-limits;
- potential provider appraisal (rejection of a potential provider for unpermitted reasons);
- tender appraisal (rejection of the tender for unpermitted reasons – the usual criterion will be either the 'lowest price' or 'economically the most advantageous' at the choice of the contracting authority);
- technical specifications being used which may be technically accurate, but which are phrased in a way contrary to the procurement rules;
- whether the open, restricted or negotiated procedure may be used to award the contract.

If a contracting authority makes a mistake in any of the required procedures, it can lay itself open to considerable difficulties, including claims for damages by aggrieved potential tenderers.

Filing procedures

28.23 Public Notices for advertising contracts (maximum 650 words) need to be placed in the OJ. The address is: The Official Journal, Office for Official Publications of the European Communities, 2 Rue Mercier, L-2985

Luxembourg. Fax (from UK) 00 352 29 29 44 637 (email: idea@opoce.cec.eu.int). There is no fee payable for the insertion, and it is sufficient to file it in English. The European Commission arranges for translation into the Community languages as appropriate, free of charge. The Notice may be faxed through but must be followed up by a hard-copy letter. The OJ is obliged to publish Notices within 12 days of the date of despatch of the Notice and to endeavour to publish Notices within 5 days of the date of despatch if requested to do so under the accelerated procedure, if sent by telex, fax or e-mail.

The open procedure
28.24 Under this procedure, the contact is advertised in the OJ and potential tenderers request the contract documents, which are sent with an invitation to tender. Upon receipt of tenders, any late tenders, those which do not comply with the requirements of the contract documents and those which are from unsuitable tenderers as prescribed in the relevant regulations and directives can be excluded. The contract is then awarded, without negotiation, in accordance with the award criteria (either lowest price or most economically advantageous tender).

Restricted procedure
28.25 Under this procedure, the open procedure is varied so that the contract advertisement requests applications to take part in the procedure. From these are selected a restricted number of not fewer than five (or all the candidates if five or fewer apply) or not more than 20 who will be invited to tender. The number must be sufficient to ensure genuine competition. Selection must be undertaken in accordance with the selection criteria and evidence of suitability provided by the candidates.

Negotiated procedure
28.26 This involves consultation and negotiation with one or more of the tenderers as to the terms of the contract. All other aspects of the restricted procedure or the open procedure (as the case may be) apply. The negotiated procedure can be used only in certain restricted circumstances, such as receipt of irregular tenders in response to an open or restricted procedure, or, in exceptional cases, where the nature of the works/supply/services does not permit prior overall pricing. In addition, in the case of intellectual services and financial services, the negotiated procedure may be used if the contract specifications cannot be established with sufficient precision to permit the award of the contract by means of the open or restricted procedure.

Public works contracts
28.27 The relevant directive is Directive 93/37,[1] which applies to public contracts for construction or civil engineering works of 5 million Euros or

---

1   SI 1991/2680 as amended by SI 1992/3279, SI 1995/201 and SI 2000/2009.

more. It also includes 'design and build' contracts. Tenders must be advertised in the OJ and strict time-limits for the publication and provision of bid documents must be specified and observed. Contracts may be awarded by open or restricted procedures, or by negotiated procedures in certain limited circumstances. Even projects below the 5 million Euros threshold must avoid matters such as a specification which indirectly discriminates. By way of example, an HEI wishes to embark upon a substantial building project, which is likely to cost about £4 million. The HEI's architects have suggested that buildings should be roofed in 'Welsh slate', as in keeping with the other roofs in the neighbourhood, but the HEI is aghast to hear that the plans should be offered to prospective tenderers with a more neutral description of the roof material. It is concerned that the required advertising procedures that it must embark upon will delay and interrupt the project itself, but that its failure to comply may lead to a withholding of funds from government. It is aware that there is on the market slate fairly similar in appearance to 'Welsh slate', but it would prefer to stipulate if possible the 'real thing'. Thus, the HEI is not allowed to put in technical specifications which refer to goods of a specific make, source, or to a particular process, and which have the effect of favouring or eliminating particular goods or contractors. This includes references to patents, trade marks, etc. If, however, the goods cannot otherwise be described by sufficiently precise and intelligible technical specifications, is it possible to use the terms otherwise banned, provided the references to such items are accompanied by the words 'or equivalent' and if that is justified because of the subject matter of the contract. There is, unfortunately, no clarification as to what an acceptable justification might be. Where 'or equivalent' is used, the HEI ought, therefore, to make it clear that it is prepared to take into account any evidence the tenderer wishes to adduce that the goods are equivalent to the named type.

Public supply contracts

28.28 Directive 93/96 relates to basic transparency, non-discriminatory technical specifications and collection of information about awards. The rules on advertising, contractual selection, contract award and time-limits, etc, do not apply to residuary services. The categorisation of services as a residuary services in Annex B of the Directive is currently subject to review. If an HEI wishes to appoint external maintenance contractors to maintain all its buildings and the fee level comes above the threshold, the contract must be put out to tender in the OJ in accordance with the relevant procedure. Employment of in-house staff to perform such services will avoid the regime which applies to contracts for the purchase, renting, leasing or hire purchase of goods by contracting authorities of 200,000 Euros or more. If an HEI has a recurrent need, for example, for meat supplies, and enters into a series of supply contracts at different times, then it should project the next 12 months' expenditure on goods of that type to ascertain whether the threshold of 200,000 Euros is exceeded. If it is, then the prescribed tendering procedure must be followed. Contracts in relation to public supplies must, as a rule, be put out to competitive tender. In other words, tendering is by an open procedure. Recourse to restricted (with pre-selection) or negotiated (with pre-selection and negotiated terms) procedures must be justified by a written statement. The UK regulations require a contracting authority which has used the negotiated procedure to submit a report to the Treasury. Finally, obligations are imposed on contracting authorities to publish, not later than 48 days after the award of a contract, basic information on the contracts which have been awarded.

Public services contracts

28.29 The relevant directives are Directive 92/50[1] and Directive 93/36,[2] which applies to priority services (part A services in the UK regulations) which include maintenance and repair services, financial services, computer and related services, insurance, data processing, accounting, market research, advertising, and architecture. Tenders for these contracts must be advertised in the OJ in accordance with the relevant procedure. The threshold is 200,000 Euros. Services such as contracts for legal services, and contracts for educational and vocational services (classified as residual services – part B services in the UK regulations) should be awarded in accordance with the rules.

Government Procurement Agreement 1994 (GPA)

28.30 In parallel with the conclusion of the Uruguay Round, on 15 April 1994 a new GPA was signed in Marrakesh, and came into force on 1 January 1996. The World Trade Organisation (WTO), the new institutional basis of the General Agreement on Tariffs and Trade (GATT), will encompass not only GATT itself but also all agreements and arrangements concluded under its auspices, such as the GPA. The new WTO GPA applies to the 15 EU Member States and to many other countries, including the USA, Japan and Canada. It is open to other governments to negotiate their accession. The agreement follows closely the lines of the EU public procurement regime and covers purchases of supplies, works and services by public bodies. It imports obligations not to discriminate against goods, works or supplies from non-EU States which are signatories to the GPA and it provides remedies for aggrieved suppliers. However, the agreement only applies to a signatory State when it guarantees mutual reciprocity with access to similar sectors between each signatory State. The thresholds are similar to EU thresholds and compliance with the EU regime will, generally, ensure compliance with the GPA. The Government is in the process of amending the current UK regulations to include a clear statement of the obligations of contracting authorities under the GPA.

---

1   SI 1993/3228 as amended by SI 2000/2006.
2   SI 1995/201 as amended by SI 2000/2009.

FEES AND AWARDS

28.31   Educational establishments and award-giving bodies have for many years distinguished in the level of fees charged, and the eligibility for awards, between those students who have a specified connection with the UK and those who do not. Students with the UK connection have often been referred to as 'home students', while those lacking the connection are referred to as 'overseas students'. We will see that 'home students' can include foreign nationals, both from within the EU and from elsewhere, provided they have a 'relevant connection'.

'Home' fees and fees awards

28.32   Educational establishments are *prima facie* entitled to charge higher fees to students who do not have a relevant connection with the UK. Local education authorities, research councils and other specified award-giving institutions are entitled to adopt criteria for eligibility based on the specified connection with the UK (and in the case of awards by the research councils and other institutions the required connection may be with Great Britain). The rules are found in the Education (Fees and Awards) Regulations 1997[1] and in the Education (Student Support) Regulations 2000.[2] The 'relevant connection' is that the student must have been:

–   ordinarily resident in the UK throughout the 3 years preceding 1 September, 1 January, 1 April or 1 July closest to the beginning of the first term of the student's course; and
–   not resident wholly or mainly for the purpose of receiving full-time education.

Such a provision on its own would offend against Art 12 of the European Treaty, so consequently there are a number of other categories of students who are eligible for the lower 'home' fees, and grants for fees but not for living expenses. To be an 'eligible student' the student must be:

–   a national of a Member State (or the child of such a national, including stepchildren and adoptees) who has been ordinarily resident within the EEA for the same 3-year period and was not so resident for any part of that period wholly or mainly for the purpose of receiving full-time education;
–   a person not ordinarily resident in the UK or an EU national (or child of such a national) who was not ordinarily resident in the EEA only because he was temporarily employed outside the UK (or in the case of an EU national employed outside the EEA), or because the student's spouse or parent was temporarily employed outside the UK or the EEA. A parent working abroad on a short, fixed-term contract will be temporarily away

---

1   SI 1997/1972 as amended by SI 1998/1965.
2   SI 2000/1121.

from the UK, as will somebody sent to work abroad from their UK-based company HQ: the problem comes when parents go to live and work in another country for a foreign employer, and even if they retain in the UK 'a family home' for holidays;[1] and, similarly, a Coventry University student was defined as 'overseas', her British father being a policeman in Hong Kong where the student had been born and educated prior to coming to the UK for HE;[2]

–   a person who is in the UK as an EEA migrant worker who has throughout the 3-year period been ordinarily resident within the EEA and was not resident there wholly or mainly for the purpose of receiving full-time education;

–   an EEA national migrant worker who is not ordinarily resident for the 3-year period only because he, or his spouse or parent, was temporarily employed elsewhere; or

–   a refugee (or spouse or child of a refugee) who is ordinarily resident in the UK and its various Islands (as defined) on the first day of the first academic year of the course.

28.33   In addition to the above 'categories of eligibility', students who are admitted to a course in pursuance of arrangements with an institution outside the UK for the exchange of students on a fully reciprocal basis may qualify for 'home fees'. The test of 'ordinary residence' in the UK means that the citizenship of the student is irrelevant. A British citizen who was resident for 2 years in, say, the US and then returned to the UK to study could be treated as liable to pay overseas fees whereas a French citizen working in Germany for a couple of years and then coming to the UK to study would be treated as eligible for home fees. Members of the UK Armed Forces are treated as being temporarily employed abroad for any period during which they serve outside the UK. 'Ordinary residence' has not been defined in statute or regulation but has been considered by the courts and interpreted to mean the place where a person is living for settled purposes as part of the regular order of his or her life.[3] Ordinary residence must not be equated simply with physical presence, because it is possible to retain ordinary residence throughout the period of a temporary absence from a place. Indeed, it is possible to be 'ordinarily resident' in two places (or even more) at the same time.[4]

Financial support

28.34   Following the implementation of the Teaching and Higher Education Act 1998, mandatory maintenance awards have been phased out and replaced

1   *R v Hereford and Worcester County Council ex parte Wimbourne* (1983) 82 LGR 251.
2   *Queen on the application of Mitchell v Coventry University and the Secretary of State for Education and Employment* [2001] ELR 594–606: not against the ECHR for UK citizens to be charged overseas fees. See also Rogerson (2000). See also concerning definitions of 'ordinary resident': *Nessa v Chief Adjudication Officer* [1999] 4 All ER 677, HL; *University College London v Newman* (1986) *The Times*, January 8, CA.
3   *Shah v Barnet London Borough Council* [1983] 2 AC 309, HL, and *Kent v University College London* (1992) 156 LGR 1003, CA.
4   *R v Nottinghamshire County Council ex parte Jain* [1989] COD 442; (1989) *The Independent*, January 23 [1990] CLY 1759.

with a system of means-tested grants and student loans, except in Scotland where the Scottish Parliament has provided for allowances to be paid to eligible students who are ordinarily resident in Scotland and has removed the requirement for Scottish HEIs to charge mandatory fees to eligible students. Under the Teaching and Higher Education Act 1998 and the Education (Student Support) Regulations 2000[1] made pursuant to it, means-tested grants are available to cover the compulsory 'home fees' which non-Scottish UK HEIs are required to charge to all eligible students; means-tested grants are also available to cover living expenses of specific categories of eligible students (such as disabled students, students who have left care and students with dependants); and student loans are automatically made available to all eligible students aged below 50 on the last day of the first academic year of the course (there are provisions which may enable eligible students who are between 50 and 55 to receive student loans).

28.35   In accordance with its obligations under Art 12 of the Treaty of Rome, an EU national or the child of an EU national who has been ordinarily resident in the EEA for the 3-year period referred to above, and was not so resident wholly or mainly for the purposes of receiving full-time education, may be eligible to receive a means-tested grant in respect of tuition fees (if he satisfies the other conditions), but is not eligible to receive a grant or student loan to cover his living costs. This is because these grants/loans in respect of living costs still fall outside EU competence, being a matter of 'educational and social policy' for the nationals of the particular Member State alone. This exception, however, only relates to EU nationals (and their children) who do not fall into any other category of eligibility as described above. Students who fall into any of these categories will be eligible to receive the special grants and loans in respect of living costs if they can satisfy the other conditions which apply. This includes EEA migrant workers and their spouses and children.

FREE MOVEMENT OF ACADEMIC STAFF AND STUDENTS

28.36   Articles 39 and 43 of the Treaty of Rome 1957 are relevant to the rights of entry and residence in the UK of academics and students who are EEA nationals and the families of EEA nationals whatever their nationality. The rights of free movement and residence possessed by students, academics and their families are found in the Treaty's directives and regulations which provide for free movement for:

- workers;
- the self-employed;
- providers and recipients of services;
- students; and
- members of the families of any of these.

---

1   SI 2000/1121.

28.37   Employees and potential employees have the right to enter the UK and remain in order to seek and take up employment. EEA students have the right to enter the UK and remain in order to pursue their studies. Both employees and students can be accompanied or joined by their families. Their position in England and Wales is governed by the Immigration (European Economic Area) Order 1994, as amended by the Immigration (European Economic Area) (Amendment) Order 1997.[1] This is designed to reflect the rights of free movement of workers, students and others found in the directives and regulations.

28.38   The Immigration (European Economic Area) Order 1994 provides that an EEA national shall be admitted to the UK on production of either a valid national identity card or passport issued by an EEA State. It provides also for the admission of non-EEA members of the family. Except in the case of students, family members are defined in the order as the EEA national's spouse, a descendant of the EEA national or the spouse who is aged under 21 years or is their dependant, or a dependent relative in the ascending line of the EEA national or the spouse. Regulation 1612/68 does, however, go further and, with Directive 68/360, requires Member States to facilitate the admission of any member of the family not falling within the definition above, if dependent on the EEA national or living under the same roof in the country from which they have come. A more distant family member would, therefore, have to invoke the Regulation in preference to the imperfect Immigration (European Economic Area) Order 1994, which provides that only the spouse and dependent children of a student are his family members. It mirrors, therefore, the more limited family rights contained in Directive 93/96. The non-EEA family members seeking to enter the UK to reside with the EEA national must first obtain an 'EEA Family Permit' which is a type of visa issued, free of charge, by the British Embassies and High Commissions Overseas.

28.39   The Immigration (European Economic Area) Order 1994 further provides that when the EEA national has been admitted, he shall be entitled to reside in the UK for so long as he remains a 'qualified person'. The definition of a 'qualified person' is:

–   a worker;
–   a self-employed person;
–   a provider or a recipient of services; or
–   a student enrolled at a recognised educational establishment in the UK for the principal purpose of following vocational training.

28.40   A qualified person is entitled to be issued a residence permit by the Home Office Immigration Department as proof of his right of residence in the UK. A family member of the qualified person is also entitled to be issued with a residence permit. In most cases, however, an EEA national working (or pursuing studies) in the UK will not have cause to approach the Immigration

---

1   SI 1994/1895 and SI 1997/2981.

Department for the issue of a residence permit. He will arrive, present his passport or identity card, reside in the UK and later take up work or studies. The student will have no cause to demonstrate that he is a qualified person by virtue of one or more of the definitions in the Immigration (European Economic Area) Order 1994. However, it is when the EEA worker or student seeks to be joined or accompanied by a non-EEA family member that it becomes necessary to acquire a residence permit proving his right of residence in order to obtain a family permit for family members coming to the UK or the residence permit for family members already here.

28.41 It is possible for a student to be a qualified person under any one or several of the headings identified above. If the student is working in addition to the studying, then he can potentially qualify as a worker; it matters not that the employment might be part-time or that the pay might be at a level which attracts family credit, so long as the employment is 'effective and genuine'. Similarly, the student might qualify as a self-employed person, pursuing a self-employed activity concurrently with his studies. Fee-paying students at a private establishment will qualify as persons receiving services. If the student cannot fall within the definition of a worker, self-employed person or provider or recipient of services, then to obtain a residence permit as a qualified person he will need to be studying full-time on a vocational course, be covered by comprehensive sickness insurance and declare an ability for self-support without recourse to public funds. These requirements in the Immigration (European Economic Area) Order 1994 reflect Directive 93/96 governing the position of students.

28.42 In conclusion, it can be stated that there is an effective regime in place for the free movement of European students and employees. In practice, the only problems that are likely to arise concern members of the family of the student or employee, who are not themselves EEA nationals.

THE HEI AS EMPLOYER

28.43 By reason of Art 39 of the European Treaty, an HEI is not entitled to refuse a position to an EU national applicant on grounds only of nationality. There is an exception for employees in the public service, but the ECJ has rightly not allowed HEIs to rely on that provision to avoid the rules where no issue of public security arises. The ECJ found that the University of Venice could be sued for discriminating against non-Italian nationals.[1] The same principle would apply in the UK if there was discrimination on immigration grounds against an EU national, or other national entitled to protection under certain EU Treaties, and hence HEIs should keep a careful eye on their recruitment procedures. In *Scholz (Ingetraut) v Opera Universitaria di Cagliari*,[2]

---

1   *Allue (Pilar) and Coonan (Mary Carmel) v Università degli Studi di Venezia* (Case C-33/88) [1989] ECR 1591.

2   (Case C-419/92) [1994] ECR I–505.

Ms Scholz argued that she had been unfairly treated under the University's recruitment procedure. The procedure gave credit for previous employment in the public service, but only if the public service was in Italy. The ECJ held that the restriction was invalid.

28.44 The issue of what amounts to discrimination on grounds of nationality or a genuine test of eligibility for employment can be difficult to resolve. For example, the ECJ found that a requirement that teachers in Ireland pass a test in the Irish language was justified, even though they would not need to use the language in their jobs.[1] More recently, in *Petrie v Universita degli Studi di Verona*,[2] the ECJ held that the Treaty did not preclude a national rule reserving eligibility for appointment to temporary teaching posts to tenured lecturers and established research staff and thereby excluding non-national foreign language assistants, who had been appointed to university teaching by competition. Universities need to be aware of the pitfalls in their dealings with potential foreign recruits and actual employees from the EEA, as much as they need to be aware of sex and disability discrimination legislation.

MUTUAL RECOGNITION OF DEGREES AND QUALIFICATIONS

28.45 The recognition of degrees between Member States is of importance to HEIs, students, potential students, employers and professional bodies. The circumstances in which a UK HEI must recognise a degree from a foreign university and vice versa, and the circumstances in which students will be able to obtain work on the basis of their UK qualification, are of vital importance. Foreign students, for example, might be dissuaded from studying in the UK if the UK qualification is not recognised abroad. Also of significance are the rules as to the length or content of courses which will determine whether or not they are recognised, and the rules concerning the recognition by professional bodies of qualifications obtained in other countries. Such questions are important for all HEIs, but those institutions offering vocational and professional courses are particularly affected. Articles 39, 43 and 47of the European Treaty provide the legal basis for the recognition of degrees. Essentially, degrees obtained by nationals of Member States in any Member State must be recognised throughout the EU if they were obtained following a post-secondary course of at least 3 years' duration. Degrees obtained in a Member State by non-EU nationals do not need to be recognised in the same way.

28.46 In the 1960s and 1970s, a series of directives provided for recognition of diplomas in relation to specific subjects, in particular the medical and allied professions: doctors, nurses, dentists, veterinary surgeons, midwives and pharmacists. Those directives required the co-ordination of training criteria so

---

1   *Groener v Minister of Education and City of Dublin Vocational Education Committee* (Case C-379/87) [1989] ECR 3967.
2   (Case C-90/96) [1998] CEC 117.

that a professional diploma was recognised only if certain subjects were included in the training. Some of these directives are still in force. For example, in 1966, the Commission challenged French legislation which permitted psychiatric nurses to obtain a general care nursing qualification based on their psychiatric nursing qualification but without complying with the minimum standards in Directive 77/453.

28.47 Instead of regulating diplomas profession by profession, however, Directive 89/48 provided for a general system. The directive uses the word 'diploma' rather than the word 'degree'. This directive was entitled 'For a general system for recognition of higher educational diplomas awarded on the completion of professional education and training of at least three years' duration'. It also provides rules for the right to use academic titles. Directive 92/51 supplemented Directive 89/48 for diplomas of shorter duration.

What degrees must be recognised?

28.48 The definition of a diploma in Art 1(a) of Directive 89/48 is:

'any diploma, certificate or other evidence of formal qualifications or any set of such diplomas, certificates or other evidence:
– which has been awarded by a competent authority in a Member State, designated in accordance with its own laws, regulations or administrative provisions; and
– which shows that the holder has successfully completed a post-secondary course of at least three years' duration, or of an equivalent duration part-time, at a university or establishment of higher education or another establishment of similar level and, where appropriate, that he has successfully completed the professional training required in addition to the post-secondary course; and
– which shows that the holder has the professional qualifications required for the taking up or pursuit of a regulated profession in that Member State ...'

28.49 There are special provisions where part of the education and training was received outside the EU. It is significant, however, that the Directive does not include any rules for minimum content requirements, and there is no prerequisite of curriculum co-ordination. The main points to be borne in mind are that the degrees are 3-year courses, that they are awarded by the HEI, on the basis of its own rules and not on the basis of any internationally co-ordinated procedure, and that they apply only to regulated professions. The last requirement is a significant limitation on the usefulness of the Directive. The most recent list of UK regulated professions is contained in the European Communities (Recognition of Professional Qualifications) (Amendment) Regulations 2000.[1]

Vocational and professional courses

28.50 Both Directives also govern professional training and professional qualifications. Directive 89/48 presupposes a higher education course of at least 3 years. Directive 92/51 governs other post-secondary education and

---

1   SI 2000/1960.

training courses, other equivalent education and training, and some secondary courses in some cases complemented by professional training and experience.

Additional requirements for some professions: aptitude tests and adaptation periods

28.51   Some regulated professions lobbied hard and were able to provide additional requirements. Lawyers' professional bodies, perhaps unsurprisingly, were the main group that insisted on additional requirements, and were widely criticised as a result. In some Member States this was no doubt for protectionist reasons, although additional requirements were agreed on the basis that while medicine or engineering require the same knowledge and skills throughout the EU, a professional lawyer requires a knowledge of the law of a particular Member State. A German national, Mr Kraus, was awarded an LLM from Edinburgh University. He tried to use the LLM in his legal training in Germany. But German law provided that he needed to obtain approval beforehand. This was expensive and time-consuming. The ECJ decided in *Kraus v Land Baden-Württemberg*[1] that such rules, where they created an obstacle to the free movement of workers, could be justified only if they tried to further an objective in the public interest and compatible with the Treaty. If such restrictions are permitted, they may go no further than what is necessary, and must be proportional. Directive 89/48 achieved a compromise by requiring an aptitude test or adaptation period for certain professions and in the case of lawyers, Directive 98/5/EC goes even further in facilitating the practice of the profession of lawyer on a permanent basis in a Member State other than that in which the legal qualification was obtained: see *Grand Duchy of Luxembourg v European Parliament and Council of the European Union.*[2]

Right to use academic titles

28.52   It is important for HEIs, graduates and employers that degrees be authentic and that their merit be known. Article 7 of Directive 89/48 makes provision for use of academic titles. The addition of the name of an institution to the degree title is optional, so it can be hard to discover a degree's origin, and even more difficult to evaluate its merit; a problem exacerbated by the international nature of the Directive. In some Member States, recognition of degrees is a matter for government, in others for the HEIs themselves. Article 7 of the Directive sets out formal rules, as follows:

–   nationals of other Member States who fulfil the necessary conditions for a regulated profession are entitled to use the professional title of the host Member State;

---

1   (Case C-19/92) [1993] ECR I–1663.
2   (Case C-168/98 7 November) (2000) unreported, ECJ.

- such nationals are allowed to use their lawful academic title, and the abbreviation for it in the language of the host State, but the host Member State may require the title to be followed by the name and location of the awarding institution; and
- where the profession is regulated by an association, nationals can only use the professional title on proof of membership, and, if membership is subject to qualification requirements, then a foreign diploma may be recognised as fulfilling any requirement for a diploma, if it fulfils the criteria in the directive.

Restrictions on the application of Directive 89/48

28.53 A significant restriction on the rights granted by the Directive is that they only apply to nationals of Member States. Thus an American citizen who has graduated in the UK is not awarded the same rights of recognition as would be a British or other EU citizen. A number of institutions are listed in the directive as being regulated professional bodies. They include the principal institutions for accountants and engineers, although the list is non-exhaustive. In *Aranitis v Land Berlin*,[1] the ECJ said that a Greek geologist wishing to practise in Germany could not rely on the Directive, because in Germany geologists practise on the basis of their degree only and so the profession was not regulated. But the other aspects of European law would still apply, for example the rules on freedom of establishment (see para **28.54**). The Directive is also limited to diplomas awarded in Member States. A strange situation arose in the case of Mr Tawil-Albertini.[2] He was a French national who obtained a doctorate in dental surgery in Beirut in 1968. His doctorate was recognised in Belgium in 1979 and he was subsequently authorised to practise dentistry in the UK and Ireland, where the authorities recognised his Lebanese qualifications. He next applied to practise in France and was refused. He sued the French Ministry and the case went to the ECJ. The Court held that, although Directive 78/686 required Member States to recognise diplomas awarded in other Member States, it did not require them to recognise diplomas from third countries, even where the diploma had already been recognised in a number of other Member States. This meant that the French national was entitled to practise in Belgium, the UK and Ireland, but not in France. See also *Hugo Fernando Hocsman v Ministrie de l'Emploi et de la Solidarite*[3] and *Jeff Erpelding v Ministrie de la Santè*.[4]

Recognition outside the terms of Directive 89/48

28.54 Quite apart from the Directive, Art 52 of the European Treaty can be used to obtain the right to use professional titles. In *Gebhard v Consiglio*

---

1   (Case C-164/94) [1996] ECR I–135.
2   *Tawil-Albertini v Ministre des Affaires Sociales* (Case C-154/93) [1994] ECR I–451.
3   (Case C-238/98) [2000] 3 CMLR 1025.
4   (Case C-16/99 14 September) unreported, ECJ.

dell'Ordine degli Avvocati e Procuratori di Milano,[1] the ECJ was faced with the issue of whether a German lawyer in Italy could use the title *avvocato* in Milan. He was not a member of the Italian Bar. The Court ruled that restrictions on the use of the title must not be discriminatory and there have to be strong public interest reasons before a restriction would be allowed. The Italian government had therefore to take into account the lawyer's qualifications and experience.

ANTI-COMPETITIVE PRACTICES

28.55 Article 81 of the European Treaty is concerned with the activities of undertakings (which includes HEIs) which in some way actually or potentially distort trade between EU Member States. The basic rule is that *any* commercial agreement, arrangement or concerted practice which may affect trade between EU Member States and which has as its *object* or *effect* an adverse effect on free competition, is void and unenforceable. 'Arrangement' has a very wide interpretation. It need not be formalised, and can even relate to an understanding between undertakings not to compete in each other's territory. The following are illustrative examples of prohibited practices:

– directly or indirectly fixing purchase or selling prices or other conditions;
– limiting or controlling production, markets, technical development or investment;
– sharing markets or sources of supply;
– applying dissimilar conditions to equivalent transactions placing contractors at a competitive disadvantage; or
– making contracts subject to supplementary obligations which have no connection with the subject of such contracts.

28.56 The following examples have been found to be in breach of Art 81:

– if one party to a technology transfer agreement is required (without an objectively justified reason) to keep out of the selling market;
– if one party to an research and development agreement is restricted in its freedom to carry out research and development independently, or in co-operation with third parties, in a field unconnected with that to which the programme relates or, after its completion, in the field to which the programme relates or in a connected field;
– where a consortium agreement to develop a common computer interface to use the Unix operating system established special criteria for membership of the consortium and placed restrictions on the admission of new members; and
– where a franchise agreement restricted competition between franchisees.

28.57 HEIs need to be particularly careful when granting or accepting exclusive arrangements in commercial agreements, particularly those relating

---

1   (Case C-55/94) [1995] ECR I–4165.

to IP licensing (including course and programme franchising, and licensing agreements) and research and development agreements. As we shall see, in connection with Art 82 (abuse of a dominant position) and the UK Competition Act 1998 (the 1998 Act), HEIs may also need to be careful when entering into exclusive arrangements with large companies who are in a dominant position in relation to the market in question; and HEIs may, themselves, be in a dominant position when it comes to specialist research courses and programmes not offered by other HEIs or not offered by other HEIs in their area, where consumer immobility may restrict the geographical extent of the market. HEIs should also note that competition law can be used as a sword by third parties or, indeed, by other HEIs, whose opportunities to compete have been infringed by unlawful anti-competitive agreements or abuse of a dominant market position.

28.58 Article 82 of the European Treaty prohibits any abuse by one or more undertakings of a dominant position in the EU or a substantial part of it. Examples of such abuse include:

– imposing unfair prices or other unfair trading conditions;
– limiting production, markets or technical developments to the prejudice of consumers;
– applying dissimilar trading conditions to equivalent transactions placing contractors at a competitive disadvantage; and
– making contracts subject to acceptance of supplementary conditions which have no connection with the subject of such contracts.

28.59 The European Treaty does not define 'dominant position', but the ECJ has held that it relates to a position of economic strength held by an undertaking which enables it to prevent effective competition in the relevant market. The 'relevant market' necessitates a consideration of the relevant product or services market and the relevant geographical market and whether that is a 'substantial part of the EU'. The relevant product market is the market for a particular product which is sufficiently differentiated from other product markets so that it is only to a limited extent interchangeable with them and not exposed to competition from other products or exposed only in a way that is hardly perceptible. ECJ decisions indicate that a single country or even part of a country (for example, southern Germany) is sufficient to constitute a 'substantial part of the EU' and the Commission has stated that a dominant position could be said to exist if a market share of 40–45 per cent is reached, although a dominant position cannot be ruled out in respect of a market share down to 20 per cent. In *Centre Belge D'Etudes de Marché Télé-marketing v Compagnie Luxembourgeoise de Télédiffusion et Information Publicité Bénélux*,[1] it was held that Art 82 applied to an undertaking even where the dominant position was attributable not to the undertaking's own activity, but to legislation which ensured that there could be little or no competition.

---

1   (Case 311/84) [1986] 2 CMLR 558.

28.60   Any contract or arrangement which offends Arts 81 and 82 will be void
and unenforceable and, in addition, heavy fines may be payable to the
Commission depending on the gravity of the infringement and any mitigating
factors. Fines for infringement of Arts 81 and 82 can be up to 10 per cent of total
annual turnover, plus periodic daily fines for continuing breach. The
Commission encourages 'whistleblowing' by exempting the first discloser of
the infringement from fines (subject to other conditions). Furthermore, the
Commission has extensive powers of investigation and inspection, including
search powers with or without notice, and can compel the production of
information and documents with fines for breach currently limited to 5000
Euros (but it is proposed to increase fines for breach of procedural rules up to
1 per cent of total annual turnover).

28.61   The increasing level of total fines for breaches of the competition rules
in recent years point to the Commission's greater stringency both in enforcing
the articles and punishing breaches: 1982 – £18m; 1988 – £62m; 1994 –
£373m. By 1999, the overall number of competition cases considered by
the Commission had increased to 1201. The Commission now has such a
backlog of outstanding work that proposals are currently in train to divest
some of the Commission's powers of enforcement onto the national
competition authorities. The scope of Art 81 is devastatingly wide. The
possibility of a large fine for infringement is significant. The precise wording of
contracts needs careful checking, but just as important are their objects and
practical effects. Otherwise, possibly many years later, unforeseeable 'effects'
may make what started out as a valid contract void and unenforceable.

28.62   If an agreement, arrangement or concerted practice is in breach of
Arts 81 or 82 the consequences can be as follows:

–   risk of heavy fines on the undertaking from the Commission for all parties
    involved in the anti-competitive behaviour;
–   the parties may have to renegotiate the agreement, in which case care is
    needed because market conditions may have changed;
–   the infringing undertaking may be liable for damages to third parties who
    suffer as a result of the unlawful conduct; or
–   independent third parties may complain to the European Commission, as
    may a party to the agreement.

28.63   Anti-competitive practices which are permitted are as follows:

–   *if the European Commission gives clearance*: achieving this can be
    time-consuming and very expensive. If granted, clearance may also be
    subject to conditions;
–   *with regard to Art 81, if the contract is 'of minor importance'*: this will be the
    case only where the aggregate market share of the participants is small
    enough to have no significant effect on competition. The Commission
    have indicated that 5 per cent is the maximum combined market share for
    horizontal agreements and 10 per cent for vertical agreements. In

addition, the combined group worldwide turnover of both parties must not exceed 200 million Euros. HEIs should be aware that use of this exemption may be unreliable in the longer term. For instance, if another group takes over the holding company of one of the parties and the group turnover limits are thus exceeded, the exemption fails and the risk of liability for Art 81 penalties revives;

– *if there is a 'block exemption' regulation available*: these are exemptions from the penalties of Art 81 granted by the Commission, in the overall interest of an efficient free market, for complete types (or blocks) of contract. However, there are two conditions: the wording of the contract must comply strictly with the block exemption; and the intention of the contract and its effect must comply strictly with the block exemption. The technology transfer block exemption, and the research and development and the vertical agreements and concerted practices block exemption are the principal ones used by HEIs, although there are several more.

Technology Transfer Licensing Agreements (Regulation 240/96)

28.64 This block exemption from Art 81 permits exclusive licensing agreements between two parties (only) which are entered into with a view to manufacture of a patentable invention and/or know-how for a period which may not exceed the patent's remaining life, and which may include a ban on 'active' selling outside the territory and a ban on 'passive' selling for a period not exceeding 5 years. Pure know-how licensing, and mixed patent and know-how licensing agreements are permitted. 'Know-how' is non-patented technical information which is secret, substantial and in any appropriate form. This exemption replaces (with a more liberal and commercial bias) the former patent licensing block exemption and the know-how block exemption. Various conditions apply and some provisions in the contract may fall foul of the exemption if they appear in the blacklist.

Research and Development Agreements (Regulations 418/85 and 2659/2000)

28.65 These are permitted on certain terms where the contract is for pure research and development, or where the research and development is for joint manufacturing or joint licensing and the object is not to restrict competition. Joint *sale* would not qualify and would have to comply with the main terms of Art 81 or be subject to a separate exemption. Again, there are various permitted clauses and various blacklisted clauses which disqualify the contract from exemption.

Vertical Agreements and Concerted Practices (Regulation 2790/ 1999)

28.66 Vertical agreements are those within undertakings at different levels in the supply chain, whereas horizontal agreements are those between undertakings at the same level in the supply chain. This new block exemption replaces a number of old exemptions relating to such things as exclusive distribution agreements, exclusive purchasing agreements and franchising. The new exemption covers multi-party agreements (cf the Technology Transfer block exemption at para **28.64**) and two decisive criteria apply when determining whether an agreement is exempted from Art 81: the level of the market share of the distributor or supplier, in the case of an exclusive franchise, distribution or supply agreement, or of the buyer in an exclusive purchase agreement; and whether or not the agreement contains any blacklisted restrictions. Market share is calculated as the Art 82 calculation in respect of 'dominant position', and in the event that the supplier's market share does not exceed 30 per cent it will not be considered to have significant market power and the agreement will be exempt if it contains no blacklisted restrictions. If the supplier's market share exceeds 30 per cent, then it can still apply to the Commission for exemption. If the share is less than 10 per cent, some blacklisted restrictions may be permissible if they do not have 'appreciable effect' on the market.

Caution

28.67 The substance of a contract is more important than what it is called. Each contract must be checked against the correct block exemption regulation, because precise details of each regulation are different. It is essential to have some mechanism for periodic review of compliance with UK and European law on commercial contracts. Market conditions can change, and what started out as a valid contract may later be void and unenforceable, with the consequent risk of fines.

Competition Act 1998

28.68 The 1998 Act prohibits anti-competitive practices in the UK by means of controls modelled on Arts 81 and 82 of the European Treaty. It affects agreements entered into after 1 March 2000 and replaces the cumbersome and complex provisions of the old legislation relating to restrictive trade practices and resale price maintenance. Its major provisions are the Chapter I prohibition and the Chapter II prohibition.

Chapter I prohibition
28.69 This prohibits agreements, decisions by associations of undertakings or concerted practices which:

– may affect trade within the UK; or

– have as their object or effect the prevention, restriction or distortion of
   competition within the UK,

unless they are excluded by the 1998 Act or are exempt. The obvious change
from Art 81 is that the 1998 Act applies to agreements which may affect trade in
the UK rather than between Member States. But since the UK is a Member State,
an agreement which falls foul of the Chapter I prohibition may also fall foul of
Art 81 if it affects trade between Member States, and double penalties may be
incurred. The Chapter I prohibition also contains a list of offending provisions
which is identical to that in Art 81. The Chapter I prohibition will only be
applicable where an agreement brings about an 'appreciable restriction' on
competition in the view of the DGFT. This is where the undertakings'
combined market share of the relevant market does not exceed 25 per cent,
unless the agreement fixes prices or shares markets or imposes minimum resale
prices. An agreement which offends the Chapter I prohibition is void (although
it may be possible to sever the terms which are void). In addition, aggrieved
third parties may claim damages and penalties may be payable to the DGFT.
There is no legal requirement to notify the DGFT of an agreement which may
fall foul of the Chapter I prohibition but, if the agreement is notified, then the
undertaking will gain provisional exemption from the date of notification.
Notification will not provide immunity from third party claims for damages.
Finally, any agreement which is exempted under an EU block exemption is also
exempted from the Chapter I prohibition. The determination of the 'relevant
market' is undertaken generally in accordance with the criteria outlined above
for determining a 'dominant position' for the purposes of Art 82, but the
geographical market may be far smaller if customers are not able or are not
likely to obtain competing products from another area due to mobility issues.
Thus, if a course or programme which is only likely to be taken up by students
living in the local area is exclusively licensed or franchised to another provider,
the combined market share of the parties may well exceed the threshold,
whereas a course of national appeal would be less likely to do so.

Chapter II prohibition
28.70   This is modelled heavily on Art 82 and prohibits any conduct on the
part of one or more undertakings which amounts to abuse of a dominant
position in a market if it may affect trade in the UK. A list of similar offending
provisions to that set out in Art 82 is also contained in the Chapter II
prohibition. 'Dominant position' relates to the UK or any part of it which, in
turn, depends on a determination of the market and the undertaking's market
share (see above). The DGFT will generally consider that an undertaking with
a market share below 40 per cent will not be individually dominant and that
with a market share above 50 per cent will be presumed to be dominant, in each
case in the absence of evidence to the contrary. There are no exemptions from
the Chapter II prohibition and only very limited exclusions. Notification for
guidance can be made to the DGFT, but it will not provide immunity from
penalties until favourable guidance or a decision is given.

Investigation and enforcement

28.71   The OFT has similar powers of investigation and enforcement as the EU Commission. Failure to co-operate is a criminal offence. It can impose fines of up 10 per cent of UK annual turnover. 'Whistleblowers' are encouraged to come forward with information and thus avoid fines. Wherever European law collides with English law, European law prevails. Any agreement or practice which contravenes European law may prove void and unenforceable, and can attract swingeing fines, even though it may comply with English domestic law. This can be the case even where the agreement or practice is between two English entities. HEIs must be able, therefore, to rely on a secure contractual framework.

Compliance review

28.72   The complexities involved between European law and English law means that specialist help is essential to avoid unforeseen problems. Preventative help can be available from many law firms in the form of a compliance review service (ie a legal health check for the academic body). The core of a compliance review for HEIs usually relates to competition law aspects on technology transfer, intellectual property licensing (including course and programme licensing and franchising), research and development agreements, and public procurement contracts. Every such agreement needs to be reviewed on a regular basis, and if necessary redrawn to ensure it complies with current European law and UK law requirements as they emerge and change. There is also a particular need to keep updated on aspects of employment law, some of which emanates from the EU, and immigration rules applying to visiting academics and students.

FUTURE DEVELOPMENTS

28.73   Some commentators are of the opinion that 80 per cent of current domestic law in the UK has derived from Brussels, either by means of regulations (which are immediately binding on all Member States with identical provisions) or directives (which can give a limited latitude in precisely how they are implemented into domestic law by the UK Parliament). It is not possible to ignore the European dimension in running an HEI. The history of the EU indicates that throughout its existence it has been moving to wider and deeper integration, initially in Western Europe but increasingly towards Central and Eastern Europe. Deeper integration involves not just monetary union, which is culminating in the European Single Currency (Euro), but also political union, and particularly the introduction of pan-European laws which may affect the powers, duties and obligations of national governments, public bodies, commercial organisations and individuals. The signing of the Treaty on European Union at Maastricht in 1992 was only the end of the beginning of the latest phase of this process. The Maastricht Treaty was particularly concerned with economic and monetary union, but contained provisions relating to a common foreign and security policy, co-operation in the fields of justice and home affairs, and the 'social chapter' (many of the provisions of which have now been incorporated into UK law). Notwithstanding the above, Europe should not be viewed simply as a source of ever more complex and intensive legislation with which HEIs have to comply on pain of litigation and fines. The single market is intended to remove barriers to trade, and to allow the free movement of goods, services, people and capital; it thus creates a number of opportunities for UK HEIs in the form of joint collaboration with European partner institutions, joint research, staff and student exchange and progression, course and programme licensing, franchising and collaboration, in addition to commercial activities and joint ventures. An HEI which fails to grasp these opportunities will be doing itself, its students and its staff a grave detriment.

Chapter 29

A NOTE ON CONSUMER LAW

David Palfreyman

INTRODUCTION

29.1   The prompting for and a key theme of this book is very much the idea of the university–student legal relationship being increasingly defined not only as one of a contract but specifically as a consumer contract for the supply of a service, with the attendant risk that, as students personally pay more in academic fees, there will be increased litigation. Or at least there will be a greater willingness to complain if the provision of that educational service falls short of the student's expectations – which may, of course, be unrealistic and unreasonable – and especially if the HEI's resources to deliver that service are stretched so far in the context of 'efficiency gains' and a declining 'unit of resource' that it is unable to live up to its own engendering of student expectations via the written 'promises' contained in the (glossy) prospectus and the oral 'guarantees' made at recruitment interviews by (over-) enthusiastic staff. Much of what is said here applies also to the HEI trading by way of selling a service in the form of research contracts or testing, or even selling manufactured products as goods (although often the latter especially will be done via a trading company: see Chapter 15).

29.2   The rise of student litigation was noted in Chapter 1 (including the growth of student consumerism in the USA, as discussed in Kaplin and Lee (1995a), p 8) and in Riesman (1998); and the general terms of the HEI–student contract have been discussed in Chapter 6. Here it is a matter of detailing the specific ways in which consumer protection legislation *might* be increasingly applied to that contract, as students come to see themselves more as consumers, all as predicted by Birtwistle and Askew (1999) and indeed for education generally in Harris (1993). Elaine Maxwell (of Elaine Maxwell and Co, Solicitors), who acts for many students in dispute with their HEIs, makes the same point:

> 'It is generally agreed that students are becoming more litigious, and this has certainly been my experience over recent years ... There are a number of factors behind this growth in *educational consumerism* ... [including the unfortunate fact that] many institutions think they can treat all students like children [while at the same time there are now many more mature students in the system who] in particular resent lecturers acting in an unprofessional manner [and who] have invested a lot in the course, and [hence who] in my experience are the most likely to complain ... *Students now have to*

invest their own money and are determined to get good value ... they now feel they are buying a product, and that product is a degree rather than the opportunity to learn.'[1]

As Geoffrey Alderman neatly put it:

'The problem is, the overriding purpose of higher education is to change the [student] customer, and the process by which this is done, and the end results, may leave the customer very dissatisfied indeed: the high grades expected and never achieved; the easy ride that was anticipated but never experienced; the cherished assumptions and ideas that were blown apart.'[2]

29.3 That said, the word is still 'might' as stressed at para **29.2**; so far consumer protection legislation has not notably been invoked in student–HEI litigation, as is also the case in the USA (although two high-profile Australian cases have referred to the Trade Practices Act 1974: *Fennell v Australia National University*[3] and *Dudzinski v Kellow* (and others, including Griffith University) (see Appendix 1 to Chapter 6).[4]

29.4 Riesman (1998; original edition 1980), in looking at the student consumerism that developed with the 'massification' of the US HE system in the 1960s and 1970s, saw the student as, if anything, *too passive a customer*. Indeed, perhaps students conspired with institutions to 'pack 'em in and pile 'em high':

'Even the most shoddy, cut-rate, and cut-throat degrees are not necessarily frauds on the student consumer. They may, in fact, be examples of collusion between academic vendor and student buyer to secure a credential at some monetary cost but almost no cost in time or effort' (p 117); and

'Where individual faculty members, desperate for students, compete for them by an automatic grade of A and by demanding minimal amounts of work, this unprofessional (though understandable) strategy can scarcely be called fraudulent, since the students are eager rather than deceived consumers' (p 358).

Riesman does not see consumer protection legislation as being able to safeguard the student, either from a college reducing quality to save money and fill places or from the students themselves wanting an easy time in terms of academic work. The State governments are 'unevenly equipped' (p 369) and lack the resources to police quality in HE, and 'court actions are also too uneven ... to serve as adequate protection against the sort of abuses that the FTC [Federal Trade Commission] has policed in the sale of other consumer products' (p 358). The most that can be achieved is to try and ensure that applicants are not misled by college 'hard-sell' recruitment and marketing material when making a very important decision affecting the rest of their lives. Instead, the protection of academic standards depends ultimately on the morale and robust integrity of the academic profession (see Kennedy (1997)).

29.5 Middlemiss (2000) also argues for the student–HEI contract to be interpreted as a consumer contract for the provision of services. He notes

---

1   From a speech given at a conference on student complaints organised by Martineau Johnson, 19 July 2000; emphasis added.
2   In *The Guardian*'s education section, 6 March 2001.
3   [1999] FCA 989 (22 July 1999).
4   [1999] FCA 390 (8 April 1999), FCA 1264 (27 August 1999).

s 25(1) of the UCTA 1977, which stresses that: 'The onus of proving that a contract is not to be regarded as a consumer contract lies on the party so contending'. He makes the further point that piecing together the terms, express and implied, of the student–HEI contract can be difficult. Indeed, it is analogous to determining the exact terms applying at any one time in the employee–employer dynamic contract of service, taking into account: job adverts; job descriptions; things said at the job interview; the letter offering the job; the statement of particulars required by ss 1–7 of the ERA 1996; the employer's staff grievances and discipline rules; works' rulebooks; staff handbooks; any trade union–employer collective agreements; terms implied by statute; terms implied by industry custom and practice; terms implied by employment case-law (Jefferson (2000), chapter 4). Finally, Middlemiss argues for the concept of reasonableness to be applied when HEIs seek to enforce express terms, adopting (as he explains) 'an approach utilised in employment law, where, in the event that an employer applies an express term unreasonably, the Court can intervene to restrict or exclude the application of an express term through superimposing an overriding implied term of reasonableness'. (Middlemiss cites *United Bank Ltd v Akhtar*;[1] but see also *Prestwick Circuits Ltd v McAndrews* [2] with *Courtaulds Northern Spinning Ltd v Sibson*[3] and *O'Brien v Associated Fire Alarms Ltd*.[4]) Such an approach would seem in keeping with the general thrust of protective consumer law.

29.6 Davis (2001) again emphasises the HEI–student contract as a consumer contract, noting Canadian experience (*Doane v Mount Saint Vincent University*[5] and citing the UK's OFT challenging unfair terms within that contract for the provision of educational services (for example, OFT *Unfair Contract Terms Bulletin 6* records South Bank University as having removed a general term giving it the right to change regulations and replacing it with one allowing such changes only at the start of each academic year; while *Bulletin 5* reports Anglia Polytechnic University as agreeing to remove a clause excluding liability for loss or damage to student property or university premises. (For discussion of the OFT interest in the HEI residential contract/licence for students, see Chapter 23.) Thus Davis sees this consumerist aspect of the HEI–student contractual relationship as 'a ticking time bomb'.

29.7 Back in 1873 and the days of *caveat emptor*, the University of Edinburgh was in conflict with a female medical student and the court still held that the University could not make an *arbitrary* decision concerning her future.[6] Also, in keeping with a consumer protectionist approach to the doctrine of contract law in more recent times, Brownsword (2000) notes that, 'wherever one looks in the modern law of contract, the notion of reasonableness seems to be at the core of its doctrinal operations [p 79] ... [it] is here, there, and everywhere [p 94]'.

---

1   [1989] IRLR 507.
2   [1990] IRLR 191, 1990 SLT 654.
3   [1988] ICR 451, [1988] IRLR 305.
4   [1968] 1 WLR 1916, [1969] 1 All ER 93.
5   74 DLR (3d) 301.
6   *Jex-Blake v Senatus Academics of the University of Edinburgh* [1873] 11 M 784.

Moreover, Brownsword further notes the creeping invasion from European law into English law (albeit not without resistance) of 'the idea of a general doctrine of good faith, in the sense of an overriding (and objective) requirement of fair dealing, [which hitherto] was not part of the lexicon of English contract law' (p 98). He concludes that 'good practice' in consumer contracting already embraces 'reasonableness', and will probably in due course 'move towards the adoption of good faith as a requirement (in substance, if not in name)' of such 'good practice' (p 121). To do so would be part of the ascendancy within 'the ideologies of contract' of 'consumer-welfarism' over 'market-individualism' in terms of proper dealing in the consumer–business (student–university) legal relationship and as 'The Tendency of the Modern Law' (chapter 6).

29.8 And 'the consumer' may not just be directly the student, or indirectly the parents, but, in fact, also the future employer or even a professional body. This last player may have real muscle to flex in this complex matrix of parties: for example, the Royal Institution of Chartered Surveyors (RICS) initially removed accreditation from 12 of its 52 HEIs offering degree courses in surveying where they were unable to guarantee that 75 per cent or more of the university's overall student intake had 17 A-level points or equivalent; it has subsequently reinstated six of them. The HEIs concerned have been told that they may appeal the RICS decision: it remains to be seen whether any will seek judicial review of it.[1]

29.9 For additional information, see: Farrington (1998), chapter 4 and especially pp 319–323 and 350–352; Harvey and Parry (2000) together with Miller *et al* (1998); Hyams (1998), pp 532 and 534–536; Birks (2000), chapter 10 and Scott and Black (2000), especially chapter 6, the last being supported by an internet home page for access to a wide range of primary material and for updating. See also Whittaker (2001b) on unfair terms in the HEI–student contract. Farrington (1998) in para 4.1 sums it up: 'The status of students has changed incredibly. The change has been from one of being in a subordinate role in the *studium generale* to consumer of services'. See also Kiloh (1998) for a wide-ranging discussion on students as 'customers, clients and consumers'. Thus, Evans and Gill (2001) is aimed squarely at the student as a newly empowered consumer, guiding him through the legal relationship with the HEI and providing, for example, a 'checklist' for students contemplating a formal complaint (pp 161–164). See also, by analogy with the school–parent(s) contract in private schools, Boyd (1998), pp 42–44, 63–65, 127, 182–183, who gives examples of the intervention of Trading Standards Officers and the OFT (Unfair Contract Terms Unit) to protect the parent-consumer: at p 64 concerning a misleading statement in a school prospectus being referred to Trading Standards under s 14 of the Trade Descriptions Act 1968 (TDA 1968); and p 127 on an OFT challenge to the 'fees in lieu of notice' rule. Kaplin and Lee (1995a), and Riesman (1998), have already been cited as a US perspective. (See also Considine (1993).)

---

1   *Estates Gazette*, 27 January 2001, p 37: note the RICS spokesperson saying that these HEIs were 'suppliers' of trained personnel for the surveying industry; see also *Estates Gazette* 16 June 2001, p 38.

29.10 There is, of course, also a strong analogy with the holiday industry (Grant and Mason (1998)), especially in the use of the prospectus/brochures and in the complexity of the service package being delivered by the supplier; and indeed with private health care (Lewis (1998)), again in terms of a complex package with no guarantee of a cure (degree) at the end of it all. The analogy with medical negligence law arises especially in the context of and complexity of deciding whether a particular medic really is a reasonably competent doctor, just as it is difficult to define exactly what is a reasonably competent academic. In the case of holiday law, the analogy is the danger of misrepresentation arising in the travel brochure – the equivalent of the HEI prospectus. That said, apart from private schooling, no other services contract has quite the extra complexity of the student–HEI contractual arrangement, in that success needs the profound involvement of the consumer in terms of putting in the effort required to take full advantage of the educational services made available by the supplier: there is no room for a passive consumer (see Palfreyman (2001)).

29.11 Yet, if in recent years UK HEIs, and possibly the academics working within them, have begun to feel threatened by the student empowered as a customer and even as a consumer, their experience is nothing compared with the extreme consumerism of the student body at the fourteenth-century University of Bologna (and to a lesser extent Padua) described in Cobban (1971):

> 'Student controls over the lecturing system were formidable. The lecturer's life proceeded in an anxious atmosphere of impending fines. A lecturer was fined if he started his lectures a minute late or if he continued after the prescribed time: indeed, if the latter occurred, the students had a statutory obligation to leave the lecture room without delay ... It would be no exaggeration to say that lecturing performance was continuously assessed by the students on both a qualitative and quantitative basis ... This whole parade of student controls was underpinned by a system of secret denunciations. That is to say, four students were secretly elected to act as spies on the doctors and were bound to report to the rectors finable irregularities arising from such matters as bad lecturing technique ... From the statutory evidence the early Bolognese system would seem to be one based on mutual mistrust and antagonisms between staff and students.'

THE LEGISLATIVE FRAMEWORK

29.12 The common law of contract and tort has been discussed elsewhere (see Chapter 6), as has the application of the HRA 1998 (Chapter 7) and the public law dimension of the student–HEI legal relationship (Chapter 9): here, the focus is on consumer protection legislation, in the form of the following:

– Supply of Goods and Services Act 1982 (SGSA 1982);
– Unfair Contract Terms Act 1977 (UCTA 1977);
– Unfair Terms in Consumer Contracts Regulations 1999 (UTCCR 1999);
– Trade Descriptions Act 1968 (TDA 1968);
– Consumer Protection Act 1987 (CPA 1987); and

– Consumer Protection (Distance Selling) Regulations 2000 (DSR 2000).

Each piece of legislation will be taken in the order of importance as listed above.

Supply of Goods and Services Act 1982 (SGSA 1982)

29.13   Section 13 of the SGSA 1982 implies into any contract to supply a service a term 'that the supplier will carry out the service with reasonable care and skill'. The word 'reasonable', besides creating work and fees for lawyers, also imports the tort standard (the test of common law negligence), rather than, for example, the contract standard of 'satisfactory quality' (once 'merchantable quality') applying to goods in s 14 of the Sale of Goods Act 1979, which is closer to strict liability. The student-consumer would need to prove failure to exercise 'reasonable care and skill' on the part of the HEI, applying 'the *Bolam* test' of professional competence from *Bolam v Friern Barnet Hospital Management Committee:*[1] '. . . the test is the standard of the ordinary skilled man exercising and professing to have that special skill . . . the ordinary skill of an ordinary competent man exercising that particular art . . .'. Thus, as an academic journal article expressed it, 'consumers are not entitled to expect perfection' (Lawson (1984)). Patients cannot expect the standard of the best doctor nor students of the top lecturer, only of the average and reasonably competent medic or academic. That does mean, however, that an HEI would probably be in breach of the implied 'reasonable care and skill' term if it left substantial teaching in the hands of unsupervised, inexperienced and untrained graduate students (or even newly appointed lecturers), who, notwithstanding youthful energy and enthusiasm, may not be deemed able to reach the required level of the competent professional academic. Similarly, an NHS Trust cannot excuse medical negligence by asserting that very junior and inexperienced surgeons were all it could afford to employ to tackle complex operations.

29.14   Section 14 of the SGSA 1982 implies a term 'that the supplier will carry out the service within a reasonable time' (for example, the HEI will not take 6 months to mark an essay, nor 2 years to process a PhD thesis: see *Charnock v Liverpool Corporation*[2] re delay in repairing a car).

29.15   Section 15 implies a term that there will be 'a reasonable charge' for the service, but *only* if a price had not already been notified/agreed at the outset (this may mean, in the context of HE, that tuition fees should not be increased way above inflation between one year of a degree course and the next: it does not mean, however, that a consumer is protected from a bad bargain when agreeing to purchase a service at an inflated and excessive price).

---

1   [1957] 2 All ER 118.
2   [1968] 3 All ER 473.

Unfair Contract Terms Act 1977 (UCTA 1977)

29.16   Section 2 of the UCTA 1997 will permit the HEI to exclude or limit its liability, perhaps in relation to the protective effect of s 13 of the SGSA 1982, only if the HEI in doing so is able to satisfy 'the requirement of reasonableness'.

29.17   Section 3 will allow the HEI to perform the contract and supply the service in a 'substantially different' way, or even 'to render no performance at all', again only if, in altering the package or partially/totally failing to supply the package, the HEI 'satisfies the requirement of reasonableness'.

29.18   Section 8 will let the HEI exclude liability for any misrepresentation only if such a term can reasonably be inserted into the student–HEI contract.

29.19   Therefore, what is 'the requirement of reasonableness' within the UCTA 1977? Section 11(1) sets it out as the reasonableness test: 'the term shall have been a fair and reasonable one to be included having regard to the circumstances which were, or ought reasonably to have been, known or in the contemplation of the parties when the contract was made'.

Unfair Terms in Consumer Contracts Regulations 1999 (UTCCR 1999)

29.20   UCTA 1977 and UTCCR 1999 clearly overlap. The latter emanates from Germany via the EU, and, if anything, is perhaps more widely applicable to HE (for discussion of consumer protection in other legal systems see Zweigert and Kötz (1998), pp 333–347. Regulation 4(1) defines 'unfair terms' as 'any term which contrary to the requirement of good faith causes a significant imbalance in the parties' rights and obligations under the contract to the detriment of the consumer'. These regulations apply only to consumer contracts and are often referred to as the 'small print' rules, since they control the use of standard terms (typically buried at the back of, say, the holiday brochure). They are enforced by a variety of regulators, notably the OFT: activities so far caught by UTCCR 1999/OFT include a dating agency, a will-making service, an internet service provider, vocational training contracts, home improvements contracts, mobile phone contracts, domestic care, nursery care, independent school education contracts, residential lettings agreements, holiday/travel brochures ... but not (yet) to any great extent the HE contract to educate, although very recently the OFT has required the amendment of terms in the residential accommodation contract at several HEIs (see Chapters 7 and 23).

29.21   The concept of 'good faith' in contract owes more to EU law than to English law: the nearest English law got to it, prior to the imposition of EU law within the UK, was the idea of 'unconscionable' behaviour on the part of one party to a contract.

29.22   Schedule 2 to the UTCCR 1994, 'Assessment of Good Faith', which provided helpful guidance to the English contract lawyer, has been deleted from UTCCR 1999:

'In making an assessment of good faith, regard shall be had in particular to –

(a)   the strength of the bargaining positions of the parties;
(b)   whether the consumer had an inducement to agree to the term;
(c)   whether the goods or services were sold or supplied to the special order of the consumer; and
(d)   the extent to which the seller or supplier has dealt fairly and equitably with the consumer.'

29.23   Schedule 2 to UTCCR 1999[1] now provides what Sch 3 to UTCCR 1994 provided, *viz* an 'Indicative and Illustrative List of Terms which may be regarded as Unfair', including of particular relevance to the form the HEI–student contract could take:

'(c) making an agreement binding on the consumer whereas provision of services by the seller or supplier is subject to a condition whose realisation depends on his own will alone' (you, Student, must do 24 modules to earn the degree of X; but I, HEI, reserve the right to close down the Department of X and transfer your modules taken to another degree course);
'(i) irrevocably binding the consumer to terms with which he had no real opportunity of becoming acquainted before the conclusion of the contract' (does the student prior to registration *really* receive *and* have chance to digest, query and renegotiate examination requirements, etc?);
'(j) enabling the seller or supplier to alter unilaterally without a valid reason any characteristics of the product or service to be provided' (for example, the requirement for a degree will be reduced from 27 modules to 24, the teaching weeks in a term will reduce from nine to eight, and the amount of assessed work per module will be reduced, so that a teaching-oriented university can provide more research time for its academics ('a valid reason'?) – even assuming, of course, that the students complained about such a reduction in work-load);
'(m) giving the seller or supplier the right to determine whether the goods or services supplied are in conformity with the contract, or giving him the exclusive right to interpret any term of the contract' (linking to . . .);
'(q) excluding or hindering the consumer's right to take legal action or exercise any other legal remedy, particularly by requiring the consumer to take disputes exclusively to arbitration not covered by legal provisions . . .'

29.24   In relation to (q) above, note the connection with Art 6(1) of the European Convention on Human Rights as incorporated into English law by the coming fully into force in October 2000 of the HRA 1998, and hence the problem for HEIs both in terms of the Visitor system being deemed compliant with the Convention and HRA 1998, and also of any proposed binding arbitration mechanism for the HEIs not being an attempt to exclude unfairly the role of the courts: see Chapters 6 and 7, plus Birtwistle (2000), Kaye (1999) and Palfreyman (2000). Scott and Black (2000), p 46 make the point that a contract term which *requires* the use of arbitration and thus excludes the jurisdiction of the courts is, in any event, unfair under the Arbitration Act 1996 (ss 89–92) and as also indicated in the UTCCR 1999.

---

1   SI 1999/2083.

29.25   Regulation 6 requires that the terms of a consumer contract must be 'expressed in plain, intelligible language' – but no guidance is given as to the criteria for determining clarity.

29.26   Whittaker (2001b) stresses that UTCCR 1999 do not apply to certain 'core terms': 'what this would mean in the education context would be that a student could not complain that overall the education which he received was not good value for money (no review on the basis of the price/quality ratio (reg 3(2)) nor that overall the focus of the course should have been differently placed or that different courses should have been offered for students in the discipline chosen (the main subject-matter of the contract (reg 3(2)) (p 209). He concludes that, whether student rights are being protected against any abuse of power (on the part of the HEI) by public law judicial review of the HEI's due process application of its regulations, or by the court's reference to the HRA 1998, or by the court's testing of the private law terms of the student–HEI contract against the good faith standards within UTCCR 1999, 'the difference between the public and private is getting smaller rather than greater' (p 217). (See also Treitel (1999), pp 248–250 and Oliver (1999).)

Trade Descriptions Act 1968 (TDA 1968)

29.27   Section 14 of the TDA 1968 creates two criminal offences relating to false descriptions of services: *knowingly* making a false description, or *recklessly* making such a statement in that the maker of the statement did not take reasonable care to check the validity of the statement ('recklessly' does not necessarily imply dishonesty – *MFI Warehouses Ltd v Nattrass*[1]). Here, s 14 of the TDA 1968 links to fraudulent or negligent misrepresentation under the Misrepresentation Act 1967. Thus, the *mens rea* (state of mind) is knowingly or recklessly making the statement; and the *actus reus* (criminal act itself) is making the statement. A 'statement' may take the form of misleading photographs, figures, etc: not just descriptive prose. The definition of services, however, can cause confusion,[2] while statements about the future as promises of services to be delivered in due course *may* not be offences if they cannot at the time of being made be statements of fact which are clearly either true or false within s 14.[3]

29.28   The HEI's defence to a charge under s 14 of the TDA 1968 would be that, despite having taken 'all reasonable precautions and exercised all due diligence', there had been a 'mistake' or matters had been 'beyond control' of the HEI (see Harvey and Parry (2000) re these defences under ss 24 and 25).

---

1   [1973] 1 WLR 307, [1973] 1 All ER 762.
2   *R v Breeze* [1973] 1 WLR 994, [1973] 2 All ER 1141, CA; *Ashley v Sutton London Borough Council* (1994) 156 JP 631; see Cartwright (1996).
3   *Becket v Cohen* [1972] 1 WLR 1593; *R v Sunair Holidays* [1973] 1 WLR 1105; *British Airways Board v Taylor* [1975] 3 All ER 307; *R v Avro plc* (1993) 157 JP 759.

Consumer Protection Act 1987 (CPA 1987)

29.29   Part III (ss 20–26) of the CPA 1987 (and its related Code of Practice)[1] covers false and misleading price indications, and could *possibly* be relevant to the HEI–student contract, perhaps especially s 21(c) which envisages hidden additional charges (for example, the degree course fee is £1075 pa but, once the student has enrolled, there will *only then* be revealed additional charges for *essential* field-courses, course materials, library/laboratory/computer use . . .).[2]

29.30   Section 39 provides the HEI with a defence of 'due diligence' similar to that in ss 24 and 25 of the TDA 1968.

29.31   Such criminal offences will normally be committed by the HEI itself, but there is often provision in consumer legislation also to prosecute 'top management' (Vice-Chancellors, in the case of HEIs) if they have connived in the committing of the offence or have negligently allowed it to happen. Similarly, lower down the scale, mere employees can also be directly prosecuted in theory, but this rarely happens in practice.

Consumer Protection (Distance Selling) Regulations 2000 (DSR 2000)

29.32   The DSR 2000[3] came into force on 31 October 2000 to provide consumer protection when contracts are arranged and concluded exclusively 'by means of distance communication': essentially, mail-order and internet purchasing. But their scope can be wider and the DTI, despite representations, did not see fit to provide an exemption for HEIs. For example, the offer and acceptance of HEI residential accommodation for a new student will almost certainly be 'negotiated' at a distance, and could be covered by these regulations if the accommodation contract (a tenancy by way of a licence or a lease – see Chapter 23) is *concluded* only in the *exclusive* use of such distance communication. In fact, even if the rent has been paid well in advance the keys to the room being physically and personally (porter/clerical officer to student) handed over on arrival at the HEI could be interpreted as the actual completion of the 'sale', and hence the sale process would probably not then be exclusively a distance communication process. Similarly, second and third-year students probably renew in person for the next year their residential accommodation contracts with the HEI. The creation of the tuition contract (see Chapter 6) will again usually be completed when the student attends 'registration' to sign up, pay fees, collect library/ID card, etc (but an HEI which 'sells' the degree course exclusively at a distance, for example, the Open University, or even a conventional HEI which does postal registration to conclude the deal, may be caught by these regulations.)

---

1   Consumer Protection (Code of Practice for Traders on Price Indications) Approved Order 1988, SI 1988/2078.
2   Ibid, Part 2, Art 2.2, concerning 'incomplete information and non-optional extras'. Note that 'top-up' fees are outlawed by ss 26 and 28 of the Teaching and Higher Education Act 1998.
3   SI 2000/2334.

29.33 If the DSR 2000 apply, the effect is merely that certain information would need to be given early in the contract creation process (especially concerning price and cancellation), and be communicated clearly. In fact, one assumes that an HEI will anyway want to be sure that its students have fully understood the rental contract they will be entering into (weekly/termly rent, any charges for heating, deposit money, terms for early vacation of the room, etc). In practice, therefore, the DSR 2000 are perhaps not as challenging to HEIs as they may seem (assuming the HEI usually proceeds on the basis of fair dealing).

CONCLUSION

29.34 While it is (hopefully) inconceivable that any UK HEI would deliberately, 'knowingly' and dishonestly set out to mislead its applicants or students, it is clear that it could (especially because of the actions of over-eager employees or agents) fail to convince a court (as have otherwise respectable holiday companies) that its false description was not a simple mistake despite all its careful checking and that it had not behaved 'recklessly'. So far, such criminal sanctions have not been applied to an HEI, but in the context of a mass HE system and amidst intensive competition between HEIs for students and their fees is it fanciful to think that, as with holidays and used cars, eventually Trading Standards Officers will interest themselves in the campus? Or will the creation of an Ombudsperson for UK HE provide the consumer protection perhaps increasingly necessary in a mass system?

29.35 Perhaps the only alternative to an Ombudsperson created by legislation in the near future, given that self-regulation is not likely to be a credible option and given that politicians will want to be seen to protect the interests of students and their parents, would be greater involvement by the OFT in the creation of a voluntary Code of Conduct on the analogy of banking or package holidays (or even introduction agencies), and backed up by, where necessary, aggressive use of s 14 of the TDA 1968 or even by new specific legislation (for example, as in the case of package holidays with the Package Travel, Package Holidays and Package Tours Regulations 1992, or as with the Estate Agents' Act 1979 and its related Orders).[1]

29.36 Thus, the UK travel industry, for example, is now regulated largely by the Package Travel, Package Holidays and Package Tours Regulations 1992,[2] which were introduced in response to EC Directive 90/314 (Package Travel, Package Holidays and Package Tours): see Grant and Mason (1998), for each at pp 455–477 and 445–454 respectively. A key feature of the 1992 Regulations is that to some degree they shift the liability of the tour operator from fault liability (the consumer must prove negligence on the part of the holiday company) towards strict liability (no excuses): the analogy here, as noted

---

1   On codes of practice generally as a means of consumer protection, see Scott and Black (2000, 42–51); plus on Ombuds-schemes see Scott and Black (2000), pp 133–140.

2   SI 1992/3288.

in para **29.13**, is with a similar contrast between the liability under s 14 of the Sale of Goods Act 1979 for items not of a 'satisfactory quality' and the lesser stringency of the fault liability arising from s 13 of the SGSA 1982 for services not provided with 'reasonable care and skill'.

29.37 Another major consumer protection aspect of the travel industry regulations is that they tightly restrain the use of exclusion/limitation clauses, and, finally, there is the absolute civil liability imposed on both tour operators and travel agents for 'any loss which the consumer suffers as a consequence' of them supplying 'misleading information' via 'descriptive matter' contained in brochures and videos. It is absolute liability because there is no due diligence defence as against criminal charges under the TDA 1968 or CPA 1987; and note that 'misleading' is, in any event, a wider term than 'inaccurate' and 'false' as used in the TDA 1968 and CPA 1987. Alongside the regulations there is, of course, the industry's own voluntary good practice guide (the ABTA *Tour Operators' Code of Conduct*): see Grant and Mason (1998), pp 478–496.

29.38 Therefore, could UK HE eventually be regulated in a similar way, with the need for regulation evolving in the transition towards a mass (or even universal) system just as the holiday industry (and its regulation) grew over recent decades? Might the talked-of Ombudsperson for UK HE model his approach on the consumer protection developed for the UK package tour industry? Perhaps the Ombudsperson will also deal with overcrowding in UK HEIs by introducing the sort of regulatory control (EC Regulation 295/91; major revision pending) now in place to police airline overbooking which leads to 'denied boarding' (or the 'bumping' of ticket-holders from a flight)? Will academic lawyers in due course produce journal articles with 'prospectuses' substituted for 'holiday brochures'?[1] It is unlikely, however, that unhappy student consumers will be able to claim damages for non-pecuniary loss (mental upset and distress over disappointment with the degree course, etc), even if they can show breach of contract by the HEI in terms of the quality of the educational experience not matching up to what the student–HEI contract promised: contract breakers are not generally liable for any distress, frustration, anxiety or displeasure they cause. It is difficult to imagine the courts finding that the contract to educate is primarily one to provide relaxation, entertainment and enjoyment by analogy with the holiday industry in *Jarvis v Swan Tours Ltd*[2] and, more usefully, in *Jackson v Horizon Holidays*,[3] or, more recently, in *McLeod v Hunter (John)*:[4] even if some HEI prospectuses seem to emphasise student night life more than expected academic activity. (See Grant and Mason (1998), pp 256–261, and McGregor (1997), paras 101–104: and note that in *Johnson v Unisys*[5] the court acknowledged that damages are not

---

1   As in Grant and O'Cain 'Lies, Damn Lies and Holiday Brochures' [1995] *Travel Law Journal* 4.
2   [1973] 1 All ER 71, CA.
3   [1975] 3 All ER 92, CA.
4   [1987] CLY 1162.
5   [1999] 1 All ER 854, [1999] ICR 809; *overturning Addis v Gramophone Co Ltd* [1909] AC 488.

awarded for such 'injury to feelings' in breach of contract cases (as long established since 1880 in *Livingstone v Rawyards Coal Co*)[1] except (it then proposed) for unfair dismissal claims (where the actual process of dismissal had been conducted by the employer in an unnecessarily and unduly harsh way) and (as already well established in *Jarvis* and *Jackson* cited above) for 'peace of mind', 'pleasurable amenity' or 'relaxation' contracts. See also *Farley v Skinner*,[2] as elaborating on those exceptional contracts where damages for annoyance might be payable, citing *Watts v Morrow*[3] and confirming *Ruxley Electronics and Construction Ltd v Forsyth*.[4]

29.39   It is also noteworthy that individuals can bring private prosecutions under, for example, s 14 of the TDA 1968. Moreover, the UTCCR 1999 gives power to non-governmental organisations, such as the Consumer's Association, to seek injunctions against the use of unfair terms: watch out if the association ever gets interested in HE.

29.40   Major's 'Charters' and Blair's 'Service First', now covering some 40 areas of government and quasi-government activity (including HE) see Barron and Scott (1992), Parlour (1996), Scott (1999), and Kiloh (1998).

29.41   Finally, a feature of consumer law is the concept of 'multi-party actions', or what in the USA would be 'a class action'. Such 'group litigation' involves a nominated judge taking on the case-management of a group of claims which all centre on similar issues of fact or law: the most famous UK example is the Thalidomide litigation of the 1960s (see Harvey and Parry (2000), pp 237–242; Miller, Harvey and Parry (1998), pp 458–481; and Hodges (2001)). While such litigation has typically involved pharmaceutical and tobacco companies and medical device manufacturers, in principle a group action could be triggered where a cohort of students have the same complaint concerning allegedly inadequate teaching, poorly resourced courses or mismanaged examinations. Indeed, it may well literally be a 'class' action: 'Diploma class sues college',[5] In this case, six HND students are claiming negligent misrepresentation under consumer protection legislation, asserting that their 2-year course did not deliver what the prospectus and other course material promised. Their lawyer, Jaswinder Gill (see Evans and Gill (2001)), sees 'the beginning of an explosion of litigation in post-16 education': 'I've got about 20–25 cases like this one coming through . . .'.

---

1   (1880) 5 App Cas 25.
2   [2001] UKHL 49, [2001] 3 WLR 899, HL; Mr Skinner, the surveyor liable (£10K damages) for not warning Mr Farley that the house he proposed to buy would be affected by aircraft noise, thereby reducing Mr Farley's 'pleasurable amenity' and inflicting on him 'mental distress and disappointment' since he had specifically asked Mr Skinner to advise on aircraft noise given that the property was near Gatwick.
3   [1991] 1 WLR 1421, CA; another property survey case.
4   [1996] AC 344, HL; £2,500 damages awarded for 'loss of amenity' when the builder constructed a swimming pool for Mr Forsyth that was too shallow compared with the depth carefully specified by Mr Forsyth in the contract.
5   *The Times Higher Educational Supplement*, 7 December 2001, p 8.

Chapter 30

A BIBLIOGRAPHICAL ESSAY ON THE VISITOR

David Palfreyman

'For corporations being composed of individuals, subject to human frailties, are liable, as well as private persons, to deviate from the end of their institutions. And for that reason the law has provided proper persons to visit, inquire into, and correct all irregularities that arise in such corporations, either sole or aggregate, and whether ecclesiastical, civil or eleemosynary.' (Sir William Blackstone, *Commentaries on the Laws of England*, 10th edn, vol I, p 480, 1787.)

INTRODUCTION

30.1 This bibliographical essay reviews the literature on the role of the Visitor under English law with respect to the chartered ('old', pre-1992) universities and colleges. It will be appreciated that the statutory ('new', ex-polytechnic universities) do not have the institution of the Visitor, being subject to judicial review as the creatures of statute. Thus, Carroll (1994) divides HEIs into the post-1992 statutory universities subject to judicial review; the traditional chartered universities and Oxbridge colleges with their Visitors; and the ancient chartered Oxford and Cambridge which, he argues, as civil rather than eleemosynary corporations have no Visitor and hence the student–university relationship is simply a matter of contract law for arbitration in the courts as for any other contract (and as for the statutory universities). See Samuels (1973) on the student–HEI contract, along with Farrington (1998) and Chapters 6, 7, 8 and 9 concerning the continuing role of the Visitor in relation to student matters, together with Chapters 10 and 11 concerning the now residual role of the Visitor in relation to staff matters.

30.2 The analysis of the literature has been divided into several sections:

- the history and evolution of the Visitor;
- the strengths and weaknesses of the Visitor as an institution;
- the jurisdiction of the Visitor;
- the Visitor's powers of enforcement and ability to award damages;
- the procedures for visitation;
- the scope for judicial review relevant to the Visitor.

30.3 A further section compares the role of the Visitor in Australia, Canada, England, New Zealand and Nigeria. Key cases relevant to the interpretation(s) set out in the texts and articles are noted at the end of this chapter.

30.4 Reference is also made to the enquiry undertaken by Lord Nolan (1996) into the governance of UK HEIs, including how they deal with student and staff complaints and problems. There is some, inevitably speculative, consideration given to the future of the Visitor – a medieval relic, a ghost clanking its chains, an anachronism awaiting abolition, or a sound model for retention within the chartered HEIs and possibly even extension into the statutory HEIs?

30.5 Thus, Samuels (1973) describes the Visitor as being 'redolent of monarchist paternalism in an isolated, unworldly community of scholars'; and Farrington (1998) concedes that the concept of visitation has 'a distinctly medieval, ecclesiastical ring', quoting McCaughlin (1983) 'an anarchaic functionary'. Farrington and Mattison (1990) compare the Visitorial Court to the other remaining vestiges of domestic tribunals left over from the Middle Ages – the Court Martial in relation to military law, the Consistory Court for Church of England ecclesiastical law, and the Court of Chivalry dealing with claims to coats of arms. Farrington (1994 edn), however, still saw the Visitor as a legal entity having 'much to commend it' and as 'perhaps a model to which the rest of the system should give close attention'. Similarly, Isaac in chapter 8 of the 1998 edition of this book, having reviewed the strengths and weaknesses of the Visitor as a fair, speedy and inexpensive mechanism for dealing with disputes, concluded that it 'is a valuable one which should not be abandoned ... [and which] generally works well. Rather than being abolished the Visitorial system should be developed and extended to all HEIs. On closer scrutiny, surprisingly few of its features are anachronistic. The majority of criticisms lie in practical considerations where new procedures and experienced personnel could straightforwardly minimise current problems. The debate has already recently moved on because of the recommendations of Lord Nolan'. (The Visitor debate post-Nolan is discussed at para **30.57**.)

30.6 As noted earlier, the Visitor is to be found in the chartered universities and in the Oxford and Cambridge colleges, but *probably* (see para **30.7**) not in the two 'ancient universities' of Oxford and Cambridge – these are civil corporations, not eleemosynary corporations. (The new universities created from the former polytechnics by statute under the Further and Higher Education Act 1992, also do not have a Visitor.) Picarda (1995 edn), p 522 notes that 'The distinction in nature between the two ancient universities and the modern [chartered] universities is to be ascribed to history rather than logic'! Picarda (1995 edn), p 519 also provides two definitions of the Visitor. First, from the *Shorter Oxford English Dictionary* (3rd edn), 'one who visits officially for the purpose of inspection or supervision, in order to prevent or remove abuses or irregularities'; and, secondly, from Mitcheson (1887), 'persons having a private or domestic judicial authority over eleemosynary, lay and ecclesiastical corporations for the correction of the life and conduct of the members and the adjudication of disputes between them'.

THE HISTORY AND EVOLUTION OF THE VISITOR

30.7   Shelford (1836), Grant (1850), Mitcheson (1887) and Williams (1910) provide historical accounts of the origin and evolution of the Visitor, all of which are echoed in the modern texts of Luxton (2001), Pettit (1993), Picarda (1999), and *Tudor on Charities* (1995). Mitcheson notes that: 'though the visitation of eleemosynary lay corporations is part of the common law of England, yet both the name and duties of the Office are derived from the canon law on which the principles of ecclesiastical visitation are based' (Mitcheson (1887), p 3).

30.8   Apart from the question of the petitioner's *locus standi*, Mitcheson's 1887 account holds good in all respects of jurisdiction, practice and procedure. He also provides a little gem in quoting the Bishop of Winchester's 1611 letter to James I, in which the author, as Visitor to St John's College, Oxford, explains his duties, noting that his visits are at his own expense ('I must visit at mine own no small charge') and beseeching His Majesty to ignore grumblings from St John about his carrying out of those duties ('a few factious fellows to cover their diverse abuses, should by causeless complaints or clamorous noise . . .') (Mitcheson (1887), pp 39–40).

30.9   Shelford ('at the expense of much labour . . . ., by a careful perusal of the reported cases', Preface) provides an early version (1043 pp) of *Tudor on Charities* or of Picarda's equally monumental work. In the section on visitation (Shelford (1836), pp 322–398), he notes that the Sovereign is the Visitor of *all* civil corporations, via the King's/Queen's Bench, and hence, on that basis, Oxford and Cambridge, the ancient universities, *do* have a Visitor despite the assertion in some textbooks that, since they are not eleemosynary, they do not (unlike their constituent colleges). He says: 'This is what is understood to be the meaning of lawyers, when they say that these civil corporations are liable to no visitation – that is, the law, having by immemorial usage appointed them to be visited and inspected by the King, their Founder, in his Majesty's Court of King's Bench, according to the rules of the common law, they ought not to be visited elsewhere, or by any other authority' (p 324).

30.10   Later, Shelford notes that 'It was adjudged that the King had an undoubted right to visit the two universities of Oxford and Cambridge' (p 333). Early editions of *Tudor on Charities* cite the Supreme Court of Judicature (Consolidation) Act 1925, s 56(2)(a) which, in turn, refers back to the Supreme Court of Judicature Act 1873, s 34, in terms of the King's/Queen's Bench having a range of miscellaneous duties (including, presumably, that of visitation to Oxford and Cambridge). The latest edition of *Tudor on Charities* (1995) continues with this interpretation. See, however, Picarda (1995 edn), pp 521–522, Pettit (1993), p 278, Farrington (1994), paras 1.14 and 2.35) and Carroll (1994) for another view. In fact, Picarda notes that 'Civil corporations are subject to the jurisdiction of the Queen's Bench Division: the Crown's prerogative to visit such corporations is exercised by the judges, administering the common law of England' (p 521). A footnote then refers to Shelford and states *Quaere* whether the court acts in the capacity of Visitor. Later, however, Picarda comments 'The Universities of Oxford and Cambridge being civil corporations do not have a Visitor: they are subject to the control of the courts' (p 522). In fact, the different interpretations are not that far apart and all this is very largely a matter of semantics: when is a Visitor not a visitor?

30.11 Shelford praises the Visitor model: 'The domestic forum of the Visitor is peculiarly adapted for determining all disputes which arise between the members of learned societies ... If the learning, morals, or proprietary qualifications of students were determinable at common law, and subject to the same review *as* legal actions, great confusion and uncertainty would follow' (1836), pp 330–331).

30.12 Thus, the Visitor watches over the endowment, the foundation, on behalf of the Founder: '... for it is fit the members that are endowed, and that have the charity bestowed upon them, should not be left to themselves (for divisions and contests will arise amongst them about the dividend of the charity), but pursue the intent and design of him that bestowed it upon them ... where they who are to enjoy the benefit of the charity are incorporated there, to prevent all perverting of the charity, or to compare differences that may happen among them, there is by law a visitational power' (Shelford (1863), p 332).

30.13 Williams follows Mitcheson and Shelford in his account of the Visitor (1910), pp 29–46, and includes a very detailed 'Appendix of Cases' (pp 120–151), many of which are Visitor cases. Williams also discusses whether Oxford and Cambridge are visited by the Crown (the most recent example, he says, being in the reign of James II): 'As the law stands at present, a civil corporation has the Crown for a Visitor, the visitation being exercised by the King's Bench Division, not by the Lord Chancellor, as in eleemosynary corporations' (p 31). However, 'There is a doubt whether Oxford and Cambridge have visitors ... The matter must be considered doubtful' (p 32). It is unclear why by 1910 what in 1836 had apparently been certain should have become doubtful, but it may be linked to the dispute detailed shortly. As for the colleges, Williams notes that 'The right of visitation is in law an incorporeal heriditament' (p 35).

30.14 The 1852 Report of the Oxford University Commission notes that: 'The University of Oxford is a corporate body ... Its privileges have been granted or renewed in many Royal Charters ... Whether there be power in any hands ordinarily to superintend this great Institution, and to reform it, when reform becomes necessary, and what is the extent of that power, if it exists, has often been a subject of dispute. Such a power has, however, been generally supposed to reside in the Sovereign, as Visitor. It has often been exercised by the Crown, and has often been recognised by the University … the right of visitation …, has never been formally denied by the University … Even if the fullest authority ever claimed by the Sovereign were demonstrated to be constitutional, the long interruption of its use might render it difficult to discover the proper mode of exercising it' (Report of the Oxford University Commissioners (1852), pp 3–4).

30.15 The material in the Report's appendices includes an opinion from the Attorney-General in 1836 that there is indeed a Visitor 'and that the power of visiting that University is in the Crown' (p D54). But the 1851 'Opinion of the Legal Advisors of the Heads of Houses and Proctors' is that the Crown possesses no such visitational authority: 'The visitatorial right, properly so called, is annexed to eleemosynary foundations alone … The University, however, is not an eleemosynary foundation, but a civil corporation, and, as such is subject to the control of the Court of Queen's Bench, which, upon complaint, acts with regard to it by mandamus, or otherwise, as it acts respecting other civil corporations. This species of control has sometimes, though inaccurately, been called Visitatorial … but where there is a Visitor a mandamus will not be granted as to any matters within his jurisdiction' (p D54).

30.16 A 'Postscript to the Evidence of the Rev J Wilkinson' (pp 245–249) discusses 'the visitatorial power of the Crown over the University' and notes that the University had on various occasions acknowledged the right of visitation. It concludes: 'the assumption by the Crown; if not of the title of Visitor, at least of the right to visit is beyond dispute. Indeed, it does not appear that the Royal right of visiting the Universities was ever questioned; on the contrary, it was gloried in as a University privilege, and urged in bar of jurisdiction by other parties'.

30.17 *R v University of Cambridge (Dr Bentley's Case)*[1] is cited: 'Dr Bentley's counsel admitted "that if the University had returned that the King was their visitor, as they might have done, it would have put an end to the dispute here" … I am contending that the University has this incident [visitation] of an eleemosynary corporation'. Counsel's view is presumably based on the acknowledged exclusivity of jurisdiction of the Visitor. More recently, in a case involving the University of Oxford the possible jurisdiction was *not* invoked by the University: see *R v Oxford University ex parte Bolchover*[2] where Bolchover claimed (unsucessfully) that the proctors had acted unfairly.

30.18 The present official stance of the University of Oxford is that it does *not* have a Visitor, although, for the purposes of attempting to demonstrate that, post-Nolan, it has an independent arbitrator of disputes, it currently argues that the proctors, a medieval office carried over the centuries into modern times, are truly independent of the 'management'/executive by definition and

---

1   (1723) 1 Str 557.
2   (1970) *The Times*, October 7.

behaviour, while the high steward is of Visitor-like gravitas: between these two officers, student and other disputes will, says the University, be dealt with impartially and fairly. If, however, the complainant remained aggrieved, there is certainly no exclusion of the courts as would be the case with a real Visitor, and hence the only practical issue is whether such a case goes direct to the Queen's Bench as the appropriate court or starts off in the county court as would most similar disputes. Or, unless in fact the Queen's Bench is not functioning *qua* court but *qua* Visitor. Hence, presumably, a judge would be despatched to Oxford or Cambridge to act as Visitor (speedy, informal, less expensive?), with the result that the decision would be final (absolute jurisdiction?) and subject only to limited judicial review by the courts. If the latter, and given that the Visitor system is generally a sound mechanism, there seems little purpose in Oxford denying that it might have such a convenient Visitor. Similarly, Cambridge at present believes itself not to have a Visitor and the 1997 case of *R v University of Cambridge ex parte Evans*[1] notes in the judgment of Sedley J that 'Cambridge University has no Visitor'. Hence the High Court in that case considered whether leave should be granted to Dr Evans to seek judicial review of the fairness of the University's promotions procedures: the judicial review route would, of course, be barred by the exclusive jurisdiction of the Visitor, had Cambridge been deemed to have one.

30.19 The better interpretation, however, is that Oxford and Cambridge do technically have a Visitor in the form of the Queen's Bench Division, but that any dispute would be dealt with by *and physically in* that court (a one-man 'court' would not helpfully be coming to Oxford!), and hence that invoking the concept of the Visitor in relation to what would in effect be judicial review of the university's procedures would make no difference to the speed/cost dimension. In disputes short of judicial review, the aggrieved student could and probably would proceed by way of the usual court hierarchy for a claim in contract or tort: there would not, in fact, be exclusive jurisdiction for the Queen's Bench Division as would, in the case of an Oxbridge college with a real Visitor, preclude a contract (and perhaps a tort) claim in relation to any alleged failure to provide the appropriate educational 'experience'.

30.20 Finally, for a US perspective see *Trustees of Dartmouth College v Woodward*.[2]

THE STRENGTHS AND WEAKNESSES OF THE VISITOR MODEL

30.21 If our friendly Visitor did not already exist, would we invent him or her? Ricquier (1978) puts it well: 'Does the Visitor matter? The question has to be asked. Recent cases upholding his jurisdiction have been greeted with

---

1   [1998] 1 EdCR 151.
2   (1819) 17 US 518, and Pound (1936).

wailing and the gnashing of teeth, and slow emergence of this antediluvian functionary into the twentieth century cannot be expected to be greeted without misgivings. There are, however, strong arguments for its retention, and indeed encouragement' (p 211).

30.22 Smith (1986) believes the Visitor to 'have a useful and important role to play in our universities ... he is invariably a person of the highest standing and authority ... disputes can then be determined swiftly, cheaply, and with the minimum of formality' (Smith (1986), p 666). *Tudor on Charities* (1995) notes that 'in recent years it has been commended as providing a practical and expeditious means of resolving disputes' (p 369), and argues that the House of Lords in recent cases has been concerned to retain the visitor's jurisdiction as a speedy, cheap and final answer to internal disputes' (p 387). The praise of Shelford (1836) has already been noted. Luxton (2001), para 1.105 refers to 'this very useful jurisdiction'.

30.23 Peiris (1987) notes that 'The rationale of the visitational jurisdiction is essentially pragmatic' and he quotes Megarry, Vice-Chancellor, in *Patel v University of Bradford Senate*:[1]

> 'In place of the formality, publicity and expense of proceedings in court with pleadings, affidavits and all the apparatus of litigation, there is an appropriate domestic tribunal which can determine the matter informally, privately, cheaply and speedily, and can give a decision which, apart from any impropriety or excess of jurisdiction, is final and will not be disturbed by the courts' (p 1499).

30.24 Lord Griffiths in *Thomas v University of Bradford*,[2] commented: 'There is also the advantage of cheapness, lack of formality, and flexibility in the visitorial procedure which is not bound by the intimidating and formalised procedures of the courts of law ... the visitorial jurisdiction is not an ancient anachronism which should now be severely curtailed, if not discontinued. If confined to its proper limits, namely, the laws of the foundation and matters deriving therefrom, it provides a practical and expeditious means of resolving disputes which it is in the interests of the universities and their members to preserve'. More recently, the Lord Chancellor expressed support for the concept of the Visitor in *Burrows v University of York*.[3]

30.25 Similarly, Lord Hardwicke LC in *Green v Rutherforth*[4] commented: 'The visitorial power, as allowed and established by the law of England, and on the grounds on which it is established, is most useful in Collleges and learned societies: and I am for supporting it as far as it is established by the constitution of this kingdom'. A few years before that case, in *A-G v Talbot*,[5] the Lord Chancellor declared the Visitor to be 'the most convenient jurisdiction; for

---

1   [1979] 1 WLR 1066, [1979] 2 All ER 582; *affirming* [1978] 1 WLR 1488, CA.
2   [1987] AC 795, at pp 824H and 825D.
3   [1999] EdCR 586.
4   (1750) 1 Ves Sen 463, at p 475.
5   [1747] 3 Atk 662.

though perhaps it may be absurd, yet it is less expensive than a suit in law or equity; and in general has been exercised in a reasonable manner'.

30.26 Howells (1989), however, queries whether the Visitor route is private and any less formal. Samuels (1973) considers the Visitor 'redolent of monarchial paternalism for an isolated unworldly community of Scholars ... inappropriate for a large place of work'. He endorses the idea of an HE advisory board which might 'exercise appellate disciplinary functions, in order to bring consistency into the university world'. This has echoes of calls, post-Nolan, for an HE Ombudsman (see para **30.57** and Chapter 8 concerning the future of the Visitor). Finally, the Report of the Oxford University Commissioners (1852) noted that 'For the settlement of internal disputes nothing can be better than the decisions of a wise Visitor. The decisions of Visitors have in point of fact been usually just and speedy' (p 183).

THE JURISDICTION OF THE VISITOR

30.27 Although in recent decades there has been some debate and confusion about the extent of the jurisdiction, there is now clarity on the boundaries, which have been confirmed along the traditional lines (with one key exception regarding academic staff contracts of employment: see Chapters 10 and 11). Thus, Farrington and Mattison (1990) noted that 'there seems to be no dispute about the exclusivity of the Visitor's unique jurisdiction' (p 79). They cited authority back to 1747: Wright J in *R v Bishop of Chester*,[1] 'Visitors have an absolute power; the only absolute one I know in England'. They also cited Lord Hardwicke LC in *A-G v Talbot*,[2] 'The powers are absolute and final, and cannot be taken away by the courts of law in this kingdom ... the most convenient jurisdiction; for though perhaps it may be sometimes absurd, yet it is less expensive than a suit in law or equity'. Farrington (1994 first edn of Farrington 1998) sees the Visitorial jurisdiction as 'a true "Alsatia in England"' (p 42). Pettit (1993) declares that the 'power of the Visitor is absolute and exclusive' (p 279).

30.28 Bridge (1970), writing in the context of the 'present unrest in the universities', saw the powers and duties of the Visitor as having been settled as early as 1692 in *Philips v Bury*[3]: 'his determinations are final and examinable in no other Court whatsoever', Sir John Holt, CJ. The Visitor should not, argued Bridge, be dismissed as being just a figurehead, having only a nominal role ('not merely a social and ceremonial adornment of the university'). Again, Lord Hardwicke is quoted from *A-G v Talbot*: 'the general powers of a Visitor are well known; no court of law or equity can anticipate their judgement, or take away their jurisdiction, but their determinations are final and conclusive'.

---

1   (1747) 1 WM Bl 22.
2   [1747] 3 Atk 662.
3   [1692] 1 Ld Raym 5, 2 TR 347, Skin 447, 4 Mod 106.

30.29   Smith (1981) traces cases from even earlier than *Philips v Bury*, such as *Daniel Appleford's Case*[1] where Appleford sought *mandamus* to restore him to his fellowship against the Warden and Fellows of New College, Oxford, only to be told by Hale CJ that 'We ought not to grant a *mandamus* where there is a visitor'. Smith's trail carries him through the eighteenth century (*R v Bishop of Chester; A-G v Talbot; St John's College, Cambridge v Todington*[2]) and the nineteenth century (*Thomson v University of London*[3]) to the twentieth century (*R v Dunsheath ex parte Meredith*;[4] *Thorne v University of London*[5]) before culminating in *Patel v University of Bradford Senate* where Megarry VC said, 'it seems to be clear that the visitor has a sole and exclusive jurisdiction, and that the courts have no jurisdiction over matters within the visitor's jurisdiction'. Smith sums up the Visitor as 'a private judge'. Smith (1986) takes the story on, noting a revival of interest in the concept of the Visitor ('A Ghost from the Past'), and citing especially *Hines v Birkbeck College*[6] concerning the overlap of membership of the foundation with the contract of employment. Does the latter 'bring the cognisance of any dispute involving such internal rules within the jurisdiction of the common law courts?'. Smith argues that it will not, on an analogy with the application of ecclesiastical law solely by the ecclesiastical courts: 'the general courts of law will not attempt to enter the jurisdiction of another which they recognise as possessing a competent authority over its own special laws and subject matter in order to enforce rights and duties derived from the law appropriate to that jurisdiction, even though they may appear at first sight to have a *prima facie* right to do so by virtue of some other relationship such as contract' (Smith (1986), p 107).

30.30   On the other hand, Smith recognises that the generality of employees are not within the jurisdiction of the Visitor. He says: 'The relationship is entirely contractual . . . Such persons may be said not to have any 'status' within the foundation itself derived from its statutes, etc, however much they appear superficially to be part of the university community' (p 569). Smith's four-part running article in the *New Law Journal* was cited by the House of Lords in *Thomas v University of Bradford*.[7]

30.31   Ricquier (1978) examining *Patel v University of Bradford Senate*, defines the jurisdiction as including anybody with *locus standi* to the internal rules of the foundation on which the Visitor arbitrates, and not just, as had been thought, corporators or actual members of the foundation. Here he agrees with Christie (1974) who had been prompted by *Herring v Templeman and Others*[8] and differs from Bridge (1970): 'It has been noted elsewhere [Christie] that the determining factor [in deciding whether a matter is within the Visitor's

---

1   (1672) 1 Mod Rep 82.
2   (1757) 1 Burr 158.
3   (1864) 33 LJ Ch 625.
4   [1951] 1 KB 127.
5   [1966] 2 QB 237, [1966] 2 All ER 338, CA.
6   [1985] 3 All ER 156.
7   [1987] AC 795, [1987] 1 All ER 834.
8   [1973] 3 All ER 569, CA; [1973] 2 All ER 581.

jurisdiction] should be not so much the status of the complainant as the subject-matter of the complaint ... the cases that go against it [this interpretation] can be discredited as being dependent on anachronistic distinctions between scholars and commoners at Oxbridge' (p 653).

30.32 Ricquier, however, does query whether the Visitor covers disputes about admission to the university, as do Smith (1986), p 568 and Picarda (1995 edn of Picarda 1999), p 529 who also accept that the jurisdiction applies to all 'of the foundation' and not just corporators. *Tudor on Charities* (1995) cites *Oakes v Sidney Sussex College, Cambridge*[1] where the Court 'declined to follow the previous view that the Visitor of an Oxford or Cambridge college has jurisdiction to determine a dispute with a scholar (ie a member of the college) but not an ordinary student' (Ricquier's point as noted earlier). Ricquier (1979) in a lengthy review of the history, role and jurisdiction of the Visitor cites a Canadian case in support of the exclusive jurisdiction line, *Vanek v Governor of the University of Alberta*;[2] a case, however, which prompted the Alberta legislation to abolish the office of Visitor altogether. He regards Sir Richard Kindersley's statement in *Thomson v University of London,* as 'the obvious starting-point for a discussion of visitational power' ('Whatever relates to the internal arrangements and dealings with regard to the government and management of the house, of the domus of the institution, is properly within the jurisdiction of the Visitor'). *Thomson v University of London* concerned the exclusive jurisdiction of the Visitor in relation to examinations and was affirmed in *Thorne v University of London*: 'the High Court does not sit as a court of appeal from university examiners' (Diplock LJ). *Langlois v Rector and Members of Laval University*[3] is also cited as a Canadian case confirming this proposition. Ricquier went on to identify the 'areas of doubt' as regards jurisdiction-overlap with the general law of the land, including trust law, where the courts can intervene since the issue is no longer solely local law, and the problems of admissions ('essentially one of discretion').

30.33 The Visitor's jurisdiction most recently (1987) and definitively came up for consideration by the House of Lords in *Thomas v University of Bradford,* here concerning not student discipline or progress as in *Patel v University of Bradford Senate* but an academic's contract of employment. Lord Griffiths, dismissing a contrary Commonwealth case, *Norrie v Senate of the University of Auckland,*[4] declared that 'the exclusivity of the jurisdiction of the Visitor is in English law beyond doubt and established by an unbroken line of authorities spanning the last three centuries'. Thus, in reviewing *Thomas v University of Bradford,* Hadfield (1987) concludes, 'The Visitor is clearly here to stay. Lewis (1987) was not so sure, noting that 'having apparently reestablished the orthodox position, the House then significantly altered the traditional understanding of the visitorial jurisdiction' by confirming that an aggrieved

1   [1988] 1 WLR 431.
2   [1975] 3 WWR 167, [1975] 5 WWR 429.
3   [1974] 47 DLR (3d) 674.
4   [1984] 1 NZLR 129.

academic employee (a member of the foundation) can utilise the Employment Protection (Consolidation) Act 1978. In fact, this ambiguity was little more than briefly academic in that the ERA 1988 promptly removed tenure, the issue at large in *Thomas v University of Bradford*, for all academic staff appointed (or even promoted) after 20 November 1987, and, via the notorious model statutes imposed by the University Commissioners set up under the ERA 1988, introduced non-Visitor mechanisms for dealing with disputes regarding the contracts of employment of academics (see Zellick (1989); Pettit (1991); Chapters 10 and 11). Pettit (1991) reviews *Pearce v University of Aston in Birmingham*[1] as a case concerning an academic in dispute over his contract of employment. (See also Khan (1993).)

30.34   Peiris (1987) and Howells (1989) also consider *Thomas v University of Bradford*, the latter contemplating 'the protection currently available to aggrieved university academics' in the context of the 1980s' universities no longer being ivory towers as they become 'more management orientated'. Hence, Howells comments, 'The appropriateness of the Visitor to resolve these disputes must be doubted'. Pitt (1990) considers the ERA 1988 'attack on tenure' and the work of the University Commissioners, now virtually complete as even the Oxbridge colleges have had their messy statutes forcibly revised to incorporate the draft model statute regarding redundancy. He notes that the Visitor may still have a role as part of the university appeal mechanism prior to a dispute reaching the courts. Hadfield (1985) considers *Re Wislang's Application*[2] concerning a dismissed lecturer.

30.35   *Tudor on Charities* (1995) quotes from *R v Committee of the Lords of the Judicial Committee of the Privy Council acting for the Visitor of the University of London ex parte Vijayatunga*:[3] 'the Visitor enjoys untrammelled jurisdiction to investigate and correct wrongs done in the administration of the internal laws of the foundation to which he is appointed; a general power to right wrongs and redress grievances'.

30.36   There is some uncertainty as to the Visitor's jurisdiction over the corporate property of the eleemosynary foundation, as discussed in Picarda (1995), pp 527–529, linking back to whether the general corporate are held on trust or not at pp 382–386, in *Tudor* (1995), pp 162/163 and 371, 374, 381 and 387, in Luxton (2001), paras 11.16–11.29 and 15.07, in Smith (1981), pp 634–637, and in Palfreyman (1998/1999 and 1999). Where the HEI is the trustee of a specific, express trust, then the jurisdiction of the Visitor certainly does *not* oust that of the courts; but it *may* to a limited degree (depending on the exact powers of the Visitor concerned) in relation to the general assets and in terms of overseeing their proper application for charitable purposes if such assets are to be seen as being held by the corporation, as it were, in trust to the

---

1   [1991] 2 All ER 461.
2   [1984] CLY 2462, NI 63.
3   [1989] 2 All ER 843, CA; [1987] 1 QB 322.

founder. *Green v Rutherforth*[1] is a key case on this complex issue. In broad terms, however, the court will find some way to assert its jurisdiction in order to ensure that the corporate assets are deployed only for appropriate charitable purposes.

THE VISITOR'S POWERS OF ENFORCEMENT AND ABILITY TO AWARD DAMAGES

30.37 Farrington in the 1994 edition of his book stated that, although the Visitor 'apparently has wide powers to grant relief . . . he or she has no power to order compensation in the nature of damages' (p 51). Lord Hailsham LC, in *Casson v University of Aston in Birmingham*[2] is quoted: 'the only substantive prayer for relief in this case is a monetary claim for compensation in the nature of damages. After considerable research, I have been unable to find any precedent in the long history of visitatorial powers in which a visitor has made such an order and in my view he has no such power'.

30.38 Farrington noted that this view was accepted by Kelly LJ in *Re Wislang's Application* and by Sir Michael Davies (1994) in the University College of Swansea case in 1993. In contrast, however, Pettit (1993) declares: 'Contrary to the view expressed by Lord Hailsham LC, the House of Lords has now said that there is no reason why the Visitor should not award damages in an appropriate case' (p 281). He cites *Thomas v University of Bradford*, which is the subject of two articles (Hadfield (1987) and Lewis (1987)), both of which note that it overruled the statement in *Casson* that the Visitor possessed no power to award damages' (Hadfield's words). *Tudor on Charities* (1995) agrees with Pettit. Farrington, however, has amended his view in the 1998 edition (para 2.224). In fact, Smith (1986), p 667, following Hailsham, also asserts an inability to award damages'. Peiris (1987), moreover, comments that 'in this state of the authorities it would certainly be rash to take for granted that the Visitor could be presumed upon to order the payment of damages for breach of contract', not least because he or she would in all probability take into account the general interest and welfare of the institution ... This erodes disconcertingly the plaintiff's legitimate interests which are protected by the common law action for contractual damages'.

THE PROCEDURES FOR VISITATION

30.39 *Tudor on Charities* (1995) agrees with Picarda (1995) on most aspects of the procedures for visitation:

– the Visitor is not obliged to proceed by way of common law rules;

---

1   (1750) 1 Ves Sen 463.
2   [1983] 1 All ER 88.

- he or she is invoked by way of petitioning for an appeal;
- the visitation is a judicial act and, hence, all relevant parties must be heard but not necessarily personally by the Visitor (in that assessors can be appointed to advise and commissaries can be sent to whom the hearing of evidence can be delegated, for example, the Crown will delegate via the Lord Chancellor to a High Court judge or even a QC) and perhaps only in writing – a point Wade and Forsyth (1994), p 537 also make.

30.40   In short, the Visitor has wide discretion over procedures, and, indeed, 'formalities should be kept to a minimum' (Picarda (1995), p 532). de Smith (1974) discusses the applicability of the rules of natural justice to Visitor procedures in the light of *R v University of Aston Senate ex parte Roffey*,[1] an interesting and controversial case: the Visitor must offer the student facing disciplinary charges the chance to offer a defence, to plead mitigating circumstances, but there needs to be no pretence that formal procedures are required as if in a court of law. Wade (1969) was critical of the legal reasoning displayed in *Roffey*: 'It was only a question of time before the high tide of litigation over natural justice reached the universities'; 'the whole legal paraphernalia' has been imported into academic life; the board of university examiners has mistakenly been viewed as a judicially reviewable statutory tribunal or government agency.

30.41   Otherwise, the only detail on the practice and procedure for Visitor appeals is the article by Picarda (1992–93). The founder has delegated to the Visitor, so can the Visitor further delegate? Broadly, no, but he or she can appoint an assessor to assist on matters of law or send a commissary. The sovereign, instead of acting via the Lord Chancellor, may appoint a commissioner. The hearing of evidence may be delegated to an examiner (but it is better not to if the material is 'hotly in dispute, because the Visitor is then deprived of the opportunity of assessing the credibility of witnesses in the box'). The Visitor can visit of his or her own accord (a 'general visitation'), but this practice has died out in modern times. Otherwise, the Visitor will be activated by an appeal, launched by petition from anybody with the necessary *locus standi* (ie 'the petitioner's interest in having a matter determined by reference to the internal laws of the foundation in question': the petitioner could be the university itself, but this is much less likely than it being an aggrieved student or academic). Thus, we have a petitioner and a respondent, and a formal petition, but thereafter the formalities are entirely within the control of the Visitor as to whether proceedings mimic court practice (for example, pleadings, discovery, interrogations, further and better particulars). Usually, 'subject to the need to conform with the principles of natural justice', the proceedings will be simple – a hearing, but one which does not necessarily involve oral evidence or, indeed, much by way of evidence (for example, if it is about the interpretation of a statute). Evidence may or may not be on oath, 'as

---

1   [1969] 2 QB 538.

the visitor may direct'. Costs and damages may be ordered. Costs were indeed awarded in *Thomas v University of Bradford (No 2)*.[1]

30.42 Mitcheson (1887) notes that the Visitor should proceed 'summarily, simply, and plainly, without the noise and formalities of a court' (p 5), and that 'visitors have in England generally adopted as closely as possible the procedure of the ecclesiastical courts; for if they are to give the parties interested a fair hearing, they can hardly adopt a more simple procedure' (p 14). Shelford (1836) also discusses powers and procedures: 'A visitor is not bound to proceed according to the rules of the common law' (p 361); his powers are 'absolute and final' (p 361); he may deprive the members of a foundation of their position if they refuse to take full part in a visitation (p 369); 'the acts of a visitor, whether right or wrong, cannot be examined in courts of law, where he has acted within the scope of his jurisdiction' (p 376); 'He may administer an oath or require an answer upon oath' (p 379). Williams echoes much of Mitcheson and Shelford (1910), noting that the Visitor cannot, apart from statute, compel the attendance of witnesses' (p 44), and that 'No precise mode of procedure is necessary, as long as substantial justice is done' (p 44). The recent case of *R v Visitor to Brunel University ex parte Jemchi*,[2] however, suggests (Sedley LJ) that a Visitor should offer an oral hearing.

JUDICIAL REVIEW OF THE VISITOR

30.43 Although there has been uncertainty even until the 1980s concerning the extent to which the Visitor is subject to judicial review, the position is now clear. Wade and Forsyth (1994) state that the Visitor is subject to judicial review for any breach in the application of the rules of natural justice in relation to procedures, and for any lack of jurisdiction and authority, but not for any error of fact or of law (here the Visitor has an 'ancient immunity'). The full range of judicial review remedies applies. Similarly, Pettit (1993) and Picarda (1995) confirm Wade and Forsyth – the jurisdiction of the Visitor is exclusive, but there is limited control by the courts by way of judicial review if the Visitor exceeds his or her jurisdiction, if there is a failure to act, and (only more recently established within case-law) clarification in certain circumstances (*not* for errors of fact or law). Picarda makes the point that, in practice, matters are likely to be clarified by way of declaration rather than the issue of an order and also comments that a Visitor could have damages awarded against him or her for exceeding his or her jurisdiction. Since there is no judicial review for error of fact, there is effectively no appeal against the decision of the Visitor. Picarda comments here that, as a result, the Visitor is unable to relieve against his or her own sentence. In relation to error of law, Pettit (1993), p 281 explains the logic in the ordinary courts nor being able to review the Visitor's interpretation and application of the internal laws of the foundation or institution – the courts are

---

1   [1992] 1 All ER 964.
2   [2001] EWCA Civ 1208, unreported, CA.

not here concerned with English law but with the *forum domesticum*, the local law of the university or college, and so they have no relevant expertise: 'The visitor is not applying the general law of the land but a peculiar, domestic law of which he is the sole arbiter and of which the courts have no cognisance'.

30.44 Wade (1993), however, queries whether such an exemption from judicial review in respect of error of law, as bestowed (or confirmed) by the House of Lords in *R v Lord President of the Privy Council ex parte Page*[1] is sustainable. It has to be noted that the Lords reversed the judgments of the lower courts, and only by a majority of three (Lords Browne-Wilkinson, Keith, Griffiths) to two (Lords Slynn and Mustill). The majority 'emphasised the considered judicial policy over 300 years in refusing to review visitors' decisions on their merits ... *certiorari* would never issue for mere error'. Wade asks whether that line of argument, dating back to *Philips v Bury*, may be 'a shibboleth', ready to be discarded as, like all else in the last 40 years (he says), it will eventually fall to the incoming tide of judicial review. Otherwise, the Visitor is, indeed, with this 'ancient immunity', in a unique position.

30.45 Smith (1993–94) also reviews *R v Lord President of the Privy Council ex parte Page* (as do Davies (1993) and Pugh (1993): see also Hadfield (1985) and Pitt (1991)), noting that the House of Lords had been unable to find 'anything inherently wrong with powers vested in an inferior court from which there could be no appeal', given that 'the rules which are under consideration are not the general laws of the realm, but the private rules of the founder, and the High Court is neither competent in such laws, nor is it directly concerned whether or not such laws are observed or enforced'. Smith is clearly more optimistic than Wade as to how much longer the Visitor can enjoy the privilege of being subject to only limited review by the ordinary courts. Certainly, as early as 1973, Fridman argued that universities:

– are *de facto* public bodies, not private and independent corporations;
– 'are totally, or almost completely financed by the public purse';
– provide 'a public service';
– are, as a result, 'amenable to the controls of administrative law'.

30.46 As will be discussed at paras **30.47–30.56**, the balance of independence/regulation and of reference to the Visitor/ordinary courts is rather different in Canada (Fridman (1973) was Dean of Law, University of Alberta), Australia and New Zealand. By way of comparison, see Baker (1992) on the scope for judicial review of the Visitors to the Inns of Court, who are themselves judges. Can the court effectively review itself if the Visitors are *de facto* judges, or are they 'mere' Visitors? The case explored by Baker is *R v Visitor to Inns of Court ex parte Calder*.[2]

---

1   [1992] 3 WLR 1112, [1991] 4 All ER 747.
2   [1993] 2 All ER 876.

A COMPARISON OF THE VISITOR IN AUSTRALIA, CANADA, ENGLAND, NEW ZEALAND AND NIGERIA

30.47 US common law has no equivalent of the Visitor and in Scotland it once existed (Farrington (1994), p 51: 'in principle the Visitorial jurisdiction in Scotland exists even though it is in desuetude'). Matthews (1980) provides a review of what he calls 'Dominion cases', noting that 'Dominion Courts while acknowledging the force of the English authorities, have shown what appears to be a reluctance to apply them' (notably in *ex parte McFadyen*,[1] an Australian case).

30.48 Willis (1979) explores *Patel v University of Bradford Senate* and 'examines its applicability to Australian universities', noting that 'the visitor's is a largely untried and unknown jurisdiction: one unwelcome, in the main, in the courts wherein it has been raised'. He considers three University of Sydney cases, including *McFadyen*, and quotes Halse Rogers J in that case: 'I think ... that probably nobody until *ex parte King* ... ever thought that there was any possibility of intervention by the visitor ... it was never contemplated by the Legislature or by anybody from the time the Act was passed ... that it did anything more than give the Governor an official connection with the University (ie the Visitor as a ceremonial feature). The conclusion is that *Patel* provides the basis for the revival of the exercise of visitatorial powers, but with what consequences it is impossible to predict' (Willis (1979), p 294).

30.49 Sadler (1980) contemplates similar territory, noting that, typically, in Australia various university acts provide for the governor to be the Visitor, and considering in particular *Murdoch University v Bloom*.[2] This was a case concerning the contractual relationship between an academic and the university. The court decided that the matter was not *domus* and, hence, not within the jurisdiction of the Visitor, but there was a strong dissenting opinion. This dispute reflected the uncertainty in English courts surrounding *Hines v Birkbeck College* until *Thomas v University of Bradford*. Sadler (1981) returns to the issue of visitatorial jurisdiction in Australia considering a range of cases dating back to 1871 and concluding that in Australia the Visitors 'consider that their jurisdiction is not appellate but is more akin to that of a court exercising supervisory jurisdiction. This view of the visitatorial role is both unsatisfactory and unprecedented'. Sadler prescribes as 'the only realistic avenue for reform' the 'detailed statutory delimitation of visitatorial jurisdiction together with the guidance of statutory criteria which visitors must take into account in exercising their jurisdiction' (the Visitor as ombudsman under statute, not as a venerable creature of common law). The Visitor, on balance, is worth preserving, says Sadler, as 'an objective independent appellate body' *providing* there is appropriate 'statutory elucidation of the visitor's jurisdiction, powers and procedures'.

---

1   [1945] 45 SR (NSW) 200.
2   (1980) unreported, 16 April.

30.50   Price and Whalley (1996) also argue for the retention of the Visitor, but only if revamped, noting recent calls for abolition in Western Australia and actual abolition in New South Wales, whereas Victoria has provided for the Visitor's jurisdiction to be concurrent with, not exclusive of, that of the courts – see the Administrative Law (University Visitor) Act 1985. Shaw (1986) is cited. They see the defects but argue for reform and renewal: 'there are real and practical ambiguities and uncertainties concerning the nature and extent of the appellate aspect of the visitorial jurisdiction . . . [hence the need] to clarify and redefine the scope of this jurisdiction in the light of such problems and contemporary needs [especially modern Administrative Law and the call for bureaucratic accountability] to enable it once again to serve the purpose for which it was originally intended' (Price and Whalley (1996), p 48). Earlier in the 1996 article they memorably described the Visitor as 'one of the earliest forms of alternative dispute resolution'. Other Australian cases include *Re University of Melbourne ex parte De Dimone*,[1] *Re Macquarie University ex parte Ong*[2] and *Bayley-Jones v University of Newcastle*,[3] in addition to those already cited.

30.51   Lewis (1985) compares England and Canada in the context of disciplinary and academic procedures for students and, with regard to the role of the Visitor, notes that in both countries the courts have been reluctant to become involved in 'purely academic assessments' – leaving the Visitor to be the sole arbiter of the soundness of that procedure by which the academic decision was reached (but not actually reviewing the decision itself). With reference to student discipline rather than academic progress, the position is similar: 'There seems a reluctance to interfere in university matters which is reflected in the marked lack of clarity and precision in the judgements'. Lewis notes that 'Some of the legislation establishing particular Canadian universities have, *perhaps unwittingly*, endowed them with a university Visitor' (emphasis added). He hopes 'that the Visitor meets the same fate in other Canadian provinces that he met in Alberta where the legislature moved swiftly to abolish him on his reentry into the legal world' (post *Vanek v Governor of the University of Alberta*[4]).

30.52   Brookfield (1985) reviews the role of the Visitor in New Zealand universities in the context of *Bell v University of Auckland*,[5] the latter having 'authoritatively defined the place of the Visitor in New Zealand law, giving to that officer a jurisdiction less exclusive of the courts than that enjoyed in England, but ascribing in some respects wider visitatorial power than was thought at least by some to exist' (p 384). As in Australia, the Governor-General was the Visitor, at least in 1860s legislation, but fairly quickly the role devolved on to the Minister of Education after a Royal Commission Report in

---

1   [1981] VR 378.
2   [1989] 17 NSWLR 119.
3   [1990] 22 NSWLR 425.
4   [1975] 3 WWR 167, [1975] 5 WWR 429.
5   [1969] NZLR 1029.

1879, before reverting to the Governor-General in the case of the 1960s' universities. The New Zealand Visitor, however, post *Norrie v Senate of the University of Auckland*,[1] is subject to full review by the courts, whatever the position in England, on the basis that New Zealand universities are publicly funded – the Visitor's jurisdiction does not so much exclude the courts as in England. On the plus side, for Visitor aficionados, 'the court has if anything expanded the Visitor's role as a judge of issues of substantive fairness'. Brookfield notes that in *Rigg v University of Waikato*[2] the Visitor exercised the quasi-judicial scope awarded in *Norrie v Senate of the University of Auckland* 'with impressive skill'.

30.53   Caldwell (1982), p 309, also writing from a New Zealand perspective, queries unquestioning deference 'to such an archaic institution ... [as being] inappropriate in a period of creativity in Administrative Law and in a time when the courts are in the process of unshackling old limitations on their right to review'. This not least because 'the modern New Zealand University... is radically different from the Oxbridge Colleges in which visitatorial jurisdiction took root'. So, 'it should therefore be subject to public scrutiny in the courts', leaving the Visitor as 'a quasi-ombudsman' in the context of the modern university 'as simply another statutory body'.

30.54   Peiris (1987) sums up the comparative position thus: 'The lines of development of English and Commonwealth law suggest varying nuances and differences of emphasis largely attributable to historical and contractual factors ... English Judges, in comparison with their colleagues in Australia and New Zealand, have conceded to the visitor ample powers' (p 377).

30.55   One reason for the difference of approach, Peiris argues, is that in Commonwealth jurisdictions 'visitors are often politicians or local worthies' and are, therefore, seen by the courts as likely to be less independent-minded than the Lord Chancellor (or his commissary) acting on behalf of the Queen who is Visitor to most English/Welsh HEIs. Moreover, as Peiris notes, at least in New Zealand, universities are 'almost invariably the creature of statute', and, as a result, are, in fact, closer to the UK statutory HEIs which, of course, do not have the Visitor model – they are fully subject to judicial review (see Carroll (1994) as regards *B v Manchester Metropolitan University ex parte Nolan*[3]). Howells (1989) considers the New Zealand situation post *Norrie v Senate of the University of Auckland* as having advantages over English law, where 'the weight of precedent' has prevented a similar rationalisation of the Visitor-courts' overlap and conflict of jurisdiction. Khan (1990 and 1991), also in considering *Norrie*, recognise the 'deep-seated origins in the common law' of the Visitor's jurisdiction and is more sympathetic to this exclusive authority continuing (as, of course, reconfirmed in the House of Lords in *Thomas v*

---

1   [1984] 1 NZLR 129.
2   [1984] 1 NZLR 149.
3   (1993) unreported, 15 July.

University of Bradford[1] and as acknowledged by the Court of Appeal most recently in *Clark v University of Lincolnshire and Humberside*:[2] see Appendix 1 to Chapter 6).

30.56 Price and Whalley (1996) refer to 'vice-regal concerns', the fear of unreasonable intervention by the Governor-General in a university's affairs, and, similarly (but rather more understandably), Ikhariale (1991) discusses the problem of such intervention in Nigerian universities in the 1980s. Robinson (1994) sees life in the Visitor yet, but possibly with 'further surprises to come'. See also Khan and Davison (1995).

THE VISITOR POST-NOLAN REPORT (1996)

30.57 What can be said of the likely future of the Visitor within English chartered HEIs in the context of:

– the non-existence of the concept not only in all countries except England and certain commonwealth common law nations, but also its non-existence even in Scotland and under US common law;

– the Visitor having been summarily executed in the province of Alberta, as described earlier, and in Victoria;

– the ambivalence of the Australian, and to a lesser degree the New Zealand, courts towards the Visitor's jurisdiction, and the calls by law academics (Caldwell (1982); Lewis (1985); Sadler (1981)) in those countries for the reform if not the termination of the Visitor;

– the absence of the Visitor in at least half of the HEIs – the statutory HEIs – and all those in Scotland;

– the two inquiries by Lord Nolan (1995 and 1996);

– an HE system within an increasingly litigious and consumerist society, where students will be making an ever-greater financial sacrifice for their education, will be ever-more conscious of value for money, will more commonly be older, part-time and vocational-orientated (see Chapters 1, 6 and 29).

30.58 Nolan (1996) refers to the Visitor and notes 'the advantage that in defined circumstances the Visitor's jurisdiction may exclude recourse to the courts' (p 107). The Nolan Report goes on, however, to state that: 'The visitorial system of hearing appeals is not by any means perfect. The process of appointing a Visitor's representative to investigate may be lengthy, visitorial law is complex, and the courts show an increasing disposition to intervene' (p 108). On balance, the Visitor is 'an outside judgement', 'an independent perspective' (p 108), and should be replicated in some way in the statutory universities ('a gap which needs to be filled' – p 109). This leads to

---

1   [1987] 2 WLR 677.
2   [2000] 1 WLR 1988.

Recommendation 9 ('Students in higher education institutions should be able to appeal to an independent body, and this right should be reflected in Higher Education Charters') and Recommendation 10 ('The higher education funding councils, institutions, and representative bodies should consult on a system of independent review of disputes'). This system might take the form of: 'a statutory panel of senior persons experienced but no longer involved in further or higher education administration, from which a conciliator or arbitrator might be drawn when required . . . [It] would supplement the Visitorial system and provide an alternative for institutions without a Visitor' (p 109).

30.59   All this is, of course, reminiscent of Samuels (1973) calling for the creation of an HE advisory board. So the Visitor seems to pass the Nolan test for public and quasi-public bodies to be seen 'to let an independent person or body review their activities if necessary' (Nolan (1996), p 102). Such independence on the part of the Visitor (as so often under-estimated by critics) led to adverse findings against the HEIs concerned in, for example, Swansea (Davies (1994)), Aberystwyth (*Jones v University College Aberystwyth*, 1995), Warwick (*The Times Higher Educational Supplement* 12 September 1997), St Anne's College, Oxford (2000) and Salford (*The Times Higher Educational Supplement* 6 June 2001), concerning procedural defects in the way the HEI dealt with the disciplinary process, student grievances or academic progress.

30.60   The CVCP (1997) had seen some advantage in trying to find a mechanism to meet Nolan criteria ('. . . to adopt a new procedure that is comparable to the visitorial jurisdiction, or a substitute for it . . . It may be possible to go a long way towards replicating the role of the Visitor, which does have the advantage of providing a relatively swift and cheap remedy . . .'), but it must not be one 'which would still leave them [HEIs] amenable to the jurisdiction of the courts'; it must be one 'that is effectively an alternative to the courts'. Hence the possibility was raised of the student–HEI contract including a term referring to *binding* arbitration under the Arbitration Act 1996, with the arbitrator being drawn from a 'Panel of Independent Persons' (such a panel might include 'independent persons who have experience in higher education, dispute resolution or related matters'). There was, however, some doubt as to whether the UTCCR 1999 might make such an arbitration clause unenforceable, especially since the NUS had already expressed concern over any such proposal to terminate students' rights to bring court actions. Moreover, public funding is not at present available for arbitration: would the HEI meet the student's legal bills, and, if so, would its cheque be open-ended? In the commercial sector, arbitration has not proved to be significantly less costly than conventional litigation, and a reformed court system may yet make litigation a speedier process than at present: hence it is not obvious that arbitration is a panacea. It may be that only new legislation could achieve the CVCP objectives of both meeting Nolan and restricting the role of the courts in the creation of a Visitor-like system for the statutory HEIs (a direction, after all, in which Nolan seems to point), or even the creation of an HE Ombudsman to replace the Visitor and to cover all HEIs. But will parliamentary time be found for such legislation?

30.61 So, post-Nolan Report (1996) the Visitor seemed to have a secure future, and perhaps even an expansionist one, subject to some elements of procedure being revamped (notably the process of actually and speedily commencing a Visitor action where somebody has to be found to act on behalf of the Queen/Lord Chancellor). Summary execution by legislation (as with the demise of the Visitor in the province of Alberta, Canada and the State of Victoria) seemed unlikely, as did a narrowing of jurisdiction in relation to interference and supervision by the courts (as in New Zealand). The recent 30 years of the 300-year or so history of the Visitor since *Philips v Bury* have seen the courts give recognition in key cases[1] to the Visitor's exclusive jurisdiction and powers: *Thorne v University of London*; *Patel v University of Bradford Senate*; *Hines v Birkbeck College*; *Thomas v University of Bradford*; *Qakes v Sidney Sussex College, Cambridge*; *Pearce v University of Aston in Birmingham*; *R v Committee of Lords of the Judicial Committee of the Privy Council acting for the Visitor of the University of London ex parte Vijayatunga*; *R v Lord President of the Privy Council ex parte Page*.

30.62 Finally, in *Clark v University of Lincolnshire and Humberside*[2] the Court of Appeal seemed readily to recognise that, had Ms Clark been challenging a chartered HEI, the Visitor would have had exclusive jurisdiction, while in *R v Visitor of the University of East Anglia ex parte Hanuman*[3] the aggrieved post-graduate student was *not* able to convince the Court of Appeal that the University's decisions concerning his academic progress involved the determination of his 'civil rights' under Art 6(1) of the European Convention on Human Rights; but this case did reach the Court of Appeal prior to the HRA 1998 coming into force on 2 October 2000 and hence an English court could yet decide the matter differently in a similar case . . . (see [2000] *Education Law Journal* pp 232–234). That said, Mr Hanuman was not notably more successful with the European Court (*Lalu Hanuman v UK*[4]). Perhaps the Visitor could risk acquiring an over-60s railcard for long-term use and for purchasing a return ticket when next challenged in the European courts. Certainly, Luxton (2001), paras 1.94–1.105 and 12.06 provides him with a cogent defence against any allegation that there could be doubt about the Visitor's independence from the HEI by drawing an analogy with how the Prison Board of Visitors in *Campbell and Fell v United Kingdom*,[5] as appointed by the Home Secretary of the day (as opposed to an HEI's Visitor usually being named in perpetuity by the long-dead Founder or in the Charter), was seen as passing the Art 6(1) test of there needing to be an impartial and independent tribunal (see Chapter 7). That said, probably the balance of academic lawyer's would *not* put money on the Visitor

---

1   Citations for the following cases can be found in the Table of Cases.
2   [2000] 3 All ER 752, [2000] ELR 345.
3   [1999] EdCR 781.
4   [2000] ELR 685.
5   (1984) 7 EHRR 165.

surviving an Art 6(1) challenge. Moreover, even if the Visitor is deemed to be compliant with the Art 6(1) requirement for an 'independent' tribunal, there is the problem of whether the Visitor is 'established by law' if that means by statute/legislation (although there is, clearly, legislation which recognises the existence of the Visitor).

30.63 On the other hand, in the event that legislation was required to establish some form of compulsory independent appeal system for the statutory universities (and possibly Oxford and Cambridge), not least to ensure that such a system then really did preclude the courts being involved (which could not be guaranteed under a voluntary arrangement) other than in the context of *Wednesbury*-style judicial review for unreasonableness, it is possible that the apparently anachronistic chartered university Visitor could be replaced by also calling upon such a panel to provide for the chartered universities a recently retired HEI administrator or manager (to sit in conjunction perhaps with a senior solicitor or barrister) as a last-resort appeal tribunal, all internal procedures having been exhausted. Thus, we may yet get for the mass HE system and 'the empowered consumer' student (see Chapter 29) an Ombuds-scheme, or even a HERO (Higher Education Regulatory Officer). For further discussion see Kaye (1999), Birtwistle (2000) and Palfreyman (2000) on the future of the Visitor. But, whatever may happen in relation to student issues, there will still be a need for the function of the Visitor in relation to academic staff disputes which fall short of being employment law matters caught by the 'Model Statutes' (see Chapters 10 and 11, and, for example, *Burrows v University of York*[1]). Therefore, could, should and would the Visitor be left with this (very) residual role?

30.64 The debate about the Visitor continues ... In one edition of *The Times Higher Educational Supplement* (6 April 2001) a news report tells of the latest thinking of UUK (formerly CVCP) – 'VCs are reluctant to evict visitor' – while an Editorial declares 'Medieval visitors have no place in modern future'. The UUK consultation document of July 2001 on the future of the Visitor proposed to leave the Visitor in place, but to install a voluntary Ombudsman system as the final stage of the chartered HEI's internal procedures (prior to a visit by the Visitor). And judicial review challenges to the Visitor under Art 6(1) seem to be making little progress. By early 2002, however, the UUK seems keen on pursuing the 'independent reviewer' route now being experimented with by Scotland.

---

1   [1999] EdCR 586; see also *Coleman v University of Leicester* (1999) unreported.

NOTES ON KEY CASES REFERRED TO IN CHAPTER 30

1. *Hines v Birkbeck College* concerned, and confirmed, the exclusivity of the jurisdiction of the Visitor in relation to employment disputes between an academic and the university (approved in *Thomas v University of Bradford*). Hoffmann J noted that the subject of the exclusivity of the Visitor 'is a subject rich in authority', and referred to *Patel v University of Bradford Senate, Casson v University of Aston in Birmingham* and *Re Wislang's Application* as well as *Thomson v University of London* and *Thorne v University of London.*

2. *Hines v Birkbeck College (No 2)* concerned the overlap between the Visitor and the court in relation to the ERA 1988, s 206, and the court applied *Pearce v University of Aston in Birmingham.*

3. In *Oakes v Sidney Sussex College, Cambridge* it was established that the Visitor's jurisdiction in relation to students depended not on the student's membership of the college (as a corporator, rather than simply *in statu pupilari*), but on whether he or she sought to enforce rights under the domestic or internal law of the college (ie all students and academics are covered). Thus, the *dictum* of Megarry Vice-Chancellor in *Patel v University of Bradford Senate* was not followed. He had held that the Visitor's jurisdiction applied only to those 'of the foundation' (for example, warden, fellows and scholars (not commoners) in an Oxbridge college context). *Thomas v University of Bradford,* however, was followed.

4. In *R v Lord President of the Privy Council ex parte Page* the House of Lords, applying *Philips v Bury* and *Thomas v University of Bradford,* reaffirmed that the decision of a Visitor was not amenble to challenge by judicial review on the grounds of error in fact or in law, but only in cases where the Visitor has acted outside his or her jurisdiction, has abused his or her powers or has acted in breach of other rules of natural justice. Lord Griffiths in his judgment clarified that an abuse of the Visitor's powers did *not* include the Visitor having made an error in the interpretation of the domestic law of the university: '*certiorari* should not lie to reverse the decision of a visitor on a question of law. The value of the visitatorial jurisdiction is that it is swift, cheap and final. These benefits will be largely dissipated if the Visitor's decision can be challenged by way of judicial review . . ., to admit *certiorari* to challenge the Visitor's decision on the grounds of error of law will in practice prove to be the introduction of an appeal by another name . . . If it is thought that the exclusive jurisdiction of the Visitor has outlived its usefulness, which I beg to doubt, then I think it should be swept away by Parliament and not undermined by judicial review'.

5. Lord Browne-Wilkinson quoted from *Philips v Bury* as 'the locus classicus of the law of Visitor . . . repeatedly applied for the last 300 years' and also cited the judgments in *R v Bishop of Chester*: 'Visitors have absolute power; the only absolute one I know of in England' (Wright, J) and 'This Court cannot control visitors' (Dennison J). In *ex parte Buller* he noted that Lord Benyon, CJ had commented that a member of a college puts himself voluntarily under a peculiar system of law, and asserts to being bound by it, and cannot thereafter complain that such a system is not in accordance with that adopted by the common law'. Thus, despite the recent growth of judicial review, it is not a concept generally applicable to the Visitor since the Visitor is not dealing with the common law, but with 'a peculiar, domestic law of which he is the sole arbiter and of which the courts have no cognisance'. Hence, if that means 'the position of the Visitor is anomalous, indeed unique', then so be it, especially since 'it provides a valuable machinery for reducing internal disputes which should not be lost'. Lords Mustill and Slynn, however, dissented from Lords Griffiths, Browne-Wilkinson and Keith, with Lord Slynn emphasising that 'there has been a considerable development in the scope of judicial review in the second half of this century' – citing Wade (1993) – which should take in the Visitor as it has other areas of legal and quasi-legal activity. See also Beloff (1999).

6. In *Patel v University of Bradford Senate* the Court of Appeal upheld the exclusivity of the Visitor's jurisdiction in relation to a student's complaint over the decision of a Board of Examiners to fail him. The Court applied *Thorne v University of London,* another complaint about examination failure (ie in a chartered university possessing a Visitor disputes about the fairness of examination decisions are solely for the Visitor and there can be no appeal from the Visitor's decision). See below for *R v Committee of the Lords of the Judicial Committee of the Privy Council Acting for the Visitor of the University of London ex parte Vijayatunga.*

7. In *Pearce v University of Aston in Birmingham,* the exclusivity of the Visitor as confirmed in *Thomas v University of Bradford,* was taken as read. The dispute was about the 'relevant date' in the ERA 1988, s 206(2), after which the Visitor's jurisdiction was excluded in relation to any employment issue between a university and its academic staff.

8. The House of Lords in *Thomas v University of Bradford* confirmed the jurisdiction of the Visitor as being exclusive 'beyond doubt' and found that the Visitor can award damages. Lord Bridge of Harwich, Lord Brandon of Oakbrook and Lord Mackay of Clashfern each concurred with the speeches of Lord Ackner and Lord Griffiths, in which the latter reviewed 'an unbroken line of authority spanning the last three centuries' and considered the articles by Bridge (1970) and

Smith (1981, 1986). The authoritative cases cited ran from *Philips v Bury*, via *Attorney-General v Talbot*, *St John's College v Todington*, *Thomson v University of London*, *Herring v Templeman and Others*, *Patel v University of Bradford Senate*, *Re Wislang's Application*, to *Hines v Birkbeck College*. Lord Griffiths noted that *Norrie v Senate of the University of Auckland*, left the Visitor in New Zealand universities 'subordinate to the courts', but advised his colleagues that 'this is not the way in which our law has developed and in my view it is not open to your Lordships to . . . adopt the New Zealand solution'.

9.   In *R v Committee of the Lords of the Judicial Committee of the Privy Council Acting for the Visitor of the University of London ex parte Vijayatunga* the Court of Appeal upheld the exclusivity of the Visitor's jurisdiction in considering matters of academic judgement (here the selection of examiners for a PhD thesis). The court noted *Thomas v University of Bradford*, concluding that the appointment of examiners was 'wholly a matter of academic judgement in which this court should not interfere'. Simon Brown J commented: '. . . the decision in *Thomas v University of Bradford*, determining as it does the exclusivity of visitatorial jurisdiction where it arises, underlies also the need for such jurisdiction to assume whatever breadth and character will best enable the visitor to discharge his ultimate function [p 343G] . . . the visitor enjoys untrammelled jurisdiction to investigate and correct wrongs done in the administration of the internal law of the foundation to which he is appointed: a general power to right wrongs and redress grievances [p 344A] . . . he may interfere with any decision which he concludes to be wrong, even though he feels unable to categorise it as *Wednesbury* unreasonable [p 344D] . . .'. Moreover, the Visitor may decline to intervene if he feels the HEI has approached an academic matter in a reasonable way, given that the Visitor has no extra expertise to add and providing that the HEI's decision was not 'clearly wrong' (p 344F) in the sense of being *Wednesbury* unreasonable.

10.   The most recent judicial comments on the Visitor are from *Clark v University of Lincolnshire and Humberside*,[1] where the Court of Appeal (re)acknowledged the exclusive jurisdiction of the Visitor in relation to disputes over the HEI–student contract.

---

1   [2000] 1 WLR 1988.

FURTHER READING

(General and Chapter by Chapter. All entries are fully detailed in the Bibliography)

GENERAL READING

(1) Areas *not* covered in this book but briefly explored in Farrington (1998):

- Animal Houses (p 143 – see also Palmer (2001) and Radford (2001) on 'animal law').

- Building Contracts (pp 146–149).

- Employment Law (chapter 5).

- Financial Audit (pp 263–271).

- Funding Councils (pp 243–263, plus *Halsbury's Laws of England*, vol 15(1) paras 571–596 and Hyams (1998): pp 50/51 and 499–507).

- Health and Safety (pp 132–146).

- Licensing of Bars, Theatres, Cinemas (pp 143–145).

- Planning Law, Listed Buildings and Building Regulations (pp 202/203).

- Property Law (pp 194–201, 207–216).

- Purchasing (pp 188–191).

- Quality Audit (pp 271–280).

- Research Councils (pp 294–295).

- VAT (pp 165–168).

    (*NB* For FE and FECs, Hyams (1998) chapter 13; Grants and Awards, Hyams (1998) pp 100–102, 153–165, including 'ordinary residence' at pp 155–157; Student Loans, *Halsbury's Laws of England*, vol 15(2) paras 839–852, Hyams (1998) pp 542/543; Students under 18, Hyams (1998) chapter 11, especially p 496 and, re '*in loco parentis*', p 474, plus Boyd (1998) on independent schools.)

(2) Useful texts (most authoritative listed first) on key areas of the law *not* covered in this book:

- Construction Law – Uff (2002).

- Employment Law – Selwyn (2000); Jefferson (2000); Anderman (2001); Duggan (1999); McMullen and Smith (2001).

- Environmental Health – Attwood (2000).

- Health and Safety – Wright (1997); James and Preece (1998); Smith et al (2000); Tolley (1998).

- Licensing (bars, theatres, cinemas, etc) – Manchester (1999); Phillips (1999).

- Listed Buildings and Conservation Areas – Mynors (1998).

- Planning Law – Grant (2000); Duxbury (1999); Blackhall (1998).

- Property Law – Sparkes (1999): leases (chapter 16), mortgages (chapter 18), boundaries (chapter 20), easements (chapter 21), covenants (chapter 22), planning and change of use (chapter 23), squatters and trespassers (chapter 25 and p 726); plus Sparkes (2001) re landlord and tenant, HMOs etc.

- Purchasing (and defective goods, shoddy services, product liability) – Harvey and Parry (2000); Miller et al (1998).

- Tax Law – Tiley (2000).

- VAT – Tolley (2000/01).

(3)   Suggested texts (most authoritative listed first) on the key areas of the law covered in this book:

- Administrative/Public Law, Due Process/Natural Justice and Judicial Review – Craig (1999); de Smith et al (1999); Cane (1996).

- Charity Law (and the Visitor) – *Halsbury's Laws of England*, vol 5(2) (2001 reissue); Picarda (1999); Luxton (2001); Warburton and Morris (1995).

- Company Law – Davies (1997); Ferran (1999).

- Consumer Law (in relation to the student–HEI contract) – Harvey and Parry (2000); Miller et al (1998); Scott and Black (2000).

- Contract Law (probably *the* most significant area of law for HEI managers) – Treitel (1999); Beatson (2002); Elliott and Quinn (2001a).

- Criminal Law – Smith and Hogan (1999).

- Discrimination Law – Fredman (2002).

- Equity and Trusts – Martin (2001).

- Law of Meetings – Shearman (1997).

- Law of Corporations – *Halsbury's Laws of England*, vol 9(2) (1998 reissue).

- Tort Law – Markesinis and Deakin (1999); Elliott and Quinn (2001b).

(4)   Education Law Journals and Education Case-Reports:

- *Education and the Law*, Carfax.

- *Education Law Journal*, Jordans.

- *Education, Public Law and the Individual*, Wiley/Hart.

- *ELAS Bulletin*, Education Law Association.

- *Education Law Monitor*, Monitor Press.

- *Education Case-Reports*, Sweet & Maxwell.

- *Education Law Reports*, Jordans.

> (*NB* On education law generally, from schools via FE to HE, see *Halsbury's Laws of England*, vol 15(1) and (2) (2001 reissue) plus Hyams (1998) and Kaye (2002, forthcoming), together with Boyd (1998), Ford et al (1999), Gilliatt (1999), Gold (2002), McEwan (1999) and Ruff (2002, forthcoming). See also Evans and Gill (2001) specifically on the legal relationship between universities and their students.)

(5)   A very good way for really keen HEI management to keep up with the law is to purchase, albeit at £150, the 2000-page, two-volume *English Private Law* edited by Peter Birks, Regius Professor of Civil Law at the University of Oxford (Oxford University Press, 2000). Subscribers will be sent paperback up-dates between editions automatically every 5 years or so. The relevant part(s) of Birks (2000) will be given below in 'Further Reading Chapter by Chapter'. In 2003 there will be a companion volume, *English Public Law* (OUP, Feldman), especially relevant to Chapters 9 and 20 of this book. Together these volumes will be the equivalent for English Law of *Gloag and Henderson: The Law of Scotland* 10th edn (1995), and a handy partial substitute for the 50 or so volumes of *Halsbury's Law of England*. Mooreover, chapter 1 of Birks is a good, concise introduction to court hierarchy, statute interpretation, case precedent and the sources of law. Finally, the HEI manager should keep an eye on the HEFCE-funded 'Active Risk Management in Education' project at www.bristol.ac.uk/armed, where many useful Units may be found on the impact of the law upon HEIs.

(6)   On HE management generally:

- Warner and Palfreyman (1996 second edition due 2003).

- The 20-volume *Managing Universities and Colleges: Guides to Good Practice* (General Editors: David Warner and David Palfreyman, Open University Press, 1999 onwards). Already published (to 2001):
  - *Managing the Academic Unit* (Bolton).
  - *Managing External Relations* (Albrighton and Thomas).
  - *Managing Financial Resources* (Thomas).
  - *Managing Information* (Elkin and Law).
  - *Managing International Students* (Humfrey).
  - *Managing Strategy* (Watson).

- *Managing Stress* (Edworthy) see also Spiers (2001).
- *Managing Students* (Gledhill).
- *Managing Quality and Standards* (Liston).

- Forthcoming (2002 and beyond):
  - *Managing Collaboration and Mergers.*
  - *Managing Conflict and Ethics.*
  - *Managing Crisis.*
  - *Managing Governance.*
  - *Managing Facilities and Outsourcing.*
  - *Managing Learning and Teaching.*
  - *Managing People.*
  - *Managing Research.*
  - *Managing Staff Development.*
  - *Managing Student Services.*

(7)   This book can be updated between editions by referring to the OxCHEPS website at www.new.ox.ac.uk/oxcheps.

CHAPTER BY CHAPTER

Chapter 2: What is a Higher Education Institution as a Legal Entity?

Birks (2000) – chapter 1 on sources of law (interpretation of statutes, case-law, precedents, court hierarchy, etc), and chapter 3 on legal personality and corporations.

Evans (2001).

Farrington (1998) – classification and categorisation of HEIs, pp 15/16; corporations, pp 18–28, 36–39; definitions, pp 2, 6; degrees, pp 58–62; HE legislation, pp 152–163; historical evolution of HE and HEIs, pp 41–48; legal status of HEIs, pp 8–15; powers of HEIs, pp 185–191; statutes and *ultra vires*, pp 32–36; statutes/ordinances/regulations, pp 39–41; university colleges, pp 53–58.

Farrington (2000a) – 'Who owns universities?' and Farrington (2000b) 'Powers of Higher Education Corporations'.

Halsbury's Laws of England, vol 15(1) paras 487–489 'university' and paras 490–494 and 511–536 re powers; plus paras 567–568 re bogus degrees.

Hyams (1998) – corporations, pp 77–80, 508–512; definitions, p 499; degrees, pp 543–545; HECs, pp 69–76.

For HEIs as charitable companies, and for the trading companies of HEIs, see Davies (1997), Ferran (1999) and Chapter 15.

For HEIs as charitable corporations, see Chapter 4.

On the law of corporations, see *Halsbury's Laws of England* (1998) vol 9(2), 'Corporations'.

On the delegation of authority and agency, see Chapter 5.

On the powers or authority of US HEIs, see Kaplin and Lee (1995a) pp 76–80.

On the legal distinction between US public and private HEIs (as firmly established in the famous *Dartmouth College* case of 1819: *Trustees of Dartmouth College v Woodward* 17 US 518 (1819) and as discussed in Rudolph (1990) pp 207–212), see Kaplin and Lee (1995a) pp 45–54, including discussion of when a private HEI's activities may become subject to public law as 'State action' via application of one more legal theories: 'delegated power' or 'public function' or 'government contracts'. *Dartmouth College* is a landmark case because it established that the institution was not a civic corporation or a public body, and its corporate property was not public property; it was a private eleemosynary, charitable corporation under the control of its trustees, and the US Supreme Court was prepared to safeguard such a private entity against legislative interference from the New Hampshire State Government. The distinction between public and private HEIs was clarified, confirming that Dartmouth College, while providing a public benefit (education), was a private charitable activity funded by the donations of supporters held in the care of its Board of Trustees. (For a detailed account of the case, see LB Richardson (1932) *History of Dartmouth College*, vol 1, pp 287–346.)

Chapter 3: Governance

AfC (1995).

Association of Governing Boards (1998).

Bargh et al (1996).

Bolton (2000) pp 10–13.

Braun and Merrien (1999).

Brown (2001).

Cabinet Office (1996).

CUC (2001).

Evans (1996), (1999) and (2000).

Farrington (1998) – generally, pp 63–98 and including delegation at pp 93–98; plus Officers, pp 110–123, and personal liability at pp 174–185; and Farrington (2000b).

Gray (1997).

Halsbury's Laws of England, vol 9(2), 'Corporations' (1998).

Hambley (1998) re personal liability.

Harpool (1996).

Harpool (1998).

Hurrell (2001).

Hyams (1994) re personal liability; (1996); (1998) especially chapter 18 re personal liability.

Palfreyman (1998) re personal liability; (2002, forthcoming); (forthcoming).

Shattock (1994); (1999); (2000); (forthcoming) re governance.

Tapper and Palfreyman (1998); (2000) pp 17–24.

TEAM (2001).

Warner and Palfreyman (1996) chapters 1, 2 and 6.

Warren (1997).

Watson (2000) especially pp 6–8.

See Chapter 4 re personal liability of charity trustees, and Chapter 15 re personal liability of company directors.

On the duties and personal liability of Trustees/Governors in a US context, see Kaplin and Lee (1995a) pp 80–87, 126–131; along with (2000) pp 81–98, and especially the 1974 *Sibley Hospital* case (*Stern v Lucy Webb Hayes National Training School for Deaconnesses and Missionaries* 381 F Supp 1003, DDC 1974) as discussed in Harpool (1996). See also Evans and Evans (1998).

Chapter 4: Charity Trusteeship

Birks (2000) chapter 4 D&G.

Birks and Pretto (2002).

Boyd (1998) chapter 17.

Farrington (1998) HEIs as charities, pp 163–172; trustee liability, pp 176–179.

Halsbury's Laws of England, vol 5(2), 'Charities' (2001 reissue).

Hyams (1998) pp 70–76, 688–690.

Luxton (2001) especially chapter 10B re exempt charities, and the text of the Trustee Act 2000 (pp 853–878).

Martin (1997) especially chapter 15 re charitable trusts; chapters 18 and 19 re duties of trustees; chapter 20 re powers of trustees; chapter 21 re the fiduciary nature of trusteeship; and chapter 23 re breach of trust.

Picarda (1999).

Warburton and Morris (1995).

Re 'total return' and 'permanent endowment', see Hill and Smith (2001) with Dutton (2001).

Re 'socially responsible investment', see Luxton (2001) and Meakin (2001).

On charity investment, see Dale and Gwinnell (1995/96), Harbottle (1995), Richens and Fletcher (1996).

On delegation of authority, agency, and vicarious liability, see Chapter 5.

On Oxbridge colleges, see Palfreyman (1995/96, 1996/97, 1998/99, 1999). See Chapter 2 of Further Reading at p 588 concerning the 1819 USA *Dartmouth College* case about an eleemosynary corporation.

On personal liability for members of councils and boards of governors, see Palfreyman (1998).

On the duties and personal liability of Trustees in a US context, see Kaplin and Lee (1995a) pp 80–87, 126–131 and especially the 1974 *Sibley Hospital* case (*Stern v Lucy Webb Hayes National Training School for Deaconesses and Missionaries* 381 F Supp 1003, DDC 1974).

On the taxation of charities, see Tiley (2000) chapter 17.

Chapter 5: Meetings

Farrington (1998) pp 98–107 summarises well the issues covered in detail within the main legal texts; see also *Halsbury's Laws of England*, vol 15(1), para 523 on committees in HECs. The definitive authority is *Shackleton on the Law and Practice of Meetings* (Shearman (1997) notably Part II). See also *Halsbury's Laws of England*, vol 9(2), 'Corporations' (1998). For a handy summary of the role of the committee secretary, see Callaghan (2000) and Joynson and Wood (1987), plus on committees generally, Stephenson in Warner and Palfreyman (1996, second edition due 2003), chapter 6. On defamation, see Clarke-Williams (2001).

Chapter 6: The Student Contract

On contract law generally, see Elliott and Quinn (2001a); Birks (2000); Beatson (1998) and Treitel (1999).

On consumer law, see Harvey and Parry (2000); Miller et al (1998); Scott and Black (2000); plus Chapter 29.

Berman (2001).

Birtwistle (1998); (2001).

Birtwistle and Askew (1999).

Davies (1996); (2000); (2001).

Greenwold (2000).

Holloway (1994).

Hyams (1998).

Kaye (1999); (2002, forthcoming).

Lewis (1983); (1985); (1998).

McManus (1998) see the chapter by Lewis on 'Litigation and the Student'; (2000).

Meredith (2000).

Middlemiss (1999); (2000).

Palfreyman (1999b); (2000); (2002, forthcoming).

Parlour and Burwood (1995).

Parry and Houghton (1996).

Piper (1994).

Rochford (1998).

Slapper (1997).

Varnham (1998).

Whincup (1993).

Whittaker (2001a); (2001b).

On study abroad safety, see Kealey (1998) and de Armars Wallace and Chan (1999).

Chapter 7: Regulating the Community: Student Complaints

See the Further Reading sections for Chapters 6, 8 and 9 (including, of course, Farrington (1998), Hyams (1998) and Harris (1999) generally on disciplinary and appeals proceedings), with Evans and Gill (2001) chapters 5, 6 and 8 (plus the 'checklist' for students making complaints, pp 161–164) for a student perspective on complaints and grievances. See also Conrick (2000) on the experience in an Irish HEI of the US and Canadian model of the HEI having an internal 'Ombuds' as a way of handling student complaints and grievances. At Nottingham Trent University there is an HEFCE-funded project concerning best practice in the management of student complaints: www.ntu.ac.uk/sss/projects/complaints-management. See also a similar project at www.bristol.ac.uk/armed, and its Unit on 'Student Discipline'.

Chapter 8: The Visitor

See, generally, Chapter 29 together with:

Farrington (1998) pp 216–235; *Halsbury's Laws of England*, vol 15(1), paras 495–497; Hyams (1998) pp 512–520; Luxton (2001) chapter 12; Picarda (1999) chapter 41; Warburton and Morris (1995) pp 369–388.

On the future of the Visitor, see Birtwistle (2000); Evans and Gill (2001) pp 125–130; Kaye (1999); Luxton (2001) paras 1.97–1.105 and 12.06; McManus (1998) chapter 9 by Lewis; Palfreyman (2000); and the relevant section of Chapter 29.

Chapter 9: Judicial Review

Cane (1996) re natural justice, see chapter 8.

Craig (1999) re natural justice, see chapter 13 re procedures at hearings (especially pp 440/441 on universities) and chapter 14 on bias.

de Smith (1999) re natural justice, see chapter 8 re hearings and chapter 11 re bias, plus on universities specifically pp 75/78.

Evans and Gill (2001) pp 139–141.

Farrington (1998) pp 236–242.

Feldman (2003, forthcoming).

Hyams (1998) chapter 14 and pp 521/522.

McManus (1998) see the chapter by Lewis on 'Litigation and the University Student'.

Palfreyman (1999b).

Schweitzer (1992).

Whittaker (2001b).

Chapters 10 and 11: Employment Law and Academics

See texts referred to in paragraph 1 of the Editors' Introduction at p 201.

Chapter 12: Intellectual Property

Bentley and Sherman (2001).

Birks (2000) chapter 6.

Cornish (1999).

Farrington (1998) chapter 6, plus a 'Model Research Agreement' on pp 300–306.

McSherry (2001).

Holyoak and Torremans (2001).

Chapter 13: Data Protection

Jay and Hamilton (1999).

Rowe (2000).

Chapter 14: The Internet

Bainbridge (2000).

Gringras (2001).

Kevan and McGrath (2001).

Lloyd (2000).

Stokes (2001).

Thomas and Calder (2001).

Chapter 15: Trading Companies

Birks (2000) chapters 3 and 16.

Farrington (1998) pp 191/192.

HEFCE (1996).

Hyams (1998) pp 72–76.

Impey (1999) on company meetings.

Shearman (1997) Part III, also on company meetings.

Topic	Davies (1997)	Ferran (1999)
1 directors' duties – – fiduciary duty of honesty, propriety, loyalty and good faith	chapter 22	chapter 5
– diligence, skill and care		chapter 6
2 floating charge	pp 89/90 and pp 326/389	pp 506–533
3 incorporation, legal personality, lifting the veil	chapter 8	chapter 1
4 insider-dealing	chapter 17	–

5	meetings	chapter 21	pp 258–271
6	nominee-directors	pp 154/155 and pp 609/610	pp 159/160
7	shadow-directors	pp 183/184	pp 155/156 and pp 482/484
8	wrongful trading	pp 151–155	pp 214–217

On agency, see Chapter 5 above.

On trading ('auxiliary enterprises') in US HEIs, see Kaplin and Lee (1995a) pp 929–945.

On trading in relation to consumer protection, misrepresentation and terms implied by relevant legislation (Sale of Goods Act 1979 and Supply of Goods and Services Act 1982), see Chapter 29 ('A Note on Consumer Law'), plus specifically on the sale of goods (rather than services) and on product liability Atiyah (2000); Bridge (1998); Markesinis and Deakin (1999) chapter 5 on product liability.

The final report of the *Company Law Review* (26 July 2001) can be seen at www.dti.gov.uk/cld/review.htm.

Chapter 16: Mergers and Acquisitions

Beasley and Pembridge (2000); note the supplementary items to the bibliography in Palfreyman et al (1998) below. Similarly, Brown (2001a), (2001b).

HEQ (1991) 45(2): an edition devoted to actual HE mergers, as cited and summarised in Palfreyman below.

Palfreyman et al (1998): including an extensive bibliography on actual HE mergers. This book's case-study material will be supplemented in Warner and Palfreyman (forthcoming) on *Managing Crisis* and on *Managing Collaboration and Mergers* in the 'Managing Universities and Colleges' series of some 20 volumes.

On mergers in US HE, see Martin et al (2001).

Chapter 17: Franchising

Adams and Pritchard-Jones (1997).

Re international disputes, Birks (2000) chapter 17D: essentially and broadly, the litigation will usually be within the jurisdiction of the country within which the contract was being performed or the alleged tortuous harm was inflicted.

HEQC (1995) and CVCP (1995).

Chapter 18: PFI

Deacon (1997).

Fox and Trott (1999).

HEFCE (2000) *Student Accommodation Projects: A Guide to PFI Contracts* (Circular 00/47).

McWilliam (1997).

NAO (1997).

Salter et al (2000).

On mortgages see Birks (2000) chapter 5.

Chapter 19: Students' Unions

Where the SU functions as a company itself, or operates in conjunction with a trading company, see Chapter 15; where it functions as an unincorporated association (and hence does not have legal personality as an artificial person), see Birks (2000) chapters 3D2 and 4G3 and Warburton (1992). For a broad discussion, see *Halsbury's Laws of England*, vol 15(2), paras 856–857 and Farrington (1998) pp 384–400; and concerning the Education Act 1994, see Hyams (1998) pp 524–527 with Hinds (1995); on SU charitable status, see Luxton (2001) paras 4.26–4.29. On the licensing of SU or HEI buildings for drink or entertainment, see Farrington (1998) pp 143–145; Manchester (1999) and Phillips (1998). See also Kaplin and Lee (1995a) paras 4.12 and 4.13 re US fraternities/sororities and student newspapers.

Chapter 20: Campus Security

Farrington (1998) pp 201/202, 401 re occupations, with p 211 re trespass.

Infield and Platford (2000) on stalking.

Smith and Hogan (1999) on criminal law, plus Feldman (2003, forthcoming).

Welham (2001) on corporate killing.

On occupier liability, see Birks (2000) chapter 14C4.

For a US perspective see Kaplin and Lee (1995a) para 4.17 on campus security and para 5.6 on public access to the campus, plus relevant update sections in Kaplin and Lee (2000).

Chapter 21: HMOs

Dymond (2000).

Farrington (1998) pp 205–207.

Sparkes (2001).

Chapter 22: Disability Legislation

Doyle (2000).

Duquette (2000).

Farrington (1998) pp 458/459.

Fredman (2002).

Hurst (2002).

Hyams (1998) pp 617–621.

Konur (2000).

O'Connor and Robinson (1999).

QAA (1999), and via www.QAA.ac.uk.

SHEFC (2000), and via www.ispn.gcal.ac.uk/teachability.

Chapter 23: Student Accommodation

Birks (2000) chapter 4B5.

Crook (1999).

Pawlowski (1993).

Sparkes (1999) chapter 17.

Sparkes (2001).

On US–HEI student housing, see Kaplin and Lee (1995a) para 4.14, as updated in Kaplin and Lee (2000).

Chapter 24: Risk Management

Bagley (1999).

Birds (2001).

Birks (2000) chapter 14E5 re product liability.

Farrington (1999) pp 209–294 re professional and product liability.

Knight and Pretty (2001).

Lowry and Rawlings (1999).

On risk management (risk avoidance, risk control, risk transfer, risk retention) in US–HEIs, see Kaplin and Lee (1995a) pp 137–142.

See the HEFCE-funded 'Active Risk Management in Education' project at www.bristol.ac.uk/armed.

Chapter 25: Alumni

See also the chapters which overlap with this one (notably Chapters 2, 3, 5, 12, 13, 14 and 15), while on the detailed rules concerning charity fund-raising campaigns see Luxton (2001), Picarda (1999) and Tiley (2001).

Chapter 26: A Note on Property

Sparkes (1999) pp 562–565; with Markesinis and Deakin (1999) pp 406–413 re bailment and the tort of conversation within the Torts (Interference with Goods) Act 1977; and, more generally, on the law of personal property, see Bridge (1996). See also Birks (2000) chapters 4C on personalty, 4F(4)(b) on lost and found, 13 on bailment and 14F on conversion.

Chapter 27: Litigation

ADR – Mackie et al (2000).

Arbitration – Marshall (2001).

Controlling Costs – *Dan Mahoney's Practical Guide to Managing Legal Costs* (2000).

Impact of the HRA 1998 and especially Article 6 of the European Convention on Human Rights – Mello (2000).

Litigation – Beecher and Lanoe (1999); Birks (2000) chapters 18 and 19; Burton (1997); Clore (1998); Fridd (2000); O'Hare and Hill (2001); Pyke (2000); Simons (1999); Waring (1999).

Mediation – Nescic and Boulle (2000); Noone (1996).

Negotiation – Tribe (1994).

Specifically on universities and litigation – Simblet (1999).

Chapter 28: EU Law

Competition Law – Whish (2001); Green and Robertson (1997).

EU HE policy – Johnson (1999).

EU law generally – Hartley (2000); Wyatt and Dashwood (2000).

HEIs as 'emanations of the State' and as 'public authorities' – Farrington (1998) pp 149–152 and Hyams (1998) pp 621–623; plus Birtwistle (2000); Kaye (1999) and Palfreyman (2000) together with Barnforth (1999); Lester and Pannick (1999) section 2.6.3 and Markus (2001).

'Ordinarily resident' – Farrington (1998) pp 377–378 and Hyams (1998) pp 155–157, plus as an interesting US analogy in terms of eligibility for reduced academic fees when attending a State HEI as an 'in-State' resident, see Kaplin and Lee (1995a) pp 434–436 and (2000) pp 268–275.

Public Procurement – Geddes (1996).

Chapters 29 and 30

For further reading on Chapter 29 (Consumer Law) and Chapter 30 (The Visitor), see the references within each chapter.

BIBLIOGRAPHY

Adams, JN and Pritchard-Jones, KV (1997) *Franchising: Practice and Precedents in Business Format Franchising* (Butterworths).

Anderman, SA (2001) *The Law of Unfair Dismissal* (Butterworths).

Association of Governing Boards (AGB) (1998) *AGB Statement on Institutional Governance* (AGB).

Association for Colleges (AfC) (1995) *Model Code of Ethics* (Association for Colleges).

Atiyah, PS (1997) *The Damages Lottery* (Hart Publishing).

Atiyah, PS (2000) *The Sale of Goods* (Butterworths).

Attwood, B (2000) *Food Law* (Butterworths).

Bagley, CE (1999) *Managers and the Legal Environment* (West).

Bainbridge, L and Sherman, B (2000) *Introduction to Computer Law* (Longman).

Baker, JH (1992) 'Judicial Review of the Judges as Visitors to the Inns of Court' *Pub L* p 411.

Bamforth, S (1999) 'The application of the Human Rights Act 1998 to public authorities and private bodies' *Cambridge Law Journal* 58(1), p 159.

Bargh, C et al (1996) *Governing Universities: Changing the Culture?* (Open University Press).

Beasley, T and Pembridge, K (2000) 'The potential for mutual-growth mergers between UK universities' *Perspectives: Policy and Practice in Higher Education* 4(2), pp 41–47.

Beatson, J (1998) *Anson's Law of Contract* (Oxford University Press).

Beloff, MJ (1999) 'Scholars, students and sanctions – dismissal and discipline in the modern university' *The Denning Law Journal*.

Bentley, L and Sherman, B (2001) *Intellectual Property Law* (OUP).

Berman, L et al (2001) 'Education negligence' *Education and the Law* 13(1), pp 51–67.

Bickel, RD and Lake, PF (1997) 'The Emergence of New Paradigms in Student–University Relations: From *In Loco Parentis* to Bystander to Facilitator' *J Coll & Univ Law* 23, 755.

Bickel, RD and Lake, PF (1999) *The Rights and Responsibilities of the Modern University: Who Assumes the Risks of College Life?* (Carolina Academic Press).

Birds, J (1997) *Modern Insurance Law* (Sweet & Maxwell).

Birks and Pretto (eds) (2002) *Breach of Trust* (Hart Publishing).

Birks, P (2000) *English Private Law* (Oxford University Press).

Birtwistle, T (1998) 'Student academic appeals: a holistic assessment' *Education and the Law* 10(1), pp 41–54.

Birtwistle, T (2000) 'Should Multiple Systems for Academic Appeals Remain? The Role of the Visitor' *Education Law Journal* 1(3), pp 135–145.

Birtwistle, T (2001) 'Higher Education and the Duty of Care: "The Law is on the move and much remains uncertain"' *Education Law Journal* 2(2) pp 87–94.

Birtwistle, T and Askew, M (1999) 'The Teaching and Higher Education Act 1998 – impact on the student contract' *Education and the Law* 11(2), pp 89–105.

Blackhall, JC (1998) *Planning Law and Practice* (Cavendish).

Bolton, A (2000) *Managing the Academic Unit* (Open University Press).

Boyd, R (1998) *Independent Schools: Law, Custom and Practice* (Jordans).

Braun, D and Merrien, FX (1999) *Towards a New Model of Governance for Universities? A Comparative View* (Jessica Kingsley).

Bridge, JW (1970) 'Keeping Peace in the Universities – The Role of the Visitor' *LQR* 86, p 531.

Bridge, M (1996) *Personal Property Law* (Blackstone Press).

Bridge, MG (1998) *The Sale of Goods* (Oxford University Press).

Brookfield, FM (1985) 'The Visitor in the New Zealand Universities' *NZ ULR* 11, p 382.

Brown, J (2001a) 'The governance of the new universities: do we need to think again?' *Perspectives: Policy and Practice in Higher Education* 5(1), p 42.

Brown, J (2001b) 'Collaboration and restructuring' *Perspectives: Policy and Practice in Higher Education* 5(4), p 93.

Brown, WO Jr (1997) 'University governance and academic tenure' *Journal of Institutional and Theoretical Economics* 153(3), pp 441–461.

Brownsword, R (2000) *Contract Law: Themes for the Twenty-First Century* (Butterworths).

Burton, F (1997) *Criminal Litigation* (Cavendish).

Cabinet Office (1996) *Spending Public Money: Governance and Audit Issues* (HMSO).

Cadbury (1994) *The Cadbury Report* (HMSO).

Cadbury Report (1992) *Report of the Committee on the Financial Aspects of Corporate Governance* (London Stock Exchange).

Caldwell, JL (1982) 'Judicial Review of Universities: The Visitor and the Visited' *Cant L Rev* 1, p 307.

Callaghan, J (2002) 'The Excellent Secretary: A Guide to Best Practice in Committee Servicing' *Perspectives: Policy and Practice in Higher Education* 6(1), p 23.

Cane, P (1996) *An Introduction to Administrative Law* (Oxford University Press).

Carroll, AJ (1994) 'The abuse of academic disciplinary power' *New Law Journal* 144, p 724.

CEF (1995) *Model Code of Conduct* (College Employers' Forum).

Charity Commission (1993) *Decisions of the Charity Commissioners, No 6* (HMSO, Royal Holloway and Bedford New College).

Christie, D (1974) 'A Problem of Jurisdiction and Natural Justice' *MLR* 37, p 324.

Clark, BR (1998a) *Creating Entrepreneurial Universities: Organisational Pathways of Transformation* (AU Press, Pergamon).

Clark, BR (1998b) 'The entrepreneurial university: demand and response' *Tertiary Education and Management* 4(1), pp 5–16.

Clarke-Williams, J (2001) *Defamation Law* (Butterworths).

Clore, J (1998) *Civil Litigation* (Cavendish).

Cobban, AB (1971) 'Medieval Student Power' *Past and Present* pp 28, 53.

Cobban, AB (1988) *The Medieval English Universities* (Longman).

Cobban, AB (1999) *English University Life in the Middle Ages* (UCL Press/Taylor & Francis).

Committee of Public Accounts (1997/98) *Governance and the Management of Overseas Courses at Swansea Institute of Higher Education* (HMSO).

Conrick, M (2000) 'Problem-solving in a University Setting: the role of the ombudsperson' *Perspectives* 4(2), p 50.

Considine, D (1993) 'The loose cannon syndrome: universities as a businesses and students as consumers' *Australian Universities Law Review* pp 24–42.

Cornish, WR (1999) *Intellectual Property Patents, Copyright, Trade Marks and Allied Rights* 4th edn (Sweet & Maxwell).

Craig, PP (1999) *Administrative Law* (Sweet & Maxwell).

Cripps, Y (1994) *The Legal Implications of Disclosure in the Public Interest* (Sweet & Maxwell).

Crook, H (1999) 'Will your Student Accommodation Agreement stand up in Court?' *UCELNET* 6, pp 4–5.

CUC (1997) *Advice on Whistleblowing* (Committee of University Chairmen).

CUC (2000) *Progress Report of the Working Party on Effectiveness of University Governing Bodies* (Committee of University Chairmen).

CUC (2001) *Guide for Members of Governing Bodies of Universities and Colleges in England, Wales and Northern Ireland* (HEFCE).

CVCP (1995) *Code of Practice: Recruitment and Support of International Students in UK Higher Education* (CVCP).

CVCP (1997) *Interim Report of the CVCP Nolan Group* (CVCP (N/97/11)).

CVCP (1997; final report, 2001) *Independent Review of Student Appeals and Staff Disputes: Interim Report of the CVCP Nolan Group* (CVCP).

Dale, HP and Gwinnell, M (1995/96) 'Time for change: charity investment and modern portfolio theory' *Charity Law and Practice Review* 3(2), pp 65–96.

Davies, K (1993) 'The justiciability question' *All ER Annual Review* 1.

Davies, Sir Michael (1994) *The Davies Report: The 'Great Battle' in Swansea* (Thoemmes Press).

Davies, MR (1996) 'Universities, academics and professional negligence' *Professional Negligence* 12(4), pp 80–108.

Davies, MR (2000) 'Admissions to Higher Education: the legal issues arising from applicants with criminal convictions' *Education and the Law* 12(3), pp 143–164.

Davies, MR (2001) 'Students, academic institutions and contracts – a ticking time bomb?' *Education and the Law* 13(1), pp 9–28.

Davies, PL (1997) *Gower's Principles of Modern Company Law* (Sweet & Maxwell).

Deacon, M (1997) 'Capital funding and the private finance initiative: panacea or poison chalice?' *Perspectives: Policy and Practice in Higher Education* 1(4), pp 133–138.

Dearing, R (1997) *Higher Education in the Learning Society: Report of the National Committee of Inquiry into Higher Education* (HMSO).

Dearlove, J (1995a) 'Collegiality, managerialism and leadership in English universities' *Journal of Tertiary Education and Management* 1(2), pp 161–169.

Dearlove, J (1995b) *Governance, Leadership, and Change in Universities* (UNESCO, IIEP).

deArmars Wallace, J and Chan, S (1999) 'ACT-TIONS – a model for student safety and institutional responsibility in study abroad' *Perspectives: Policy and Practice in Higher Education* 3(4), pp 123–127.

de Mello, R (2000) *The Human Rights Act 1998* (Jordans).

de Smith, SA (1974) 'Aston's Villa – Replay for Visitors?' *CU* 33, p 23.

de Smith, SA et al (1999) *Principles of Judicial Review of Administrative Action* (Sweet & Maxwell).

DfEE (1993) *The Charter for Higher Education* (HMSO).

Doyle, B (2000) *Disability Discrimination: Law and Practice* 3rd edn (Jordans).

Duggan, M (1999) *Unfair Dismissal: Law, Practice and Guidance* (CLT Professional Publishing).

Dutton, J (2001) 'Endowed Charities: A Total Return Approach to Investment?' *Charity Law and Practice Review* 7(2), pp 131–136.

Duquette, C (2000) 'Experiences at university: perceptions of students with disabilities' *Canadian Journal of Education and Work* 30(2), pp 123–141.

Duxbury, RMC (1999) *Planning Law and Procedure* (Butterworths).

Dymond A (2000) *Houses in Multiple Occupation: Law and Practice in the Management of Social Housing* (Lemos & Crane).

Edworthy, A (2000) *Managing Stress* (Open University Press).

Elleven, RK, Lumsden, DB and Kern, CW (1997a) 'Student legal issues confronting metropolitan colleges and universities: a 10 years look ahead' *Education and the Law* 9(1), pp 41–50.

Elleven, RK, Lumsden, DB and Kern, CW (1997b) 'A comparison of student legal issues perceptions held by chief student and chief legal affairs offices: a study of metropolitan universities in the US' *Education and the Law* 9(3), pp 225–232.

Elliott, C and Quinn, F (2001a) *Contract Law* (Longman).

Elliott, C and Quinn, F (2001b) *Tort Law* (Longman).

Evans, EM and Evans, WD (1998) '"No Good Deed Goes Unpunished": Personal Liability of Trustees and Administrators of Private Colleges and Universities' *Tort and Insurance Law Journal* 33, p 1107.

Evans, GR (1996) *Raising Concerns and Handling the Consequences in Further and Higher Education: a Handbook* (Council for Academic Freedom and Academic Standards).

Evans, GR (1999) *Accountability in Higher Education* (SRHE/Open University Press).

Evans, GR (2001) 'University Autonomy and State Control: Legal Implications of the Historical Invasions of Oxford and Cambridge' *Education Law Journal* 2(3), pp 134–143.

Evans, GR and Gill, J (2001) *Universities and Students: A Guide to Rights, Responsibilities and Practical Remedies* (Kogan Page).

Farrington, DJ (1997) *Handling Student Complaints*, UCoSDA Briefing Paper 48 (UCoSDA).

Farrington, DJ (1998) *The Law of Higher Education* (Butterworths).

Farrington, DJ (2000a) 'Who owns universities?' *Perspectives: Policy and Practice in Higher Education* 4(1), pp 21–24.

Farrington, DJ (2000b) 'Powers of Higher Education Corporations' *Education Law Journal*.

Farrington, DJ and Mattison, F (1990) *Universities and the Law* (Conference of University Administrators, Reading).

FEFC (1994a) *Report of Inquiry into Derby Tertiary College Wilmorton* (FEFC).

FEFC (1994b) *Report of Inquiry into St Phillip's Roman Catholic Sixth Form College* (FEFC).

Feldman, D (2003, forthcoming) *English Public Law* (Oxford University Press).

Ferran, E (1999) *Company Law and Corporate Finance* (Oxford University Press).

Fine, R (1997) *Being Stalked* (Chatto & Windus).

Ford, J et al (1999) *Education Law and Practice* (Legal Action Group).

Fox, J and Nicholas, T (eds) (2002) *The PPP Handbook* (Jordans).

Franks Report (1996) *University of Oxford: Report of Commission of Inquiry* (Oxford University Press).

Fredman, S (2002) *Discrimination Law* (OUP).

Fridd, N and Widdie, S (2000) *Basic Practice in Court, Tribunals and Inquiries* (Sweet & Maxwell).

Fridman, GHL (1973) 'Judicial Intervention into Universities' Affairs' *Chitty's U* 21, p 181.

Furmston, MP (1992) *Universities and Disclaimers of Liability* (CVCP N/92/112 (29/5/92)).

Geddes, A (1996) *Public and Utility Procurement* (Sweet & Maxwell).

Gilliatt, J (1999) *Teaching and the Law* (Kogan Page).

Gold, R (2002) *Running a School: Legal Duties and Responsibilities* (Jordans).

Grant, D and Mason, S (1998) *Holiday Law* (Sweet & Maxwell).

Grant, J (1850) *The Law of Corporations* (Butterworths).

Grant, M (2000) *Planning Law* (Sweet & Maxwell).

Gray, H (1997) 'Higher education institutions as corporations' *Perspectives: Policy and Practice in Higher Education* 1(3), pp 78–80.

Greenbury Report, The (1995) *Directors' Remuneration* (HMSO).

Greenwold, J (2000) 'Lawyers in the Classroom: the new law of educational negligence' *Education and the Law* 12(4), pp 246–257.

Griffiths, JAG (1997, and subsequent editions) *The Politics of the Judiciary* (Fontana).

Gringas, C (2001) *Laws of the Internet* (Butterworths).

Hadfield, B (1987) 'The Visitor Stays – Thomas v University of Bradford' *Pub U*, p 320.

Hall, J (1990) 'Confidentiality on the Campus' *Education and the Law* 2(1), p 117.

Hall, J (1994) 'College Governors – Understanding the Checks and Balances' *Education and the Law* 6(4), p 187.

Halsbury's Laws of England vol 5(2) on 'Charities' (Butterworths, 2001 reissue).

Halsbury's Laws of England vol 9(2) on 'Corporations' (Butterworths, 1998 reissue).

Halsbury's Laws of England vol 15(1) and (2) on 'Education' (Butterworths, 2001 reissue).

Hambley, E (1998) *Personal Liability in Public Service Organisations: A Legal Research Study for the Committee on Standards in Public Life* (HMSO).

Harbottle, M (1995) *Investing Charity Funds* (Jordans).

Harbrugh, J and Brilke, B (1998) 'Travel in the Younger Set is a part of education: the liability of universities for the death or injury of students' *International Travel Law Journal* 2, pp 78–99.

Harpool, D (1996) 'The Sibley Hospital Case: Trustees and Their Loyalty to the Institution' *J Coll & Univ Law* 23, 255.

Harpool, D (1998) 'Minimum Compliance with Minimum Standards: Managing Trustee Conflicts of Interest' *J Coll & Univ Law* 24, 465.

Harris, B (1999) *Disciplinary and Regulatory Proceedings* (Barry Rose).

Harris, N (1993) *Law and Education: regulations, consumerism and the education system* (Sweet & Maxwell).

Hart, C (2001/02) *Civil Litigation* (Jordans).

Hartley, TC (2000) *Foundations of European Law* (Oxford University Press).

Harvey, BW (1999) 'University Law in Theory and Practice' *Perspectives: Policy and Practice in Higher Education* 3(1), pp 19–22.

Harvey, BW and Parry, DL (2000) *The Law of Consumer Protection and Fair Trading* (Butterworths).

HEFCE (1996) *HEIs Related Companies: Recommended Practice Guidelines* (HEFCE).

HEFCE (2000) *Better Accountability for Higher Education* (HEFCE).

HEQ (1991) 'Mergers in Higher Education' *Higher Education Quarterly* 45(2) (entire issue).

HEQC (1995) *Code of Practice for Overseas Collaborative Provision in Higher Education* (HEQC).

Hill, J and Smith, J (2001) 'Permanent Endowment and Total Return' *Charity Law and Practice Review* 7(2), pp 125–130.

Hinds, W (1995) 'The Education Act, 1994: the student union provisions' *Education and the Law* 7(2), pp 133–142.

Hodges, C (2001) *Multi-Party Actions* (Oxford University Press).

Holloway, J (1994) 'The Rights of Individuals who receive a defective education' *Education and the Law* 6(2), pp 207–219.

Howells, GG (1989) 'Employment Disputes within Universities' *CJQ* 8, p 152.

Hurrell, B (2001) 'Governance codes' *Perspectives: Policy and Practice in Higher Education* 5(1), p 17.

Hurst, A (2002) 'Teaching for Diversity and Retention: The Example of Students with Disabilities' in S Ketteridge et al *The Effective Academic* (Kogan Page).

Hyams, O (1994) 'The potential liabilities of governors of education institutions' *Education and the Law* 6(2), pp 191–205.

Hyams, O (1996) 'Higher and further education dismissals and redundancies – problem areas and their consequences for corporations and governors' *Education and the Law* 8(2), pp 137–152.

Hyams, O (1998) *Law of Education* (Sweet & Maxwell).

Hyams, O (2000) *Employment in Schools: A Legal Guide* (Jordans).

Ikhariale, MA (1991) 'The institution of the Visitor in English and overseas universities: problems of its use in Nigeria' *International and Comparative Law Quarterly*, p 699.

Impey, D (1999) *Company Meetings* (Jordans).

Infield, P and Platford, G (2000) *The Law of Harassment and Stalking* (Butterworths).

James, I and Preece, D (1998) *Health and Safety Management* (Jordans).

Jarratt Report, The (1985) *Report of the Steering Committee for Efficiency Studies in Universities* (CVCP).

Jay, R and Hamilton, A (1999) *Data Protection Law and Practice* (Sweet & Maxwell).

Jefferson, M (2000) *Principles of Employment Law* (Cavendish).

Johnson, N (1999) 'From vocational training to advocation: the development of a no-frontiers education policy for Europe' *Education and the Law* 11(3), pp 199–213.

Joynson, M and Wood, J (1987) *The Committee Business* (CUA/AUA).

Kaplin, WA (1979) *The Law of Higher Education* 1st edn (Jossey-Bass).

Kaplin, WA (1985) *The Law of Higher Education* 2nd edn (Jossey-Bass).

Kaplin, WA and Lee, BA (1995a) *The Law of Higher Education* 3rd edn (Jossey-Bass).

Kaplin, WA and Lee, BA (1995b) *Cases, Problems and Materials: An Instructional Supplement to the Law of Higher Education* (Jossey-Bass).

Kaplin, WA and Lee, BA (1997) *A Legal Guide for Student Affairs Professionals* (Jossey-Bass).

Kaplin, WA and Lee, BA (2000) *Supplement to the Law of Higher Education* (NACUA).

Kaye, T (1999) 'Academic judgement, the university visitor and the Human Rights Act 1998' *Education and the Law* 11(3), pp 165–186.

Kaye, T (2002, forthcoming) *Education Law* (Blackstone).

Kealey, D (1998) 'Unusual pains: liability and study abroad' *Journal of International Education* 7, pp 7–9.

Kennedy, D (1997) *Academic Duty* (Harvard University Press).

Kevan, T and McGrath, P (2001) *E-Mail, the Internet and the Law* (EMIS Professional Publishing).

Khan, AN (1997) 'Canadian visiting academics: tenure implications' *Education and the Law* 9(2), pp 109–122.

Khan, AN (1998) 'Canadian education: discrimination based on or because of sexual orientation' *Education and the Law* 10(4), p 253.

Kiloh, G (1998) 'Customers, Clients and Consumers' *Perspectives: Policy and Practice in Higher Education* 2(2), p 46.

Knight, RF and Pretty, DJ (2001) *Reputation and Value: The Case of Corporate Catastrophe* (Oxford Metrica).

Konur, O (2000) 'Creating enforceable civil rights for disabled students in higher education: an institutional theory perspective' *Disability and Society* 15(7), pp 1041–1063.

Lester, Lord and Pannick, D (1999) *Human Rights Law and Practice* (Butterworths).

Lever, J (QC) (1995) *Independent Inquiry Report* (University of Portsmouth).

Lewis, CB (1983) 'The Legal Nature of a University and the Student–University Relationship' *Ottawa Law Review* XV, pp 37–49.

Lewis, CB (1985) 'Procedural Fairness and University Students: England and Canada Compared' *The Dalhousie Law Journal* 9(3), pp 13–27.

Lewis, CB (1998) 'Litigation and the university student' McManus, *Education and the Courts* (Sweet & Maxwell).

Lewis, CJ (1987) 'Universities, Visitors and the Courts' *CLJ* 46, p 384.

Lewis, D (2001) *Whistleblowing at Work* (Athlone Press).

Lewis, D, Ellis, C-A, Kyprianou, A and Homewood, S (2001) 'Whistleblowing at work: the results of a survey of procedures in further and higher education', in *Education and the Law* 13(3), p 214.

Lloyd, IJ (2000) *Information Technology Law* 3rd edn (Butterworths).

Lowry, J and Rawlings, P (1999) *Insurance Law: Doctrines and Principles* (Hart Publishing).

Luxton, P (2001) *The Law of Charities* (Oxford University Press).

Mackie, K et al (2000) *Commercial Dispute Resolution: An ADR Practice Guide* (Butterworths).

Manchester, C (1999) *Entertainment Licensing* (Butterworths).

Markesinis, BS and Deakin, SF (1999) *Tort Law* (Oxford University Press).

Marshall, E (2001) *Gill: The Law of Arbitration* 4th edn (Sweet & Maxwell).

Martin, J (1997) *Hanbury and Martin: Modern Equity* (Sweet & Maxwell).

Martin, J et al (2001) *Merging Colleges for Mutual Growth* (Johns Hopkins).

Matthews, TG (1980) 'The Office of the University Visitor' *University Qld U* 11, p 152.

Meakin, R (2001) 'Socially Responsible Investment by Charities' *Charity Law and Practice Review* 7(2), pp 137–150.

McCaughlin, S (1983) 'Up against the Law. The University Visitor' *Legal Services Bulletin* 8, p 140.

McEwan, V (1999) *Education Law* (CLT Professional Publishing).

McGregor, H (1997) *McGregor on Damages* (Sweet & Maxwell).

McManus, R (1998) *Education and the Courts* (Sweet & Maxwell).

McManus, R (2000) *Education Law Journal* 1(4), p 200.

McMullen, J and Smith, I (2000) *Breach of the Employment Contract and Wrongful Dismissal* (Butterworths).

McSherry, C (2002) *Who Owns Academic Work?: Battling for Control of Intellectual Property* (Harvard University Press).

McWilliam, J (1997) 'A commissioner's tale: Avery Hill Student Village, University of Greenwich' *Public Money and Management* 17(3), pp 21–24.

Meredith, P (2000) *Education and the Law* 12(3), p 139.

Middlemiss, J (1999) 'Liability of universities for students under the law of contract' *Judicial Review* 19(3), pp 170–183.

Middlemiss, S (2000) 'Legal Liability of Universities for Students' *Education and the Law* 12(2), pp 69–91.

Miller, CJ, Harvey, BW, Parry, DL (1998) *Consumer and Trading Law: Cases and Materials* (Oxford University Press).

Mitcheson, RE (1887) *Opinion on the English Law and Practice of Visitation of Charities*.

Mynors, C (1998) *Listed Buildings, Conservation Areas and Monuments* (Sweet & Maxwell).

NACUA (1989) *Student Legal Issues* (NACUA).

NACUA (1994) *The Formbook* (NACUA).

NACUA (1996) *Deformation Issues in Higher Education* (NACUA).

NAO (1995) *Severance Payments to Senior Staff in the Publicly Funded Education Sector* (HMSO).

NAO (1997) *The PFI Contracts for the Bridgend and Fazakerley Prisons* (HMSO).

NAO (1997a) *Report of the Comptroller and Auditor General, Governance and Management of Overseas Courses at Swansea Institute of Higher Education* (HC222) (The Stationery Office).

NAO (1997b) *Report of the Comptroller and Auditor General, University of Portsmouth* (HC4 Session 1997–98, January) (The Stationery Office).

NAO (1998) *Report of the Comptroller and Auditor General, Scottish Higher Education Funding Council Investigation of Misconduct and Glasgow Caledonian University* (HC680 Session 1997–98, January) (The Stationery Office).

Neave, D (1998) 'Review of "Higher Education and the Law"' *Education and the Law* 10(2/3), pp 197/198.

Nelson, C and Watt, S (1999) *Academic Key Words: A Devil's Dictionary for Higher Education* (Routledge).

Nescic, M and Boulle, L (2000) *Mediation: Principles, Process, Practice* (Butterworths).

Nolan, Lord (1995) *First Report of the Committee on Standards in Public Life* (HMSO).

Nolan, Lord (1996) *Second Report of the Committee on Standards in Public Life* (HMSO).

Nolan, Lord (1997) *Third Report of the Committee on Standards in Public Life* (HMSO).

Noone, C (1996) *Mediation* (Cavendish).

O'Connor, U and Robinson, A (1999) 'Accession or Exclusion? University and the Disabled Student: A Case-Study of Policy and Practice' *Higher Education Quarterly* 53(1), pp 88–103.

O'Hare, J and Hill, RN (1999) *Civil Litigation* (Sweet & Maxwell).

Oliver, D (1999) *Common Values and the Public–Private Divide* (Butterworths).

Olivier, N (1999) *Corporate Campus* (South End Press).

Oxford (1995) *Commission of Inquiry: Framework Document* (University of Oxford).

Oxford (1996) *Governance* (University of Oxford).

Palfreyman, D (1989) 'The Warwick Way: a case study of innovation and entrepreneurship with a university context' *Journal of Entrepreneurship* 1(2), pp 207–219.

Palfreyman, D (1995/96) 'Oxbridge Fellows as Charity Trustees' *The Charity Law and Practice Review* 3(3), pp 187–202.

Palfreyman, D (1996/97) 'The Oxford Colleges and their College Contributions Scheme' *The Charity Law and Practice Review* 4(1), pp 51–65.

Palfreyman, D (1997) 'Gift horses – with strings attached!' *Perspectives: Policy and Practice in Higher Education* 1(4), pp 133–138.

Palfreyman, D (1998) 'Unlimited personal liability for members of Councils and Boards of Governors?' *Education and the Law* 10(4), pp 245–252.

Palfreyman, D (1998/99) 'Oxford Colleges: Permanent Endowment, Charity Trustee-ship, and Personal Liability' *The Charity Law and Practice Review* 5(2), pp 85–134.

Palfreyman, D (1999a) 'Is Porterhouse really "a Charity"?' *The Charity Law and Practice Review* 6(2), pp 151–166.

Palfreyman, D (1999b) 'The HE–student legal relationship, with special reference to the USA experience' *Education and the Law* 11(1), pp 5–23.

Palfreyman, D (2000) 'The University of Barchester, Cokestown University, Ipswich Cathedral Choir School, Gas Street Comprehensive School and the European Convention on Human Rights: a link? *Education and the Law* 12(2), pp 93–104.

Palfreyman, D (2001) *The Oxford Tutorial* (OxCHEPS).

Palfreyman, D (2002, forthcoming) *The University–Student Legal Relationship: Contract and Consumer Law, Tort and Educational Malpractice* (OxCHEPS).

Palfreyman, D (forthcoming) 'Proper Governance in the English Chartered University' *Education and the Law*; and also available as an OxCHEPS Occasional Paper.

Palfreyman, D and Warner, DA (1998) *Higher Education and the Law: A Guide for Managers* (Open University Press).

Palfreyman, D, Thomas, H and Warner, DA (1998) *How to manage a merger, or avoid one* (Heist Publications).

Palmer, J (2001) *Animal Law* (Shaws).

Parlour, JW (1996) 'Student charters in higher education' *Education and the Law* 8(3), p 229.

Parlour, JW and Burwood, LRV (1995) 'Students' Rights' *Education and the Law* 7(2), pp 63–78.

Parry, G and Houghton, D (1996) 'Plagiarism in UK universities' *Education and the Law* 8(3), p 201.

Pawlowski, M (1993) 'When is a Tenancy not a Tenancy?' *L&T Rev* 3(3).

Peiris, GL (1987) 'Visitorial Jurisdiction: The Changing Outlook on an Exclusive Regime' *AALR* 16, p 376.

Perlman, B (1988) *The Academic Intrapreneur* (Praeger).

Pettit, PH (1991) 'Academic Tenure and the Education Reform Act 1988' *MLR* 54, p 137.

Pettit, PH (1993) *Law of Trusts* (Butterworths).

Phillips, G and Scott K (2001/02) *Employment Law* (Jordans).

Phillips, H and Claricoat, J (1995 Summer) 'The sale of chattels held on charitable trusts' *Christie's Bulletin* pp 1–9.

Phillips, J (1999) *Licensing Law Guide* (Butterworths).

Picarda, H (1992–3) 'Practice and Procedure on Visitorial Appeals' *Charity Law and Practice Review* 1, p 63.

Picarda, H (1999) *The Law and Practice Relating to Charities* (Butterworths).

Piper, DW (1994) *Are Professors Professional? – the organisation of university examinations* (Jessica Kingsley).

Pitt, G (1990) 'Academic Freedom and Education Reform: The Tenure Provisions of the Education Reform Act 1988' *IUF* 19, p 33.

Pollock, F and Maitland, FW (1923) *The History of English Law* (Cambridge University Press).

Pound, R (1936) 'Visitorial Jurisdiction over Corporations in Equity' *Harvard Law Review* 49(3), pp 369–453.

Price, DM and Whalley, PWF (1996) 'The university Visitor and university governance' *Journal of Higher Education Policy and Management* 18(1), pp 45–57.

Pyke, J (2000) *A–Z of Civil Litigation* (Sweet & Maxwell).

QAA (1999) *Code of Practice: Students with Disabilities* (QAA); and also via www.QAA.ac.uk.

Radford, M (2001) *Animal Welfare in Britain* (OUP).

Richens, NJ and Fletcher, MJG (1996) *Charity Land and Premises* (Jordans).

Report of the Oxford University Commissioners (1852).

Ricquier, WTM (1978) 'The University Visitor' *DaJU* 4, p 647.

Ricquier, WTM (1979) 'Failed Students and Access to Justice' *Pub U*, p 209.

Riesman, D (1998) *On Higher Education; the academic enterprise in an era of rising student consumerism* (New Brunswick, NJ: Transaction Publishers).

Rochford, F (1998) 'The relationship between the student and the university' *Law and Education* (Australia and New Zealand) 3(1), pp 23–25.

Rogerson, P (2000) 'Habitual Residence: The New Domicile?' *ICLQ* 49, p 86.

Rowe, H (2000) *Data Protection Act, 1998: A Practical Guide* (Tolley).

Ruff, A (2002, forthcoming) *Education Law: Cases and Materials* (Butterworths).

Rudolph, F (1990) *The American College and University: A History* (University of Georgia Press).

Ryder, A (1996) 'Reform and higher education in the enterprise era' *Higher Education Quarterly* 50(1), pp 54–70.

Sadler, RT (1980) 'The University Visitor in Australia: Murdoch University v Bloom' *Mon UR* 7, p 59.

Sadler, RT (1981) 'The University Visitor: Vistorial Precedent and Procedure in Australia' *U Tas UR* 7, p 2.

Salter, B et al (2000) 'Managing the Private Finance Initiative' *Perspectives: Policy and Practice in Higher Education* 4(3), pp 68–73.

Samuels, A (1973) 'The Student and the Law' *Journal of the Society of Public Teachers Law* 12, p 252.

Saunders, N (1999) 'The Human Rights Act, 1998: research, freedom of speech and academic freedom' *Education and the Law* 11(3), pp 187–197.

Schweitzer, TA (1992 Winter) 'Academic challenge cases: should judicial review extend to academic evaluations of students?' *The American University Law Review* pp 261–272.

Scott, C and Black, J (2000) *Cranston's Consumer and the Law* (Butterworths).

Selwyn, N (2000) *Selwyn's Law of Employment* (Butterworths).

Shattock, ML (1994) *The UGC and the Management of British Universities* (Open University Press).

Shattock, ML (1999) 'Governance and management in universities: the way we live now' *Journal of Education Policy* 14(3), pp 271–282.

Shattock, ML (2000) 'Strategic Management in European Universities in an age of increasing institutional self-reliance' *Tertiary Education and Management* 6(2), pp 93–104.

Shattock, ML (forthcoming) *Managing Governance* (Open University Press).

Shaw (1986) 'Disputes within Universities: the Visitor or the Courts?' *The Australian Universities Review* 29(1).

Shaw, R and Smith, D (1979) *The Law of Meetings. Their Conduct and Procedure* (Macdonald & Evans).

Shearman, I (1997) *Shackleton on the Law and Practice of Meetings* (Sweet & Maxwell).

SHEFC (1999) *The Guide for Members of Governing Bodies of Scottish Higher Education Institutions and Good Practice Benchmarks* (SHEFC).

SHEFC (2000) *Teachability: Creating an Accessible Curriculum for Students with Disabilities* (SHEFC); and also via www.ispn.gcal.ac.uk/teachability.

Shelford, U (1836) *Law of Mortmain* (Longman).

Sheridan, L (1993/94) 'Cy-près Application of three Holloway pictures' *Charity Law and Practice Review* 2(3), pp 181–184.

Siedentop, L (2000) *Democracy in Europe* (Penguin).

Simblet, A (1999) 'Litigation with Universities' *Litigation* 17(2), p 47.

Simons, A (1999) *A Practical Guide to the Small Claims Court* (Tolley).

Skinner, M (2001) 'The AUA Code of Professional Standards' *Perspectives: Policy and Practice in Higher Education* 5(3), pp 63–67.

Slapper, G (1997) 'Judging the Educators: Forensic Evaluation of Academic Judgement' *Education and the Law* 9(1), pp 5–12.

Slaughter, S and Leslie, LL (1997) *Academic Capitalism: Policies, and the Entrepreneurial University* (The Johns Hopkins University Press).

Smith, I et al (2000) *Health and Safety – The Modern Legal Framework* (Butterworths).

Smith, JC and Hogan, B (1999) *Criminal Law* (Butterworths).

Smith, PM (1981) 'The Exclusive Jurisdiction of the University Visitor' *LQR* 97, p 610.

Smith, PM (1986) 'Visitation of the Universities: A Ghost from the Past' *NLJ* 136, pp 484, 519, 567, 665.

Smith, PM (1993/94) 'The Jurisdiction of the University Visitor: How Exclusive is Exclusive?' *Charity Law and Practice Review* 2, p 103.

Soley, L (1995) *Leasing The Ivory Tower: The Corporate Takeover of Academia* (South End Press).

Sparkes, P (1999) *A New Land Law* (Hart Publishing).

Sparkes, P (2001) *A New Landlord and Tenant* (Hart Publishing).

Spiers, C (2001) *Managing Stress in the Workplace* (Butterworths).

Sporn, B (1999) *Adaptive University Structures: An Analysis of Adaption to Socio-Economic Environments of US and European Universities* (Jessica Kingsley).

Stokes, S (2001) *Art & Copyright* (Hart Publishing).

Tapper, T and Palfreyman, D (1998) 'The Collegial Tradition' *Higher Education Quarterly* 52(2), pp 142–161.

Tapper, T. and Palfreyman, D (2000) *Oxford and the Decline of the Collegiate Tradition* (Woburn Press).

Taylor Report (2001) *New Directions for Higher Education Funding* (UUK).

TEAM (2001) 'Special Issue on Governance Seminar' *Tertiary Education and Management* 7(2), pp 89–224.

Thomas, G and Calder, K (2001) 'Specialisms for generalists' *Perspectives: Policy and Practice in Higher Education* 5(2), p 48.

Thomas, P (ed) (1975) *Universities and the Law* (Legal Research Institute of Manitoba).

Tiley, J (2000) *Revenue Law* (Hart Publishing).

Tolley (1998) *Tolley's Office Health and Safety Handbook* (Tolley).

Tolley (2000/01) *Tolley's Value Added Tax, 2000–01* (Tolley).

Torremans, P (2001) *Hollyoak and Torremans: Intellectual Property Law* 3rd edn (Butterworths).

Treitel, GH (1999) *The Law of Contract* (Sweet & Maxwell).

Tribe, D (1994) *Negotiation* (Cavendish).

Tur, T (2001) *Oxford Magazine* No 1792, p 21.

Uff, J (1999) *Construction Law* (Sweet & Maxwell).

Underhill, T and Hayton, DJ (1995) *Law of Trusts and Trustees* (Butterworths).

Varnham, S (1998) 'Liability in Higher Education in New Zealand: Cases for Courses' *Law and Education (Australia and New Zealand)* 3(1), pp 2–18.

Wade, HWR (1969) 'Judicial Control of Universities' *LQR* 85, p 468.

Wade, Sir William (1993) 'Visitors and Error of Law' *LQR* 109, p 155.

Wade, WHR and Forsyth, CF (1994) *Administrative Law* (Oxford University Press).

Warburton, J (1992) *Unincorporated Associations* (Sweet & Maxwell).

Warburton, J and Morris, D (1995) *Tudor on Charities* (Sweet & Maxwell).

Waring, M (2001/02) *Commercial Litigation* (Jordans)

Warner, DA and Crosthwaite, E (1995) *Human Resources in Higher and Further Education* (SRHE/Open University Press).

Warner, DA and Palfreyman, D (1996, 2nd edn due 2002) *Higher Education Management: The Key Elements* (Open University Press).

Warner, DA and Palfreyman, D (2001) *The State of UK Higher Education: Managing Change and Diversity* (Open University Press).

Warren, RC (1994) 'The collegiate ideal and the organisations of the new universities' *Reflections on Higher Education* 6, pp 34–55.

Warren, RC (1997) 'Corporate temperance in higher education' *Perspectives: Policy and Practice in Higher Education* 1(3), p 82.

Watson, D (2000) *Managing Strategy* (Open University Press).

Wellam, M (2001) *Corporate Killing – The New Law* (Butterworths).

West, E (2000) *Companies Limited by Guarantee* (Jordans).

Whincup, MH (1993) 'The Exercise of University Disciplinary Powers' *Education and the Law* 5(1), pp 19–31.

Whish, R (2001) *Competition Law* 4th edn (Butterworths).

Whittaker, S (2001a) 'Public and Private Law-Making: Subordinate Legislation, Contracts and the Status of "Student Rules"' *Oxford Journal of Legal Studies* 21(1), pp 103–128.

Whittaker, S (2001b) 'Judicial Review in Public Law and in Contract Law: the Example of "Student Rules"' *Oxford Journal of Legal Studies* 21(2), pp 193–217.

Williams, J (1910) *The Law of the Universities* (Butterworths).

Willis, P (1979) 'Patel v University of Bradford Senate' *MUUR* 12, p 291.

World Bank, The (1994) *Higher Education: The Lessons of Experience* (World Bank).

Wright, F (1997) *Law of Health and Safety at Work* (Sweet & Maxwell).

Wyatt, D and Dashwood, A (2000) *European Law* (Sweet & Maxwell).

Zellick, G (1989) 'British Universities and the Education Reform Act 1988' *Pub U*, p 513.

Zellick, G (1994) *Final Report of the Task Force on Student Disciplinary Procedures* (CVCP).

Zweigert, K and Kötz, H (1998) *Comparative Law* (Oxford University Press).

CONTACT DETAILS FOR CONTRIBUTORS

The websites for the various law firms contributing to this book are as follows.

Eversheds	www.eversheds.com
Linnells	www.linnells.co.uk
Manches	www.manches.co.uk
Martineau Johnson	www.martineau-johnson.co.uk
Mills & Reeve	www.mills-reeve.com
Pinsent Curtis Biddle	www.pinsentcurtis.com
Shakespeares	www.shakespeares.co.uk
Travers Smith Braithwaite	www.traverssmith.com

INDEX

References are to editors' introductions (§), paragraph numbers and
chapter appendices

Abandonment   26.3–26.4
Abuse of a dominant position   28.58,
    28.70
Abuse of power   3.13–3.14, 9.15,
    9.26
Academic appeals
    cheating   7.53
    codes of practice   7.48–7.49
    complaints   7.48, 7.51, 7.55–7.56
    discipline   7.48–7.54
    misconduct   7.48
    natural justice   7.50, 7.53
    penalties   7.53
    procedure   7.53
    Quality Assurance Agency   7.48–
        7.49
    Visitor   7.51–7.52, 7.54
Academic freedom   §10.2–10.4,
    10.14–10.16
    Canada   §10.4
    Human Rights Act 1998   10.16
    intellectual property   10.15
    Model Statute   11.6
    research   10.16
    United States   §10.3
    Visitor   10.14
Acceptance   6.9, 6.15
Access to courts or tribunals   7.19
Accidents   §6.19
Accommodation. See also Leased
    premises, Licences, Multiple
    occupation, houses in
    distance selling   29.32
    Private Finance Initiative   §18.3
Account, action for an   27.60
Accountability
    accounts   3.25
    annual reports   3.25–3.26
    board of governors   3.4

Cambridge University   5.28–5.30
    Funding Council   3.25
    governance   3.1, 3.4, 3.15
    governing bodies   3.4, 4.21
    meetings   3.25
    Public Accounts Committee   3.25
Accounts
    accountability   3.25
    charities   4.17
    due diligence   16.32
    Private Finance Initiative   18.5
Acknowledgement of service   9.50
Acquisitions. See Mergers and
    acquisitions
Adaptation periods   28.51
Administrative courts   7.4–7.5, 9.50
Administrators. See Management
Admissions   6.4, 6.13, 27.68
ADR. See Alternative dispute resolution
Adversarial proceedings   7.33,
    27.11–27.13, 27.15
Advertising   25.31
Advice
    charities   4.24, 4.26, 4.27
    governing bodies   4.24
    Private Finance Initiative   18.33
    risk management   24.16
    trustees   §4.2, 4.24, 4.26, 4.27
Affinity products and services   25.29
Age for entering into contracts   6.15
Agency
    authority   5.23, 5.27
        actual   5.23
        apparent   5.23
        implied   5.23
        ostensible   5.23
    information technology   5.28–5.30
    third parties   5.24
    vicarious liability   5.19, 5.25

Allocation to tracks 27.32
Alternative dispute resolution 6.36,
    27.48–27.51. *See also* Arbitration
  advantages of 27.51
  conciliation 8.25
  litigation §27.4, 27.18
  mediation 8.21, 8.25, 27.50
  mini-trials 27.50
  purpose of 27.49
Alumni
  affinity products and services
    25.29
  advantages of 25.1
  associations §25.1, 25.2–25.5
  benefits of 25.4–25.5
  charitable giving 25.6–25.19
  confidentiality 25.29
  data protection 25.20–25.38
  direct marketing 25.34
  endowments 25.5
  host mailings 25.28, 25.29
  internet 25.33
  location-based advertising 25.31
  outsourcing 25.36–25.37
  power to form and administer
    25.3
  taxation 25.6–25.19
  unsolicited telephone calls 25.30
Annual reports 3.25–3.26, 4.17
Anti-competitive practices
  block exemptions 28.63, 28.64,
    28.66–28.69
  cautions 28.67
  clearances 28.63
  Competition Act 1998 28.68–
    28.69
  compliance review 28.72
  concerted practices 28.66
  contracts 28.60–28.61, 28.63,
    28.65–28.66
    minor importance, of 28.63
  dominant position 28.57–28.59,
    28.66, 28.70
    abuse of 28.58, 28.70
    definition 28.59, 28.70
  EC law 28.55–28.72
  enforcement 28.71
  exclusive arrangements 28.57
  exemptions 28.63, 28.66–28.70
  fines 28.60–28.62, 28.71

  inspections 28.60
  investigations 28.60, 28.71
  know how 28.64
  licensing 28.64
  notifications 28.69
  permitted 28.63
  product market 28.59
  prohibited practices 28.69–28.70
    examples of 28.55–28.56
  relevant market 28.59, 28.69
  research and development
    agreements 28.65
  technology transfer licensing
    28.64
  trading companies §15.5
  vertical agreements 28.66
Apologies 5.14
Appeals. *See also* Academic appeals
  arbitration 27.43
  complaints 7.56
  Court of Appeal 27.25
  courts App 6(1)
  discipline 7.26, 7.46, 7.48–7.54,
    §9.9, 11.76
  dismissal 11.76
  employment 10.11
  fair trials 7.20, 7.24
  Nolan Committee §6.7–6.8, §9.4
  permission 27.25
  time-limits 7.46
  Visitor 30.63
Applicants §6.2, 6.23
Aptitude tests 28.51
Arbitration 27.41–27.46
  advantages 27.46
  agreements 27.41
  appeals 27.43
  arbitrators, increased power of
    27.45
  autonomy of the parties 27.42
  binding 8.21
  complaints §9.4
  courts, supportive role of 27.43
  definition 27.8
  disadvantages 27.46
  enforcement 27.46, 27.62
  expenses 27.46
  flexibility 27.44
  franchising 17.39
  Human Rights Act 1998 8.21

Arbitration – *cont*
  objects of   27.41
  privacy   27.46
  simplicity   27.46
  specialisation   27.46
  Visitor   8.20, 8.21, 30.60
  Working Group   §9.4
Arrest   20.11–20.14
Articles of association   15.26, 19.27
Articles of treaties   28.8
Assignment of intellectual property
  12.46–12.50
Association Agreements   28.5
Audits   1.33, 1.34, 3.17, §9.9
Australia   1.14, 30.48–30.50
Awards   28.31–28.35

Bailment   26.4–26.5
Ballots   5.5, 19.4
Banking   16.40
Bargaining power, inequality of
  6.28–6.30
Barriers to trade   28.73
Barristers' immunity   §6.25
Berne Convention   12.21
Best practice   §3.4, §3.6–§3.7, §3.9
Bias. *See* Impartiality
Block exemptions   28.63, 28.64,
  28.66–28.69
Board of governors. *See also* Chair
  accountability   3.4
  appointment   3.4, 3.23–3.24
  Cadbury Committee   3.23
  composition   3.4, 3.23–3.24
  conflicts of interest   3.21–3.22
  fiduciary duties   3.33
  functions of   3.10
  governance   3.10, 3.17–3.18
  Nolan Committee   3.24
  personal liability   3.32–3.33
  trustees   §4.3
Board of Visitors   §8.4
Bodies corporate   4.18
Bonds   18.35
Books   1.12–1.14
Borrowing. *See* Loans
Breach of the peace   20.13
Brochures   29.9–29.10

Buildings. *See also* Occupiers' liability
  leased premises   23.16–23.18
  Private Finance Initiative   18.26–
    18.27
  students' union   19.11–19.17
Bullying   7.13
Business transfers. *See* Transfers of
  undertakings

Cadbury Committee   3.1, 3.23
Cambridge University
  agency   5.28–5.30
  CAPSA   5.28–5.30, 24.28
  charities   4.10–4.11
  judicial review   9.12
  Visitor   §8.2, 30.6, 30.13, 30.15–
    30.19
Canada   1.14
  academic freedom   §10.4
  intellectual property   §10.4
  Visitor   30.51
Cancellation of contracts   6.14
Canon law   8.2, 30.7
Capability   10.19
Capacity to enter into contracts   6.15
Capital gains tax   25.8, 25.10
CAPSA   5.28–5.30, 24.28
Case management   27.18–27.19,
  27.35
Case-book   1.39
Causation   §6.26, 6.24, 6.26–6.27
Cautions   28.67
Caveat emptor   29.7
CCTV   20.20–20.22
Central Europe   28.5, 28.73
Chair
  committees   5.2
  governance   3.18
  meetings   5.1–5.2
  principal and   3.18
  removal of   5.2
  role of   5.1–5.2
  voting   5.2
Chancellor   §3.4
Chancery Division   27.24
Charges   7.31
Charities
  abuse of status as   4.15
  accounts   4.17

Charities – *cont*
advantages of status of   2.5, 19.12
advice   4.24, 4.26, 4.27
alumni   25.6–25.19
annual reports   4.17
assets of   4.20, 4.27
benefits received by donors   25.17
Cambridge University   4.10–4.11
capital gains tax   25.8, 25.10
Charity Commissioners   4.11,
    4.13–4.15, 4,19, 4.24, 4.27–4.28,
    15.3
Common Investment Fund   4.28
controls   4.15–4.16
corporations   4.27, 5.29–5.30
data protection   25.11
declarations   25.11–25.13
    cancellation of   25.12
deeds of covenant   15.12–15.13,
    25.14–25.16
definition   4.2–4.3
deposits   25.15
directors   4.18
donations   19.13–19.17
due diligence   16.24
education   4.4–4.7, 4.19
ex gratia payments   4.19
exempt   4.10–4.17, 4.28, 15.3–
    15.5, 19.11–19.12, 19.30, 25.6
fees   4.5
funding   4.19
fund-raising   15.5, 25.19
Gift Aid   15.12–15.13, 25.9, 25.16
giving   25.6–25.19
governing bodies   4.18–4.20, 4.26
income tax   25.10
inheritance tax   25.7
Inland Revenue   4.17
insurance   4.26
investment   §4.2, 4.20, 4.27–4.28
jurisdiction   4.10–4.11, 4.13
legal entity   §2.3, 2.5
loan covenants   25.15
management   4.18, 4.20
Oxford University   4.10–4.11
payroll giving   25.18
personal liability   3.35, §4.1–§4.4,
    4.1–4.29
public, benefit of the   4.6, 4.15
purposes, charitable   4.2–4.9, 4.19

regulation   4.10–4.17
scholarships   4.7
staff   4.16
statutory institutions   4.27
Students' Union   19.11–19.17,
    19.30
tax relief   4.17, 15.3–15.5, 18.36,
    19.12, 25.6–25.19
trading companies   2.5, 4.17,
    §15.6, 15.2–15.5
trustees   3.35, §4.1–§4.4, 4.1–4.29
    associations   4.18
VAT   15.14
Visitor   4.16
wills, legacies from   4.8–4.9, 4.14
Chartered institutions   1.21, 1.24–
    1.25
corporations   2.1
Council   3.19
governance   3.6, 3.19
governing bodies   3.25
judicial review   7.3, 9.19
legal entity   §2.1, §2.3–§2.4
litigation   27.2
mergers and acquisitions   16.12,
    16.13, 16.18
personal liability   3.41, 3.44, 3.49
powers of   2.1, 2.3
public bodies   7.3
Visitor   2.2, 7.3, §8.1–§8.5, 8.1–
    8.26, 30.6
Charters   1.3, 1.10, 29.40
Chattels   26.1–26.6
Cheating
academic appeals   7.53
defamation   5.18
Oxford University's Statement to
    Students   1.37
plagiarism   5.18
Checks and balances   3.16–3.20
Choice of law   17.35, 17.40,
    17.42
Civil law   §2.3, 3.32
Civil Procedure Rules 1998   9.50,
    27.10, 27.71
Civil rights and obligations   7.17–
    7.18, 9.43–9.44
Claim forms   9.49–9.50
Clamping   20.9–20.10
Class actions   6.30, 29.41

Clearances 28.63
Clearing 6.12
Close circuit television 20.20–20.22
Clubs 1.37
Codes of practice
  academic appeals 7.48–7.49
  close circuit television 20.20
  complaints 8.20
  consumer law 29.29, 29.35
  disability discrimination 22.9,
    22.25
  dismissal 11.72
  franchising §17.4
  freedom of expression 19.6, 29.19
  governance §3.6
  Greenbury Code 3.2
  harassment §7.4
  internet 14.5
  meetings 5.6
  personal liability 3.47
  quality assurance 7.48–7.49, 7.55,
    7.59
  Visitor 8.20, 8.22
Collective agreements 16.20
Commissary 8.2, 8.14, 8.15, 30.41
Commissioners
  dismissal 10.20
  employment 10.17–10.26
  good cause, meaning of 10.19
  powers and duties of 10.17–10.26
  statutes 10.18–10.23
Commissioning editors 5.22
Committees
  audit 3.17
  Chair 5.2
  defamation 5.14
  delegation 5.19
  governance 3.2, 3.17
  governing bodies 3.24
  meetings 5.9, 5.11
  nomination 3.24
  Public Accounts Committee 3.25
  redundancy 11.67, 11.70
  remuneration 3.2, 3.17
Community
  higher education institutions as
    2.8–2.10
Companies. *See also* Corporations,
    Directors, Mergers and acquisitions,
    Trading companies
  articles of association 19.27

charitable status 19.30
company secretaries 5.12, 15.29
drink and 19.32
format 19.26
guarantee, companies limited by
    19.26
legal entity §2.3–§2.4
meetings 5.12
members 19.29
memorandum of association
    19.27
personal liability 3.42, 3.45
special purpose 18.14
spin-out 12.48–12.50
students' union 19.25–19.33
Company secretaries 5.12, 15.29
Compensation. *See* Damages
Competition. *See* Anti-competitive
    practices
Complaints 7.55–7.59 *See also*
    Visitor
  academic appeals 7.48, 7.51, 7.55
  alternative dispute resolution
    6.36
  appeals 7.56
    academic 7.48, 7.51, 7.55–7.56
  arbitration §9.4
  Chancellor's Court §3.4
  codes of practice 8.20
  contracts §6.1, 6.2, 6.21
  decision-taking 7.55–7.56
  delay in dealing with §6.6
  disability discrimination 22.15
  discipline 7.58–7.59
  dismissal 11.75
  examinations 1.37
  fair trials 7.20
  governance §3.4, §3.6
  harassment 7.58
  misconduct 11.75
  multiple occupation, houses in
    21.13
  Oxford University's Statement to
    Students 1.37–1.38
  procedure 6.36, App 6(2), 7.55
  protection from §6.6–§6.9
  public procurement 28.22
  Quality Assurance Agency 6.36,
    7.55–7.56
  risk management 24.15

Complaints – *cont*
  students' union   19.4
  types of   7.56
  Visitor   8.20, 8.25
Compromise   27.17, 27.27, 27.71
Computers
  hacking   14.8
  internet   14.8
  misuse   14.8
  Oxford University's Statement to
     Students   1.37
  software   12.15, 12.59
Concerted practices   28.66
Conciliation   8.25
Conditional offers   6.9
Conditions of contracts   6.17–6.19,
   11.27
Conduct   1.37, 3.31, 7.27, 7.48,
   11.71–11.76, 11.84, 11.87
Confederation   16.6
Confidentiality *See also* Secrecy
  alumni   25.39
  data protection   §13.3–13.4
  disability discrimination   22.25
  research   §10.5
  United States   §10.5
Conflicts of interest
  board of governors   3.21–3.22
  directors   15.28
  disclosure   3.21–3.22
  governance   3.4, 3.14, 3.21–3.22
  governing bodies   3.21, 4.21
  intellectual property   11.2–11.3
  interests, register of   3.22
  Nolan Committee   3.21
  personal liability   3.33
  research   §10.4
  safeguards against   3.21–3.22
  statutory institutions   3.21
  trading companies   §15.7, 15.30
Conscience, freedom of   7.16
Consideration   6.15
Consultants   11.41
Consumer law   29.1–29.41
  brochures   29.9–29.10
  caveat emptor   29.7
  charters   29.40
  codes of practice   29.29, 29.35
  consumerism, growth of   1.3–
   1.11, 1.13, §6.1, 6.2, 29.2–29.4,
   29.11, 29.34

  contracts   §6.1, 6.2, 29.1, 29.5–
   29.7, 29.38
  criminal offences   29.31, 29.37
  distance selling   29.32–29.33
  due diligence   29.30, 29.37
  EC law   29.36
  fees   29.15
  holiday industry   29.10, 29.35–
   29.37
  Human Rights Act 1998   29.12
  legislative framework   29.12–
   29.33
  litigiousness, growth in   29.2–29.3
  ombudsperson   29.34–29.35,
   29.38
  private prosecutions   29.29
  prospectuses   29.9–29.10
  representative actions   29.41
  satisfactory quality   29.13, 29.36
  skill and care   29.13
  supply of goods and services
   29.13–29.15
  trade descriptions   29.27–29.28
  unfair contract terms   6.28–6.30,
   29.5–29.9
  United States   29.2–29.3
Continuing Professional
   Development   1.15
Contracts   1.12, 5.20
  acceptance   6.9, 6.15
  admissions   6.4, 6.13
  age   6.15
  anti-competitive practices   28.60–
   28.61, 28.63, 28.65–28.66
  binding   6.8, 6.11, 6.15
  breach of   6.20–6.36
  cancellation   6.14
  capacity   6.15
  case-law   App 6(1)
  clearing   6.12
  complaints   §6.1, 6.2, 6.21
  conditions   6.17–6.19, 11.27
  consideration   6.15
  consumer law   §6.1, 6.2, 6.28–
   6.30, 29.1, 29.5–29.7, 29.38
  damages   6.22, 6.24–6.27
  disability discrimination   §22.6
  discipline   §6.2, §7.2–§7.3, 7.26
  disclaimers   6.34
  dismissal   11.2–11.58

Contracts – *cont*
  distance, concluded at   6.14, 29.32
  due diligence   16.28
  duration of   6.16
  education experience   §6.2–§6.5
  educational malpractice   §6.26–
    §6.28
  employment   6.6, 10.3, 10.11–
    10.13, 10.24–10.26, 11.2–11.58,
    12.38, 16.20
    franchising   17.17–17.18
    transfer of undertakings   17.22
  exclusion clauses   6.28, 6.34, 20.5
  existence of   6.3–6.19
  fair trials   7.18
  fees   §6.9, 6.15, 6.17
  fixed-term   11.2, 11.14–11.17,
    11.37, 11.70–11.93
  formation of   6.8–6.15
  franchising   17.5–17.45, 17.28–
    17.29
    privity of   17.8–17.11
    student   17.6–17.7
    terms of   17.12–17.43
  frustration   11.19
  implied terms   6.17–6.19
  information   6.14
  intellectual property   11.38,
    11.44–11.45
  judicial review   6.23, 7.4, 9.20–
    9.23, 9.25, 9.27, 9.29, 9.38, 9.41
  matriculation   6.4
  mental capacity   6.15
  mergers and acquisitions   16.3–
    16.9, 16.13–16.16
  method of making   6.8–6.15
  minor importance of   28.63,
  Model Statute   11.1–11.58
  more than one   6.4–6.6
  obligations, types of   6.4–6.5,
    6.17–6.18, 7.2
  offer   6.6, 6.9, 6.15, 6.22, 6.24–
    6.25
    conditional   6.9
    informal   6.10–6.11
  overseas students   §6.1, 6.11
  parties to   6.7
  postgraduate admissions   6.13
  prevention of breach of   6.31–6.36
  Private Finance Initiative   18.26–
    18.27

  privity of   17.8–17.11
  public service contracts   28.29
  public supply contracts   28.28
  public works contracts   28.27
  redundancy   11.12, 11.22, 11.27
  references   6.38
  registration   6.17
  remedial action   6.31–6.36
  remedies   6.21–6.27
  research and development   28.65
  risk management   24.20–24.26
  services for   10.3
  skill and care   6.18
  specific performance   6.22
  standard terms   6.29
  students   §6.1–§6.30, 6.1–6.40,
    App 6(1), App 6(2), 7.2, 17.6–
    17.7
    backgrounds of   6.2
    overseas   §6.1, 6.11
    relationship between HEIs and
      6.3–6.5, 7.2
  students' union   19.21–19.22
  termination   6.16
  terms   6.17–6.19, 6.29, 10.3,
    11.27, 17.12–17.43
  third parties   4.23
  time for making   6.8–6.15
  transfer of undertakings   16.20
  UCAS   6.7, 6.9
  ultra vires   4.23
  unconscionability   §6.15
  unfair terms   6.19, 6.28–6.30
  unincorporated associations
    19.10
  United States   §6.10–§6.19
  vertical agreements   28.66
  vicarious liability for breach of
    5.21–5.22
  Visitor   6.21–6.22
  warranties   3.40
  wrongful dismissal   11.48–11.58
Co-operation agreements   16.8
Copyright
  Berne Convention   12.21
  criteria for protection   12.20
  database extraction right   12.25
  fair dealing   12.58
  franchising   17.15, 17.19
  freedom of expression   12.4

Copyright – *cont*
  licensing   12.60, App 6(2)
  moral rights   12.24
  multiple rights   12.22
  photocopying   App 6(2)
  related forms of protection   12.23
  seeking protection   12.21
  Universal Copyright Convention
    12.21
Corporations. *See also* Companies
  charities   4.27, 5.29–5.30
  charter, created by   2.1
  criminal offences   4.25
  definition   2.1
  fair trials   7.20
  governance   3.1, 3.18
  legal entity   §2.2–§2.4, 2.1
  personal liability   3.29–3.44, 3.47
  powers of   2.1
  statute, created by   2.1
Corrections   5.14
Correspondence   7.14
Costs   6.21, 7.5
  damages   27.40
  franchising   17.23
  injunctions   27.40
  judicial review   9.49–9.52
  litigation   27.39–27.40
  security, for   27.40
  summary judgments, applications
    for   27.40
  Visitor   8.6, 8.25
Council   1.12, 3.19
Court of Appeal   27.25
Criminal offences
  charges   7.43–7.45
  consumer law   29.31, 29.37
  corporate killing   §6.21
  corporations   4.25
  discipline   7.43–7.45
  fair trials   9.44
  hacking   14.8
  harassment   §7.4
  health and safety   20.8
  insurance   3.48, 4.26
  multiple occupation, houses in
    21.35
  occupations   20.17–20.18
  personal liability   3.30–3.31, 3.48,
    4.26

  pornography   14.10
  sexual offences   §6.19
  statutory offences   3.30, 4.25
  trade descriptions   29.27–29.28
  United States   §6.19
  Zellick Report   7.44

Damages. *See also* Compensation
  causation   6.24, 6.26–6.27
  contracts, breach of   6.22, 6.24–
    6.27
  costs   27.40
  declarations   27.57
  definition   27.53
  disability discrimination   22.20
  dismissal   10.21, 11.1, 11.48–
    11.58
  educational malpractice   §6.26–
    §6.27, 6.27
  expenses   6.25
  injunctions   27.56
  interim   27.40
  judicial review   7.5, 9.16, 9.17,
    9.42
  loss of future earnings   1.9
  measure of   6.25
  mitigation   6.25
  negligence   6.27
  offers   6.24–6.25
  Oxford University's Statement to
    Students   1.37
  personal injuries   6.27
  public procurement   28.22
  purpose of   27.53
  racial discrimination   7.61
  references   §6.23, 6.38
  risk management   §24.4
  sex discrimination   7.61
  special needs, failure to diagnose
    6.27
  trespass to land   20.14
  Visitor   §8.2, 8.6, 30.37–30.38
Data protection   §13.1–§13.5
  13.1–13.13, 25.20–25.38
  access   13.10, 13.22, 13.24
  affinity products and services
    25.29
  alumni   25.20–25.38
  close circuit television   20.20–
    20.21

Data protection – *cont*
  conditions   25.20
  consent   25.21–25.29, 25.32,
    25.33
  data controllers   13.1, 13.22,
    20.21
    definition of   13.2
  data protection principles   13.6,
    13.23, 25.36–25.37
  data subjects, rights of   13.10,
    13.22, 13.24
  definitions   13.2–13.6
  degree results, confidentiality of
    §13.3–§13.4
  direct marketing, right to object
    to   25.34
  EC law   25.32
  EEA, transfer of data out of   25.32
  e-mails   §13.2
  exemptions   13.11
  freedom of information   §13.2,
    13.14, 13.22–13.25
  host mailings   25.28, 25.29
  Human Rights Act 1998   25.26
  indemnities   25.38
  Information Commissioner
    13.20–13.21, 25.26
    notification of   13.5
    powers of   13.12
  Information Tribunal   13.16
  internet   14.2, 14.7, 14.9, 25.33
  job interviews   §13.5
  location advertising   25.31
  manual records   13.8
  notification   13.25, 25.26
  Office of the Information
    Commissioner   13.12
  outsourcing   25.36–25.37
  personal data   13.23, 25.26
    categories of   13.7
    definition of   13.3, 13.22
    objecting to processing of
      25.35
    sensitive   13.7
  processing   13.4
  registration   25.26
  risk management   §24.3
  safe harbour   25.32
  sensitive personal data   13.7,
    25.21

  students' union   19.29
  Telephone Preference Service
    25.24
  third parties, sharing data with
    25.29
  transfer of data outside EEA
    25.32
  transitional relief   13.9
  unsolicited telephone calls   25.30
  wrongful dismissal   11.1, 11.48–
    11.58
Databases   11.59, 12.25, 14.11
Dearing Report
  governance   §3.6, 3.6
  governing bodies   3.27
  staff or student representatives
    3.27
Decision-making
  complaints   7.55–7.56
  delegation of   9.32
  discretion of   9.35
  evidence, in line with the   9.37–
    9.38
  governance   3.7, 3.9–3.12, 3.14
  governing bodies   3.10
  heard, right to be   9.42
  impartiality   9.48
  improper purpose, must not be in
    pursuit of a   9.38
  judicial review   9.6–9.7, 9.11,
    9.17–9.21
    decision must exercise mind of
      body   9.34
    delegation of   9.32
    discretion of   9.35
    evidence, in line with the   9.37–
      9.38
    heard, right to be   9.42
    impartiality   9.48
    improper purpose, must not be in
      pursuit of a   9.38
    legitimate expectations   9.41
    properly constituted body, for
      9.31
    proportionality   9.40, 9.51
    reasons for   9.45–9.46
  legitimate expectations   9.41
  meetings   5.13–5.18
  mind of body, exercising   9.34
  properly constituted body, for
    9.31

Decision-making – *cont*
  proportionality   9.40, 9.51
  public law   7.3
  reasons   7.39, 9.45–9.46
  United States   §6.18–§6.19
  Visitor   7.3, 8.16
  whistleblowing   3.27
Declarations
  charitable giving   25.11–25.13
  damages   27.57
  incompatibility, of   7.9
  judicial review   9.20
  taxation   25.11–25.13
Deeds of covenant   15.12–15.13,
    25.14–25.16
Defamation
  apologies   5.14
  cheating   5.18
  committees   5.14
  corrections   5.14
  definition   5.13
  fair comment   5.14
  innuendo   5.13
  intention   5.14
  internet   14.1, 14.12–14.16
  justification   5.14
  libel   5.13
  malice   5.14
  meetings   5.13–5.18
  Oxford University's Statement to
      Students   1.37
  plagiarism   5.18
  qualified privilege   5.14, 5.16–5.18
  references   5.15, 5.16, §6.23
  slander   5.13
  United States   5.17
Definition of university   §2.1
Degradation   1.37
Degrees. *See also* Mutual recognition of
    degrees and qualifications
  bogus   §2.1
  leased premises   23.29
  withholding   23.29
Delay
  complaints   §6.6
  reasons   7.40
  Visitor   8.7, 8.14
Delegation   5.19–5.27
  committees   5.19
  decision-making   9.32
  governance   3.18, 3.20

  judicial review   9.32
  litigation   27.66
  powers   2.4
  statutory institutions   2.4
  United States   5.21
Demonstrations
  occupations   §20.1, 20.17–20.18
  Oxford University's Statement to
      Students   1.37
  use of force   §20.1
Deposits   25.15
Design   11.26
Detinue   26.5
Diplomas, recognition of   28.48–
    28.49
Direct effect   28.9, 28.10
Direct marketing   25.34
Directives   28.10, 28.14–28.17,
    28.46–28.47, 28.50, 28.53–28.54
Directors
  charities   4.18
  conflicts of interest   15.28
  de facto   15.18
  duties of   15.28
  fiduciary duties   4.21, 15.28
  nominees   §15.3
  personal liability   15.18, 15.28
    analogy with   3.38–3.40, 3.42,
      3.49
  shadow   15.18, 19.31
  students' union   19.29–19.31
  wrongful trading   15.18
Disability discrimination   7.12,
    §22.1–§22.8, 22.1–32
  adjustments, reasonable   7.64,
      22.9, 22.17, 22.25, 22.27–22.28
  alternative work   §22.2
  code of practice   22.9, 22.25
  complaints   22.15
  confidentiality   22.25
  consultation   22.11
  contracts   §22.6
  damages   22.20
  disability
    definition of   22.4–22.5
    statements   22.21
  discrimination, meaning of   22.25
  dismissal   11.78
  employment   22.4, 22.6–22.15
  guidance   22.9

Disability discrimination – *cont*
  Human Rights Act 1998 §22.1,
    22.31–22.32
  job interviews 22.6
  justification 22.8, 22.26
  leased premises 22.12, 22.17,
    22.28
  less favourable treatment 22.7,
    22.17, 22.25–22.26
  mental disabilities §22.4–§22.5
  multi-facted HEIs 22.2
  multiple occupation, houses in
    §22.1
  numbers of disabled students
    §22.7
  practical steps 22.10
  premises, adjustments to 7.64,
    22.9, 22.17, 22.25, 22.27–22.28
  public authorities 22.31–22.32
  remedies 22.15, 22.29
  services, provision of 22.16–
    22.20, 22.24
  Special Educational Needs and
    Disability Act 2001, impact
    of 22.21–22.30
  small employers 22.6
  staff §22.2
  timetable 22.30
  trading companies 22.6
  United States §22.2–§22.5
  vicarious liability 22.14
  victimisation 22.13, 22.24
Discipline 7.25–7.47
  academic appeals 7.48–7.54
  adversarial hearings 7.33
  appeals 7.26, 7.46, 7.48–7.54,
    §9.69, 11.76
  cases on §9.7–§9.9
  charges, specificity of 7.31
  complaints 7.58
  composition of the tribunal 11.75
  conduct of proceedings 7.42
  contracts §7.2–§7.3, 7.26
  criminal charges, related 7.43–
    7.45
  criminal offences 7.27, 7.43–7.45
  dismissal 11.32, 11.35, 11.73,
    11.75–11.76
  equality of arms 7.35
  evidence, disclosure of 7.32–7.33

  fair trials 7.18–7.20, 7.24, 7.34,
    9.44
  function of 7.25, 7.27
  hearings 7.34–7.38
  Human Rights Act 1998 7.34–
    7.35
  internal hearings 7.35, 7.38
  judicial review 7.47, §9.7, 9.10,
    9.25–9.29
  leased premises 23.33
  legal representation 7.35–7.36
  misconduct, definition of 7.27
  mitigation 7.41
  Model Statute 11.33
  natural justice 7.30
  oral hearings 7.34
  order of procedure 7.37
  Oxford University's Statement to
    Students 1.37
  penalties 7.41
  procedure 7.29, 7.37, 7.42, 7.66
  proportionality 7.35, 7.41
  reasons 7.39–7.40
  regulations 2.9
  remedies 7.25
  risk management 24.21
  separation of roles 7.37
  staff 1.15
  standard of proof 7.38
  Visitor 30.51
  witnesses 7.37, 7.42
  Zellick Report 7.44
Disclaimers 6.34, 20.16
Disclosure. *See also* Whistleblowing
  conflicts of interest 3.21–3.22
  governance 3.23–3.27
  judicial review 9.38, 9.42, 9.51
  litigation 27.33
Discovery 27.69
Discrimination 7.5, 7.60–7.64. *See*
  also Disability discrimination,
  Racial discrimination, Sex
  discrimination
  dismissal 11.78
  EC law 28.43–28.44
  fair trials 7.20
  Human Rights Act 1998 7.12
  judicial review 9.47
  nationality 28.43–28.44
  positive 7.61

Discrimination – *cont*
  public procurement   28.19, 28.20,
    28.27
  risk management   §24.4, 24.23
Dismissal   10.1–10.2. *See also*
    Redundancy, Unfair dismissal,
    Wrongful dismissal
  academic staff   11.7–11.19
    definition   11.7
  ACAS code of practice   11.72
  alternative employment   11.13
  appeals   11.76
  Commissioners   10.20
  complaints   11.75
  consent by   11.18
  contracts of employment   11.2–
    11.58
  damages   10.21, 11.1, 11.48–11.58
  definition   11.9–11.12
  disability discrimination   11.78
  discipline   11.32, 11.35, 11.73,
    11.75–11.76
  EC law   11.17
  fixed-term employment   11.2,
    11.14–11.17, 11.37, 11.70–11.93
    definition of   11.16
    renewal of   11.15
  frustration   11.19
  good cause for   10.19, 11.29–
    11.34, 11.36, 11.38
    definition   11.30–11.33
    mental capacity and   11.39–
      11.41
    misconduct   11.71–11.76
  hearings   10.1
  ill-health   11.77–11.78
  incapacity   11.77–11.78
  medical examinations   11.78
  mental capacity   11.39–11.41
  misconduct   11.30–11.31, 11.71–
    11.76
  mitigation   11.75
  Model Statute   §11.1, 11.1–11.93
  notice   11.35
  pensions   11.41
  procedure   §11.1, 11.1–11.93
  reasonableness   11.1, 11.42–11.47
  reasons for   11.20–11.34
  reorganisations   11.38
  restrictions   11.35–11.47
  staff   1.15

  academic   11.7–11.19
  substantial reason, some other
    11.38
  suspension   11.75
  timescale for   11.75
  transfer of undertakings   16.20
  Visitor   10.10
  witness statements   11.75
Dissolution   3.43–3.45
Dispute resolution. *See also* Alternative
    dispute resolution, Litigation
  franchising   17.35–17.39
  risk management   24.15, 24.23
Distance, contracts concluded at a
    6.14
Distance learning   17.44
Distance selling   6.14, 29.32–29.33
Domain names   12.33–12.34, 14.11
Dominant position   28.57–28.59,
    28.66, 28.70
Donations   19.13–19.17
Drinking   §6.5, §6.22
Due diligence
  accountancy   16.32
  charities   16.24
  compliance with laws   16.27
  constitution   16.24
  consumer law   29.30, 29.37
  contractual arrangements   16.28
  employment   16.26
  environment   16.31
  financial   16.32
  insurance   16.29
  intellectual property   16.30
  legal   16.24–16.30
  litigation   16.27
  mergers and acquisitions   §16.3,
    16.17, 16.22–16.32, 16.41–16.42
  property   16.25
  transfer of undertakings   16.26
Duration of contracts   6.15

Eastern Europe   28.5, 28.73
EC law   §28.1–28.3, 28.1–28.73
  academic staff, free movement of
    28.36–28.42
  anti-competitive practices   28.55–
    28.72
  articles   28.8

EC law – *cont*

Association Agreements   28.5
awards   28.31–28.35
barriers to trade   28.73
Central Europe   28.5, 28.73
consumer law   29.36
data protection   25.32
designs   12.26
direct effect   28.9, 28.10
directives   28.10
discrimination   28.43–28.44
discussions   28.11
dismissal   11.17
Eastern Europe   28.5, 28.73
emanations of the state   2.6
employer, HEIs as   28.43–28.44
entry, rights of   28.36–28.42
European Community or European
    Union   28.12
European Convention on Human
    Rights   28.4
European Court of Justice   28.3
European Economic Area   28.4
European Higher Education Area
    §28.3
family members   28.38
fees   28.31–28.35
fixed-term employment   11.17,
    11.80
free movement of academic staff and
    students   28.36–28.42
health and safety   20.7
identity cards   28.38, 28.40
mutual recognition of degrees and
    qualifications   §28.2, 28.45–
    28.54
nationality discrimination   28.43–
    28.44
opinions   28.11
package holidays   29.34
passports   28.38, 28.40
patents   12.19
Private Finance Initiative   §18.5,
    18.17–18.21
public bodies   2.6
public procurement   28.13–28.30
qualified persons   28.39–28.40
recommendations   28.11
regulations   28.9
remain, right to   28.36–28.42

residence permits   28.40–28.41
staff, free movement of   28.36–
    28.42
students, free movement of
    28.36–28.42
trade marks   12.32
transfer of undertakings   17.30
Treaty of Rome   28.12, 28.36
Treaty on European Union   28.2,
    28.7, 28.12, 28.73
    unfair contract terms   6.30,
        29.20
vocational training   28.2
working hours   §28.2
Education
    charities for purposes of   4.4–4.7,
        4.19
    experience   §6.2–6.5
    Human Rights Act 1998   7.11
Educational malpractice   §6.24–6.28
    breach of duty of care   §6.25
    causation   §6.26
    compensation   §6.27
    contracts   §6.26–6.28
    damages   §6.26–6.27, 6.27
    examinations   §6.25
    personal liability   §6.25
    remoteness   §6.26
    special relationships   §6.25
    standard of care   §6.24, §6.26
    tort   §6.26
    United States   §6.24
E-mails
    data protection   §13.2
    harassment   14.17
    internet   14.1–14.3, 14.16
    threats   14.16
Employment   §10.1–10.9, 10.1–
    10.26. *See also* Dismissal, Health
    and safety, Redundancy, Staff,
    Transfer of undertakings, Vicarious
    liability
    academic freedom   §10.2–10.4,
        10.14–10.16
    appeals   10.11
    Commissioners, powers and duties
        of   10.17–10.26
    contracts   6.6, 10.3, 10.11–10.13,
        10.24–10.26, 17.17–17.18
    services for   10.3
    terms of   10.3

Employment – *cont*
  disability discrimination   22.4,
    22.6–22.15
  due diligence   16.26
  EC law   28.43–28.44
  fiduciary duties, breach of   10.24–
    10.26
  franchising   17.17–17.18
  hearings, right to   10.1, 10.11
  intellectual property   10.4
  inventions   12.39
  job interviews   §13.5
  judicial review   10.11
  Model Statute   11.1–11.58
  offers   6.6
  office-holders   10.12
  procedural protection   10.11–
    10.13
  public law   10.11–10.13
  redundancy   §10.7
  references   5.15, 5.16, §6.23, 6.38,
    §24.3
  research   10.4
    confidentiality of   §10.5
  services, contracts for   10.3
  sex discrimination   §10.1
  stress   1.15, §6.22
  students' union   19.20
  tenure   §10.6
  termination of   §11.1, 11.1–11.93
  transfer of undertakings   10.3,
    17.33
  United States   §10.2
  Visitor   10.5–10.16
  whistleblowing   §10.8
  working hours   §28.2
Endowments   25.5
Enforcement of orders   27.62
Entertainment   1.37
Entry, rights of   28.36–28.42
Environment   16.31, §24.3
Equal opportunities   1.37, 6.33, 7.62
Equality of arms   7.22, 7.35
Errors. *See* Mistakes
European Convention on Human
    Rights   7.7–7.8
  Council of Europe   28.4
  EC law   28.4
  fair trials   6.21, 9.43
  judicial review   9.42, 9.47
  Visitor   5.21, §8.4, 8.18, 10.10
European Court of Justice   28.3
European Economic Area   28.4
European Higher Education Area
    §28.3
European Union. *See* EC law
Eviction   §23.1
Evidence
  decision-making   9.37–9.38
  discipline   7.32–7.33
  judicial review   9.37–9.38
    consideration of the   9.36
    decision must accord with the
      9.37–9.38
  witnesses   7.37, 7.42, 11.75
Ex gratia payments   4.19
Examinations
  building works during   23.18
  cheating   1.37
  complaints   1.37
  educational malpractice   §6.25
  leased premises
    building works during   23.18
    marks, withholding   §23.3
  Oxford University's Statement to
    Students   1.37
  religion   7.16
  security   §20.8
Exchange rate   28.18
Exclusion clauses   6.28, 6.34, 20.5
Exclusive possession   23.3, 23.6–
    23.10, 23.30
Exemptions   28.63, 28.66–28.70
Expenses   6.25, 21.28
Expert determination   17.38
Expression, freedom of. *See* Freedom of
    expression
Expulsion   §9.7–§9.9, 9.25, 9.29

Fair comment   5.14
Fair trials
  access to courts or tribunals   7.19
  appeals   7.20, 7.24
  civil rights and obligations   7.17–
    7.18, 9.43–9.44
  complaints   7.20
  compliance with   7.23
  contracts   7.18
  corporations   7.20
  criminal offences   9.44

Fair trials – *cont*
  discipline   7.18–7.20, 7.24, 7.34,
    9.44
  discrimination   7.20
  equality of arms   7.22
  European Convention on Human
    Rights   6.21, 9.43
  higher education corporations
    7.20
  Human Rights Act 1998   6.31,
    7.17–7.24, 7.34, 9.36
  independent and impartial
    tribunals   7.17, 7.20, 9.43
  internal hearings   7.18, 7.20, 7.24
  judicial review   7.19–7.20, 9.36,
    9.42–9.44, 9.50
  legal representation   7.22
  notices of hearings   7.21
  oral hearings   7.19, 9.43
  prevention of breach of contract
    6.31
  proportionality   7.22
  public hearings   7.17, 7.21
  reasons   9.46
  Visitor   6.21, 7.19–7.20, §8.4,
    8.18, 10.10, 30.62
Family Division   27.24
Family life, right to respect for   7.14
Family members   28.38
Fees
  charities   4.5
  consumer law   29.15
  contracts   §6.9, 6.15, 6.17
  debtors   §6.9, §23.3
  EC law   28.31–28.35
  freedom of information   13.17
  multiple occupation, houses in
    21.20
  Oxford University's Statement to
    Students   1.37
  part-time students   1.3
  residence   28.32
Fiduciary duties
  board of governors   3.33
  contracts of employment   10.24–
    10.26
  council   1.12
  directors   4.21, 15.28
  governing bodies   3.37, 4.21
  personal liability   3.33, 3.37, 3.40,
    3.49

  trustees   §4.2–4.3
Field trips   §6.19
Finance   18.34–18.36
Finders   26.2
Fines   28.60–28.62, 28.71
Fixed-term employment
  capability   11.84, 11.87
  conduct   11.84, 11.87
  consultation   11.83
  definition of   11.16
  dismissal   11.2, 11.14–11.17,
    11.37, 11.70–11.93
    unfair   11.60, 11.79–11.80,
      11.82–11.87
    wrongful   11.49
  EC law   11.17, 11.80
  Model Statute   11.88–11.89
  redundancy   11.89–11.93
  renewal of   11.15
  unfair dismissal   11.60, 11.79–
    11.80, 11.82–11.87
  waiver   11.79–11.87
  wrongful dismissal   11.49
Floodlighting   20.16
Force. *See* Use of force
Foreign community   2.8–2.9
Foundations   §2.3
Franchising   §17.1–17.4, 17.1–17.45
  arbitration   17.39
  choice of law   17.35, 17.40, 17.42
  codes of practice   §17.4
  contracts   17.5–17.45, 17.28–
    17.29
    privity of   17.8–17.11
    student   17.6–17.7
    terms of   17.12–17.43
  copyright   17.15, 17.19
  costs, exposure to   17.23
  definition   17.1–17.4
  delivery
    completing   17.28–17.29
    control of   §17.1–§17.2, 17.22–
      17.27
  dispute resolution   17.35–17.39
  distance learning   17.44
  drafting   17.45
  expert determination   17.38
  funding   17.12
  information technology   17.44
  intellectual property rights   17.13–
    17.21

Franchising – *cont*
  international   17.3–17.4
  jurisdiction   17.40–17.41
  Learning and Skills Council   17.44
  licensing   17.20–17.21
  management   17.7
  negotiation, structured   17.37
  payments   17.12
  principal obligations   17.12
  privity of contract   17.8–17.11
  problems with   17.4
  quality control   §17.1–§17.2,
    17.22–17.27
  staff   17.30–17.34
  students,
    contracts   17.6–17.7
    liability to   17.24
  termination of   17.27–17.34
  terms of   17.12–17.43
  transfer of undertakings   17.30–
    17.34
  UK based HE/FE franchise   17.2
  ultra vires   17.25–17.26
Free movement of academic staff and
    students   28.36–28.42
Freedom of establishment   28.53
Freedom of expression   7.15, 9.22,
    12.4
  codes of practice   19.6, 20.19
  'reasonably practicable'   19.6–19.7,
    20.19
  students' union   19.6–19.8
Freedom of information   13.14–
    13.26, App 13
  access   13.15
  compliance, costs of   13.17
  data protection   §13.2, 13.14,
    13.22–13.25
  enforcement   13.21
  exemptions   13.17, 13.19, App 13
  fees   13.17
  Information Commissioner
    13.20–13.21
  Information Tribunal   13.16
  public authorities   13.15–13.21
    definition of   13.15, 13.18
  publication schemes   13.20
  requests for information   13.17,
    13.22

  right to know   13.14
  time for compliance   13.17
Freedom of thought, conscience and
    religion   7.16
Frustration   11.19
Funding   1.1, 1.9. *See also* Private
    Finance Initiative
  accountability   3.25
  charities   4.19
  finance   18.34–18.36
  franchising   17.12
  Funding Council   3.25, 3.43
  governance   3.7
  misapplied funds, personal liability
    for   3.34–3.42
  personal liability   3.34–3.42
  whistleblowing   3.26
Fund-raising   15.5, 25.19

Gagging clauses   §3.6
GATT   28.30
Gift Aid   15.12, 25.9, 25.16
Good cause
  dismissal   10.19, 11.29–11.34,
    11.36, 11.38
    definition   11.30–11.33
    mental capacity and   11.39–
      11.41
    misconduct   11.71–11.76
    unfair   11.66
Good faith
  governance   3.14–3.15
  unfair contract terms   29.7, 29.21–
    29.22
Good practice   §3.4, §3.6–§3.7, §3.9
Governance   §3.1–§3.12, 3.1–3.49
  abuse of power   3.13–3.14
  accountability   3.1, 3.4, 3.15
  audit committees   3.17
  best practice guidance   §3.4,
    §3.6–§3.7, §3.9
  board of governors   3.17
    chair of   3.18
    functions of   3.10
  Cadbury Committee   3.1
  chair, principal and   3.18
  Chancellor's Court   §3.4
  chartered universities   3.6, 3.19
  checks and balances   3.16–3.20

Governance – *cont*
  code of practice   §3.6
  committees   3.2, 3.17
  complaints   §3.4, §3.6
  conflicts of interest   3.4, 3.14,
    3.21–3.22
  controls   3.14–3.20
    improved   3.16–3.20
  corporations   3.1, 3.18
  Council   3.19
  Dearing Report   §3.6, 3.6
  decision-making   3.7, 3.9–3.12,
    3.14
  delegation   3.18, 3.20
  disclosure   3.23–3.27
  effective   3.9–3.12
  funding   3.7
  gagging clauses   §3.6
  good faith   3.14–3.15
  governing bodies,
    accountability of   3.4
    appointment of members of   3.4
    board   3.10, 3.17
    Council   3.19
    decision-making   3.10
    lay members of   3.18
    reduction in size of   3.19
    role of   §3.1, §3.4, §3.7–§3.11,
      3.18
  Greenbury Committee and Code
    3.2
  independence   §3.7, 3.1–3.2
  interests, register of   §3.3
  Jarratt Report   3.1
  liability   3.28–3.49
  media treatment   3.5
  Nolan Enquiry   §3.2–§3.4, §3.6,
    3.2–3.5
  personal liability   3.28–3.49
  principal,
    chair and   3.18
    role of   3.18
  propriety   3.13–3.14
  public life, principles of   3.3–3.4
  remuneration committees   3.2,
    3.17
  risk management   24.2, 24.4
  safeguards   3.13–3.14
  Scotland   §3.7
  scrutiny   3.1–3.8
  secrecy   §3.6, 3.13
  self-interest   3.13, 3.14
  separation of powers   3.14–3.14
  standards   3.3–3.4
  statutory institutions   §3.4,
    3.5–3.6, 3.20, 3.49
  transparency   3.2, 3.14–3.15,
    3.23–3.27
  Vice-Chancellor,
    remuneration of   3.17
    role of   3.19
  whistleblowing   §3.6
Governing bodies. *See also* Board of
  governors
  accountability of   3.4, 4.21
  advice   4.24
  appointment of members of   3.4
  charities   4.18–4.20, 4.26
  chartered institutions   3.25
  conflicts of interest   3.21, 4.21
  Council   3.19
  Dearing Committee   3.27
  decision-making   3.10
  fiduciary duties   3.37, 4.21
  governance,
    accountability of   3.4
    appointment of members of   3.4
    board   3.10, 3.17
    Council   3.19
    decision-making   3.10
    lay members of   3.18
    reduction in size of   3.19
    role of   §3.1, §3.4, §3.7–§3.11,
      3.18
  independence   §3.7
  lay members of   3.18
  nomination committees   3.24
  personal liability   3.28, 3.34–3.41,
    3.49, 4.21–4.23
  reduction in size of   3.19
  representatives on staff and
    student   3.27
  role of   §3.1, §3.4, §3.7–§3.11,
    3.18
  skill and care   5.29
  staff representatives   3.27
  statutory institutions   3.25, 3.34
  student representatives   3.27
  students' union   19.4–19.5
  trustees   4.21
  ultra vires   4.22

Government Procurement
    Agreement   28.30
Grants   21.30–21.31, 28.34
Greenbury Committee and Code   3.2
Grievance procedure   8.3, 8.5
Group actions   6.30, 29.41
Guarantee, companies limited by
    15.24, 19.26
Guidance
   best practice   §3.4, §3.6–§3.7, §3.9
   disability discrimination   22.9
   governance   §3.4, §3.6–§3.7, §3.9
   mergers and acquisitions   16.3
   multiple occupation, houses in
      21.5–21.6, 21.15

Hacking   14.8
Halls of residence   21.12–21.13,
   21.34, 23.22
Harassment   1.15
   codes of practice   §7.4
   complaints   7.59
   criminal offences   §7.4
   e-mails, threats in   14.17
   Oxford University's Statement to
      Students   1.37
Hazing   §6.3–§6.4
Head tenancy schemes   21.34,
   23.31–23.32
Health and safety   20.7–20.10
   clamping   20.9–20.10
   corporate killing   §6.21
   criminal offences   20.8
   EC law   20.7
   parking controls   20.9–20.10
   sport   §6.21
   students' union   §19.1, 19.19
   teleworkers   20.8
Heard, right to be   9.42
Holiday industry   29.10, 29.35–
   29.37
Home, right to respect for   7.14
Home community   2.8–2.9
Homeworkers   20.8
Host mailings   25.28, 25.29
Houses. *See* Multiple occupation
   houses in
Human rights. *See* European
   Convention on Human Rights,
   Human Rights Act 1998

Human Rights Act 1998   1.10, App 1,
   §7.1, 7.6–7.24. *See also* European
   Convention on Human Rights, Fair
   trials
   academic freedom   10.16
   arbitration   8.21
   close circuit television   20.22
   consumer law   29.12
   correspondence   7.14
   data protection   25.26
   declarations of incompatibility
      7.9
   disability discrimination   §22.1,
      22.31–22.32
   discipline   7.34–7.35
   discrimination   7.12
   education, right to   7.11
   family life, right to respect for
      7.14
   freedom of expression   7.15
   home, right to respect for   7.14
   inhuman or degrading treatment
      7.13
   judicial review   9.1, 9.3, 9.17,
      9.23, 9.28, 9.33, 9.36, 9.40,
      9.50–9.51
   legal representation   7.35
   ombudsman, establishment of
      1.11, 8.23
   precedent   7.8
   private life, right to respect for
      7.14
   proportionality   9.40
   public bodies   2.6, 7.7, 7.39
     courts and tribunals, as   7.8
   reasons   7.39
   statutory legislation   7.9
   thought, conscience and religion,
      freedom of   7.16
   torture   7.13
   unfair contract terms   29.24, 29.26
   Visitor   2.2, 8.1, 8.4, 8.12, 8.18–
      8.19, 8.24–8.26
Hours of work   §28.2

Identity cards   28.38, 28.40
Illegality   9.15
Ill-health, dismissal for   11.77–11.78
Immunity   §6.25

Impartiality
  decision-making   9.48
  independent and impartial
    tribunals   7.17, 7.20, §8.4,
      8.19, 9.44
  judicial review   9.48
  test for   9.48
  Visitor   §8.4, 8.9, 8.19
Implied terms   6.17–6.19
Incapacity, dismissal for   11.77–
  11.78
Income tax   25.10
Independence
  governance   §3.7, 3.1–3.2
  governing bodies   §3.7
  independent and impartial
    tribunals   7.17, 7.20, §8.4,
      8.19, 9.44
  Visitor   §8.4, 8.19
Informal offers   6.10–6.11
Information. *See also* Freedom of
  information, Information
  technology
  contracts   6.14
  prevention of breach of contract
    6.34
Information Commissioner
  data protection   25.26
  freedom of information   13.20–
    13.21
  Information Tribunal   13.16
  notification of   13.5
  powers of   13.12
Information technology. *See also*
  Computers, Internet, Software
  agency   5.28–5.30
  domain names   12.33–12.34
  franchising   17.44
  Oxford University's Statement to
    Students   1.37
Inheritance tax   25.7
Inhuman or degrading treatment
  7.13
Injunctions   6.22
  costs   27.40
  damages   27.56
  judicial review   9.17, 9.20
Inland Revenue   4.17
Innuendo   5.13
Inquisitorial litigation   27.11, 27.15

Insolvency   3.43–3.45, 15.18
Inspections   28.60
Insurance
  charities   4.26
  criminal offences   3.48, 4.26
  due diligence   16.29
  excess   3.48, 4.26
  exclusions   4.26
  insurance   4.26
  litigation   §27.5
  Oxford University's Statement to
    Students   1.37
  personal liability   3.48, 4.26
Intellectual property   1.25, §12.1–
  §12.6, 12.1–12.66, App 12(1),
  App 12(2). *See also* Copyright,
  Patents, Trade marks
  academic freedom   10.15
  acquisition   12.35
  assignment   12.46–12.60
  awareness, creating   12.62
  Canada   §10.4
  capturing   12.63
  conflicts of interest   12.2–12.3
  consultants   12.41
  content of agreements   12.52
  contract staff   12.41
  contracts   12.44–12.45
    additional terms   12.45
    employment of   12.38, 17.17–
      17.18
  course of employment   12.38
  creation   12.35
  databases   12.59
  definition   12.3
  designs   12.26
  domain names   12.33–12.34
  due diligence   16.30
  employment   10.7, 12.38
  experimental use   12.58
  formalities   12.51, 12.53
  franchising   17.13–17.21
  importance of   12.3
  infringement of third party rights
    12.57
  intangibility   12.9
  internet   14.11
  inventions   12.39
  know how   28.64
  lecturing staff   12.38–12.39

Intellectual property – *cont*
 licensing   12.46–12.50, 17.15,
  17.20–17.21
 management   12.61–12.64
 mixed sources   12.43
 monopoly rights   12.6, 12.8
 narrower rights   1.27
 national character   12.10
 outside contributors   12.42
 ownership   12.36–12.61, 17.14–
  17.21
 Oxford University's Statement to
  Students   1.37
 registration   12.8, 12.55
 reproduction rights   12.5
 research   §12.3, §12.4, 12.38–
  12.39, 12.58
  staff   12.38–12.39
 Research Assessment Exercise
  1.25
 royalties   12.47
 sale   12.47
 scope of protection   12.4–12.7
 selection of viable   12.64
 software   12.59
 sources, variety of creators or
  12.37
 spin-out companies   12.48–12.50
 sponsorship   §12.3
 staff   12.38–12.39, 12.41
 stamp duties   12.54
 students   12.40
 third party owned materials   17.15
 types of   12.11–12.34
 United States   §12.2
Interception of communications
 14.10. *See also* Surveillance
Interests. *See also* Conflicts of interest
 governance   §3.3
 register of   §3.3, 3.22
 self-interest   3.13, 3.14
Internet   14.1–14.17
 codes of conduct   14.5
 computer misuse   14.8
 copyright   14.11
 data protection   §13.2, 14.2, 14.7,
  14.9, 25.33
 databases   14.11
 defamation   14.1, 14.12–14.15
 digital rights management   14.17

 domain names   12.33–12.34,
  14.11
 e-mail   §13.2, 14.1–14.3, 14.17
 hacking   14.8
 harassment   14.16
 intellectual property   14.11
 interception of communications
  14.10
 patents   14.11
 pornography   14.10
 risk management   14.6, 24.6
 service providers   14.11, 14.13
 theft of data   14.9
 threatening e-mails   14.16
 trade marks   14.11
 United States   14.3–14.4, 14.13,
  14.17
Interviews
 data protection   §13.5
 disability discrimination   22.6
 job   §13.5, 22.6
 risk management   24.23
Inventions   12.39
Investigations   28.60, 28.71
Investments
 charities   §4.2, 4.20, 4.27–4.28
 ethical/socially responsible   4.20
 standard investment criteria   §4.2,
  4.27
 trustees   §4.2, 4.20, 4.27–4.28
Irrationality   9.29

Jarratt Report   3.1
Job interviews
 data protection   §13.5
 disability discrimination   22.26
Joint liability   3.32
Joint ventures   16.1, 16.6–16.7,
  16.13–16.16
Journals   1.12
Judgments, summary   27.40
Judicial review   27.61
 abuse of power   9.15, 9.26
 acknowledgement of service   9.50
 Administrative Court   9.50
 applications for   9.4
 Cambridge University   9.12
 chartered institutions   7.3, 9.19
 Civil Procedure Rules 1998   9.50
 claim forms   9.49–9.50

Judicial review – *cont*
  contracts   6.23, 7.4, 9.20–9.23,
      9.25, 9.27, 9.29, 9.38, 9.41
  costs   7.5, 9.49–9.52
  damages   7.5, 9.16, 9.17
  data protection   9.42
  decision-taking   9.6–9.7, 9.11,
      9.17–9.21
    decision must exercise mind of
        body   9.34
    delegation of   9.32
    discretion of   9.35
    evidence, in line with the   9.37–
        9.38
    heard, right to be   9.42
    impartiality   9.48
    improper purpose, must not be in
        pursuit of a   9.38
    legitimate expectations   9.41
    properly constituted body, for
        9.31
    proportionality   9.40, 9.51
    reasons for   9.45–9.46
  declarations   9.20
  delegation   9.32
  development of   9.2–9.5
  discipline   7.47, §9.7, 9.10, 9.25–
      9.29
  disclosure   9.38, 9.42, 9.51
  discretion   9.35
  discrimination   9.47
  education cases   9.5
  employment   10.11
  European Convention on Human
      Rights   9.42, 9.47
  evidence
    consideration of the   9.36
    decision must accord with the
        9.37–9.38
  expulsion   §9.7, 9.25, 9.29
  fair trials   7.19–7.20, 9.36, 9.42–
      9.44, 9.50
  freedom of expression   9.22
  grounds   9.15–9.19
  growth of   9.4
  heard, right to be   9.42
  Human Rights Act 1998   9.1, 9.3,
      9.17, 9.23, 9.28, 9.33, 9.36, 9.40,
      9.50–9.51
  illegality   9.15
  impartiality   9.48

  improper purpose, must not be in
      pursuit of a   9.38
  injunctions   9.17, 9.20
  irrationality   9.29
  legitimate expectations   9.41
  litigation   27.23
  mandatory orders   9.17, 9.20
  natural justice   9.20, 9.25
  nature of   9.6–9.14
  Oxford University   9.12
  permission   9.52
  private schools   9.20
  procedural unfairness   9.15, 9.31,
      9.42
  procedure   6.23, App 6(1), 9.3,
      9.15, 9.31, 9.42, 9.49–9.52
  prohibiting orders   9.17, 9.20
  proportionality   9.40, 9.51
  public bodies   2.7, 9.6, 9.12, 9.18–
      9.19, 9.23
    public functions, exercising
        9.19, 9.23
  quashing orders   9.17, 9.20
  reasons   9.45–9.46
  reducing risk of   9.30–9.48
  remedies   9.15–9.20
    exhaustion of internal   9.12–
        9.13
  staff   §9.6
  standing   9.51
  statutory institutions   7.3,
      §9.1–§9.9, 9.1–9.52
  students   9.24–9.29
  students' union   §19.2
  test for determining whether
      institution amenable to   9.19
  time-limits   App 6(1)
  ultra vires   9.33
  Visitor   2.2, §8.3, 8.12, 8.25, 9.12,
      9.28, 30.43–30.46
  Wednesbury unreasonableness
      9.37
Judiciary, attitudes of   §7.5
Jurisdiction
  charities   4.10–4.11, 4.13
  franchising   17.40–17.41
  litigation   27.9, 27.21–27.25
  Visitor   4.10, 6.22, App 6(1),
      7.51–7.54, §8.1, 8.3, 8.13, 10.5–
      10.10, 20.32–30.36, 30.43

Jurisdiction – *cont*
  Visitor – *cont*
   Australia   30.49–30.50
   New Zealand   30.55
Justification for defamation   5.14

Know how   28.64

Law reports   1.12
Learning and Skills Council   17.44
Leased premises
  building works   23.16–23.18
  control   23.10, 23.31
  degrees, withholding   23.29
  disability discrimination   22.12,
    22.17–22.18
  discipline   23.33
  dwellings   23.11–23.13
  eviction   §23.1
  examinations
    building works, during   23.18
    marks, withholding   §23.3
  exclusive possession   23.3, 23.6–
    23.10, 23.30
  halls of residence   23.22
  head tenancy agreements   23.31–
    23.32
  intention of the parties   23.5
  licence, or   §23.1–§23.3, 23.1–
    22.34
  noise   23.16–23.19
  notice to quit   23.25
  nuisance   23.19, 23.27
  quiet enjoyment   §23.1, 23.15–
    23.18
  re-entry, rights of   23.14–23.15
  repossession   23.23–23.25
  services   23.9
  terms of the agreement   23.14–
    23.21
  unfair contract terms   §23.2,
    23.26–23.32
Leasing   18.34, 18.36
Lecturers and intellectual property
    12.38–12.39
Legacies from wills   4.8–4.9, 4.17
Legal entity, higher education
    institutions, as   §2.1–§2.4, 2.1–
    2.10

charitable status   §2.3, 2.5
chartered institutions   §2.1,
    §2.3–§2.4
civil law   §2.3
community   2.8–2.10
corporation, as   §2.2–§2.4, 2.1
definition of university   §2.1
foundations   §2.3
legal personality   §2.2
powers   2.2–2.4
public bodies   2.6–2.7
registered companies   §2.3–§2.4
statutory institutions   §2.1,
    §2.3–§2.4
unincorporated associations   §2.3
university, use of term   §2.1
Legal personality   §2.2
Legal problems in HEIs
  externally, dealt with   1.29–1.30
  frequency of   1.23–1.27
  increase or decrease in   1.27
  internally, dealt with   1.29
  questionnaire on   1.22–1.34
  types of   1.23–1.26
Legal representation
  discipline   7.35–7.36
  fair trials   7.22
  Human Rights Act 1998   7.35
  Visitor   6.21
Legitimate expectations
  decision-making   9.41
  judicial review   9.41
  meetings   5.11
Liability. *See also* Personal liability
    Vicarious liability
  limitation of   3.36, 3.38, §15.2,
    15.17–15.20
  students' union   19.18–19.24
  trading companies   §15.2, 15.17–
    15.20
Libel   5.13
Licences. *See also* Licensing
  exclusive possession   23.3, 23.6–
    23.10, 23.30
  halls of residence   23.22
  leased premises   §23.1–§23.3,
    23.1–22.34
  possessory   23.6
Licensing
  anti-competitive practices   28.64

Licensing – *cont*
  copyright   12.60, App 6(2)
  drink   19.32
  franchising   17.20–17.21
  intellectual property   12.46–12.50,
    17.15
  multiple occupation, houses in
    21.2, 21.32
  security   §20.8
  students' union   19.32
  technology transfer licensing
    28.64
Liens   26.6
Limitation of liability   3.36, 3.38,
    §15.2, 15.17–15.20
Limitation periods. *See* Time-limits
Listing   27.37
Litigation   §27.1–§27.5, 27.1–27.71
  admissions   27.68
  adversarial litigation   27.11–27.13,
    27.15
  allocation to tracks   27.32
  alternative dispute resolution
    §27.4, 27.18
  case management   27.18–27.19,
    27.35
    conferences   27.35
  Chancery Division   27.24
  chartered institutions   27.2
  Civil Procedure Rules 1998   9.50,
    27.10, 27.71
  consumer law   29.2–29.3
  costs   27.39–27.40
  Court of Appeal   27.25
  court structure   27.15, 27.22–
    27.23
  debtors   §6.9
  defence   27.31
  definition   27.8
  delegation   27.66
  disclosure   27.33
  discovery   27.69
  dispute, identifying the   27.64
  documents   27.69
  due diligence   16.27
  enforcement of orders   27.62
  evidence, preparation of   27.34
  external disputes   27.6
  Family Division   27.24
  future of   27.70–27.71

inquisitorial litigation   27.11,
    27.15
insurance   §27.5
internal disputes   27.5
judicial review   27.23
jurisdiction   27.9, 27.21–27.25
lawyers, time for involving   27.67
listing   27.37
litigiousness amongst students
    1.3–1.11, §6.11–§6.12
locations of courts   27.24
overriding objective   27.16
Part 36 offers and payments   27.36
particulars of claim   27.31
pre-action protocol   27.27, 27.28
procedural law   27.10
procedure   27.26–27.40
Queen's Bench Division   27.24
remedies, exhaustion of   §27.3
risk management   24.16
safeguards for HEIs   27.63–27.69
service   27.30
settlement   27.17, 27.27, 27.71
starting proceedings   27.29
stay of proceedings   §27.4
structure   27.21–27.25
substantive law   27.10
time-limits   27.30, 27.65
trials   27.38
types of dispute   27.4–27.7
United States   §6.11–§6.12, §27.2–
    §27.3
Visitor   27.2, 27.4
without prejudice   27.68
Woolf reforms   27.15, 27.20,
    27.70
Loans
  charitable giving   25.15
  borrowing, costs of   18.34–18.35
  mergers and acquisitions   16.40
  statutory corporations   2.4
  taxation   15.10, 25.15
  ultra vires   2.4
Local authorities   21.1–21.2, 21.5,
    21.9, 21.12–21.35
Location-based advertising   25.31
Locus standi. See Standing
Loss of earnings   1.9
Lost property   26.2

Madrid Protocol and Agreement
  12.32
Malice   5.13
Malpractice. *See* Educational malpractice
Management. *See also* Governance
  charities   4.18, 4.20
  Continuing Professional
    Development   1.15
  franchising   17.7
  intellectual property   12.61–12.64
  legal literacy   1.15
  legal qualifications of   1.28
  multiple occupation, houses in
    21.27–21.28, 21.32–21.33
  Nolan Committee   1.11
  public procurement   28.16
  students' union   §19.1
  trading companies   §15.1
  Visitor   1.11, 8.3
Mandatory orders   9.17, 9.20
Manual records   13.8
Matriculation   6.4
Media   3.5
Mediation   8.21, 8.25, 27.50
Medical examinations   11.78
Meetings   §5.1, 5.1–5.30
  accountability   3.25
  chair, role of   5.1–5.2
  codes of conduct   5.6
  committees   5.9, 5.11
  common law   §5.1, 5.2–5.6, 5.12
  company law   5.12
  company secretaries   5.12
  convention, procedure based on
    §5.1, 5.1, 5.6, 5.8
  debates   5.6
  decision-making   5.8–5.11
  defamation   5.13–5.18
  delegation   5.9
  discussion   5.6, 5.8
  disorder   5.1
  intra vires   5.9
  irregularities, dealing with   5.10
  legitimate expectations   5.11
  minutes   5.8
  motions   5.1, 5.6–5.7
  natural justice   5.11
  notice of   5.3
  polls   5.5
  procedure   §5.1, 5.6–5.7, 5.11
  public   3.25

  proxies   5.5
  quorum   5.4, 5.10
  secret ballots   5.5
  Standing Orders   5.6
  trading companies   15.27
  ultra vires   5.9–5.10
  voting   5.2, 5.5
Memorandum of association   15.26,
  19.27
Mental disabilities
  contracts   6.15
  disability discrimination   §22.4–
    §22.5
  dismissal   11.39–11.41
  Oxford University's Statement to
    Students   1.37
  stress   1.15, §6.22, §24.3, §24.4
Mergers and acquisitions   §16.1–
  §16.4, 16.1–16.42
  banking   16.40
  chartered institutions   16.12,
    16.13, 16.18
  confederation   16.6
  conference on   §16.2
  constitution and structure   16.33
  constitutional   16.3–16.9
  consultation   16.18, 16.38
  contractual arrangements   16.3–
    16.9, 16.13–16.16
  co-operation agreements   16.8
  due diligence   §16.3, 16.17,
    16.22–16.32, 16.41–16.42
  external approval   16.18
  feasibility   16.42
  global partnerships   §16.2
  guidance   16.3
  inquiries, making proper   16.17
  joint ventures   16.1, 16.6–16.7,
    16.13–16.16
  legal framework   16.2–16.18
  loans   16.40
  pensions   16.39
  powers   16.10–16.12
  principal officers   16.36
  process of transfer, achieving
    16.3–16.8
  redundancies   16.37
  reorganisation   16.37
  security   16.40
  staff consultation   16.38
  statutory institutions   16.13

Mergers and acquisitions – *cont*
   structure   16.33
   timescale   16.34
   trade unions   16.38
   transfer of undertakings   16.1,
      16.11, 16.19–16.21, 16.37–16.38
   transitional issues   16.35
Mini-trials   27.50
Minority shareholdings   15.30
Minutes   5.8
Misconduct
   academic appeals   7.48
   complaints   11.75
   discipline   7.27
   dismissal for good cause   11.71–
      11.76
   personal liability   3.31
   public office, in   3.31
Mitigation   6.25, 7.41
Model Statute
   academic freedom   11.6
   application of   11.7–11.19
   contracts of employment   11.1–
      11.58
   discipline   11.33
   dismissal   §11.1, 11.1–11.93
   fixed-term employment   11.88–
      11.89
   guiding principles   11.6
   interpretation   11.6
   redundancy   11.8, 11.20–11.34,
      11.67–11.70
   unfair dismissal   11.59–11.78
   wrongful dismissal   11.48–11.58
Monitoring   7.14, 24.11–24.12
Monopolies   12.6, 12.8
Moral rights   12.24
Motions   5.1, 5.6–5.7
Multi-party actions   6.30, 29.41
Multiple occupation, houses in
   §21.1, 21.1–21.35
   charter   21.22
   complaints   21.13
   control orders   21.28
   control provisions   21.18–21.22
   criminal offences   21.35
   definition   21.3–21.14, 21.32
   disability discrimination   §22.1
   effect of being   21.15–21.2
   expenses   21.28
   fees   21.20
   grants   21.30–21.31
   guidance   21.5–2.6, 21.15
   halls of residence   21.12–21.13,
      21.34
   head tenancy schemes   21.34
   licensing   21.2, 21.32
   local authorities   21.1–21.2, 21.5,
      21.9, 21.12–21.35
   management   21.27–21.28, 21.32–
      21.33
      regulations, imposition of
         21.27
   overcrowding   21.26
   planning   21.14
   registration   21.15–21.22
   removal expenses   21.28
   renovation   21.30
   repair   21.23, 21.30
   shared houses   21.3–21.11
   social problems   21.1
   special control provisions   21.21
   statutory universities   21.1
   works, powers to require   21.23–
      21.25
Mutual recognition of degrees and
   qualifications
   adaptation periods   28.51
   additional requirements   28.51
   aptitude tests   28.51
   diplomas, recognition of   28.48–
      28.49
   directives   28.46–28.47, 28.50,
      28.53–28.54
   EC law   §28.2, 28.45–28.54
   freedom of establishment   28.53
   professional bodies   28.53
   professional courses   28.50
   titles, right to use academic
      28.52, 28.54
   training   28.46, 28.50
   vocational courses   28.50

Nationality discrimination   28.43–
   28.44
Natural justice
   academic appeals   7.50, 7.53
   discipline   7.30
   judicial review   9.20, 9.25
   meetings   5.11

Natural justice – *cont*
  Visitor   §8.3, 30.40, 30.43
Negligence   §6.2. *See also*
  Educational malpractice
  accidents   §6.19
  barristers   §6.25
  damages   6.27
  drunkenness   §6.22
  field trips   §6.19
  immunity   §6.25
  references   6.38
  security   20.1
  special needs   6.27
  sport   §6.21
  United States   §6.12
  vicarious liability   5.21, §6.21
New Zealand   1.14, 30.52–30.53,
  30.55
Noise   23.16–23.19
Nolan Committee   1.11
  annual reports   3.26
  appeals   §6.7–§6.8, §9.4
  board of governors   3.24
  conflicts of interest   3.21
  governance   §3.2–§3.4, 3.6,
    3.2–3.5
  public bodies, appointment to
    3.24
  Visitor   §6.8, §8.1, 8.1, 8.15,
    30.57–3.64
  whistleblowing   3.26
Nuisance   23.19, 23.27

Occupations
  criminal offences   20.17–20.18
  possession orders   20.17
  security   20.17–20.18
  trespass   20.18
  use of force   §20.1
Occupiers' liability   20.2–20.6
  access routes   20.6
  allurements   20.3
  children   20.3
  exclusion of liability   20.5
  reasonableness   20.3, 20.5
  trespassers   20.3–20.5
  visitors   20.3, 20.5
  warnings   20.3, 20.5–20.6
Offers   6.6, 6.9–6.11, 6.15, 6.22,
  6.24–6.25

Office of the Information
  Commissioner   13.12
Office-holders   10.12
Ombudsman   1.11, 7.65
  consumer law   29.34–29.35, 29.38
  creation of   §8.5, 8.20, 8.23
  Human Rights Act 1998   1.11,
    8.23
  public bodies   2.7
  Visitor   §8.5, 8.20, 8.23, 30.63
Openness   3.2, 3.14–3.15, 3.23–3.27
Opinions   28.11
Oral hearings   7.19, 9.43
Outsourcing   25.36–25.37
Overcrowding   21.26
Overriding objective   27.16
Overseas students   §6.1, 6.11
OxCHEPS   1.39
Oxford University
  charities   4.10–4.11
  judicial review   9.12
  security   §20.1–§20.2
  Statement to Students   1.37–1.38
  trade marks   §12.1
  Visitor   §8.2, 30.1, 30.6, 30.1,
    30.6, 30.13–30.19, 30.26

Parents   1.8
Paris Convention   12.17, 12.32
Parking control   20.9–20.10
Part 36 offers and payments   27.36
Particulars of claim   27.31
Part-time students   1.3, 19.3
Passports   28.38, 28.40
Patents   12.12–12.34
  applications in every country
    12.16
  European Patent Convention
    12.19
  exclusions   12.15
  industrial application, capable of
    12.15
  internet   14.11
  novelty   12.13
  obviousness   12.14
  Paris Convention   12.17
  Patent Cooperation Treaty   12.18
  patentability   12.12
  protection, seeking   12.16
  software   12.15

Payroll giving   25.18

Penalties   7.41, 7.53

Pensions   11.41, 16.39

Personal injuries   6.27

Personal liability
avoidance of   3.46–3.47
board of governors   3.32–3.33
breach of duty   3.33
charities   3.35, §4.1–§4.4, 4.1–4.29
chartered institutions   3.41, 3.44, 3.49
codes of conduct   3.47
companies   3.42, 3.45
conflicts of interest   3.33
corporation members   3.29–3.44, 3.47
criminal offences   3.30–3.31, 3.48, 4.26
directors   15.18, 15.28
analogy with   3.38–3.40, 3.42, 3.49
dissolution   3.43–3.45
educational malpractice   §6.25
fiduciary duties   3.33, 3.37, 3.40, 3.49
Funding Councils   3.43
governance   3.28–3.49
governing bodies   3.28, 3.34–3.41, 3.49, 4.21–4.23
heads of   3.30–3.33, 3.48
insolvency   3.43–3.45
insurance   3.48, 4.26
joint civil liability   3.32
limitation of   3.36, 3.38
misapplied funds   3.34–3.42
misconduct in public office   3.31
public bodies   3.28
relief from   3.40
standards   3.28
statutory institutions   3.33, 3.49
statutory offences   3.30
third parties   4.23
transfer of   3.43
trustees   3.29, 3.40, 3.49
charities   3.35, §4.1–§4.4, 4.1–4.29
limiting liability of   3.36
quasi, liability as   3.35–3.36
ultra vires   3.40, 4.22
warranties   3.40

wrongful trading   15.18

Personal property   26.1–26.6
abandonment   26.2–26.4
bailment   26.4–26.5
chattels   26.1–26.6
detinue   26.5
finders   26.2
liens   26.6
lost property   26.2
treasure trove   26.3

PFI. *See* Private Finance Initiative

Photocopying   App 6(2)

Pinochet case   5.11

Plagiarism   5.18

Planning   21.14

Plant and machinery   18.34

Plays   1.37

Police
Oxford University's Statement to Students   1.37
security   20.11
United States   §20.1
University   1.37

Polls   5.5

Polluter pays   16.31

Pornography   14.10

Possession of land   27.59

Possession orders   20.17

Postgraduates   6.13

Powers of higher education institutions. *See also Ultra vires*
chartered institutions   2.1, 2.3
delegation   2.4
legal entity   2.2–2.4
statutory institutions   2.1, 2.3–2.4
subjective test   2.3

Pre-action protocol   9.49, 27.27, 27.28

Precedent   7.8

Pregnancy   §9.9

Prevention of breach of contract   1.33, 6.31–6.36
clarity   6.35
complaints   6.36
disclaimers   6.34
equal opportunities   6.33
exclusion clauses   6.34
fair trials   6.31
Human Rights Act 1998   6.31
information   6.34

Prevention of breach of contract – *cont*
  policy, knowing the   6.33
  procedure   6.31–6.32, 6.35
  publication   6.34
Principals
  chair   3.18
  governance   3.18
  legal qualifications of   1.28
  mergers and acquisitions   16.36
  role of   3.18
Prison Board of Visitors   §8.4
Privacy   9.8, 27.46. *See also* Private
  life, right to respect for
Private Finance Initiative   §18.1–
  §18.5, 18.1–18.37
  accommodation   §18.3
  accounting   18.5
  achieving transactions, method of
    18.7
  advice   18.33
  anatomy of   18.15–18.28
  ancillary services   18.26–18.27
  assets   18.8
  best and final offer stage   18.23
  buildings   18.26–18.27
  contracts   18.26–18.27
  definition   18.2
  EC law   §18.5, 18.17–18.21
  form of the transaction   18.24–
    18.25
  mechanics   18.21–18.23
  payment mechanism   18.16
  position of HEIs   18.3
  procedure   18.21–18.23
  public procurement   §18.5, 18.12–
    18.13, 18.17, 18.31
    conventional   18.12, 18.31
  regulatory framework   18.10
  risk   18.4–18.6
  services   18.8
  special purpose companies   18.14
  timetable   18.28
  VAT   §18.4
  Visitor   30.39–30.43, 30.61
Private law   1.18
Private life, right to respect for   7.14
Private prosecutions   29.29
Private schools   9.20
Privity of contract   17.8–17.11
Procedure
  academic appeals   7.53

clarity   6.35
complaints   6.36, App 6(2), 7.55
discipline   7.29, 7.27, 7.42, 7.66
dismissal   §11.1, 11.1–11.93
  unfair   11.66
employment   10.11–10.13
judicial review   6.23, App 6(1),
  9.3, 9.15, 9.31, 9.42, 9.49–9.52
litigation   27.26–27.40
meetings   §5.1, 5.1, 5.6, 5.8
prevention of breach of contract
  6.31–6.32, 6.35
Private Finance Initiative   18.21–
  18.23
procedural unfairness   9.15, 9.31,
  9.42
public procurement   28.19, 28.24–
  28.26
redundancy   11.68
unfair dismissal   11.45–11.47,
  11.66
Visitor   8.14
wrongful dismissal   11.52–11.58
Professional bodies   28.53
Professional courses   28.50
Profits, extraction of   15.11–15.13
Prohibiting orders   9.17, 9.20
Promises   §6.13
Promotion   §9.6
Property. *See also* Buildings
  Intellectual property, Occupiers'
  liability
  due diligence   16.25
  possession of land   27.59
  security   20.16
  Visitor   30.36
Proportionality
  decision-making   9.40, 9.51
  discipline   7.35, 7.41
  fair trials   7.22
  Human Rights Act 1998   9.40
  judicial review   9.40, 9.51
Prospectuses   29.9–29.10
Protests. *See* Demonstrations
Proxies   5.5
Public Accounts Committee   3.25
Public bodies
  appointment   3.24
  chartered institutions   7.3

Public bodies – *cont*
  courts, as   7.8
  definition   13.15, 13.18
  disability discrimination   22.31–
    22.32
  EC law   2.6
  emanations of the State   2.6
  freedom of information   13.15–
    13.21
  Human Rights Act 1998   2.6,
    7.7–7.8
  judicial review   2.7, 9.6, 9.12,
    9.18–9.19, 9.23
  legal entity   2.6–2.7
  local authorities   21.1–21.2, 21.5,
    21.9, 21.12–21.35
  multiple occupation, houses in
    21.1–21.2, 21.5, 21.9, 21.12–
    21.35
  Nolan Committee   3.24
  obligations of   7.2
  ombudsman   2.7
  personal liability   3.28
  public function, carrying out a
    8.12, 9.19, 9.23
  racial discrimination   7.62
  reasons   7.39
  regulation   2.7
  tribunals, as   7.8
  Visitor   2.7, 8.12, 8.18
Public Concern at Work   §10.8
Public hearings   7.17, 7.21
Public interest disclosure. *See*
  Whistleblowing
Public law   1.18
  decision-making   7.3
  employment   10.11–10.13
  remedies   7.3
  United States   §9.5
  Visitor   7.3
Public life, principles of   3.3–3.4
Public procurement
  aggregation   28.20
  complaints   28.22
  contracting authorities   28.16
  damages   28.22
  directives   28.14–28.17
  discrimination   28.19, 28.20,
    28.27
  EC law   28.13–28.30

  exchange rate   28.18
  filing procedures   28.23
  GATT   28.30
  Government Procurement
    Agreement   28.30
  management supervision by the State,
    subject to   28.16
  negotiated procedure   28.26
  open procedure   28.24
  Private Finance Initiative   §18.5,
    18.12–18.13, 18.17, 18.31
  procedure   28.19, 28.24–28.26
  public services contracts   28.29
  public supply contracts   28.28
  public works contracts   28.27
  purchasing power   28.13
  regulations   28.14–28.17
  restricted procedure   28.25
  technical specifications   28.21,
    28.27
  third party claims   28.22
  thresholds   28.18–28.21
  time-limits   28.15
  urgency   28.15
  World Trade Organisation   28.30
Public service contracts   28.29
Public supply contracts   28.28
Public works contracts   28.27
Publication   6.34

Qualifications   10.19. *See also*
  Mutual recognition of degrees and
  qualifications
  legal   1.28
  management of, legal   1.28
  principals of, legal   1.28
Qualified privilege   5.14, 5.16–5.18
Quality assurance   6.36, 7.48–7.49,
  7.55, 7.59, §17.1–§17.2, 17.22–
  17.27
Quashing orders   9.17, 9.20
Queen's Bench Division   27.24
Questionnaires   1.22–1.34
Quiet enjoyment   §23.1, 23.15–
  23.18
Quorum   5.4, 5.10

Racial discrimination   7.60
  claims, prevention of   7.63
  damages   7.61

Racial discrimination – *cont*
  equal opportunities   7.62
  exemptions   7.61
  positive discrimination   7.61
  public bodies   7.62
  religion   7.16
  students' union   19.24
  time-limits   7.61
  vicarious liability   5.25
Reasonableness
  arrest   20.11
  dismissal   11.1, 11.42–11.47
  judicial review   9.37
  occupiers' liability   20.3, 20.5
  unfair contract terms   6.29, 29.5,
    29.7, 29.16–29.19
  unfair dismissal   11.44–11.45,
    11.64
  use of force   §20.3–§20.7
  Visitor   30.53
  Wednesbury unreasonableness
    9.37, 30.43
Reasons
  applicants, rejection of   6.23
  decision-taking   7.39, 9.45–9.46
  delay   7.40
  discipline   7.39–7.40
  dismissal   11.20–11.34
  fair trials   9.46
  Human Rights Act 1998   7.39
  judicial review   9.45–9.46
  public bodies   7.39
  unfair dismissal   11.61–11.63,
    11.66
Recommendations   28.11
Rectification   27.55
Redundancy   §10.7
  'activity'   11.25
  collective   11.90–11.93
  committees   11.67, 11.70
  consultation   11.69–11.70, 11.90–
    11.93
  contracts of employment   11.12,
    11.22, 11.27
  definition   11.20–11.22, 11.27
  dismissal   10.2
  early warnings   11.69
  employers, different kinds of
    11.27
  fixed-term employment   11.89–
    11.93

  mergers and acquisitions   16.37
  Model Statute   11.8, 11.20–11.34,
    11.67–11.70
  procedure   11.68
  reallocation of duties   11.27
  recommendations   11.67, 11.70
  redeployment   11.27
  reorganisations   11.38
  selection   11.67–11.69
  terms and conditions, different
    11.27
  test   11.23
Re-entry, right of   23.14–23.15
References   5.15, 5.16, §6.23, 6.38,
    §24.3
Registration
  contracts   6.17
  data protection   25.26
  designs   12.26
  multiple occupation, houses in
    21.15–21.22
  trade marks   12.29
  VAT   15.14
Regulation
  charities   4.10–4.17
  public bodies   2.7
Regulations   28.9, 28.14–28.17
Religion, freedom of   7.16
Remain, right to   28.36–28.42
Remedies. *See also* Damages
    Declarations
  account, action for an   27.60
  applications   6.23
  contracts, breach of   6.21–6.27
  disability discrimination   22.15,
    22.29
  exhaustion of internal   9.15–9.20,
    §27.3
  injunctions   6.22, 9.17, 9.20,
    27.40, 27.56
  judicial review   9.15–9.20
  litigation   §27.3
  mandatory orders   9.17, 9.20
  offers, compliance with   6.22
  possession of land   27.59
  prohibiting orders   9.17, 9.20
  public law   7.3
  quashing orders   9.17, 9.20
  rectification   27.55
  restitution   27.58

Remedies – *cont*
  specific performance 6.22, 27.54
  tracing orders 27.58
  Visitor 6.22, 8.1
Remoteness §6.26
Removal expenses 21.28
Remuneration
  committees 3.2, 3.17
  Greenbury Report 3.2
  Vice-Chancellor 3.17
Renovation 21.30
Reorganisations 11.38, 16.37
Repair 21.23, 21.30
Repossession 23.23–23.25
Representative actions 6.30, 29.41
Representatives
  Dearing Committee 3.27
  governing bodies, on 3.27
  staff 3.27
  student 3.27
  whistleblowers 3.27
Reproduction rights 12.5
Research
  academic freedom 10.16
  confidentiality of §10.5
  conflicts of interest §10.4
  employment, research §10.5, 10.4
  intellectual property §12.3, §12.4,
    12.38–12.39, 12.58
  Oxford University's Statement to
    Students 1.37
  Research Assessment Exercise
    1.25
  statutory institutions 1.25
  United States §10.5
Research and development
  agreements 28.65
Residence
  fees 28.32–28.33
  grants 28.35
  permits 28.40–28.41
Resolutions 15.30
Restitution 27.58
Risk management
  advice 24.16
  CAPSA IT project 24.28
  complaints 24.15
  contracts 24.20–24.28
  control of risks 24.9, 24.18, 24.25
  core business §24.5

  cost implications 24.14
  damages §24.4
  data protection §24.3
  discipline 24.21
  discrimination §24.4, 24.23
  dispute resolution 24.15, 24.23
  documentation, review of 24.23
  environment §24.3
  governance 24.2, 24.4
  identification of risk 24.7
  incorporation of terms 24.23
  insurance §24.1–§24.6, 24.1–
    24.29
  internal controls 24.4
  internet 14.6
  interviews 24.23
  lawyers, use of 24.19
  legal 24.13–24.25
  litigation 24.16
  measuring risks 24.8, 24.24
  methodology 24.23
  monitoring 24.11–24.12
  plans, formulating, communicating
    and implementing 24.10,
    24.25
  Private Finance Initiative 18.4–
    18.6
  process 24.5–24.12
  reduction of risk, options for 24.9
  references §24.3
  reputation, damage to 24.14
  reviews 24.20–24.25
  risk assessment §24.2
  scope of review, identifying the
    24.6
  self-assessment 24.23
  stress §24.3, §24.4
  students' union 19.18–19.21
  training 24.19
Royalties 12.47

Safety. *See also* Health and safety
  Oxford University's Statement to
    Students 1.37
  United States §6.19
Satisfactory quality 29.13, 29.36
Scholarships 4.7
Scotland
  governance §3.7
  grants 28.34
Scrutiny 3.1–3.8

Secrecy. *See also* Privacy
  ballots   5.5, 19.4
  gagging clauses   §3.6
  governance   §3.6, 3.13
Security
  arrest   20.11–20.14
  close circuit television   20.20–
    20.22
  costs for   27.40
  disclaimers   20.16
  examinations   §20.8
  floodlights   20.16
  guards   20.11–20.15
  licences   §20.8
  mergers and acquisitions   16.40
  negligence   20.1
  occupations   20.17–20.18
  Oxford University   §20.1–§20.2
  police   20.11
  property   20.16–20.18
  unfair contract terms   20.16
  United States   §6.19
  use of force   §20.1–§20.7, 20.13–
    20.15
  vicarious liability   20.14
Self-defence   §20.7
Self-interest   3.13, 3.14
Separation of powers   3.14
Service providers   14.11, 14.13
Settlement   27.17, 27.27, 27.71
Sex discrimination   7.60
  claims, prevention of   7.63
  damages   7.61
  employment   §10.1
  pregnancy   §9.9
Sexual offences   §6.19
Shared houses   21.3–21.11
Shares, companies limited by   15.23
Sickness, dismissal for   11.77–11.78
Slander   5.13
Small print   29.20
Societies   1.37
Software   12.15, 12.59
Solicitors
  audits   1.33, 1.34
  preventive law   1.33
  selection of   1.31–1.34
    questionnaire on   1.33–1.34
  tenders   1.31
Special needs, failure to diagnose
  6.27

Specific performance   6 22, 27.54
Sponsorship   12.3
Sport   §6.21
Staff. *See also* Dismissal
  Employment, Redundancy
  capability   10.19
  charities   4.16
  definition   10.19
    academic, of   11.7
  disability discrimination   §22.2
  discipline   1.15
  dismissal   1.15
  EC law   28.36–28.42
  franchising   17.30–17.34
  free movement of   28.36–28.42
  governing bodies, representatives
    on   3.27
  intellectual property   12.38–12.39,
    12.41
  judicial review   §9.6
  lecturers   12.38–12.39
  mergers and acquisitions   16.38
  promotion   §9.6
  qualifications   10.19
  representatives   3.27
  students' union   19.20
  transfer of undertakings   16.20
  Visitor   8.3
  whistleblowers   3.27
Stalking   1.15, §7.4
Stamp duties   12.54
Standard forms   8.25
Standard of care   4.3, §6.26
Standard of proof   7.38
Standard terms   6.29
Standards   3.3–3.4, 3.28
Standing
  judicial review   9.51
  Visitor   30.8
Standing Orders   5.6
Statute. *See* Model Statute
Statutory institutions   1.21, 1.24
  charities   4.27
  conflicts of interest   3.21
  corporations   2.1
  delegation   2.4
  governance   §3.4, 3.5–3.6, 3.20,
    3.49
  governing bodies   3.25, 3.34
  judicial review   7.3, §9.1–§9.9,
    9.1–9.52

Statutory institutions – *cont*
   legal entity   §2.1, §2.3–§2.4
   loans   2.4
   mergers and acquisitions   16.13
   multiple occupation, houses in
     21.1
   personal liability   3.33, 3.49
   powers   2.1, 2.3–2.4
   research   1.25
   ultra vires   2.4
   Visitor   §9.4, 30.1
Statutory interpretation   7.9
Stay of proceedings   §27.4
Stress
   employment   1.15, §6.22
   risk management   §24.3, §24.4
Students
   consumerism   1.3–1.11, §6.1
   contracts   §6.1–§6.30, 6.1–6.40,
     App 6(1), App 6(2), 7.2, 17.6–
     17.7
   EC law   28.36–28.42
   franchising,
     contracts   17.6–17.7
     liability to   17.24
   free movement   28.36–28.42
   governing bodies, representatives
     on   3.27
   higher education institutions and,
     relationship between   6.3, 7.2
   intellectual property   12.40
   judicial review   9.24–9.29
   litigiousness of   1.3–1.11
   overseas   §6.1, 6.11
   part-time   1.3, 19.3
   postgraduates   6.13
   representatives   3.27
   whistleblowers   3.27
Students' union
   affiliations   19.4
   buildings   19.19
   charities   19.11–19.17, 19.30
   complaints   19.4
   contracts   19.21–19.22
   data protection   19.29
   definition   19.1–19.3
   directors   19.29–19.31
   donations   19.13–19.17
   duty of care   19.22–19.23
   employment   19.20

   financial affairs   19.4
   freedom of expression   19.6–19.8
   governing bodies   19.4–19.5
   health and safety   §19.1, 19.19
   incorporation, reducing risks by
     19.25–19.33
   judicial review   §19.2
   legal status of   §19.1–§19.3, 19.1–
     19.33
   liability   19.18–19.24
   licensing   19.32
   management   §19.1
   membership   19.4, 19.29
   Oxford University's Statement to
     Students   1.37
   part-time students   19.3
   President   19.4
   property   §19.3
   racial discrimination   19.24
   risk   19.18–19.21
   running an incorporated   19.28
   secret ballots   19.4
   staff   19.20
   status   19.9–19.10
   tortious liability   19.21
   unfair contract terms   19.21
   unincorporated associations   19.9–
     19.10, 19.21
   VAT   §19.2
Summary judgments   27.40
Supervision   §6.3–§6.5
Supply of goods and services   29.13–
   29.15
Surveillance   §20.1, 20.20–20.22

Taxation
   alumni   25.6–25.19
   capital gains tax   25.8, 25.10
   charities   4.17, 15.3–15.5, 18.36,
     19.12, 25.6–25.19
   declarations   25.11–25.13
   deeds of covenant   15.12–15.13,
     25.14–25.16
   finance   15.9
   Gift Aid   15.12, 25.9, 25.16
   income tax   25.10
   inheritance tax   25.7
   leasing   18.36
   loans   15.10, 25.15
   off-the-shelf schemes   15.7

Taxation – *cont*
  payroll giving   25.18
  profits, extraction of   15.11–15.13
  trading companies   15.2–15.5,
    15.7–15.13
Technology transfer licensing   28.64
Telephone Preference Service   25.24
Teleworkers   20.8
Tenancies. *See* Leased premises
Tenders   1.31
Tenure   §10.6
Termination of contracts   6.16
Termination of employment   §11.1,
    11.1–11.93. *See also* Dismissal
Terminology   1.20–1.21
Terms of contracts   6.17–6.19, 6.28–
    6.30, 10.3, 11.27, 17.12–17.43. *See
    also* Unfair contract terms
Textbooks   1.12–1.14
Theft   1.37, 14.9
Thought, freedom of   7.16
Threats in e-mails   14.17
Time-limits   27.65
  appeals   7.46
  judicial review   App 6(1)
  litigation   27.30
  public procurement   28.15
  racial discrimination   7.61
  service   27.30
Titles, right to use academic   28.52,
    28.54
Tortious liability   19.21
Torture   7.13
Tracing orders   27.58
Trade descriptions   29.27–29.28
Trade marks   12.27–12.32
  distinctiveness   12.30
  domain names   12.33–12.34
  EC law   12.32
  foreign applications   12.32
  geographical terms   12.30
  internet   14.11
  Madrid Protocol and Agreement
    12.32
  Oxford University   §12.1
  Paris Convention   12.32
  registered   12.29
  unregistered   12.28
Trade unions   16.20, 16.38

Trading companies   §15.1–§15.7,
    15.1–15.30. *See also* Directors
  articles of association   15.26
  charities   2.5, 4.17, §15.6, 15.2–
    15.5
  commercial reasons for   15.6
  commercialisation, debates on
    §15.7
  company secretaries   15.29
  conflicts of interest   §15.7, 15.30
  corporate personality   §15.2
  disability discrimination   22.6
  guarantee, limited by   15.24
  incorporation   15.22
  insolvency   15.18
  limitation of liability   §15.2,
    15.17–15.20
  management   §15.1
  meetings   15.27
  members   15.27
  memorandum of association
    15.26
  minority shareholdings   15.30
  off-the-shelf   15.22
  powers of the HEIs   15.15
  public limited   15.25
  reasons for setting up   15.2–15.7
  relationship between HEIs and
    15.16
  resolutions   15.30
  shares, limited by   15.23
  starting   15.21–15.26
  subsidiaries   15.15
  taxation   15.2–15.5, 15.7–15.13
  types of   15.23–15.25
  ultra vires   15.15
  unfair competition   §15.5
  United States   §15.4
  VAT   15.2, 15.7, 15.14
  veil of incorporation   §15.2, 15.19
  vicarious liability   §15.1
  wrongful trading   15.18
Training
  Continuing Professional
    Development   1.15
  EC law   28.2
  management   1.15
    risk   24.19
  mutual recognition of degrees and
    qualifications   28.46, 28.50

Training – *cont*
  vocational   28.2, 28.50
Transfer of undertakings   10.3
  application of regulations   16.19
  collective agreements   16.20
  consultation   16.20
  contracts of employment   16.20,
    17.33
  dismissal   16.20
  due diligence   16.26
  EC law   17.30
  economic entities   17.31
  franchising   17.30–17.34
  interpretation   17.31
  mergers and acquisitions   16.1,
    16.11, 16.19–16.21, 16.37–16.38
  staff   16.20, 17.30–17.34
  terms and conditions   16.20
  trade unions   16.20
Transparency   3.2, 3.14–3.15, 3.23–
  3.27
Travel industry   29.10, 29.35–29.37
Treasure trove   26.3
Treaty of Rome   28.12, 28.36
Treaty on European Union   28.2,
  28.7, 28.12, 28.73
Trespass to land
  damages   20.14
  occupations   20.18
  occupiers' liability   20.3–20.5
Trustees
  advice   §4.2, 4.24, 4.26, 4.27
  bodies corporate   4.18
  charities   3.35, §4.1–§4.4, 4.1–
    4.29
    assets of   4.20
    duties of trustees of   4.19–4.20
    persons who are trustees of
      4.18
  duties of   §4.1–§4.4, 4.1–4.29
  duty of care   §4.2, 4.27
  fiduciary duties   §4.2–§4.3
  governing bodies   4.21
  insurance   4.26
  investment powers   §4.2, 4.20,
    4.27–4.28
  limiting liability of   3.36, §4.2
  mistakes   §4.4
  personal liability   3.29, 3.35–3.36,
    3.40, 3.49, §4.1–§4.4, 4.1–4.29
  powers of   §4.1–§4.4, 4.1–4.29

  protection of   §4.4
  quasi, liability as   3.35–3.36
  skill and care   4.27
  standard of care   §4.3
  Trustee Act 2000   4.27–4.29
  ultra vires   4.22
Tuition fees. *See* Fees
Turnover   1.1

UCAS   6.7, 6.9
UCELNET   1.12, 1.29
Ultra vires
  contracts   4.23
  franchising   17.25–17.26
  governing bodies   4.22
  judicial review   9.33
  loans   2.4
  meetings   5.9–5.10
  personal liability   3.40, 4.22
  statutory institutions   2.4
  trading companies   15.15
  trustees   4.22
Unconscionability   §6.15
Unfair competition   §15.5
Unfair contract terms   6.19
  consumer law   29.5–29.9
  consumers   6.28, 6.30
  EC law   6.30, 29.20
  exclusion clauses   6.28
  good faith   29.7, 29.21–29.22
  Human Rights Act 1998   29.24,
    29.26
  indicative list of terms   29.23
  leased premises   §23.2, 23.26–
    23.32
  negligence   6.28
  plain, intelligible language   29.25
  reasonableness   6.29, 29.5, 29.7,
    29.16–29.19
  representative actions   6.30
  security   20.16
  small print   29.20
  standard terms   6.29
  students' union   19.21
  Visitor   30.60
Unfair dismissal   10.20
  continuity of employment   11.59
  dismissal, definition of   11.60,
    11.65

Unfair dismissal – *cont*
 fixed-term contracts   11.60,
   11.79–11.80, 11.82–11.87
 good cause   11.66
 Model Statute   11.59–11.78
 procedure   11.45–11.47, 11.66
 reasonableness   11.44–11.45,
   11.64
 reasons   11.61–11.63, 11.66
 waiver   11.79–11.87
Unincorporated associations
 charities   4.18
 constitution of   19.10
 contracts   19.10
 legal entity   §2.3
 students' union   19.9–19.10, 19.21
Union. *See* Student's union
United States
 academic freedom   §10.3
 books   1.13
 confidentiality   §10.5
 consumer law   29.2–29.3
 consumerism, growth in   1.10,
   1.13
 contracts   §6.10–§6.19
 criminal offences   §6.19
 data protection   25.32
 decision-taking   §6.17–§6.18
 defamation   5.17
 delegation   5.21
 disability discrimination   §22.2–
   §22.5
 drinking   §6.5
 educational malpractice   §6.24
 employment   §10.2
 hazing   §6.3–§6.4
 intellectual property   12.2
 internet   14.3–14.4, 14.13, 14.18
 litigation   §27.2–§27.3
 litigiousness in   §6.11–§6.12,
   29.2–29.3
 negligence   §6.12
 police forces   §20.1
 private institutions   §9.5
 promises   §6.13
 public institutions   §9.5
 public law   §9.5
 research, confidentiality of   §10.5
 security   §6.19

 sexual offences   §6.19
 supervision   §6.3–§6.5
 tenure   §10.6
 trading companies   §15.4
 unconscionability   §6.15
 vicarious liability   5.21
 Visitor   30.47
Unsolicited telephone calls   25.30
Universal Copyright Convention
   12.21
Universities
 definition of   §2.1
 legal entity   §2.1
 use of term   §2.1
Universities and Colleges Education Law
   Network (UCELNET)   1.12,
   1.29
Use of force
 occupations   §20.1
 reasonableness   §20.3–§20.7
 security   §20.1–§20.7, 20.13–
   20.15
 self-defence   §20.8
 weapons   20.15

VAT
 charities   15.14
 input tax   15.14
 Private Finance Initiative   §18.4
 registration   15.14
 standard-rated   15.14
 students' union   §19.2
 taxable activities   15.14
 trading companies   15.2, 15.7,
   15.14
 zero-rated   15.14
Veil of incorporation   §15.2, 15.19
Vertical agreements   28.66
Vicarious liability
 agency   5.19, 5.24
 commissioning editors   5.22
 contracts   5.21–5.22
 course of employment   5.25–5.26
 disability discrimination   22.14
 'frolic of his own'   5.25–5.26, 6.38
 negligence   5.21, §6.21
 references   6.38
 racial discrimination   5.25
 security guards   20.14
 sport   §6.21

Vicarious liability – *cont*
  trading companies   §15.1
  United States   5.21
Vice-Chancellor   3.17, 3.19
Victimisation   22.13, 22.24
Visas   §10.8
Visitor   30.1–30.64
  academic appeals   7.51–7.52, 7.54
  academic freedom   10.14
  Alsatia   2.2
  alternatives to   8.20–8.25
  appeals   30.63
  appointment, justification for   8.2
  arbitration   8.20, 8.21, 30.60
  Australia   30.48–30.50
  background   8.2–8.3
  benefits of   8.4–8.10, 30.21–30.26
  bibliographical essay on   30.1–30.64
  Cambridge University   §8.2, 30.1, 30.6, 30.13, 30.15–30.19
  Canada   30.51
  canon law   8.2, 30.7
  cases   30.13
  charities   4.16
  chartered institutions   2.2, 7.3, §8.1–§8.5, 8.1–8.26, 30.6
  code of practice   8.20, 8.22
  Commissary   8.2, 8.14, 8.15, 30.41
  complaints   8.20, 8.25
  conciliation   8.25
  costs   8.25
    reduced   8.6
  damages   §8.2, 8.6, 30.37–30.38
  decision-making   7.3
    inconsistency in   8.16
  definition   30.6
  delay   8.7, 8.14
  discipline   30.51
  dismissal   10.10
  drawbacks of   8.11–8.17, 30.21–30.26
  employment   10.5–10.16
  errors of law   30.43–30.44
  European Convention on Human Rights   5.21, §8.4, 8.18, 10.10
  evolution of   30.7–30.20
  fair trials   6.21, 7.19–7.20, §8.4, 8.18, 10.10, 30.62

  finality of decisions   8.12
  future of   §8.5, 30.57–30.64
  grievance procedure   8.3, 8.5
  group of   8.25
  hearings   30.41–30.42
  history   30.7–30.20
  Human Rights Act 1998   2.2, 8.1, 8.4, 8.12, 8.18–8.19, 8.24–8.26
  impartiality   §8.4, 8.9, 8.19
  identity of   8.2
  independent and impartial tribunal, as   §8.4, 8.19
  informality   8.5
  judicial review   2.2, §8.3, 8.12, 8.25, 9.12, 9.28, 30.43–30.46
  jurisdiction   4.10, 6.22, App 6(1), 7.51–7.54, §8.1, 8.3, 8.13, 10.5–10.10, 30.32–30.36, 30.43
    Australia   30.49–30.50
    New Zealand   30.55
  knowledge of institution and higher education, insufficient   8.15
  legal representation   6.21
  litigation   27.2, 27.4
  literature on role of   30.1–30.64
  management   8.3
  mediation   8.25
  natural justice   §8.3, 30.40, 30.43
  New Zealand   30.52–30.53, 30.55
  Nolan Committee   §6.8, §8.1, 8.1, 8.15, 30.4, 30.57–30.64
  Ombudsman   §8.5, 8.20, 8.23, 30.63
  Oxford University   §8.2, 30.1, 30.6, 30.13–30.19, 30.26
    Statement to Students   1.38
  powers   §8.1
  preferred rights   8.17
  Prison Board of Visitors   §8.4
  privacy   8.8
  procedure   8.14, 30.39–30.43, 30.61
  property   30.36
  public bodies   2.7, 8.12, 8.18
  public function, carrying out a   8.12
  public law   7.3
  remedies   6.22, 8.1
  renaming of   8.25
  replacement of   30.57–30.64
  resource, as a useful   8.10

Visitor – *cont*
  role of   1.11, 2.2, §8.1–§8.5, 8.1–
    8.26
    literature on   30.1–30.64
  speed   8.7
  staff   8.3, 30.33–30.35
  standard forms   8.25
  standing   30.8
  statutory institutions   §9.4, 30.1
  timetables   8.25
  unfair contract terms   30.60
  United States   3–47
  updating concept of   8.20, 8.24–
    8.25
  Wednesbury unreasonableness
    30.53
Vocational training   28.2
Voting   5.2, 5.5

Warnings   20.3, 20.5–20.6
Warranties   3.40
Weapons   20.15
Wednesbury unreasonableness   9.37,
    30.53
Wheel-clamping   20.9–20.10
Whistleblowing
  decision-making   3.27
  employment   §10.8
  Funding Council   3.26

governance   §3.6
Nolan Committee   3.26
Oxford University's Statement to
    Students   1.37
Public Concern at Work   §10.8
staff or student representatives
    3.27
Wills, legacies from   4.8–4.9, 4.14
Without prejudice rule   27.68
Witnesses   7.37, 7.42, 11.75
Woolf reforms   27.15, 27.20,
    27.70
Work permits   §10.9
Working hours   §28.2
Works, powers to require   21.23–
    21.25
World Trade Organisation   28.34
Wrongful dismissal
  contracts of employment   11.48–
    11.58
  damages   11.1, 11.48–11.58
  fixed-term contracts   11.49
  Model Statute   11.48–11.58
  procedure   11.52–11.58
Wrongful trading   15.18
WTO. See World Trade Organisation

Zellick Report   7.44